BIOLOGICAL FOUNDATIONS OF PSYCHIATRY
Volume 1

Biological Foundations of Psychiatry
Volume 1

Edited by

Robert G. Grenell

Section on Neurobiology
Institute of Psychiatry and
Human Behavior
University of Maryland Hospital
Baltimore, Maryland

Sabit Gabay

Biochemistry Research Laboratory
Veterans Administration Hospital
Brockton, Massachusetts

Raven Press • New York

Raven Press, 1140 Avenue of the Americas, New York, New York 10036

Made in the United States of America

International Standard Book Number 0–911216–96–0
Library of Congress Catalog Card Number 74–15664

Sponsored by the Society of Biological Psychiatry

Contents of Volume 1

LEVELS OF CONSCIOUSNESS

Contents of Volume 2

INTEGRATION

Contributors for Volumes 1 and 2

A. Michael Anch
Sleep Laboratories
Department of Psychiatry
Baylor College of Medicine
Houston, Texas 77025
and
Veterans Administration Hospital
Houston, Texas 77211

Ronald J. Bradley
Neurosciences Program and Department
of Psychiatry
University of Alabama
Birmingham, Alabama 35294

Remi J. Cadoret
Department of Psychiatry
University of Iowa
College of Medicine
Iowa City, Iowa 52242

J. A. Deutsch
Department of Psychology
University of California, San Diego
La Jolla, California 92037

J. C. Eccles
Department of Physiology
State University of New York Medical
School
Buffalo, New York 14220

Seymour Ehrenpreis
New York State Research Institute for
Neurochemistry and Drug Addiction
Wards Island
New York, New York 10035

Daniel L. Ely
Department of Physiology
University of Southern California
School of Medicine
Los Angeles, California 90007

John P. Flynn
Department of Psychiatry
Yale University School of Medicine
New Haven, Connecticut 06508

Charles E. Frohman
The Lafayette Clinic and Department of
Psychiatry
Wayne State University School of Medi-
cine
Detroit, Michigan 48202

David Galin
Langley Porter Neuropsychiatric Institute
University of California, San Francisco
and
Institute for the Study of Human Con-
sciousness
San Francisco, California 94143

Mark A. Geyer
Department of Psychiatry
University of California, San Diego
La Jolla, California 92037

Jacques S. Gottlieb
The Lafayette Clinic and Department of
Psychiatry
Wayne State University School of Medi-
cine
Detroit, Michigan 48202

R. G. Grenell
Section of Neurobiology
Institute of Psychiatry and Human Be-
havior
University of Maryland Hospital
Baltimore, Maryland 20014

Robert G. Heath
Department of Psychiatry and Neurology
Tulane University School of Medicine
New Orleans, Louisiana 70112

James P. Henry
Department of Physiology
University of Southern California
School of Medicine
Los Angeles, California 90007

Williamina A. Himwich
Nebraska Psychiatric Institute
University of Nebraska College of
Medicine
Omaha, Nebraska 68106

Leo E. Hollister

Veterans Administration Hospital and Stanford University School of Medicine
Palo Alto, California 94304

Ismet Karacan

Sleep Laboratories
Department of Psychiatry
Baylor College of Medicine
Houston, Texas 77025
and
Veterans Administration Hospital
Houston, Texas 77211

M. Kinsbourne

Hospital for Sick Children
555 University Avenue
Toronto, Ontario, Canada M5G 1X8

H. S. Koopmans

Department of Psychology
Columbia University
New York, New York 10027

Abel Lajtha

Neurosciences Department
Institute for Information Systems
University of California, San Diego
La Jolla, California 92093

Robert B. Livingston

Neurosciences Department
Institute for Information Systems
University of California, San Diego
La Jolla, California 92093

Paul D. Maclean

Laboratory of Brain Evolution and Behavior
National Institute of Mental Health
National Institutes of Health
Bethesda, Maryland 20014

Arnold J. Mandell

Department of Psychiatry
University of California, San Diego
La Jolla, California 92037

D. McCulloch

Section of Neurobiology
Institute of Psychiatry and Human Behavior
University of Maryland Hospital
Baltimore, Maryland 20014

James L. McGaugh

Department of Psychobiology
School of Biological Sciences
University of California
Irvine, California 92664

James Olds

Division of Biology
Beckman Laboratories 216–76
California Institute of Technology
Pasadena, California 91125

Karl H. Pribram

Department of Psychology
Stanford University
Stanford, California 94305

John D. Rainer

722 W. 168th Street
New York, New York 10032

Charles Shagass

Department of Psychiatry and Eastern Pennsylvania Psychiatric Institute
Temple University
Philadelphia, Pennsylvania 19104

Arthur K. Shapiro

Department of Psychiatry Special Studies Laboratory
Payne Whitney Clinic
New York Hospital
Cornell University Medical College
New York, New York 10021

John R. Smythies

Neurosciences Program and Department of Psychiatry
University of Alabama
Birmingham, Alabama 35294

David N. Teller

New York State Research Institute for Neurochemistry and Drug Addiction
Wards Island
New York, New York 10035

Ming T. Tsuang

Department of Psychiatry
University of Iowa College of Medicine
Iowa City, Iowa 52242

H. Weil-Malherbe

National Institute of Mental Health
William A. White Building,
St. Elizabeths Hospital
National Institutes of Health
Washington, D.C. 20032

Robert L. Williams

Sleep Laboratories
Department of Psychiatry
Baylor College of Medicine
Houston, Texas 77025
and
Veterans Administration Hospital
Houston, Texas 77211

Arthur Yuwiler

Neurobiochemistry Laboratory
Brentwood Veterans Administration
  Hospital
Los Angeles, California 90023
and
Department of Psychiatry
University of California, Los Angeles
Los Angeles, California 90024

Foreword

Biological psychiatry is an interdisciplinary science concerned with studies of the basic foundations of behavior, including the abnormal behavior characteristic of the mentally ill.

All human behavior is mediated by events in the nervous system and, as I have pointed out elsewhere, a disembodied psyche is a scientifically meaningless concept—like the grin of the Cheshire cat without the cat. This, of course, should not imply that one cannot effectively study behavior without reference to its genetic, biochemical, and neurological determinants; but Freud himself emphasized that psychoanalysis was a therapy that he hoped in time would be superceded by advancements of basic biomedical knowledge.

Unfortunately we are still far from understanding the biological determinants of most of our behavior, including the problems psychiatrists are called upon to treat. But, just as basic biomedical research has shed much light on many clinical problems in medicine, it is expected that biological psychiatry will contribute increasingly to the ultimate advancement of clinical psychiatry, despite our ignorance which is not to be overcome by hypothetical verbal systems. As P. W. Medewar has said, "The case against a psychological system of treatment such as psychoanalysis does not really rest on the fact that it is inefficacious—for that must be true of a great many forms of medical treatment—but on the fact that belief in psychoanalysis is an important impediment to the discovery of true causes of mental illness."

Julian Huxley has pointed out that we are, of course, organizations with two aspects—a material aspect, when seen objectively from the outside, and a mental aspect, when experienced subjectively from the inside. We are simultaneously and indissolubly both matter and mind. Huxley considers the possible evolution of mind from simple organisms to man and the survival value of mental process by natural selection. He argues that mind cannot be a useless epiphenomenon. It would not have evolved unless it had been of biologic advantage in the struggle for survival. He holds that the mind-intensifying organization of animals' brains, based on the information received from the sense organs and operating through the machinery of interconnected neurons, is of advantage for the simple reason that it gives a fuller awareness of both outer and inner situations. It therefore provides a better guidance for behavior in the chaos and complexity of the situations with which animal organisms can be confronted. It endows the organism with better operational efficiency. Consciousness and behavior are emergent properties of complex nerve nets that have evolved as organs of survival.

To date, the contributions of physiology and biochemistry to the relief of psychiatric disorders have been modest ones. This would be expected from the complexities of the problems, the relative paucity of research support (until very recently), and the short time that such research has had to advance. There are, however, some important contributions. Thus the severe psychosis characteristic of pellagra due to vitamin B deficiency has disappeared throughout the South with the discovery of its cause and the use of vitamins. The psychosis of general paresis, sometimes indistinguishable in symptoms from schizophrenia, has virtually disappeared in many places since the discovery of its relation to earlier spirochete infection and the treatment of syphilis with antibiotics. Feeblemindedness accompanying the rare disease phenylketonuria is now understood to be genetically determined resulting in the lack of a specific enzyme; this can be successfully treated by preventing the ingestion of the amino acid phenylalanine that cannot be normally metabolized due to the enzyme deficit. Downs disease (mongolism), another of many genetically caused mental disorders, and many other forms of defective behavior are also coming to be understood in terms of enzyme or endocrine deficits. The new field of psychopharmacology has made important empirical advances—tranquilizer drugs have been responsible for a reduction in the patient populations of mental hospitals.

Most of us would agree that biology in its broad sense embraces the basic sciences of medicine and one might ask, if biology is the basic science of medicine, what is the technology of medicine? Lewis Thomas, President of Memorial Sloan-Kettering Cancer Center, has spoken of three technologies in medicine: high technology, half-way technology, and nontechnology. Representatives of high technologies are immunology, enabling us to prevent diseases such as small pox, diphtheria, and polio; prevention of dental caries by fluoridation of water; insecticides to eliminate malaria and yellow fever; and antibiotics for the treatment of the most serious bacterial infectious diseases. Other examples of high technologies are hormones to treat endocrinological diseases such as diabetes and basic knowledge of metabolism to prevent or correct nutritional problems. There have also been developed surprisingly effective drugs for the treatment of specific symptoms such as pain. The point of all this is that the high technology of medicine has primarily evolved from the free exercise of human curiosity, that is, from basic science. These valuable things are byproducts of exploring minds aiming to understand nature as a foundation for medical technologies. The social good of this kind of high technology is obvious and the more specific and advanced the technology, the less expensive it becomes. For example, care of a case of typhoid fever before typhoid vaccination or chemotherapeutic treatment might well cost, at today's prices, $10,000, and tuberculosis, before the use of isoniazid and streptomycin, was a major killer and its cost for patient care was enormous. Following the discovery of these drugs in the late 1940s, vastly expensive tuberculosis hospitals simply became obsolete.

The half-way technology of medicine is seen in the burgeoning activities of surgeons involved in the removal and replacements of living or artificial parts with elaborate manipulations of immunosuppressive drugs to prevent or slow rejection of the transplants. If we knew more of the basic science of immunology, transplantation could become a reliable, simpler, and less expensive process. And, if we knew more about the chemistry of vascular disease, we could perhaps prevent the very diseases that require transplantation.

The surgical and radiational attack on cancer is also half-way technology. We would not need these if we had more knowledge of the basic disease processes to enable us to prevent malignancies or treat them with specific chemotherapy and by immunization. Decisions as to who will and who will not be treated, because the half-way technology is so complicated and expensive, raise harrowing ethical problems. Polio is now treated by high technology by discovery of its viral agent and successful immunization by inoculation. Twenty years ago it was treated by half-way technology—iron lungs—a frightfully expensive and tortuous procedure. Fifty years ago it had no technology.

Thomas points out the existence of a vast soggy area of the nontechnology of medicine which accounts for a substantial fraction of the cost of today's medicine. These are supportive treatments that the physician uses because he cannot do anything else. These would include treatment of diseases such as arthritis and emphysema, and of a host of psychosomatic disorders. Nontechnologies consume the largest portion of the physician's time, often stated to be as much as 70 to 80%. The ultimate in nontechnology is psychoanalysis.

Biological psychiatry aims to bring to bear on psychiatric problems the armamentaria of physics, chemistry, cell biology, neurophysiology, psychopharmacology, and genetics. From such approaches much has been learned, and much more will be learned, about behavior, both normal and abnormal, from which one may hope to see emerge advances in high technology for treatment of the mentally ill. As examples of high technology in this field, we have mentioned the treatment of psychoses due to pellagra, general paresis, and the brain-damaging phenylketonurea. To these should be added mongolism, which can be detected *in utero* by amniocentesis, and the defective embryo aborted. There are some 1,500 diseases associated with genetics, and of these, 415 have been linked to a single dominant gene and 300 to recessive genes (each of which is a harmless carrier until mating links two similar recessive alleles together). Many of the 1,500 disorders are a result of polygenic factors and many are associated with major behavior disturbances.

Today there is a growing body of information obtainable from amniocentesis and from blood and urinary determinations of parents and the newborn that can inform prospective parents of the likelihood they may have highly defective offspring or, as in some cases, an embryo certain to become a mongoloid child. Many of these fortunately rare genetic disorders show serious mental defects to that negative eugenics; i.e., the genetics of disease is especially pertinent to biological psychiatry. Schizophrenia is now clearly known to involve a strong genetic component but this has not yet yielded a new therapeutic technology, although one may expect it to do so in time. At present, psychosurgery is still experimental and needs more research. Its potentialities of developing into a high technology for psychiatric medicine are great, despite the hysterical opposition of some to its use.

These two volumes ably review many aspects of the rapidly advancing field of biological psychiatry and should serve as a guide to the oncoming generations of investigators.

Hudson Hoagland
President Emeritus
The Worcester Foundation for
Experimental Biology
Shrewsbury, Massachusetts

Editorial Preface

The title of this two-volume set has been chosen with care. It serves to indicate what we feel the nature of the contents to be, as well as to indicate what it is not. It should be understood, then, that the discussions presented deal with particular aspects of the biological foundations of behavior and its disorders. These volumes are not, nor were they intended to be, a textbook of "biological psychiatry." Such a book might follow, but it would, of necessity, have to be of a markedly different character. It would be a straight-forwardly clinical text, case oriented and designed to discuss the analysis and treatment of mental disorders on the basis of a medical rather than a psycho-analytic model.

It also must be pointed out that we are aware of serious omissions that interfere with both the continuity and the totality of the presentation. Such lacunae were not desired, nor were the areas of discussion they concern by any means less important. They occur only because of the realistic limita-tions of size. We have not been able to deal with all the phases of how genetic, environmental, and evolutionary factors influence brain structure and behavior of the individual; or with all the problems of consciousness and altered states thereof; or with myriad basic questions concerning relevant problems of synaptic activity, neurotransmitters, neuro- and other hormones, etc. The list could go on almost ad infinitum. We hope to deal with such problems, as well as with others, in more detail in future publica-tions.

Despite these difficulties, we have attempted to present certain major conceptual areas and "foundation stones" as a continuum. Thus we have begun with Dr. Rainer's basic discussion of genetics. It is out of these funda-mental, molecular, and genetic properties that the individual structural entities and functional mechanisms develop, which, in their relationship to the environment, form the core of the behavioral patterns of the organism.

The organismic-environmental continuum involves the operation of each on the other, and, at least from one point of view, brings us to questions concerning sensory processing, learning, memory, motivation, and so on. That is, we are led to inquire into cognitive mechanisms of the conscious organism, and, ultimately, into their malfunction, deficit, and disorder. Thus we have chosen to follow the genetic introduction with discussions dealing with such issues.

However, such physiological and psychophysiological considerations are not alone sufficient to clarify all the behavioral processes concerned. Both the organism and its environment undergo constant change during development.

Volume 2, primarily involving biochemistry and pharmacology, is devoted to problems either of or related to mental disorder. It is here that we begin to look at the application of the basic biological concepts and data to dysfunction and disease. Perhaps the greatest value of such attempts, at the present time, is to make clear the vast ignorance of both the basic scientist and the clinician, and to suggest the many paths of investigation that remain to be discovered and followed.

The final two chapters in Volume 2 deal with more theoretical aspects of the brain-mind system. The chapter by Grenell and McCulloch is a brief attempt to demonstrate the fundamental relationship of information processing to normal and abnormal behavior. The last chapter (Pribram) suggests what we hope ultimately will be the case; namely, that the time will come when such terms as "biological psychiatry" and "psychoanalytic" will no longer be needed; that biological and psychoanalytic concepts will not be considered as inimical and unrelenting, impossibly different views, but that one will be able to explain the other, and Freud's own predictions will be validated.

These volumes are the first in a series to be published under the aegis of the Society of Biological Psychiatry. We trust any omissions will be remedied in future volumes to appear as part of this major educational undertaking.

Many people have been invaluable in the production of this work. We must express our gratitude to the Society: to the other members of the Society's Committee on Publication of Educational Materials (Drs. David Kennard, Robert Heath, and John Paul Brady); to our contributing authors who agreed to help despite their 24-hour work days; and to numerous devoted people at Raven Press—particularly to Mrs. Virginia Martin, without whom many problems might never have been solved.

R. G. Grenell
and
S. Gabay

Pages from The History of the
Society of Biological Psychiatry

George N. Thompson

University of California, School of Medicine, Irvine, California 92664

Biological psychiatry is rooted deeply in the past. Some of its early origins may be traced to the Physiological Psychology of Wundt, Pavlovian Psychology, and even the early historical researches of Imhotep, Hippocrates, and other physicians interested in the biological foundations of psychiatry. We need not review the cultist excursions of psychiatry into the many ideologies of inventive minds. Through all of these offshoots, there has persisted through the centuries a fundamental series of truths that make up the central core of what we have named biological psychiatry.

The early part of the 20th century saw the development of great interest, coupled with the rapid expansion of socialist governments and, consequently, social sciences, in purely psychic speculations. The soma was almost abandoned. Despite the great interest of both scientists and the community in the social aspects of psychiatry, a small nucleus of "organically oriented" psychiatrists continued to stress the importance of the fundamental basic sciences in understanding and treating disorders of behavior and thinking.

One motivating purpose led to the founding of the Society of Biological Psychiatry, an innovation that occurred in Los Angeles, California. In 1944 two scientists who were both neurologists and psychiatrists, and who also were both research workers and clinicians, had intense interest in clinical cerebral localization of all psychological functions, as well as neurological aspects of human activity. They considered that all mental functioning had its origin in cerebral neuronal activity. This was, of course, not a new concept but was one that had long been neglected in psychiatric practice.

At the time of their completion of a textbook of psychiatry[1] with co-authorship, one of the authors, Thompson, proposed to the other, Nielsen, that there was no adequate forum for scientists with interests in the organic aspects of psychiatry to meet, exchange ideas, and express their points of view. There were in existence at that time (1944) a few organizations with specific localized interests but none with a broad comprehensive interest in the "neuronal basis of human behavior." Thompson's proposal was quickly adopted and a select group of nine founders were invited to form the nucleus of what was to become an international research organization and which was destined to profoundly influence the direction that psychiatry would take in the future. The original two scientists, George N. Thompson and Johannes M. Nielsen, expanded their number to nine.

It is of interest that all of the original nine were professors of psychiatry or psychiatry and neurology at their respective medical schools.

Many difficulties were encountered by this young organization, which held its first organizational meeting in the living room of Nielsen and Thompson at the Fairmont Hotel in San Francisco in June 1945. Nielsen served as its president for its first two years and Thompson served as its secretary-treasurer for 25 years and then as its President.

From its inception, the naming of the organization was a matter of particular interest to the "founding fathers." No less than 50 names were considered but always the name "Society of Biological Psychiatry" met with the greatest approval. I recall Spafford Ackerly from Louisville, Kentucky, saying, at a discussion of names, "Society of Biological Psychiatry—I like that." Numerous attempts were made by members to change the name, but it survived.

Rapidly the Society merged into itself related groups, The National Society of Medical Psychiatry, the Electroshock Research Association, the Carbon Dioxide Research Association, and others. The Society maintained a close liason with neurology and psychiatry by meeting just before the meeting of the American Psychiatric Association or the American Neurological Association on alternate years, but also met in conjunction with other groups. Research has always been stressed and its functions have encompassed both basic and clinical research.

The international nature of the Society was exemplified by its emblem with the words "International Research" and by its international membership. The schematic brain designed by James Papez, an early member, graces that emblem. Biological psychiatrists of all the world joined its ranks and attended its meetings. The founding members were neurologists, psychiatrists, and neurosurgeons. With the recognition of the contributions of other sciences to biological psychiatry, members in other fields were added rapidly, the only specific requirement (other than contributions to research), being an M.D. or a Ph.D. degree in a related field. The Society now numbers among its members neurologists, psychiatrists, neurosurgeons, psychologists, biochemists (including neuropsychopharmacologists), enzymologists, physicists, and others. It is through the interrelated efforts of these workers that the Society has achieved its greatness.

In response to a request from the American Psychiatric Association, the purposes of the Society were expressed in an article in the *American Journal of Psychiatry,* "The Society of Biological Psychiatry"[2]. It was specifically stated that membership should be limited to scientists interested in the biological basis of human behavior.

Although the Society of Biological Psychiatry itself is international in membership, it became apparent that scientists of many countries wished to have their own Societies and meetings. The first such Society was founded by one of our members, Dr. Schaude, who moved to Amsterdam and then founded the Dutch Society of Biological Psychiatry. There rapidly followed organizations of the Mexican, Argentinean, Japanese, and Scandinavian Societies which are actively sponsoring research and holding meetings.

It is a tribute to the energies and genius of the late Dr. Edmundo Fischer and his colleagues in Argentina that the Primero Congreso Mundial de Psiquiatria Biologica was organized and held in September 1974, in the beautiful city of Buenos Aires. At this congress, the World Federation of Biological Psychiatry was formed.

Significant milestones in the progress of the Society of Biological Psychiatry movement have been:

1. The establishing of committees to give impetus to research and other activities (1958).
2. The establishing of the annual A. E. Bennett Neuropsychiatric Foundation Research Awards in both basic and clinical psychiatry to encourage young workers in research in biological psychiatry (1958).
3. The Annual Foreign Guest Speaker Award sponsored by the Manfred Sakel Foundation of New York City (1959).
4. The amalgamation of other organizations, e.g., The American Society of Medical Psychiatry, into the Society, while maintaining its identity and purposes (1963–64).
5. The establishing of the Annual Gold Medal Award for the individual who has contributed most to the development of the science of Biological Psychiatry (1965).
6. The establishing of foreign and corresponding memberships (1969).
7. Joint meetings with other groups, e.g., The American Electroencephalographic Society, The Pavlovian Society, The American Medical Association, The American Psychiatric Association, The American Neurological Association, The American Neuropathological Association, The Canadian Neurological Association, International Psychosomatic Developmental Association, and others.
8. Liaison of the Society of Biological Psychiatry with newly established foreign Societies of Biological Psychiatry (1960–1975).

The founders of the Society always recognized that to survive, an organization must have a cause and a continuing developing purpose. There is a neverending cause and purpose of this Society, its continuing sponsorship of neverending and never completely achieved research—research into the biological basis of human behavior. In 1971 this writer wrote[3]: "It was with the hope of shining light on mental science and showing in true order and perspective the biological basis of human behavior, that this Society was founded. The Society was dedicated to scientists interested in the neuronal basis of human behavior." There has been no change from these objectives in the direction and goals of the Society.

At the time of organization of this Society, we said (1): "Psychiatry has developed an enormous superstructure and a tremendously complex culture without a foundation of material substance. It has been too poetic and too little factual." It is to be noted that the Society has set out and is attempting to build a foundation under that superstructure.

It has been noted that at the time of the founding of the Society, most of the interest of biologically oriented psychiatrists was in the field of cerebral localization. We searched for cerebral areas, cortical and subcortical, that mediated mental and personality function. At that time we hoped that, in time, the mapping of the entire cerebrum would solve all problems of mental illness. Here I quote from "Perspectives in Biological Psychiatry" (3):

> We were impressed by the finger-agnosia syndrome of Gerstmann; hemiachromatopsia, the loss of color recognition in one-half of the visual field; loss of the sense of motion; the simultanagnosia of Wolpert; the apperceptive blindness of the senile of Arnold Pick (atrophy of the occipital lobes causing total loss of power of identification through all senses.) The symbolic functions concerned with revisualization in the angular gyrus, Riddoch's syndrome of loss of interest and attention in homonymous half visual fields, Anton's syndrome of unawareness of blindness, Hughlings Jackson's "dreamy states" from irritation of the calcarine area 19, Henschen's postulate that all visual hallucinations are due to irritation of secondary and tertiary visual areas, Wernicke's area for recognition of sounds, astereognosis, or tactile agnosia, the dramatic anosagnosia of Babinski, the ideational apraxia of Nielsen [4] the complicated agnosias, such as the visual agnosias for symbols, the language formulation areas of the cortex, agraphia, alexia, all stimulated our belief that further mapping of the brain would solve psychiatric problems still unsolved.
>
> The importance of the frontal lobes relative to intellect and personality, Kleist's data concerning the "higher psychic functions of the orbital area," the evidence that the fundamental problems of personality are located in the hypothalamus, and Thompson's [5] discovery of the cerebral area essential to consciousness added weight to the importance of deeper brain structures in mental function. James Papez's discovery (following Karl Kleist) of the importance of the cingulate gyrus in emotion, and of the functions of the limbic system was another landmark in the cerebral localization of mental function.

We note that a marked change in the direction of research occurred, from the mapping of cortical areas, to the biochemistry of the brain. A new science of psychopharmacology was born. A rapid progression of discoveries of psychopharmacological agents occurred with dizzying speed. There rapidly appeared upon the horizon the phenothiazines, reserpine, lithium, imipramine, butyrophenone, *d*-lysergic acid, meprobamate, monoamine oxidase inhibitors, amphetamine, benzodiazepine, diphenylhydantoin, thioxanthene, the tricyclic antidepressants, and others. Other therapies, insulin coma, and electroconvulsive treatment rapidly diminished in frequency of use and in research.

The development of these agents in treatment brought forth a new question or resurrected an old one: How and why do these agents alter mental function? Is all mental illness the result of biochemical or faulty metabolism or due to genetic errors in biochemistry?

With the development of psychopharmacologic agents, and as a part of this development, there occurred an increased interest in the hormones and then the enzymes of the brain. Startling discoveries were the correlations of mental disease with discoveries of enzyme functions. The historical perspectives of this Society point to great advances in the future. We can now say with confidence, as did Ingham, that all psychology is physiology. The recent statement by a prominent psychoanalyist that "biological psychiatry seems to be the force of the future" (anonymous), points to the directions that history has taken us. We are the disciples of history and the truth of science is our leader.

The importance of molecular biology on the future of biological psychiatry is almost beyond any perspective. The importance of chemical shifts within individual nerve cells indicates possibilities for the future.

As Dr. Spafford Ackerly indicated when he said, "Biological Psychiatry— I like that," so have others, as evidenced by the recently organized Societies in many countries. Likewise, the titles of recent meetings show the impact of biological psychiatry on psychiatry as a whole. In October, 1969, Loyola University Medical Center's symposium was entitled, "The Brain and Human Behavior." A recent meeting in Baltimore was entitled, "Discoveries in Biological Psychiatry." The California Institute of Technology gave a conference entitled, "Biological Bases of Human Behavior." I cannot end this historical summary without expressing a moving *bienvenido* to all including scientists from another hemisphere. "The international character of our Society and its membership has been stressed by our emblem with international research underlining the neuronal connections of an early member's brain drawing, that of Dr. James Papez. The Society of Biological Psychiatry has elected to membership a group of Russian scientists. I received most interesting letters of appreciation from them, and was quite moved by a letter from Professor I. S. Beritashvili, of the Institute of Physiology, Georgian Academy of Sciences, who wrote in part, "I wish to thank you very much for the great honour you have done me in electing me a corresponding member of the Society of Biological Psychiatry . . . Please convey my sincere gratitude to the Council of the Society for the great honour they have done me . . . May the Society of Biological Psychiatry be as successful in the cognition of behavior of normal and diseased minds as your countrymen have been in the cognition of the moon."

The future of scientific psychiatry is the future of biological psychiatry.

REFERENCES

1. Nielsen, J. M., and Thompson, G. N. (1947): *The Engrammes of Psychiatry.* Thomas, Springfield, Ill.
2. Thompson, G. N. (1954): The society of biological psychiatry. *Am. J. Psychiatry,* 111:5.
3. Thompson, G. N. (1971): Perspectives in biological psychiatry. *Biol. Psychiatry,* 3:3–8.
4. Nielsen, J. M. (1941): *A Textbook of Clinical Neurology.* Hoeber, New York.
5. Thompson, G. N. (1951): Cerebral area essential to consciousness. *Bull. LA Neurol. Soc.,* 16:4.

Biological Foundations of Psychiatry,
edited by R. G. Grenell and S. Gabay.
Raven Press, New York © 1976.

Introduction

J. C. Eccles

Department of Physiology, State University of New York, Medical School, Buffalo, New York 14220

More than ever before, brain research is being recognized as the ultimate scientific challenge confronting mankind. Every since the realization of his existence, man has been trying to understand what he is, the meaning of his life, and how to conquer and control the land, air, and water that are the bases of his existence of this small planet. And now it would be agreed that the brain is central to the life of man. But for man's brain, no cosmological or environmental problems would exist. "The whole drama of the cosmos would be played out before empty stalls. . . ." A better understanding of the brain is certain to lead man to a richer comprehension of himself, of his fellow man, and of society, and, in fact, of the whole world with its problems. However, the whole story of the wonderful development of man and his brain has a somber side as well. It is as if evolution has overplayed the biological story by developing a system so complex and subtle that it had within it the threat of malfunction on a scale that could overwhelm all of the inbuilt biological controls that ensured the stable and normal functioning of brains of even the higher animals. It is here that we encounter the problem of biological psychiatry, which is the theme of this handbook. The marvelous creative process of evolution has resulted in human brains which are so subtle and sensitive in their functioning that psychiatric disorders become more and more of a problem for the highly developed societies in our most sophisticated civilizations.

The human brain is without any qualification the most complexly organized structure in the universe. The brains of higher mammals appear to be not greatly inferior in structure and in most aspects of operational performance. Yet there is something very special about the human brain. It has a performance in relationship to culture, to consciousness, to language, to memory, that uniquely distinguishes it from even the most highly developed brains of other animals. It is certainly beyond our comprehension how these subtle properties came to be associated with a material structure that owes its origin to the biological process of evolution. Our brains give us all our experiences and memories, our imaginations, our dreams. Furthermore, it is through our brains that each of us can plan and carry out actions and so achieve expression in the world as, for example, I am doing now in writing this account. For each of us, our brain is the material basis of our personal identity—distinguished by our selfhood and our character. In summary, it gives for each of us the essential "me." Yet when all this is said, we are still only at the beginning of comprehending the mystery of our being.

In the various sections of this handbook, it will be appreciated that it is convenient in the first place to investigate the brain of man as we would a machine, but, of course, a special kind of machine of a far higher order of complexity in performance than any machine designed by man—even the most complex of computers. There are several major fields of study. First, there are structural studies—the components from which it is built and how they are related to each other. Second, there are functional studies—the neurochemistry and biophysics of the simplest components, the nerve cells. Third, there are operational studies—the synaptic linkage of individual nerve cells into levels of organization from the simplest to the ever-more complex. However, we are still at a very early stage of our attempt at understanding the brain, which is the last of all the frontiers of knowledge that man can attempt to overpass and encompass. Vigorous and exciting new disciplines emerge in such fields as neurogenesis, neurocommunications, neurochemistry, and neuro-pharmacology.

NEUROANATOMY: NEURON, SYNAPSE, AND NEUROGENESIS

It was first proposed by Ramón y Cajal, the great Spanish neuroanatomist, that the nervous system is made up of neurons, which are isolated cells, not joined together in some syncytium (the reticular theory of Gerlach), but each one independently living its own biological life. This concept is called the *neuron theory*. This theory achieved a functional meaning when Sherrington developed the concept of the synapse by means of which one nerve cell communicated with another by having its axonal branches terminating in synaptic knobs on dendrites of a neuron next in series. The new technique of electron microscopy has illuminated the structure of the neuron and the synapse in a manner beyond the wildest dreams of Ramón y Cajal and Sherrington.

The individuality of the neuron is strikingly shown by the continuity of the membrane that completely encloses it, even at the zones of functional contact. The intactness of the membrane even holds at the so-called gap junction, where there is tight apposition at the synaptic contact. The membranes of each component can be traced right through this intimate apposition. With the chemical transmitting synapses, there is, of course, a synaptic cleft of 200 to 300 Å across, completely separating the synaptic ending from the recipient neuronal surface.

Other important new discoveries arising from electron microscopy are the synaptic vesicles, which can now be accepted as packages of the specific chemical transmitter substances. Electron microscopy is even giving evidence that relates to the manner in which these vesicles are organized in the synaptic knob so that they are available for ejecting their contents into the synaptic cleft when there is activation by the presynaptic impulse. Electron microscopy also gives intriguing evidence as to how the synaptic vesicles are recharged after they have ejected their contents into the synaptic cleft. In that way, the synaptic knob becomes the seat of an on-going biological process of transmitter generation, storage, and release.

The building of the nervous system provides the most wonderful example of organic growth. As we study each stage in the development of the brain from the earliest embryonic period onward, we are confronted by a most dramatic story. The primitive cells of the neural plate multiply, eventually forming nerve cells that grow connections to other nerve cells. It is an almost infinitely complex programmed performance, as if there were some supremely intelligent conductor in command. Yet, it is believed that this development up to every detail of the fully formed brain is the result of the genetic instructions coded in deoxyribonucleic acid (DNA) and also of the various secondary instructions that at all stages of development guide the neuronal growth by specific chemical sensing. All of this detailed connectivity is established before there is any organized activity of the brain.

Research work on the building of the nervous system is now being carried out at a high level of scientific expertise. The growth of fragments isolated from embryonic brain is under intensive study. Electron microscopic investigations aid greatly in evaluating the stages of development of nerve cells. Various kinds of chemical, viral, and radiation lesions are used in order to destroy specific components of the developing nervous system and to study the reactions to such lesions. Powerful techniques of radiolabeling have now been applied with great success to the understanding of neurogenesis in sites that are particularly favorable for rigorous investigation. Radioisotopes are incorporated in nuclei of germinal cells prior to the mitosis that generates neuroblasts; nerve cells developed from these neuroblasts can be identified over long periods of time by the radiolabel they carry. Thus, we are beginning to understand how defects arise in brain development. From this will come the rational treatment of congenital defects in the brain arising from mutational, enzymatic, or genetic disorders.

NEUROPHYSIOLOGY: IMPULSES AND SYNAPTIC TRANSMISSION

Investigations on the functional performance of the nervous system have been carried out for many decades, but only in the last 20 years have the microelectrode techniques been effectively utilized. These techniques are now the most important in all investigations concerning the operation of the nueronal machinery, both in localized regions of interaction and also in the long and complex neuronal pathways at all levels of the brain. The various modes of communication between nerve cells across their regions of close contact (the synapses) are now well understood. There are several regions of the brain, such as the cerebellum, which are fairly well understood structurally and functionally. For example, in the cerebellum all the neuronal constituents are recognized, and their synaptic connections have been established. However, much more investigation is required as to the organization of the neuronal systems operating more widely and in the more complex integrations. This is even true for the afferent and efferent pathways of the cerebellum. But it is at the highest level of the brain, the cerebral cortex, that the greatest challenges exist.

A most important development for the future is concerned with the analysis of the firing frequencies of the individual nerve cells. These are the basic units of the brain, both structurally and functionally, the total for the human brain being in the order of some tens of thousands of millions. In any one zone of the brain there are, of course, multitudes of similar nerve cells so that the observations of single cells can be regarded as a valid sampling procedure. Our laboratory has been particularly concerned with this study of the individual units as evidenced by their impulse discharges. These discharges are unitary signals, and one can in the first instance think of the nervous system as being made up of this multitude of units that communicate by impulse transmission. That is, one must regard the nervous system as being designed essentially for the purpose of conveying and integrating information that is encoded in these patterns of impulse discharge.

It will be appreciated that there are many practical applications of these electrophysiological investigations. For example, electrical recording from the brain produces the electroencephalogram, which provides information about brain disorders, such as epilepsy. This information is of great value in the diagnosis, localization, and treatment. Another important application is in the electrical recording from peripheral nerves and muscles, which leads to a diagnosis and understanding of many disorders of movement.

PHARMACOLOGY: CHEMICAL TRANSMITTERS

A survey of the contributions to this field of scientific investigation shows how central neuropharmacology is to so much of psychiatric practice. One feels there is an almost unlimited future in the discovery of more and more effective pharmacological controls of mental disorders. Basically, we have the concept that the neuronal surfaces are covered by receptor sites for specific molecules. Some of these receptor sites are, of course, functionally effective at synapses in giving the selective response to the respective transmitter substances. However, it has now been clearly shown that neuronal surfaces have specific receptor sites not related to synaptic actions, being, in fact, related to molecules that are not at all involved in synaptic actions on those particular neurons. These new insights into the pharmacological properties of neuronal membranes have been developed primarily by the techniques of neuropharmacology with the electrophoretic application of substances to the exteriors of neuronal surfaces. The responses of the neurons are assayed by the changes in their background firing frequency. This technique is one of great subtlety and has completely transformed out concepts of the actions of drugs upon nerve cells.

This work has, of course, been specially applied to the problem of identification of specific substances that act as synaptic transmitters in the central nervous system. Several of these transmitters are now known with reasonable assurance: acetylcholine, glycine, γ-aminobutyric acid, and norepinephrine. Many more have yet to be discovered or more convincingly displayed, such as dopamine, serotonin, glutamate, and the polypeptide, substance P. There is a most important field of investigation in studying the manufacture, emission, and removal of these nervous transmitters. Essentially we still operate conceptually with the key–lock model, both of transmitter action at the *receptor sites* on surface membranes of nerve cells and of its simulation or blocking by pharmacological agents. The most sophisticated example of this key–lock concept is in the molecular models that Smythies constructs for the various membrane receptors and in the ionic channels they control.

There is an immense future in this field of pharmacological control of neuronal systems. One can predict with assurance that there will be great successes in the efforts to develop specific chemical substances that have unique controlling action upon particular aspects of brain function. The great improvements in anesthetics can be mentioned, and already there are very effective controls of epileptic seizures, of parkinsonism, and of the peripheral paralysis of myasthenia gravis.

Because so much of this handbook is concerned with the drug treatment of psychiatric disorders, it is necessary only to make passing reference to the tremendously important new developments in this field. It is a great challenge to discover chemical substances that have specific actions upon classes of neurons so that the responses of these neurons can be raised or lowered by the applied drug. There is the general belief that more specificity of drug action may be obtained by utilizing pharmacological substances that are not the actual synaptic transmitters, but which are analogs of these transmitters. It is a great challenge to organic chemists to develop a systematic understanding of the way in which the molecular structure relates to drug action, and in that way to develop "tailor-made" molecules with highly specific therapeutic functions.

Of course, grave dangers are associated with the introduction of new drugs in psychiatric treatment, as witness the introduction of LSD into this country. The specific pharmacological actions of hallucinogens, for example, are utilized by individuals with a consequent development of psychotic disorders and even destruction of their personalities. Nevertheless, in this respect, one can have hope that substances will be discovered that can effectively counteract drug addiction. The more knowledge we have in this field the more we will be able to control these disorders.

Neurochemistry is developing in an amazing manner through the utilization of the many microchemical procedures and radiotracer techniques. These techniques are so refined that investigations can be carried out even on single cells. Some aspects of neurochemistry are very closely related to neurophysiology and neuropharmacology because they are concerned with the molecular structure of membranes, with chemical transport of specific protein, for example, along nerve fibers, and with the synaptic receptor sites and associated channels for transport of such ions as sodium, calcium, potassium, and chloride. Other key problems of neurochemistry concern the manufacture both of the specific synaptic transmitters and of the specific receptor sites for these transmitters. Neurochemistry will ultimately illuminate the problems of trophic influences between nerve cells and the surface sensing that is postulated as forming the basis of all the specific connectivities that are established between nerve cells in the process of neurogenesis. Moreover, there are many other fields of neurochemical investigation in which studies are made of enzyme systems and metabolic cycles. The brain has a very high metabolism, which is, to a large extent, concerned with the operation of pumps that actively move such ions as potassium and sodium across the surface membranes of nerve cells. These ionic pumps are involved in maintaining the correct ionic composition of nerve cells and the associated electrical potentials across their surface membranes. Metabolic energy is also required for pushing the trophic substances along the fibers. Despite the high metabolism of the nervous system, about 20% of the basal metabolic rate, the average energy per nerve cell is extremely low, about 3×10^{-10} w.

NEURONAL CONNECTIVITY

Neurocommunication is essentially concerned with the transfer and integration of information. The patterns of impulse frequency referred to under the section on Neurophysiology provide the raw material for theoretical developments of neurocommunications theory. However, it must be recognized that the nervous system does not operate simply by single lines of communication, but rather by multitudes of lines in parallel; superimposed upon this is an amazing complexity of dynamic loop operations with all manner of feedback controls and cross-linkages. In considering neurogenesis, we have to envisage principles of design that extract precision of performance from a structure operating with much background noise, much as in tape recorders and gramophone records, and the many aberrancies of connectivities that would be expected of a biological system that has grown in the manner outlined. Furthermore, attempts are being made to understand the mode of operation of neuronal systems through the construction of computer models designed to give simulated performance and at the same time to embody the principles of design that have been discovered in the neuronal systems.

It is of special interest to biological psychiatrists that fundamental new concepts are being developed with regard to the neuronal connectivities in the cerebral cortex. It has been recognized for more than a decade that in some regions of the cerebral cortex the neurons are arranged in columns that subserve specific integrational purposes. For example, these columns have been demonstrated in the somesthetic cortex and in the visual cortex, where they are specified for sensory modalities or for orientations of lines in the visual field. Recently, neuroanatomists, particularly Szentágothai, have been analyzing the neuronal connectivities in these columns and have proposed that they are analogous to integrating microcircuits of electronics, but, of course, they are much more complex. It can be recognized that these columns act as powerful amplification units with a great deal of vertical excitatory action between the neurons in the column. Furthermore, it is recognized that each column contains inhibitory neurons that act upon adjacent columns. Thus, we can envisage the cerebral cortex as being made up of a mosaic of columns of the order of 1,000,000 for the human cerebrum, each one of which is a power unit with inhibitory action upon adjacent columns and, of course, transmission of its own excitatory level to other columns by virtue of its efferent association fibers. In addition to this neuronal mosaic from laminae 3 to 6, there is a finer, more superficial mosaic arrangement in the columns of laminae 1 and 2. There has been little physiological investigation relating to these new anatomical insights. However, it can be appreciated that there is evident need of experimental investigations, both anatomical and functional. In order to understand further the mode of operation of the cerebral cortex in all of its transcendent performances, one can anticipate many decades of investigation in this most important of all scientific endeavors.

MEMORY AND BEHAVIOR

Investigations on memory have tended to develop in two quite separate ways. One line of investigation is physiological and has a counterpart in neuroanatomy. It is concerned with the effect of use and disuse on synaptic efficacy and an attempt to correlate such changes with the growth and breakdown of synapses. In the incredibly complex communication system of the brain, each memory must involve some stabilization of specific channels within it. Some sensory input, something seen or heard, for example, would thus be able to trigger a whole series of patterned activities which are much the same as those produced by an earlier input of the same kind. One can say that this replaying in the brain results in the remembrance in the mind. The other line of investigation is particularly concerned with the postulated chemical mechanisms of memory and seeks to discover specific chemical molecules that have a unique relationship, each with a specific memory. This work can be criticized because it is not effectively correlated with neuroanatomy and neurophysiology, and because it provides no basis for recall, which is the essence of memory. Nevertheless, the chemical investigations are of importance because with any explanation of memory there must be some neuronal change that has a chemical and metabolic basis. For example, there is now good evidence that long-term memories cannot be laid down if the enzymes responsible for protein synthesis in the brain are inactivated. As is to be expected, even the ribonucleic acid (RNA) responsible for the production of these enzymes is also essentially concerned in the laying down of long-term memory traces.

One of the most important lines of investigation on the neuronal mechanism for memory utilizes electron microscopic studies for revealing the synaptic changes responsible for memory. There have been several good investigations of this type that demonstrate atrophy of synapses under conditions of prolonged disuse. It is more difficult to design experiments that will display the effects of increased synaptic usage. Such changes as synaptic hypertrophy or increased synaptic function by the formation of secondary synapses would be expected. Hitherto great difficulties have been encountered in designing and employing suitable experimental methods for giving prolonged synaptic usage to specific regions. The experimental design should enable comparisons to be made between control areas and areas subjected to prolonged intense activity. Another possibility is that increased usage of synapses does not itself promote the synaptic hypertrophy, but this is a result of a conjunction of synaptic action on a neuron, one type of synapse acting to call forth a hypertrophy in another type by some conjunction process. Theories of this kind are very attractive because they allow for much more specificity in synaptic growth and therefore in the learning process. However, the experimental evidence is still indirect. The design of experiments for direct testing has proved to be rather difficult. There is no need for a special account of behavior in this introduction because so many of the contributions are written by experts in the field.

THE BRAIN–MIND PROBLEM

During the last decade, remarkable studies have been made by Sperry and his associates on patients in whom uncontrollable epilepsy made it necessary to cut the great commissure (the corpus callosum) connecting their two cerebral hemispheres. In all subjects, the speech center was in the left hemisphere, which was the dominant hemisphere, as is almost always the case. It was shown that all conscious experiences of the subject were derived from neuronal events in this dominant hemisphere. The minor hemisphere could program a wide variety of skilled responses, but none of these goings-on in that hemisphere gave conscious experience to the subject. Evidently, the speech and associated ideational areas of the dominant hemisphere are the only parts of the brain that give conscious experiences to the subject. This remarkable finding is of the greatest importance both neurologically and philosophically.

Consequently, there is strong evidence that we have to associate the dominant hemisphere, i.e, the speech hemisphere, with the amazing property of being able to give rise to conscious experiences in perception, and also to receive from them in the carrying out of willed movements. Moreover, the most searching investigation discloses that the minor hemisphere does not have in the smallest degree this amazing property of being in liaison with the conscious mind of the subject with respect to either giving or receiving. One would predict with assurance that in subjects with the rarely occurring right hemispheric representation of speech, the right hemisphere would be dominant, as revealed after the callosal transection, and would be solely associated with the conscious experiences of the subject.

The unique association of speech and consciousness with the dominant hemisphere gives rise to the question: Is there some special anatomical structure in the dominant hemisphere that is not matched in the minor hemisphere? In general, the two hemispheres are regarded as being mirror images at a crude anatomical level, but recently it has been discovered that in about 80% of human brains there are asymmetries with special developments of the cerebral cortex in the regions both of the anterior and posterior speech areas. However, apart from such differences at a macrolevel, one must assume that there are specially fine structural and functional properties as the basis for the linguistic performance of these speech areas. Undoubtedly, most exciting work awaits the investigation of these areas by electron microscopic techniques. It can be anticipated that eventually there will be electrophysiological analysis of the on-going events in the speech areas of conscious subjects whose brains are exposed for some therapeutic purpose. In the evolution of man, there must have been most remarkable developments in the neuronal structure of the cerebral cortex, which have made possible the evolution of speech. One can imagine that progressively more subtle linguistic performance gave primitive men the opportunities for very effective survival, which may be regarded as a strong evolutionary pressure. As a consequence, there were the marvelously rapid evolutionary changes transforming in 1 to 2 million years a primitive ape to the present human race.

In a remarkable new conceptual development arising from study of split-brain subjects, Levy-Agresti and Sperry have proposed that the dominant and minor hemispheres have a division in their operational tasks. It is suggested that this division of tasks enables each hemisphere to perform its particular general mode of processing information before there is synthesis and eventual appearance as conscious experience. Because neural events in the minor hemisphere do not give the subject conscious experiences directly, we have to postulate that the neuronal machinery involved in these specific operational tasks works at an unconscious level, which would be in good agreement with the psychiatric concept of the unconscious mind. For example, in listening to music it can be envisaged that initially immense and complex operational tasks such as decoding, synthesizing, and patterning are carried out in the temporal lobe of the minor hemisphere. Communication via the corpus callosum to the liaison areas of the dominant hemisphere with the consequent conscious experiences presumably is delayed until these most sophisticated neural operations have been carried out in the special musical centers. In their operational function, these centers can be regarded as being analogous to the speech centers, but as yet they await a systematic and comprehensive neurological investigation.

The split-brain investigations have, in the opinion of the author, falsified the psychoneural identity hypothesis. It is demonstrated that the minor cerebral hemisphere, with its on-going activities that can be categorized as displaying memory, understanding even at a primitive verbal level, and concepts of spatial relationships, does not give any conscious experiences to the subject, who remains in conscious liaison only with neural events in the dominant hemisphere. Evidently, the concept of psychoneural identity has lost its primitive simplicity of identification of neural activities of the brain in general with conscious experiences derived therefrom. In particular, sophisticated, intelligent, and learned activities of the minor hemisphere do not achieve liaison to the consciousness of the subject. Moreover, as Sperry has realized, the problems must be approached at a new level of understanding, the holistic approach. This occurs only in special regions of the cerebral cortex and in special states of these regions. Moreover, psychoneural parallelism must be rejected, for according to this view the mental states are ineffective, being mere spin-offs of neural activities that they cannot influence.

Evidently, immense and fundamental problems are involved in the evolution of the brain, which occurred as man was gradually developing his means of communication through speech. One can imagine that speech and brain development went on together in the evolving process, and that from these two emerged the cultural performance of man. Over hundreds of millenia, there must have been a progressive development of language from its primitive form as expressive cries to a language that became a gradually more and more effective means of description and argument. In this way, by forging linguistic communication of ever-increasing precision and subtlety, man must gradually have become a self-conscious being aware of his own identity or selfhood. As a consequence, he also became aware of death, as witnessed so frequently and vividly in other members of the tribal group whom he recognized as beings like himself. We do not know how early in the story of man this tragic and poignant realization of death-awareness came to him, but it was at least a hundred thousand years ago, as evidenced by the ceremonial burial customs.

EPILOGUE

At the present time, we can think of the total problem of brain operation as a pile of disconnected fragments of a jigsaw puzzle with only a relatively few fragments pieced together to give a meaningful understanding; but every year many more intelligible pictures emerge as pieces of the puzzle are put into position, and special successes occur when various small organized regions are seen to fit together giving a still larger understanding. At present, it can be stated that all of the various fields of investigation outlined above are being very effectively pursued in many laboratories throughout the world, but much more effort could be fruitfully used. It is important to recognize that brain research is not a restricted field of scientific investigation. It involves a study of the most complex structure in nature, the understanding of which will require the highest intellectual efforts, not only of experts in the various biological disciplines specified here, but also of theoreticians from all the physical sciences, particularly in the fields of mathematics, chemistry, biophysics, and bioengineering.

Biological Foundations of Psychiatry,
edited by R. G. Grenell and S. Gabay.
Raven Press, New York © 1976.

Genetics in Behavior and Psychiatry

John D. Rainer

722 W. 168th St., New York, N.Y. 10032

I. HISTORY OF THE RELATION BETWEEN GENETICS AND PSYCHIATRY

Psychiatry has not always been considered a biologic discipline; if its foundation in scientific biology seems assured today, much of the credit must go to the increased appreciation of the role of genetics in the behavioral sciences. Genetics of course is now firmly based in biophysics and biochemistry, in cell biology, population dynamics, and ultimately in the grand cybernetic scheme of evolution.

The development of psychiatry as a responsible medical specialty actually took place during the same decades that saw the rise of modern genetics. Both of them moved from inexact, sometimes fanciful, eclecticism to more scientifically oriented disciplines based on observation, classification, and experimental technique. But until comparatively recently, the two fields remained separated, partly because the unifying concepts that could define the interactions between man and nature had not clearly emerged, partly because human genetics had yet to develop its more powerful techniques, and partly because many behavioral scientists felt that genetics could only interfere with their melioristic aims. Thus, in the mental sciences, hereditary and environmental influences were for many years considered antithetical and mutually exclusive, the ancient dichotomies of nature and nurture, of matter and mind, reigned, and biologic and psychologic disciplines remained distinct.

It is the nature of history to date progress according to the names of its major synthesizers; yet pre-Mendelian genetics goes back at least to Aristotle and pre-Kraepelinian psychiatry to Hippocrates and Galen. Before the rediscovery and confirmation in 1900 of Mendel's observations made 35 years earlier, cytologists had described the fertilization of the ovum and recognized the role of the chromosomes in cell division and Weissman had formulated the germ-plasm theory. Darwin had already established the general principles of evolution, although its mechanisms still remain to be understood completely.

Among early psychiatrists, such figures as Morel and Magnan contributed to the clinical system put together by Kraepelin, whose scheme provided subsequent generations with a first approximation to a descriptive nosology for biologic investigation to build upon. Yet when it came to etiology, the pendulum swung back and forth, for many years dividing behavioral scientists into biologically and psychologically minded groups, since heredity and environment were thought of as separate and distinct forces. In the United States, the major role was usually given to psychogenic or environmental forces and Watson's behaviorism and Meyer's psychobiology stressed the predominant role of external influences in molding behavior and lifestyle. When psychoanalysis moved from Europe to America before and after World War II, there was a tendency to stress its concern with trauma and conflict and to overlook the attention of such pioneers as Freud (1958, 1964) and Jones (1951) to inborn differences. There were a few psychoanalysts of that generation who did consider constitutional predispositions; Hartmann (1950) studied inborn characteristics of the ego, and Rado (1956) considered genetics and physiology as the foundation stones of the science of psychodynamics.

Clinical psychiatric research provided some early American family and twin studies of the major psychoses by Rosanoff, Handy, Plesset, and Brush (1934) and by Pollock, Malzberg, and Fuller (1939), which aimed at assessing the genetic role. However, it was the publication of Kallmann's *The Genetics of Schizophrenia* (1938) based on his Berlin family study, and of his paper "The Genetic Theory of Schizophrenia" (1946) based on his New York State twin investigation, that first sharply divided and then gradually alerted American psychiatrists to the essential interacting role of genetic factors. In the course of his influential career, first in Germany and then at the New York State Psychiatric Institute, Kallmann and his associates studied and wrote on many subjects, among which were schizophrenia, affective psychoses, male homosexuality, various forms of mental deficiency, genetics of aging and longevity, tuberculosis and its association with schizophrenia, early total deafness, chromosome disarrangements, and genetic counseling (Kallmann, 1953a; Rainer, 1966).

European psychiatry had developed its own tradition of psychiatric genetics, particularly in Germany, England, and Scandinavia. A major center developed at the Max Planck Institute in Munich, which was founded by Kraepelin; genetics there grew under Rüdin and Schulz, whose names are associated with the earliest family-risk studies in psychotic disorder. Through this school passed many well-known figures including Kallmann and Slater. In England the Galton Laboratory under Fisher, Haldane, and Penrose pioneered in biometric aspects of human genetics, while the Psychiatric Genetics Research Unit of the Medical Research Council at the Maudsley Hospital flourished under Slater's direction and influence.

Political events and the horror of Nazi pseudoeugenics put into disrepute the scientific exploration of genetic contributions to behavior, and in some areas, notably the problem of intelligence, there is still much heated misunderstanding. However, new biologic techniques and sophisticated conceptual frameworks have more recently made the role of genetics in psychiatry one that is constructive and fully compatible with human rights, values, and individuality. These new developments are described in more detail; they include mathematical and experimental models of genetic diversity in populations, the concept of interaction among genes, the contributions of chromosomal (cytogenetic) studies to the understanding of concerted gene action, the elaboration of the structure of the DNA molecule and the genetic code, and the still unfathomed mechanisms for controlling gene expression according to the needs of the changing organism in its changing environment.

Psychiatric and behavioral genetics is now beginning to draw on these broadening conceptions while turning its attention to some of its own neglected paths. These new directions include the experimental study of individual differences in strains of animals, from drosophila to dogs, and recognition of individual differences in humans from the neonatal period on, measured in behavioral terms or according to metabolic and pharmacologic distinctions. Investigations of families and twins have been supplemented by enzyme analysis and linkage studies in search of genetic markers and by adoption studies and longitudinal observations to tease out the role of the environment. The number of reviews and textbooks in psychiatric genetics (Kallmann, 1962; Rosenthal and Kety, 1968; Rosenthal, 1970; Slater and Cowie, 1971;

Erlenmeyer-Kimling, 1972) and behavior genetics (Fuller and Thompson, 1960; Vandenberg, 1965; Ehrman, Omenn, and Caspari, 1972; Thiessen, 1972) has grown almost geometrically in the past two decades and attests to the healthy rapprochement that has brought genetics and the behavioral sciences together toward a common biologic goal.

II. GENETICS TODAY—CURRENT AREAS OF RESEARCH

A. Cytogenetics

One of the more recent and most graphic segments of human genetic research has been the still-developing field of cytogenetics. When, in the mid 1950s, it became feasible to demonstrate human chromosomes in laboratory preparations, the way was cleared for the dramatic elucidation of certain classic deficiency syndromes with physical and behavioral characteristics. At the same time, new avenues of research began to open, promising better knowledge of gene localization, metabolic intermediaries, and eventually the general effect of chromosomes on behavior.

It was during the 35 years in the latter half of the nineteenth century during which Mendel's findings remained obscured that Waldeyer and others described chromosomes—specially staining thread-like bodies in the cell nucleus that were replicated in the process of cell division and were distributed to the daughter cells as exact duplicates. In the formation of germ cells, each cell received only half of the chromosomes in the parental cells. These facts turned out to be consistent with the statistical findings of Mendel, and thus it became possible to combine data derived from breeding experiments with the microscopic study of cells and chromosomes.

More recently, an important chance discovery foreshadowed later developments in this field when Barr and Bertram (1949) described an important morphologic difference between interphase cells of females and of males. First described in neurons of the cat, but soon observed in more easily obtained cells in other mammals including man, a densely staining basophilic chromatin mass could be seen on the inner surface of the nuclear membrane in females, but not in males. The laboratory determination of sex chromatin in the human is generally performed by examining a smear of buccal mucosal cells, scraped gently from the inside of the mouth, placed on slides, fixed, and stained. From 100 to 200 cells are counted, and the chromatin mass is visible as a lens-shaped body. Depending on the stain used, the source of the specimen, and the laboratory, from 30 to 60% of the cells of a normal female show the dark-staining mass, referred to as sex chromatin or a Barr body. In 1954 a corresponding sex difference was discovered in polymorphonuclear leucocytes, where an additional small lobe is found in approximately 2% of cells in females and in less than 0.2% of cells in males. Because of its shape, this small lobe was called a "drumstick."

In the normal female with two X chromosomes, the sex chromatin body appears to consist of all or part of one X chromosome—the one that replicates late in cell division—which has been modified, suppressed, or totally "inactivated." This process ensures only a single active X chromosome in each cell. According to Lyon (1962), this inactivation takes place in all cells in the early life of the female embryo, it being a matter of chance whether the paternally derived or maternally derived chromosome is inactivated in any given cell. Henceforward, the female is a "mosaic" with approximately 50% of her cells having the paternal X active, the other 50%, the maternal.

Subsequently, Tjio and Levan (1956) made use of improved methods for observing human chromosomes microscopically to report the correct number as 46. Previously *in vivo* preparations usually contained few mitotic cells, and these suffered from degenerative changes as well as superimposition of chromosomes, making accurate count difficult. In fact for many years it was believed that man had 48 chromosomes.

With the introduction of tissue culture methods, there became available a source of many cells in the process of mitotic division, the stage in which the chromosomes are distinguishable. Since the process quickly goes on to cell division and the chromosomes again become indistinct, treatment of the culture with colchicine to arrest the cells in the metaphase stage was instituted. Then, to avoid clumping, suspension of the cells in hypotonic solution was found to swell the nuclei, spreading the chromosomes and separating them before final fixation and staining of the cells in slide or cover-slip preparations.

Scanning the field under low power, it is possible to see "spreads," chromosomal complements in which each chromosome is revealed as an X-shaped or V-shaped body, actually a single chromosome in the process of dividing with each chromatid still joined to its replica at the centromere.

These procedures were first applied to skin biopsy material; they are now most practically used with lymphocytes of peripheral blood. In 72 hr in appropiate media and proper temperature, such cultures will have divided; the rate of such division being increased considerably by the addition of phytohemagglutin at the outset. This substance apparently acts as an antigenic stimulus to the proliferation of lymphocytes.

After preparing the slides, the spreads can be photographed under oil immersion and the chromosomes cut out and arranged in standardized order, to produce a visual representation of the chromosome complement, or karyotype. The chromosomes can be distinguished by size and position of the centromere (median, submedian, or toward one end, with the chromosomes correspondingly termed metacentric, submetacentric, and acrocentric).

The original standardization took place soon after the early discoveries, at a meeting in Denver (Denver Report, 1960). The first 22 pairs, the autosomes, were divided into seven groups, labelled A to G, the 23rd pair representing the sex chromosomes, XX in women, XY in men. The original description of the chromosomes was as follows.

"*Group 1–3.* (A) Large chromosomes with approximately median centromeres. The three chromosomes are readily distinguished from each other by size and centromere position.

Group 4–5. (B) Large chromosomes with submedian centromeres. The two chromosomes are difficult to distinguish, but chromosome 4 is slightly longer.

Group 6–12. (C) Medium-sized chromosomes with submedian centromeres. The X-chromosome resembles the longer chromosomes in this group, especially chromosome 6, from which it is difficult to distinguish. This large group presents the major difficulty in identification of individual chromosomes.

Group 13–15. (D) Medium-sized chromosomes with nearly terminal centromeres (acrocentric chromosomes). Chromosome 13 has a prominent satellite on the short arm. Chromosome 14 has a small satellite on the short arm. No satellite has been detected on chromosome 15.

Group 16–18. (E) Rather short chromosomes with approximately median (in chromosome 16) or submedian centromeres.

Group 19–20. (F) Short chromosomes with approximately median centromeres.

Group 21–22. (G) Very short acrocentric chromosomes. Chromosome 21 has a satellite on its short arm. The Y-chromosome is similar to these chromosomes." (Subsequent investigations revealed that satellites are carried by all the acrocentric chromosomes except the Y, although they cannot always be seen; therefore, the use of satellites to distinguish between acrocentric chromosomes is probably not reliable.)

Further conferences were held in London in 1963, in Chicago (Chicago Conference, 1966) and in Paris (Paris Conference, 1972) in order to increase the specificity of chromosome identification. Chromosomes were further identified by the presence of secondary constrictions, and autoradiography (incorporation of radioactive thymidine into replicating chromosomes) was used to determine the time sequence of chromosome replication and hence further specify the chromosomes within a given group. These were among the methods suggested at the earlier of these conferences; in Chicago a standard nomenclature was adopted for describing the human karyotype. Finally new staining techniques were developed that make each chromosome individually recognizable by disclosing banded regions.

Quinacrine mustard stain yields fluorescent bands, whereas various modifications of Giemsa stain reveal corresponding dark and light regions. Aside from their value in identifying normal chromosomes, these banded areas can be used to trace segments translocated from one chromosome to another; they are adding also to the growing understanding of the chemical nature and the function of the chromosomal regions.

The classic forms of human karyotype anomalies were described soon after the chromosome techniques were developed and even before the classification system was standardized. The first group of such aberrations was marked by the presence from birth of an abnormal number of chromosomes (aneuploidy), either fewer than the normal complement of 46 (hypodiploidy) or more (hyperdiploidy).

These conditions can arise by a process known as nondisjunction, usually in the formation of the gamete (sperm or ovum) that united in the conception of the given individual. Although usually in such germ-cell formation, one chromosome of each pair goes into the sperm or ovum, the two chromosomes of a given pair may for reasons not fully understood remain together. A germ cell with an extra chromosome combining with a normal gamete will give rise to a zygote (fertilized ovum) with three instead of two of the given chromosomes, a condition known as trisomy.

The earliest trisomic condition to be described and clinically the most significant example is Down's syndrome, formerly known as mongolism. It had been known for a long time that babies with this defect were often born to older mothers; a uterine defect, however, tended to be ruled out by the fact that dizygotic twins were discordant, whereas monozygotic pairs had almost a 100% concordance rate. Lejeune, Gautier, and Turpin, (1959) using the new tissue culture methods clarified the picture by their discovery that a series of patients with Down's syndrome had 47 instead of 46 chromosomes and that the additional chromosome was one of the smallest chromosomes, No. 21 in the conventional numbering system. This trisomic condition, arising presumably by nondisjunction in oögenesis, is associated with a chromosome imbalance that results in the typical intellectual, morphologic, and biochemical abnormalities in the Down's syndrome complex.

Two rarer trisomies involving the autosomes are represented by the D-trisomy (Patau, Smith, Therman, Inhorn, and Wagner, 1960) and the E-trisomy (Edwards, Harnden, Cameron, Crosse, and Wolfe, 1960), both resulting in serious birth anomalies in infants who usually live less than 1 year. The former is characterized by microphthalmos, cleft lip and palate, and polydactylia; the latter by micrognathia, low set ears, overlapping of fingers, and other skeletal and cardiac defects.

Even though all cases of Down's syndrome are essentially marked by a trisomy of G group chromosome 21, important modifications of the process can be observed. For one thing, the extra chromosome may be lost in one cell during the very early cell divisions of the zygote; two cell lines may then persist, one with 46 and one with 47 chromosomes. The individual will be known as a mosaic; clinically he may be intermediate between normal and fully symptomatic. Although few persons (all women) with full Down's syndrome have had children, it is possible that relatively asymptomatic mosaicism may cause an increased risk of affected offspring in such parents.

A second modification results from a translocation of chromosome 21 to one of the larger chromosomes, usually in the D group. If the zygote started as a trisomy and there are two other No. 21 chromosomes present (*de novo* translocation), the infant has Down's syndrome, even if his total chromosome count would be 46 if the D/21 translocation were counted as a single chromosome. Alternatively, a translocation in a normal zygote would yield 45 chromosomes by simple count and would result in a normal individual. However, such a person, with a balanced translocation, would have an increased risk of having affected children since it would be possible to form a gamete with both a normal chromosome 21 and the double (translocation) chromosome.

Numerically the risk of a second affected child for a mother who has had one child with Down's syndrome is of the same order of magnitude as any other woman of the same age (1 in 600 overall, up to 1 in 50 in mothers over 45). There may be some increase attributed to a genetic tendency to nondisjunction in some families, but even if the normal risk were doubled, it would still remain relatively low for the younger age group. With a balanced D/21 translocation in the mother, on the other hand, the risk of an affected child regardless of her age is about 10%; in the father it is about 2%, with a risk also of the children being such carriers themselves. Karyotype examination is essential in counseling such families; if a patient is a carrier or the mother is over 40, it is possible now by amniocentesis followed by culture and examination of fetal cells to rule out Down's syndrome in the fetus or give the parents an opportunity to decide on abortion.

Turning to the X and Y chromosomes, a series of syndromes have been described ranging from absence of a sex chromosome (the 45, X Turner's syndrome) to the addition of extra X or Y chromosomes to the normal male or female complement. These variations occur as a result of a process of nondisjunction in gamete formation.

Even before karyotyping was possible, Turner's syndrome was noted to be marked by the absence of Barr bodies in phenotypic females. These persons tended to be short, with sexual underdevelopment, webbing of the neck, and possible cardiac defects. Similarly a group of males with eunuchoid habitus, atrophic testicular tissue, and some gynecomastia, were noted to have Barr bodies, counter to their phenotypic sex. These anomalous situations were clarified when the Turner's female proved to have only one X chromosome, and the Klinefelter's male to have two X chromosomes in addition to his Y chromosome. A third chromosomal abnormality is represented by females, often amenorrheic, sometimes intellectually retarded, with an XXX chromosome pattern and two Barr bodies in typical cells. These findings, consistent with the Lyon hypothesis of inactivation of all X chromosomes in excess of one, also established the essential role of the Y chromosome in determining maleness.

Since the descriptions of the classic syndromes, a variety of more complex pictures have been reported, such as XXXY individuals who are males with severe mental deficiency, and many cases of mosaicism. It has been estimated that one in every 150 newborn infants has an identifiable chromosome aberration.

In addition to the study of abnormal human karyotypes and their relationship to clinical syndromes, the techniques of cytogenetics have been used in cell hybridization, a powerful and intriguing method for localizing on individual chromosomes the genes determining particular enzymes. Until this technique was demonstrated, such linkages could only be established statistically by careful analysis of many pedigrees. Although still useful, this traditional approach has now been supplemented by the growth *in vitro* of hybrid cells. These are actually cells formed by fusion between cells derived from donors either of the same species or of different species. Under virus induction, the membranes of both cells break down and a cell is formed with all the chromosomes of both cells; as this unstable cell type replicates itself, chromosomes are lost. Normal cells can be fused with mutant cells, which are incapable by themselves of synthetizing a given enzyme and hence are unable to live in a medium lacking an essential nutrient. By noting the pattern of chromosome loss as the hybrid cell line ceases to be viable in such a medium, it is possible to determine which chromosome carried the given gene in the normal donor cell.

B. Biochemical Genetics

Early in the century, Garrod (see Harris, 1970) coined the designation "inborn errors of metabolism." He foresaw by many decades the relation of inheritable gene-borne disorders to blocks in enzyme controlled pathways of intermediary metabolism—later known as the "one gene–one enzyme" hypothesis. Among the genetic defects of this nature subsequently identified are galactosemia and phenylketonuria. Although the faulty enzymes in the major psychiatric syndromes have not been identified, the two syndromes noted above include marked mental retardation.

Another area of biochemical genetics in which metabolic blocks are of importance to the psychiatrist is pharmacogenetics. For example patients with genetic defects in pseudocholinesterase may respond to succinylcholine administration with profound apnea. In other examples, isoniazid is inactivated slowly in individuals who lack a hepatic enzyme, isoniazid acetylase, and genetic differences in the inactivation of tricyclic antidepressants, of phenothiazines, and of diphenylhydantoin are being described.

C. Molecular Genetics

Ever since the rediscovery of Gregor Mendel's work at the turn of the century, it was clear that individual hereditary traits are determined by paired particles (later called genes), which remain unchanged throughout life, independently separate during gamete formation, and are transmitted via the ovum and sperm, respectively, to combine again in the zygote. The sum total of the genetic constitution of an individual, as thus established in the zygote and duplicated in every somatic cell, is referred to as the genotype and his appearance and physiologic state at any given time as his phenotype. If an individual receives the same (or an essentially indistinguishable) gene from each parent at a given locus, such an individual is termed a homozygote, and assuming the proper environment he will exhibit the characteristics associated with the action of that gene. On the other hand, he may receive a different gene (allele) at the given locus from each parent; he is then termed a heterozygote and may either exhibit traits that are intermediate to those associated with the homozygote for either gene or he may display the same trait as a homozygote. In the latter case, the trait is known as dominant; a trait that is not expressed in an easily discernible manner in a heterozygote is known as recessive. A dominant gene is transmitted in pedigrees in the direct line of descent through the affected parent in each generation and appears in approximately 50% of that parent's offspring. Recessive traits require inheritance from both parents who are rarely affected themselves, since they are usually heterozygotes. A child of two heterozygotes has a 25% risk of being a homozygote and thus of being affected. Transmission of the gene is chiefly along collateral lines, from heterozygote to heterozygote.

In the case of a gene carried on the X chromosome, the trait can be transmitted from father to daughter or from mother to daughter or son, if dominant, whereas an X-linked recessive trait will usually be transmitted from father to grandson via a heterozygous (carrier) daughter, with relatively few females affected.

It has to be emphasized that genes produce traits only through a long series of steps that may be modified at every level by environmental forces and requirements, both pre- and postnatal, as well as by the action of other genes, so that the effects described above may vary from complete expression to total lack of penetrance. There are many traits, particularly those involving variations within the range of normal in such characteristics as height or intelligence, but also in graded pathologic syndromes such as cleft palate, in which the genetic contribution is made by the resultant effect of many genes. These genes may either all be of minor intermediate effect (multifactor inheritance), or they may modify the effect of single major genes.

In 1944 what Watson (1970) later termed "Avery's bombshell" opened the modern era with the proof of the genetic role of nucleic acids, particularly deoxyribonucleic acid (DNA). The structure of this molecule was described by Watson and Crick (1953a, b). Two sugar (deoxyribose)-phosphate-sugar chains are twisted about each other, forming a double helix. To each sugar is attached a nucleotide base—a purine (adenine or guanine) or pyrimidine (cytosine or thymine). From a sugar on one chain to the corresponding sugar on the other, there is a hydrogen bond linkage that may only take place between either adenine on one chain and thymine on the other, or guanine on one and cytosine on the other. A DNA molecule may consist of thousands of such nucleotide linkages.

This model made it possible to understand the basic cellular processes— replication, transcription, and translation. In cell division the DNA strands separate and each then reforms its missing half from the surrounding materials with the aid of specialized enzymes. In doing so, the base pairs (adenine-guanine, cytosine-thymine) are preserved; hence the sequence in the two daughter chains is the same as that in the original one.

The base sequence is of paramount importance, since it represents the code that is transcribed to a single stranded molecule, messenger ribonucleic acid (mRNA), which is then found in the cytoplasm in juxtaposition to structures known as ribosomes. As the ribosomes move along the length of the mRNA, the code is translated into a chain of amino acids. This takes place as the proper amino acids are carried one by one to each codon (sequence of three bases) by specialized transfer RNA molecules. The code has been deciphered by ingenious experimental means, and it appears that throughout all living matter on Earth, each sequence of three bases calls for one amino acid alone. After a chain of amino acids is completed, it may join with other such polypeptide chains and assume the configuration of a protein. The mRNA molecule undergoes enzymatic degradation after it has completed its role as template.

In the above scheme, a change in the nucleotide sequence in the DNA arising from an error during replication constitutes a mutation; a modified polypeptide or protein may be produced, and if sufficiently different biologically from the original, a loss of enzyme activity may result, as in phenylketonuria. If the gene determines a structural polypeptide, an abnormal variant may be produced; hemoglobin S, found in sickle cell disease, for example, differs from normal hemoglobin A by a single amino acid (valine instead of glutamic acid) at a specific point (position 6) in the beta chain.

D. Population Genetics

Mendelian population genetics stems from a formula propounded in 1908 known as the Hardy-Weinberg law, which says, in brief, that under certain ideal conditions (a large stationary population, random mating, no selective advantage of one phenotype over another, and no further mutation), a population will in one generation reach an equilibrium that can be predicted from the frequencies of the various genes in the population. In particular considering a single locus with two possible alleles A and A' occurring with frequencies p and q, respectively, the equilibrium proportions will be p^2 for AA individuals (homozygotes), $2pq$ for AA' individuals (heterozygotes) and q^2 for A'A' individuals (homozygotes). Henceforward this genetic structure would ideally remain unchanged through the generations. Actually, of course, change does occur because of random variation (genetic drift) in small populations, because of an excess of homozygotes caused by assortative mating, and under the pressures of selection and mutation.

Even though the Hardy-Weinberg law may define the theoretic structure of a population, modern pedigree analysis to test genetic hypotheses concerning specific attributes must consider problems of ascertainment, of penetrance thresholds, and of environmental effects. Corrections must be made for modes of ascertainment—complete or incomplete—which are differently applicable to dominant or recessive conditions. Quantitative techniques that apply to polygenic inheritance yield results that mimic single-gene transmission if there is a threshold for clinical manifestation. The most sophisticated models today include such parameters as the population and gene frequencies, the variance owing to environment, and the degree of manifestation in heterozygotes; using computer techniques observed data from pooled pedigrees can then be matched to hypothetical models of genetic transmission. Methods such as these illustrate the complexity, as well as the force, of current approaches to exploring the interaction of genes with each other and with the environment on the level of population dynamics.

III. GENE–ENVIRONMENT INTERACTION

Since historically the main difficulties in the application of genetics to psychiatry center about the role of the environment, it may be helpful to describe some models of gene-environment interaction before turning to the current status of genetic findings in psychiatric disorder. These models can put the biologic data already described into the proper interactional framework, and should make it more comfortable, conceptually and in practice, to avoid the time-worn dichotomies that have held back biologic-genetic thought in the behavioral sciences.

It is helpful to consider the role of genetics in psychiatry at a series of organizational levels. These levels can range from the subatomic, the molecular, intracellular, and cellular to the tissue, organ and organismic, the neurologic and psychodynamic, the family, social, demographic, and ecologic, and on the broadest time scale the level of evolutionary change.

At the level of gene function, the transcription and translocation process whereby the coded DNA molecule governs the synthesis of proteins has already been described. There is no doubt that this complex machinery has developed over millenia by an evolutionary process. What is obviously necessary is a mechanism whereby the process can be controlled, so that cells may differentiate in their functions and work together within an organism to meet its needs within a changing milieu. One model for such feedback control was proposed by Jacob and Monod (1961) for the bacterial cell. An operator gene may code for a particular enzyme, but its action may be repressed or induced depending on the presence and quantity of the substrate on which the given enzyme normally acts, or of the end product that it normally helps to synthetize. This repression or induction is governed by the interaction of a repressor protein, produced by a separate regulatory gene, with the given substrate or end product. Thus when enzymes are needed to metabolize a specific food molecule or to manufacture a needed substance, they are produced, and, when they are not necessary, their production is turned off. This feedback mechanism ensures a regulation of the genes by their surroundings. More complex mechanisms undoubtedly play roles in higher organisms; hormones, for example, are believed to regulate DNA-governed enzyme synthesis in insects and in mammals, acting either on the chromosomes or at the cell surface.

A growing science of immunogenetics typifies another form of interaction between genes and environment. It is generally believed that the lymphoid cell contains a vast number of genes (DNA regions), each of which can code for a different antibody. If this is the case, a control mechanism must exist whereby the presence of an antigen informs the gene controlling the corresponding antibody to function. Again evolution has molded an adaptive mechanism by which genes extend, rather than limit, the organism's dealings with its environment.

Jumping to a more complex level of interaction in this systems-approach scheme, observers of infants and children verified the description of individual differences among children, found these differences to interact with maternal attitudes in shaping subsequent behavior patterns, and began to study the details of the interaction in a longitudinal framework. As Anna Freud (1966) wrote "inherent potentialities of the infant are accelerated in development, or slowed up, according to the mother's involvement with them, or the absence of it." Personality attributes have been measured along various dimensions, among them sleep, feeding, and sensory responses, activity and passivity, motor behavior, and specific reaction patterns. One group for example, has identified nine temperamental qualities in early infancy that tend to persist at least during the first 2 years (Thomas, Chess, Birch, Hertzig, and Korn, 1963). These are activity level, rhythmicity, approach-withdrawal, adaptability, intensity of reaction, threshold of response to stimulation, quality of mood, distractibility, and attention span and persistence. Heredity alone cannot determine these constitutional variations since the process of interaction begins from the moment of conception, and prenatal and perinatal influences come into the picture. But with more refined observations and genetic analysis applied to the data, increasing insight into gene-environment interaction at this complex neurophysiologic level should result.

In the field of psychosomatic disorder, a number of paradigms have been described that combine the action of hereditary, constitutional, early nurtural, and social influences. Mirsky has studied the etiology of peptic ulcer and found that both newborns and healthy adults varied in the degree of secretion of pepsinogen, as measured in urine and blood. This variation appears to be genetically determined. Under conditions of environmental deprivation, in particular basic army training, only among those rated as hypersecretors did he find signs and symptoms of duodenal ulcer. According to Mirsky (1960) infants who are functional hypersecretors, presumably on genetic grounds, show a strong hunger that is insatiable by the average mother; the mother therefore is perceived as rejecting. Later in life, these dependent wishes persist, and they can be revived when environmental stress threatens loss of support. The resultant anxiety, by pathways as yet not certain (hypothalamic, autonomic, hyperexcretion of pepsinogen, hyperchlorhydria, hypermotility, hyperadrenalism), may precipitate the ulcer in the predisposed individual.

Another model for interaction is provided by the observations of Spitz (1965) on the pathogenesis of infantile eczema. He observed a group of infants and their mothers and found that the children who developed this condition in the second 6 months of life were marked both by a set of hyperactive cutaneous reflexes at birth and by mothers whose own anxiety and repressed hostility led them to deprive their children of skin contact. Thus a congenital, perhaps hereditary, predisposition had to be matched by a specifically stressful environment to lead by pathways as yet unknown to a psychosomatic disorder. The eczema almost always cleared up with the increased motility and independence of older babyhood.

On a still broader scale gene-environment interaction is displayed in the dynamics of population change, and in fact underlies the major unifying concept of biology, adaptation by evolution. Both the natural and man-made environment exert positive and negative selection pressures, which respond to and modify the genetic structures of the population and the individuals within it. Two examples are the use of tools which appears to have preceded biologic changes in the hand, brain, and face (Washburn, 1959), and the selective advantage of the sickle-cell heterozygote (who is relatively resistant to falciparum malaria), which has kept the gene at an equilibrium frequency in malarial regions despite negative selection against the homozygote.

IV. GENETICS OF PSYCHIATRIC DISORDERS AND MODES OF INVESTIGATION

On the basis of the foregoing conceptual and factual background in modern biologic genetics, it is possible to survey the existing data and the direction of research in psychiatric genetics without risking the connotation of narrow fatalism, which may have formerly characterized this discipline. At the present stage of knowledge, methodology is at least as important as definitive conclusions; this section is therefore organized according to modes of investigation.

A. Molecular and Biochemical Defects

The most clear evidence for the genetic basis of a disease would be of course to isolate a faulty enzyme, determine the amino acid substitutions, and trace the mutation in the DNA segment responsible. It has been said that there is no twisted thought without a twisted molecule; the speaker was not referring to the DNA helix but the metaphor was a prophetic one.

Until it becomes possible to spot errors in the genetic code representing a particular gene by direct methods, the closest approach is to identify the enzyme deficiency by electrophoretic methods or by studying the course and products of intermediary metabolism. Such information is available for example, in the amino-acidurias, typified by phenylketonuria (PKU). Phenyl-pyruvic acid was first discovered in 1934 by Følling in the urine of children with mental defect and a wide range of physical signs and symptoms: small stature, light skin, blue eyes, widely spaced teeth, hyperactive reflexes, and occasionally seizures. Traced to a deficiency in the liver enzyme phenylalanine hydroxylase, the condition is generally inherited through an autosomal recessive gene. With an incidence at birth of about one in 10,000, the condition may account for as many as 1% of cases in institutions for mental deficiency. Heterozygotes may be detected by their response to a phenylalanine loading test, whereas affected infants are routinely picked up by the Guthrie test, and after false-positive results are ruled out, may develop normally if placed on a phenylalanine-free diet.

Another example of metabolic disease with psychiatric symptoms is hyper-uricemia (Lesch-Nyhan disease). Mental and physical retardation, neurologic signs, and specifically self-mutilation are found (the child bites and destroys his fingers and lips). It appears to be inherited as a X-linked recessive trait.

B. Chromosomal Anomalies

More complex than those associated with the individual gene or its direct product are the syndromes stemming from chromosomal anomalies, e.g. trisomy, monosomy, translocation, and deletion. The mechanisms have already been described. The congenital malformations associated with abnormalities in the autosomal complement are typified by the most common, Down's syndrome or mongolism. This syndrome accounts for up to 10% of institutionalized mentally retarded patients.

Sex chromosomal anomalies form a second large group of hitherto obscure syndromes, now associated with a defect in genetic expression. At this point most descriptions of behavior deviations in this group are based on cases reported because of physical or mental symptoms severe enough to be noted, and any conclusion must therefore be tentative. Large-scale screening programs in infants may give a more realistic picture of the incidence of persons with such anomalies in the population and their subsequent fate. Such programs, to be sure, have built-in hazards, i.e. ascertainment of an otherwise normal infant with a chromosomal anomaly poses the dilemma of whom to tell, and how to observe, without traumatizing the parents and the child and perhaps creating a self-fulfilling prophecy. Yet until such life histories are studied, the role of the karyotype in determining behavior will not be clearly evaluated, nor its interaction with biologic, social, and educational forces completely understood.

In Klinefelter's syndrome, there is conflicting evidence regarding psychiatric disorder associated with the extra X chromosome. It would appear, however, that persons with this anomaly have, more often than expected by chance, weak libido, mental subnormality, and nonspecific personality disorders ranging from inadequate personality and delinquency to schizophrenia-like behavior. Still, since the karyotype occurs in two to three per 1,000 male newborns, the chromosomal abnormality has to interact with other factors in the precipitation of overt behavior disorder. It is possible that in some cases the chromosome anomaly lowers the threshold for the manifestation of an otherwise determined psychosis by adding an additional biologic or social burden; the combined biologic factors may be aggravated by the social handicap of dysplastic body frame or eunuchoid habitus.

Another male karyotypic anomaly has attracted a good deal of medical-legal as well as theoretical interest, namely the 47, XYY genotype (National Institute of Mental Health, 1970). First described in a normal male from a family marked by abnormal karyotypes, it was soon reported to occur with apparently increased frequency in inmates confined to institutions for delinquents, particularly associated with mental subnormality. Since then persons with the anomaly have been characterized as emotionally unstable and irresponsible, with little depth of feeling, evincing episodic violence from early childhood or adolescence, impulsive often with signs and symptoms of a convulsive diathesis, and often the only delinquent member in their family. The relatively high incidence of this anomaly among newborns (estimated as 1 in 200 to 1 in 2,000) and the description of adults with the chromosome defect who show no history of impulsive violence make it clear that legal and preventive considerations require more knowledge about the developmental process in male children with an extra Y chromosome. Only a few direct observations from childhood have been made (Cowie and Kahn, 1968), including a pair of twins with dissimilar courses (Rainer, Abdullah, and Jarvik, 1972) whose study suggests some of the possible biologic and intrafamilial determinants of the more overt manifestations.

In females, an extra X chromosome has been associated with menstrual disturbances, and sometimes with mild retardation and social withdrawal. No specific behavior correlate can be definitely ascribed to this group, and the positive findings described may be limited to the subgroups found in institutions.

Turner's syndrome, marked by the absence of the second sex chromosome

(45, X) is associated with short stature, webbing of the neck, sexual infantilism, and a variety of other physical anomalies. The ovaries are reduced to streaks of fibrous tissue. The girls react less than might be expected to their sexual immaturity and body defects; many have been described as stable, placid, and maternal in temperament. Although not generally retarded, they appear to show a discrepancy between normal verbal and low-performance IQ, with a specific defect in space-form appreciation. This is a notable example of a specific cognitive correlate of a chromosomal defect.

There are some reports, finally, of chromosome aberrations in schizophrenia. An excess of X trisomies (Raphael and Shaw, 1963) or at least of mosaicism involving X chromosome aneuploidies (Kaplan, 1971) has been described among schizophrenic females; with the trisomies and to a lesser extent the mosaics marked by a more severe course than schizophrenics with normal karyotype (Vartanyan and Gindilis, 1972). If these observations are confirmed, the nature of the aggravating role of a coincidental trisomy in a schizotypal individual needs further consideration.

C. Linkage Analysis

One of the strongest pieces of evidence for single gene transmission of a trait or illness is to establish genetic linkage. Evidence for linkage depends essentially on demonstrating that distribution of the trait in families and populations is consistent with its determination by a gene that is on the same chromosome as, and at a short distance from, a known marker gene. If two genes are on different chromosomes, there will be families in which both happen to be present, but the phenotypic manifestations that they respectively transmit will occur in the various members of such families either together (coupling) or separately (repulsion) in equal proportions. Even if the genes are on the same chromosome but far apart, there will be no consistent relationship between them because of the phenomenon of crossing over during meiosis. But if the genes are closely linked on the same chromosome, the likelihood of crossing over between them will be low; hence in a given family the traits will tend to be inherited together in most members or apart in most members. There will, in other words, be a reduced frequency of recombination involving genes at the two loci, and in principle linkage is suggested by the detection of such pedigrees. Complete analysis of this phenomenon is no problem under experimental circumstances, where crossbreeding of informative animals may lead to mapping of many chromosomes. In humans, it is necessary to find informative families who carry the two genes in question, and to determine the proportion of family members in whom apparent recombination has taken place and to calculate the likelihood that a deviation from 50% is caused by linkage.

There is evidence for example that manic-depressive illness may be transmitted by a dominant gene on the X chromosome, linked in some families with the known X-borne genes for color blindness (Winokur and Tanna, 1969; Mendlewicz, Fleiss, and Fieve, 1972) and in others with the Xg blood group. Since linkage in this instance is to genes on the X chromosome, there are certain patterns of inheritance in pooled families that would be expected, the chief one being the absence of father-to-son transmission. These patterns have been found in many, but not in all, families reported, thus indicating that the X-linked variety represents probably one mode of inheritance in a genetically heterogeneous syndrome.

It is important not to confuse linkage with association. If two traits are linked, they may exist in a family usually together or usually apart; if they are associated, they will tend to exist together. Such associations have been posited, for example, between duodenal ulcer and blood type O; they may represent the result of pleiotropic (many-faceted) expression of the same gene, or of two genes facilitating each other's expression on some metabolic or phenotypic level.

D. Pedigree Studies

In the case of well-defined pathologic syndromes, the study of individual pedigrees may suggest genetic transmission, particularly if a clear dominant or X-linked pattern is discernible. In Huntington's chorea for example, the disorder is transmitted by a dominant autosomal gene from either parent to a child of either sex with a 50% risk. Even here, however, such factors as the clinical heterogeneity and the late manifestation of symptoms has obscured the inheritance pattern when not carefully considered. In accumulating pedigrees, there is the danger of seeing only the more dramatic instances of illness, or of equating familial with genetic. The older literature abounds in such descriptions as the Kallikak family with a variety of sociopathic and psychologic disorders whose etiology is far from clear. Pedigree studies may therefore serve to generate hypotheses that have to be supplemented by the study of representative samples with proper statistical methods of correcting for biased ascertainment.

E. Family Risk Studies

The pedigree method may be extended to collections of families, where studies of risk (sometimes referred to as contingency methods) are designed to compare the expectancy for a given condition in the relatives of affected individuals with that in the general population. In this type of investigation, it is important that the affected individuals be diagnosed according to uniform criteria and that they represent a consecutive series of patients (or a random sample thereof). They may then be designated as index cases, or probands. All relatives in the desired categories must then be located and diagnoses made.

Because the aim is to determine not the incidence (new cases) nor the prevalence (total cases) but rather the expectancy rate (cases that may arise during the lifetime of the relatives), it would be necessary to wait many years; more practically a correction method is applied. A simplified method often used is the Weinberg abridged method. In this method, a manifestation age interval is determined on clinical grounds; in schizophrenia, for example, it is usually taken at 15 to 45 years. The number of cases found among a given category of relatives (the numerator) is then related to a denominator, which is not the total number of relatives in that category, but rather that number diminished by all of those who have not reached the earliest manifestation age and half of those still within the manifestation period. This method yields a risk figure that represents the expectancy of developing the given condition for those who will live through the manifestation period. Such a risk figure can then be compared with similarly obtained risk figures for other groups of relatives and with those for the general population. The latter rates have been determined in many cases by total or sample population studies or by studying the relatives of control patients.

This method has been most useful in determining empirical risks for illness in given classes of relatives; such results by themselves can not rule out non-hereditary forms of familial transmission. (To be sure in an interaction theory, the aim is not to rule these out but to include them in a total synthesis.) Nor can contingency risk data substantiate one form of genetic transmission rather than another, even if biases of ascertainment are properly corrected for, in a biologic system where polygenic inheritance is possible and where penetrance and expressivity are determined by many threshold factors of a genetic, organic, and environmental nature.

The contingency method of genetic investigation nevertheless provided many of the early data in the major psychoses (and less convincingly in some neuroses) that served as the rationale and the groundwork for other types of investigation later on.

In schizophrenia research the rediscovery of Mendel's quantitative approach to genetics and the Kraepelinian description of dementia praecox led to a variety of family risk studies, first in Germany and then in the United States. Rüdin (1916) reported on the siblings of almost 1,000 patients from the Munich psychiatric clinic; the schizophrenia rate in the group of siblings ranged from 4.48% where neither parent was affected to 22.72% where both were psychotic or alcoholic. Schulz (1932) refined the diagnosis of the index cases and reexamined Rüdin's results on 660 cases. He noted that the schizophrenia rate was higher for siblings of index cases with insidious onset and no precipitating course, and lower for those with acute onset and benign course. This finding foreshadowed a good deal of later discussion on genetic loading with respect to type or severity of disease.

In his large family study conducted in Berlin, Kallmann (1938) investigated the families of 1,087 patients, representing all the schizophrenia case records available in the Herzberge hospital in Berlin for the years 1893 to 1902. The cases were chosen by reviewing personally the charts of all admissions, and the diagnoses were made without reference to the hospital's diagnosis or to any notes on hereditary conditions in the family of the patient. Kallmann omitted patients who developed symptoms only after the age of 40, as well as those with neurological symptoms associated with syphilis or alcohol. He then divided the index cases into hebephrenic, catatonic, paranoid, and simple categories and undertook the task of tracing their siblings and descendants, both direct and collateral. For children of index cases, the overall schizophrenia rate corrected for age distribution was 16.4%, but it ranged from about 20% each for hebephrenic and catatonic cases (nuclear) to about 10% each for paranoid and simple ones (peripheral). For siblings the overall rate was 11.5%, with about 13% in the nuclear group and about 9% in the peripheral. It should be noted that Kallmann made clear in his discussion that a genetic factor is necessary for schizophrenia but not sufficient, and that both the penetrance and the phenotypic manifestation depend on "the individual interplay among genetic, constitutional, and environmental factors."

In another mammoth investigation, only recently reported by Reed, Hartley, Anderson, Phillips, and Johnson (1973), the investigators followed for over four generations the relatives of 99 psychotic probands in the Warren (Pennsylvania) State Hospital. The overall rates for psychosis in parents, siblings, and children were similar (about 18%), but there were two notable findings: no correlation with respect to schizophrenia or manic-depressive illness between the diagnosis of the index case and the affected relatives, and the observation, unlike that in most other studies, that psychotic mothers produced about twice as many psychotic offspring as did psychotic fathers.

The findings in other family studies of the same period but in different countries were much the same. For example Garrone (1962) in Geneva studied 4,000 index cases and their families and found a rate of 14.7% in siblings. His risk figures for parents and children were also similar to the German and American studies. In all of these studies, the risk for relatives was significantly higher than the general population rate, which has been variously determined from less than 1 to a high of 2, and rarely 3%.

With regard to the mode of inheritance, Kallmann (1938) suggested that a single gene was responsible for schizophrenia and that this gene was autosomal recessive in nature and could be modified by other genes conferring a greater or lesser degree of resistance. Other investigators have provided such hypotheses as dominant inheritance with incomplete penetrance in heterozygotes, two-gene models, a polygenic form of inheritance with a threshold, and a heterogeneity model specifying a variety of separate genes, dominant or recessive, any one of which might be involved in the etiology of schizophrenia. In all of these models, environmental stress is presumed to be an interacting factor. Using various genetic models compatible with the data, theories as to the exact mode of inheritance of schizophrenia must remain inconclusive until the biochemical and physiologic nature of the inherited vulnerability factor is identified.

Family risk data have also contributed to the study of the genetics of affective disorder. Kraepelin had observed large numbers of relatives of manic-depressive patients who had the same disorder: a variety of studies in Germany, Scandinavia, and Great Britain indicated a range of 10 to 15% risk of affective disorder in parents, siblings and children of manic-depressive patients with no appreciable increase in schizophrenia in this group. The general population rate for manic-depressive psychosis has been calculated as 0.4%, with rates of 0.8 and up to 1.6% in special populations. Kallmann (1953b) and Stendstedt (1952), postulated an autosomal dominant type of inheritance with incomplete penetrance.

Based on the classification (Leonhard, 1959) of affective disease into manic-depressive disease (bipolar illness) and recurrent depression (unipolar illness), more recent studies have indicated a considerably higher rate of disorder in the relatives of bipolar patients. Unipolar patients generally have unipolar relatives, but there is some disagreement on whether bipolar patients may have unipolar relatives or are limited to bipolar ones.

It is well known that there is an excess of female patients in the affective psychoses, and it has recently been suggested that sex distribution in patients and their relatives is consistent with an X-linked genetic transmission. For such transmission it would be necessary to show (1) the illness is twice as common in the female; (2) affected females have affected parents and affected children who are female and male in equal proportions; (3) they have affected siblings who are female and male in the proportion 3:1; (4) affected males have affected parents or children who are exclusively female (no male-to-male transmission); however, they have affected siblings who are female and male in equal proportion. These criteria have not been met precisely for either group, but Perris (1960) has approximated them in the unipolar group, but not the bipolar, whereas Reich, Clayton, and Winokur (1969) have demonstrated them in the relatives of the bipolar psychosis group. Some further corroboration of the latter two findings has come from the linkage studies previously described.

In the case of neuroses, there are a number of reviews (Inouye, 1972; Slater and Cowie, 1971) describing an increase in neurotic illness and neurotic personality traits of a like kind among relatives of obsessional neurotics, anxiety neurotics, and hysterics, with much stronger evidence for the first than the last of these. From a biologic point of view, these data are insufficient to establish a clear pattern of genetic transmission in neurotic illness and problems of diagnosis and separation of environmental stress factors are increased many fold compared with studies in the psychoses.

F. Twin-Study Method

If there is one technique that has been associated with the application of genetics to medicine and particularly to psychiatry, it is the study of twins. Galton was the pioneer in the use of twins as a means of separating genetic and environmental influences. Monozygotic (identical) twins and dizygotic (fraternal) twins differ in degree of genetic relationship, the former deriving from the same fertilized ovum and, barring a rare chromosome loss, starting embryonic life with the same genetic substance, the latter derived from two separate fertilized ova and genetically not more nor less similar than two full siblings born at different times. In both cases, unless the twins are separated at birth (a rare occurrence), they share the same physical environment.

Whether the social and affectional environment is equal in both instances has often been the subject of critical comment. There are numerous instances in which parents choose to differentiate their twins and treat them differently, but these are by no means confined to dizygotic pairs. As a result of circulatory variations, monozygotic pairs may, in fact, be subject to more disparate influence during intrauterine life than dizygotic pairs. Moreover parents are often unsure of what type of twins they have, and similar patterns of family dynamics occur in both types. Actually the drive to differentiate the twins may be more marked in pairs that look most alike. Finally behavioral differences interact with physical ones in the continuous process of development.

In applying the twin-family method, the index cases are twins, and data are obtained on their co-twins, siblings, and if desired other relatives. Comparisons can then be made between pairs in a graded series, namely monozygotic twins, dizygotic twins of the same sex, dizygotic twins of opposite sexes, full siblings, half-siblings, and step siblings. This procedure makes it possible to study intrafamily variations with a minimum of uncontrolled variables.

It is important to avoid certain common misconceptions concerning twin studies. Carefully stated genetic hypotheses should not be questioned simply because some pairs of dissimilar monozygotic twins have been found. Genes actually determine a norm of reaction, the exact expression of which depends on many interactions taking place before, at, and after birth, and 100% concordance in a series of monozygotic twin pairs is not to be expected in a clinical syndrome of any complexity. With many pathways from genetic structure to the expression of behavioral traits, small but crucial influences upon the process of interaction at critical points during all states of development may lead to wide divergence in phenotypes.

In the use of twins to determine concordance rates, it is essential that the condition to be investigated be no more prevalent in twins than in singletons, that a consecutive series of monozygotic and dizygotic twins (or a complete random sample thereof) be studied, and that the diagnoses of illness and zygosity be made independently.

In addition to the statistical approach using concordance rates, more intensive studies of twins in the fields of biochemical and clinical investigation are possible. Longitudinal data from selected pairs of monozygotic twins, comparing their reactions and patterns under different conditions of physical health or defect, accidental trauma, family role assignment, or even planned differences in management or separation at birth are most illuminating. Such observations, indeed, are perhaps most valuable in suggesting crucial environmental factors that stand out when hereditary predisposition is most similar.

In schizophrenia early classic twin studies in Europe, Japan, and the United States between 1928 and 1961 agreed very closely in the concordance rates for monozygotic twins (about 65% without age correction) dizygotic twins (about 12%) and full siblings (about the same as dizygotic twins).

In the large investigation of Kallmann (1946) based on a series of over 900 index cases, concordance rates for monozygotic and dizygotic twins were 69 and 10%, respectively; with age correction these figures correspond to the well-known expectancy rates of 86 and 14%. Subsequent findings were foreshadowed in some of the details of Kallmann's series, where the overall risks given above obscured the wide range of rates the variation of which depended on the severity of illness in the index case. If the index case showed little or no deterioration, the monozygotic twin expectancy rate was as low as 26%, the dizygotic 2%, whereas for those with extreme deterioration the rates were as high as 100 and 17%, respectively.

More recent twin studies in England, Scandinavia, and the United States have been marked by various methodologic refinements. Notable among these was the fact that they turned, for a source of index cases, either to all twins in the population, looking afterward for those with schizophrenia, or at least to a group that included clinic and day hospital patients as well as more static or chronic patients on the wards. In either case, acute patients or those with less chronic severity could now enter the study as index cases along with the more typical chronic ones. Other refinements included the use of newer methods of zygosity analysis, particularly blood groups, thus reducing possible sources of error, although it has been shown that the older similarity methods were quite accurate and any rare errors could not have been crucial even in the older investigations.

Among these newer studies, one of the largest based on personal survey was reported by Kringlen (1967). Ascertaining all of the 25,000 pairs of twins born in Norway between 1901 and 1930, a list made possible by the existence of a Central Birth Registry, Kringlen proceeded to search their records and seek out their co-twins. Concordance rates for those pairs with schizophrenia in one twin ranged from 25 to 38% for monozygotic pairs, 4 to 10% for dizygotic. The higher figure derived from less strict diagnostic criteria and hence included less severe illness in either twin. Gottesman and Shields (1972) studied all twins admitted either as outpatients or as short-stay inpatients at the Maudsley Hospital in London between 1948 and 1964. They reported overall concordance rates of 50% for monozygotic twins, 10% for dizygotic, although in more detailed breakdown the rates they found also varied with severity. For example, if length of hospitalization of the index case was taken as the criterion, the monozygotic rates were 70% with more than 1 year in the hospital, 33% with less than a year. Similar results were reported in Denmark by Fischer, Harvald, and Hauge (1969). Even in a survey of 274 pairs in which one or both had a diagnosis of schizophrenia, taken from a register of 15,909 male veterans of the relatively healthy Armed Forces (Allen, Cohen, and Pollin, 1972), concordance rates of 27.4% for monozygotic, 4.8% for dizygotic twins were reported. All of these figures continue the trend toward lower absolute concordance rates for both types of twins in nonchronic schizophrenia, but the discrepancy between mono-zygotic and dizygotic concordance rates is maintained in every group.

Out of all the twin studies, old and new, there has developed no consensus as to specific predictive factors distinguishing the affected from the non-affected twins in the discordant pairs. In a study at the National Institute of Mental Health (Pollin and Stabenau, 1968) designed to examine a group of discordant pairs, it seemed in general to be the smaller and physiologically less competent twin at birth who later developed schizophrenia. Such diver-gence could be based on neurologic differences or on the fact that the weaker twin was assigned an overdependent, overprotected role within the family, a theory favored by the investigators, or on some combination of both.

Twin studies in affective disorder were largely conducted before the dis-tinction was generally made between bipolar and unipolar syndromes. In one of the largest studies reported, Kallmann (1953b) located 27 monozygotic and 58 dizygotic pairs; concordance for the former group was 100%, for the latter 25.5%, with 22.7% concordance in siblings. Since the index cases were all admitted to a mental hospital, only severe cases were included, and the perfect concordance rate for monozygotic twins was considered by the investigator himself as a biased one. Other twin studies in England and Scandinavia also demonstrated a large discrepancy between concordance rates in the two kinds of twins.

Zerbin-Rüdin (1969) examined the twin studies in the literature and at-tempted to separate the bipolar and unipolar cases. She found indeed that of the completely concordant pairs, only five out of 50 monozygotic pairs and three out of 20 dizygotic represented one bipolar member and one still of the unipolar variety. The others were largely both unipolar or both bipolar, strongly suggesting separate genetic predispositions.

In neurotic illness, Shields and Slater (1971), studied outpatient twins with the diagnosis of neurosis or personality disorder. In this group, 29% of monozygotic co-twins had the same diagnosis as the index case, as contrasted with 4% of dizygotic co-twins. Anxiety states showed higher concordance than other neurotic syndromes; hysteria on the other hand showed little evidence for genetic basis. Other studies of neurotic patients as well as psychologic tests of personality seem to agree that anxiety has the highest genetic component, obsessional states next, and hysteria least of all.

G. Adoption Studies

While the study of twins went a long way to provide the kind of data that could be used to separate genetic and environmental contributions to the distribution of mental disorder, there were still some objections to it on methodologic grounds. One of these was the assumption, believed by some to be a fair one but by others to be strongly unwarranted, that monozygotic twins and dizygotic twins had similar environmental treatment. With the paucity of twins with psychiatric diagnosis reared apart from infancy, a number of investigations in the 1960s turned to another method, the study of adoptive parents and adopted offspring.

These investigations have strengthened the evidence regarding the genetic contribution to the major psychoses for those previously unconvinced. In schizophrenia two studies, by Heston and Denney (1968) in Oregon and by Rosenthal, Wender, Kety, Schulsinger, Welner, and Østergaard (1968) in Denmark, indicated higher rates for schizophrenia and related psychopathology in the adopted children of schizophrenic parents than in a control series of adopted children of nonschizophrenic parents, although both groups were not reared by their biologic parents. In fact in the Oregon study, the proportion of children whose biologic mothers were schizophrenic and who were themselves schizophrenic at the time of study (early adulthood) although raised from infancy in adoptive homes, was 16%, precisely the risk figure for offspring in earlier family studies. In the control group, none of the children were so affected.

The converse of this research design is represented by studying the parents, biologic and adoptive, of schizophrenic patients. Wender, Rosenthal, and Kety (1968), in a preliminary survey in the United States, found considerably less psychopathology in the adoptive parents of schizophrenic patients than in the biologic parents of a matched group of patients. In Denmark, where both the biologic and adoptive families of the same adoptee patients could be traced and studied, Kety, Rosenthal, Wender, and Schulsinger (1968) found more schizophrenia and related syndromes in the biologic relatives of patients than in the biologic relatives of controls. Actually a good part of this increase was due to affected paternal half-siblings in the biologic families, tending to rule out special maternal effects. In the adoptive families, there was a lower prevalence of disorder in relatives of both patients and controls.

Schulsinger (1972), who worked on both of the Danish schizophrenia studies, also conducted a study of adoptees with the diagnosis of psychopathy.

Again there was a preponderance of similarly diagnosed individuals among the biological relatives of the index cases, as compared with the biological relatives of a matched control group of nonpsychopathic adoptees and with both groups of adoptive families. A study of alcoholism using the same Danish register of adoptees led to similar conclusions (Goodwin, Schulsinger, Hermansen, Guze, and Winokur, 1973). Data on affective disorder have not yet been reported.

H. Longitudinal Studies

Whatever contributions family risk, twin-family, and adoptive studies can make to knowledge of empirical risk, genetic involvement, and environmental influence, the developmental course of psychiatric illness and early signs of a predictive nature that occur as nature and nurture interact, can only be revealed by longitudinal observations. Such an approach also avoids confusing precursor signs with the effects of illness. Using high-risk populations from which to choose the children to be followed makes for economy and precision, and genetic relationship to an affected person—in practice, being the child of one or two such patients—is the only consistent risk-producing factor. There are a good number of such studies currently in progress in schizophrenia, differing according to the age at which the children are first observed and the kinds of observations made. The increased marriage and fertility rate in schizophrenia makes such studies doubly significant; their theoretical potential is matched by the practical importance of spotting early vulnerability as a prelude to searching for preventive strategies.

Longitudinal studies can be retrospective, too, of course, as the backgrounds in home and school of patients can be compared with their twins, their siblings, or their classmates. However, any findings here may easily be biased by retrospective falsification, poor memory, and *ad hoc* theorizing.

V. GENETIC CONTRIBUTIONS TO HUMAN VARIATION

A. Aging and Senility

The lifespan of offspring was related to that of their parents (Pearl and Pearl, 1934) by comparing the forebears of two groups of persons, one still living at the age 90 years or more, and the other group chosen at random. It was found that the parents and grandparents of the index cases lived significantly longer than those of the control group.

The twin method has been adapted to the developmental problem of aging by Kallmann (1961) and various colleagues, who in 1945 first collected over 1,600 twin index cases over the age of 60. Of those twins who died, monozygotic pairs showed lifespans significantly closer to each other than dizygotic pairs, and in all cases lifespans were also positively correlated with that of siblings and parents. Decline of intellectual function also showed less intrapair difference in monozygotic than in dizygotic twins (Jarvik, Kallmann, Falek, and Klaber, 1957).

Subsequent cytogenetic studies of peripheral blood lymphocytes showed an excess of chromosome loss in aged women over younger women; this difference did not appear in the men studied (Jarvik and Kato, 1970). This finding suggested, but of course did not establish, a similar loss of chromosomes in glial cells with a possible effect on intellectual function in aging.

In senile psychosis, the twins studied by Kallmann and Jarvik who developed that syndrome showed significantly greater concordance in the monozygotic pairs. Larsson, Sjögren, and Jacobson (1963) in Sweden found an increase of senile psychosis in first-degree relatives of index patients; and cytogenetic studies by Nielsen, Jensen, Lindhardt, Stottrup, and Sondergaard (1968) and Jarvik, Altshuler, Kato, and Blumner (1971) indicated a positive association between senile psychosis and chromosome loss, particularly X-chromosome loss, in females.

B. Intelligence and Mental Defect

Some of the genetically transmitted forms of mental deficiency with an enzymatic, metabolic, or chromosomal basis have been described. It has been estimated that from 2 to 3% of the population is found to have IQ values below 70. About half of this number is accounted for by Down's syndrome, rare recessive genes, and such events as birth injuries, traumata, or severe early infectious disease. Even among these, there are intelligence differences that must be explained on environmental or other genetic grounds.

The remaining 1% is believed to represent the low end of a distribution whose variances are due to both polygenic and environmental influences. The relative role of these two is under continuous debate, and there is probably more controversy today about the role of heredity in intelligence than in any other area of psychiatric genetics. Involved in the debate are such matters as the value of compensatory or head-start programs in early-childhood education, the problem of underprivileged groups, and innumerable school policies. Underlying the divergence are a number of serious difficulties: measuring intelligence apart from environmental influence, determining the role of very specific environmental deprivation on the one hand and of genes on the other on individual development, and the extrapolation of these findings to statements about population groups.

There is little doubt that intelligence scores, largely IQs, show positive correlation with genetic closeness; a thorough survey of the literature (Erlenmeyer-Kimling and Jarvik, 1963) made this clear, and these similarities persist in longitudinal studies of twins and in twins separated early in life. However, it is a common fallacy that if a trait has a significant genetic component, differences between groups with respect to that trait must be genetically determined. Actually this would only be true if all pertinent environmental valuables were identical in the two groups. As this is almost certainly not the case in the ethnic and socioeconomic groupings currently discussed, nor can it easily be brought about in a short time, many have found the arguments for the genetic conditioning of differences in racial and class IQ averages to be unconvincing.

In the case of those on the defective end of the spectrum without specific syndromes, Reed and Reed (1965) have concluded that 5/6 of such persons have at least one parent or an aunt or uncle similarly retarded. Another way in which they presented their conclusions was that the 1 to 2% of the population composed of fertile retardates produced 36% of the retardates of the next generation, so that if only normal people with normal siblings had reproduced in the previous generation, only 0.5% of the population in the United States, or 500,000 persons, would be retarded instead of triple that number as at present.

C. Patterns of Sexual Choice

Current controversy over the diagnostic status of male homosexuality turns attention to the question of genetic contribution to sexual choice patterns. Based on findings that male homosexuals had more brothers than sisters, early investigators wondered whether a female chromosome constitution might be implicated. With the advent of sex chromatin and karyotype studies, no abnormalities were found, although, on the basis of late maternal age at their birth, Slater (1962) speculated that some chromosomal aberrations might be found in certain homosexual males. Klinefelter's syndrome includes some cases with homosexual behavior, but is not generally associated with homosexuality. Some attention has been given to reports of abnormal male hormone excretion, or to prenatal effects of female hormone administration, but the pathways to behavioral manifestation are not at all clearly established.

Twin studies in a group of somewhat atypical (many psychotic or psychopathic) male homosexual subjects by Kallmann (1952) indicated a substantially higher concordance rate in monozygotic twins. Kallmann interpreted this finding in the context of a postulated polygenically controlled disturbance in psychosexual maturation patterns. One may speculate that among these patterns with a possible genetic component may be the rate of maturation of personality development, and the ability to perceive and respond to sexual stimuli, to recognize satisfaction and success, and to utilize these experiences as integrating forces in sexual role development. At vulnerable points, a pattern of behavior may be initiated that can be reinforced (or diverted) by accidental or family influences. Such influences were sought in a psychoanalytically oriented study of a number of monozygotic twin pairs discordant for homosexual behavior (Rainer, Mesnikoff, Kolb, and Carr, 1960). Among the areas that seemed to influence homosexual choice were the twins' relationship with their parents, frustration in heterosexual contacts, and poor masculine identification, often based on covert expression of the parents' super-ego defects (Kolb, Rainer, Mesnikoff, and Carr, 1961).

VI. ETHICAL ISSUES IN PSYCHIATRIC GENETICS

With increased knowledge about genetics has come greater public interest in the field, and people have come to expect answers to many questions, theoretical and practical. The concept of normality has been extended to genetic normality, and people are wondering about their chromosome constitution and their recessive genes. The scientific understanding and careful exploitation of new findings in genetics may lead to the betterment of the health and happiness of individuals and their families through prevention and treatment. At the same time, however, the premature or unthinking application of genetic concepts may cause people undue concern, arouse unreasonable expectations, or create social problems.

For the future, perhaps not too distant to be concerned about today, are the implications of genetic engineering—correction of mutational defects on the level of the DNA molecule, replacement of genes, human cloning, and so on. Artificial insemination, with choice of donor sperm, production at will of male or female children, and *in vitro* fertilization, are more immediate technical processes with possibilities for good or harm. These developments will demand the utmost in social and scientific responsibility.

At present the general upsurge in applied medical genetics has been in the areas of genetic screening and genetic counseling. Underlying these activities is the vague concept of normality. It is not easy to forget the nefarious programs that have, in the past, been instituted in the name of pseudoscientific theories. Today, with the major advances in the real science of genetics, couples often measure their own worth against a poorly defined standard of genetic perfection. The concept of normalcy leaves some thorny questions unanswered. Is the heterozygote for a recessive gene healthy? What about limitations on his choice of mate? Should the heterozygote for a dominant trait in its preclinical stage, such as Huntington's chorea, know of his future fate, if tests are found for such determination? How does one weigh the relative importance of individual happiness, health of immediate offspring, and social benefit, short- and long-term? What of genes that are harmful in double dose but confer a benefit to the heterozygote? They could be decreased by screening, counseling, or even sterilization, or increased by medical advances that reduce the homozygote's genetic disadvantage—which is to be preferred?

VII. GENETIC COUNSELING AND THE ROLE OF PSYCHIATRY

Genetic counseling today involves not only taking an accurate medical and family history, but obtaining all necessary laboratory tests. Amniocentesis may yield fetal cells or fluid for enzyme study, which in some conditions (mainly rare ones) may foretell the fate of the given embryo. Many parents today ask for such a test "to see if my child will be normal," and it must be explained that only certain indications exist for such a procedure.

Genetic screening programs of newborns, or of prospective parents, have been activated for Tay-Sachs disease and for sickle cell anemia. These programs, however, raise the serious need for informed consent with proper explanation and genetic counseling for all involved; these provisions would seem to be minimum measures for preventing undue anxiety, misunderstanding, or trauma.

Turning to specific psychiatric disorders, counseling in schizophrenia is largely limited to persons with schizophrenic relatives or to schizophrenic adults who contemplate marriage or parenthood. In the latter groups, it is clear that genetic counseling cannot be divorced from psychiatric management, and it is generally agreed that the counselor should ideally be a psychiatrist as well. The risks of parenthood may then be discussed in terms of the health of the parents as well as of genetic risks for future offspring.

Similar considerations arise in the case of manic-depressive psychosis. With evidence for dominant inheritance, many prospective parents themselves may have mild or severe recurring illness, and if X-linkage is confirmed, it may even be possible in some families to determine in advance which members are likely to be vulnerable to the psychosis. At the same time, the psychiatrist will be aware of the need for careful diagnosis, have knowledge of alternate forms of the same disorder, and be able to assess the role of new treatment methods as they affect the advice given by genetic counselors.

The psychiatrist who is in touch with biological advances in genetics, must not overlook his responsibility to apply these to patients with humane understanding according to his knowledge of human feeling and motivation. The guilt, recrimination, and sense of worthlessness felt by parents who are led to believe they are genetically abnormal must be appreciated, and counseling has to be psychotherapeutically oriented.

The new science of genetics in psychiatry has already achieved much and will open many more pathways in the future to understanding and control. As biologists we must place our new knowledge in its evolutionary perspective, as social-minded students of pathology, we must consider it within its environmental settings, and as humane clinicians, we must apply and interpret it in the broadest traditions of ethical medicine.

REFERENCES

Allen, M. G., Cohen, S., and Pollin, W. (1972): Schizophrenia in veteran twins: A diagnostic review. *Am. J. Psych.,* 128:939–945.

Barr, M. L., and Bertram, E. G. (1949): A morphological distinction between neurons of the male and female, and the behavior of the nucleolar satellite during accelerated nucleoprotein synthesis. *Nature,* 163:676–677.

Chicago Conference (1966): Standardization in human cytogenetics. *Birth Defects: Original Article Series, The National Foundation,* p. 2.

Cowie, J., and Kahn, J. (1968): The XYY constitution in a pre-pubertal child. *Br. Med. J.,* 1:748–749.

Denver Report (1960): A proposed standard system of nomenclature of human mitotic chromosomes. *Am. J. Hum. Genet.,* 12:384–388.

Edwards, J. H., Harnden, D. G., Cameron, A. H., Crosse, V. M., and Wolff, O. H. (1960): A new trisomic syndrome. *Lancet,* 1:787–790.

Ehrman L., Omenn, G., and Caspari, E., editors (1972): *Genetics, Environment and Behavior.* Academic Press, New York.

Erlenmeyer-Kimling, L., editor (1972): *Genetics and Mental Disorders.* International Arts and Sciences Press, New York.

Erlenmeyer-Kimling, L., and Jarvik, L. (1963): Genetics and intelligence: A review. *Science,* 142:1477–1479.

Fischer, M., Harvald, B., and Hauge, M. (1969): *Br. J. Psych.,* 115:981–990.

Følling, A. (1934): Über Ausscheidung von Phenylbrenztraubensäure in den Harn als Stoffwechselanomalie in Verbindung mit Imbezzillität. *Z. Physiol. Chem.,* 227:169–176.

Freud, A. (1966): *Normality and Pathology in Childhood,* p. 233. Hogarth Press, London.

Freud, S. (1958): The disposition to obsessional neurosis, a contribution to the problem of choice of neurosis. In: *Standard Edition, Vol. 12,* pp. 317–326. Hogarth Press, London; originally published in 1913.

Freud, S. (1964): Analysis terminable and interminable. In: *Standard Edition, Vol. 23,* pp. 216–254. Hogarth Press, London; originally published in 1937.

Fuller, J. L., and Thompson, W. R. (1960): *Behavior Genetics.* Wiley, New York.

Garrone, G. (1962): Étude statistique et génétique de la schizophrénie a Geneve de 1901 a 1950. *J. Genet. Hum.,* 11:89–219.

Goodwin, D. W., Schulsinger, F., Hermansen, L., Guze, S. B., and Winokur, G. (1973): Alcohol problems in adoptees raised apart from alcoholic biological parents. *Arch. Gen. Psych.,* 28:238–243.

Gottesman, I. I., and Shields, J. (1972): *Schizophrenia and Genetics: A Twin Study Vantage Point.* Academic Press, New York.

Harris, H. (1970): *Garrod's Inborn Errors of Metabolism.* Oxford University Press, London.

Hartmann, H. (1950): Comments on the psychoanalytic theory of the ego. *Psychoanal. Study Child,* 5:74–96.

Heston, L. L., and Denney, D. (1968): Interactions between early life experience and biological factors in schizophrenia. In: *The Transmission of Schizophrenia,* edited by D. Rosenthal and S. S. Kety. Pergamon Press, Oxford.

Inouye, E. (1972): Genetic aspects of neurosis: A review. *Int. J. Ment. Health,* 1:176–189.

Jacob, F., and Monod, J. (1961): Genetic regulatory mechanisms in the synthesis of proteins. *J. Mol. Biol.,* 3:318–356.

Jarvik, L. F., Altshuler, K. Z., Kato, T., and Blumner, B. (1971): Organic brain syndrome and chromosome loss in aged twins. *Dis. Nerv. Syst.,* 32:159–170.

Jarvik, L. F., Kallmann, F. J., Falek, A., and Klaber, M. M. (1957): Changing intellectual functions in senescent twins. *Acta Genet. Stat. Med.,* 7:421–430.

Jarvik, L. F., and Kato, T. (1970): Chromosome examinations in aged twins. *Am. J. Hum. Genet.,* 22:562–572.

Jones, E. (1951): *Essays in Applied Psychoanalysis.* Hogarth Press, London; originally published in 1930.

Kallmann, F. J. (1938): *The Genetics of Schizophrenia.* Augustin, New York.

Kallmann, F. J. (1946): The genetic theory of schizophrenia. *Am. J. Psych.,* 103:309–322.

Kallmann, F. J. (1952): Comparative twin study of the genetic aspects of male homosexuality. *J. Nerv. Ment. Dis.,* 115:283–298.

Kallmann, F. J. (1953a): *Heredity in Health and Mental Disorder.* Norton, New York.

Kallmann, F. J. (1953*b*): Genetic principles in manic-depressive psychosis. In: *Depression,* edited by P. Hoch and J. Zubin. Grune and Stratton, New York.

Kallmann, F. J. (1961): Genetic factors in aging: Comparative and longitudinal observations in a senescent twin population. In: *Psychopathology of Aging,* edited by P. Hoch and J. Zubin. Grune and Stratton, New York.

Kallmann, F. J., editor (1962): *Expanding Goals of Genetics in Psychiatry.* Grune and Stratton, New York.

Kaplan, A. R. (1971): Association of schizophrenia with non-Mendelian genetic anomalies. In: *Genetic Factors in "Schizophrenia,"* edited by A. R. Kaplan. Charles C. Thomas, Springfield, Ill.

Kety, S. S., Rosenthal, D., Wender, P. H., and Schulsinger, F. (1968): The types and prevalence of mental illness in the biological and adoptive families of adopted schizophrenics. In: *The Transmission of Schizophrenia,* edited by D. Rosenthal and S. S. Kety. Pergamon Press, Oxford.

Kolb, L. C., Rainer, J. D., Mesnikoff, A., and Carr, A., (1961): Divergent sexual development in identical twins. In: *Third World Congress of Psychiatry, Proceedings, Vol. 1.* University of Toronto Press and McGill University Press, Montreal.

Kringlen, E. (1967): *Heredity and Environment in the Functional Psychoses.* Universitetsforlaget, Oslo.

Larsson, T., Sjögren, T., and Jacobson, G. (1963): Senile dementia: a clinical sociomedical and genetic study. *Acta Psych. Scand.,* Suppl. 167.

Lejeune, J., Gautier, M., and Turpin, R. (1959): Etudes des chromosomes somatique de neuf enfants mongolien. *C.R. Academie Science (Paris),* 148:1721–1722.

Leonhard, K. (1959): *Aufteilung der Endogenen Psychosen.* Akademie Verlag, Berlin.

Lyon, M. (1962): Sex chromatin and gene action in the mammalian X-chromosome, *Am. J. Hum. Genet.,* 14:135–148.

Mendlewicz, J., Fleiss, J. L., and Fieve, R. R. (1972): X-linkage in manic-depressive illness. *J. Am. Med. Ass.,* 222:1624–1627.

Mirsky, I. A. (1960): Physiologic, psychologic and social determinants of psychosomatic disorders. *Dis. Nerv. Syst., Monograph Suppl.,* 21:50–56.

National Institute of Mental Health (1970): *Report on the XYY Chromosome Abnormality.* U.S. Government Printing Office, Washington.

Nielsen, J., Jensen, L., Lindhardt, H., Stottrup, L., and Sondergaard, A. (1968): Chromosomes in senile dementia. *Br. J. Psych.,* 114:303–309.

Paris Conference (1972): Standardization in human cytogenetics. *Birth Defects; Original Article Series, The National Foundation,* p. 8.

Patau, K., Smith, D. W., Therman, E., Inhorn, S. L., and Wagner, H. P. (1960): Multiple congenital anomaly caused by an extra autosome. *Lancet,* 1:790–793.

Pearl, R., and Pearl, R. DeW. (1934): *The Ancestry of the Long-Lived.* Johns Hopkins Press, Baltimore.

Perris, C. (1966): A study of bipolar (manic-depressive) and unipolar recurrent depressive psychoses. *Acta Psych. Scand.* Suppl. 194.

Pollin, W., and Stabenau, J. R. (1968): Biological, psychological, and historical differences in a series of monozygotic twins discordant for schizophrenia. In: *The Transmission of Schizophrenia,* edited by D. Rosenthal and S. S. Kety. Pergamon Press, Oxford.

Pollock, H. M., Malzberg, B., and Fuller, R. G. (1939): *Heredity and Environmental Factors in the Causation of Manic-Depressive Psychoses and Dementia Praecox.* State Hospital Press, Utica.

Rado, S. (1956): Adaptational psychodynamics, a basic science. In: *Psychoanalysis of Behavior, Volume 1.* Grune and Stratton, New York.

Rainer, J. D. (1966): The contributions of Franz Josef Kallmann to the genetics of schizophrenia. *Behav. Sci.,* 11:413–437.

Rainer, J. D., Abdullah, S., and Jarvik, L. F. (1972): XYY karyotype in a pair of monozygotic twins: a 17-year life-history study. *Br. J. Psych.,* 120:543–548.

Rainer, J. D., Mesnikoff, A., Kolb, L. C., and Carr, A. (1960): Homosexuality and heterosexuality in identical twins. *Psychosom. Med.,* 22:251–259.

Raphael, T., and Shaw, M. W. (1963): Chromosome studies in schizophrenia. *J. Am. Med. Ass.,* 183:1022–1028.

Reed, S., Hartley, C., Anderson, V. E., Phillips, V. P., and Johnson, N. A. (1973): *The Psychoses: Family Studies,* Saunders, Philadelphia.

Reed, E. W., and Reed, S. C. (1965): *Mental Retardation, A Family Study.* Saunders, Philadelphia.

Reich, T., Clayton, P., and Winokur, G. (1969): Family history studies: V. The genetics of mania. *Am. J. Psych.,* 125: 1358–1369.

Rosanoff, A. J., Handy, L. M., Plesset, I. R., and Brush, S. (1934): The etiology of so-called schizophrenic psychoses with special reference to their occurrence in twins. *Am. J. Psych.,* 90:247–286.

Rosenthal, D. (1970): *Genetic Theory and Abnormal Behavior.* McGraw-Hill, New York.

Rosenthal, D., and Kety, S. S., editors (1968): *The Transmission of Schizophrenia.* Pergamon Press, Oxford.

Rosenthal, D., Wender, P. H., Kety, S. S., Schulsinger, F., Welner, J., and Østergaard, L. (1968): Schizophrenics' offspring reared in adoptive homes. In: *The Transmission of Schizophrenia,* edited by D. Rosenthal and S. S. Kety. Pergamon Press, Oxford.

Rüdin, E. (1916): *Zur Vererbung und Neuentstehung der Dementia Praecox.* Springer, Berlin.

Schulsinger, F. (1972): Psychopathy, heredity and environment. *Int. J. Ment. Health,* 1:190–206.

Schulz, B. (1932): Zur Erbpathologie der Schizophrenie. *Zeitschrift für die gesamte neurologie und psychiatrie,* 143:175–293.

Shields, J., and Slater, E. (1971): Diagnostic similarity in twins with neurosis and personality disorders. In: *Man, Mind and Heredity,* edited by J. Shields, and I. I. Gottesman. Johns Hopkins Press, Baltimore.

Slater, E. (1962): Birth order and maternal age of homosexuals. *Lancet,* 1:69–71.

Slater, E., and Cowie, V. (1971): *The Genetics of Mental Disorder.* Oxford University Press, London.

Spitz, R. A. (1965): *The First Year of Life,* pp. 224–242. International Universities Press, New York.

Stenstedt, A. (1952): A study in manic-depressive psychosis: clinical, social and genetic investigations. *Acta Psych. Neurol. Scand.,* Suppl. 79.

Thiessen, D. D. (1972): *Gene Organization and Behavior.* Random House, New York.

Thomas, A., Chess, S., Birch, H. G., Hertzig, M., and Korn, S. (1963): *Behavioral Individuality in Early Childhood.* New York University Press, New York.

Tjio, J. H., and Levan, A. (1956): The chromosome number of man. *Hereditas,* 42:1–6.

Vandenberg, S., editor (1965): *Methods and Goals in Human Behavior Genetics.* Academic Press, New York.

Vartanyan, M. E., and Gindilis, V. M. (1972): The role of chromosomal aberrations in the clinical polymorphism of schizophrenia. *Int. J. Ment. Health,* 1:93–106.

Washburn, S. L. (1959): Speculations on the interrelations of the history of tools and biological evolution. In: *The Evolution of Man's Capacity for Culture,* edited by J. N. Spuhler. Wayne State University Press, Detroit.

Watson, J. D. (1970): *Molecular Biology of the Gene.* Benjamin, New York.

Watson, J. D., and Crick, F. H. C. (1953a): Molecular structure of nucleic acids. A structure for deoxyribose nucleic acid. *Nature,* 171:737–738.

Watson, J. D., and Crick, F. H. C. (1953b): Genetical implications of the structure of deoxyribonucleic acid. *Nature,* 177:964–967.

Wender, P., Rosenthal, D., and Kety, S. S. (1968): A psychiatric assessment of the adoptive parents of schizophrenics. In: *The Transmission of Schizophrenia,* edited by D. Rosenthal and S. S. Kety. Pergamon Press, Oxford.

Winokur, G., Clayton, P., and Reich, T. (1969): *Manic-Depressive Illness.* Mosby, St. Louis.

Winokur, G., and Tanna, V. L. (1969): Possible role of X-linked dominant factor in manic-depressive disease. *Dis. Nerv. Syst.,* 30:89–94.

Zerbin-Rüdin, E. (1969): Zur Genetik der depressiven Erkrankungen. In: *Das Depressive Syndrom,* edited by H. Hippius and H. Selbach. Urban & Schwarzenberg, Munich.

Biological Foundations of Psychiatry,
edited by R. G. Grenell and S.
Gabay. Raven Press, New York ©
1976.

Sensory Processing, Perception, and Behavior

Robert B. Livingston

Neurosciences Department and Institute for Information Systems, University of California San Diego,
La Jolla, California 92093

I. INTRODUCTION

Many the wonders
But none more wonderful than man
Who has learned the art of speech
and windswift thought
and living in neighborliness.
He faces no future helpless, only death.
And he has contrived refuge from illnesses
once beyond all cure.

Chorus in *Antigone* by Sophocles

One of the principal aims of psychiatry is to comprehend human experience and behavior in their fullest dimensions. Accepting this aim thrusts us into the same deep, searching endeavor that has absorbed the talents of a great host of individuals in humanistic as well as scientific disciplines. Philosophers, poets, playwrights, and novelists have been exploring these problems alongside clinicians and basic medical scientists.

When we look up from our medical pursuits, we are both excited and impressed by the insights into problems that we are attempting to understand as conveyed, for example, in the sonnets and the plays of Shakespeare. The humanists do not assess complicated processes piecemeal in the way that scientists are wont to do. They depend rather on intuitive imagination, delving into their own subjective feelings and observing with keen eyes the behavior and testimony of others. They portray human experience and behavior through vignettes of individual personages, interlocked with one another in dramatic form. And they succeed best when they create robust characterizations that are so thoroughly integrated that the imagined individual's purposes, values, and attachments transport the drama and compel the tragic and comic outcomes. The greatest of these geniuses seems not only to understand individual human beings thoroughly but also to be able to predict the consequences of a given character in given circumstances wonderfully well. This is a necessary element to the success of their art.

These considerations attract us to inquire what may be missing in the traditional scientific treatment of our subject matter, the mechanisms governing human sensory processing, perception, and behavior. Perhaps we are too isolated within our individual disciplinary extractions. Adequate information may be at hand, in the discipline next door, or perhaps floating as bits and pieces of a mosaic that could be assembled if only we could communicate adequately among the various disciplines. Perhaps we are insufficiently daring in making theoretical assumptions needed to bridge the gaps in our knowledge. Altogether, it seems, the facts that we think we understand seem small and shrivelled, and sparse when compared with an idealized portrait of the whole, like dried seeds rattling in a gourd.

We agree that complexity begets emergent properties that cannot be predicted from knowledge of mechanisms based at some lower level of analysis no matter how adequately the lower level mechanisms are understood. The corollary of this insight is that regularities do appear at successively greater levels of complexity from molecules, cells, organs, organisms, to societies, and so on without our being able to provide a deductive account of how it is that those successive regularities make their appearance. The playwright of course operates without the constraints of a scientific discipline, but still, he reasons through much of what we despair of sorting out; and we yield him credit for his portrayal through our own intuitive assessments.

The scientist is not expected to be a philosopher, poet, playwright, or novelist. But perhaps we can identify one shortcoming in traditional scientific presentations that would benefit our own accounting if we only had the requisite daring. As scientists, we may be too shy about making inferences, and yet what we can put together without peradventure of doubt may not be entirely satisfying.[1] Even when all the fragments of the scientific objective are mastered, serious gaps remain in relation to practical problems and, in the final analysis, these must be filled in imaginatively by the practitioner. A somewhat more comprehensive whole might be pieced together by resorting to selected literature throughout all pertinent neurosciences fields including the social sciences, but the feeling of unity of the subject matter might by then have strayed off.

What may take us some measure toward remedying this difficulty is for an author to assume greater than ordinarily allowed liberty in attempting to assemble information from different disciplines and from different levels of scientific discourse. With care, this might be done in a rather personal synoptic way so as to account, approximately, for the complicated whole as perceived in an integrated manner, as all of a piece.

There are obviously grave dangers in this, for both reader and author. Any such view is bound to be wrong in many detailed respects, and it may be quite misleading on the grand scale. As everyone readily understands, there are not yet enough facts known to put the details together into complete wholes to comprehend the basics of most clinical problems in the rest of

---

[1] Kenneth E. Boulding made a somewhat facetious comment on this problem which epitomizes what we are saying: "Science might almost be defined as the process of substituting unimportant questions which can be answered for important questions which cannot" (1).

medicine, much less in psychiatry. The bulk of information transmitted in this synoptic fashion is more likely to have a briefer than usual half-life of reputability, and may possibly deserve no existence at all in terms of scientific respectability. Nevertheless, such an account might be of some assistance to someone, a stranger to most of the details, to be presented a view, even if it is tentative, even if it succeeds only in helping the reader secure an interest in, an overview of, a difficult subject matter taken as a whole. If an abiding interest can be established, the reader will soon cultivate his own way of navigating through the moot shoals, and he will soon establish his own authority from studying patients and fribbling as most of us do with the sprawling literature.

This chapter, then, is an attempt to communicate some of the majesty and transcendent beauty of sensory processing, perception, and behavior. Conceptual liberties are taken freely, without further apologies. This is in part because of the broad interdisciplinary span of the subject matter within which only an amateur standing can be claimed for most, because of the enormity of the literature and detail involved, much of which is too burdensome to transmit and a good deal of which is unsettled anyhow, and, finally, because of the wide gaps in our knowledge which, according to the arguments just given, must be imaginatively bridged conceptually now, even though they will undoubtedly require engineering reconstruction as better information and wiser interpretations come forward.

> *We may suppose that in the time run through by a course of action focussed upon a final consummatory event, opportunity is given for instinct, with its germ of memory however rudimentary and its germ of anticipation however slight, to evolve under selection that mental extension of the present backward into the past and forward into the future which in the highest animals forms the prerogative of more developed mind. Nothing, it would seem, could better ensure the course of action taken in that interval being the right one than memory and anticipatory forecast: and nothing, it would seem, could tend to select more potently the individuals taking the right course than the success which crowns that course, since the consummatory acts led up to are such— e.g. the seizure of prey, escape from enemies, attainment of sexual conjugation, etc.—as involve the very existence of the individual and the species.*

> Sir Charles Sherrington, *Integrative Action of the Nervous System* (1906)

II. BEHAVIOR AND EVOLUTION

A. Perception in Relation to Behavior and Evolution

Organisms are built for action. They are self-organizing systems and, given substrate, they spontaneously move, secrete and grow. The metabolic engines of life yield behavior even in a stimulus-monotonous environment. A point of importance is that without behavior there could be no evolution. Even single-celled organisms and plants are not exempt from that dictum.

To succeed in evolution, organisms must survive to reproductive age and they must also successfully reproduce. Put another way around, living systems possess survival and reproductive capacities that are indispensable to the furtherance of evolution. That sounds like a tautology, but really it is not. We are accounting for a chain of progressive successions, not recurrences as in a circle. Fecundity offers the surplus, and diversity offers the variations which are winnowed and selected according to their possession of behavioral traits which are useful for survival and reproduction, and which only after behavioral success can contribute to continuing evolution.

It is by means of this progressive and creative selection procedure acting on the basis of *behavior* that successful genetic lines are shaped into divergent species which because of their diversity may have members who possess particular advantages for one or another environment, or better still, general adaptive capacities which make them able to fit into a variety of environments, including rapidly changing ones. We shall examine behavior and its role in evolution in order to understand better the place of perception in relation to behavior and ultimately the role of sensory processing as contributory to perception.

It will be observed that we are proceeding from behavior to perception to sensory mechanisms rather than the other way around. This is the opposite of tradition. Our reasons are clear. The question may rightly be asked, "Sensation for what?" For perception, and ultimately behavior. And behavior for what? Behavior is that expressive process which is instrumental in the selection processes of evolution. *It is precisely behavior that is selected for, and only secondarily are perceptions and sensory processes at stake* because they are not manifest, lying as they do behind behavior. It is important to remember that *sensory processing and perception may be in error, and frequently are in error, without the fault being tested, as long as the behavior remains tolerably successful.* In fact, perception and sensory processing will not ordinarily be corrected unless and until the behavior is discovered to be in error (2).

All this may seem problematical because of our habit of thinking that sensory input governs behavior rather exclusively. On the contrary, *sensory input does not guide behavior in any exclusive way.* As we shall try to establish, *all behavior may be considered a search for internal satisfactions in which sensory input plays only a prognosticatory and consequence-tallying role.* The contents of conscious and unconscious processing of the momentary flux which includes past experiences, expectations, purposes and sensation are all shaped together in anticipatory projection of forthcoming behavioral advantages. In this total flux, sensation is only one part, and it is not often a dominant part (3).

As we shall take pains to emphasize throughout this chapter, the S→R paradigm, which stands for "stimulus leads to response," is too exclusive. It fails to reflect more than an artificial and modest portion of behavior, behavior limited to times when the internal state of that organism is peculiarly set for just that outcome.

1. The Interdependence of DNA, Morphogenesis, and Behavior

Simpson (4) has concluded that "the major (if not the only) non-random, orienting factor in the process of evolution is reasonably identified as adaptation." Deoxyribonucleic acid (DNA), bodily structure, and behavior are complementary agents that respond to the requirements for adaptation. Continuity and heritability in evolution are due, as is now commonly appreciated, to an appropriate elaboration, according to chance, of the DNA molecule. Appropriateness of the changes that take place in the DNA is defined by the results of selective demands imposed on survival and reproductive capacities, as defined by structure and behavior. These latter must be sufficiently effective for the protection and delivery of the DNA. The interdependent molecule, structure, and behavior thus vault over one another in cartwheel fashion in an endless succession of generations.

Each of our direct ancestory, therefore, (a) comported herself and himself adequately to reach reproductive age and (b) succeeded in reproducing what could carry the DNA and certain structural and behavioral competences forward into succeeding generations. We find ourselves contemporary witnesses standing, with the most recent links in our hands, contemplating a chain of successfully behaving organisms that reaches back in a direct line all the way between ourselves and some fateful catalyst in a primeval sea, and which bears a complicated network of kinship with all other forms of life. This direct line spans some three or four thousand million years—an unbroken record for the successful elaborations of DNA and parallel successful progressions in structure and behavior.

We are fitted for life according to the history of that chain. The behavioral selection pressures that were applied to our ancestors and the talents that emerged in them by virtue of the chance changes in their DNA have conclusively shaped our nervous system, its limitations and its potentialities, including all means by which we perceive, discriminate, and comport ourselves.

Through the combined operations of "chance and necessity," a phrase introduced into this very context by Sophocles (see Monod, ref. 5, for an entrancing explanation of the contemporary biological explanations of these processes), there emerged new forms of life that possessed increasingly broader ranges of behavioral alternatives. This increase in freedom of behavior provides a reasonable definition of "higher forms" of life. By this process, behavior has become increasingly less reflexive and imperious and increasingly creatively adaptive.

2. The Emergence of Higher Nervous Processes

Even single-celled organisms must provide appropriate linkages between "receptor" elements on their cellular surface and "effector" elements among their organelles. Their receptors are prototypical for all of our sensory apparatus and their effectors for all of the means by which we behave. Sensorimotor linkages are internal, intracellular in the beginning, and by evolutionary progression, gradually lengthened and complicated—as in multicellular nervous and endocrine systems presented by higher forms. Yet, in common with single-celled organisms, all we can do is to discriminate among a paltry few of the total potential stimuli in our environment and then either relax, contract, or secrete.

The magnificent potentialities of human behavior arise, simply stated, from the longer circuiting of these fundamental linkages. The choices of efferent (effector) output are determined internally, and they depend strictly on the momentary internal state of the organism. There is never a direct path from stimulus to response. Even the monosynaptic path for stretch reflexes which arcs between certain muscle receptors, the spinal cord, and returns to the same muscle, is susceptible to modulations and interventions which can converge on that synaptic relay from many remote regions of the neuraxis (6). Whether an otherwise adequate stimulus elicits a response depends strictly on the internal state of that neuraxis, not simply the integrity of the reflex arc *per se*. There is, in short, never a direct linkage between stimulus and response, even when the path is confined within a single cell.

It took about half of all the time of evolution for chemical aggregates to produce successful single cells, and about half of all the remaining time for cells to produce successful multicellular organisms (7). This latter step required, first and foremost, controls for the subordination of parts on behalf of the whole. What it allowed was an almost unlimited variation in specialization of parts, particularly among nervous mechanisms, receptors, effectors, and the increasingly elaborate central circuitry which provided for the integrity of the organism as a whole and for internal sensorimotor linkages through central circuits.

The biosphere became quickly populated by multicellular species. The highest of these, in terms of degrees of behavioral freedom, ergo the most creatively adaptable, is mankind which has successfully occupied all terrestrial environments, using direct and artificial means. Indeed, mankind has been nearly, but not quite, as successful in adapting to various parts of the biosphere, as some single-celled organisms such as some of the blue-green algae. If mankind, or the blue-green algae, were to become entirely successful by way of adaptation, there would be no pressure for their further speciation.

During the evolutionary ascent of man, there have been developed increasingly adaptive linkages among receptors, the mechanisms accounting for the internal state, and effector mechanisms. As we shall see, these three components are mutually strongly interdependent throughout evolution, development, and behavior.

The broader ranges of behavioral alternatives that have emerged during the evolution of higher forms have been governed by increasingly complicated internal mechanisms including those which we subsume, without fully understanding them, under the headings of consciousness, perception, judgment, and volition. The origins of these processes, which in man are exceedingly involved, must have been quite humble, and they undoubtedly obtained an early start in evolution. The advantage for successful coping and reproductive behavior of having central circuitry that is capable of providing additional alternatives to otherwise largely reflexive behaviors is obvious. See below how this is achieved so as to preserve reflexes and yet to allow an increasing range of alternatives (8).

Further advantage accrues when the central representation for such alternatives begins to be subject to controls that can be applied in accordance with the results of a broad range of past experiences. This requires that experience, at least biologically significant experience, leaves its trace. The weighted average of such traces, when related to experiences that correspond with incoming sensory signals, can then be introduced in such a manner as to improve the probabilities of successful behaviors in the future. This, in any event, is what seems to happen in respect to memory trace effects that modify ongoing behavior in higher forms.

Continually more powerful advantage stems from adding additional display space in the central nervous system, thus providing a further enrichment of memory stores together with improved interactive processes so that more discriminative selections can be arranged. This may be supposed to come about through comparisons being made among incoming sensory data, expanded representations of the internal state, together with representations of the present potential alternatives for behavior, all being influenced by an assortment of past similar experiences, including the important biological outcomes elicited on those earlier occasions. This description seems logical enough but it begins to beggar the imagination; it therefore deserves being analyzed later in respect to its various component mechanisms.

3. The Ascendancy of Higher Nervous Processes

Advantages, even slight in the beginning, tend to be accelerated in evolutionary perfection at least until some limitations are met. So far as we know, the usefulness of cognitive processes such as consciousness, perception, judgment, and volition have not begun to meet any limits. There has instead been a remarkable qualitative as well as quantitative expansion, practically an explosion, of these higher nervous processes during the most recent one-tenth of one percent of the history of evolution, coinciding with the emergence of *Homo sapiens sapiens*. Mankind and the contemporary higher apes (gorilla, chimpanzee, and orangutan) apparently separated from common ancestors approximately four and one-half to five million years ago (9). Within that short span of evolutionary time, higher nervous processes accelerated vastly in their scope and potentialities.

Evolution has accumulated in mankind an awesome degree of freedom of behavior, e.g., to study mankind, the environment, even evolution itself, and to begin learning what it would take to design and control the future course of evolution by means of deliberate biological interventions. This is probably the most important fact known to science (10), and it is certainly the most significant event in all of evolutionary history.

Evidence from cave painting and expert tool-making, suggestive of cognitive processes underlying symbolization and language formation, supported by inferences from fossil skull structures carry the point of emergence of spoken language somewhere between 50,000 and 500,000 years ago (11). The importance of this momentous event to the cognitive history of mankind cannot be overestimated. It enabled the dissemination and storage, independent of any single nervous system, of experiences that have cultural and survival values for the group. It provided an expanded cognitive grip on cultural integration. The obviously uncertain span of dates reflects a presumably extended period when, it must be supposed, the ululations of the anthropoids (presumably localized in the cephalic brainstem) either were transformed into or were superordinated by verbal symbolizations employed in accordance with phonetic and syntactical rules (presumably neocortical in representation) (11–14).

Written language began with primitive astronomical and other prognosticatory notations about 50,000 years ago, but developed its own practical rules only later, between about 3000 and 1500 B.C. at nearly the same time in both Asia and the Mediterranean region. The first library of clay tablets was assembled in Assyria during the Reign of Assurbanipal, about 650 B.C. (15). Mathematics dates from a practical treatise written by an Egyptian priest before 1000 B.C. It received more theoretical treatment in the form of propositions and deductive reasoning in the hands of Ionian Greeks beginning with Thales and Pythagoras in the 7th and 6th centuries B.C., respectively (15). Literature, theater, and music (including musical notation) developed shortly; much later, such advantages as moveable type and, more recently, cinema, radio, and video transmission, and the assistance of computers for engineering, mathematical and cognitive processing, and notation. The importance of these cultural advances stems from their extraordinary power for detailed and permanent documentation and ultimately practically unlimited and instantaneous dissemination of information about ideas, objects, and events. Each such advance represented at the time an uncanny supplementation to the powers of individual and collective consciousness, perception, and judgment, and a significant instrument for the binding of cultural integrity.

The difficult problem of emergence of consciousness has been thoughtfully considered by a great number of authors. We find ourselves in essential harmony with the views advanced by Sellars (16) and Herrick (10), and extensively treated in Herrick's biography of Coghill (17). Briefly put, *consciousness can be considered a co-emergent property of nervous organiza-*

tion. The contents of consciousness and the degrees of its elaboration will obviously depend on the design and capacity of any given nervous system. The central biological advantage is that consciousness of imagery, and the powers this conveys for the sorting of such images in the process of internal trial and error discrimination and ratiocination prior to behavioral exposure, and for taking apart and reassembling images in novel configurations, the biological foundation for creativity, have contributed enormously to the advancement of behavioral competence.

There has been an unfortunate tendency generally in Western civilization and more particularly in Western science to neglect the importance of subjective as well as objective information relating to human behavior. Just because the subjective experience is not easily accessible in animals does not warrant the relatively wholesale rejection of that information in the study of human experience and behavior. We adhere to the view given by Hamilton (18), a psychiatrist, that "Subjective phenomena, *as these are experienced by the persons who report their occurrence,* do not need to be translated into anything else in order to be dealt with as objectively as we deal with all other biological phenomena."

B. Evolution and Development of Cognitive Skills

Some of the mystery of cognitive processing can be dispatched at the outset by our recognizing the key biological step taken to alter behavior from being purely reflexive to being facultatively longer-circuiting in character. We have stressed how indispensable effective behavior is in the history of evolution. This notion helps us to appreciate that even slight contributions that make behavior more effective are favored during evolution. What took place required the safeguarding of reflexes while adding more complex behavioral possibilities. This process involved the *insertion* of new pathways-of-access into the interneuronal pool through which the reflex patterns were being transmitted.

1. Evolutionary Insertion of Longer-Circuiting Pathways

The increase in freedom of behavior which serves as a useful definition of higher evolutionary forms came about by the insertion or infusion of longer-circuiting nervous system pathways into the central relay junctions used by more primitive reflex systems. This represented an additional interposition between sensory input and motor output. The determinative switchings and final behavioral controls take place within the interneuronal pools that surround the motor neurons serving effector organs. Because of the heterogeneous nature of pathways converging upon these "executive neurons" in the spinal cord and brainstem, Sherrington (19) referred to them as "final common paths." Access of longer-circuiting pathways to processes taking place at this important junction does not eliminate reflex responses. Higher nervous control of effector organs is *integrated* with reflex patterns. But the evolutionary achievement of such access provided, in principle, for an unlimited panoply of higher nervous system options to become available to behavior.

The central key to this evolutionary advancement lies in precisely how the most direct reflexive and the longer-circuiting pathways can share in the necessary integrative processes. Sensory incoming signals, arising from a variety of receptors, conveyed along nerve fibers having different conduction velocities, are distributed upward and downward along the spinal cord and brainstem by ascending and descending branches of the incoming fibers. The time-space display of these incoming signals is thought to control choices of message routing via second-order neurons by way of reflex responses and sensory projections passing centralward (20–22).

Multiple descending influences which come directly from cortex via the pyramidal tract and from many other cortical and subcortical stations via the remaining descending systems, collectively called extrapyramidal, distribute impulses within both sensory and motor nuclei and thereby apply indirect and direct influences upon ascending sensory signalling, reflex outflow, and the more elective aspects of motor performance (6, 23, 24). Interneurons residing in brainstem and spinal cord aggregations constituting sensory and motor nuclei, in the respective dorsal and ventral horns of the spinal cord, make contributions by way of their own spontaneous activity and impulses via short and intermediate range relays and recurrent feedback projections wholly contained within those cellular aggregations (6, 25).

Both *analysis,* characteristic of sensory trajectories, and *synthesis,* embodied in the confluent funneling through the final common path to efferent organs, are accomplished by these kinds of neuronal means. The important evolutionary "invention" that enabled insertion of higher level controls took place gradually, with increasing power of governance from higher centers (26). Ultimately the entire design and control potential of the human cerebrum became functionally insinuated into the interneuronal junctions at all sensorimotor integrative stations strung along the entire brainstem and spinal cord.

The critical switching that allows such higher nervous processes to affect behavior takes place at sites that are juxtaposed among the reflexive short-circuiting paths, the intermediately longer-circuiting visceral sensory signalling and visceral motor relays, and the longest-circuiting awesome processes of cerebration. The forces of evolution that have led to higher forms have been selectively expressed in accordance with advantages gained by creatures that utilized these higher nervous pathways to best strategic advantage. The essence of this advantage rests on improved conscious and unconscious prognostications for behavior: this means improved sensory processing, perception, decision making, and motor control command. Sensory input data play upon each of these processes from imperious reflexes to the most exalted of considered judgments, but the payoff, for the individual and for the species, still depends, strictly and exclusively, on the success or failure of the emitted behavior.

Even the most elaborate, longest-circuiting pathway does not come under the culling influence of evolutionary selection except insofar as it adds to or detracts from successful behavior. This is a point of utmost philosophical and practical importance. It cannot be known whether what transpires in the way of sensory processing and perceptual experience supports a "true," "veridical," or "objective" image of the outside world or any event in it. Images can be sometimes discovered to be false. No images can be found to be "true," although we often act as though they were true with certitude, even to the harm of others.

Although scientists try to obtain facts and to verify them in a variety of ways, in the end, they are up against observations such as dial readings and other perceptions that are affected by past experiences, expectations, and purposes (1, 2, 27, 28). There is no way to check for error in perceptions except through the examination of behavioral outcomes. What needs to be added to this universal fact is that perceptions are individually idiosyncratic, depending on past history, expectations, and purposes, and that perceptions compared across cultures show even greater differences (29–32). According to these differences, the world and events in it are seen differently, responded to differently, and have different significances with respect to the attachment of values. The red fields of battle, the green tables of diplomacy, and the gray towers of justice represent primitive means that have been created to deal with problems that arise from perceptual differences, among other sources of conflict.

The insertion of roundabout circuits for optional additional behaviors would allow for practically unlimited ramifications except for three factors. (a) It is necessary to have the system operate holistically, with parts subordinated to the objectives of the whole organism. This requires the centralization of what might be called "approach/avoidance" orientation and "go/no go" behavior-releasing mechanisms. In the case of vertebrate brains, these latter appear to be located in the region of the posterior hypothalamus (17, 33–36). (b) It is beneficial to have behavioral release that is based on incoming sensory data made relatively promptly so that the behavior will be in time with the event. The turnaround time thus needs to be kept short. (c) It is also beneficial that behavioral release be unambiguous; this is not always the case and the behavior may oscillate indeterminably (37). All three of these factors place constraints on the systems organization of brain mechanisms involved in sensory processing and perception (3).

We have considered some of the evolutionary advantages of higher nervous processes, their ascendancy and their widespread distribution. We have not, however, provided reasons that might help explain how this spectacular biological ornamentation may have originated. The question is: By what biological means might human cognitive skills have become possible?

2. The Evolutionary Route Taken By Mankind

Attention has focussed on the explosive expansion of the human brain during the relatively short evolutionary period when humankind and the great apes took different paths to the present. Many reasons have been given for this unique organ development. One of the most persuasive of these is the notion that a large fraction of brain development was put off until after birth. The human infant is remarkably immature when compared with any other animals. The turtle is independent from hatching. The newborn zebra is on its feet within a few minutes and can keep up with the herd within a few hours. The young monkey is able to ambulate and climb shortly after birth.

The human offspring, in contrast, spends about 20% of its total lifespan in gradually decreasing dependence on the parental generation. The human infant is born with certain perceptual skills relating to visual and auditory space (38, 39). It learns with extraordinary rapidity (40), and does not seem to be motivated by reinforcement so much as by an intrinsic predilection for problem-solving, even within the first postnatal days (38). The human babe seems more precocious at least in sensory skills than previously credited. Some of these skills seem to disappear later, perhaps from neglect of their cultivation, or possibly because of some central reorganization. Some of the disappearing sensory skills come back later in a different context, related to different perceptual strategies (38).

The child spends a great deal of time developing a succession of constituent components of his ultimate (adult) perceiving, behaving self. This process begins with brain operations such as nutritive, visceral, and skeletal reflexes and the perceptual skills just mentioned. Gradually added to these are mental operations that arise through the development of the child's own body image, with isolation of external objects and persons, and some beginning conceptions relating to the constancy of objects (41). Still later appears a more comprehensive awareness of the self which is characterized by longer-range purposes, consistent and persisting values, and lasting affectional attachments. Altogether this ensemble of emergent character can be said to constitute an integrated, whole, self-organizing system that can be defined briefly as a *brain-mind-self* complex (42).

This characterological development merges with what Bronowski (43) calls "the long childhood," a period of several years of dependent apprenticeship that instills special social and cultural skills based on the culture and setting within which the child is immersed. An Eskimo child and one in the Kalahari Desert will be learning radically different family activities, languages, and methods of coping with their habitats. The rate of learning during this apprenticeship is extraordinary. Among a great many other cognitive skills, the child is learning a language, an elaborate system of values, including codes for decorum, and is in both specific and global aspects becoming rapidly aculturated, that is, becoming firmly committed according to a given culture.

The child is born with an incompletely developed brain. Although the vast majority of neurons are already present, a small fraction of microneurons are still being produced. These find their way into cortical structures and provide processes and synaptic junctions in an unusual way during the mind-brain-self development period (44). Altman has suggested that this micro-neuronal architecture may represent the establishment of circuitry specifically relating to early learning experiences. Many cells are still migrating into surface layers of the cerebral cortex, neurons are also migrating into the hippocampus, and other limbic structures are undergoing rapid maturation late during gestation and continuing for months postnatally (45). The cerebellum is perhaps the most immature region, and its fine structure is affected by limb mobility and other factors postnatally (46). It may well be that sensorimotor skills representing unconscious proprioception are being assembled in the process of cerebellar maturation (47, 48).

The child's brain grows at a prodigious rate during this entire time. It doubles in volume within 6 months after birth and doubles again by the end of the 4th year. Roughly half of the increase in volume is due to proliferation of neuronal processes and the other half to myelination of axons which contributes importantly to nerve impulse conduction velocity and reliability (49, 50). Myelination, which occurs rapidly from the end of the first trimester during gestation, continues at a high rate throughout childhood and adolescence and thereafter at a slow rate into old age (51).

a. The child's brain development and aculturation

No other animal has either such a long period of dependent apprenticeship or such a spectacular brain development, with its attendant elaboration of circuitry that is being built up during the period of acquisition of cognitive operations embracing an entire culture. There is reason to presume that these two features—brain growth and aculturation—are interactive in some ways and that the brain circuits being laid down are affected in that process according to specific experiences relating to a specific environment. Fine synaptic modeling is considered fundamental to learning (52, 53), and brain morphogenesis during a prolonged period of exposure to significant novel experiences can be expected to be modeled in accordance with the ongoing experiences. The prodigious rate of learning seems to continue throughout the period of rapid brain growth and beyond, into adolescence, after which there is a decline in rate of oxygen consumption to adult levels (54, 55). It has been demonstrated in rats that "enriched" as compared with "impoverished" environments yield larger brains with increased cortical thickness and an increase in fine processes (56–58). It is well recognized, also, that chronic undernutrition during this period of rapid growth slows the maturational process and leads to measurable deficits in the number of brain cells and the volume occupied by nerve processes and synaptic structures (55, 59–63). Later feeding apparently cannot make up for such deficits.

b. Evolutionary selection processes thought to favor late brain development

Given the facts of notable immaturity of the human infant, postponement of a great deal of human brain development until the early postnatal months and years, and the extraordinary morphogenic plasticity of the developing brain during the prolonged infancy and childhood, we may take the liberty of presuming how the hominid line sprang ahead of its cousins the great apes. Larger brains had already demonstrated strong evolutionary advantages. The size of the brain, however, was probably limited by the risk to mother and offspring as a consequence of difficulty in delivering the larger head. One choice: build more spraddle-legged women. A way around such an impasse could be the following compromise: much of the brain growth would be postponed until after birth. This would entail delivery of an immature infant requiring more care-giving by adults. Nervous and endocrine changes in both parents and offspring would be required to accommodate this close generational interdependence.

The child would be born with more general rather than specific capacities built into its brain circuitry at the time of birth. The period of rapid, vulnerable brain growth coupled with rapid learning experiences would be reflected in an enormously expanded capacity to adapt to a specialized environment. The general capacity for learning would be substituted for built-in guidance governing behavior. It may well have been such factors expressing themselves in mankind, in contrast to the higher apes, that enabled the hominid line to become adapted to all terrestrial environments.

c. Evolutionary contributions to human reproductive success

Mammalian life could not have emerged and succeeded without there being achieved adequacy of behavior involved in the obligate cooperation necessary for fertilization and also the generational contributions for carrying the unborn and for providing tissue for nutrition of the newborn. This requires perceptual and behavioral activities, influenced by endocrine secretions, that will ensure the necessary cooperation, mutual trust and altruism, making them all conducive to internal satisfactions. We can provide only a few examples from the massively scaled and intricate pattern of nervous, endocrine and behavioral activities involved. The Neurosciences Third Study Program presented a resume, organized by Donald Pfaff, from which the following items are drawn (64).

Nervous and endocrine systems evolved early in evolution and have remained interdependent, with nervous mechanisms controlling endocrine activities and *vice versa*. Hypothalamic regulation of six anterior pituitary hormones involves the discharge into the portal-hypophyseal vessels of various releasing and inhibiting peptides by the hypothalamus (65). Anterior pituitary hormonal effects on target endocrine glands in turn contribute part of the feedback control of hypothalamic initiatives; other controls return by way of nervous pathways that are themselves affected by the history of hormonal levels (66). The two posterior pituitary hormones are secreted directly into the general circulation by nerve endings of cells lying in the hypothalamus. Altogether, five of the pituitary hormones, four anterior and one posterior, contribute directly to reproductive behavior, and the remaining pituitary hormones probably also contribute indirectly.

Prenatal hormonal conditions establish the basic psychosexual orientation of the individual. High concentrations of androgenic hormones affect sexual and social development of the adult genetic female monkey and human if the androgenic conditioning is given during gestation (67, 68). Perinatal exposure to testicular secretions modifies tissue differentiation in genitourinary systems and in specific parts of the spinal, brainstem, and higher nervous centers (69, 70). They alter the normally cyclic hypothalamic controls to being tonic (71), diminish hypothalamic responses to female hormones (72, 73), and increase responsiveness of the adult spinal cord to androgens (74).

> All tissues, central and peripheral, mediating reproduction in males are active simultaneously. In females, on the other hand, there is a sequential activation of the various tissues affecting reproduction. Growth of uterine tissues precedes a major burst of gonadotropic activity, which precedes display of sexual behavior, which precedes ovulation. The sequential, rather than simultaneous, nature of female reproductive function is compatible with divergent thresholds to estrogen activation among the various tissues mediating reproduction. This, in turn, is compatible with the absence of perinatal hormones serving to render such thresholds more uniform in adults. (69)

Sex hormone concentration at critical times of perinatal and prepubertal stages of development apparently affect the generation of specific steroid "receptors" in nerve cells in various parts of the nervous system (75). The neuroendocrine control of mating reflexes in both sexes is affected by early hormonal sensitization and later hormonal stimulation. Peripheral and central trajectories of the sensory and motor pathways involve spinal reflexes, brainstem activation, and limbic-hypothalamic emotional and appetitive governance (76). Without doubt, tumescence and other peripheral tissue changes alter the responsiveness of sensory end-organs, and the signals sent centralward are also affected by the influence of hormonal titres on higher centers.

3. The Distinctiveness of Symbolization and Cultural Evolution

It is frequently assumed that cultural evolution is something separate from biological evolution. Rather, as Medawar (77) has emphasized, cultural evolution is a further expression of biological evolution and it is clearly based on evolutionary advances of biological functions. Cultural evolution would not have occurred and could not be sustained except perforce of the evolutionary advantages spawned by the biological systems that underlie symbolization. Cognitive processes in general involve representation of objects and events in central neural processes; symbolization involves the re-representation outside the body by something artificial that is taken to substitute for an internal image.

The great advantage of symbolization derives from its arbitrariness and flexibility, and also from its external public manifestation through gestures, vocalizations, and markings, opening symbolizations to becoming mutually agreed upon and widely shared. It is obvious that symbolization, so germinal in the acceleration of biological evolution through cultural advances, is utterly dependent on mechanisms involved in sensory processing and perception, and, further, that the development of symbolization provides an effective feedback stimulation acting toward the perfection of perceptual skills and a simultaneous increase in the freedom and economy of central nervous imagery and memory stores, as well as their flexibility in representation of a practically unlimited variety of cognitive contents.

It is sometimes mistakenly assumed that because the higher apes can be *conditioned* to utilize symbols prepared and presented to them by scientists that the ape brain's competences are approximating ours in respect to symbolization. That is not correct, as White (78) has taken pains to show. The distinction in cognitive powers lies in the failure of the higher apes, or any other animal, independently of man, to generate and assign symbols for objects, events, or processes. The apes are tool-users to a degree, in both the physical and cognitive meaning of that phrase; but they do not create novel tools nor do they perfect, safeguard, or store given tools. Neither do they assign symbols and elaborate on them for communication and record-keeping purposes in ways that human societies characteristically do.

It is probably correct that the considerable capacities for social imitation seen in many monkeys and higher apes represent the biological foundations for further evolution of cognitive processes. But it may be supposed, on the basis of arguments given, that it required the combination of prolonged infantile dependence, with rapid brain growth, with biologically significant social learning experiences, to achieve the cultural and linguistic advances shared by all mankind. Of these, the most important elements would appear to be the timing of *rapid brain growth postnatally,* the built-in auditory and visual spatial *perceptual capacities,* the *nervous and endocrine developments* that account for intimate, prolonged *interdependence* and the powerful bonds of *attachment* between generations, and the almost aggressive *problem-solving and play propensities* of the newborn child and infant. The "long childhood" of cultural apprenticeship then has its biological and cultural momentum pretty well assured.

What is so distinctive about cultural evolution, and sets it apart in terms of the rate of change that it manifests is simply this: Whereas, with genetic inheritance, we can benefit only in accordance with the DNA contributions from our own direct ancestors, with cultural evolution, we can, in principle, benefit from any contribution put into symbolic form by any person, from anywhere, living or dead.

III. PERCEPTION

> *The truth is that Experience is trained by* both *association and dissociation, and that psychology must be writ* both *in synthetic and in analytic terms. Our original sensible totals are, on the one hand, subdivided by discriminative attention, and, on the other, united with other totals—either through the agency of our own movements, carrying our senses from one part of space to another, or because new objects come successively and replace those by which we were at first impressed. The 'simple impression' of Hume, the 'simple idea' of Locke are both abstractions, never realized in experience. Experience, from the very first, presents us with concrete objects, vaguely continuous with the rest of the world which envelops them in space and time, and potentially divisible into inward elements and parts. These objects we break asunder and reunite. We must treat them in both ways for our knowledge of them to grow; and it is hard to say, on the whole, which way predominates.*

> William James, *The Principles of Psychology, 1890*

A. Perception in the Train of Behavior

Perception lies in the train of brain events which contribute to behavior. Perception consists of more than can be acted out, and behavior consists of more than is organized through perceptual processes: for example, in reflex responses, in reaction to central brain stimulation, in automatisms of which we are unconscious, and so on. Perception may be in error, as when the hunter perceives a deer but shoots a man.

Perception represents the outcome of evolutionary selections that have found advantage through conscious awareness of certain brain events, the awareness of which has in the past improved behavioral outcomes. Perception does not come as an evolutionary dowry of ready-made percepts; instead, inherited mechanisms involved in sensory input, such as spatial orientation, contribute to adequate initial behavior. Sensory processing and perceptual mechanisms are readily conditionable and develop within the individual according to the outcomes of successful and unsuccessful experiences. Thus, the transformations that take place at each nuclear relay along sensory and particularly associative paths involved in complex perceptual image formation reflect evolutionary history plus that of the individual. From time to time, perceptual experiences may be radically altered, but changes are ordinarily modest, and at any given time our perception is quite persuasive of the nature of a "reality" within which we behave.

Sensation involves subjective experiences that arise from the stimulation of sensory endorgans. Sensory processing involves much more than the straightforward relay of sensory-evoked impulses to higher brain centers. A necessary part of that processing demands that comparisons be made with memory stores in order for a recognizable sensation to be encountered. There is, moreover, a great deal of sensory signalling that never reaches consciousness. We shall explore, therefore, the nature of perceptual consciousness, as established in accordance with past experiences, expectations, and purposes, and the ways by which ongoing sensory processing may articulate with more complicated perceptual experience. Perception involves subjective awareness, but includes many other-than-sensory data sources. It constitutes an internal model of the world. Perception is an ongoing experience in consciousness, usually coherent and convincing, and, as relating to behavior, compelling. Perception includes the total mental contents of our contemporary existence, including images as we experience them from present stimuli, and images that we may call up to consciousness from previous experiences or imaginings. Perception includes the motor options of which we are aware.

Although we know from practical experience that perception can be subject to error (Descartes, refs. 79 and 80, based his entire philosophy of universal doubt on such evidence), perception nonetheless provides our only access to "reality." Sensation, interpreted through perceptual modes, is our primary means of contact with our existence, our place in space-time, and our experience with objects, events, and nature in general (1, 2, 81–83). We can "know" something to be contrary to our perception, in which case we say we are experiencing an illusion, but our perception, even with its errors, is always first-hand. In hallucinations, we have no other awareness.

1. The Contents of Perception

Perception includes, foremost, all evidence available to consciousness concerning our internal state. This is the primary content of our awareness (84). This is what the physician is inquiring about when he asks, "How are you feeling?" Subjective responses, congruently given, constitute the most important and consistent source of information in medical science relating to a patient's health status, and it constitutes an early warning system relating to any change in health status. Feeling states appear to arise from activity that occurs in gray matter close to the walls of the ventricular system, the floor of the fourth ventricle, the cylinder of periaqueductal gray matter, the walls and floor of the third ventricle, and cortical and subcortical structures relating to the limbic system which sits bilaterally astride the cephalic brainstem and rings the ventricular channels that open into the lateral ventricles.

Perception includes the entire arena of conscious thought processes. We arrive at conscious judgments in our perceptual apparatus: we "perceive" what is the best choice among options available to us. Thus, if we have the option of playing tennis but "do not feel up to it," we reach a conscious decision based on approach/avoidance, go/no go considerations, including any pertinent past experiences relating to our court opponent and the social pressures for or against playing. It is this perceptual apparatus that has to make the choice as to whether we will respond to some visceral craving or not, in given circumstances. It is here that decorum and values and social context have conscious access to our behavior. The whole focus of aculturation bears precisely on this seat of awareness. This is also the station for conscious application of our educational skills. In short, everything of which we are conscious comes together in perception. It is from this locus of consideration that our volition is generated (85).

2. The Requirements for Purposeful Behavior

Aristotle recognized that purposeful behavior required coincidence of two internal conditions: appetite and emotion. You may have a great thirst, but a foul and noisome water source may be rejected because of emotional revulsion. You may also have the emotional willingness, but insufficient appetite, to eat or drink even highly "appetizing" nutrients. Penfield (86), on the basis of stimulation of exposed cortex in waking patients, came to the conclusion that voluntary activity was not generated from neocortex. Instead, he felt, volition sprang from some deeper subcortical source which he called the "centrencephalon," without implying anatomical precision. Later he suggested that the centrencephalon probably resides somewhere in the cephalic brainstem (87). We consider that volition is closely connected with or coexistent with mechanisms that release behavior, mechanisms located within the upper midbrain and posterior inferior diencephalon—the ventral cephalic brainstem, the site of go/no go decision making (84, 88).

This is perhaps a somewhat alien idea because of the commonplace belief that our voluntary activities are assumed to be guided by cortex. But all visceral regulation, respiratory, cardiovascular, thermal, etc.—appetitive in starting activity and "satietive" in stopping activity—resides in the brainstem reticular formation subadjacent to the periventricular mechanisms enumerated above that relate to internal feeling states (see ref. 88). Thus, the "respiratory center" in the medulla oblongata has mechanisms for inspiration and expiration that are reciprocally related to one another and that are modulated by afferent input from vagus and intercostal nerves, from carotid body and carotid sinus afferents, and from local cerebrospinal fluid gas saturation (89, 90). The reticular neurons in this location command the reciprocal effectors of respiration. The appetitive tides of the moment in respiratory regulation follow one another rapidly, compared with the tides of thirst and hunger, mechanisms that are governed primarily by way of the hypothalamus.

We are suggesting that another location of reticular formation in the ventral cephalic brainstem is engaged in making go/no go decisions in relation to somatic just as reticular formation serves an analogous function with regard to visceral activities. It is probably the same station that is involved in unconscious as well as conscious release of behavior, hence governing go/no go for all somatic behavior. For example, during a game of squash the knife edge decision whether to go or not to go after a difficult shot is probably executed unconsciously by the same locus that discriminates between going and not going to the theater.

The apparatus we have designated go/no is conceived to act on the basis of a convergent flow of information relating to internal feeling states, contexts respecting optional behaviors, the momentary flux of purposes and expectations, and the weighted average of past experiences, unconsciously as well as consciously evaluated. Parallel to this decision-making system, and interdependent with it in respect to outcomes, are unconscious and conscious mechanisms relating to like/dislike and approach/avoidance attitudes and those generally related to the focus of emotions.

Regions of brain found to yield positive reinforcements occupy most of the hypothalamus and extend throughout the cortical and subcortical structures that make up the limbic system (91–94). The brain regions that appear to represent pain, which provide strong aversion and which on stimulation are negatively reinforcing, relate to the dorsolateral parts of the cephalic midbrain, and adjacent posterior hypothalamus and inferomedial thalamus (95–99). The limbic system is thought to be the main locus for emotional experience and expression (100) involving e-motion, or ex-motion, i.e., the outward expression of the internal state. The limbic system together with projections from the frontal lobes, thought to underlie planning of behavior, have their combined main outlets in a small medial zone of the cephalic end of the midbrain, in close proximity to negatively reinforcing (pain) representation (101, 102). All this convergence would seem to congregate go/no go decision-making specifically in relation to whether the action should be one of approach or avoidance. Thus we can now speak, in a preliminary way, about the two indispensable factors necessary for purposeful action that were recognized long ago by Aristotle, namely, appetite and emotion. We also have progressed toward being able to account for the contents and the biological purposes of perceptual experiences.

3. Perception in Critical Situations

Given that we have a measure of understanding of how purposive behavior is organized, what can we say about the impact of perception on behavior in critical situations when there is some urgency relating to survival? Kilpatrick (103) has contributed to this subject in a context that is pertinent to psychiatry. He seeks to understand, on the basis of laboratory research work, how perceptions interact with incoming sensations, specifically in the context of disasters.

> *A complex predictive equation is involved in any instance of behavior. Included in this equation is the person's assessment of 'what is out there,' and the assessment of 'what is out there' depends in large degree on where the person is, what he is attending to, and his experience in decoding patterns of nervous*

impulses of that kind. Included also in the equation is the person's perception of himself; including, among other things, his purposes, his ability to act in certain ways, and his relationships with others. Somehow these perceived attributes of 'other' and 'self' are brought into relationship in the perceptual process. Emerging from this relational process is a prognosis or 'best bet,' unique for the individual, as to the probable consequences of the total situation as perceived. (103)

Kilpatrick (103) believes that the following principles are likely to be operating in the disaster situation: (a) events will be interpreted in accordance with an already established perceptual scheme; (b) actions will tend to be appropriate to the situation *as perceived* although actually perhaps illogical or inappropriate; (c) the individual may isolate himself or herself from the event in favor of familiar perceptual organizations and familiar, previously reliable behavior patterns, even though they are not appropriate for the given occasion; (d) the individual's suggestibility will be high; (e) conflicting and noncorresponding perceptual cues will induce emotional depression which, if the conflicts are resolved, will be followed by elation; and (f) perceptual reorganization will be most effectively accomplished through actions undertaken by the individual faced with a disaster.

It appears also that advanced intellectual knowledge of the situation does not help perceptual reorganization when the ongoing sensory information does not correspond with that individual's past experiences, expectations, and purposes, that is, if it does not correspond with some stable perceptual construct of that individual. Cues generated through action are at first related to previous perceptual constructions and only later can they be related to new hypotheses internally formed to accommodate the conflicting and noncorresponding sensations encountered in the critical situation. The acting-out to test the new assumptions concerning that situation may lead then to a more appropriate perception. Only after such hypotheses are generated can acting-out result in any progressive adaptation. Intellectual cues provided at that time have been shown to speed the perceptual learning process (103).

4. The Localization of Perceptual Processes

It is not yet possible to specify precisely what brain mechanisms are involved in perceptual processing. Studies of brain injuries and brain stimulation, even when engaging conscious and articulate individuals, cannot unambiguously localize brain events involved in cognitive processes. It is possible that such events are fairly widely distributed and that they may represent aggregate functions involving many widespread anatomical sites perhaps including up and down along the neuraxis. Nonetheless, research carried out on experimental animals and studies conducted on patients with surgical severance of the principal cerebral commissures (as a means of helping to control severe intractable epilepsy) indicate that much of our perceptual processing is selectively relegated to one or the other of the two cerebral hemispheres (104–107).

In animal and human studies it has been shown that different aspects of experience can be represented in the two hemispheres at the same time, even supporting stable contrary conditioning to the same stimulus (104, 107). Sperry (107) and colleagues, studying humans with disconnected left and right hemispheres, found two distinctive modes of perception, involving complementary specializations in the two sides of the brain (Fig. 1). A series of important communications on this subject appears in *The Neurosciences Third Study Program* (106).

It has long been recognized that the left cerebral hemisphere is dominant for speech in most individuals. To a slight degree, a few percent only, this is reversed among right-handed individuals (105). All senses except possibly olfaction appear to be differently affected in terms of the kinds of features that are extracted by the two hemispheres. The right ear, which projects predominantly into the left hemisphere, can be employed advantageously for speech; and the left ear, which projects to its contralateral hemisphere, is better at discriminating in music (108, 109). Semmes (110) demonstrated that complex perceptual tasks can be remembered accurately without employment of language and that tactile form perception may be disturbed in patients with brain injury who do not have peripheral sensory deficits. In such individuals, Milner (105) has shown that the right hemisphere is superior to the left in the discrimination and remembrance of spatial patterns.

Right temporal lobe deficits lead to impairment in visual recognition tasks that may be ascribed to faulty visual memory (111). Following removal of the right hippocampus, there is impairment of visual localization; after removal of the left hippocampus, patients show impairment of verbal memories (111). Right frontal lobe deficits lead to faulty performance in the temporal ordering of nonverbal events (105). Children appear to utilize both hemispheres in language functions during early development, prior to their commitment of language characteristically to the left hemisphere. Early damage to speech areas in a child's left neocortex may induce a representation of speech in the *right* hemisphere. The results of such "cognitive crowding" are manifestations of cerebral plasticity, but those individuals are likely to be below average in general intelligence (112).

Berlucchi has found asymmetries by examining *normal* subjects with respect to visual discriminations, using very brief exposures to the two visual half-fields of noncorresponding, conflicting images (113). Broadbent (114) has conducted a similar study with normal subjects in relation to conflicting or competing auditory stimuli.

In sum, then, it appears that the two hemispheres have some degree of specialization for memory storage and perceptual discrimination that is evident when the two hemispheres are separated or are put into opposition with

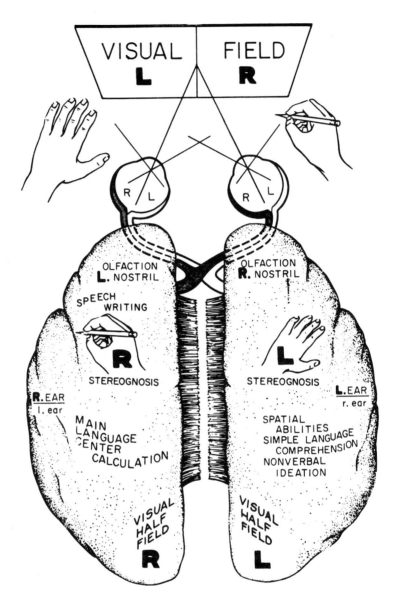

FIG. 1. Functional specialization in surgically separated cerebral hemispheres in man. Brain commissurotomy has been performed for the relief of severe intractable epilepsy. Careful testing shows that each hemisphere can function independently for certain positive operations and can act in opposition to the other hemisphere to reveal response dominance. The large corpus callosum is sectioned in its entirety, including, presumably, the hippocampal commissure. The massa intermedia of the thalamus, when present, and the anterior commissure are also severed. Each disconnected hemisphere retains a full set of cortical and subcortical connections, except for the severed interhemispheric connections. Normal perceptual transfer between hemispheres is lacking: objects seen in the contralateral visual field or identified by the contralateral hand, and even odors identified through one (the ipsilateral) nostril are not recognized or remembered by the uninformed hemisphere. In general, the left hemisphere provides the main language center, including auditory and visual imagery relating to language, and motor commands relating to speech and writing. The left hemisphere deals with calculation, analytical functions, serial ordering, and logical thought processes. The right hemisphere is more competent than the left in regard to spatial perception, recognition by palpatation of three dimensional objects, nonverbal forms of ideation, and the recollection and recognition of faces, paintings, and maps. Visualization and memory storage in the right hemisphere is ordinarily related to the object as a whole. Some simple stereotypal gestural language is also stored and controlled in the right hemisphere. (From Sperry, ref. 107.)

one another. The left hemisphere has to do with analysis, logic, language, mathematics, in sequential operations. The right hemisphere performs holistic, synthetic, syncretic operations dealing with music, form, pattern, perceptions-as-a-whole (107). Yet, in normal subjects, when two different cognitive tasks are carried out simultaneously, there is some distinct loss of efficiency (114). Interference between the two hemispheric projections appears to be the rule when the commissures are intact. *Even though there is a conspicuous degree of hemispheric specialization, the normal human brain performs best as a single-channel system.*

Not all commissural systems are equivalent with regard to perceptual processing in learning and memory situations. Doty (115, 116) has reviewed this subject, which originated with Russian studies, and has also reported experiments conducted by himself and collaborators. Evidence indicates that while the corpus callosum, the main interhemispheric commissure, provides readout of memories stored in the contralateral hemisphere, it actively suppresses the formation of memory stores in the hemisphere contralateral to the one engaged in an ongoing experience. This suppression of interhemispheric transfer of engrams has the effect of doubling the capacity of neocortex for memory storage. The anterior commissure, however, which interconnects the two temporal lobe regions, apparently participates in bilateral memory storage (116). This would affect predominantly the phylogenetically older cortical systems. Altogether, this line of research suggests that *there may be some specialized neurons that are involved in particular ways in learning and memory and in the utilization of memory stores in sensory processing and perceptual functions.*

B. Perception in Relation to Sensory Processing

1. Access to Consciousness

To this point, our consideration of perception has included only vague allusions as to where these complicated processes may take place, except for the obvious fact that we localize them very strictly within the brain. The question of where the processing of events responsible for conscious experiences occurs has long been moot. Someone, asked how much space a thought would occupy, replied sagely, "About the size of a human head." We acknowledge, however, that it is possible for next neighboring cells to be engaged independently in conscious and unconscious processes. This is the case for visceral adjacent to somatic sensory signals. Fibers representing each of these sensory paths accompany one another closely throughout spinal, brainstem, thalamic, and cortical representations, and yet the visceral afferent signals may be entirely unavailable to consciousness whereas the somatic signals are readily accessible (117).

The visceral ascending signals are indisputably active, but they do not, save in exceptional circumstances, contribute to conscious experiences. The explanation ordinarily provided to define *referred sensations,* where somatic sensation is provoked by visceral disorder, depends on the idea that such juxtaposed neuronal paths are subject to spilling over from visceral to activating the adjacent somatic sensory channels. Consciousness, as mentioned earlier, has not apparently had many evolutionary payoffs in respect to visceral sensory processing. Most sensory input from visceral organs has become isolated from, or perhaps has never gained access to, consciousness. In a similar manner, binocular and monocular cells in neighboring columns of visual cortical representation are apparently able to process information that is selectively and separably available to consciousness. Furthermore, it is a commonplace clinical observation that a child with a squint may develop alternating amblyopia, invoking suppression of the visual image from one eye at a time, alternately. This requires at least that neighboring cells in the lateral geniculate body, and perhaps also other cells farther along the chain of cortical representations, must be able privately and independently to contribute to consciousness while the other nearby cells are effectively suppressed from consciousness.

The problem of access of certain cellular events to consciousness is thus found to be quite precise, discrete, and plastic. There is no reason, in principle, why consciousness should involve aggregated populations or comprehensive sectors of the brain; it might be and probably is, very highly selective among neighboring fiber tracts and cells in all sensory projection systems. Consciousness might also be capable of shifting about, as many have suggested, not only as it apparently can in alternating amblyopia of squint, but also perhaps by shifting up and down the neuraxis to lower and higher levels, depending perhaps on focus of attention and also perhaps on specialized experiences, as those involved in training to make rapid perceptual decisions and in the control of finely detailed and phrased motor performances, as in musical instrument playing.

2. Organization of Sensory Systems

The structure of sensory systems has traditionally been held to be relatively straightforward. The discovery by Magendie and Bell of the functional distinctions between the posterior (dorsal) sensory and anterior (ventral) motor roots confirmed the proposition that individual peripheral nerve fibers were not conducting to *and* from the neuraxis. It was likely, on the basis of their observations, that sensory and motor messages would also be conducted centrally along separate channels. What seemed to be needed was to explore sensory pathways in an inward direction to discover the manner and levels by which sensory and motor mechanisms are articulated. Neurologists developed the canny knack of identifying deficits in sensory and motor pathways, working in each case backwards from the periphery. A few, like Jackson (118), took a special interest in "dreamy states" and other psychical phenomena originating from central epileptic episodes. Psychiatrists found their brain domains progressively shrinking as the neurological sciences moved inwards. One direction for the future of both disciplines, undoubtedly, will be to consolidate both their conceptual and their technical means of finding access to regions of overlap in the still relatively unexplored central frontiers.

The introduction of aniline dyes and methods for selective silhouetting of nerve cells using metallic impregnation and the discovery of methods to follow degenerating processes made it possible to chart conduction pathways throughout the peripheral and central nervous system. Early studies had indicated that interneuronal contacts are polarized so as to commit the direction of impulse signalling from collateral and terminal axons to dendrites and cell bodies of the succeeding neurons. Well-defined neuroanatomical entities, such as circumscribed nuclei and closely packed large, myelinated fiber bundles, yielded, by the end of the first quarter of this century, a convincing map of both sensory and motor pathways, flowing to and from their localized areas of cortical representation and the vast sheets of association cortex. The scheme at that time was better defined and more readily understandable than what we need to address in this accounting. Now, at the beginning of the last quarter of this century, there are many more questions, but also far better means for investigating them, with respect to how and where perception and sensory processing take place.

Erlanger and Gasser (119, 120) introduced electronic amplification and oscilloscopic recording that permitted exquisite time resolution of nervous system events, especially with respect to the explosive axonal impulse. Increasingly subtle patterns of coding information in axonal spikes are being explored (121). Slower potentials, as exhibited by the electro-encephalogram, discovered about the same time, have not been so easily resolved in relation to their underlying sources and contributions. The story of slow potential contributions to neural integration is being actively pursued (122). *Fantastically small* DC *gradients (of the order of $10\mu V/\mu m$) are being found capable of contributing to neuronal processing of messages.*

Adrian (123) and Zotterman (124) showed that single fibers recorded by fine electrodes inserted into nerves would respond to cutaneous stimulation in anesthetized or decerebrate animals at about the same threshold as one would find for conscious perceptual threshold in alert human subjects. Dusser de Barrenne (125) used strychnine to elicit specific behaviors that allowed him to follow the ascending sensory pathways. Adrian (126), and later Marshall et al. (127), followed such pathways to their corresponding areas of cortical representation by means of electrical recording. The basic plan for sensory processing, as now understood, was discovered in this way. The sensory receptors initiated impulses that travelled along ascending sensory pathways, with access to motor sources of reflex responses along the way, and relays to topographic cortical representations. Associationism, stemming from philosophical notions, was supported by the functional organization of cortical association areas.

3. The Waking Brain

The above studies were usually carried out with animals under surgical levels of anesthesia, or with the brain stem transected at the midbrain level or thereabouts (decerebrations). As a consequence of Hess' introduction of methods for central stimulation in waking, behaving animals (128) and the work of Magoun and colleagues on the reticular activating system (see ref. 129), it became apparent that the classical ascending sensory pathways were only part of the ascending impulse traffic elicited by sensory stimuli. Moreover, with the use of nitrous oxide–oxygen (laughing gas) to induce an analgesic (pain-relieved) state rather than an anesthetic (all sensation-relieved) state, it was possible to show that of five major ascending trajectories of impulses generated by tooth pulp stimulation one pathway was differentially affected by the volatile analgesic, leaving the others more or less intact (96, 98).

Was that brainstem path affected by the analgesic agent the indispensable afferent ingredient for pain sensation? If so, pain sensibility was not being conducted in by way of the classical sensory pathways. An equivalent dose of nitrous oxide–oxygen analgesia obliterated pain in human subjects stimulated through amalgam fillings seated against the tooth pulp in normal teeth. If some critical part of the perceptual formula for the perception of pain was removed by the analgetic gas, while leaving intact the classical trigeminal pain pathway, then we have much more to learn about sensory information transmission and sensory processing. Perhaps this evidence will help us understand the commonplace neurosurgical failure to relieve intractable pain by tractotomies even though the pathological specimen may indicate that the classical pain pathway was effectively interrupted.

4. Transactional Mechanisms

Neurochemistry took its origins from the isolation of constituents by Thudichum in England (130) and was further advanced by Folch-Pi in America (131). Loewi in America (132) and Dale in England (133) built a convincing case for chemical transmission across synapses. *There are now seven well-proven chemical transmitters and a half-dozen more that are putative neurotransmitters* (134). Many are small, relatively ubiquitous molecules.

Electron microscopy showed that areas of transmitter discharge are actually confined to small loci within the terminal axonal endings (135) and, more remarkably, that some synapses appear to be transmitting in the reverse orientation, contrary to the supposedly normal polarization of synapses, i.e., from soma and dendrites of the nominally "receiving" neuron to the terminal axon of the nominal "sender" (136–139). What does this imply for circuitry? In some synaptic regions, first demonstrated in the olfactory system, synaptic patches are found to be sending and receiving chemical transmitters across closely adjacent parts of the same pair of membranes (137). *Neurotransmitters are being found to induce appreciable biological effects at extremely low concentrations, in the range of 10^{-10} M.* In addition, *there are also electrical synapses and other junctions that may permit other kinds of active exchanges between nerve cells and between neurons and glia* (140).

The *action potential,* the all-or-nothing, explosive nerve impulse, *now appears to be only one of several means of sending messages of biological importance within and among brain cells:* there are two-way transport systems, fast and slow, along axons and dendrites; messages can penetrate cells without ionic or chemical invasion, by allosteric interactions and by other means of obtaining intercellular cooperativity; macromolecular systems that account for localized membrane structural specificity and the extracellular spaces between neurons respond to low DC potential changes by changing intercellular distances; organelle operations such as intracellular transport, transduction, and other more spectacular means of event coupling, have been found to be susceptible to alteration through the experiences of the whole animal; enzyme systems, chemomechanical and chemoelectrical coupling, both in both directions, subtle homeostatic mechanisms, and circuitously interdependent metabolic controls are similarly subject to modulation; hormones that signal and amplify both near and remote processes—*all of these control processes and functional linkages pose complexities and subtleties for integration that would have been unimaginable only a few years ago.* These mechanisms are analyzed in terms of nervous system functions in a recent publication by Schmitt et al. (141). In a relatively short time, sensory processing mechanisms have advanced from being intuitively straightforward and based largely on concepts of *interactions* to a highly sophisticated congeries involving *transactions.*

Transactions occur among multiple, mutually interdependent systems in simultaneous action. In the case of sensory systems the pertinent transactions operate integratively among a cascade of levels of increasing complexity. Terms such as allosterism, cooperativity, amplification, transport, and transduction are receiving new meaning now in contexts pertinent to behavior. They are being applied to dynamic transactional neuronal and glial operations extending all the way from recognition systems on the glycoproteinaceous "fuzz" that makes up the mosaic of neuronal surfaces involved in embryogenesis and repair to the balance of controls engaging the metabolic engines that govern chemical and electrical operations, to the activities involved in the coupling between receptors and effectors that are interacting with the outside world. It is a new conceptual ball game.

It is still necessary to consider action sequences among cells that are passing throughout the nervous system; but their sufficiency for explaining overall integrative processes as reflected in conscious experience and behavior must be supposed more tentatively than has heretofore generally been admitted. At present we have more in the way of plasticity and dynamic qualities to explain sensory processing than we can constrain from flying into conceptual fragments. Nonetheless, there are certain general principles that can be recognized as contributing to sensory processing in systematic ways: spontaneous activity, localization of stimulus maxima, lateral inhibition, parallel processing, feedback loops for the hierarchal coordination of subsystems, central control of sensory receptors, and central sensory transmission, plus a few useful neurophysiological metaphors: gate theories, ideas of corollary discharge, and notions of holographic images.

IV. SENSORY PROCESSING

All integrative processes are directive. At every step from lower to higher levels something new is added. The higher patterns are not made by simple additive assembly of the properties of the lower, and the laws of their operation are not identical with those of the lower. This is as true of a chemical reaction as of the creative imagination of a philosopher or a poet.

C. Judson Herrick, *The Evolution of Human Nature* (1956)

A. Ontogeny of Perception

Organisms perceive the world in terms of objects for which sensory processing provides detailed information relating to the "what" and the "where" of those objects. Recognition of objects requires that a comparison be made between the sensory signals arising from the object and similar experiences previously stored in memory. As Piaget (142) has shown, *it takes some years for the child's perception of objects to develop to the level familiar to us in the testimony and behavior of adults.* Building on reflexes centered on assimilation, the child begins to exploit *things,* and by that process begins to organize primitive ideas about things. Further organization of such ideas contributes to the *structuring of stable images* relating to things. Such images finally become so structured that even if objects only roughly and erroneously resemble already well-developed images, the objects may nevertheless be perceptually incorrectly interpreted as conforming (143). *The remembered images misstructure ongoing sensory experiences and show great resistance to being corrected.*

The first stages in the process of exploration of objects have been well described by Bower (38). Infants on the first day of life can learn; indeed, learning in the period before and during language development is probably superior than at any other age (40, 144). This may be accounted for by the extremely rapid growth of the brain during this period. The newborn infant demonstrates a propensity for playing sensorimotor games and for problem-solving. Siqueland and Lipsitt (145) report that infants in the first day of life can develop a head-turning response that is specific to one side or the other depending on whether a bell or buzzer is sounded. Contingencies can then be reversed, demonstrating rapid discrimination reversal that occurs "with a facility unsurpassed by any nonhuman primate."

Each time contingencies are changed, the response activity rate of the infant goes up: The infant seems to be "testing hypotheses" and responds with new hypotheses to each new challenge. Unless the learning situation is interactive and rapidly progressing, the infant will, apparently, lose interest and cease to interact with a given problem. Much early learning of this sort occurs without identifiable reinforcement, as in *imprinting* in animals (see ref. 146). Older infants continue to detect and to exploit contingencies connecting any response with any reinforcement, and they gradually cease to respond to stimuli that are not specifically connected with reinforcements (38).

Newborn infants orient correctly in the direction of visual and auditory stimuli and show some depth perception even in the first days of life (39, 147). Very young infants make use of optical expansion information and manifest a corresponding coordinated defense response to approaching objects (148). The child's growing sensory system is calibrated into its growing motor system from the outset, posing a deep methodological problem because neither system remains continuously invariant for very long, a desideratum for developing standards against which learning can be measured.

Infants in the first week of life apparently have elaborate built-in mechanisms for initiating some distinctive forms of apprehension of objects. Thereafter, such abilities undergo repeated metamorphic alterations in the process of growing older. Each metamorphosis involves a retreat from previously manifested skill acquisitions followed by the reappearance of skills needed to solve similar problems but in accordance with different thinking strategies (41, 142). Early infantile capabilities for perception and learning change considerably in the course of the first year of life along with changes in their reaction to systematic reinforcement.

B. Sensory Mechanisms Underlying Perception

1. Stimulus Identification and Localization

Successful adaptation to environments containing many objects requires that sensory data provide a current internal model suitable for working among previously experienced objects and a model for gaining acquaintance with unfamiliar objects. Both the process of identifying, classifying, and relating the stored images of experienced objects to suit ongoing behavior, and the process of sensorial exploration to assemble new and revised images by which behavior can be organized suitably in conjunction with unfamiliar objects, involve many steps that cannot be accomplished by sensory input alone. They require that incoming sensory data call up and sort for closest resemblance to previously stored and classified information from past experience. Quick access to such highly select and more-or-less appropriately matched, stored information for perceptual and behavioral purposes is an obvious requirement for successful behavior. Yet, essentially nothing is known about the neurophysiological processes that occur as this call-up and comparison are accomplished. Heuristic theories abound, but none to date specifies the underlying mechanisms in any detail. The process clearly involves comparisons, and at a relatively abstract level of cognitive processing; and this all takes place prior to consciousness. The key steps involve rapid matching and hypothesis formation followed by hypothesis testing, first internally, while the sorting is still going on, and eventually hypothesis testing by means of behavior.

Despite difficulties, some headway can be made, in part at a neurological level, approaching gross systems involved in sensory reintegration from the "hash" of incoming sensory impulses, and at finer structural levels that characterize neural activity and architecture. For example, a neurological case can be made in the visual system for the assumption that neocortical representations of vision provide information concerning the "what" of visual targets, whereas the superior colliculus is more concerned with directing gaze in relation to vestibular, neck, eye muscle, and retinal localization of events that contribute to specifying the "where" of visual targets in relation to the perceiver.

Examples of fine functional and architectural analyses are given by Szentágothai (149–151), Sholl (152), the Scheibels (153–155), Ramón-Moliner (156), and Ramón-Moliner and Nauta (157). Coupled with neurophysiological investigations, their approach provides a useful opportunity for our understanding of integrative processes. This combination is well exemplified in the monograph on the cerebellum by Eccles, Ito, and Szentágothai (158). Something comparable is overdue relating to integrations occurring along sensory pathways.

The discipline of arguing from fine architectural organizations found its origins in the enterprising investigations of Ramón y Cajal (see particularly ref. 159), but speculations relating to the operations of networks based on neuroanatomical observations really originated with Lorente de Nó (160–162). He developed general notions about neuronal coupling and about processes such as "delay lines" and "reverberating circuits." It now appears that a subpopulation of neurons within such networks (about 10% of the total) may be especially capable of modification through experience and that these especially modifiable units may be instrumental in generating the rapid turn around of sensory data processing and comparisons by such networks that are so critically necessary for survival. An excellent evaluation of present knowledge of such mechanisms and their role in brain operations is available in a recent report of a Neurosciences Research Program Work Session edited by Szentágothai and Arbib (163). Perhaps the most powerful single mechanism for early stimulus identification and localization depends on lateral inhibition which will be dealt with in the next section.

2. The Powers of Lateral Inhibition

Lateral inhibition in sensory systems was first described by Ernst Mach (164). Kuffler (165) defined this process as it affects cells in the retina. With ON-center/OFF-surround cells a local light elicits increased impulse generation, but activity is reduced when the light is projected into the immediately surrounding area. OFF-center/ON-surround cells behave in contrary fashion, being diminished in activity by localized light and activated when the light falls into the immediate surround. Similar lateral inhibiton occurs in all sensory systems. Figure 2 illustrates lateral inhibition in relation to stimuli falling on the skin. Although a large area of skin may be deformed or displaced, the effects of lateral inhibition maximize the neuronal discharge pattern generated by the stimulus and localize it to the central focal point of application of the stimulus.

The activity of nerve cells in relation to the phenomenon of lateral inhibition has been well demonstrated in studies on the light receptors of the horseshoe crab, *Limulus,* by Hartline and others (166). Exactly how lateral

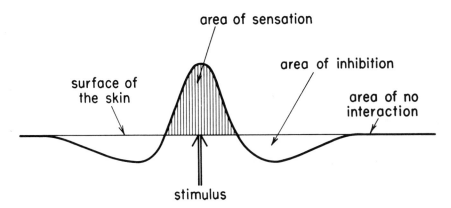

FIG. 2. Lateral inhibition: an area of sensation produced by a local stimulus, and its surrounding area of inhibition. In all sensory systems, in retina, cochlea, olfactory bulb, taste, and skin sensory channels, the boundaries of a stimulus are characteristically sharpened by such an inhibitory surround. The principle is illustrated here for stimulation of the skin. The point of stimulus contact induces local activation, which is spatially confined by inhibitory activities imposed on the central transmission pattern by the neighboring circuits. The net effect is to sharpen outlines and edges, and to exaggerate adjacent contrasts. Similar sharpening effects induced by lateral inhibition occur along central sensory relays and within higher centers. Thus visual acuity, pitch discrimination, odor and taste specification, and skin localization become sharpened through sensory processing that occurs all along the ascending sensory pathway. Perceptual projection is subjectively assigned to the locus of maximum activation. A further effect is that while disparity (contrast) is augmented along all of the margins of, say, a photic stimulus, at the same time the background differences between the illuminated area within the stimulus field and that representing the dark expanse outside the stimulus are only minimally differentiated. Local change of state is exaggerated, sharply localized spatially, and polarized according to the direction of the imposed differences. But unchanging areas, both inside and outside the stimulus boundaries, do not greatly burden the brain with messages. (From von Békésy, ref. 170.)

inhibition is achieved is still obscure, but the phenomenon is widespread throughout the nervous system. The immediate effect is simultaneously to exaggerate amplitude and to narrow the spatial extent, to narrow and *sharpen* boundaries. It also minimizes the amount of central signal transmission necessary to locate the edges and discontinuities imposed on sensory fields by stimulus objects. The emphasis given to edges is strengthened by similar tuning and sharpening effects at successive relays along all ascending sensory pathways. The net effect is that, for example, a radiologist can see more in the way of faint lines and borders than any mechanical image identifier can extract from the same X-ray film unless the physical imaging system has built into it some analogous edge-intensifying processors.

A row of retinal ganglion cells having ON-center/OFF-surround can be connected so as to provide impulse responses relating to a straight-line bar of light extended in any direction in accordance with the physical arrangement of connections between the cells. A row of cells having OFF-center/ON-surround can provide for active responses to dark lines in any similarly given direction. The two lines in juxtaposition would reinforce each other. Hubel and Wiesel (167–169) pioneered in the analysis of such projections in visual systems. *The net effect is to localize and enhance responses elicited by objects, and to specify sharply their discontinuities and boundaries.* In the case of auditory, cutaneous and other sensory channels, the effects are analogous —to sharpen tuning, to confine, and to specify the loci of greatest displacement.

If a vibrating rounded needle is applied to the skin, it can induce oscillations that extend throughout large regions of flesh and bony structures of the body, but because of the narrowing effects of lateral inhibition, the subjective experience is that of a single confined point of vibration (170). Experienced observers, stimulated by two vibrating needles arranged in such a way that the displacement waves have a precedence that occurs at one of the points, will perceive a single source of vibration that lies somewhere between the two points of stimulation. If the vibrating points are placed on two fingertips, the precedence of vibrational displacement can be so arranged that the single locus of perceived vibration migrates back and forth between the two fingertips. If the fingers now are spread apart, then the "phantom vibrating source" is obliged to travel a greater distance and therefore must travel back and forth at a greater velocity. If two such vibrating points are placed on the two hands, the single vibrating locus, as perceived, can be obliged to course greater distances through space between the two sites of stimulation.

In this way, von Békésy (170) has suggested, tactile stimulus interpretations may become projected as originating from somewhere *outside* our bodies, as is taken for granted in our perceptual interpretations in vision and hearing. This is accomplished, he believes, by mechanisms of lateral inhibition operating all along the ascending sensory pathways. Once again, our sensory interpretive processes appear to be operating to solve problems, to provide

FIG. 3. Sensory substitution: a video camera drives cutaneous stimulation as a substitution for vision in a blind subject. The subject wears a 6 g TV camera complete with lens system and electronic drive circuit attached to the frame of his eyeglasses. Everywhere his "gaze" is directed, the camera takes in the "visual" field. Wires lead to an electrical stimulus drive circuit held in the subject's right hand. A matrix containing an array of 256 concentric silver electrodes, held in his left hand, can be applied to the skin of his abdomen. After a relatively few hours of practice, using active head movements in "viewing," the subject becomes unaware of the abdominal stimulation via the electrodes and instead "projects" images as arising from within the spaces scanned by his camera "eye." It is essential that the individual actively direct the camera, by head or hand movements, in order for his subjective experience to project "real objects, out there." (From Bach y Rita, ref. 171.)

simplifying hypotheses, and to test them—creating images that can account for the phenomena on some kind of simplest hypothetical basis as prognostication for behavior.

Similar lateral inhibition edge-enhancing effects resulting from skin stimulation have been put to practical use by Bach y Rita (171) in the form of "sensory substitution." For blind persons, he has designed a video camera system that can stimulate multiple points on the skin by local indentation, vibration, or electrical activation. In this way, patterns of skin stimulation corresponding to images formed via the video system are employed as the means for somesthetic substitution in place of the visual loss. Patterns projected on the skin have no "visual meaning" unless the individual is behaviorally active in directing the video camera using head, hand, or body movements. When the blind person actively directs the video camera, after only a few hours of experience, he or she no longer interprets the skin sensations as messages relating to skin but rather as images projected into the space that is being explored by bodily directed "gaze" of the video camera (171).

Lateral inhibitory mechanisms that operate along the channels from skin to perceptual access (cortex?) serve to establish a perceived image that is sufficiently definite that it carries prognostic value for behavior: it quickly becomes conditioned and attached to behavioral programs so that the individual acts out upon and into the perceived space. The image is projected outside the body just as it is in vision. At that point of experience, cutaneous stimulus source substitution for visual input is accomplished.

C. Sensory Signal Processing
1. Complex "Instantaneous" Comparisons With Stored Images

It is well known that the images developed through vision, by virtue of the various lines of projection of light between objects and the retina, must be interpreted in accordance with perceptual notions of perspective whether these are innate, as Gibson's (172) studies suggest, or acquired, as implied by the experiments of Held (173), for example. A rectangular table surface, seen in perspective, will have a trapezoidal shape, and a round table top will project as an elipse. Right-angled architecture, seen in perspective, will have correspondingly modified acute and obtuse angles. There is a difference, then, between the way objects are constructed and the way in which they are projected on the retina. The problem is: How are sensory input data processed so as to be perceived in ways that are appropriate for behavior? That this is no simple matter is vouchsafed by the fact that the problem of perspective was not grasped for purposes of artistic representation until the Renaissance: when it was introduced, by Alhazen, it spread quickly throughout European civilization and had many stimulating repercussions, for example by contributing to the analysis and development of optical systems such as the telescope (see ref. 43).

Persons who are blind from birth have become acquainted with objects through bodily movements and palpation. They have therefore not been required to adjust to the many different appearances of objects when projected from different angles. On this account, blind persons provided with cutaneous sensory substitution have to adjust to accommodating these various perspectives and interpreting them in ways useful for behavior. One such subject exclaimed to Bach y Rita (174), on beginning to understand this variety and complexity of spatially projected images, that sighted persons live in a "very distorted world."

By the same token, sighted persons become strongly attached to making automatic perceptual assumptions in relation to the structure of objects such as, for example, to the rectilinearity of many man-made objects. Thus they learn to make false assumptions respecting distorted rooms and trapezoids painted to resemble windows (2, 175). *A rotating trapezoid is perceived as an oscillating window, and a distorted room is seen as rectilinear, even at the expense of obviously noncorresponding sensory signals.* For instance, a cube attached to the frame of a rotating trapezoid, assumed to be a rectilinear window, will seem to orbit through free space as the window is perceived (erroneously) to oscillate. The window will also seem to oscillate when seen from the side, whereas seen from the same point of view in an inclined mirror at the same time, it is seen to be rotating. In the distorted room, *the observer retains the erroneous image even when he knows it to be erroneous,* and will perceive a marble rolling uphill, and a person doubling in height while walking from one corner of the room to another. These and other demonstrations, introduced by Ames, are commonly displayed and talked about, but they are usually put aside as illusions, something somehow "contributed by the mind." Nevertheless, they pose central and profoundly challenging questions to be answered in terms of the nervous system processes by which such assumptions are organized and so compellingly and speedily introduced into our perceptual experiences.

Ames and his followers have provided many examples of such automatic and forceful assumptions that dominate our everyday perceptual life. These assumptions are largely acquired and they have deep significance for our comprehending the foundations of human knowledge and particularly, for our understanding cross-cultural discrepancies in perception. Dewey was so impressed by Ames' work that he declared it to be "by far the most important work done in the psychological-philosophical field during this century" (143). We know only that most of such compelling assumptions are acquired, that they vary across cultural boundaries in accordance with differences in experiences and in accordance with culturally idiosyncratic social significances that are attached to objects and events, and that they are highly resistant to change. When change does occur, it is to another set of perceptual assumptions. Change does not occur without the subject taking action in the given noncorrespondent situation. The consequences of repeated actions reveal, after some time, but quite abruptly, the nature of the situation. At that instant a different perception obtrudes itself. Now the new percept will, in turn, modify—perhaps inappropriately—perceptual experiences into the future (175). Three different examples are given to illustrate the scope of this problem.

(i) Campbell has shown that there are cultural differences in perception of a simple "T" stimulus pattern in which both the upright and horizontal bars are equal in length. Subjects are asked whether one line is longer than the other. When this stimulus is presented to people in The Netherlands they tend on the average to perceive the horizontal bar as being the longer of the two lines. People in Switzerland, presented with the same stimulus and instructions, tend on the average to perceive the vertical bar as being the longer of the two lines. It is presumed that the Dutch, accustomed to seeing distant horizontal land- and seascapes habitually assume that such lines represent great distances compared with vertical lines in their perceptual environment. Swiss, on the other hand, living amidst steep mountains and valleys, with mostly nearby horizons, habitually assume that vertical distances are apt to be greater than horizontal in their perceptual environment.

(ii) Kilpatrick invited subjects to inspect three small model rooms which could be viewed monocularly from the same swivel seat. Each of the rooms could be (and usually is) assumed to be rectilinear from the point of view provided. One room is left-right distorted, with the left wall approximately twice the size of the right, and with floor, ceiling and back wall slanted narrowing to the right. A second is up-down distorted, with the ceiling twice the size of the floor, and with all three walls slanted inward correspondingly. The third model room is constructed rectilinearly. Subjects viewing these three rooms usually testify that they are similar and rectilinear.

If the subject is then given a pointer and asked to touch a tiny symbol (a bug) painted on the left back region of the left-right distorted room, he or she will fail to reach sufficiently far back to touch the spot, and will have to stretch farther and farther. During this "extra reaching" experience, the subject usually giggles, a sign of subjective discovery of a not discomfitting noncorrespondence between assumptions and events. Then the subject is asked to touch a mark on the right wall. The pointer is repeatedly and unexpectedly stubbed against the back wall and the right wall, until, by withdrawing the arm and pointer more and more, the target can eventually be met. Repeated challenges of alternately touching the "bug" and the "mark" result in improved gestures until, after several trials, correct behavioral responses *and* subjective experiences which correspond to the actual structure of room obtain simultaneously. The subject now perceives the room as left-right distorted, and "sees" it according to its designed perspectives. The behavior is now correspondingly correct. This much may perhaps be expected.

Finally, the subject is invited to inspect the three rooms once more: now, they are all three perceived as left-right distorted rooms looking alike although one is actually up-down distorted and another is rectilinear in shape. Lessons from this study suggest that we perceive not only according to our past experiences, but that we learn to perceive and ultimately to accommodate our behavior to novel configurations only through acting-out in them, and that when we have succeeded in learning a new perceptual solution we have imposed on our behavior a new set of assumptions that may in turn interfere with our future perceptual prognostications.

(iii) Since the experiments of Stratton in 1896 (176, 177), there have been many studies on the perceptual effects of distorting lenses. Left-right reversals, up-down reversals, and the combination of left-right plus up-down

reversals can be introduced. Interestingly, it takes some days longer to accommodate to left-right reversals than to up-down reversals, but both can be
successfully accommodated for behavioral purposes of bicycle riding, fencing,
etc. Similarly, prismatic wedges before the eyes cause vertical lines to appear
bowed at first, but the bowing is perceptually straightened if the wedges continue to be worn. If either of these kinds of lens systems is removed after
accommodation has occurred, then a period of reaccommodation takes place
before normal vision is restored.

For example, accommodation to left-right and up-down reversal (a one-
power telescope lens) involves perceptual restoration of a normal orientation
for behavioral purposes of left-right and up-down intentions. When the
glasses are removed, the world is once again left-right and up-down reversed,
even though the retinal images are now *correctly* projected. With the prismatic
wedges, removal is followed by bowing of the lines in the opposite direction.
It takes a rather shorter time to accommodate to normal vision again than it
did to learn to accommodate to wearing the distorting lenses. Repetition of
use and disuse of the lens complexes demonstrates some savings.

Perhaps the most astonishing accommodation to change of visual input relates to experiments by Kohler (178) in which he used blue and yellow half-
lenses in eye glasses so that the left halves were blue and the right halves
yellow. At first, objects seen with the gaze directed to the right were yellow
and those to the left blue; but after only a few days of wearing the glasses,
the chromatic scale returned nearly to normal. This meant that the visual input was *altered with regard to color perception somewhere on the way to perceptual centers, strictly in accordance with the direction of the gaze.* Again,
as might now be anticipated when the glasses were removed, there were complementary color changes, associated with direction of gaze, which returned
to normal color perception after an appreciable period of time.

What can be said about how such mechanisms may operate in terms of
sensory processing? The most important clues, probably, relate to behavior in
that the noncorrespondence with past experiences is discovered only by action,
and that the stored images are corrected only after behavior achieves success
at which moment the perception itself is suddenly projected in a form appropriate in prognosticatory terms for the desired behavior. *Behavior is not
only the goal of sensory processing, it is important in the shaping of sensory
processing.* It appears that "instantaneous" comparisons being made between
incoming sensory data and stored perceptions run along all right in any given
experiential context until some "hitch" occurs, as Ames' thought described
this matter (143).

"In any given context" suggests that memory stores may be "filed" or
"accessible" according to given contexts and that some delay in matching
stored percept to sensory input should be experienced when the context is
suddenly altered. We experience a hitch on discovering that events did not
turn out according to our perceptual prognostications: we reach too short of

the "bug" target with the pointer or, far worse, we shoot a man when we are perceiving a deer. This does not correspond with our expectation, and it defeats our purpose. Experiencing a hitch provides an opportunity for learning; it is, some would say, the only way for adults to learn: in the latter event, a brutal lesson, but one that might become generalized for other persons and occasions.

It seems that the *context* of experience then will link together our accumulated stores of similar images for comparison readiness, images which, if matched by events, will allow the behavior to proceed apace. There is no biological need for better perception. But when something unexpected occurs, or when we reach the end of the road of similar experiences, we proceed into ambiguous territory on the basis of rehearsed methods for exploration of oncoming events and novelties. These methods call for more tentative behavior and draw upon relatively abstract notions concerned with likely or potential expectations.

In both familiar and unfamiliar contexts, ongoing behavioral programs apparently attract a "running prognosticating commentary" of expectations according to the weighted averages of stored experiences, which is more or less accurately and completely "matched" by our ongoing sensory experiences. We can proceed with perception rather far according to our purposes and expectations and contrary to incoming sensory data (143). If a "hitch" occurs, if an event obtrudes itself that does not correspond to the "running prognosticating commentary," if the elevator goes *down* when we pushed the "up" button, we are suddenly alerted, our midbrain reticular activating system arouses the entire forebrain and spinal column in readiness for action: our EEG tracing becomes highly activated, our pupils dilate, our palpebral fissures open wider, our stretch reflexes increase tension, our sphincters pucker, we may have an arrest of peristaltic action and a wave of abrupt vasodilation and sweating or piloerection. Our memory stores are probably alerted, too, that the context has been altered as well. If something sufficiently startling occurs, the reactions are all the more widespread and remarkable, including putting down of memory stores relating to the occasion itself.

When we heard that President Kennedy was assassinated, we couldn't help recognizing subjectively the changes in context for all the U.S. and all of our futures, including various far-fetched potential scenarios. At the same time, entirely unconsciously, all of the details associated with our hearing the news —where we were, with whom, how exactly we heard, even the appearance of the knobs on the radio or TV instrument and the detailed setting where we heard the news—were automatically stored in our memories. It is as though a generalized "now store" order had been dispatched to notify the whole brain to capture all of the associated events, directly or indirectly related (84).

Indeed, something of that exact sort may well occur, with the frontal limbic midbrain area inducing a generalized arousal that might include a physiological signal manifesting that "something important just happened: all recently activated circuits should be reinforced so as to capture the details of that occasion." Kety (179) has proposed that such an order might provide a widespread release of norepinephrine, either by discharge into the blood stream or by nervous dispatch. It might otherwise constitute a specialized nervous discharge, perhaps allied to or identical with the arousal mechanisms itself (53, 84, 88, 179, 180). The main point is that a generalized order of this sort would store in memory everything that had just occurred without any particularly selective process, linking all recent events, internally and externally experienced.

The nature of such a storage mechanism is different from traditional postulates relating to memory storage which have concentrated on activation primarily or solely along the specifically affected pathways themselves. A generalized order does not need to specify anything except to reinforce those synapses that had just been active so that they would be more likely to fix in that special configuration, to retain the pattern, in effect, the total image of the event. This would be perhaps the simplest possible biological signal, arising as we may suppose, from the upper midbrain region where both positive and negative reinforcement systems are in closest proximity and from which area generalized arousal is already known to be dispatched.

This would account for the well-known fact that any sensory, motor, visceral, or somatic event can be consolidated into a stored configuration, including generalizations which embrace everything experienced on that given occasion. If events are repeated, such as bell associated with food, in the pavlovian paradigm, the generalizations which at first included the room, table, harness, experimenter, and all, will gradually fade; when the only experience regularly followed by food is the bell, timed as if in a cause-effect relationship, the salivation response becomes increasingly specific to bell alone.

2. Feedback and Feedforward Controls

Feedback control has been utilized in hydraulic and mechanical systems since antiquity. It received formal mathematical treatment in 1868 by Maxwell. The year before this, Helmholtz described a sensation relating to the "intensity of the effort of will" which he thought would account for visual perceptual stability during voluntary eye movements, in contrast to the perception of environmental motion when the eye ball is displaced passively (181). More recently, since the advent of cybernetics, systems engineering, and bioengineering, both feedback and feedforward systems have been actively investigated to significant advantage in both biological and engineering fields. Present concepts are well documented in two recent monographs of the Neurosciences Research Program, on *Central Control of Movement,* chaired by Evarts (182) and *Conceptual Models of Neural Organization,* edited by Szentágothai and Arbib (163).

In fact, it appears that there are several general neurological strategies involved in feedback mechanisms: (i) The most usually described is that of muscle afferents and other *proprioceptive sensory neurons* disposed in muscle, tendons, joint surfaces, and joint capsules, along fascial plains, and, to a lesser degree, distributed through skin and subcutaneous tissues. Activity from the muscle spindle, the most elaborate sensory organ aside from the eye and the ear, is differentially affected by active and passive movement of the muscle; the others are affected by any such movement. (ii) Knowledge of the effects of movement in the environment returns by way of a variety of sensory pathways. The old adage "Practice makes perfect" is not correct: *It is only practice, the results of which are known, that contributes to motor skill development* (183). Both perceptual skill development and motor training are involved in all learned motor coordinations. In the development of expressive skills such as playing a musical instrument, or effectual skills such as removing an appendix, practice allows improvement of perceptual habits, of internal images, and of motor commands. Additionally (iii), there are internal feedback loops which are not so obvious, and which are more subtle, plastic, and ubiquitous. For these, the following discussion is pertinent.

The interneurons in sensory and motor nuclei in spinal cord and brainstem contribute to ascending messages that ultimately are routed back toward motor centers. The bulk of these are referred to as *flexor reflex afferents,* representing wide-ranging sensory and central fields *that have access to flexor motor responses all along the neuraxis* (184). These include intersegmental and interlimb paths (185), plus the nine main spinocerebellar paths, in addition to other projections to cephalic brainstem and cerebral cortex including the sensorimotor cortex (186). They do not mainfest sensory modality specificity; the receptive fields represented by individual ascending units are large and may include a whole limb or more than one limb, and they can therefore provide only crude spatial discrimination; they are relayed by spinal and brainstem interneurons which in turn may be strongly facilitated or inhibited by descending pathways. They are generally excited by the pyramidal tract and inhibited by reticulospinal projections (184).

The interneurons concerned act simultaneously as reflex centers in the transmission path between local sensory input and motor output; as controllers of ascending messages of a quite nonspecific sort destined to influence flexor motor activities but only weakly influenced for this purpose by sensory input; and as relays conveying quite specific information from motor cortex to the final common path, the individual motor unit. Thus, interneuronal pools all along the neuraxis provide feedback to higher centers that may be ultimately reflected both in widespread flexion responses and in discrete motor activities (182).

An obvious central feedback loop is the *cerebellar-cerebral* path which is believed to monitor cortical output and to send back to the cortex corrective information based on unconscious proprioception and perhaps also on learned sensorimotor performance habits. This recurrent pathway can apply corrective internal influences affecting behavior before peripheral information from proprioception and from receptors involved in monitoring changes in the environment can have any effect. This internal control obviously involves both sensory and motor characteristics and is also very likely on logical grounds to be implicated in the formation and storage of images relating to both perception and motor command. It would therefore likely play an instrumental role in the development of conscious and unconscious prognostications relating to behavior. Other acknowledged feedback loops pass between cortex and thalamus and between thalamo-cortical and cortico-thalamic circuits (187). These make up a large percentage of the mass of the thalamus (188), the remainder being occupied with conveying the classical sensory relays to cortex.

It must now be obvious that the brain is not readily divided up into strictly sensory and motor pathways and functions. Instead, as we have tried to emphasize, the system is built for action: the perceptual correlates of experience including knowledge of our bodies and of objects and events in the outside world and consciousness of whatever degrees of freedom we have for selecting among behavioral options, are not seated in some circumscribed region in cortex. They are probably highly selectively interpenetrating vertically and horizontally throughout rather extended regions of the central nervous system. If we are not mistaken, what gives rise to partial conscious access to these activities relates not so much to their location as to evolutionarily selected individually determined past payoffs for the existence of awareness and for the advantages of conscious interventions that have taken place and been reinforced among numerous interdependent pathways and centers all of which are geared to contribute toward successful behavior. An adaptive organism must be capable of bringing sensory data and action programs together in such a way as to provide effective behavioral outcomes, and that is all that is necessary. The internal model of which we are partly conscious, of our bodies and of the world about us, represents only a small share of this complicated correlation process. It represents that share of the internal model for which there has been developed, on the basis of past payoffs, specifically, payoffs for the effects of this awareness on the successes and failures of behavior. It is toward this behavioral goal that feedback from multiple sources makes its contribution.

Feedforward is anticipatory. It relates to the utilization of an internal model to organize activities, without waiting for feedback (189). If the movement is ballistic, that is, launched so as to be carried through regardless of feedback or before feedback can return, feedforward is serving alone. This is true for many gestures in sports such as the tennis serve or the golf swing, and the control must be extremely precise. More usually, feedforward control is combined with corrective influences from feedback during the course of the movement; feedforward provides approximate control and feedback contributes to making the action more precise. Vestibular and postural maintenance systems can operate in this way, with muscle spindle and joint receptors providing feedback that generates some limb-by-limb control.

In general, with both feedback and feedforward, the subordinate parts of the whole system assume some degree of autonomy. This distributes control to locales where it can have the shortest turnaround time and provide the most precise control. This also relieves higher centers of some burden of activity. One example illustrates some of the advantages when a vestibulo-spinal and local limb reflex mechanism combination provides an animal with accurately timed and quantified postural support via each individual limb in conditions of walking, running, jumping in darkness or on uneven ground (190). Of course, these local control loops must be subordinated to hierarchical "override" whenever the purposes of the whole animal demand an unusual program. An earlier section dealt with lateral inhibition and related some of the important functional consequences of lateral inhibition with respect to sensory processing and perceptual experience. Remember that similar inhibitory processes operate with both feedback and feedforward mechanisms and with them contribute to sharpening and confining the spatial domains of images being processed, and characterizing such images in increasingly abstract forms (see ref. 191). Such sensory processing also takes place in relation to the descending controls that modulate ascending sensory transmission.

3. Central Control of Sensory Transmission

It is now generally appreciated that an equivalent of about 10% or so of the total number of afferent and ascending sensory channels is dedicated to centrifugal control of sensory receptors and ascending sensory relays (192–198). These descending projections can inhibit or facilitate receptor activities and sensory relay transmission. There is a downward cascade, from cortex to thalamus to brainstem to spinal cord, or the equivalent, in each of the sensory systems. The descending route roughly parallels the classical ascending sensory pathways. There are also indirect trajectories via the brainstem reticular formation.

Whereas in invertebrates it is common for individual peripheral sense receptors to receive centrifugal controls, in higher forms this has been largely reduced in favor of centrifugal operations occurring at spinal rather than peripheral levels. Some peripheral sense organs receive sympathetic innervation which can modulate receptivity (199). Some hormones and other circulating factors have effects not only on responsivity of receptors but also of neurons in central reflex arcs and ascending central relays (199–201).

Muscle spindles constitute a system *par excellence* for central control of afferent input. The small-diameter gamma-efferent motoneuron that innervates an internal (intrafusal) muscle in the spindle does not directly affect contraction of the larger muscle housing the spindle. Rather it alters the rate of firing of afferent nerve fibers that have their end organs in the spindle. The largest diameter afferent, Ia, has a monosynaptic excitatory influence on the alpha-motoneuron serving the muscle containing the spindle. This is the main control affecting muscle tension and stretch reflexes. Thus, discharge of the small gamma-efferent motoneuron causes changes that affect several afferents, one of which contributes to the firing of the large-diameter alpha-motoneurons that induce contractions in the larger, encompassing muscle. The spindle afferents inform the central nervous system of the mechanical situation of the muscle over a wide range of phasic and static conditions of its stretch. The rate of firing of spindle afferents supplies information as to the *length* of the spindle, whereas the rate of increase or decrease of their firing indicates the *velocity of change* of length.

The gamma-motor innervation of the intrafusal muscle in the spindle provides a *controlled bias* to this afferent response system so that it will have a broad dynamic range of responses for even subtle changes within any given length of the spindle (202–205). Spindle afferent information is widely distributed, not only to the corresponding spinal segment but also to many spinal and brainstem levels and to selected regions of the cerebellum, basal ganglia, and cerebral cortex (206). Altogether, this central control of sensory signalling represents a precise and widely projected feedback of information to the central nervous system as to the disposition and dynamics of all skeletal muscles. Since the gamma-motoneuron can be activated by many different central loci, this whole afferent input system is brought under the control of the central nervous system itself (207).

It is evident that the retina, in all vertebrates studied, including mammals and specifically man, receives efferents that terminate in the region of the relay between bipolar cells and ganglion cells, ending on the amacrine cells which play some kind of modulating role at that synaptic relay (208). For some time there was doubt about the existence of efferents to the retina in mammals (209), and it is not yet established whence these optic centrifugal cells originate. In the birds, efferent control to the retina is served by a thalamic nucleus, which in turn receives a topographic representation of the retina via the optic tectum (analogous functionally to the superior colliculus in mammals) (210–214). Miles (215–219) has conducted anatomical, physiological, and behavioral studies on this system. He showed that birds with bilateral destruction of the isthmo-optic nucleus could not distinguish as well as intact birds food and non-food particles in dim light (220). In the bird, the efferent projections to the retina represent only about 1% of the total number of optic nerve fibers, whereas in mammals the percentage is higher. Centrifugal fibers in the normal human optic nerve represent about 10% of the total (221–223).

In the cochlea and vestibular sensory receptor systems, efferent fibers discovered by Rasmussen (224–227) have synaptic connections to the actual receptor units themselves, the hair cells. In the cochlea there are also nerve-to-nerve endings on the terminal boutons of afferent fibers which articulate synaptically with the hair cells (228). Galambos in 1956 (229) and others later (230, 231) demonstrated that central stimulation in the region of the origin of the olivocochlear bundle, the source of these efferent fibers, suppresses the acoustic nerve responses to sounds. Subsequent studies, reviewed by Worden (232), have revealed how complex may be the effects of such efferent impulses. Dewson (233) has shown that section of the crossed portion of the olivocochlear bundle in monkeys results in those animals showing impaired discrimination of spectrally complex sounds presented along with a masking tone. The deficit is not apparent without the masking tone. He also found that stimulation of the efferent bundle improved the temporal resolving power of the cochlea (234). Something of the same sort of centrifugal control seems to be exerted on olfactory mechanisms (235).

Altogether, it is evident that the central nervous system can exercise many discriminative controls affecting sensory input. Emphasis has been placed here on the controls affecting receptors because such an early influence would absolutely preclude unmodulated sensory data from reaching perceptual centers. This is a radical piece of information, for it implies the possibility of initial bias affecting data destined for perception at the very beginning of the generation of sensory signals. It thereby hangs a question mark in front of all discussions dealing with epistemology. The matter could be rationalized if it were argued that the perceiving organism "knows" what efferent signals it generates, and therefore it could, in principle, subtract from or add to the resultant centrally projected signal in order to correct it accordingly. This remains a theoretical possibility, to be sure, but it appears not to be operative inasmuch as *animals are found to behave in correspondence with the resultant effects of centrifugal alterations to incoming signals.* If they have to utilize information from sensory control commands, they seem not to utilize that information in their expressed conduct. And we can infer from human subjective testimony relating to the Ames' demonstrations that such information does not appear to correct perceptual experience either.

It is obvious that the central nervous system has command over receptors in other prior and overriding ways: pinching the nostrils, closing the eyes, covering the ears, moving the sense organs to other sources of stimuli, etc. There are also intermediate sites of intervention that are affected by central command: changes in the tissue and chemical milieu surrounding receptors as affected by various hormonal physiological and behavioral states, contraction and relaxation of middle ear muscles, pupillary control, and so on. The pupil is an especially fascinating organ that exhibits a certain degree of natural unrest, manifests "noise" generated centrally that affects both pupils simultaneously, and displays certain quantifiable servo-loop responses (236). Beyond this, the pupil is also an exquisite instrument for reflecting emotional states and expectations (237).

Therefore, there is no ambiguity that the nervous system can control its own input in a wide variety of ways. Most of the external controls and those manifested peripherally, such as the pupillary response and middle ear muscle reflexes, have long been recognized as sensory controls and have been taken for granted (or dismissed) in relation to sensory processing. What is new is that the brain can control its own input using covert means—centrifugal central pathways that have no outward display except in relation to behavior and that need to be analyzed using central recording. It is found that these controls can influence sensory receptor thresholds (199), the extent and distribution of sensory-evoked responses (238–240), and activities taking place along circuits relating to sensory systems (241–243). It is also obvious that some of the sensory discriminatory processes involved can operate at the very earliest stages of sensory processing (244) (see Fig. 4).

Clearly, the cortex is not the first step in sensory processing, nor does it appear to be the last step. Something fairly complicated seems to be taking place all along both ascending *and* descending pathways that relates to sensory processing and that contributes, during wakefulness, to perception.

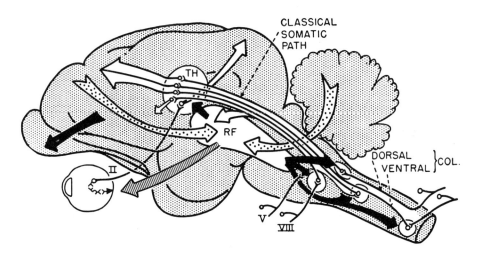

FIG. 4. Central control of sensory receptors and central sensory transmission. An overall scheme of brain modulating its own input is illustrated. Certain regions of neocortex, the frontal lobe of the cerebellum, and the phylogenetically ancient limbic cortex can strongly influence conduction in the extraclassic ascending sensory pathways coursing through the central cephalic reticular formation (French, et al., 242), shown by cerebral and cerebellar dotted arrows. The reticular formation can in turn (*black arrows*) inhibit olfactory relay in the olfactory bulb, somatosensory relay in the dorsal and ventral columns and trigeminal relays, as well as auditory and vestibular relays. The reticular formation can also inhibit the relay of all modalities through the thalamus, and it can both inhibit and facilitate retinal events. There appears to be a dedication to centrifugal control channels that is roughly equivalent to 10% of all incoming sensory ascending fibers. The full biological significance with respect to sensory signal processing and perception of this centrifugal control mechanism is only beginning to be understood. The fact of its existence in so many species and its power to modulate input is evidence for its evolutionary value. An important fact is that such influences may take place prior to the raw sensory data having access to mechanisms that are presumably available to consciousness. Central sensory control can thus offer pre-conscious modification of perceptual experience. (From Hernández-Peón, reproduced by French, ref. 245.)

There is some degree of erosion or augmentation and sharpening of information that started into the nervous system. There is, moreover, an intrusion into the participating circuits of additional influences from stored information that relates to past experiences, expectations, and purposes. Just how and where this information is introduced is not yet clear, but evidence suggests that it may be having conspicuous effects at least above midbrain levels (246–248) and perhaps all the way down to the receptor surfaces or at least the first central synaptic relays (249, 250). The perceptual shaping seems to be all of a piece in the same way that behavior is integrated. Perception and behavior serve the interests of the organism as a whole, serving internal satisfactions, contributing to updating an internal model of the world developed by that organism, and thereby contributing to its successful behavior.

This is what one might introspectively expect would take place within the waking brain: a reduction of data from the assaulting avalanche of stimuli impinging on sensory receptors, a modification of this input in accordance with stable central images, and an organization of prognostications for behavior based on past experiences, expectations, and purposes. Part of these transformations are accounted for through activity of centrifugal sensory control mechanisms. The brainstem reticular formation contributes not only to the maintenance of consciousness but also, in its role as an additional descending control of ascending sensory input, to the contents of consciousness (197, 198). Much more is to be learned about these centrifugal mechanisms influencing perception for the particular benefit of psychiatry.

V. SENSATION

I have learned from some persons whose arms or legs have been cut off, that they sometimes seemed to feel pain in the part which had been amputated, which made me think I could not be quite confident that it was a certain member which pained me, even though I felt pain in it. . . . In the same way, when I feel pain in my foot, my knowledge of physics teaches me that this sensation is communicated by means of nerves dispersed through the foot, which being extended like cords from there to the brain, when they are affected in the foot, at the same time affect the inmost portion of the brain which is their extremity and place of origin, and there excite a sensation of pain represented as existing in the foot. . . . If there is any cause which excites, not in the foot but in some part of the nerves which are extended between the foot and the brain, or even in the brain itself, the same action which usually is produced when the foot is detrimentally affected, pain will be experienced as though it were in the foot.

René Descartes, *Discourse de la Méthode* (1637)

How does an animal receive stimuli? What mechanisms account for the transformation of physical and chemical events in the environment into nerve impulses? What are the characteristics of different receptors located in special sense organs and scattered throughout the body and within the brain itself? There is no ambiguity about peripheral nerves being distinguishable as *afferent* and *efferent*, incoming and outgoing, but once the central nervous system is reached, the problem becomes increasingly difficult. *The spinal interneuron is both afferent and efferent. And so, in principle, are all other neurons entirely contained within the central nervous system.* The roles of traditionally sensory (e.g., dorsal columns) and motor (e.g., pyramidal tract) neurons are coming under increasing question as to their contributions above and beyond their ostensible "sensory" and "motor" functions (251). A question consequently intrudes as to how far centralward do we carry the notion of sensory pathways? To what destiny are they thought to be aimed? Other questions arise as to the purity of the different sensory modalities because they begin to invade one another's domains early in their central trajectories. At what levels and where are the biological systems located that are involved in the decoding of incoming messages? How are such messages utilized, in consciousness, and in behavior? What is meant by the notion of *utility* in respect to sensory signalling? How do these sensory and perceptual issues relate to psychiatry? These are some of the questions that we shall attempt to address in the following sections.

A. Sensory Transduction and Encoding

1. Sensory Receptors and Receptor Systems

Some sensory end-processes are relatively isolated, others are arranged side by side, densely crowded together in a compact tissue of receptors. Some of the latter involve complicated neural networks disposed within the sensory end-organ. The simplest systems include bare nerve endings and encapsulated endings such as those found in glabrous and hairy skin, along the walls of hollow viscera and blood vessels, along mesenteric and fascial surfaces, tendons, joints, and joint capsules. Intermediately complicated endings are associated with specialized receptor cells such as those in the taste buds. More complicated sensory mechanisms are bound up in muscle spindles and still others are distributed as sensory epithelia in particular parts of blood vessels (the aortic and carotid bodies) and in specialized parts of auditory and vestibular organs. The most complicated sense organs are olfactory and visual receptors, being in each case associated intimately with outward extensions of brain tissue. In a strict sense the olfactory tracts and optic nerves are not bona fide nerves. The brain apparently just cannot wait to hear from them and to begin processing olfactory and visual messages, so it meets them at their origins.

The obvious fact is that all sensory receptors are buried in tissue. Even the chemoreceptors in the olfactory epithelium are covered with cilia that may exquisitely and specifically be receptive (252) but their ciliary lash-up is embedded in mucus. Bare nerve endings are always surrounded by cells that must contribute to their mechanical and chemical environs. Many receptors are encased in capsules and specialized end-organs contributed by peripheral glia, and other cells. The retina is most curiously disposed, with the light receptors located externally, farthest from incoming light. Light has to traverse not only the translucent cornea, lens, and vitreous humor but also a tangle of blood vessels, which you can see with the ophthalmoscope, and all of the 10 or so layers of fibers and ganglion, bipolar, amacrine, and horizontal cells. The light receptors are even pointing their sensory detectors away from the source of light.

Withal, the receptors in each of these various systems are cunningly selected so as to be so highly sensitive that they can probably detect only one odorous molecule, one photon, and to respond to extremely small displacements. Hair cells in the cochlea are activated when the tympanic membrane is vibrating only about half the diameter of the hydrogen molecule.

Only one specific kind of molecule is identified with the interaction of stimulus with activation mechanisms of the receptor: photons interact with rhodopsin. An early retinal potential is generated by charge displacements that occur in or near the rhodopsin molecule whenever that molecule undergoes a spectral transition as we shall relate below (253–255). What is universal in sense receptors is the development of some kind of potential in the receptor directly or indirectly associated with the nerve membrane—the *generator potential*—which is then transformed into a conducted nerve impulse, the spike (256). From the point of spike generation centralward, sensory signalling is organized in terms of nervous processes that have nothing to do with the particular sensory modality that set the whole process in train, except for two facts: (i) The particular sensory stimulus triggers nerve impulses which are conveyed along those particular fibers that are connected in sequence as relays along relatively modality-specific pathways. On account of this functional connection sequence starting with a particular sense-organ, the pathway is called a *labeled line*. Although other modalities may intrude, the entire chain seems to be preferentially responsive to the stimulus modality at the head of the line. (ii) The morphology—the axonal-dendritic-somatic architecture—of the chains of relays engaged in transmitting the different modalities is somewhat specially organized, presumably favoring the extraction of distinctive features relating to the stimulus.

Another universal feature of sense receptors is that they are biological systems with the dynamic properties, vulnerabilities, etc., that this implies. They exhibit turnover of cell surfaces, cell contents, such as the rhodopsin-containing discs in rods and cones, and even the receptor cells themselves, as in the case of taste and olfactory receptors. It is likely that the bare and encapsulated nerve endings in skin are similarly undergoing turnover which may give rise to misunderstandings about the number of different varieties of nerve endings, some of them being juvenile and degenerative forms of one and the same type of ending (252). It should also be borne in mind that some of the special properties of sensory systems may reside not exclusively in the nature of the receptor but be contributed to according to the characteristics of the surrounding tissue which undoubtedly partially shapes stimulus impact on the receptor.

Finally, most receptors give rise to generator potentials that are depolarizing to the resting membrane. An exception is the photoreceptors, both rods and cones. These are hyperpolarized, and their membrane resistances are correspondingly increased (255, 257). This is rationalized at present by the anti-intuitive conception that photoreceptors (of vertebrates, at least) are depolarized or excited in the dark, and suppressed or repolarized by light. This would require that they continually release synaptic transmitter substance in the dark and cease doing so or do so in diminished amounts when they are exposed to light. In this connection, it is commonplace that some receptors are "spontaneously active," that is, active continuously in a steady-state condition. The advantage of this is clear. It is obviously easier to obtain subtle differences in the rate or other characteristics of impulse discharge than it is by changing abruptly from no activity to modest activity. Moreover, if there is a certain rate or pattern of discharge at rest, diminution of a given stimulus state, as by relaxation of muscle tone, can be followed by diminution of the rate or some other change in pattern of the receptor discharge.

a. Somesthetic receptors

The receptor—meaning the nerve terminal and whatever associated non-neural transducer cells may be involved—plus the centrally conducting axonal processes and the cell body constitute a *sensory unit*. This is the primary afferent, the first neuron in the order of succession in sensory processing. Each unit has a receptive field within which it may be activated by stimuli of adequate intensity and quality. An area of skin, for example, may be innervated by a single unit, or there may be discontinuous areas relating to such a unit. There may be large as well as small receptive fields. There are differences in threshold and responsivity depending on where within a given receptive field the unit is activated (258). The peripheral branches of adjacent receptors may be interlaced to some extent, providing overlapping of their receptive fields. Density of packing of peripheral sensory receptors differs from one skin region to another, being especially dense in the fingertips and sparse in the skin over the back and in most subcutaneous areas. Endings also show different rates of adaptation to stimulation; some respond only to transients, on or off, with a short burst of impulses, whereas others discharge a steady rate of firing of impulses in accordance with a steady intensity of stimulation following transient accelerations and decelerations of firing rate accompanying increases and decreases of stimulus intensity.

Different sense organs discharge in response to different incident stimuli: mechanical changes in pressure, stretch, shearing force, temperature, electrical potential change, chemical substances such as the release of histamine into the tissue, fluid that accumulates within blisters, and so on. These changes may yield alterations in the static properties of the nerve ending, in its capacitance, resistance, etc. There may be chemical intermediaries as well, this being uncertain. Such changes lead to generator current flow that triggers further local depolarization sufficient to induce a full-scale action potential that will be conducted centralward.

Mechanical receptors, both free nerve endings and a variety of encapsulated endings, serve touch and pressure detection in the skin. Some of the most sensitive are activated by movement of hairs. Mechanoreceptors in joints, joint capsules, tendons, fascial plains, and even skin can serve, along with vestibular receptors in the inner ear, position sense, and kinesthesis. Stretch receptors of muscles probably do not contribute to conscious sensations. Pressure and shearing force detectors lie in hollow viscera, gastrointestinal tract, urinary tract, etc., and in the carotid and aortic and other pressor receptors in vascular and pulmonary beds, including, e.g., carotid sinus receptors. Hair cell mechanoreceptors are responsible for responses in the cochlea subserving hearing. There are separate thermoreceptors for warmth and cold (259), special receptors sensitive to the partial pressure of CO_2, O_2, H^+ (89), central osmoreceptors sensitive to ion concentrations in extracellular fluid, and receptors especially sensitive to blood levels of certain critical nutrients (260, 261). Of course, all cells are more or less sensitive to each of these potential stimuli; some are specialized, however, and located strategically, as in the case of O_2 detectors in the carotid body which is suffused with arterial blood. Situated as the carotid body and sinus are, they can help in the regulation of oxygen supply and blood pressure controlled at an adequate level for the brain. Extremes of mechanical force or of temperature and the presence of certain chemicals released by incipient or actual tissue destruction can give rise to nervous activity in several kinds of nerve endings, nociceptors, subserving pain (21, 124, 258).

The pacinian corpuscle is a form of encapsulated sensory nerve ending that has been closely studied. It is rather ubiquitously distributed, being found in skin, on fascial surfaces, in association with muscle sheaths, in mesentery, and elsewhere. It is a rapidly adapting mechanoreceptor. Its capsule, made up of a number of cells, is elipsoid in shape, and it may be 1 or 2 mm in size. It contains internal lamellae that are hemicentric on the inside; the intralaminar spaces are filled with a turgid fluid containing collagen fibrils; the whole capsule is scarcely compressible, and any pressure exerted on its surface from any direction will be distributed along the bare nerve ending and final node of Ranvier embraced by the capsule (262).

Loewenstein (263) has investigated this nerve terminal with and without its capsule. When the capsule is indented with increasing forces, there are first nonpropagating generator potentials, followed, if sufficient force is applied, by a propagated nerve impulse in the associated nerve fiber. If the lamellae are carefully removed, the response is similar, but if pressure is applied to the node of Ranvier, local generator potentials are precluded from eliciting a nerve impulse. If the nerve is sectioned and allowed to degenerate for a few days, the generator potential itself disappears.

By extrapolation, it is presumed that many other sensory end-organs are similarly activated. The generator potential which can be recorded at many such endings, has properties like those that excite muscle at the end-plate (excitatory end-plate potential, EPP) and at postsynaptic junctions in dendrites and nerve cell bodies (excitatory postsynaptic potential, EPSP). Tetrodotoxin, which at low concentrations blocks sodium ion conduction, can block the nerve impulse generation without greatly affecting the generator potential (256).

It is probable that the nerve impulse is dependent upon outward flow of current at the critical first node of Ranvier, just as is thought to be the case for the generation of nerve impulses at the initial segment of the axon as it leaves the cell body (264). The axon hillock, where cell body excitability generates a nerve impulse, is different from the nerve terminal by not being mechanically excitable (265). All of this means that the nerve fiber has distinctive specializations of structure for functional advantages, at each location, the axon hillock, the nodes of Ranvier, and at nerve terminals. Other specializations of nerve membrane are associated with synapses and other functionally important interneuronal and neuromuscular junctions, and even at glial-axonal junctions associated with myelin (266).

i. Visceral sensory receptors

Sensory receptors are abundant throughout the viscera and mesenteries. They include all types of nerve endings seen in skin and subcutaneous tissues except, naturally, for the specialized cutaneous endings associated with hairs. There are abundant pacinian corpuscles which may be seen to advantage here because they stand out visibly in the thin loops of mesentery. Sheehan (267) found pacinian corpuscles to be congregated near blood vessels at the roots of mesentery and considered that they might be responsive to circulatory pressure. Nerve endings in viscera are readily activated by adequate stimuli, i.e., stretch of the walls of a hollow viscus, strain on the mesentery, stress applied to the walls of blood vessels. When viscera are exposed, even light air blowing across them or a slight vibration of the operating table will set of a thunderous discharge of visceral afferent nerves recorded by electrical amplification and monitored by a loudspeaker.

It is interesting, therefore, that the viscera which are sending impulses centralward in large and meaningful patterns relating to the state and economy of their points of departure, e.g., relating to cerebral perfusion, the degree of distension or collapse of the lungs, the degree of distension of gut, etc., do not reach consciousness except vaguely and perhaps acutely only when life-threatening circumstances arise in the head or the abdominal or thoracic cavities. These afferents pass to the spinal cord and synapse in the dorsal horn, sending collaterals and second-order impulses along ascending sensory pathways in quite orthodox fashion.

Their cell bodies reside in the dorsal root ganglia along with all somatic afferent cells. They lie, in their roots of entry and central trajectories, in close proximity to somatic afferent activity, which is presumably the basis for referred sensation. Yet the lungs and gut can be cut, burned, crushed, and otherwise severely assaulted, with associated serious tissue destruction and accompanied by abundant nerve impulses discharges, without a flicker of conscious evidence of such events. On the other hand, distension of bowel or blood vessel or traction on mesentery and especially distension of the ureter or uterus, however, will elicit plainly distressing although rather poorly localized pain (268). The pain may be referred to some somatic locations, e.g., gallbladder distension may be accompanied by acute shoulder pain. The innervation of liver and gallbladder capsules is from the same cervical spinal cord levels at which brachial plexus nerves from the shoulder make their entrance.

It appears that evolution has "conditioned" us to be unresponsive in consciousness to visceral afferent signalling which is ordinarily of an "internal housekeeping" nature. Perhaps because never before experienced, by reason of protection behind the somatic body wall, the cutting, burning, etc., of internal viscera have no evolutionary significance. But when bowel or ureter obstruction or gallbladder distension occurs, which are more commonplace associations of life-threatening danger, the visceral afferent signals are switched into consciousness even though the actual tissue damage may be less than with the cutting, burning, etc. This underlines again the selective nature of consciousness and its specialized role reserved for the shaping of behaviors that may be more successful as a consequence of conscious intervention.

This evidence emphasizes the *discriminative selection of impulses for representation in consciousness from among closely neighboring sensory paths.* It exemplifies the lesson that *natural selection selects on the basis of behavioral outcomes and not on internal structures or functions excepting in relation to those outcomes.* This in no way denies the importance to the central nervous system of information derived from visceral afferent input relating to homeostatic and vegetative reflex controls (269). Visceral afferent impulses do have their covert but vitally important roles.

b. Taste and olfactory receptors

Taste and olfaction are not particularly similar except for being chemoreceptor systems responsive to environmental stimuli. Taste is really a *chemical touch system,* because it depends on physical contact with the object that is to be chemically appreciated. Like other kinds of touch, chemical-touch-taste is conveyed along with other somesthetic modalities from the tongue and fauces through the brainstem and upwards via the thalamus to neocortex. Olfaction, by contrast, receives its chemical signals by air transport that is swept into the upper chambers of the nasal passages. Its first-order neurons are very short, debouching through the cribriform plate into an outward extending plexus of brain, the olfactory bulb and tract. The olfactory tract delivers messages relating to olfactory cues to medial and lateral regions of phylogenetically old cortex and associated subcortical structures. It represents the only sensory modality that is not relayed through thalamus to neocortex. It bypasses the thalamus altogether.

Taste nerve endings invade one or more taste buds and innervate many of the taste cells in each cluster (270). There are interactions between individual taste cells and between coinnervated taste buds. It is interesting that the taste cells have a short half-life of only about 10 days and are continually being replaced. The rapid turnover makes it all the more remarkable how consistent are averaged nerve bundle responses to a wide variety of cations and taste stimuli. The taste cells respond to thousands of different types of chemicals, some of which are synthetic and not naturally occurring (271). Salts are probably adsorbed with very weak binding strength by the cation to a receptor surface, perhaps on the protruding microvilli. Binding characteristics help to account for hierarchies of activation of nerve impulses by various cations. Sweet- and bitter-evoking responses probably originate from complexing between the stimulus molecule and some proteinaceous receptor molecule (272). These are probably all surface reactions; it is doubtful that any taste molecules need to cross the cell membrane in order to have their stimulating effects. More likely, the receptor molecule undergoes a conformational change that increases receptor membrane permeability locally and starts the process of initiating a nerve impulse.

Clinically, four qualities of taste are detected on the tip of the tongue: sweet, salt, sour, and bitter. Sour is most readily appreciated along the sides of the tongue and bitter most posteriorly. Nerve fibers can be recorded singly in animals, by being teased from a bundle, and averaged responses can be recorded from a large bundle of fibers, such as the chorda tympani. Taste cells, single nerve fibers, and averaged responses all display a lack of strict specificity but each instead exhibits a range of specificities. It is likely that a particular quality of taste is not conveyed by a single class of fibers; yet quantitative responses corresponding to quite repeatable subjective experiences have been recorded from the chorda tympani nerve in human subjects undergoing surgery for otosclerosis (273). Humans differ greatly in their sensitivities to basic taste substances and their hierarchies of sensitivities to different qualities. The magnitude of subjective sweetness bears a logarithmic relationship to the absolute concentration of a sweetener, and the relative sweetness of different sweeteners changes in direct relationship to the concentration of sucrose (274).

Olfactory receptors consist of cell bodies lying in the olfactory epithelium, a densely packed bed of receptor units interspersed with sustentacular cells. The former have cilia and the latter microvilli forming a pink velvety surface covered with mucus. Blast cell replacement of olfactory cells ceases in adults but the cilia and receptor surfaces continue to turn over rapidly throughout life (275). The olfactory receptor cell surface that is exposed to the nasal cavity exhibits a fuzzy electron microscopic appearance suggestive of mucopolysaccharides which may constitute selective receptor surfaces. There are prominent vacuoles, signs of pinocytosis, and many mitochondria present (276), suggesting a high rate of metabolic activity and probably also an active replacement of cell membrane by eversion of vesicles. The membrane of receptor cells narrows along the base of the epithelium to form a slender axon that projects through the cribriform plate to synapse with both tufted and mitral cells in the olfactory bulb. The tufted cells project axons along the olfactory tract and anterior commissure to the contralateral olfactory tract and bulb, contributing inhibitory effects to the opposite side. This provides direct lateral inhibition from one olfactory bulb to the other and may, for example, assist a bloodhound running a scent to distinguish unambiguously which nostril is receiving the stronger concentration of odor.

A negative potential shift occurs in recordings from the olfactory epithelium, the electro-olfactorogram, when odorous air is passed across the olfactory epithelium (277). The amplitude of this response increases in logarithmic fashion with increasing odor concentrations. This potential persists even when sufficient cocaine has been applied to block conduction in the olfactory nerves, suggesting that it resembles other generator potentials. In unanesthetized epithelia, extracellular recording from individual olfactory nerve fibers shows bursts of spikes in response to odor-bearing air (278). The olfactory units are not particularly odor selective; they do, however, respond to a number of odorants but with different numbers of nerve impulses. Evidently odor discrimination involves a complicated signal-sorting process. The mitral and tufted cells, granular cells, and neuropile representing the communicating network in the bulb are arranged in some 26,000 glomeruli. Interneurons and axon collaterals from the major neuronal types provide lateral inhibition across and between glomeruli in ways that contribute to sharpening borders of activity (279). This process becomes increasingly sharpened, stage by stage along the central projections (280).

The mitral cells constitute proper second-order neurons in the olfactory pathway. Granule cell interneurons provide modulatory influences on transactions taking place within the bulb. The olfactory tract is made up of myelinated fibers which project, as well as to the contralateral bulb, to medial frontal cortex, anterior and medial temporal cortex, and parts of the amygdala. There are apparently no direct fibers to the hippocampus or septum. The olfactory system does, however, project by a series of relays to hippocampus, septum, and hypothalamus, and ultimately to the frontal-limbic midbrain area (280). Olfactory cortex of dogs, in areas analogous to frontal and temporal lobe mesocortex, is necessary and sufficient for olfactory discriminations (281). The olfactory system constitutes an impressive chemical discrimination mechanism. Quite subtle structural changes can be detected in molecular configurations, as among various musks, for example. Organic chemists, with practice, can readily recognize an extended series of alcohols, aldehydes, and acids. An incredibly small quantity of odiferous material can be detected, 0.00000004 mg per liter of air of mercaptan, for example.

It used to be supposed that birds had little or no olfactory sense, but Wenzel (282) has shown that grain-eating birds show increased olfactory bulb electrical activity with exposure to grain odors; vultures and raptorial birds show similar activity with exposure to meat and offal; and pigeons, which are omniverous, show increased activity with each of these test exposures. Olfaction and taste combine to provide suitable selections of food to fulfill nutritive needs (283), and both can be effectively conditioned to specific appetitive reactions (281). Olfaction and taste stimuli put into action important salivatory and other digestive mechanisms important for the acceptance and digestion of food. Olfactory signals play an important role in sexual functions for monkeys and other animals (284), and presumably also for mankind.

c. Auditory and vestibular receptor systems

Both the labyrinth (with its semicircular canals, utricle, and saccule) and the cochlea contain orderly clusters and rows of receptors, hair cells that respond to shearing forces applied to their protruding cilia. Differences in orientation of hair cells in the receptors account for the differences in polarization of microphonic potentials in response to this shearing force which involves displacement between the base supporting the receptor and a gelatinous structure into which the cilia project. In the utricle and saccule, this gelatinous material contains calcium carbonate granules, the otoliths, which have much greater specific gravity than the surrounding endolymphatic fluid. Hence, the otoliths and their gelatinous embedding are attracted by gravity and are therefore affected according to various directions of acceleration.

The semicircular canals have bulbous enlargements within which are located sensory organs consisting of a crista within which hair cells are fixed, and a gelatinous cupola that crowns the hair cells and that is in turn moved by displacement of the endolymph, as in angular acceleration. Since the utricle and saccule respond to accelerations in any direction, and the semicircular canals to angular accelerations controlled by the orientation of the canals, the utricle and saccule contribute unique sensory data relating to linear accelerations.

The arrangements of cilia provide a directional orientation for the receptors; e.g., hair cells in the crista of the horizontal canals are oriented with the kinocilium (the largest of the cilia) toward the utricle, whereas hair cells in the other two canals are oriented oppositely with respect to the kinocilium and the utricle. Motion of the cilia is excitatory in one direction and inhibitory in the other. This results in increased firing in nerve fibers arising from the horizontal crista during utriculopetal movement of the cupola and decreased firing of fibers serving the other cristae. The contralateral semicircular canals are fixed in the skull oppositely and are therefore affected oppositely during accelerations. The hair cells are correspondingly oppositely activated and suppressed. This means that, with cancellation in the brainstem of most of the primary afferent effects from the two sides of the head when movements have exactly opposite effects, higher nervous system levels need to process only information relating to the stimulus asymmetries and they can be spared much of the lower impulse traffic.

The cochlea is constructed with a basilar membrane which is particularly stiff at the basal positions and more compliant near the apex (285). The transduction of mechanical vibrations to nerve impulses apparently involves movement of the basilar membrane and the attached organ of Corti which rides upon the basilar membrane, in relation to the tectorial membrane, the gelatinous roof into which the receptor hair cell cilia protrude. For reasons of architecture and due to oxygen-requiring work performed by the stria vascularis, there is a standing potential across the basilar membrane that is approximately twice that of a cell's resting membrane potential. This large potential may contribute to the cochlear microphonic potential that is generated when the basilar membrane is vibrated (286). The microphonic potential is independent of the compound action potential of the eighth nerve; for example, it reverses polarity with the stimulus whereas the neural response does not. [See Békésy (287) for thorough studies of the cochlea.]

Afferent nerve terminals attach themselves to the hair cells in locations that appear in electron micrographs to implicate chemical transmitter communication, with the receptor discharging vesicular contents to activate postsynaptic structures in the afferent terminal bouton (228, 288, 289). In both vestibular and auditory receptors, there are also numerous *efferent* fibers, arising from cells in the brainstem (225, 290), which project to the hair cells and attach themselves to the terminals of the afferents. Evidently, these efferents can suppress the hair cells directly and can interfere with afferent nerve excitation at its point of departure by effecting postsynaptic inhibition (291).

It has been shown that stimulation of the crossed fibers in the efferent complex reduces the afferent nerve discharge and at the same time releases an enhanced cochlear microphonic potential response to acoustic stimulation (229, 231, 292). Activation of the uncrossed efferent fibers, in contrast, results in a lesser reduction in the nerve response and no increase in the cochlear microphonic (293–295). If strychnine or the related alkaloid brucine is injected, the efferent controls are transiently blocked (296). Similar inhibitory effects are understood to occur in relation to vestibular efferent controls (297).

Naturally there is a great deal of curiosity attached to what may be the functional role of the efferent projections to the vestibular and auditory systems and, altogether, considerable study has been devoted to this problem. There are approximately 120 uncrossed olivocochlear fibers and 450 crossed fibers. There are additional reticulocochlear fibers, at least in rodents (298). Among the outer hair cells, as a consequence of abundant branching, there are an estimated 40,000 efferent endings (299, 300). These cover a preponderance of the synaptic surface of the outer hair cell receptors ending directly on those cells (289). Among inner hair cells, efferent fibers terminate mainly on the afferent boutons, on the postsynaptic afferent take-off.

Worden (301) has reviewed experiences with electrical stimulation of the olivocochlear bundle, pointing up the complexity of efferent fiber influences on receptors and on neural discharge. There is evidence to suggest that the bundle can function as a general control of afferent input, perhaps acting to suppress background noise and to improve signal-to-noise ratios (233, 234), but these questions are not resolved. It is proving about as difficult to learn what the centrifugal, efferent projections do for perception as it has been all along to understand the functions of the ascending, sensory contributions.

d. Visual receptor system

The vertebrate retina is made up of three distinctive cellular layers. The outermost, farthest from the source of light stimulation, is made up of rods and cones. In the vicinity of the visual axis, the innermost two layers are parted, baring the receptor cells which are packed more closely together there for greater acuity of vision. Rod receptors, especially sensitive in dim light vision, are locally replaced by cones capable of discriminating color. From this central visual area, the fovea, we derive our sharpest vision and most concentrated color appreciation. Where the optic nerve root enters the back of the eyeball, there is a "blind spot" perforce of the absence there of light receptors.

The two inner cell layers consist of bipolar cells and ganglion cells, the latter representing third-order units along the visual path. At the level of the synaptic junction between light receptors and bipolar cells are horizontal cell interneurons. At the level of synaptic junction between bipolar cells and ganglion cells are amacrine cell interneurons. It is interesting that in the retinas of frogs, rabbits, and pigeons, through-put of visual information is less direct; that is, more integrative connections are found along the path, involving greater participation in the relay process by the interneurons (302). And physiological evidence in the frog indicates that retinal discrimination and preliminary decision-making, e.g., bug detection, is already well advanced within the retina (303–305).

We have already introduced the integrative implications of lateral inhibition as manifested by ON-center/OFF-surround and OFF-center/ON-surround ganglion cells in the retina. We have also mentioned the fact that in the dark retinal receptors are evidently continuously releasing chemical transmitters and that this process is interrupted by incident light stimulation. We need now to consider briefly the nature of the process of transduction of light into neuronal signals and the nature of color vision.

Light receptors consist of columnar cell bodies that project via a narrow cilia-like neck to an outer segment that contains rhodopsin, a globular protein that is attached in regular arrays to membranous bilayer discs that are stacked within the outer segment. Incident light is thought to produce a dipole by shifting hydrogen from the hydroxyl group to the nitrogen, yielding a *cis* to *trans* isomerization that involves rotation around a single bond (254). This requires that rhodopsin be attached to the membrane, and its consequence— in less than half a microsecond—is an early receptor potential (306) which has a peak action spectrum at the same wave length as rhodopsin (253). The amplitude of this early receptor potential is linearly related to the number of rhodopsin molecules excited by the incident light. Montal (307) has succeeded in incorporating rhodopsin in artificial membranes so that the detailed nature of this process can be more readily unraveled. Because the early receptor potential can be obtained in fixed and frozen retinas, and because of its short latency, it is considered not to involve a membrane response. The dipole effect would be sufficient to induce later membrane effects which turn out, unexpectedly, to involve hyperpolarization (255).

Tomita (255, 257, 308) has succeeded in microelectrode penetration of single cone receptors. By scanning the incident light spectrum, he found that 74% of the population of cones respond with greatest signal-to-noise ratios in the red, 16% in the blue, and 10% in the green spectral ranges. Rushton (309), using reflectance from retinal pigments in the intact human eye, succeeded in determining light absorption in normal human subjects and in all known types of defective color vision. Marks et al. (310) showed that single cones in excised human or monkey retinas yield three different pigments as determined by spectral absorbance, and their spectral distributions coincide with the normal pigments as defined by Rushton's reflectance studies (309). Rushton found that in each of the color defectives there is a loss or anomaly in one or more of the three cone pigments, and that the observed defects in vision are not due to abnormal processing of neural responses initiated by normal pigments.

Thus, ganglion cells in the retina convey to the superior colliculus (for eye motor control and other reflex responses), to visual cortex (for refined color and form discrimination), and to the hypothalamus (for neuroendocrine signaling purposes) information that is already considerably processed in the retina. The even more elaborate retinal processing that takes place in the retinas of some lower and intermediate forms (frogs, rabbits, pigeons, and ground squirrels) illustrates the principle of peripheral distribution of decision-making for purposes of economizing on higher centers. In vision, at least, one may presume from these observations that when more elaborate and extensive higher centers become available, decision-making can be somewhat shifted centralward.

B. Sensory Mechanisms

1. The Classical Sensory Pathways

Figure 5 illustrates diagrammatically the ascending somatic sensory and auditory-vestibular pathways. There are two main classical ascending pathways in the somatosensory system, a phylogenetically older spinothalamic route and the dorsal column-medial lemniscus projections which appear in rudimentary form in reptiles and which enlarge greatly in relation to other somesthetic paths in mammals. Both of these systems relay in the ventral basal part of the thalamus and project in each hemisphere onto two major areas of neocortex. They convey somewhat different messages concerning the body wall and objects impinging on it, and this is of help to the neurologist in diagnosing spinal lesions.

In general, the lemniscal system is considered to be the more discriminative of the two paths. The trigeminal nerve, subserving sensation from the face is similarly divided into a phylogenetically older trigeminothalamic path and a more discrete, phylogenetically newer system which projects upwards from the main sensory and anterior nuclei of the fifth cranial nerve. A third, still less specific system for somesthesia ascends from spinal to cortical levels largely by way of the spinal and brainstem reticular formation and is relayed through the thalamus via the intralaminar and other nonspecific thalamic projections. This third projection system contributes most extensively to association areas, and in lesser degree to the basal ganglia and the limbic system. Finally a fourth projection system includes independent traffic of ascending impulses that pass through the pulvinar-posterior region of the thalamus and thence to proximal association areas of neocortex as depicted by stippling in Fig. 5 (311).

a. Spinothalamic pathways

The spinothalamic system that ascends in the anterolateral part of the spinal cord consists of two phylogenetically distinctive projections, a paleo-spinothalamic and a neospinothalamic system. They are composed mostly of smaller diameter myelinated and less fully myelinated fibers, as compared with the dorsal column-lemniscal pathway, and they are less precisely organized topographically. As the great Arctic explorer and humanitarian Nansen (312) showed, the incoming dorsal root fibers bifurcate on entering the spinal cord and send processes ascending and descending to provide synaptic relays along several spinal segments. Many of the second-order neurons, after being affected by spinal afferent input plus various activities contributed as a result of the convergent influences on the local interneuronal pools, cross the midline in the anterior white commissure and ascend in the anterolateral portion of the spinal cord. Ascending fibers at successively higher segmental levels fall into line along the medial side of this pathway. Some of these fibers send collaterals into the reticular formation of the spinal

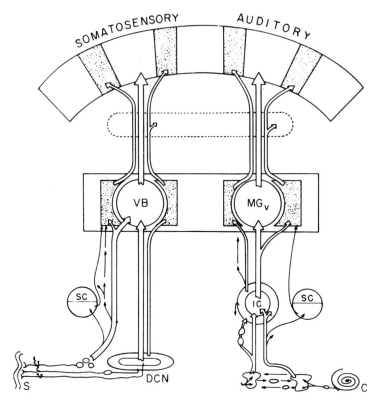

FIG. 5. Ascending somatic sensory and auditory pathways schematized. Peripheral receptors and other elements of the somatosensory (S, skin) and auditory (C, cochlear) systems are depicted at the bottom, with ascending projections rising through spinal, brain stem and thalamic relays to neocortex. Somatic fibers travel upwards along two main paths, spinothalamic on the left, with some ascending polysynaptic spinal relays coursing through the reticular formation and superior colliculus with the more direct and discrete dorsal column, medial lemniscal pathway on the right. Both of these ascending pathways relay to cortex by way of the ventrobasal thalamus (VB) and via associated intralaminar and reticular nuclei of the thalamus and the pulvinar posterior associative thalamic relay systems (*stippled*). Thence projections pass to the somatosensory cortex (*clear*) and adjoining association areas of neocortex (*stippled*). The ascending auditory pathway has greater bilaterality of projection stemming from two-way commissural paths in the medulla. It has ascending relays mainly via the inferior colliculus (IC) [and, in lesser part, also by way of the superior colliculus (SC)], thence to the medial geniculate body (MG$_v$) and onto the classic auditory area in neocortex. There are other more diffusely projecting and pulvinar associative relays for acoustic signals which are projected into primary auditory cortex (*clear*) and proximal association areas of neocortex (*stippled*). Influences on basal ganglia motor mechanisms are indicated by the projections to the dotted oval below cortex. Not shown: somatosensory and auditory descending corticifugal projections which course downward in an approximately parallel stream of projections to influence each of the layers of ascending relays and also many of the peripheral receptors. The descending sensory control system constitutes approximately 10% of the number of channels contained in the ascending system. (From Graybiel, ref. 311.)

cord and brainstem on their way to the ventral basal part of the thalamus where they terminate.

Other fibers belonging to this sector of the cord ascend no farther than the bulb or pons or midbrain, contributing terminally to the brainstem reticular formation. In each quadrant of the spinal cord are other ascending fibers that take a swift up-and-down course, being relayed in the bulbar reticular formation. These constitute the ascending limb of the spino-bulbo-spinal reflex system. The bulb itself is one of the great convergent centers of the brain, receiving from many remote areas including all of the major functional divisions of the nervous system and conveying powerful facilitatory and inhibitory messages into the spinal cord that have widespread motor and sensory influences (129, 185, 190, 313, 314).

The phylogenetically oldest portion of the spinothalamic pathway projects to equally old elements of the medial and posterior thalamus, the central lateral, parafascicularis and paracentralis nuclear groups. This pathway combines with ascending reticular projections in contributing to generalized arousal of the forebrain. These ascending projections represent convergent paths for multiple sensory modalities. They therefore are not supposed to convey discrete, modality-specific information. They could and very likely do convey information relating to the occurrence of *change of state,* internal and external, for which *arousal* may be an appropriate reaction. They also may convey information about the *intensity* of any given stimulation.

The combination of spinothalamic projections contributes to cerebral information relating to touch, temperature, and pain sensations. Spinothalamic mechanisms are very closely allied to the spinal and brainstem reticular formation; indeed, they probably represent an evolutionary derivative of the reticular formation selected for providing a more rapid and somewhat more discretely organized and modality-specific pathway alternative to the diffusely projecting reticular formation. They convey light touch that is not very accurately localized and, in addition, thermal information and signals relating to pain perception.

(i) *Thermal sensibility.* Thermosensitive receptors exist in the skin, in various areas of the circulatory system and viscera, and within the central nervous system. Central receptors are found in the spinal cord, but not in the bulb. They are located in the pons, midbrain and in the preoptic, anterior hypothalamic region.

> *Irrespective of the initial temperature, warmth receptors respond with an overshoot of their discharge on sudden warming and with a transient inhibition on cooling, whereas cold receptors respond in the opposite direction from that of warm receptors, temporarily overshooting frequency on cooling and showing transient inhibition on warming. In addition to this dynamic behavior, there are also typical differences in the static frequency curves of both types of cutaneous receptors, the temperature of the maximum discharge being much lower for cold receptors than for warmth receptors . . . by combination of the static discharges from cold and warmth receptors, unequivocal information is obtained at any temperature. (315)*

Impulses elicited by warmth and cold follow the spinothalamic pathway travelling in the anterolateral quadrant of the spinal cord, and can be recorded from cells in the thalamus and in somatosensory cortex. The sensation of warmth apparently cannot be explained simply by inhibition of cold receptors and corresponding cold pathway activity. Thermoregulatory reflexes from both cold and warmth exposure can be elicited during sleep when no conscious sensations or conscious behavioral responses are in evidence. Warming the preoptic area in the anterior hypothalamus activates responses to counteract warming and inhibits responses to counteract cooling. Cooling the hypothalamus has opposite effects. In waking rats and monkeys, a shift of local hypothalamic temperature will trigger operant behavior aimed at reducing the thermal displacement (315).

(ii) *Pain mechanisms* (see 21, 22, 83, 316, 317). Small, generally unmyelinated C-fibers and small myelinated delta fibers, among cutaneous afferents, include populations that respond at low thresholds to noxious stimuli. The C-fibers responding to noxious stimuli appear to contribute to central subjective experiences relating to long-latency, long-lasting pain that may be poorly localized and deliver a subjective sensory quality of burning. The delta fibers appear to contribute to shorter latency, more discrete, and better localized sensations. If a peripheral nerve is blocked by pressure, conduction in delta fibers is interfered with before there is loss of conduction in the fine, unmyelinated fibers. As pressure is increased, there is first a loss of discriminative touch, followed by disappearance of discomfort from sharp pricking stimuli (along with failure of the delta fiber conduction), leaving tickle-touch, thermal sensibility, and a worsened, long-lasting, burning quality of pain. Loss of conduction in large diameter fibers appears to "release" greater central perturbations from small fiber activation by noxious stimuli. Further pressure eliminates conduction even in the fine fibers. This sequence of sensory loss is reversed when local anesthetics are used to block the nerve. The initial loss is for the long-lasting, burning pain, later the localized, sharp, pricking pain, and lastly discriminative touch sensations (22, 316, 317).

Collins et al. (318) stimulated and recorded from human peripheral nerves during graded electrical excitation. When only large beta fibers were activated at various frequencies, the subjective experience was not painful. When beta plus delta fibers were stimulated, localized, sharp, pricking sensations were added. And when the larger fibers were blocked by a local cooling, stimuli strong enough to evoke activity in C-fibers yielded unbearable pain. There may be a quality of "release" operating here as well as the direct effects of stimulating C-fibers. Burgess and Perl (319) and Perl (320) have analyzed delta fiber responses in cats and monkeys, finding that 17% of the fibers responded preferentially to cutaneous stimuli that are generally considered painful when applied to humans. The receptive fields of these fibers were small, and the loci of most active responses to pricking and penetration of the skin were scattered within those fields. These units were unresponsive to extremes of temperature.

Dorsal root fibers enter the spinal cord, with some ascending two or three segmental levels in the superficial Lissauer's tract before synapsing in the substantia gelatinosa. Shallow incisions cutting Lissauer's tract reduce pain sensibility in the corresponding segments. The substantia gelatinosa is a neuronal pool which is readily inhibited by large diameter afferent fibers and by descending controls affecting relay through the pool, thus reducing crossed ascending responses in the anterolateral quadrant of the spinal cord (321). Stimulation of the anterolateral quadrant elicits pain in conscious human subjects, and section of that quadrant yields partial or complete analgesia for the contralateral side of the body for all levels caudal from two or three segments below the incision.

It is presently held that pain sensibility depends on integrity of the paleospinothalamic projections to intralaminar and other diffusely projecting nuclei of the thalamus and to the dorsolateral portion of the anterior midbrain (99, 322–324). These are very powerful negative reinforcement loci. Pain sensation probably does not depend on the centrum medianum, or on the neospinothalamic relay through the ventral basal thalamus, or on neocortex. Stimulation of these latter regions does not evoke subjective pain in conscious humans, whereas stimulation of the spinothalamic and trigeminothalamic tracts in the brain stem and the dorsolateral region of the anterior midbrain gives rise to intolerable pain (99).

As Descartes learned from contemporary testimony, following amputation, perception of an absent limb may persist indefinitely. And sometimes the phantom is painful. The existence of phantom sensation seems incredible to laymen because they assume that without sense receptors it should be impossible to have explicit sensations. The phantom may be quite complete as regards sense of position, movement, itching, tickling, and other sensations in addition to pain in all its details. It is evident that phantom sensation is convincing to the amputee and that children and others unacquainted with the phenomenon provide similar, detailed testimony. Many amputees, immediately following the limb removal, while the anesthesia is wearing off, may assume that the operation has not been performed because their sensations are so perfectly intact and compelling. There are several reasons for recognizing an organic basis for this disturbing perception.

There is a systematic foreshortening of parts of the phantom, roughly corresponding to the areal extent of central representation of the limb. The hand and foot are nearly normal size, the forearm and lower leg are shortened between the bordering joints, and the upper part of each extremity is especially foreshortened. The phantom foot reaches somewhat above the ankle and the phantom arm reaches only to the brim of the pelvis. Phantom limbs following spinal transection are, however, normal in length. Bors (325) had two patients who had had foreshortened lower extremities following amputation but whose phantoms were restored to normal length by later spinal transection. Phantom sensations may be modified by interventions to the stump and to the sympathetic outflow to the stump (22, 316, 317).

It is likely that phantom sensation is due to the commitment, as a consequence of abundant experience, of central neural pathways—spinal, brainstem, thalamic, cortical, limbic, basal gangliar and cerebellar—which, of course, are not amputated along with the limb. They remain behind, with their spontaneous activity, as before, and with their access to conscious and unconscious elements of experience. All they lack are the peripheral axonal processes of the severed nerves and the peripheral end-organs, a really small share of the total nervous system commitment engaged on behalf of that body image by past experiences. Pain experienced in the phantom is particularly bewildering because the natural targets of therapy seem to be missing. To paraphrase Descartes, knowing the above information, we can no longer be confident that it is a certain member which pains us even though we feel pain in it.

Another clinical point of importance to the interpretation of pain relates to patients with partial nerve injury followed by intractible, burning pain. This syndrome, causalgia, classically described by Mitchell more than a century ago (326), represents abnormal and excessive activity among reflex, central, sensory, and motor pathways. The full-blown clinical picture includes not only bizarre symptoms of excruciating, burning, lancinating pain, but also local atrophy of muscle and skin, sometimes osteomalacia, changes in pigmentation, hair growth, curvature and thickness of the nails, and remarkable excesses of perspiration (316, 317, 326). There are also important instances of minor causalgias with lesser degrees of similar pathophysiology. And the same principles may be applicable to a wide variety of clinical syndromes involving the notion of a "vicious circle," with or without pain (117, 316).

Analysis of these pain syndromes indicates clearly that at least part of their mechanisms must be assigned to altered internal activities and reflex responses, a central excitatory state that is "cyclonic" in its power to engulf and to facilitate the spread of normal incoming sensory signals and the "release" of both visceral and somatic reflex patterns in excess. Noordenbos (327) has contributed the important idea that large fibers may act to inhibit activity in small fibers. The large fibers, having greater velocity, arrive first at the spinal relay centers, e.g., the substantia gelatinosa and the dorsal horn gray matter more generally, and can there inhibit the penetration and dissemination of signals coming along via the smaller fiber systems. This idea is supported by evidence from many sorts of pathological processes in which the large myelinated fibers are damaged or lost.

Melzack and Wall (321) have devised a theory which has a good deal of indirect evidence in its support and which has led to a number of reasonably successful techniques for pain therapy. However, the actual anatomical and physiological situation is so complicated that the Melzack and Wall "gate-control theory" remains largely conceptual. Bascially, they reason that the through-transmission of nerve impulses from peripheral nerve activity to spinal mechanisms is controlled by a gating mechanism in the dorsal horn. This gate-control system is influenced by a variety of inputs: from activity in large-diameter afferent fibers which inhibit the spread and relay of small-diameter afferent fiber impulses, tending to close the "gate," while small fiber activities open the gate; from centrifugal impulses that also influence the gate; and from some of these descending influences which can be acted upon by unconscious and conscious cognitive processes to alter the spinal gating mechanisms.

Melzack and Wall (21) later particularized a portion of the descending, centrifugal control of pain transmission by invoking a *central control trigger* whereby incoming signals are swiftly identified, localized, evaluated in accordance with past experiences, and inhibited *prior to the action of the gate* in checking or releasing pain signals to higher centers. The central control trigger represents a cognitive hand on the gate. This addendum to their theory again depends on large-diameter afferent fibers which, to activate the central control trigger, must transmit signals up the dorsal columns, which does not require any synaptic delay because these include first-order neurons ascending by this route, the lemniscal and some other brainstem and higher cerebral circuits, with a quick turn-around descending command that operates on the gate at the spinal level, and perhaps also at other higher levels, to permit or to exclude the noxious signals from gaining access to consciousness. Here Malzack and Wall are up against the questions we have addressed earlier in this chapter, namely, how is it possible to affect nearly instantaneous recognition-evaluation-decision-and-action systems?

We would put some of these recognition mechanisms along the ascending pathways on the grounds that the learning and practice of both sensory and motor skills seem to result in earlier and earlier recognition and response, and presumably this involves further downstream decision-making. Bicycle riding is such a skill that becomes enduringly automatic, possibly at lower spinal, brainstem and cerebellar levels, thus freeing the higher centers from much neuronal processing and decision-making. Indeed, after the skill is well entrenched, if conscious attention is suddenly focused on the decision making processes involved in turning the front wheel of the bicycle to maintain balance, the rider soon realizes, perhaps looking up from the pavement, that the decisions are better made by "lower" centers. The earlier such turn-around is possible, the better for the Melzack and Wall gate-control theory, and for many other problems relating to perception and behavior.

b. Dorsal column-lemniscal pathway

The dorsal columns are composed of relatively large diameter first-order neuronal projections that relay prior to or in the dorsal column nuclei at bulbar level. They include the longest nerve fibers in the body, extending from toe to the base of the neck, with the cell body lying in the corresponding dorsal root ganglion. There is great fidelity of representation of location, spatial form and extent of vibration, two-point sensibility, and fine temporal ordering of events. As befitting this fidelity, there is great orderliness of the fiber distribution within the dorsal columns and their bulbar nuclei (328).

The relay in the dorsal column nuclei is complicated. Only some 20% of synaptic terminals there degenerate after the dorsal columns are sectioned. In the dorsal column nuclei there is strong lateral inhibition, contributing to spatial sharpening of sensory information at that level. This is provided by the main afferent input to the nucleus, the dorsal column fibers, whereas a further sharpening at the thalamic relay level is provided not by the ascending input but by descending, recurrent collaterals from thalamocortical, next-order projections (329).

A further extrinsic inhibition affecting the dorsal column cells can be observed even after the dorsal columns have been sectioned. This is done by applying noxious stimuli somewhere on the body. This latter inhibition is largely presynaptic. Gentle tactile stimuli can provide a facilitation in the dorsal column nuclear relay that is also independent of the dorsal column input. Clearly, some of these integrative effects come about through the action of other ascending sensory pathways. There are also corticifugal influences on the dorsal column nuclei, both direct and indirect. The most direct are those from collaterals of the pyramidal tract (329, 330). These descending sensory relay control mechanisms are largely inhibitory. They are topographically organized, and they interact actively with the intrinsic lateral inhibition. From this evidence it can be appreciated that this, the most faithful and straightforward of relay systems, is nonetheless involved in complicated transactions. Even the adjoining, apparently equivalent cuneate and gracile nuclei differ from each other in organization in the cat: the former nucleus representing upper thoracic and cervical levels, conveys representation of muscle afferents, but the latter, representing lower thoracic and lumbosacral levels, does not (329).

The lemniscal system including the trigeminal lemniscus conveys a quite precise neuronal transform of stimulus attributes from dorsal column relay to the ventral basal portion of the thalamus and thence by thalamocortical relay, still preserving remarkable spatial and temporal fidelity, to neocortex where the body image is well represented. The body form has been topologically preserved in the dorsal columns and the dorsal column nuclei (328), and throughout the medial lemniscus and thalamocortical projections. Lateral inhibition also contributes to the spatial resolution throughout this system.

The ventral basal thalamus receives the lemniscal and spinothalamic tracts, now aggregated into a single topographic pattern representing the contralateral side of the entire body scheme. Poggio and Mountcastle (331) have shown that the thalamocortical relay is highly reliable. The ventrobasal region of the thalamus also receives abundant projections of descending corticothalamic fibers stemming from both the first and second somatosensory fields of cortical representation. These descending influences also conform to somatotopology. Their dominant effect is inhibitory (332, 333).

Lesions in the somatic sensory area I cause defects in somatic sensibility in humans (334). Electrical stimulation of this area in conscious human subjects elicits bizarre sensory experiences referred to local regions of the contra-lateral side of the body (335). Woolsey has investigated the projections of body topography of a variety of animals from sense organs through thalamo-cortical projections to its two dimensional display in cortex (336–338). *Specificity for modality as well as accurate spatial and temporal information is preserved in cortical display* (339). Powell and Mountcastle (340) have shown that these specific patterns are preserved in arrays of cellular columns within the sensory cortex, and that lateral inhibition is still continuing to sharpen representations even within the cortex (341).

In the superior bank of the Sylvian fissure resides a second sensory field, somatic sensory area II. This is much smaller in extent than somatic sensory area I. It preserves dermatomal topology, although with greater overlapping. *Somatic sensory area II is distinguished in an important respect in that it involves representation of both halves of the body.*

c. Auditory mechanisms

Most auditory first-order neurons exhibit spontaneous activity. They are differently sensitive to sounds of specific frequencies, with considerable sharp-ening of tuning when compared with the mechanical tuning curve of the cochlea (342). At the onset of a continuing auditory stimulus, there is an increase in firing rate of correspondingly tuned units which soon adapt to an approximately steady discharge (343). The tuning curves for each unit show a narrow frequency for greatest sensitivity which widens slightly for higher frequencies and widens more broadly for lower frequencies, as stimulus intensity is augmented. The lopsided triangular-shaped tuning curves for second- and third- and higher order neurons show a progressively narrower response area as units are tested along the ascending auditory pathway (344, 345).

Figure 5 illustrates the auditory pathway in highly schematic form. Pro-jections from the two ears involve considerable crossing and recrossing within the bulb and more conspicuous bilaterality of upward projection than any other sensory system. Yet, as already indicated, for purposes of message interpretation, the contralateral cerebral hemisphere is functionally pre-dominant. The inferior colliculus is a major way-station along the ascending auditory path. Prior to the inferior colliculus, auditory signals are relayed in the nucleus of the lateral lemniscus, an event that is prominent enough to be recorded as a far-field evoked potential (see below). From the inferior colliculus, which is a convergent site for many modalities and has the highest metabolic rate in the entire brain, suggesting great activity and presumably also importance, auditory projections travel by way of the brachium of the inferior colliculus to the medial geniculate body (MG_v).

Galambos et al. (346) have succeeded in cutting this brachium bilaterally in cats and find that acoustic evoked potentials are still about the same amplitude and only 2 or 3 msec delayed in latency when compared with potentials evoked before the brachium was cut. The prime difference is that the cortical evoked potential is now eliminated by a surgical level of barbiturate anesthesia although not with chloralose anesthesia. Galambos interprets these findings as meaning that a medial, extralemniscal brainstem pathway is of importance in signalling neocortex about auditory events in the waking state. A boy who died at age 10 comprehended spoken speech, learned from conversation, and, when measured 2 years prior to death, had a vocabulary of at least 175 words. His audiogram, taken on several occasions, showed his hearing to be within normal limits. His brain showed severe degeneration of both the medial geniculate body and auditory cortex. The authors were driven to conclude that an extralemniscal pathway and nonauditory cortex were instrumental in such hearing and auditory language as the boy comprehended (347). It therefore is likely that the extralemniscal pathway that activates auditory cortex as demonstrated by Galambos et al. may convey more than simply change of state and intensity information.

By recording from scalp at the vertex and from skin over the mastoid process, and by using a computer of averaged transients to sum responses hundreds of times following each stimulus in a rapid train of clicks or tone pips, and by using very rapid oscilloscopic beam sweeps to display the averages, Jewett has shown that it is possible to record far-field acoustic responses that are thought to relate to the events taking place in a succession of stations along the auditory pathway (246, 348–351). Most recently, Buchwald and Huang (352) have succeeded in assigning each of the specific far-field responses, I to V, to specific brainstem sites.

> *The resultant data indicate that the primary generator of potential 1 is the acoustic nerve; of potential 2, the cochlear nucleus; of potential 3, neurons of the superior olivary complex activated by projections crossing the midline; of potential 4, neurons of the ventral nucleus of the lateral lemniscus and preolivary region activated equally by crossed and uncrossed projections; and of potential 5, neurons of the inferior colliculus activated by crossed projections.* (352)

This new, noninvasive technique for analysis of activity taking place along the auditory pathway has provided an objective means for appraising the state of function of the entire sensory column devoted to acoustic signalling. It has been used with infants (350), patients in coma (353, 354), and persons with various central hearing deficits. It is especially practical because it can quickly inform the examiner about the integrity of auditory brainstem pathways from bulb to thalamus and about, by extrapolation, the functional state of the brainstem more generally. This makes it useful for determining the functional state of brainstem pathways in deep narcosis as distinguished from destructive lesions. The technique is already proving promising for the analysis of a variety of problems ranging from nutritional and early developmental problems to vascular disorders, trauma, neoplasms, degenerations, and infections—whatever—affecting this vital brain channel.

If a steady loud noise is sounded in the presence of animals who have electrodes implanted at various stations along the auditory pathway, it is possible to determine (a) what steady as well as transient changes are elicited by the sound and (b) how the succession of stations along the ascending auditory pathway responds during the course of sensory processing of a steady sound stimulus (355). At the onset of the sound, there is a transient large-amplitude initial response representing cochlear activation which is relatively quickly attenuated as a consequence of contraction of the middle ear muscles. Then, for about half an hour, there is a measurable, gradual, somewhat uneven relaxation of the middle ear muscles and a corresponding rise in cochlear activity. The muscles are not fatigued, for they can be readily induced to contract fully; there is instead a slow, somewhat unsteady diminution in the amount of middle ear muscle tension. The initial transient large-amplitude responses and the diminution due to middle ear muscle contraction followed by gradual relaxation can be seen in the cochlear nuclei (the first central auditory relays), in the nucleus of the lateral lemniscus, the inferior colliculus, and the medial geniculate body, with decreasing amplitudes of overall responses in that ascending order (355).

The central auditory pathway responses to steady state noise stimulation are by no means steady: dynamic changes are occurring throughout the duration of steady stimulation. In association with the decline in the tension of the middle ear muscles, the lower auditory pathways show increased averaged electrical activity. The lesser amplitude of responses at successively higher stations suggests that the brain is sparing of its own involvement at higher levels. Indeed, the medial geniculate (the thalamic relay) response is only a transient event at onset and cessation of the stimulus: the averaged electrical activity during the long continued sound stimulus is scarcely different from background levels, if at all. The auditory cortex, surprisingly, shows *diminished* averaged electrical activity for the duration of the sound stimulus (355).

In addition to attenuation of auditory responses to steady sound stimulation as a consequence of middle ear muscle contractions, there is some internal, neuronal sensory control which is evidenced on discontinuation of the sound stimulus. When the sound is stopped, each of the brainstem relay stations shows a profound reduction in averaged electrical activity, below control background levels for those nuclei. This lasts for some minutes, showing gradual recovery. Such a pattern suggests that the central control of sensory transmission has been inhibiting responses to the loud sound, and that there is some hysteresis in this control operation. Both middle ear attenuation and central control would be operating to reduce the occupation of higher centers with the incoming signals. One other observation of note is that the medial, extralemniscal auditory pathways that pass through the reticular formation show only transient changes in averaged electrical activity with onset and offset of the long-continuing stimulus. It is as if those channels were more interested in change of state than in steady stimulus conditions (355).

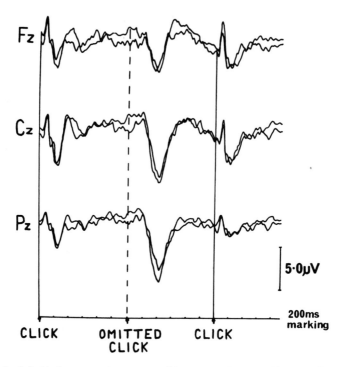

FIG. 6. Cerebral electrical responses to an expected but nonoccurring event. High amplification recording from vertex and mastoid permits tracing averages of 64 responses in human subjects who have been presented a train of clicks or tones at regular intervals (in this case, at an interval of 1.1 sec). An occasional member of the train is then simply omitted. The subject anticipates a stimulus at each interstimulus interval and is asked to count the number of times the stimulus does not occur. A large positive wave at 300 msec (P_3) following the nominal stimulus onset occurs regularly in the absence of any stimulus being presented (!). This is obviously a brain event, perhaps a perception, the recognition of a difference, perhaps the "aha" experience associated with finding what the subject was looking for (namely, the absence of the click or tone pip), or maybe the resolution of prior uncertainty. Similar electrical events at this 300 msec time interval have been recorded in relation to a wide variety of detection and problem-solving auditory test experiences, and also in reasonably comparable visual and tactile tasks. This 300 msec event therefore appears to be a central activity aroused by the task, regardless of the particular sensory pathway. (From Galambos, ref. 351.)

If a subject is asked to keep track of the number of times a signal in a regular train of acoustic stimuli is omitted from the train, a large positive wave occurs regularly at about 300 msec following the anticipated (but not occurring) signal (246, 247, 351). This phenomenon is illustrated in Fig. 6. This response obviously represents a major brain event relating to expectations when attention is focussed on a non-event. Interest derives from the fact that this warrants a synchronized brain event that does not have an external triggering stimulus; nor does there need to be any overt response. Large-amplitude waves at this latency can be recorded following the delivery of information for which the subject was primed and seeking (351). Such an electrical brain wave accompanies many different signal detection tasks, and the size of the response will vary with the subject's *confidence* in his or her decision. The response is made even larger if the subject is informed in an auditory discrimination task by light signals that his decision was *incorrect*. The presentation of completely irrelevant, and, even more effectively, surprising sensory (visual or auditory) events, also yields a large amplitude 300 msec positive wave. Similar-looking, relatively long-latency, large-scale positive waves can be seen at 300 msec following stimulation of visual, auditory, and somesthetic discrimination tasks—making it likely that similar brain events follow similar mental tasks (351). Although these new methods are not themselves as yet fully perfected, it looks as if *the discriminating brain employs a similar task-oriented operation for each of the sensory inputs*—an operation that exhibits measurable by-products. Some mental activities can now be triggered by the senses and objectified outside the head.

d. Vestibular mechanisms

The vestibular apparatus contributes centrally to spinal, brainstem, cerebellar, and cerebral events. They have mostly unconscious reflex effects but there are contributions of which we are aware, our subjective appreciation of our head in space, the subjective influences of vestibular disturbances known as motion sickness, with some strong visceral component, and the indirect results of vestibular mechanisms on our posture and equilibrium.

Vestibular projections to brainstem and spinal cord are organized so as to maintain the head position constant in any given situation. Vestibular and tonic neck and other axial controls act in concert. Vestibulo-ocular reflexes (VOR) provide for adjustments of eye movements to maintain a constant position of the retina in response to positional changes or movements of the head. Extensive feedback and feedforward controls operate in these circuits (47). The feedforward controls make extensive use of the cerebellum.

The VOR starts with semicircular canal and otolith stimuli, followed by second-order vestibular neurons to the eye motor nuclei, III, IV and VI, strung along the brainstem. The actions of the vestibular system are systematically facilitatory and inhibitory, with four groups of vestibular neurons influencing six groups of oculomotor nuclei, interactions now analyzed anatomically and physiologically (see ref. 47). The phylogenetically oldest part of the cerebellum, the flocculus, contributes to the VOR by receiving primary vestibular afferents—arising directly from the vestibular apparatus—and providing inhibitory patterns of influence on second-order vestibular neurons engaged in ocular control. It is thought that this operation contributes to feedforward VOR mechanisms. Lesions of the flocculus impair the VOR (356).

Vestibulospinal reflexes (VSR), like the VOR, involve primary vestibular afferents, second-order vestibular neurons arising from vestibular nuclei, and spinal motor neurons. There are fast medial and lateral excitatory vestibulospinal influences and slower medial inhibitory vestibulospinal influences, but in this case no additional loop through the cerebellum (47). The most rapid trajectories are bilaterally facilitatory to both flexors and extensors, probably connect monosynaptically with the motor neurons, and induce a short-latency muscular response (190). A second excitatory peak, immediately following, appears to be contributed by vestibulo-reticulo-spinal projections. These latter responses are delayed in their start in the bulb and are both facilitatory and inhibitory in their motor effects. Both categories of direct and reticular-relayed VSR projections are conveyed in the ventral quadrants of the spinal cord. These vestibular evoked responses can be blocked by prior stimulation of most spinal nerves, but are markedly enhanced locally by slight weight-bearing movements of the corresponding limb. This latter combination of vestibular and limb afferent controls contributes to local stability and strength of the limb in posture and locomotion (190). This VSR control system seems to function in relation to local limb afferent input in ways that are analagous to the VOR control system in relation to afferent input from the retina, to improve prehension of the limb and eye upon the outside world.

e. Visual mechanisms

The pineal melatonin-forming mechanism is controlled by lighting: the relevant enzyme, hydroxyindole-O-methyltransferase (HIOMT) is sustained at a high level in blind animals and in animals kept in continuous light (357). This tonic neuroendocrine control involving the pineal gland is mediated by retinal projections to the suprachiasmatic nuclei of the hypothalamus where relays project caudally via the medial forebrain bundle to the tegmentum of the midbrain and then presumably by way of reticulo-bulbo-spinal projections, and finally via sympathetic outflow to the superior sympathetic ganglion and thence to the pineal gland (358). These roundabout projections appear to be instrumental in the phasic timing of circadian rhythms in relation to the diurnal flux of environmental light. Destruction of the suprachiasmatic nuclei eliminates both pineal and pituitary diurnal rhythms. The effect is not simply visual; otherwise the rhythms would become free running, as they do following blinding. The visual contribution seems to be to link an entrained rhythm to an environmental rhythm. Moreover, the suprachiasmatic nuclei seem to play an essential role in the endogenous control of diurnal rhythms as exhibited behaviorally as well as endocrinally (359, 360).

The main projections from retina to the brain go by way of the lateral geniculate bodies (thalamic relays) to neocortex, for detailed vision, and to the tectal and pretectal regions, for governing the direction of gaze and for the control of the pupil. One question to put to the neocortical system is: How do we see binocularly? How do we achieve a single image of objects using two eyes rather than two images? How is the seam between the two half-fields of vision which are independently projected onto the two hemispheres made both matching and invisible? How do we see stereoscopically, taking advantage of information from each of the eyes and integrating their discrepancies systematically so as to discover depth cues?

The optic chiasma in humans is abundantly crossed; approximately half of the ganglion cells in the retina, those on the nasal side of each retina, project to the contralateral hemisphere. In passing through the lateral geniculate body, a thalamic relay, the fibers from each eye are isolated from one another in distinctive layers. Superimposed on the physical separations are inhibitory influences which preclude interaction between fibers from the separate eyes (361). At the level of occipital neocortex, however, there are many neurons that receive input from both eyes. This binocularity as expressed in single neurons was first demonstrated by Hubel and Wiesel in 1959 (362). More recent work by them and others suggests that practically all simple visual units in the cat cortex receive excitatory input from both eyes (363). Stereopsis, that is, depth perception, involves monocular as well as binocular cues. The binocular cues depend on a certain acceptable degree of disparity between the two occipitally projected images, one from each eye, disparate according to the separateness of images focussed on the two corresponding half-retinae. Julesz (364), using random-dot stereograms, has shown that binocular depth judgment does not depend upon recognition of form—hence such judgment may be extracted by processes taking place early in the visual projection sequence.

By virtue of the phenomena of lateral inhibition, simple visual cortical cells have small-sized visual fields and highly specified stimulus parameters for their optimal activation. Units responding to images projected onto the two retinae of the cat will indicate by discrete changes in their firing rates that optical disparity changes of as little as 2 min of arc have occurred (361). There is a very strong suppression of activity in response to the image projected in one eye if the image is slightly inappropriately located in reference to the corresponding region of the other eye. This laboratory disparity detection is only about 10 times broader than the *minimum* detectable by man. Thus binocular disparity is signalled by neurons that are suppressed when specific bars of light, moving in specific directions, are projected on the two retinae with a certain measure of disparity between the two otherwise identical stimuli.

Binocular fusion may require similar formations: it, too, results in inhibition of units activated binocularly but with discrepant disparities. The process results in a reduction in the number of units responsive to the same contour but with different disparities to those units that can "tolerate" a particular disparity, hence a binocular fusion of that given contour (361). The various processes of inhibition (lateral inhibition along single channels and disparity inhibition among binocular units) not only sharpen images and resolve ambiguities of potential double vision, but they also contribute by this means to depth perception. Furthermore, all of the cumulative inhibition pares down the total amount of signalling with which later sensory processing may cope. It is a simplifying, abstracting process.

Hubel and Wiesel (365) had shown early that some visual cortical cells are "simple" in their response characteristics, while other neurons, which presumably derive information from special constellations of simple neurons, are "complex" in their response characteristics. These cortical units seem to be arranged in columns such that all of the cells in a given column share the same field and orientation and are "interested" in similar parameters among stimuli projected within that field. Both simple and complex neurons have been found to be interested in disparity, and neurons concerned with similar disparity specificities are arranged in columnar form together (366). Such units are activated by disparities relating to objects projected on the two eyes, with disparities linked to a given plane of view, but not to planes in front of or behind that plane. Some complex neurons in the visual cortex are arranged presumably to generalize for disparity but at the same time to be specific for orientation and direction of the object. Other units respond over wide ranges of both disparity and field.

What has been presented thus far must be reckoned in reference to eye movements which themselves produce changes in disparity of projected images. A correlation between eye movements and retinal imagery as projected on visual cortex is competently accomplished by the seeing person, but not yet adequately understood in terms of the relevant circuitry. This requires that the visual cortex have up-to-date and accurate information relating to the position of the eyes. This derives from eye muscle afferents and also from cortical command in the frontal lobes (area 8). More remote still are problems relating to how a synthesis is obtained for perceiving the three-dimensionality of objects and events that may have myriad contours. At some stages the built-in mechanisms are sufficient, but beyond those, learning mechanisms must provide interpretive skills that were left unordained by the experience of the species. (See Fig. 7.)

There is some evidence that vision is not limited to the perspectives of Euclidean geometry but can utilize also, or perhaps instead, a geometry of central perspective, involving perceptual vector analysis (368). An example, given by Johansson, is the ability of subjects to perceive a dozen lights attached to an actor's body, against a dark background, as a "person involved in definable actions," whereas the lights cannot be meaningfully interpreted when the individual is in repose. Such perception involves the interpretation of the consequences of locomotor activity in continuous perspective transformations. The perceiving subject, meanwhile, must know reasonably accurately when and how much at what velocity he or she moved eyes, head, and body in relation to the visual cues presented. This requires that visual information must interact with signals from other sense organs relating to vestibular, neck, trunk, and limb movements, and sometimes auditory and olfactory cues as well. *The perception of objects and events in our environ-*

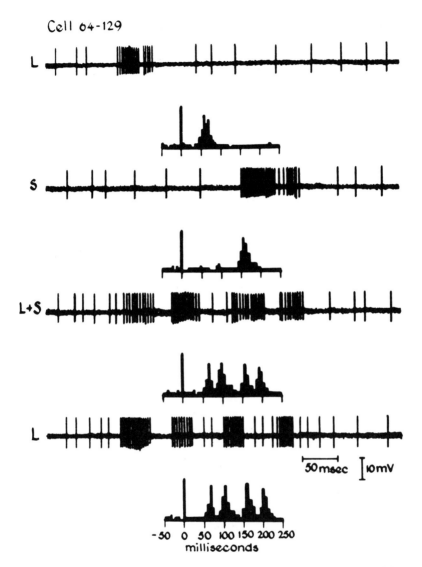

FIG. 7. Conditional modification of a single visual cortical cell response pattern as elicited by visual stimuli. Along line L, the cell displays its responses to presentation of a dark horizontal bar. The histogram below represents the sum of 20 trials. At S the same cell responds to an electric shock applied to the contralateral hind limb, and the sum of 20 trials is graphed beneath. When L and S are combined, the resulting responses and the histogram are conspicuously different from what would be expected with any simple addition of the two events. After 40 combined stimulus trials, the cell is tested with the visual stimulus alone. The response now looks more like the pattern elicited by the previously paired stimuli than it did prior to the pairing. Cells that are capable of transient modification of their response patterns in this way are relatively infrequently encountered. They represent about 10% of the total of cortical cells which respond to more than one modality of stimulation. In other experiments it has become evident that "plasticity" of this kind may be seen in a small proportion of neurons in various nuclei all along the neuraxis and not simply at cortical levels. (From Morrell, ref. 367.)

ment depends upon the utilization of relative constancies, and perspective transformations, that are abstracted from information entering the optical flow and that engage transactionally with other sensory systems as well as with past experiences, expectations and purposes. This demands continuous intersensory processing based upon previous intersensory learning.

2. "Extra-Classical" Sensory Pathways

We have already dealt with the fact that phylogenetically older, more medially located pathways are activated *pari passu* along with activation of the classical sensory paths. It is these older pathways that we refer to as "extra-classical" because they were not recognized until certain more obvious sensory trajectories had already become embedded in the literature—had become *the* sensory path—hence "classical!" The older paths were late to be recognized for two reasons: (a) they are not anatomically or physiologically discrete, and (b) they tend to be eliminated functionally with most anesthetic agents and following truncation of the neuraxis.

In the pioneer days of investigation of sensory (and motor) pathways, it had been necessary to use anesthetics or to decerebrate or otherwise eliminate higher forebrain processes in experimental animals. It was not until Hess (369) showed that it is feasible to implant electrodes under surgical anesthesia and thereafter to use them for stimulation (and recording) purposes that the *waking* brain could be investigated. Another factor delaying this evidence was that it was found, unexpectedly but gratifyingly, that *in anesthetized animals both peripheral and central neurons respond with impulses de novo or changes in rate of firing of impulses in reaction to sensory stimuli at thresholds that closely approximate those encountered when such stimuli are administered to conscious human subjects.* It came as a surprise originally that sensory systems will respond from receptors to cortical fields when animals are deeply anesthetized. It came as a reverse surprise, later, when animals with implanted electrodes were studied without central anesthesia, to learn that *in the absence of anesthesia, impulses occurring along sensory pathways are less consistent, of lower amplitude (generally) and far more widespread than the previous findings with anesthetized animals had indicated.*

The phylogenetically older pathways are more difficult to decipher because they are made up by a majority of smaller neurons with shorter processes and having axons with less myelin. More importantly, they are far less discrete in their receptive reach with dendrites and similarly less discrete with their axonal presentations. Finally, they interlace with one another and fail to make up discrete nuclei and tracts. Figure 8 illustrates, in two different species, some of the characteristics of these diffusely receiving and projecting neurons. In the upper half of the figure, the Scheibels have depicted a microscopic section of the bulb of a young kitten, showing the convergence of

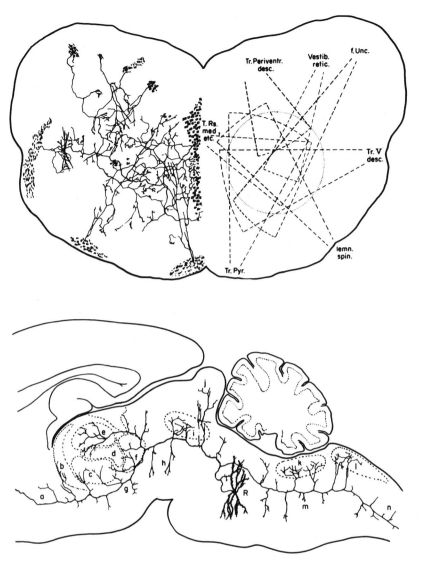

FIG. 8. Illustrations of some of the morphological characteristics of diffusely projecting neurons in two different species. Upper: A transverse section through the upper third of the medulla oblongata of a 10-day old kitten. The overlapping convergences of terminating and collateral fibers which enter the core of the reticular formation to form synapses are shown. *Left*, fibers traced from microscopic sections; *right*, some of the overlapping sectors which include, clockwise, fibers descending from the periventricular system (possibly relating to feeling states), projections from vestibular nuclei (relating to orientation and movement), roof nuclei of the cerebellum (probably concerned with sensorimotor coordination), the descending root of the trigeminal (representing facial sensation), the spinal lemniscus (conveying spinothalamic impulses for pain, temperature and touch sensibility), the pyramidal tract (relating to cortical motor control), and medial reticular projections (diffusely projecting systems projecting onto diffusely projecting systems). Lower: A sagittal section through the brain of a young rat. The axonal trajectory of a single neuron with its cell body located in the nucleus reticularis giganto-cellularis, R, is depicted. The rostrally coursing axonal component supplies collaterals to inferior colliculus, the region of the IIIrd and IVth cranial nerve nuclei, midbrain reticular formation, posterior nuclear groups in the thalamus (governing somatosensory relays), diffusely projecting nuclei of the thalamus, ventral thalamic nuclei (relaying basal gangliar and cerebellar projections to motor cortex), hypothalamus, and basal forebrain region. The posteriorly directed component sends collaterals into the pontine and bulbar reticular formation, the hypoglossal nucleus (XII), the dorsal column nuclear relay (n. gracilis) and the intermediate gray reticular formation of the spinal cord. (From Scheibel and Scheibel, ref. 370.)

collaterals from fibers of passage in sensory and motor tracts passing through the bulb. These collaterals converge centrally into fields of available terminal arborizations that are approximately described by the wedges drawn in dashed lines on the right. These overlapping fields of representation are infiltrated by dendrites and are the seat of cell bodies belonging to diffusely projecting neurons (370).

In the lower part of Fig. 8 is shown a longitudinal section from the brain of a young rat. It traces the dendrites, cell body, and a single long axon in its main distributions up and down the neuraxis, contributing terminals to sensory and motor and association nuclei on either side of the midline over an enormous length of brainstem and spinal cord. Such large cells are frequent but not predominant: the majority are equally astonishingly small and short. They communicate locally instead of sending impulses over long distances. These reticular neurons are the cells which Allen presciently called the "left-over cells" of the spinal cord and brain stem, left over, that is, after the better-defined structures had all been named (371). It was in relation to this anatomical "manure pile" that Magoun and his colleagues began their successful search for "ponies" that would bind psychology and neurophysiology together (see refs. 3, 129, 193, 242, 250, 313).

These cells and their processes defy easy categorization and functional definition. They are involved and "interested" in a multitude of functions, and to some degree they may be plastic in their functional connections. They represent a convergent pool, larger by far than the interneuronal pools we have been describing in the dorsal horn and in all central sensory relay nuclei. But they are similar in the elementary sense that they are all *interneurons, par excellence.* We call them "extra-classical" out of respect for the traditional terminology that has distinguished extra-pyramidal pathways from the pyramidal tract in motor systems. The "extra-pyramidal" motor mechanisms like the extra-classical sensory pathways, are phylogenetically old: they had for eons to suffice for all vertebrate motor functions, until quite recently, until the pyramidal tract made its appearance in mammals.

The extra-classical sensory pathways similarly had to suffice for sensory signalling to higher brain centers. They include first of all a matrix tissue of reticular formation, diffusely projecting upwards and downwards along the nervous system, pleurisynaptic, serving both sides of the neuraxis, crossing and recrossing the midline, literally stitching the nervous system together. These pathways also include paleospinothalamic projections, the phylogenetically more recent neospinothalamic projections, in contrast with the newest dorsal column-medial lemniscus pathways, emergent in the mammals, all of which have already been described.

The combination in functional entirety means that sensory signals are parallel-processed by phylogenetically, structurally and functionally distinguishable projections. They have different evoked response wave forms and latencies. It must be remembered, too, that there are descending, corticifugal projections that parallel the classical ascending pathways, and other descending projections which travel by way of the reticular formation, all of which can rightly be called extra-classical descending sensory control pathways. It is prudent at this time to be somewhat reserved as to how much of what modality may be conveyed by what parts of this multi-part projection array. An instance that is apropos was cited earlier of the 10-year-old boy who died without classical auditory cortex and thalamic projection (from a birth injury) but who could nonetheless handle a limited vocabulary and learn by means of what must be presumed to be medial extra-classical auditory projections. Also, in considering pain mechanisms, above, we pointed out that one of five parallel processing paths was knocked out by nitrous oxide-oxygen anesthesia at a dose level that eliminated pain perception in man, but which left touch and other sensibilities in the human subjects.

There is a great deal more we need to understand about each of these various systems to put them together into a coherent, understandable and not-too-oversimplified version of the brain in all of its transactional glory. This much may be said to advantage with respect to differences in interpretation of experimental studies relating to sensory and perceptual mechanisms. The experimentalist can find what he or she seeks to find with his or her microelectrode: that is, if the person is looking for stable relays from sensory receptors to cortical projection areas, there are plenty of stable units there. It is easier to find such stability in anesthetized animals, but even in waking animals there are *many units, particularly in the dorsal column-lemniscal path* which *show a beautiful consistency* all along the various sensory projections. If the search is made in the *neospinothalamic pathway, there is greater variability,* and *in the paleospinothalamic path, still greater variability, and in the reticular ascending core, almost no modality or localizing specificity,* perhaps nothing much more than a signal that something changed, somewhere.

And if an investigator is looking for units that will show plasticity or instability, he can readily find them. They are there, in abundance. *It is not an either/or situation but a situation in which both types of characteristics exist in the nervous system.* Undoubtedly, both are essential for successful performance of the brain.

A further point of importance is that even in the most stable pathways, such as the dorsal column-lemniscal projections, about 10% of all of the units encountered show a remarkable degree of plasticity. Stability cannot be hoked up: it is there. And such unitary and relay stability may be instrumental in stabilizing our sensory processing. But as we have learned, the stability of our sensations, and even more so of our perceptions, depends upon far more involved and dynamic factors than fidelity of transmission of signals that are strictly imitative of the sensory receptor's activations. No one is better qualified to describe this stability/instability, specificity/nonspecificity problem than Mountcastle:

Each of us believes himself to live directly within the world that surrounds him, to sense its objects and events precisely, and to live in real and current time.

I assert that these are perceptual illusions.

Contrarily, each of us confronts the world from a brain linked to what is "out there" by a few million fragile sensory nerve fibers, our only information channels, our lifelines to reality. They provide also what is essential for life itself: an afferent excitation that maintains the conscious state, the awareness of self.

Sensations are set by the encoding functions of sensory nerve endings, and by the integrating neural mechanics of the central nervous system. Afferent nerve fibers are not high-fidelity recorders, for they accentuate certain stimulus features, neglect others. The central neuron is a storyteller with regard to the nerve fibers, and it is never completely trustworthy, allowing distortions of quality and measure, within a strained but isomorphic spatial relation between "outside" and "inside." Sensation is an abstraction, not a replication, of the real world. (372)

*   *   *

And men should know that from nothing else but from the brain come joys, delights, laughter and jests, and sorrows, griefs, despondency and lamentations. And by this, in an especial manner we acquire wisdom and knowledge, and see and hear and know what are foul and what are fair, what sweet and unsavory. . . . And by the same organ we become mad and delirious and fears and terrors assail us, some by night and some by day, and dreams and untimely wanderings, and cares that are not suitable and ignorance of present circumstances, desuetude and unskillfulness. All these things we endure from the brain, when it is not healthy. . . . or when it suffers any other preternatural and unusual affliction.

Hippocrates, *On the Sacred Disease*

REFERENCES

1. Boulding, K. E. (1956): *The Image*. University of Michigan Press, Ann Arbor.
2. Ames, A., Jr. (1955): *An Interpretive Manual for the Demonstrations in the Psychology Research Center, Princeton University: The Nature of Our Perceptions, Prehensions and Behavior*. Princeton University Press, Princeton, New Jersey.
3. Livingston, R. B. (1962): How man looks at his own brain: An adventure shared by psychology and neurophysiology. In: *Psychology: A Study of a Science, Study II. Empirical Substructure and Relations with Other Sciences, Vol. 4 Biologically Oriented Fields: Their Place in Psychology and in the Biological Sciences*, edited by S. Koch, pp. 51–99. McGraw-Hill, New York.
4. Simpson, G. G. (1952): *The Meaning of Evolution*. Yale University Press, New Haven, Connecticut.
5. Monod, J. (1971): *Chance and Necessity*. (Translated from *Le Hasard et la Necèssité* by Austryn Warnhouse.) Knopf, New York.
6. Eccles, J. C. (1973): *The Understanding of the Brain*. McGraw-Hill, New York.
7. Calvin, M. (1967): Chemical evolution of life and sensibility. In: *The Neurosciences: A Study Program*, edited by G. C. Quarton, T. Melnechuk, and F. O. Schmitt, pp. 780–800. Rockefeller University Press, New York.
8. Livingston, R. B. (1970): Some general aspects of brain function. In: *Control Processes in Multicellular Organisms, A Ciba Foundation Symposium*, edited by G. E. W. Wolstenholme and J. Knight. Churchill, London.
9. Zuckerhandl, E. (1963): Perspectives in molecular anthropology. In: *Classification and Human Evolution*, edited by S. L. Washburn, pp. 243–272. Aldini, Chicago.
10. Herrick, C. J. (1956): *The Evolution of Human Nature*. University of Texas Press, Austin.

11. Critchley, M. (1960): The evolution of man's capacity for language. In: *Evolution after Darwin, Vol. 2, The Evolution of Man, Culture and Society,* edited by S. Tax, pp. 289–308. University of Chicago Press, Chicago.
12. Lenneberg, E. H. (1964): *New Directions in the Study of Language.* MIT Press, Cambridge, Massachusetts.
13. Lenneberg, E. H. (1967): *Biological Foundations of Language.* John Wiley & Sons, New York.
14. Lenneberg, E. H., ed. (1974): Language and brain: Developmental aspects. *Neurosci. Res. Prog. Bull.,* 12:513–656.
15. Barnes, H. E. (1935): *The History of Western Civilization.* Harcourt, Brace, New York.
16. Sellars, R. W. (1938): An analytic approach to the mind-body problem. *Philos. Rev.,* 47:461–487.
17. Herrick, C. J. (1949): *George Ellett Coghill, Naturalist and Philosopher.* University of Chicago Press, Chicago.
18. Hamilton, G. V. (1948): *A Research in Marriage.* Lear, New York (quoted from Herrick, ref. 10).
19. Sherrington, C. S. (1947): *The Integrative Action of the Nervous System.* Yale University Press, New Haven. A reprinted edition of the 1906, Charles Scribner's Sons edition, with a forward to the 1947 edition by Sir Charles.
20. Fulton, J. F. (1926): *Muscular Contraction and the Reflex Control of Movement.* Williams & Wilkins, Baltimore.
21. Melzack, R., and Wall, P. D. (1965): Pain mechanisms: A new theory. *Science,* 150:971–979.
22. Melzack, R. (1973): *The Puzzle of Pain.* Baisc Books, New York.
23. Bodian, D. (1967): Neurons, circuits, and neuroglia. In: *The Neurosciences: A Study Program,* edited by G. C. Quarton, T. Melnechuk, and F. O. Schmitt, pp. 6–24. Rockefeller University Press, New York.
24. Eccles, J. E. (1953): *The Neurophysiological Basis of Mind, the Principles of Neurophysiology.* Clarendon Press, Oxford.
25. Schmidt, R. (1973): Control of the access of afferent activity to somatosensory pathways. In: *Handbook of Sensory Physiology, Vol. 2, Somatosensory System,* edited by A. Iggo, pp. 151–206. Springer, Berlin.
26. Edinger, L. (1900): *Vorlesungen uber den Bau de nervosen Centralorgane des Menschen und der Thiere.* F. C. W. Vogel, Leipzig.
27. Cantril, H., Ames, A. A., Jr., Hastorf, A. H., and Ittelson, W. H. (1949): Psychology and scientific research. *Science,* 110:461–464, 491–497, 517–522.
28. Russell, B. (1948): *Human Knowledge, Its Scope and Limitations.* Simon and Schuster, New York.
29. Bronfenbrenner, U. (1970): *Two Worlds of Childhood, U.S. and U.S.S.R.* Russell Sage Foundation, New York.
30. Carroll, J. B., ed. (1956): *Language, Thought and Reality, Selected Writings of Benjamin Lee Whorf.* John Wiley & Sons, New York.
31. Livingston, R. B. (1963): Perception and commitment. *Bull. At. Scientists,* 19:14–18.
32. Livingston, R. B. (1973): Neurosciences and education. *Prospects,* 3:415–437.
33. Hess, W. R. (1954): *Diencephalon, Autonomic and Extrapyramidal Functions.* Grune & Stratton, New York.
34. Hess, W. R. (1957): *The Functional Organization of the Diencephalon.* Grune & Stratton, New York.
35. Hess, W. R. (1969): *Hypothalamus and Thalamus, Experimental Documentation,* 2nd Edition. Georg Thieme, Stuttgart.
36. Wyrwicka, W. (1964): Electrical activity of the hypothalamus during alimentary conditioning. *Electroencephalogr. Clin. Neurophysiol.,* 17:164–176.
37. Grastyán, E., Karmos, G., Vereczkey, L., and Kellenyi, L. (1966): The hippocampal electrical correlates of the homeostatic regulation of motivation. *Electroencephalogr. Clin. Neurophysiol.,* 21:34–53.
38. Bower, T. G. R. (1941): *Development in Infancy.* W. H. Freeman, San Francisco.

39. Wertheimer, M. (1962): Psychomotor coordination of auditory-visual space at birth. *Science,* 134:1692.
40. White, B. L. (1971): *Human Infants—Experience and Psychological Development.* Prentice Hall, Englewood Cliffs, New Jersey.
41. Piaget, J. (1971): *Biology and Knowledge: An Essay on the Relations Between Organic Regulations and Cognitive Processes.* University of Chicago Press, Chicago.
42. Livingston, W. K., Cantril, H., and Livingston, R. B. Brain, mind and self. (*In press.*)
43. Bronowski, J. (1973): *The Ascent of Man.* Little, Brown and Company, Boston.
44. Altman, J. (1967): Postnatal growth and differentiation of the mammalian brain, with implications for a morphological theory of memory. In: *The Neurosciences: A Study Program,* edited by G. C. Quarton, T. Melnechuk, and F. O. Schmitt, pp. 723–743. Rockefeller University Press, New York.
45. Sidman, R. L. (1970): Cell proliferation, migration, and interaction in the developing mammalian central nervous system. In: *The Neurosciences Second Study Program,* edited by F. O. Schmitt, pp. 100–116. Rockefeller University Press, New York.
46. Szentágothai, J. *Personal communication.*
47. Ito, M. (1974): The control mechanisms of cerebellar motor systems. In: *The Neurosciences Third Study Program,* edited by F. O. Schmitt and F. G. Worden, pp. 293–303. The MIT Press, Cambridge, Massachusetts.
48. Llinás, R. R. (1969): *Neurobiology of Cerebellar Evolution and Development.* A.M.A. Institute for Biomedical Research, Chicago.
49. Muralt, A. Von (1946): *Die Signalübermittlung im Nerven.* Birkhäuser, Basel.
50. Staempfli, R. (1954): Saltatory conduction in nerve. *Physiol. Rev.,* 34:101–112.
51. Yakovlev, P. I., and Lecours, A.-R. (1967): The myelogenetic cycles of regional maturation of the brain. In: *Regional Development of the Brain,* edited by A. Minkowski. Blackwell Scientific, Oxford.
52. Bullock, T. H., ed. (1966): Simple systems for the study of learning mechanisms. *Neurosci. Res. Prog. Bull.,* 4:105–233.
53. Livingston, R. B., ed. (1966): Brain mechanisms in conditioning and learning. *Neurosci. Res. Prog. Bull.,* 4:235–347.
54. Sokolov, L. (1972). Circulation and energy metabolism of the brain. In: *Basic Neurochemistry,* edited by R. W. Albers, B. Agranoff, R. Katzman, and G. J. Siegel, pp. 299–325. Little, Brown and Company, Boston.
55. Herschkowitz, N., and Rossi, E. (1972): Critical periods in brain development. In: *Lipids, Malnutrition and the Developing Brain,* edited by K. Elliott and J. Knight, pp. 107–119. Elsevier, Amsterdam.
56. Diamond, M. C., Rosenzweig, M. R., Bennett, E. L., Lidner, B., and Lyon, L. (1972): Effects of environmental enrichment and impoverishment on rat cerebral cortex. *J. Neurobiol.,* 3:47–64.
57. Diamond, M. C. (1976): Effects of differential environment on the anatomy of the rat forebrain. In: *Brain Mechanisms Relating to Learning,* edited by R. B. Livingston. Elsevier, Amsterdam. (*In press.*)
58. Kretsch, D., Rosenzweig, M. R., and Bennett, E. L. (1960): Effects of environmental complexity and training on brain chemistry. *J. Comp. Physiol. Psychol.,* 53:509–519.
59. Dobbing, J. (1972): Vulnerable periods of brain development. In: *Lipids, Malnutrition and the Developing Brain,* edited by K. Elliott and J. Knight, pp. 9–29. Elsevier, Amsterdam.
60. Livingston, R. B., Calloway, D. H., MacGregor, J. S., Fisher, G. J., and Hastings, A. B. (1975): U.S. poverty impact on brain development. In: *Growth and Development of the Brain,* edited by M. A. B. Brazier, pp. 377–394. Raven Press, New York.
61. Shneour, E. A. (1974): *The Malnourished Mind.* Anchor Press, Doubleday, Garden City, New York.
62. Winick, M., Rosso, P., and Brasel, J. (1972): Malnutrition and cellular growth in the brain: Existence of critical periods. In: *Lipids, Malnutrition and the Developing Brain,* edited by K. Elliott and J. Knight, pp. 199–212. Elsevier, Amsterdam.

63. Winick, M., ed. (1974): *Nutrition and Fetal Development.* John Wiley & Sons, New York.
64. Pfaff, D., ed. (1974): Hormonal factors in brain function. In: *The Neurosciences Third Study Program,* edited by F. O. Schmitt and F. G. Worden, pp. 547–646. The MIT Press, Cambridge, Massachusetts.
65. Guillemin, R., and Burgus, R. (1972): The hormones of the hypothalamus. *Sci. Am.,* 227:24–33.
66. Ganong, W. F. (1974): Brain mechanisms regulating the secretion of the pituitary gland. In: *The Neurosciences Third Study Program,* edited by F. O. Schmitt and F. G. Worden, pp. 549–563. The MIT Press, Cambridge, Massachusetts.
67. Goy, R. W., and Goldfoot, D. A. (1974): Experimental and hormonal factors influencing development of sexual behavior in the male rhesus monkey. In: *The Neurosciences Third Study Program,* edited by F. O. Schmitt and F. G. Worden, pp. 571–581. The MIT Press, Cambridge, Massachusetts.
68. Money, J. W., and Ehrhardt, A. A. (1968): Prenatal hormonal exposure: Possible effects on behaviour in man. In: *Endocrinology and Human Behaviour,* edited by R. P. Michael, pp. 32–48. Oxford University Press, London.
69. Feder, H. H., and Wade, G. N. (1974): Integrative actions of perinatal hormones on neural tissues mediating adult sexual behavior. In: *The Neurosciences Third Study Program,* edited by F. O. Schmitt and F. G. Worden, pp. 583–586. The MIT Press, Cambridge, Massachusetts.
70. Goldman, B. (1974): The hypothalamic-pituitary-gonadal axis and the regulation of cyclicity and sexual behavior. In: *The Neurosciences Third Study Program,* edited by F. O. Schmitt and F. G. Worden, pp. 587–591. The MIT Press, Cambridge, Massachusetts.
71. Harris, G. W. (1964): Sexual hormones, brain development and brain function. *Endocrinology,* 75:627–648.
72. Clemens, L. G., Shryne, J., and Gorski, R. A. (1970): Androgen and development of progesterone responsiveness in male and female rats. *Physiol. Behav.,* 5:673–678.
73. Gerall, A. A., and Kennedy, A. M. (1970): Neonatally androgenized females' responsiveness to estrogen and progesterone. *Endocrinology,* 87:560–566.
74. Hart, B. L. (1968): Neonatal castration: Influence on neural organization of sexual reflexes in male rats. *Science,* 160:1135–1136.
75. McEwen, B. S., Denef, C. J., Gerlach, J. L., and Plapinger, L. (1974): Chemical studies of the brain as a steroid hormone target tissue. In: *The Neurosciences Third Study Program,* edited by F. O. Schmitt and F. G. Worden, pp. 599–620. The MIT Press, Cambridge, Massachusetts.
76. Pfaff, D. W., Diakow, C., Zigmond, R. E., and Kow, L.-M. (1974): Neural and hormonal determinants of female mating behavior in rats. In: *The Neurosciences Third Study Program,* edited by F. O. Schmitt and F. G. Worden, pp. 621–646. The MIT Press, Cambridge, Massachusetts.
77. Medawar, P. B. (1957): *The Uniqueness of the Individual.* Basic Books, New York.
78. White, L. A. (1960): Four stages in the evolution of minding. In: *Evolution After Darwin, Vol. 2, The Evolution of Man, Culture and Society,* edited by S. Tax, pp. 239–253. University of Chicago Press, Chicago.
79. Descartes, R. (1637): *Discours de la Méthode, pour bien conduire sa raison, et chercher la vérité dans les sciènces; plus la Dioptrique, les Météores et la Géométrie, qui sont des essais de cette méthode.* Leyden.
80. Descartes, R. (1955): *Philosophical Works of Descrates.* (Translated by Elizabeth S. Haldane and G. R. T. Ross.) Dover Publications, New York.
81. Allport, F. H. (1955): *Theories of Perception and the Concept of Structure, a Review and Critical Analysis With an Introduction to a Dynamic-Structural Theory of Behavior.* John Wiley & Sons, New York.
82. Boring, E. G. (1942): *Sensation and Perception in the History of Experimental Psychology.* Appleton-Century-Crofts, New York.
83. Keele, K. D. (1957): *Anatomies of Pain.* Charles C Thomas, Springfield, Ill.
84. Livingston, R. B. (1967): Brain circuitry relating to complex behavior. In: *The Neurosciences: A Study Program,* edited by G. C. Quarton, T. Melnechuk, and F. O. Schmitt, pp. 499–515. Rockefeller University Press, New York.

85. Ittelson, W. H. (1962): Perception and transactional psychology. In: *Psychology: A Study of a Science, Study II. Empirical Substructure and Relations with Other Sciences. Vol. 4. Biologically Oriented Fields: Their Place in Psychology and in Biological Science,* edited by S. Koch, pp. 660–704. McGraw-Hill, New York.

86. Penfield, W., and Rasmussen, T. (1950): *The Cerebral Cortex of Man, A Clinical Study of Localization of Function.* Macmillan, New York.

87. Penfield, W. (1958): *The Excitable Cortex in Conscious Man.* Liverpool University Press, Liverpool.

88. Livingston, R. B. (1967): Reinforcement. In: *The Neurosciences: A Study Program,* edited by G. C. Quarton, T. Melnechuk, and F. O. Schmitt, pp. 568–577. Rockefeller University Press, New York.

89. Hornbein, T. F. (1965): The chemical regulation of ventilation. In: *Physiology and Biophysics,* edited by T. C. Ruch and H. D. Patton, pp. 803–819. W. B. Saunders, Philadelphia.

90. Young, A. C. (1965): Neural control of respiration. In: *Physiology and Biophysics,* edited by T. C. Ruch and H. D. Patton, pp. 788–802. W. B. Saunders, Philadelphia.

91. Olds, J. (1958): Self-stimulation of the brain. *Science,* 127:315–324.

92. Olds, J. (1962): Hypothalamic substrates of reward. *Physiol. Rev.,* 42:554–604.

93. Valenstein, E. S. (1970): Stability and plasticity of motivation systems. In: *The Neurosciences Second Study Program,* edited by F. O. Schmitt, pp. 207–217. Rockefeller University Press, New York.

94. Vallenstein, E. S. (1973): *Brain Control; A Critical Examination of Brain Stimulation and Psychosurgery.* John Wiley & Sons, New York.

95. Delgado, J. M. R., Roberts, W. W., and Miller, N. E. (1954): Learning motivated by electrical stimulation of the brain. *Am. J. Physiol.,* 179:587–593.

96. Kerr, D. I. B., Haugen, F. P., and Melzack, R. (1955): Responses evoked in the brain stem by tooth stimulation. *Am. J. Physiol.,* 183:253–258.

97. Melzack, R., and Haugen, F. P. (1957): Responses evoked at the cortex by tooth stimulation. *Am. J. Physiol.,* 190:570–574.

98. Melzack, R., Stotler, W. A., and Livingston, W. K. (1958): Effects of discrete brainstem lesions in cats on perception of noxious stimulation. *J. Neurophysiol.,* 21:353–367.

99. Nashold, B. S., Jr., Wilson, W. P., and Slaughter, D. G. (1969): Sensations evoked by stimulation in the midbrain of man. *J. Neurosurg.,* 30:14–24.

100. MacLean, P. D. (1970): The triune brain, emotion, and scientific bias. In: *The Neurosciences Second Study Program,* edited by F. O. Schmitt, pp. 336–349. Rockefeller University Press, New York.

101. Nauta, W. J. H. (1964): Some efferent connections of the prefrontal cortex in the monkey. In: *The Frontal Granular Cortex and Behavior,* edited by J. M. Warren and K. Akert, pp. 397–409. McGraw-Hill, New York.

102. Nauta, W. J. H. (1966): Brain mechanisms in conditioning and learning, summarized by Robert B. Livingston. *Neurosci. Res. Prog. Bull.,* 4:320–325.

103. Kilpatrick, F. P. (1961): Perception in critical situations. In: *Explorations in Transactional Psychology,* edited by F. P. Kilpatrick, pp. 316–320. New York University Press, New York.

104. Gazzaniga, M. S. (1970): *The Bisected Brain.* Appleton-Century-Crofts, New York.

105. Milner, B. (1974): Hemispheric specialization: Scope and limits. In: *The Neurosciences Third Study Program,* edited by F. O. Schmitt and F. G. Worden, pp. 75–89. The MIT Press, Cambridge, Massachusetts.

106. Milner, B., ed. (1974): Hemispheric specialization and interaction. In: *The Neurosciences Third Study Program,* edited by F. O. Schmitt and F. G. Worden, pp. 1–89. The MIT Press, Cambridge, Massachusetts.

107. Sperry, R. W. (1974): Lateral specialization in the surgically separated hemispheres. In: *The Neurosciences Third Study Program,* edited by F. O. Schmitt and F. G. Worden, pp. 5–19. The MIT Press, Cambridge, Massachusetts.

108. Kimura, D. (1961): Cerebral dominance and perception of verbal stimuli. *Can. J. Psychol.,* 15:166–171.

109. Kimura, D. (1964): Left-right differences in the perception of melodies. *Q. J. Exp. Psychol.*, 16:355–358.
110. Semmes, J. (1965): A non-tactual factor in astereognosis. *Neuropsychologia*, 3:295–315.
111. Corsi, P. M. Human memory and the medial temporal region of the brain. Unpublished Ph.D. Thesis, McGill University, cited in Milner, ref. 105.
112. Hebb, D. O. (1942): The effect of early and late brain injury upon test scores, and the nature of normal adult intelligence. *Proc. Am. Philos. Soc.*, 85:275–292.
113. Berlucchi, G. (1974): Cerebral dominance and interhemispheric communication in normal man. In: *The Neurosciences Third Study Program*, edited by F. O. Schmitt and F. G. Worden, pp. 65–69. The MIT Press, Cambridge, Massachusetts.
114. Broadbent, D. E. (1974): Division of function and integration of behavior. In: *The Neurosciences Third Study Program*, edited by F. O. Schmitt and F. G. Worden, pp. 31–41. The MIT Press, Cambridge, Massachusetts.
115. Doty, R. W. (1974): Interhemispheric transfer and manipulation of engrams. In: *Cellular Mechanisms Subserving Changes in Neuronal Activity*, edited by C. D. Woody, pp. 153–159. Brain Information Service, Los Angeles.
116. Doty, R. W. (1976): "Ionic" versus "molecular" memory—are there mnemonic neurons? In: *Brain Mechanisms Relating to Learning*, edited by R. B. Livingston, Elsevier, Amsterdam. (*In press.*)
117. Livingston, R. B. (1972): Neural integration. In: *Pathophysiology, Altered Regulatory Mechanisms in Disease*, edited by E. D. Frolich, pp. 569–598. J. B. Lippincott, Philadelphia.
118. Jackson, J. H. (1888): On a particular variety of epilepsy ("intellectual aura"), one case with symptoms of organic brain disease. *Brain*, 11:179–207.
119. Erlanger, J., and Gasser, H. S. (1937): *Electrical Signs of Nervous Activity*. University of Pennsylvania Press, Philadelphia.
120. Gasser, H. S., and Erlanger, J. (1926): The role played by the sizes of the constituent fibers of a nerve trunk in determining the form of its action potential wave. *Am. J. Physiol.*, 80:522–547.
121. Perkel, D. H., and Bullock, T. H. (1968): Neural coding. *Neurosci. Res. Bull.*, 6:221–348.
122. Adey, W. R. (1969): Slow electrical phenomena in the central nervous system. *Neurosci. Res. Prog. Bull.*, 7:75–180.
123. Adrian, E. D. (1928): *The Basis of Sensation, the Action of the Sense Organs*. Christophers, London.
124. Zotterman, Y. (1939): Touch, pain and tickling: An electrophysiological investigation on cutaneous sensory nerves. *J. Physiol.*, 95:1–28.
125. Dusser de Barrenne, J. G. (1916): Experimental researches on sensory localisations in the cerebral cortex. *Q. J. Exp. Physiol.*, 9:355–390.
126. Adrian, E. D. (1947): *The Physical Background of Perception*. Clarendon Press, Oxford.
127. Marshall, W. H., Woolsey, C. N., and Bard, P. (1941): Representation of tactile sensibility in the monkey's cortex as indicated by cortical potentials. *J. Neurophysiol.*, 4:1–24.
128. Hess, W. R. (1932): *Die Methodik der lokalisierten Reizung und Ausschaltung subkortikaler Hirnabschnitte*. Georg Thieme, Leipzig.
129. Magoun, H. W. (1963): *The Waking Brain, 2nd Edition*. Charles C Thomas, Springfield, Ill.
130. Thudichum, J. L. W. (1884): *A Treatise on the Chemical Constitution of the Brain*. Baillière, Tindall and Cox, London.
131. Folch-pi, J., and Lees, M. (1951): Proteolipides, a new type of tissue lipoproteins: their isolation from brain. *J. Biol. Chem.*, 191:807–817.
132. Loewi, O. (1936): The chemical transmission of nerve action. In: *Nobel Lectures, Physiology or Medicine, 1922–1941*, pp. 416–429. Elsevier, Amsterdam.
133. Dale, H. H. (1936): Some recent extensions of the chemical transmission of the effects of nerve impulses. In: *Nobel Lectures, Physiology or Medicine, 1922–1941*, pp. 402–413. Elsevier, Amsterdam.

134. Cooper, J. R., Bloom, F. E., and Roth, R. H. (1974): *The Biochemical Basis of Neuropharmacology, 2nd Edition.* Oxford University Press, New York.
135. Peters, A., Palay, S. L., and Webster, H. DeF. (1970): *The Fine Structure of the Nervous System: The Cells and Their Processes.* Harper and Row, New York.
136. Rall, W., and Shepherd, G. M. (1968): Theoretical reconstruction of field potentials and dendrodendritic synaptic interactions in olfactory bulb. *J. Neurophysiol.* 31:884–915.
137. Rall, W. (1970): Dendritic neuron theory and dendro-dendritic synapses in a simple cortical system. In: *The Neurosciences Second Study Program,* edited by F. O. Schmitt, pp. 552–565. Rockefeller University Press, New York.
138. Shepherd, G. M. (1970): The olfactory bulb as a simple cortical system: Experimental analysis and functional implications. In: *The Neurosciences Second Study Program,* edited by F. O. Schmitt, pp. 539–552. Rockefeller University Press, New York.
139. Shepherd, G. M. (1974): *The Synaptic Organization of the Brain, An Introduction.* Oxford University Press, New York.
140. Brightman, M. W., and Reese, T. S. (1969): Junctions between intimately apposed cell membranes in the vertebrate brain. *J. Cell Biol.,* 40:648–677.
141. Schmitt, F. O., Schneider, D. M., and Crothers, D. M., eds. (1975): *Functional Linkage in Biomolecular Systems.* Raven Press, New York.
142. Piaget, J. (1953): *The Origin of Intelligence in the Child.* Routledge and Kegan Paul, London.
143. Cantril, H., ed. (1960): *The Morning Notes of Adelbert Ames, Jr.* Rutgers University Press, New Brunswick.
144. Lipsitt, L. P. (1969): Learning capacities of the human infant. In: *Brain and Early Behavior Development in the Fetus and Infant,* edited by R. J. Robinson, pp. 227–249. Academic Press, London.
145. Siqueland, E. R., and Lipsitt, L. P. (1966): Conditioned head-turning in human newborns. *J. Exp. Child Psychol.,* 3:356–376.
146. Hess, E. H. (1973): *Imprinting: Early Experience and the Developmental Biology of Attachment.* Van Nostrand Reinhold, New York.
147. Aronson, E., and Rosenbloom, S. (1971): Space perception in early infancy, perception within a common auditory-visual space. *Science,* 172:1161–1163.
148. Ball, W., and Tronick, E. (1971): Infant responses to impending collision: optical and real. *Science,* 171:818–820.
149. Szentágothai, J. (1973): Neuronal and synaptic architecture of the lateral geniculate nucleus. In: *Handbook of Sensory Physiology, Vol. VII/3, Part B. Central Processing of Visual Information,* edited by R. Jung, pp. 141–176. Springer, Berlin.
150. Szentágothai, J. (1973): Synaptology of the visual cortex. In: *Handbook of Sensory Physiology, Vol. VII/3, Part B. Central Processing of Visual Information,* edited by R. Jung, pp. 269–324. Springer, Berlin.
151. Szentágothai, J. (1970): Glomerular synapses, complex synaptic arrangements, and their optional significance. In: *The Neurosciences Second Study Program,* edited by F. O. Schmitt, pp. 427–443. Rockefeller University Press, New York.
152. Sholl, D. A. (1956): *The Organization of the Cerebral Cortex.* Methuen, London.
153. Scheibel, M. E., and Scheibel, A. B. (1966): Patterns of organization in specific and nonspecific thalamic fields. In: *The Thalamus,* edited by D. P. Purpura and M. D. Yahr, pp. 13–46. Columbia University Press, New York.
154. Scheibel, M. E., and Scheibel, A. B. (1969): Terminal patterns in cat spinal cord, III. Primary afferent collaterals. *Brain Res.,* 13:417–443.
155. Scheibel, M. E., and Scheibel, A. B. (1970): Elementary processes in selected thalamic and cortical subsystems—the structural substrates. In: *The Neurosciences Second Study Program,* edited by F. O. Schmitt, pp. 443–457. Rockefeller University Press, New York.
156. Ramón-Moliner, E. (1968): The morphology of dendrites. In: *The Structure and Function of Nervous Tissue, Vol. 1,* edited by G. H. Bourne, pp. 205–207. Academic Press, New York.

157. Ramón-Moliner, E., and Nauta, W. J. H. (1966): The isodendritic core of the brain stem. *J. Comp. Neurol.*, 126:311–335.
158. Eccles, J. C., Ito, M., and Szentágothai, J. (1967): *The Cerebellum as a Neuronal Machine*. Springer, New York.
159. Ramón y Cajal, S. (1909): *Histologie du Système Nerveux de l'Homme et des Vertébrés*. Maloine, Paris.
160. Lorente de Nó, R. (1922): La corteza cerebral del ratón, primera contribución, la corteza acústica. *Trab. Lab. Invest. Biol. Univ. Madrid*, 20:41–78.
161. Lorente de Nó, R. (1932): Vestibulo-ocular reflex arc. *Arch. Neurol. Psychiatr.*, 30:245–291.
162. Lorente de Nó, R. (1938): Analysis of the activity of the chains of internuncial neurons. *J. Neurophysiol.*, 1:207–244.
163. Szentágothai, J., and Arbib, M. A. (1974): Conceptual models of neural organization. *Neurosci. Res. Prog. Bull.*, 12:307–510.
164. Mach, E. (1959): *The Analysis of Sensation and the Relation of the Physical to the Psychical*. Dover Publications, New York.
165. Kuffler, S. W. (1953): Discharge patterns and functional organization of mammalian retina. *J. Neurophysiol.*, 16:37–38.
166. Ratliff, F., and Hartline, H. K. (1959): The response of Limulus optic nerve fibers to patterns of illumination on the receptor mosaic. *J. Gen. Physiol.*, 42:1241–1255.
167. Hubel, D. H. and Wiesel, T. N. (1962): Receptive fields, binocular interaction and functional architecture in the cat's visual cortex. *J. Physiol.*, 160:106–154.
168. Hubel, D. H., and Wiesel, T. N. (1968): Receptive fields and functional architecture of monkey striate cortex. *J. Physiol.*, 195:215–243.
169. Hubel, D. H., and Wiesel, T. N. (1970): Cells sensitive to binocular depth in area 18 of the macaque monkey cortex. *Nature (Lond.)*, 225:41–42.
170. von Békésy, G. (1967): *Sensory Inhibition*. Princeton University Press, Princeton, New Jersey.
171. Bach-y-Rita, P. (1972): *Brain Mechanisms in Sensory Substitution*. Academic Press, New York.
172. Gibson, J. J. (1966): *The Senses Considered as Perceptual Systems*. Houghton Mifflin, Boston.
173. Held, R. (1970): Two modes of processing spatially distributed visual stimulation. In: *The Neurosciences Second Study Program*, edited by F. O. Schmitt, pp. 317–324. Rockefeller University Press, New York.
174. Bach-y-Rita, P. *Personal communication.*
175. Kilpatrick, F. P., ed. (1961): *Explorations in Transactional Psychology*. New York University Press, New York.
176. Stratton, G. M. (1896): Some preliminary experiments on vision without inversion of the retinal image. *Psychol. Rev.*, 3:611–617.
177. Stratton, G. M. (1897): Vision without inversion of the retinal image. *Psychol. Rev.*, 4:341–360, 463–481.
178. Kohler, I. (1962): Experiments with goggles. *Sci. Am.*, 206:62–72.
179. Kety, S. S. (1970): The biogenic amines in the central nervous system: Their possible roles in arousal, emotion, and learning. In: *The Neurosciences Second Study Program*, edited by F. O. Schmitt, pp. 324–336. Rockefeller University Press, New York.
180. Livingston, R. B. (1964): Cited in: Some brain structures and functions related to memory, edited by W. J. H. Nauta. *Neurosci. Res. Prog. Bull.*, 2:25–27.
181. MacKay, D. M. (1970): Perception and brain function. In: *The Neurosciences Second Study Program*, edited by F. O. Schmitt, pp. 303–316. Rockefeller University Press, New York.
182. Evarts, E. V., ed. (1971): Central control of movement. *Neurosci. Res. Prog. Bull.*, 9:1–170.
183. Bartlett, F. C. (1947): The measurement of human skill. *Br. Med. J.*, 1:835–838, 877–880.
184. Oscarsson, O. (1970): Functional organization of spino-cerebellar paths. In:

Handbook of Sensory Physiology, Vol. 2, Somatosensory System, edited by A. Iggo, pp. 339–380. Springer, Berlin.

185. Shimamura, M., and Livingston, R. B. (1963): Longitudinal conduction systems serving spinal and brain stem coordination. *J. Neurophysiol.,* 26:258–272.

186. Grampp, W., and Oscarsson, O. (1968): Inhibitory neurons in the Group I projection area of the cat's cerebral cortex. In: *Structure and Function of Inhibitory Neuronal Mechanisms,* edited by C. von Euler, S. Skoglund, and U. Söderberg, pp. 351–356. Pergamon Press, Oxford.

187. Chang, H.-T. (1950): The repetitive discharges of corticothalamic reverberating circuit. *J. Neurophysiol.,* 13:235–257.

188. Hassler, R. (1966): Thalamic regulation of muscle tone and the speed of movement. In: *The Thalamus,* edited by D. Purpura and M. D. Yahr, pp. 419–438. Columbia University Press, New York.

189. MacKay, D. M. (1973): Visual stability and voluntary eye movements. In: *Handbook of Sensory Physiology,* edited by R. Jung. Springer, New York.

190. Gernandt, B. E., Katsuki, Y., and Livingston, R. B. (1957): Functional organization of descending vestibular influences. *J. Neurophysiol.,* 20:453–469.

191. Reichardt, W., and MacGinitie, G. (1962): Zur Theorie der lateralen Inhibition. *Kybernetik,* 1:155–165.

192. Escobar, A., ed. (1964): *Feedback Systems Controlling Nervous Activity.* Sociedad Mexicana de Ciéncias Fisiologicas, Mexico, D. F.

193. Hernández-Peón, R., Scherrer, H., and Jouvet, M. (1956): Modification of electrical activity in cochlear nucleus during "attention" in unanesthetized cats. *Science,* 123:331–332.

194. Hernández-Peón, R., Guzmán-Flores, C., Alcaraz, M., and Fernández-Guardiola, A. (1957): Sensory transmission in visual pathway during "attention" in unanesthetized cats. *Acta. Neurol. Lat. Am.,* 3:1–8.

195. Hernández-Peón, R. (1961): Reticular mechanisms of sensory control. In: *Sensory Communication,* edited by W. A. Rosenblith, pp. 497–520. John Wiley & Sons, New York.

196. Livingston, R. B. (1959): Central control of receptors and sensory transmission systems. In: *Handbook of Physiology, Section 1, Vol. 1, Neurophysiology,* edited by J. Field, H. W. Magoun, and V. E. Hall, pp. 741–760. American Physiological Society, Washington, D.C.

197. Livingston, R. B. (1958): Central control of afferent activity. In: *Reticular Formation of the Brain,* edited by H. H. Jasper, L. D. Proctor, R. S. Knighton, W. C. Noshay, and R. T. Costello, pp. 177–185. Little, Brown and Company, Boston.

198. Towe, A. L. (1973): Somatosensory cortex: descending influences on ascending systems. In: *Handbook of Sensory Physiology, Vol. 2, Somatosensory System,* edited by A. Iggo, pp. 701–718. Springer, Berlin.

199. Loewenstein, W. R. (1956): Modulation of cutaneous mechano-receptors by sympathetic stimulation. *J. Physiol.,* 132:40–60.

200. Dell, P., Bonvallet, M., and Hugelin, A. (1954): Tonus sympathique, adrénaline et controle réticulaire de la motricité spinale. *Electroencephalogr. Clin. Neurophysiol.,* 6:599–618.

201. Gordon, G., and Miller, R. (1973): Identification of cortical cells projecting to the dorsal column nuclei of the cat. *Q. J. Exp. Physiol.,* 54:85–98.

202. Matthews, P. B. C. (1964): Muscle spindles and their motor control. *Physiol. Rev.,* 44:219–288.

203. Matthews, P. B. C. (1972): *Mammalian Muscle Receptors and their Central Actions.* Arnold, London.

204. Ottoson, D., and Shepherd, G. M. (1971): Transducer properties and integrative mechanisms of the frog's muscle spindle. In: *Handbook of Sensory Physiology, Vol. 1, Principles of Receptor Physiology,* edited by W. R. Loewenstein, pp. 442–499. Springer, Berlin.

205. Shepherd, G. M. (1970): The olfactory bulb as a simple cortical system: Experimental analysis and functional implications. In: *The Neurosciences Second Study Program,* edited by F. O. Schmitt, pp. 539–552. Rockefeller University Press, New York.

206. Eldred, E., Granit, R., and Merton, P. A. (1953): Supraspinal control of the muscle spindles and its significance. *J. Physiol.*, 122:498–523.
207. Granit, R., and Kaada, B. R. (1952): Influence of stimulation of central nervous structures on muscle spindles in cat. *Acta Physiol. Scand.*, 27:130–160.
208. Van Hasselt, P. (1973): The centrifugal control of retinal function. A review. *Ophthalmol. Res.*, 4:298–320.
209. Brindley, G. S. (1970): *Physiology of the Retina and Visual Pathway*, 2nd edition. Arnold, London.
210. Cragg, B. G. (1962): Centrifugal fibers to the retina and olfactory bulb, and composition of the supraoptic commissures in the rabbit. *Exp. Neurol.*, 5:406–427.
211. Cowan, W. M. (1970): Centrifugal fibres to the avian retina. *Br. Med. Bull.*, 26:112–118.
212. Holden, A. L. (1968): Antidromic activation of the isthmo-optic nucleus. *J. Physiol.*, 197:183–198.
213. Honrubia, F. M., and Elliott, J. H. (1970): Efferent innervation of the retina. II. Morphologic study of the monkey retina. *Invest. Ophthalmol.*, 9:971–976.
214. Honrubia, F. M., and Elliott, J. H. (1968): Efferent innervation of the retina. I. Morphological study of the human retina. *Arch. Ophthalmol.*, 80:98–103.
215. Miles, F. A. (1970): Centrifugal effects in the avian retina. *Science*, 170:992–995.
216. Miles, F. A. (1972): Centrifugal control of avian retina. I. Receptive field properties of retinal ganglion cells. *Brain Res.*, 48:65–92.
217. Miles, F. A. (1972): Centrifugal control of avian retina. II. Receptive field properties of cells in the isthmo-optic nucleus. *Brain Res.*, 48:93–113.
218. Miles, F. A. (1972): Centrifugal control of avian retina. III. Effects of electrical stimulation of the isthmo-optic tract on receptive field properties of retinal ganglion cells. *Brain Res.*, 48:115–129.
219. Miles, F. A. (1972): Centrifugal control of avian retina. IV. Effects of reversible cold block of the isthmo-optic tract on receptive field properties of cells in the retina and isthmo-optic nucleus. *Brain Res.*, 48:131–145.
220. Rogers, L. J., and Miles, F. A. (1972): Centrifugal control of avian retina. V. Effects of lesions of the isthmo-optic nucleus on visual behaviour. *Brain Res.*, 48:147–156.
221. Wolter, J. R. (1965): The centrifugal nerves in human optic tract, chiasm, optic nerve and retina. *Trans. Am. Ophthalmol. Soc.*, 63:678–707.
222. Wolter, J. R., and Lund, O. E. (1968): Reaction of centrifugal nerves in the human retina. *Am. J. Ophthalmol.*, 66:221–232.
223. Sacks, J. G., and Lindenberg, R. (1969): Efferent nerve fibers in the anterior visual pathways in bilateral congenical cyctic eyeballs. *Am. J. Ophthalmol.*, 68:691–695.
224. Rasmussen, G. L. (1964): Anatomic relationships of the ascending and descending auditory systems. In: *Neurological Aspects of Auditory and Vestibular Disorders*, edited by W. S. Fields and B. R. Alford, pp. 1–19. Charles C Thomas, Springfield, Ill.
225. Rasmussen, G. L. (1960): Efferent fibers of the cochlear nerve and cochlear nucleus. In: *Neural Mechanisms of the Auditory and Vestibular Systems*, edited by G. L. Rasmussen and W. Windle, pp. 105–115. Charles C Thomas, Springfield, Ill.
226. Smith, C. A., and Rasmussen, G. L. (1963): Recent observations on the olivo-cochlear bundle. *Ann. Otol. Rhinol. Laryngol.*, 72:489–506.
227. Gacek, R. R. (1960): Efferent component of the vestibular nerve. In: *Neural Mechanisms of the Auditory and Vestibular Systems*, edited by G. L. Rasmussen and W. Windle, pp. 276–283. Charles C Thomas, Springfield, Ill.
228. Engström, H., Ades, H. W., and Hawkins, J. E. (1962): Structure and functions of the sensory hairs of the inner ear. *J. Acoust. Soc. Am.*, 34:1356–1363.
229. Galambos, R. (1956): Suppression of auditory nerve activity by stimulation of efferent fibers to cochlea. *J. Neurophysiol.*, 19:424–437.
230. Fex, J. (1974): Neuroexcitatory processes of the inner ear. In: *Handbook of Sensory Physiology, Vol. 5/1: Auditory System*, edited by W. Keidel and W. D. Neff, pp. 585–646. Springer, Berlin.

231. Desmedt, J. E. (1962): Auditory evoked potentials from cochlea to cortex as influenced by activation of the efferent olivo-cochlear bundle. *J. Acoust. Soc. Am.,* 34:1478–1496.
232. Worden, F. G. (1971): Hearing and the neural detection of acoustic patterns. *Behav. Sci.,* 16:20–30.
233. Dewson, J. H., III (1968): Efferent olivocochlear bundle, some relationships to stimulus discrimination in noise. *J. Neurophysiol.,* 31:122–130.
234. Dewson, J. H., III (1967): Efferent olivocochlear bundle, some relationships to noise masking and to stimulus attenuation. *J. Neurophysiol.,* 30:817–832.
235. Kerr, David I. B., and Hagbarth, K.-E. (1955): An investigation of olfactory centrifugal fiber system. *J. Neurophysiol.,* 18:362–374.
236. Stark, L. (1968): *Neurological Control Systems, Studies in Bioengineering.* Plenum, New York.
237. Hess, E. (1965): Attitude and pupil size. *Sci. Am.,* 212:46–54.
238. Hearst, E., Beer, B., Sheatz, G., and Galambos., R. (1960): Some electrophysiological correlates of conditioning in the monkey. *Electroencephalogr. Clin. Neurophysiol.,* 12:137–152.
239. Marsh, J. T., McCarthy, D. A., Sheatz, G., and Galambos, R. (1961): Amplitude changes in evoked auditory potentials during habituation and conditioning. *Electroencephalogr. Clin. Neurophysiol.,* 13:224–234.
240. Galambos, R., and Sheatz, G. C. (1962): An electroencephalograph study of classical conditioning. *Am. J. Physiol.,* 203:173–184.
241. Adey, R., Segundo, J., and Livingston, R. B. (1957): Corticifugal influences on intrinsic brainstem conduction in cat and monkey. *J. Neurophysiol.,* 20:1–16.
242. French, J. D., Hernández-Peón, R., and Livingston, R. B. (1955): Projections from cortex to cephalic brainstem (reticular formation) in monkey. *J. Neurophysiol.,* 18:74–95.
243. Frommer, G. P., and Livingston, R. B. (1963): Arousal effects on evoked activity in a "non-sensory" system. *Science,* 139:502–504.
244. Coulter, J. D., Maunz, R. A., and Willis, W. D. (1974): Effect of stimulation of sensorimotor cortex on primate spinothalamic neurons. *Brain Res.,* 65:351–356.
245. French, J. D. (1958): Cortifugal connections with the reticular formation. In: *Reticular Formation of the Brain,* edited by H. H. Jasper, L. D. Proctor, R. S. Knighton, W. C. Noshay, and R. T. Costello, pp. 491–505. Little, Brown and Company, Boston.
246. Picton, T. W., Hillyard, S. A., Krausz, H. I., and Galambos, R. (1974): Human auditory evoked potentials. I. Evaluation of components. *Electroencephalogr. Clin. Neurophysiol.,* 36:179–190.
247. Picton, T. W., and Hillyard, S. A. (1974): Human auditory evoked potentials. II. Effects of attention. *Electroencephalogr. Clin. Neurophysiol.,* 36:191–199.
248. Galambos, R. (1974): The human auditory evoked response. In: *Sensation and Measurement,* edited by H. R. Moskowitz, B. Scharf, and J. C. Stevens, pp. 215–221. D. Reidel, Dordrecht-Holland.
249. Hernández-Peón, R., Jouvet, M., and Scherrer, H. (1957): Auditory potentials at cochlear nucleus during acoustic habituation. *Acta Neurol. Lat. Am.,* 3:144–156.
250. Hernández-Peón, R. (1960): Neurophysiological correlates of habituation and other manifestations of plastic inhibition (internal inhibition). In: *The Moscow Colloquium on Electroencephalography of Higher Neurons Activity,* edited by H. H. Jasper and G. D. Smirnov, pp. 101–114. The EEG Journal, Montreal.
251. Hyvärinen, J. (1973): CNS: Afferent mechanisms with emphasis in physiological and behavioral correlations. *Ann. Rev. Physiol.,* 35:243–272.
252. Sinclair, D. C. (1967): *Cutaneous Sensation.* Oxford University Press, London.
253. Cone, R. A. (1967): Early receptor potential, photoreversible charge displacement in rhodopsin. *Science,* 155:1128–1131.
254. Cohen, R. A., and Brown, P. K. (1967): Dependence of the early receptor potential on the orientation of rhodopsin. *Science,* 156:536.
255. Tomita, T. (1970): Electrical activity of vertebrate photoreceptors. *Q. Rev. Biophys.,* 3:179–222.

256. Loewenstein, W. R., Terzulo, C. A., and Washizu, Y. (1963): Separation of transducer and impulse-generating processes in sensory receptors. *Science,* 142: 1180–1181.

257. Toyoda, J., Hashimoto, H., Anno, H., and Tomita, T. (1970): The rod response in the frog as studied by intracellular recording. *Vision Res.,* 10:1093.

258. Maruhashi, J., Mizuguchi, K., and Tasaki, I. (1952): Action currents in single afferent nerve fibres elicited by stimulation of the skin of the toad and the cat. *J. Physiol.,* 117:129–151.

259. Zotterman, Y., ed. (1967): *Sensory Mechanisms.* Elsevier, Amsterdam.

260. Anand, B. K., Dua, S., and Singh, B. (1961): Electrical activity of the hypothalamic "feeding centers" under the effect of changes in blood chemistry. *Electroencephalogr. Clin. Neurophysiol.,* 13:54–59.

261. Anand, B. K. (1970): Regulation of visceral activities by the central nervous system. In: *Control Processes in Multicellular Organisms, A Ciba Foundation Symposium,* edited by G. E. W. Wolstenholme and J. Knight, pp. 356–383. Churchill, London.

262. Spencer, P. S., and Schaumburg, H. H. (1973): An ultrastructural study of the inner core of the Pacinian corpuscle. *J. Neurocytol.,* 2:217–235.

263. Loewenstein, W. R. (1960): Biological transducers. *Sci. Am.,* 203:98–108.

264. Libet, B. (1970): Generation of slow inhibitory and excitatory postsynaptic potentials. *Fed. Proc.,* 29:1945–1956.

265. Gray, J. A. B., and Ritchie, J. M. (1954): Effects of stretch on single myelinated nerve fibres. *J. Physiol.,* 124:84–99.

266. Livingston, R. B., Pfenninger, K., Moor, H., and Akert, K. (1973): Specialized paranodal and interparanodal glial-axonal junctions in the peripheral and central nervous system: A freeze-etching study. *Brain Res.,* 58:1–24.

267. Sheehan, D. (1933): The clinical significance of the nerve endings in the mesentery. *Lancet,* 1:409–410.

268. Livingston, W. K. (1935): *The Clinical Aspects of Visceral Neurology.* Charles C Thomas, Springfield, Ill.

269. Livingston, R. B. (1955): Some brain stem mechanisms relating to psychosomatic functions. *Psychosom. Med.,* 17:347–354.

270. Biedler, L. M. (1963): Dynamics of taste cells. In: *Olfaction and Taste,* edited by Y. Zotterman, pp. 133–144. Pergamon Press, Oxford.

271. Biedler, L. M., and Reichardt, W. E. (1970): Sensory transduction. *Neurosci. Res. Prog. Bull.,* 8:461–560.

272. Dastoli, F. R., Lopiekes, D. V., and Price, S. (1968): A sweet-sensitive protein from bovine taste buds, purification and partial characterization. *Biochemistry,* 7:1160–1164.

273. Diamant, H., Funakoshi, M., Strom, L., and Zotterman, Y. (1963): Electrophysiological studies on human taste nerves. In: *Olfaction and Taste,* edited by Y. Zotterman, pp. 193–204. Pergamon Press, Oxford.

274. Schutz, H. G., and Pilgrim, G. J. (1957): Differential sensitivity in gustation. *J. Exp. Psychol.,* 54:41–48.

275. Andres, K. H. (1970): Anatomy and ultrastructure of the olfactory bulb in fish, amphibia, reptiles, birds and mammals. In: *Taste and Smell in Vertebrates,* edited by G. E. W. Wolstenholme and J. Knight, pp. 177–196. Churchill, London.

276. de Lorenzo, A. J. D. (1963): Studies on the ultrastructure and histophysiology of cell membranes, nerve fibres and synaptic junctions in chemoreceptors. In: *Olfaction and Taste,* edited by Y. Zotterman, pp. 5–18. Macmillan, New York.

277. Ottoson, D. (1956): Analysis of the electrical activity of the olfactory epithelium. *Acta Physiol. Scand. (Suppl. 122),* 35:1–83.

278. Gesteland, R. C., Lettvin, J. Y., and Pitts, W. H. (1965): Chemical transmission in the nose of the frog. *J. Physiol.,* 181:525–559.

279. Leveteau, J., Daral, G., and MacLeod, P. (1969): The role of olfactory nucleus in interbulbar inhibition. In: *Olfaction and Taste IV,* edited by D. Schneider, pp. 135–141. Verlag, Stuttgart.

280. Adey, W. R. (1970): Higher olfactory centres. In: *Taste and Smell in Vertebrates,* edited by G. E. W. Wolstenholme and J. Knight, pp. 357–378. Churchill, London.

281. Allen, W. F. (1935): Olfactory and trigeminal conditioning reflexes in dogs. *Am. J. Physiol.*, 118:532–540.
282. Wenzel, B. M. (1967): Olfaction perception in birds. In: *Second International Symposium on Olfaction and Taste,* edited by T. Hayashi, pp. 203–217. Pergamon Press, London.
283. Richter, C. P. (1943): Total self-regulatory functions in animals and human beings. *Harvey Lect.*, 38:63–103.
284. Pfaff, D. W., and Pfaffman, C. (1969): Olfactory and hormonal influences on the basal forebrain of the male rat. *Brain Res.*, 15:137–156.
285. Békésy, G. von, and Rosenblith, W. A. (1951): The mechanical properties of the ear. In: *Handbook of Experimental Psychology,* edited by S. S. Stevens, pp. 1075–1115. John Wiley & Sons, New York.
286. Tasaki, I., and Spyropolous, C. S. (1959): Stria vascularis as source of endocochlear potential. *J. Neurophysiol.*, 22:149–155.
287. Békésy, G. von (1960): *Experiments in Hearing (Research Articles from 1928 to 1958).* McGraw-Hill, New York.
288. Smith, C. A. (1961): Innervation pattern of the cochlea: The internal hair cell. *Ann. Otol. Rhinol. Laryngol.*, 70:504–527.
289. Smith, C. A., and Sjöstrand, F. S. (1961): Structure of the nerve endings on the external hair cells of the guinea pig cochlea as studied by serial sections. *J. Ultrastruct. Res.*, 5:523–556.
290. Gracek, R. R. (1960): Efferent component of the vestibular nerve. In: *Neural Mechanisms of the Auditory and Vestibular Systems,* edited by G. L. Rasmussem and W. Windle, pp. 276–284. Charles C Thomas, Springfield, Ill.
291. Goldstein, M. H., Jr. (1974): The auditory periphery. In: *Medical Physiology, 13th Edition, Vol. 1,* edited by V. B. Mountcastle, pp. 383–411. C. V. Mosby, St. Louis.
292. Fex, J. (1962): Auditory activity in centrifugal and centripetal cochlear fibres in cat, a study of a feedback system. *Acta Physiol. Scand. (Suppl. 189),* 55:1–68.
293. Fex, J. (1965): Auditory activity in uncrossed centrifugal cochlear fibres in cat, a study of a feedback system II. *Acta Physiol. Scand.*, 64:43–57.
294. Desmedt, J. E., and LaGrutta, V. (1963): Function of the uncrossed efferent olivo-cochlear fibres in the cat. *Nature*, 200:472–474.
295. Sohmer, H. (1966): A comparison of the efferent effects of the homolateral and contralateral olivo-cochlear bundles. *Acta Otolaryngol.*, 62:74–87.
296. Desmedt, J. E., and Monaco, P. (1960): Suppression par la strichnine de l'effect inhibiteur centrifuge éxérce par le faisceau olivo-cochleaire. *Arch. Int. Pharmacodyn. Ther.*, 129:244–248.
297. Klinke, R., and Galley, N. (1974): Efferent innervation of vestibular and auditory receptors. *Physiol. Rev.*, 52:316–357.
298. Rossi, G., and Cortesina, G. (1963): Research on the efferent innervation of the inner ear. *J. Laryngol. Otol.*, 77:202–233.
299. Spoendlin, H. H., and Gacek, R. R. (1963): Electronmicroscopic study of the efferent and afferent innervation of the organ of Corti in the cat. *Ann. Otol. Rhinol. Laryngol.*, 72:660–686.
300. Spoendlin, H. H. (1966): *The Organization of the Cochlear Receptor.* Karger, Basel.
301. Worden, F. G. (1966): Attention and auditory electrophysiology. In: *Progress in Physiological Psychology, Vol. 1,* edited by E. Stellar and J. M. Sprague, pp. 45–116. Academic Press, New York.
302. Dowling, J. E. (1968): Synaptic organization of the frog retina: An electron microscopic analysis comparing the retinas of frogs and primates. *Proc. R. Soc. Lond.* [Biol.], 170:205–228.
303. Lettvin, J. Y., Maturana, H. R., McCulloch, W. S., and Pitts, W. H. (1959): What the frog's eye tells the frog's brain. *Proc. Inst. Radio Engr.*, 47:1940–1951.
304. Maturana, H. R., Lettvin, J. Y., Pitts, W. H., and McCulloch, W. S. (1960): Physiology and anatomy of vision in the frog. *J. Gen. Physiol. (Suppl.)*, 43:129–175.

305. Lettvin, J. Y., Maturana, H. R., Pitts, W. H., and McCulloch, W. S. (1961): Two remarks on the visual system of the frog. In: *Sensory Communication,* edited by W. A. Rosenblith, pp. 757–776. John Wiley & Sons, New York.
306. Brown, K. T., and Murakami, M. (1964): A new receptor potential of the monkey retina with no detectable latency. *Nature,* 201:626–628.
307. Montal, M., and Korenbrat, J. I. (1973): Incorporation of rhodopsin proteolipid into bilayer membranes. *Nature,* 246:219–221.
308. Brown, K. T., and Murakami, M. (1964): Biphasic form of early receptor potential of the monkey retina. *Nature,* 204:739–740.
309. Rushton, W. A. H. (1975): Visual pigments and color blindness. *Sci. Am.,* 232: 64–74.
310. Marks, W. B., Dobelle, W. H., and MacNichol, E. F., Jr. (1964): Visual pigments of single primate cones. *Science,* 143:1181–1183.
311. Graybiel, A. M. (1974): Studies on the anatomical organization of posterior association cortex. In: *The Neurosciences Third Study Program,* edited by F. O. Schmitt and F. G. Worden, pp. 205–214. The MIT Press, Cambridge, Massachusetts.
312. Nansen, F. (1887): The structure and combination of the histological elements of the central nervous system. *Bergens Mus. Aarsberetning,* 1886:27–214.
313. Magoun, H. W. (1950): Caudal and cephalic influences of the brain stem reticular formation. *Physiol. Rev.,* 30:459–474.
314. Gernandt, B. E., Iranyi, M., and Livingston, R. B. (1959): Vestibular influences on spinal mechanisms. *Exp. Neurol.,* 1:248–273.
315. Hensel, H. (1973): Cutaneous thermoreceptors. In: *Handbook of Sensory Physiology, Vol. 2, Somatosensory System,* edited by A. Iggo, pp. 79–110. Springer, Berlin.
316. Livingston, W. K. (1943): *Pain Mechanisms.* Macmillan, New York.
317. Bonica, J. J. (1953): *The Management of Pain.* Lea and Febiger, Philadelphia.
318. Collins, W. F., Nulsen, F. E., and Randt, C. T. (1960): Relation of peripheral nerve fiber size and sensation in man. *Arch. Neurol.,* 3:381–385.
319. Burgess, P. R., and Perl, E. R. (1967): Myelinated afferent fibres responding specifically to noxious stimulation of the skin. *J. Physiol.,* 190:541–562.
320. Perl, E. R. (1968): Myelinated afferent fibres innervating the primate skin and their response to noxious stimuli. *J. Physiol.,* 197:593–615.
321. Melzack, R., and Wall, P. D. (1962): On the nature of cutaneous sensory mechanisms. *Brain,* 85:331–356.
322. Albe-Fessard, D., and Besson, J. M. (1973): Convergent thalamic and cortical projections—the non-specific system. In: *Handbook of Sensory Physiology, Vol. 2, Somatosensory System,* edited by A. Iggo, pp. 489–560. Springer, Berlin.
323. Mehler, W. R. (1962): The anatomy of the so-called "pain tract" in man, an analysis of the course and distribution of the ascending fibers of the fasciculus antero-lateralis. In: *Basic Research in Paraplegia,* edited by J. D. French and R. W. Porter, pp. 26–55. Charles C Thomas, Springfield, Ill.
324. Melzack, R., Stotler, W. A., and Livingston, W. K. (1958): Effects of discrete brainstem lesions in cats on perception of noxious stimulation. *J. Neurophysiol.,* 21:353–367.
325. Bors, E. *Personal communication.*
326. Mitchell, S. W. (1872): *Injuries of Nerves and Their Consequences.* J. Lippincott, Philadelphia.
327. Noordenbos, W. (1959): *Pain.* Elsevier, Amsterdam.
328. Glees, P., Livingston, R. B., and Soler, J. (1951): Die intraspinale Verlauf und die Endigungen der Sensorischen Wurzeln in die Nucleus Gracilis und Cuneatus. *Arch. Psychiatr. Z. Neurol.* 187:190–204.
329. Gordon, G. (1973): The concept of relay nuclei. In: *Handbook of Sensory Physiology, Vol. 2, Somatosensory System,* edited by A. Iggo, pp. 137–150. Springer, Berlin.
330. Guzmán-Flores, C., Buendia, N., Anderson, C., and Lindsley, D. B. (1962): Cortical and reticular influences upon evoked responses in dorsal column nuclei. *Exp. Neurol.,* 5:37–46.

331. Poggio, G. F., and Mountcastle, V. B. (1960): A study of the functional contributions of the lemniscal and spinothalamic systems to somatic sensibility: Central nervous mechanisms in pain. *Bull. Johns Hopkins Hosp.,* 106:266–316.

332. Towe, A. L., and Jabbur, S. J. (1961): Cortical inhibition of neurons in dorsal column nuclei of cat. *J. Neurophysiol.,* 24:488–498.

333. Jabbur, S. J., and Towe, A. L. (1961): Cortical excitation of neurons in dorsal column nuclei of cat, including an analysis of pathways. *J. Neurophysiol.,* 24:499–509.

334. Critchley, M. (1953): *The Parietal Lobes.* Edward Arnold, London.

335. Penfield, W., and Rasmussen, T. (1950): *The Cerebral Cortex of Man, A Clinical Study of Localization of Function.* Macmillan, New York.

336. Woolsey, C. N., and Fairman, D. (1946): Contralateral, ipsilateral and bilateral representation of cutaneous receptors in somatic areas I and II of the cerebral cortex of pig, sheep, and other mammals. *Surgery,* 19:684–702.

337. Woolsey, C. N. (1958): Organization of somatic sensory and motor areas of the cerebral cortex. In: *Biological and Biochemical Bases of Behavior,* edited by H. F. Harlow and C. N. Woolsey, pp. 63–81. University of Wisconsin Press, Madison.

338. Rose, J. E., and Woolsey, C. N. (1958): Cortical connections and functional organization of the thalamic auditory system of the cat. In: *Biological and Biochemical Bases of Behavior,* edited by H. F. Harlow and C. N. Woolsey, pp. 127–150. University of Wisconsin Press, Madison.

339. Werner, G., and Witsel, B. L. (1968): Topology of the body representation in somatosensory area I of primates. *J. Neurophysiol.,* 31:856–869.

340. Powell, T. P. S., and Mountcastle, V. B. (1959): Some aspects of the functional organization of the cortex of the postcentral gyrus of the monkey, a correlation of findings obtained in a single unit analysis with cytoarchitecture. *Bull. Johns Hopkins Hosp.,* 105:133–162.

341. Mountcastle, V. B., and Powell, T. P. S. (1959): Neural mechanisms subserving cutaneous sensibility, with special reference to the role of afferent inhibition in sensory perception and discrimination. *Bull. Johns. Hopkins Hosp.,* 105:201–232.

342. Weiss, T. F. (1964): A model for firing patterns in auditory nerve fibers. *Tech. Report No. 418, Res. Lab. of Elect.,* M.I.T.

343. Kiang, N. Y. S., Watanabe, T., Thomas, E. D., and Clark, L. F. (1962): Stimulus coding in the cat's auditory nerve. *Ann. Otol. Rhinol. Laryngol.,* 71:1009–1026.

344. Katsuki, Y., Suga, N., and Kanno, Y. (1962): II. Neural mechanisms of the peripheral and central auditory system in monkeys. *J. Acoust. Soc. Am.,* 34:1396–1410.

345. Katsuki, Y. (1961): Neural mechanism of auditory sensation in cats. In: *Sensory Communication,* edited by W. A. Rosenblith, pp. 561–583. John Wiley & Sons, New York.

346. Galambos, R., Meyers, R. E., and Sheatz, G. (1961): Extralemniscal activation of auditory cortex in cat. *Am. J. Physiol.,* 200:23–28.

347. Landau, W. M., Goldstein, R., and Kleffner, F. R. (1960): Congenital aphasia, a clinicopathalogical study. *Neurology,* 10:915–921.

348. Jewett, D. L. (1970): Volume conducted potentials in response to auditory stimuli as detected by averaging in the cat. *Electroencephalogr. Clin. Neurophysiol.,* 28:609–618.

349. Jewett, D. L., and Williston, J. S. (1971): Auditory-evolved far fields averaged from the scalp of humans. *Brain,* 94:681–696.

350. Hecox, K., and Galambos, R. (1974): Brain stem auditory evoked responses in human infants and adults. *Arch. Otolaryngol.,* 99:30–33.

351. Galambos, R. (1974): The human auditory evoked response. In: *Sensation and Measurement,* edited by H. R. Moskowitz et al., pp. 215–221. D. Riedel, Dordrecht-Holland.

352. Buchwald, J. S., and Huang, C.-M. (1975): Far-field acoustic response: origins in the cat. *Science,* 189:382–384.

353. Starr, A., and Achor, L. J. (1975): Auditory brainstem responses in neurological diseases. *Arch. Neurol.,* 32:761–768.
354. Starr, A. (1975): Clinical relevance of auditory brainstem responses. In: *Evoked Responses,* edited by J. E. Desmedt. (*In press.*)
355. Starr, A., and Livingston, R. B. (1963): Long-lasting nervous system responses to prolonged sound stimulation, in waking cats. *J. Neurophysiol.,* 26:416–431.
356. Di Giorgio, A. M., and Guilio, L. (1974): Reflessi ocularidi origire otolitica ed influenza del cervalletto. *Boll. Soc. Ital. Biol. Sper.,* 25:145–146.
357. Axelrod, J., Wurtman, R. J., and Snyder, S. H. (1965): Control of hydroxyindole-O-methyltransferase in the rat pineal gland by environmental lighting. *J. Biol. Chem.,* 240:949–954.
358. Moore, R. Y. (1974): Visual pathways and the central neural control of diurnal rhythms. In: *The Neurosciences Third Study Program,* edited by F. O. Schmitt and F. G. Worden, pp. 537–542. The MIT Press, Cambridge, Massachusetts.
359. Stephan, F. K., and Zucker, I. (1972): Rat drinking rhythms, central visual pathways and endocrine factors mediating responsiveness to environmental illumination. *Physiol. Behav.,* 8:315–326.
360. Stephan, F. K., and Zucker, I. (1972): Circadian rhythms in drinking behavior and locomotor activity of rats are eliminated by hypothalamic lesions. *Proc. Natl. Acad. Sci. USA,* 69:1583–1586.
361. Pettigrew, J. D. (1972): The neurophysiology of binocular vision. *Sci. Am.,* 227:84–95.
362. Hubel, D. H., and Wiesel, T. N. (1959): Receptive fields of single neurons in the cat's striate cortex. *J. Physiol.,* 148:547–591.
363. Henry, G. H., Bishop, P. O., and Coombs, J. S. (1969): Inhibitory and subliminal excitatory receptive fields of simple units in cat striate cortex. *Vision Res.,* 9:1289–1296.
364. Julesz, B. (1971): *Foundations of Cyclopean Perception.* University of Chicago Press, Chicago.
365. Hubel, D. H., and Wiesel, T. N. (1962): Receptive fields, binocular interaction and functional architecture in the cat's visual cortex. *J. Physiol.,* 160:106–154.
366. Hubel, D. N., and Wiesel, T. N. (1970): Stereoscopic vision in macaque monkey: cells sensitive to binocular depth in area 18 of the macaque monkey cortex. *Nature,* 225:41–42.
367. Morrell, F. (1967): Electrical signs of sensory coding. In: *The Neurosciences: A Study Program,* edited by G. C. Quarton, T. Melnechuk, and F. O. Schmitt, pp. 452–469. Rockefeller University Press, New York.
368. Johansson, G. (1975): Visual motion perception. *Sci. Am.,* 232:76–88.
369. Hess, W. R. (1932): *Die Methodick der lokalisierten Reizung und Ausschaltung subkortikaler Hirnabschnitte.* Georg Thiene, Leipzig.
370. Scheibel, M. E., and Scheibel, A. B. (1969): Anatomical basis of attention mechanisms in vertebrate brains. In: *The Neurosciences: A Study Program,* edited by G. C. Quarton, T. Melnechuk, and F. O. Schmitt, pp. 577–602. Rockefeller University Press, New York.
371. Allen, W. F. (1932): Formatio reticularis and reticulo-spinal tracts, their visceral functions and possible relationships to tonicity and clonic contractions. *J. Wash. Acad. Sci.,* 22:490–495.
372. Mountcastle, V. B. (1975): The view from within: Pathways to the study of perception. *Johns Hopkins Med. J.,* 136:109–131.

Biological Foundations of Psychiatry,
edited by R. G. Grenell and S. Gabay.
Raven Press, New York © 1976.

Hemispheric Specialization: Implications for Psychiatry

David Galin

Langley Porter Neuropsychiatric Institute, University of California, San Francisco, and the Institute for the Study of Human Consciousness, San Francisco, California 94143

I. INTRODUCTION

The two cerebral hemispheres in humans are specialized for different cognitive functions, and when they are surgically disconnected, they each appear conscious, i.e., two separate conscious minds in one head. Not only are they separate minds, but because of their specialization they are different, not duplicate minds. This conclusion is the most dramatic and most important to come out of all the great volume of studies of commissurotomy patients done in the last decade by R. W. Sperry and his colleagues at the California Institute of Technology; J. E. Bogen, M. Gazzaniga, J. Levy, C. Trevarthen, R. Nebes, H. Gordon, and others. These conclusions are extensively documented (1–11). Bogen (12) has summarized the main propositions very elegantly, and with proper historical perspective, under the title of "Neowiganism":

> The essentials of this theory and its implications were first developed by A. L. Wigan in a book called *The Duality of the Mind* published in 1844. Wigan was first led to his theory by the postmortem observation of a man whom he had known well before the man's death from unrelated causes. At autopsy, one cerebral hemisphere was found to be totally absent. Wigan was not only astounded by this finding, but had the wits to see its meaning: only one hemisphere is required to have a mind or to be a person. Therefore Wigan concluded: If only one cerebrum is required to have a mind, possession of two hemispheres (the normal state) makes possible or perhaps even inevitable the possession of two minds; and however synchronous these two minds may be most of the time, there must inevitably be some occasion when they are discrepant. This provides the anatomical-physiologic basis for that division of self, that internal struggle which is characteristic of so much of mankind's ill health and unhappiness. This magnificent speculation was accorded very little notice at the time. . . . What Wigan did not know (was that) . . . whereas the two hemispheres of a cat or monkey may sustain two duplicate minds, the lateralization typical of man requires that the two minds must *necessarily* be discrepant. "Neowiganism" means that . . . each of us is possessed of two minds which differ in content, possibly even in goals, but most certainly in respect to mode of organization. The evolutionary advantage of having two different minds is obvious; possession of two independent problem solving organs increases mightily the likelihood of a creative solution to a novel problem. At the same time there is an enormous increase in the likelihood of internal conflict. And so we have man, the most innovative of species and at the same time the most at odds with himself.

EEG experiments in our laboratory with normal people have demonstrated lateral specialization in the intact brain (13–15). It is not an artifact caused by the radical surgery or preoperative neurologic disorder. Our study of how these two half-brains cooperate or interfere with each other in normal intact people has just begun. This chapter briefly reviews experiments and clinical observations that have direct implications for psychiatry, and discusses some questions and opportunities for research which arise from them. The purpose of this review is not to "neurologize" psychiatric concepts; it is to suggest that our present understanding of the hemispheric disconnection syndromes and hemispheric specialization can provide a useful framework for developing research and theory.

II. A NEUROPHYSIOLOGICAL CONTEXT FOR UNCONSCIOUS PROCESSES

A. Hemispheric Specialization for Different Cognitive Modes

Our understanding of lateral specialization is based on studies of behavioral deficits produced by unilateral lesions (16–18) and cerebral disconnections (2, 19) and most recently from studies of normal subjects (13–15, 28–40). It is generally agreed that in typical right handers language processes and arithmetic depend primarily on the left hemisphere and that the right hemisphere is particularly specialized for spatial relations and some musical functions.[1] For example right temporal lobectomy produces a severe impairment on visual and tactile mazes; left temporal lesions of equal extent produce little deficit on these tasks, but specifically impair verbal memory. In the "split-brain" patients the left hemisphere is capable of speech, writing, and calculation, but is severely limted in problems involving spatial relationships and novel figures. The right hemisphere has use of only a few words[2] and can perform simple addition only up to 10, but it can easily perform tasks involving complex spatial relations and musical patterns.

This lateralization of cognitive function has been demonstrated in normal subjects with EEG techniques (13, 14, 28, 29), evoked potentials, (15, 30–35), and with studies of left/right visual field differences in perception and reaction time (36–40). For example, we have examined the EEGs of normal subjects performing verbal and spatial tasks to determine whether there were differences in activity between the two hemispheres (13–15). We found a relatively higher alpha amplitude (a measure of idling) over the right hemisphere during the verbal tasks, and relatively more alpha over the left hemisphere during the spatial tasks. In other words the hemisphere expected to be less engaged in the task has more of the idling rhythm. Other investigators have confirmed our observations on changes in alpha asymmetry in studies that contrasted verbal and musical tasks (28, 29). We also found changes in the asymmetry of flash-evoked potentials as subjects switched from verbal to spatial tasks (15). Other laboratories using the evoked potential method have reported that responses to speech sounds were larger in the left hemisphere than in the right (33) and that responses to complex visual forms were larger on the right than on the left (35). Another large group of studies with normal subjects has made use of the different hemispheric projections of the left and right visual fields and has found for example that the left and right hemispheres have opposite superiorities in

---

[1] Here and in the following discussions I am referring to the lateralization characteristics of right-handers. The situation with left-handers is more complex, and has been summarized very well by Hécaen and Ajuriaguerra (20); see also 21–24.

[2] Very little expressive language, comprehension of syntax at about the level of a 2 year old (25, 26). See Smith (27) for a report of modest recovery or relearning following left hemispherectomy.

discriminative reaction times to stimuli such as letters and faces (39, 40).

It is important to emphasize that what most characterizes the hemispheres is not that they are specialized to work with different types of material (the left with words and the right with spatial forms); rather, each hemisphere is specialized for a different cognitive style, the left for an analytical, logical mode for which words are an excellent tool, and the right for a holistic, gestalt mode, which happens to be particularly suitable for spatial relations, as well as music. The difference in cognitive style is explicitly described in a recent paper by Levy, Trevarthen, and Sperry (8) (see also refs. 9, 42):

> Recent commissurotomy studies have shown that the two disconnected hemispheres, working on the same task, may process the same sensory information in distinctly different ways, and that the two modes of mental operation, involving spatial synthesis for the right and temporal analysis for the left, show indications of mutual antagonism (41). The propensity of the language hemisphere to note analytical details in a way that facilitates their description in langauge seems to interfere with the perception of an over-all Gestalt, leaving the left hemisphere 'unable to see the wood for the trees.' This interference effect suggested a rationale for the evolution of lateral specialization . . .

B. The Hemispheric Disconnection Syndrome

Sperry et al. (1) have summarized the hemispheric disconnection syndrome as follows:

> The most remarkable effect of sectioning the cerebral commissures continues to be the apparent lack of change with respect to ordinary behavior. (They) . . . exhibit no gross alterations of personality, intellect or overt behavior two years after operation. Individual mannerisms, conversation and bearing, temperament, strength, vigor and coordination are all largely intact and seem much as before surgery. Despite this outward appearance of general normality in ordinary behavior . . . specific tests indicate functional disengagement of the right and left hemispheres with respect to nearly all cognitive and other psychic activities. Learning and memory are found to proceed quite independently in each separated hemisphere. Each hemisphere seems to have its own conscious sphere for sensation, perception, ideation, and other mental activities and the whole inner realm of gnostic experience of the one is cut off from the corresponding experiences of the other hemisphere—with only a few exceptions . . .

To understand the method of testing and interviewing each half of the brain separately, two points of functional anatomy must be kept in mind. The first is that since language functions (speech, writing) are mediated predominantly by the left hemisphere in most people, the disconnected right hemisphere cannot express itself verbally. The second point is that the neural pathways carrying information from one side of the body and one-half of the visual field cross over and connect only with the opposite side of the brain. This means that sensations in the right hand and images in the right visual space will be projected almost entirely to the *left* hemisphere. Similarly, the major motor output is crossed, and the left hemisphere controls mainly the movements of the right hand.[3] Therefore, patients with the corpus callosum sectioned can describe or answer questions about objects placed in their right hands, or pictures flashed to the right visual field with a tachistoscope, but are unable to give correct verbal reports for test items presented to the left hand or the left visual field (they will in fact, often confabulate). However, the mute right hemisphere can indicate its experience through various nonverbal responses, as for example, by manual selection of the proper object from an array.

C. Dyscopia versus Dysgraphia

Dr. Joseph Bogen, one of the surgeons who performed the split-brain operations, has published some results from drawing tests that he conducted with his patients after the operation (3). These tests illustrate in a simple way the basic difference between the two hemispheres in their capacities for holistic processes.

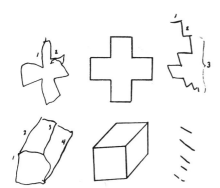

FIG. 1. Drawing test by a patient who had undergone the split-brain operation. Drawings were made by the right hand (right) and left hand (left) of the model (center). (From Bogen, ref. 3.)

Figure 1 shows two geometric designs, a cross and a cube, which Bogen asked the patients to copy, and samples of their productions with the right and left hands. The copies with the left hand (controlled by the right hemisphere) are fairly good representations of the model, although the draughtsmanship is crude. The essence of the form is preserved. The patient was very reluctant to try the task with his right hand (controlled by the left hemisphere) protesting that it was too difficult, that he was never good at drawing, etc., although he had just done the left-hand copies without hesitation. The right hand's copy of the cross preserves the *elements* of the form (a sequence of connected right angles) but the essence of the form, the con-

---

[3] Ipsilateral motor control is weak and variable; it is minimal for fine movement and distal control, but improves postoperatively in some cases, confounding interpretations of tests based on lateralized output.

FIG. 2. Drawing by another split-brain patient of the same models shown in Fig. 1. Right- and left-hand drawings are also as in Fig. 1. (From Bogen, ref 3.)

figuration or gestalt, is lost. The attempt to copy the cube with the right hand shows the same phenomenon; the most basic elements, the lines, are given without the articulation that constitutes the form. Figure 2 shows similar examples from another patient.

In contrast to the successful left-handed performance on the drawing tests, these patients were unable to write the date or the day of the week from dictation with their left hands. With their right hands, which could not copy forms, they could easily write spontaneously or to dictation. This lateral dissociation between copying and writing showed very little recovery in those patients who had a normal childhood neurological development. It was less persistent in those brain injuries dated from birth to early childhood, presumably because early injury leads to compensation by other brain structures, and less lateral specialization. Figure 3 shows characteristic disability in the writing and drawing of a patient 5 years after commissurotomy (3).

> With his left hand he drew what looks as if it might be a "P" and then stopped and shook his head. He was asked what this was and said, "I was trying to write my name (Bill)." He was then asked to write something with his right hand and he wrote the sentence in the upper right hand corner. He was then asked to attempt again with his left hand and produced only the small scrawl which is seen in the upper left hand corner. He was then shown a model of the Greek cross; he copied it with his left hand. The arrow which was added later indicates that he started at the top of the figure and drew the entire

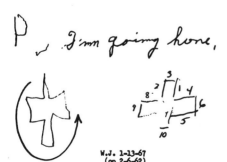

FIG. 3. Sample of the drawing test by a third split-brain patient. Also of right- and left-handed writing ability. (From Bogen, ref. 3.) See text.

figure with a single continuous line. He was then asked to copy the same model wtih his right hand; he drew the strokes in the order indicated. He finished only the first six strokes; he was then urged to continue and he added the seventh. When persuaded to add some more, he put in the concluding three strokes and then stopped. When asked if he was done, he said, "Yes."

Bogen's description highlights the difference in the processes by which the two hands copy the Greek cross. The left hand executes the figure in a smooth continuous motion; it is a gestalt. The right hand, which had shown some improvement in the 5 years since surgery, proceeded part by part, as indicated by the sequence of the strokes.

D. Dissociation of Experience

The dissociation between the experiences of the two disconnected hemispheres is sometimes very dramatic. Sperry and his associates have photographed some illustrative incidents. One film segment shows a female patient being tested with a tachistoscope as described above. In the series of neutral geometrical figures being presented at random to the right and left fields, a nude pinup was included and flashed to the right (nonverbal) hemisphere. The girl blushes and giggles. Sperry asks, "What did you see?" She answers, "Nothing, just a flash of light," and giggles again, covering her mouth with her hand. "Why are you laughing then?" asks Sperry, and she laughs again and says, "Oh, Dr. Sperry, you have some machine!" The episode is very suggestive; if one did not know her neurosurgical history one might see this as a clear example of perceptual defense and think that she was "repressing" the perception of the conflictful sexual material—even her final response (a socially acceptable nonsequitur) was convincing (see also ref. 6, pp. 723–733, especially p. 732).

A different patient was filmed performing a block design task; he is trying to match a colored geometric design with a set of painted blocks. The film shows the left hand (right hemisphere) quickly carrying out the task. Then the experimenter disarranges the blocks and the right hand (left hemisphere) is given the task; slowly and with great apparent indecision it arranges the pieces. In trying to match a corner of the design the right hand corrects one of the blocks, and then shifts it again, apparently not realizing it was correct: the viewer sees the left hand dart out, grab the block to restore it to the correct position—and then the arm of the experimenter reaches over and pulls the intruding left hand off-camera.

E. Psychiatric Implications

There is a compelling formal similarity between these dissociation phenomena seen in the commissurotomy patients and some phenomena of interest to clinical psychiatry; for example, according to Freud's early "topographical" model of the mind, repressed mental contents functioned in a separate realm that was inaccessible to conscious recall or verbal interrogation, functioning according to its own rules, developing and pursuing its own goals, affecting the viscera and insinuating itself in the stream of ongoing consciously directed behavior (43, 44).

In later psychoanalytic models, the division of the mental apparatus was based on differences in the formal organization of thought and the control of emotional energy (primary versus secondary processes), rather than primarily on the basis of accessibility to conscious awareness (44–46). According to Klein (47) these different formulations have never been adequately synthesized,[4] and several theorists and experimentalists (47, 50–57) have continued to explore the interactions between (a) cognitive organization, (b) affective controls, and (c) variations in states of consciousness.

Freud had reluctantly abandoned the attempt to relate the functioning of the parts of the mental apparatus to specific anatomical locations because the neurology of the time was insufficient (44, pp. 107–109). It may be useful to reconsider these questions now, in the context of our present understanding of the hemispheric disconnection syndromes and the specialization of the two hemispheres for different cognitive modes.

Certain aspects of right-hemisphere functioning are congruent with the mode of cognition psychoanalysts have termed primary process, the form of thought that Freud originally assigned to the system Ucs (44, p. 119; compare particularly with ref. 58, p. 53–55).

1. The right hemisphere primarily uses a nonverbal mode of representation, presumably images: visual, tactile, kinesthetic, auditory etc. (3, 4, also 8, pp. 74–75).

2. The right hemisphere reasons by a nonlinear mode of association rather than by syllogistic logic; its solutions to problems are based on multiple converging determinants rather than a single causal chain (3, 4, 8, 9). It is much superior to the left in part-whole relations, e.g., grasping the concept of the whole from just a part.

3. The right hemisphere is less involved with perception of time and sequence than the left hemisphere (59–64).

4. There is considerable evidence that the right hemisphere does possess words, but the words are not organized for use in propositions (see discussion by Bogen, ref. 4, pp. 146–147; also ref. 25). For example, a patient with a total left hemispherectomy may be able to sing lyrics of a song, but not be able to use the same words in a sentence (27, 65). Therefore, when the right hemisphere did express itself in language, we might expect its use of words to reflect its characteristic holistic style. Because it deals more effectively with

---

[4] Although Arlow and Brenner (45) claim the "structural theory" is in direct conflict with the "topographical theory" and should replace it rather than be reconciled with it, others disagree (48, 49, 52).

complex patterns taken as a whole than with the individual parts taken serially, we might expect metaphors, puns, double-entendre, and rebus, i.e., *word-pictures*. The elements in these verbal constructions do not have fixed single definitions (are not clearly bounded), but depend on context, and can shift in meaning when seen as parts of a new pattern. This is the sort of language that appears in dreams and slips of the tongue extensively described in *The Psychopathology of Everyday Life* (66). The right hemisphere is also particularly adept in the recognition of faces (67, 68) which carry much of the meaning in informal and colloquial speech (cf. Brenner's example, 58, p. 55, "He's a great one"; see also 69, 70 for appearance of poetry following an aphasiogenic left-hemisphere lesion).

When the two hemispheres are surgically disconnected the mental process of each one is inaccessible to deliberate conscious retrieval from the point of view of the other. However, the operation does not affect them so symmetrically with respect to overt behavior; Sperry and his collaborators have found that "in general, the postoperative behavior of (the commissurotomy patients) has been dominated by the major (left) hemisphere . . ." except in tasks for which the right hemisphere is particularly specialized (6, 8). In these respects there seems to be a clear parallel between the functioning of the isolated right hemisphere and mental processes that are repressed, unconscious, and unable to directly control behavior.

Anecdotal observations of the patients suggest that the isolated right hemisphere can sustain emotional responses and goals divergent from the left (e.g., assaulting with one hand and protecting with the other), although how often this occurs is questionable (7, p. 107; see also 11). However, systematic experiments with split-brain monkeys do provide direct support for the possibility of conflicting motivations (71, 72):

> The split hemispheres can experience reinforcing events independently . . . at the moment one hemisphere is experiencing a particular stimulus as an effective reinforcer the other hemisphere is either oblivious of this assigned value or free to respond negatively to its own experience (71) . . . the probability that a hemisphere will control a response is directly related to its history of obtaining reinforcers. The hemisphere which is most successful in earning reinforcement comes to dominate.

All of the above considerations lead us to examine the hypothesis that in normal, intact people mental events in the right hemisphere can become disconnected functionally from the left hemisphere (by inhibition of neuronal transmission across the corpus callosum and other cerebral commissures) and can continue a life of their own. This hypothesis suggests a neurophysiological mechanism for at least some instances of repression and an anatomical locus for some of the unconscious mental contents.

This hypothesis requires that parts of the transmission from one hemisphere to the other can be selectively and reversibly blocked. This does not seem implausible; selective gating has already been demonstrated in the central control of sensory input for all sensory modalities (73–75). Stimulation of callosal fibers can inhibit as well as excite neuronal discharge in the contralateral cortex (76–78); noting these reports, Bogen (5) proposed ". . . certain kinds of left-hemisphere activity may directly suppress certain kinds of right-hemisphere action. Or they may prevent access to the left hemisphere of the products of right hemisphere activity." Presumably there is reciprocity; right-hemisphere processes could interfere with or suppress certain left-hemisphere activity.

F. How Integrated Are the Two Hemispheres Under Normal Conditions?

We do not know what is the usual relation between the two hemispheres in normal adults, but we can speculate on several arrangements. One possibility is that they operate in alternation, i.e., taking turns, depending on situational demands. When one hemisphere is "on" it inhibits the other. A variant of this relationship might be that the dominating hemisphere makes use of one or more of the subsystems of the other hemisphere, inhibiting the rest. The inhibition thus may be only partial, suppressing enough of the subordinate hemisphere as to render it incapable of sustaining its own plan of action. We have some observations of intact people consistent with this view from EEG studies (13, 14), lateral eye movement studies (79–82), and studies of behavioral interference (23, 24, 83–86, see also ref. 3, p. 102 for evidence of this kind of inhibition in cases of lesions). Such a relation of reciprocal inhibition of cognitive systems may be based on the left/right reciprocal inhibition so characteristic of the sensorimotor systems around which the whole brain is built. Another variant is the one hypothesized above; one hemisphere dominates overt behavior, but can only disconnect rather than totally inhibit (disrupt) the other hemisphere, which remains independently conscious. The fourth possible condition, in which the two hemispheres are fully active and integrated with each other, is the condition that Bogen associates with creativity, man's highest functioning (5); unfortunately this does not seem to occur very often. In fact he suggests that one of the reasons that the commissurotomy patients appear so normal to casual observation is because the activities of daily life do not demand much integration of holistic and analytic thought.

If the usual condition then is either alternation between the two modes, or parallel but independent consciousness with one of them dominating overt behavior, what factors determine which hemisphere will be "on"? Which will gain control of the shared functions and dominate overt behavior? There are two factors suggested by experiments with split-brain monkeys and humans. One could be called "resolution by speed"; the hemisphere that solves the problem first gets to the output channel first. This seems the most likely explanation for the observations in the human patients that "when a hemisphere is intrinsically better equipped to handle some task, it is also easier for that hemisphere to dominate the motor pathways (8, 26).

For example, Sperry and his collaborators have found that, although "in general the post-operative behavior of (the commissurotomy patients) has been dominated by the major (left) hemisphere . . . ", the right hemisphere dominated behavior in a facial recognition task (8). Recognition of faces requires a perception of the gestalt and is relatively resistant to analytic verbal description (67, 87). Therefore it could be anticipated that the disconnected right hemisphere might be better than the left at recognizing faces. Different photographs were projected simultaneously to the left and right visual fields of commissurotomy patients. When the patients were asked to select the one they had seen from a row of samples they pointed to the face that had been shown to the right hemisphere.

A second factor determining which hemisphere gets control could be called "resolution by motivation"; the one who cares more about the outcome preempts the output. This is demonstrated in a series of ingenious experiments with split-brain monkeys by Michael Gazzaniga (71, 72). Each hemisphere was taught a visual discrimination task; two designs were displayed in front of the monkey, and if he pressed the correct one he was rewarded with a drink of fruit juice. Optical apparatus was used so that different cues could be projected to each hemisphere at the same time from the same apparent location in space. In this way it could be arranged so that both hemispheres saw the correct cue in the same place (calling for the same response) or in different places, calling for competing responses. After each hemisphere had independently learned the discrimination and was picking the correct cue nearly every time, the monkey was tested in a conflict situation, with each hemisphere seeing the correct cue in a different place. All of the animals showed a clear dominance of one of the hemispheres in this situation, i.e., they responded consistently with the correct response for that hemisphere. Then the hemispheres were again trained separately, but with different reward conditions; the cue for the nondominant hemisphere was still rewarded every time it was selected, but the cue for the dominant hemisphere was rewarded only once every six times it was selected. When tested again in the conflict situation the dominance was changed; the monkey consistently chose the cue which was correct for the previously nondominant hemisphere. Gazzaniga concludes: "Cerebral dominance in monkeys is quite flexible and subject to the effects of reinforcement. . . . The hemisphere which is most successful in earning reinforcement comes to dominate." I am proposing that this may apply to intact humans as well. As the left hemisphere develops its language capability in the 2nd and 3rd year of life it gains a great advantage over the right hemisphere in manipulating its environment and securing reinforcements. It seems likely to me that this is the basis for the suzerainty of the left hemisphere in overt behavior in situations of conflict with the right hemisphere.

G. Factors Contributing to a Unity of Consciousness

In spite of their different modes of organization, the two hemispheres are usually not in conflict. There are many unifying factors besides the cerebral commissures, which may also account for the surprisingly ordinary appearance of the commissurotomy patients outside of special laboratory test situations. Sperry et al. (1) describe some of the unifying influences:

> Some of these are very obvious . . . like the fact that these two separate mental spheres have only one body so they always frequent the same places, meet the same people, see and do the same things all the time and thus are bound to have a great overlap of common, almost identical, experience. The unity of the eyeball as well as the conjugate movements of the eyes causes both hemispheres to automatically center on, focus on, and hence probably attend to, the same items in the visual field all the time."

The sense of personal unity is a compelling subjective experience, and may derive in part from these factors. Sir Charles Sherrington (88) states it elegantly:

> This self is a unity . . . it regards itself as one, others treat it as one, it is addressed as one, by a name to which it answers. The Law and the State schedule it as one. It and they identify it with a body which is considered by it and them to belong to it integrally. In short, unchallenged and unargued conviction assumes it to be one. The logic of grammar endorses this by a pronoun in the singular. All its diversity is merged in oneness.

But we have good reason to believe that the experience of mental unity is to some extent an illusion, resulting in fact from exactly the conventions of language and law that Sherrington cites. "The strength of this conviction (of unity) is no assurance of its truth" (4, p. 156 ff). One of the most striking features of the commissurotomy syndrome is that the patients (at least the hemisphere that can be interviewed) do not experience their obvious duality; they do not notice anything missing after the operation (1):

> These people do not complain spontaneously about a perceptual division or incompleteness in their visual experience. . . . One can compare the visual experiences of each hemisphere to that of the hemianopic patient who, following accidental destruction of one visual cortex, or even hemispherectomy, may not recognize the loss of one half of visual space until this is pointed out in formal tests.
>
> There is no indication that the dominant mental system of the left hemisphere is concerned about or even aware of the presence of the minor system under most ordinary conditions except quite indirectly as, for example, through occasional responses triggered from the minor side. As one patient remarked immediately after seeing herself make a left-hand response of this kind, "Now I know it wasn't me that did that!"

H. Conditions Favoring the Development of Separate Streams of Consciousness

There are several ways in which the two hemispheres of an ordinary person could begin to function as if they had been surgically disconnected, and decrease their exchange of information.

The first way is by active inhibition of information transfer because of conflict. Imagine the effect on a child when his mother presents one message verbally, but quite another with her facial expression and body language; "I am doing it because I love you, dear," says the words, but "I hate you and will destroy you" says the face. Each hemisphere is exposed to the same sensory input, but because of their relative specializations, they each emphasize only one of the messages. The left will attend to the verbal cues because it cannot extract information from the facial gestalt efficiently; the right will attend to the nonverbal cues because it cannot easily understand the words (8). Effectively a different input has been delivered to each hemisphere, just as in the laboratory experiments in which a tachistoscope is used to present different pictures to the left and right visual fields. I offer the following conjecture: In this situation the two hemispheres might decide on opposite courses of action; the left to approach, and the right to flee. Because of the high stakes involved each hemisphere might be able to maintain its consciousness and resist the inhibitory influence of the other side. The left hemisphere seems to win control of the output channels most of the time (6), but if the left is not able to "turn off" the right completely it may settle for disconnecting the transfer of the conflicting information from the other side. The connections between hemispheres are relatively weak compared to the connections within hemispheres (5) and it seems likely that each hemisphere treats the weak contralateral input in the same way in which people in general treat the odd discrepant observation that does not fit with the mass of their beliefs; first we ignore it, and then if it is insistent, we actively avoid it (89).

The mental process in the right hemisphere, cut off in this way from the left hemisphere consciousness, which is directing overt behavior, may nevertheless continue a life of its own. The memory of the situation, the emotional concomitants, and the frustrated plan of action all may persist, affecting subsequent perception and forming the basis for expectations and evaluations of future input.

But active inhibition arising from conflicting goals is not the only way to account for a lack of communication between the two hemispheres, and a consequent divergence of consciousness. In the simplest case, because of their special modes of organization and special areas of competence, the knowledge that one hemisphere possesses may not translate well into the language of the other. For example parts of the experience of attending a symphony concert are not readily expressed in words, and the concept "Democracy requires informed participation" is hard to convey in images.

What may be transmitted in such cases may be only the conclusion as to action and not the details on which the evaluation was based.

I. Defensive Maneuvers and Modes of Representation of Thought

Horowitz (57) has proposed a model for defensive maneuvers based on interactions between different modes of representation of ideas. His two main categories, an "image" mode and a "lexical" or verbal mode, can to some extent be related to right and left hemisphere processes.[5]

Horowitz stresses the distinction between thought form (e.g., image versus lexical) and thought organization (e.g., primary versus secondary process). Failure to make this distinction has led to erroneous assumptions. For example regressive, concrete, and primary process thinking often occurs in the form of visual images. "This frequent occurrence of image form with regressive content organization leads to tacit assumptions such as (1) primary process thought is represented in images and secondary process thought is represented in words; (2) thought in images is more primitive than thought in words; or (3) thought in images is concretistic and thought in words is abstract. Such assumptions are unwarranted collapses of differing categories."

However, each mode of representation does have "intrinsic organizational tendencies" that make it most appropriate for the expression (or concealing) of various contents. According to Horowitz, images are particularly suited to express the immediate quality and intensity of "complicated affective states which are hard to articulate, such as the patient's sense of psychic disintegration." He also suggests that at least in some persons censorship operates less keenly over images than over lexical representation. He cites attempts by Freud, Jung, and Kubie "to use this property of image formation to skirt defensive processes and gain access to repressed mental contents," by instructing patients to think in images rather than in words. He also notes that emotional responses to images tend to be greater than to purely lexical representations of the object names. "Ferenczi attempted to use this to obtain more emotional insight in obsessional patients, demanding that they visualize their memories and fantasies."

The strength of Horowitz's formulation is that it suggests very explicit designations of the cognitive processes which make up a defensive maneuver. He proposes that defenses operate by controlling the entry and exit of information from one mode of representation to another (57):

---

[5] The third category is an "enactive" mode, in which movements, postures, or patterns of muscle tension express an intention, an attitude, or a memory. Horowitz does not make much use of this category in the development of his model, and it seems to me that such proprioceptive representations could be subsumed under the category of images. His three categories are closely related to Bruner's (90), but instead of Bruner's emphasis on the abstract-concrete dimension, Horowitz emphasises the different qualities that these modes of representation give to conscious experience.

Various types of control at boundaries could accomplish any defensive aim. For example, inhibition of entry into *any* system of representation would accomplish *repression* if the information was internal (e.g. memory), or *denial* if the information was external (e.g. perceivable). *Isolation* could be accomplished by inhibition of translation between one system and another. For example, a warded-off idea or affect that gained representation as an image would be inhibited from translation to lexical representation. This maneuver would reduce conceptual meanings or implications and hence lower emotional response.

In the development of these ideas Horowitz is led to propose an elaboration of Freud's topographical model of the mind, but without going so far as to suggest neuroanatomical referents (57):

> Each mode constitutes a way in which information can be represented in conscious experience . . . some memories are multiply coded. They may be transformed into conscious experience in any system of representation or in several modes simultaneously, whatever best suits the problem at hand.
>
> Some memories are not multiply coded. When they are activated they will gain conscious status only in a specific mode, even if this modal system is not the major form of current conscious experience. A traumatic perception, a primal scene for example, may be quickly repressed. If repression was rapid, the primal scence information was represented in consciousness mainly as visual or auditory images. The information out-of-consciousness is therefore coded in a form that will gain consciousness only as visual or auditory images. The repression has interrupted translation to other modes . . . these considerations suggest the elaboration of the topographic point of view from the systems conscious, preconscious, and unconscious to such heirarchies within separable systems for representation. A given set of ideas and feelings may be functionally conscious in one mode of representation, functionally preconscious in another, and functionally unconscious in a third.

This formulation is consistent with the hypothesis that I suggested previously; if mental processes of the right hemisphere were functionally disconnected from the left, they could be conscious from the point of view of the right and unconscious from the point of view of the left.

Expanding Horowitz's model to incorporate some neuroanatomical referents does not require that the lexical and image modes be exclusively assigned to left and right hemisphere processes. Each hemisphere clearly has some capacity in each mode, and the differences appear to be in the relative predominance of one mode or the other.

III. OPPORTUNITIES FOR RESEARCH

In the preceding sections, I have reviewed some of the literature on hemispheric specialization and the commissurotomy syndrome. I have proposed that in intact people the cognitive specialization of the two hemispheres can lead to the development of separate realms of awareness. I believe that this can provide a useful framework for thinking about the interaction of cognitive structures, defensive maneuvers, and variations in states of consciousness. In the following discussions, reports from several other areas that support this approach or that provide opportunities for testing its usefulness in clinical and laboratory research are reviewed.

A. Hemispheric Specialization and the Expression of Unconscious Processes

After the two hemispheres in man or monkey are surgically disconnected, one side tends to dominate the behavior (6, 8, 72). In the human cases, the left hemisphere usually has preemptive control over the main stream of body activity as well as of propositional speech. If repression in normal intact people is to some extent subserved by a functional disconnection of right hemisphere mental processes, we might expect to see the expression of unconscious ideation through whatever output modes are not preempted by the left hemisphere.

1. *Somatic and autonomic expression.* One possibility for expression is through somatic representations, psychosomatic disorders, and somatic delusions. We might expect these symptoms to show a predominance on the left side of the body because of the crossing of the sensorimotor pathways. In Ferenczi's paper on hysterical stigmata, he reports just this in a discussion of a case of left hemianesthesia (91, see also ref. 92):

> One half of the body is insensitive in order that it shall be adapted for the representation of unconscious fantasies, and that 'the right hand shall not know what the left hand doeth.' I derive support for this conception from the consideration of the difference between right and left. It struck me that in general the hemianesthetic stigma occurs more frequently on the left than on the right; this is emphasized too in a few textbooks. I recalled that the left half of the body is *a priori* more accessible to unconscious impulses than the right, which, in consequence of the more powerful attention-excitation of this more active and more skillful half of the body, is better protected against influences from the unconscious. It is possible that—in right-handed people—the sensational sphere for the left side shows from the first a certain predisposition for unconscious impulses, so that it is more easily robbed of its normal functions and placed at the service of unconscious libidinal fantasies.

Unfortunately, Ferenczi provides no quantitative documentation for his assertion of the prevalence of left-sided hysterical symptoms and this report must be considered an opportunity for research rather than support for our hypothesis.

Another channel for somatic expression of right hemisphere attitudes is the autonomic nervous system. In studies of normal humans, Varni et al. (93) concluded, "Asymmetry of autonomic activity is typical rather than atypical." The cerebrum participates extensively in visceral control (94, 95) and asymmetrical cerebral activity may be reflected through asymmetrical autonomic activity (96).

Studies of autonomic activity fall into two classes; those in which the autonomic response is used merely as an indicator of some CNS process that is the main focus of interest (such as "attention" or "anxiety"), and those in which the autonomic variable itself is the focus of interest, such as blood pressure or heart rate in studies of cardiovascular regulation. In the indicator category, autonomic activity may be even more useful than our EEG alpha asymmetry measure as a sign of lateral cerebral specialization (13–15), because the EEG can sample only those areas on the dorsal convexity of the brain. The autonomic variables probably reflect activity in just those areas of the brain that are not reached by the scalp EEG; the orbital and cingulate cortex, and the deep medial structures of the temporal lobe such as the hippocampus and amygdala (94, 95). If a person is presented with stimulus material from an area of known conflict, asymmetry in skin conductance responses or digital blood flow might indicate that the two hemispheres had different affective reactions to the material. We are currently pursuing experiments along this line.

Consideration of left/right asymmetry may be useful for the second category of research too, where the autonomic variable is of interest in itself rather than as an "indicator." There is some evidence of lateral specialization in visceral control just as in the realm of cognition. For example, we know that the right vagus affects primarily the heart rate, whereas the left vagus affects primarily the strength of contraction, and hence systolic pressure (97). Similar asymmetry has been shown for the sympathetic innervation of the heart (98, 99). (To my knowledge, there are no reports concerning the possibility of functional asymmetries in the abdominal vagus or sympathetics.) If this lateral specialization in visceral control is extensive it may help in explaining psychosomatic symptom choice, e.g., hypertension versus tachycardia or dysrhythmia. Just as there appear to be individual differences in cognitive style, with a predominance of the mode of the left or right hemisphere (100–103), so there may be a preferred visceral mode. We might expect those psychosomatic symptoms that are the expression of unconscious right hemisphere processes to appear in the right hemisphere visceral mode, as the stigma of hysteria are alleged to appear in the left side of the body (91).

2. *Dreams.* In periods of inactivity the right hemisphere might seize the opportunity to express itself, as in daydreams, which occur during pauses in the stream of waking behavior, and in dreams at night. Freud called dreams the "royal road to the unconscious." Is there any link between the right hemisphere and dreams? Is there any evidence that the two hemispheres do not contribute symmetrically to dreams?

The mode of cognition in dreaming is usually of the "primary process" type; mainly nonverbal, image representations, with nonsyllogistic logic, and violations of ordinary temporal sequencing. The parallel between aspects of right hemisphere mentation and primary process thinking has been detailed in Sec. II E. of this paper.

Humphrey and Zangwill (104) described three patients who spontaneously reported cessation of dreaming following posterior brain injuries. All three had left homonymous hemianopsia indicating injury to the right hemisphere visual pathways. Impaired visual imagery in the waking state was also found. They cite four other cases in older neurological literature of depression of dreaming and waking visual imagery, usually associated with right parieto-occipital lesions. Bogen observed that following section of the corpus callosum, several patients reported that they no longer had any dreams, in contrast to frequent vivid dreaming before the operation (4). One interpretation of this observation is that since the report of nondreaming was made by the left (verbal) hemisphere, which no longer had access to the right hemisphere's experience, the right (nonverbal) hemisphere may still be enjoying its dreams.

Austin (105) studied dream reports of people classified as divergent and convergent thinkers (convergent types are those who excel at rational analysis but do relatively poorly on open-ended tests requiring mental fluency and imaginativeness). Convergers tend to specialize in the physical sciences and divergers tend toward the arts. These "types" are consistent with the cognitive specializations of the left and right hemispheres (4). Austin found that divergers were much more likely to report dreams when awakened in a REM period, and that when convergers did report dreams they were much shorter than the dreams of the divergers. Austin interprets this finding in a manner similar to the interpretation of the reports of loss of dreams by Bogen's "split-brain" patients: the convergers are having the dreams, but are not able to recall them. In this case the failure to recall is not because of a lesion but because of what Austin calls their "intellectual bias" against "the emotional and nonrational, which reinforces their capacity for logical construction at the expense of combinatory play."

In our laboratory we are currently looking for direct evidence on whether or not the right hemisphere is more actively engaged in dream cognition than the left, by studying the EEG asymmetry in REM sleep. In the enormous body of EEG studies on sleep and dreaming, there has been almost no attention given to the question of hemispheric asymmetry in the EEG patterns characterizing the stages of sleep or to the possibility that the two hemispheres make different contributions to the mental activity of sleep. The analysis of the neurological mechanisms relating to sleep have usually been directed toward the vertical organization of the CNS: brainstem mechanisms interacting with cerebral mechanisms. The additional complication of the lateral specialization of the cerebrum for different cognitive modes which is superimposed on this vertical system has not yet been studied.

B. Hemispheric Differences in Coping Strategies and Affective Reactions

1. *Denial of illness.* Anosognosia is the term most commonly used to refer to the condition in which a patient with a gross neurological deficit (a hemiplegia or a hemianopia) is unaware of his disability, shows an attitude

of indifference, or frankly denies it. It is also variously reported as "la douce indifference" (106), "la belle indifference" (107), and "anosodiaphoria" (109). Critchley describes the range of this fascinating and frequent symptom as follows (109):

> . . . hemiplegics may show a diversity of mental attitudes towards their disability. One patient may apparently be unaware of the fact of immobility. Or he may grudgingly admit to some mild degree of disability and then proceed to advance some inadequate excuse. . . . Or again, a hemiplegic patient may stoutly deny the fact that he is paralysed . . . he may declare that he is moving his limbs when he is not. He may deny the ownership of the paralysed limb. Nay, more; he may even proclaim that the limbs belong to some other person, real or imaginary, alive or dead.
>
> Discussion still reigns nevertheless as to the meaning of these facts. Do they, for example, apply particularly to the consequences of disease of the non-dominant hemisphere? . . . Are they but arresting instances of a general underlying tendency to avoid looking unpleasant facts in the face—illustrating in this way the 'denial syndrome' of Weinstein and Kahn (110)? We must admit that while the problems are not yet wholly settled, we cannot avoid noting the frequency with which such patients display a disability of the non-dominant (right) hemisphere . . .

These and related symptoms are discussed in detail in his chapter "Disorders of the Body Image" (111). He presents the indifference reaction as a simple extension of the unilateral spatial neglect, or imperception, which is one of the commonest signs of parietal disease (111, pp. 226ff, 340ff, 396), and which is also demonstrable in animals (112). However, according to Weinstein and Kahn (110), in the human cases anosognosia may be due to psychosocial factors such as social attitudes toward illness or the symbolic significance of the disability, rather than due to a specific brain lesion. In their view the indifference is a motivated reaction to the deficit, which in its more florid form appears as denial. They interpreted the euphoric reaction as just another variety of the denial reaction, the particular type depending on the defensive character style of the premorbid personality. However, they too agree that anosognosia is much more common following right hemisphere lesions than left (4.5 to 1 in their series). We are thus lead to the conclusion that denial is a characteristic way for the intact left hemisphere to cope with a right hemisphere lesion. This is consistent with the model proposed in the previous sections; the denial could be sustained by an inhibition of information transfer across the corpus callosum from the damaged right side.

Is there a coping strategy or emotional reaction that is characteristic following left hemisphere injury? In a recent study, Gainotti (107, 108) reported on 150 cases of unilateral cerebral lesions. He compared the incidence of the indifference reaction and the "catastrophic reaction" described by Kurt Goldstein. The incidence of catastrophic reactions was 62% with left lesions, only 10% with right lesions. In contrast, the incidence of "la belle indifference" was 33% with right lesions, only 11% with left lesions ($p < 0.01$).

2. *Asymmetry of affective reaction to intracarotid Amytal.* Another type of evidence suggests that there may be a particular quality of affective reaction associated with injury to each hemisphere. Terzian and Cecotto made this observation in the course of administering the Wada carotid amytal test (113, 114). This is a procedure generally used prior to neurosurgery to establish which hemisphere is dominant for language in ambiguous cases, such as when the patient is left handed, or ambidextrous (115). A small quantity of the anesthetic is injected into one common carotid artery. This results in anesthetizing only the ipsilateral hemisphere, producing a contralateral hemiplegia and, if it happens to be the side dominant for speech, a complete aphasia. The symptoms last only for a few minutes. Terzian observed that a certain number of his patients had a marked emotional reaction as the anesthetic was wearing off. He describes is as follows (114):

> . . . Amytal on the left side provokes . . . a catastrophic reaction in the sense of Goldstein. The patient . . . despairs and expresses a sense of guilt, of nothingness, of indignity, and worries about his own future or that of his relatives, without referring to the language disturbances overcome and to the hemiplegia just resolved and ignored. The injection of the same dose in the contralateral carotid artery of the same subject or in subjects not having received the left injection, produces on the contrary a complete opposite emotional reaction, an euphoric reaction that in some cases may reach the intensity of maniacal reaction. The patient appears without apprehension, smiles and laughs and both with mimicry and words expresses considerable liveliness and sense of well-being.

In a subsequent paper, Alema, Rosadini, and Rossi (116) reported that this specifically lateralized affective response was seen best in patients with no brain damage; in cases with unilateral damage it was seen only on the intact side, and in cases of diffuse or bilateral damage it was not seen at all. (The indications for performing the test on the patients with no brain damage were not reported). These extraordinary observations were confirmed by Rossi and Rosadini (117) and by Hécaen and Ajuriaguerra (20), but disputed by Milner (118), who studied the emotional response of 104 patients undergoing the Wada test. She reported only rare depression, and no systematic asymmetry in the euphoria. She related the emotional reaction to the temperament of the patient. Neither Milner nor Rossi were able to account for their divergent results. At this point we must await further studies to resolve these conflicting reports.

Another provocative study was carried out by Hommes and Panhuysen (119, 120) on the effects of unilateral carotid amytal in patients hospitalized for depression, with no known brain damage. This report is difficult to evaluate because of many methodological limitations which the authors themselves acknowledge. Nevertheless, because of their implications, their results should be noted.

First, they found much more dysphasia following right-hemisphere injections in this depressed population than would be expected in the general population. Second, when they ranked their patients in terms of left hemispheric dominance for speech they found there was a strong negative correlation with depth of clinical depression (preamytal); the most depressed had the least left dominance for speech. The authors conclude: "It is therefore possible that . . . the level of functional dominance of the left hemisphere is reduced by the process that leads to depression." They found an elevation of mood with injection on either side, although it was sometimes much more marked on one side. They point out that the patients were already depressed, and a further depressive reaction following left injection might be inconspicuous.

The interpretation of the affective reaction to unilateral amytal is especially difficult because it occurs not at the peak of the disability, but as the anesthetic is wearing off, or with doses too small to produce EEG and gross neurological symptoms. Is the affect originating from the injected side, as a reaction to the drug, or from the uninjected side, as the balance of dominance between them is shifted? In other respects the reported amytal emotional asymmetry is similar to that seen following permanent unilateral lesions, described in Sec. III B-1 *Denial of Illness;* depressive catastrophic reactions more frequent with left lesions, indifference or euphoria with right lesions.

C. Unilateral Electroconvulsive Shock Treatment (ECT)

1. *Comparison of therapeutic response to left and right hemisphere treatment.* In the past 10 years, there have been numerous reports that the post-treatment confusion and memory disturbance that commonly follows conventional bitemporal ECT can be minimized by using a unilateral technique; the electrodes are applied only on one side of the head, usually the right. Most authors report no loss in therapeutic effectiveness in relieving the symptoms of depression (121-127), although some report that unilateral treatment requires more sessions for equivalent results (128–131). If hemispheric specialization and interaction are related to the organization and integration of personality, then it seems reasonable to expect that which hemisphere gets the shock treatment might effect the therapeutic outcome. What is the evidence for any such differential effect?

Although a substantial literature on unilateral ECT has developed, only a few studies have compared the efficacy of unilateral shock to the left and right hemispheres. Most studies have only compared efficacy of right hemisphere ECT to the conventional bilateral ECT, or have been primarily concerned with the nature and extent of the memory loss and confusion, which are usually held to be unrelated to therapeutic effect (132). As is usual in clinical outcome studies, gross differences in treatment procedure, patient selection, method and time of evaluation make the comparison of one report with another very difficult. [A summary of methodologic problems in ECT studies is given by Costello (123, 133).] Nevertheless, a careful reading of this clinical literature does suggest a differential role of the two hemispheres in response to ECT.

Three studies compared the therapeutic effect of left, right, and bilateral ECT in depressives, and included a blind follow-up evaluation at least 1 month after the last treatment (121, 122, 124). Halliday et al. (121) and Cronin et al. (122) both found ECT to the left hemisphere to be significantly less effective in relieving depression than ECT to the right. The third study by Fleminger et al. (124), which seems generally comparable, found no difference between the treatments.

Three other studies also compared outcome in left, right, and bilateral ECT and found no difference between the groups (123, 125, 134), but they differ substantially in method from those cited above. Two of these mention therapeutic effect only in passing; their patient groups included schizophrenics with depressives, and evaluation was based entirely on the number of treatments given (125) or number of treatments plus the discharge summary (134). The third (123) rated improvement only to the day following the last treatment, and the authors themselves caution that because of the lack of follow-up and because of high variances in the self-report inventories used their conclusion should be considered exploratory.

The study by Cronin et al. (122) found both right and bilateral treatment were superior to left ECT. They emphasized that the difference was not apparent until after the eighth treatment, and had increased further at follow-up 1 month later.

The study by Halliday et al. (121) tends to show that right ECT was more effective than left or bilateral ECT according to overall clinical assessment 3 months after the end of treatment. Although they point out that a significantly greater number of patients receiving left ECT relapsed and/or dropped out of the study, their overall conclusion was: "There was no significant difference in the effect on depression on the three types of ECT." It is worthwhile to consider their results in detail. Five of the patients who dropped out were known to have relapsed under treatment (three with left ECT, one with right ECT, one with bilateral ECT), but because they were not assessed at the end of the study in the same formal manner as the others, Halliday did not include them in his summary table. With these patients added to the appropriate "worse" groups, the results are shown in Table 1. The effects of left ECT and bilateral ECT seem to be similar. The tendency for right ECT to produce superior results (better versus no better) does not reach the $p = 0.05$ level of confidence by the Fischer Exact Probability Test, but the tendency for left ECT to make patients worse (worse versus not worse) is significant at $p = 0.05$. It would seem important to repeat this study with a larger sample.

Halliday et al. (121) note that the seizure produced by the treatment was wholly or preponderantly unilateral in only one-third of the cases. We might hypothesize that the effect in those cases that had bilateral fits was more

TABLE 1. Comparison of unilateral and bilateral ECT

Condition	Left ECT n = 14	Right ECT n = 17	Bilateral ECT n = 18
Recovered	4 (28.5)	8 (47.0)	5 (27.8)
Improved	5 (35.7)	6 (35.3)	7 (38.9)
No change	0 (0)	2 (11.8)	0 (0)
Worse	5 (35.7)	1 (5.9)	6 (33.3)

Numbers in parentheses represent percentages.
Adapted from Halliday et al., ref 121.

similar to the effect of bilateral ECT. Therefore, in comparing left and right ECT for therapeutic efficacy, the comparison should be restricted to those patients who had unilateral seizures.[6] The difference between the unilateral treatment groups could be washed out by the inadvertent addition of what may be in effect bilateral treatment. If this is correct, then research on methods to confine the seizure to one hemisphere would be very important.

2. *Field dependence and lateralization of brain function: Effects of unilateral ECT.* A recent study by Silverman and his colleagues compared the effects of left and right ECT in terms of the cognitive style concept field dependence (100, 135). Although not explicitly concerned with therapeutic outcome, this suggests a way to understand the clinical empirical results of Cronin et al. (122) and Halliday et al. (121) in terms of changes in balance between the two specialized hemispheres.

Field dependence is measured by a variety of tests, but most commonly with the rod-and-frame test. The subject sits facing a rod surrounded by a tilted frame, and is asked to adjust the rod to vertical. People with a strong tendency to be influenced by the frame (the context or "field") and thus to miss the vertical, are called field dependent. Field dependence has been related to a great many personality and psychophysiological variables such as responsiveness to social cues, defensive style (denial versus intellectualization), and symptom choice in psychosomatic illness (135-138). In general it is the field-dependent who come out on the pathological, more primitive, less desirable end of the continuum. This may be due to the fact that all the field-dependence tests are set up requiring the subject to be as field independent as he can. There are none that I know of in which the person is asked to be as responsive to context as possible. In other words, these tests can reveal only an inability to operate in a field-independent mode on demand, not the relative ability to perform in either mode, or the preference for one mode over the other.

Silverman and his colleagues concluded, in reviewing a series of studies,

---

[6] What is reported simply as a "bilateral seizure" may have begun unilaterally and spread to include the other side. Therefore, it may not be symmetric in its effects. The EEG could be used to evaluate the extent and duration of the afterdischarge and postictal depression on each side.

that extreme field-dependent subjects had a pattern of deficits that might signify a subclinical cerebral injury; left/right confusion, primitive drawings in the draw-a-person test, poor mirror-tracing, and embedded-figures performance, and a paradoxical response to amphetamine. In another experiment using a paired-associates learning test with word pairs and form pairs, they found that the field-dependent subjects showed relative deficiency on the words section, suggesting a relative deficit in left hemisphere functioning. In order to directly test the relation between left and right cerebral dysfunction and field-dependent performance on the rod-and-frame test they studied a group of right-handed depressed patients who were undergoing unilateral ECT. They hypothesized that if field-dependence was related to left hemisphere dysfunction then patients who had ECT on the left, rather than on the right, should have increased rod-and-frame error scores. The results were extraordinarily consistent; all 12 patients who had left ECT showed more field dependence on the posttreatment test. But the more startling result was that all 12 patients who had right ECT showed less field-dependence, i.e., fewer errors (100). In discussing this result, Silverman suggests that it is possible that ". . . right ECT decreases a subject's ability to respond to a stimulus field such that the more peripheral elements of the field are not attended to. In the case of the rod-and-frame task, it is the frame which is both peripheral as well as the major source of interference in performing the task. Thus, with the distracting influence of the frame attenuated the rod can be more accurately brought to true vertical" (135). Thus, field dependence is seen to be associated with a relative right hemisphere dominance, rather than a left hemisphere dysfunction per se.

In summary examination of the literature on unilateral ECT for depression suggests that the two hemispheres differ in the response to treatment, and that it may be useful to consider the effect of this treatment in terms of changing the balance or interaction between the two hemispheres. The results of Halliday et al. (121), Cronin et al. (122), and Cohen et al. (100) are certainly consistent with the observations discussed in previous sections: the frequency of depressive reaction after amytal injection of the left hemisphere, and after lesions of the left hemisphere, and the report of Hommes and Panhuysen (119, 120) that their depressed patients showed less than usual left dominance.

IV. LIFESTYLE

Several authors have suggested that not only can an individual's cognitive style be elaborated into a lifestyle, but that an entire culture may reflect a particular cognitive style. It may be useful to consider how the development of a particular pattern of hemispheric balance or dominance in an individual may be affected by the social context in which he grows up. A cultural emphasis on one or the other mode of knowing and validating experience could interact with genetic and individual determinants. Each of the following papers describes two main cognitive types, more or less congruent with the left-hemisphere-analytic and right-hemisphere-holistic modes.

Deikman (56) specifically addressed psychiatric problems. He proposed that there are two fundamental modes of consciousness, each with its own character style and each adaptive under certain limiting conditions. He makes use of this model to explicate the goals and methods of mystical disciplines, the results of experimental meditation, and LSD experiences.

An anthropological paper by Lee (103) describes a Pacific island culture (the Trobrianders) which is characterized by "a non-linear codification of reality." Proceeding mainly from a Whorfian analysis of their language structure, she contrasts their holistic world view with the linear analytic style of our Western culture.

Cohen (101) defines "analytic" and "relational" styles which she believes characterizes American middle-class (white) and ghetto (black) subcultures. She explores the effect of this difference on the children in the schools. The educational system embodies the middle-class, linear, analytic style in every aspect; in the architecture, the seating plans, the division of the day into discrete periods, and the emphasis on the left hemisphere skills (verbal, computational) in the curriculum. She believes this leads to a true "culture conflict" for children with the "relational" style.

Bogen et al. (102) also maintain that subcultures can be characterized by their predominant cognitive style. They explicitly propose that "cultural differences can be interpreted in part as a result of asymmetry in hemispheric utilization." This conclusion is based on a demographic study ($n = 1,220$) which included tests involving verbal abstraction (WAIS similarities) and spatial synthesis (Street Gestalt Completion). The results were analyzed in terms of urban-rural, black-white, male-female populations and included a group of rural Hopi indians.

Domhoff (92) offers a psychoanalytic discussion of the polarization of right and left as good and bad. He gives an excellent historical and anthropological bibliography of the ubiquitous characterization of the right as good, male, strong, bright, and the left as bad, female, weak, mysterious.

V. CONCLUSION

In this chapter I have proposed that our present knowledge of the two hemispheres' cognitive specialization and potential for independent functioning provides a useful framework for thinking about the interaction of cognitive structures, defensive maneuvers, and variations in states of awareness.

A brief review was presented of the evidence that the left hemisphere is specialized for an analytic, linear mode of information processing, and that the right hemisphere is specialized for a holistic, gestalt mode. The commissurotomy syndrome was described, particularly with respect to observations which indicate that each disconnected hemisphere is independently conscious, and that in general the left hemisphere in these patients seems to dominate their postoperative behavior. A parallel was noted between the functioning of the isolated right hemisphere and mental processes that are repressed, unconscious, and unable to directly control behavior. The congruency between some aspects of the right hemisphere cognitive mode and some aspects of primary process thinking was discussed; both depend mainly on nonverbal image representations, with nonsyllogistic logic, and are more concerned with multiple simultaneous interactions than with temporal sequencing.

These considerations led to the hypothesis that in normal intact people mental events in the right hemisphere can become disconnected functionally from the left hemisphere (by inhibition of neuronal transmission across the corpus callosum) and can continue a life of their own. This hypothesis suggests a neurophysiological mechanism for at least some instances of repression, and an anatomical locus for some unconscious mental contents.

If repression is to some extent subserved by a functional disconnection of right hemisphere mental processes, we might expect that unconscious ideation would be expressed primarily through channels that are not preempted by the dominant verbal left hemisphere. This notion led us to review several studies which suggest that the right hemisphere plays a special role in dreaming, and that it might be fruitful to look for lateral asymmetries in the autonomic nervous system and in psychosomatic symptoms.

Another group of studies were reviewed that concern the differences between the two hemispheres in the affective reactions or coping strategies that appear following cerebral injuries or in the course of the intracarotid amytal test. Denial of illness or euphoria is seen most often following right lesions, and "catastrophic" or depressive reactions most often following left lesions. At present the evidence for these differences pertains only to reactions to injury; we do not know whether or to what extent the two hemispheres in the intact brain may each subserve characteristic defensive styles or affective tone.

Finally, the literature on unilateral ECT for the relief of depression was reviewed. It was concluded that the therapeutic effect may depend on which hemisphere gets the treatment. It is suggested that the therapeutic effect can be understood in terms of changing the balance between the specialized hemispheres.

Early attempts to integrate neurology and psychodynamics were not very fruitful, perhaps premature. Since then the two disciplines have developed extensively, but quite separately, without much cross-fertilization. In this chapter I have juxtaposed a variety of observations and concepts from neuropsychology and psychiatry. I believe these are complementary rather than competing formulations. The work discussed here seems to indicate a profitable direction for developing research and theory.

ACKNOWLEDGMENTS

This research was supported in part by U.S. Public Health Service Career Development Award MH28457 from the National Institute of Mental Health and Grant NS 10307 from the National Institute of Neurological Diseases and Stroke.

REFERENCES

1. Sperry, R. W., Gazzaniga, M. S., and Bogen, J. E. (1969): Interhemispheric relationships; the neocortical commissures; syndromes of hemisphere disconnection. In: *Handbook of Clinical Neurology, Vol. 4*, edited by P. J. Vinken and G. W. Bruyen, pp. 273–290. North Holland, Amsterdam.
2. Sperry, R. W., (1973): Lateral specialization of cerebral function in the surgically separated hemispheres. In: *The Psychophysiology of Thinking*, edited by F. J. McGuigan and R. A. Schoonover, pp. 209–229. Academic Press, New York.
3. Bogen, J. E. (1969): The other side of the brain 1. Dysgraphia and dyscopia following cerebral commissurotomy. *Bull. Los Angeles Neurol. Soc.*, 34:73–105.
4. Bogen, J. E. (1969): The other side of the brain II: An appositional mind. *Bull. Los Angeles Neurol. Soc.*, 34:135–162.
5. Bogen, J. E., and Bogen, G. M. (1969): The other side of the brain III: The corpus callosum and creativity. *Bull. Los Angeles Neurol. Soc.*, 34:191–220.
6. Sperry, R. W. (1968): Hemisphere deconnection and unity in conscious awareness. *Am. Psychol.*, 23:723–733.
7. Gazzaniga, M. S. (1970): *The Bisected Brain*. Appleton-Century-Crofts, New York.
8. Levy, J., Trevarthen, C. and Sperry, R. W. (1972): Perception of bilateral chimeric figures following hemispheric deconnexion. *Brain*, 95:61–78.
9. Nebes, R. (1971): Superiority of the minor hemisphere in commissurotomized man for perception of part-whole relations. *Cortex*, 7:333–349,
10. Nebes, R. D. (1974): Hemispheric specialization in commissurotomized man. *Psychol. Bull.*, 81:1–14.
11. Gordon, H., and Sperry, R. W. (1969): Lateralization of olfactory perception in the surgically separated hemispheres of man. *Neuropsychologia*, 7:111–120.
12. Bogen, J. E. (1971): Final panel (part IV). In: *Drugs and Cerebral Function, Cerebral Function Symposium*, edited by W. L. Smith, pp. 263–272. Charles C Thomas, Springfield, Ill.
13. Galin, D., and Ornstein, R. (1972): Lateral specialization of cognitive mode: An EEG study. *Psychophysiology*, 9:412–418.
14. Doyle, J. C., Galin, D., and Ornstein, R. (1974) Lateral specialization of cognitive mode: II. EEG frequency analysis. *Psychophysiology*, 11(5):567–578.
15. Galin, D., and Ellis, R. R. (1975): Asymmetry in evoked potentials as an index of lateralized cognitive processes: Relation to EEG Alpha Asymmetry. *Neuropsychologia*, 13:45–50.
16. Milner, B. (1971): Interhemispheric differences in the localization of psychological processes in man. *Br. Med. Bull.*, 27:272–277.
17. Luria, A. R. (1966): *Higher Cortical Functions in Man*. Basic Books, New York.
18. Zangwill, O. L. (1960): *Cerebral Dominance and its Relation to Psychological Function*. Oliver and Boyd, Edinburgh.
19. Geshwind, N. (1965): Disconnexion syndromes in animals and man. I. *Brain*, 88:237–294; also II. *Brain*, 88:585–644.

20. Hécaen, H., and Ajuriaguerra, J. (1964): *Lefthandedness*. Grune and Stratton, New York.
21. Silverman, A. J., Adevai, G., and McGough, W. E. (1966): Some relationships between handedness and perception. *J. Psychosom. Res.* 10:151–158.
22. James, W. E., Mefferd, R. B., and Wieland, B. A. (1967): Repetitive psychometric measures: Handedness and performance. *Percept. Mot. Skills*, 25:209–212.
23. Levy, J. (1969): Possible basis for the evolution of lateral specialization of the human brain. *Nature*, 224:614–615.
24. Miller, E. (1971): Handedness and the pattern of human ability. *Br. J. Psychol.*, 62:111–112.
25. Gazzaniga, M. S., and Hillyard, S. A. (1971): Language and speech capacity of the right hemisphere. *Neuropsychologia*, 9:273–280.
26. Levy, J., Nebes, R., and Sperry, R. W. (1971): Expressive language in the surgically separated minor hemisphere. *Cortex*, 7:49–58.
27. Smith, A. (1966): Speech and other functions after left (dominant) hemispherectomy. *J. Neurol. Neurosurg. Psychiatry*, 29:467–471.
28. McKee, G., Humphrey, B., and McAdam, D. (1973): Scaled lateralization of alpha activity during linguistic and musical tasks. *Psychophysiology*, 10:441–443.
29. Schwartz, G., Davidson, R. J., Maer, F., and Bromfield, E. (1973): Patterns of hemispheric dominance in musical, emotional, verbal and spatial tasks. Presented at the Society of Psychophysiology Research Annual Meeting, New Orleans.
30. Buchsbaum, M., and Fedio, P. (1969): Visual information and evoked responses from the left and right hemispheres. *Electroencephalogr. Clin. Neurophysiol.*, 26:266–272.
31. Buchsbaum, M., and Fedio, P. (1970): Hemispheric differences in evoked potentials to verbal and non-verbal stimuli in the left and right visual fields. *Physiol. Behav.*, 5:207–210.
32. McAdam, D. W., and Whitaker, H. A. (1971): Language production: Electroencephalographic localization in the normal human brain. *Science*, 172:499–502.
33. Morrell, L. K., and Salamy, J. G. (1971): Hemispheric asymmetry of electrocortical responses to speech stimuli. *Science*, 174:164–166.
34. Wood, C., Goff, W. R., and Day, R. S. (1971): Auditory evoked potentials during speech perception. *Science*, 173:1248–1251.
35. Vella, E. J., Butler, S. R., and Glass, A. (1972): Electrical correlate of right hemisphere function. *Nature New Biol.* 236:125–126.
36. White, M. J. (1969): Laterality differences in perception; a review. *Psychol. Bull.*, 72:387–405.
37. Filbey, R. A., and Gazzaniga, M. S. (1969): Splitting the normal brain with reaction time. *Psychonomic Sci.*, 17:335.
38. McKeever, W. F., and Huling, M. (1970): Left cerebral hemisphere superiority in tachistoscopic word recognition performance. *Percept. Mot. Skills*, 30:763–766.
39. Rizzolatti, G., Umilta, C., and Berlucchi, G. (1971): Opposite superiorities of the right and left cerebral hemispheres in discriminative reaction time to physiognomical and alphabetical material. *Brain*, 94:431–442.
40. Berlucchi, G., Heron, W., Hyman, R., Rizzolatti, G., and Umilta, C. (1971): Simple reaction times of ipsilateral and contralateral hand to lateralized visual stimuli. *Brain*, 94:419–430.
41. Levy, J. (1970): Information processing and higher psychological functions in the disconnected hemispheres of human commissurotomy patients. Unpublished thesis, California Institute of Technology.
42. Semmes, J. (1968): Hemispheric specialization: A possible clue to mechanism. *Neuropsychologia*, 6:11–26.
43. Freud, S. (1953): *Interpretation of Dreams, standard ed., Vols. 4 and 5*. Hogarth Press, London.
44. Freud, S. (1948): The unconscious. *Collected Papers, Vols. 4 and 5*. Hogarth Press, London.
45. Arlow, J. A., and Brenner, C. (1964): *Psychoanalytic Concepts and the Structural Theory*. International Universities Press, New York.
46. Freud, S. (1927): *The Ego and the Id*. Hogarth Press, London.

47. Klein, G. S. (1959): Consciousness in psychoanalytic theory: Some implications for current research in perception. *J. Am. Psychoanal. Ass.*, 7:5–34.
48. Gill, M. (1963): Topography and systems in psychoanalytic theory. *Psychol. Issues. Vol. 3* (2), Monograph #10.
49. Kubie, L. (1958):*Neurotic Distortion of the Creative Process.* Univ. of Kansas Press, Lawrence, Kansas.
50. Rapaport, D. (1967): States of consciousness: A psychopathological and psychodynamic view. In: *Collected Papers of David Rapaport, Chap. 33,* edited by Merton M. Gill, Basic Books, New York.
51. Fischer, C. (1957): Study of the preliminary stages of the construction of dreams and images. *J. Am. Psychoanal. Ass.*, 5:5–60.
52. Fischer, C., and Paul, I. H. (1959): The effect of subliminal visual stimulation on images and dreams: A validation study. *J. Am. Psychoanal. Ass.*, 7:35–83.
53. Shevrin, H. (1973): Brain wave correlates of subliminal stimulation, unconscious attention, primary and secondary process thinking, and repressiveness. *Psychol. Issues, Vol. 8* (2), Monograph 30, pp. 56–87.
54. Piaget J. (1973): The affective unconscious and the cognitive unconscious *J. Am. Psychoanal. Ass.*, 21(2):249–261.
55. Rubenfine, D. L. (1961). Perception, reality testing and symbolism. *Psychoanal. Study Child,* 16:73–89.
56. Deikman, A. (1971): Bimodal consciousness. *Arch. Gen. Psychiatry,* 25:481–489.
57. Horowitz, M. J. (1972): Modes of representation of thought. *J. Am. Psychoanal. Ass.,* 20(4):793–819.
58. Brenner, C. (1973): *An Elementary Textbook of Psychoanalysis,* International Universities Press, New York.
59. Efron, R. (1963): Effect of handedness on the perception of simultaneity and temporal order. *Brain,* 86:261–284.
60. Efron, R. (1963): The effect of stimulus intensity on the perception of simultaneity in right and left-handed subjects. *Brain,* 86:285–294.
61. Efron, R. (1963): An extension of the Pulfrich stereoscopic effect. *Brain,* 86:295–300.
62. Efron, R. (1963): Temporal perception, aphasia and deja vu. *Brain,* 86:403–424.
63. Carmon, A., and Nachshon, I. (1971): Effect of unilateral brain damage on perception of temporal order. *Cortex,* 7:410–418.
64. Swischer, L., and Hirsch, I. J. (1972): Brain damage and the ordering of two temporally successive stimuli. *Neuropsychologia,* 10:137–152.
65. Zangwill, O. L. (1967): Speech and the minor hemisphere. *Acta Neurol. Psychiat. Belgica,* 67:1013–1020.
66. Freud, S. (1926): *Psychopathology of Everyday Life.* Macmillan, New York.
67. Hécaen, H. (1962): Clinical symptomatology in right and left hemispheric lesions. In: *Interhemispheric Relations and Cerebral Dominance,* edited by V. B. Mountcastle. Johns Hopkins Press, Baltimore.
68. DeRenzi, E., and Spinnler, H. (1966): Visual recognition in patients with unilateral cerebral disease. *J. Nerv. Ment. Dis.,* 142:515–525.
69. Fischer, E. D., and Mann, L. B. (1952): Shift of writing function to minor hemisphere at the age of seventy-two years. Report of case with advanced left cerebral atrophy. *Bull. Los Angeles Neurol. Soc.,* 17:196–197.
70. Critchley, M. (1967): Creative writing by aphasiacs. In: *Neurological Problems,* edited by J. Chordoski, pp. 275–286. Pergamon Press, New York.
71. Johnson, J. D., and Gazzaniga, M. S. (1971): Reversal behavior in split-brain monkeys. *Physiol. Behav.,* 6:707–709.
72. Gazzaniga, M. S. (1971): Changing hemisphere dominance by changing reward probability in split-brain monkeys. *Exp. Neurol.,* 33:412–419.
73. Livingston, R. B. (1959): Central control of receptors and sensory transmission systems. In: *Handbook of Physiology—Neurophysiology I.* edited by H. W. Magoun, Chap. 31, pp. 741–760. Am. Physiol. Soc., Washington, D.C.
74. Whitfield, I. C. (1967): *The Auditory Pathway.* Williams & Wilkins, Baltimore.
75. Pribram, K. (1971): *Languages of the Brain,* Prentice-Hall, Englewood Cliffs, N.J.

76. Asanuma, H., and Osamu, O. (1962): Effects of transcallosal volleys on pyramidal tract cell activity of cat. *J. Neurophysiol.,* 25:198–208.
77. Hossman, K. A. (1969): Untersuchungen uber transcallosale potentiale an der akuten corpus callosum katze. *Dtsch. Z. Nervenheilk,* 195:79–102.
78. Eidelberg, E. (1969): Callosal and non callosal connections between the sensory motor cortices in cat and monkey. *Electroencephalogr. Clin. Neurophysiol.* 26:557–564.
79. Galin, D., and Ornstein, R. (1974): Individual differences in cognitive style: I. Reflective eye movements. *Neuropsychologia,* 12:367–376.
80. Kocel, K., Galin, D., Ornstein, R., and Merrin, E. L. (1972): Lateral eye movement and cognitive mode. *Psychonomic Sci.,* 27:223–224.
81. Kinsbourne, M. (1972): Eye and head turning indicates cerebral lateralization. *Science,* 176:539–541.
82. Bakan, P. (1969): Hypnotizability, laterality of eye-movements and functional brain asymmetry. *Percept. Mot. Skills,* 28:927–932.
83. Brooks, L. R. (1970): An extension of the conflict between visualization and reading. *Q. J. Exp. Psychol.,* 22:91–96.
84. Deutsch, D. (1970): Tones and numbers: Specificity of interference in immediate memory. *Science,* 168:1604–1605.
85. den Hyer, K., and Barrett, B. (1971): Selective loss of visual information in STM by means of visual and verbal interpolated tasks. *Psychonomic Sci.,* 25:100–102.
86. Nebes, R. (1971): Handedness and the perception of the part-whole relationship. *Cortex,* 7:350–356.
87. Rondot, P., and Tzavaras, A. (1969): La prosopagnosie apres vingt annees d'etudes cliniques et neuropsychologiques. *J. Psychol. Norm. Path.* 66:133–165.
88. Sherrington, C. (1947): *The Integrative Action of the Nervous System,* p. xvii. Cambridge University Press, Cambridge.
89. Stent, G. (1972): Prematurity and uniqueness in scientific discovery. *Sci. Amer.* 227(6): 84–93.
90. Bruner, J. S. (1964): The course of cognitive growth. *Am. Psychol.,* 19:1–15.
91. Ferenczi, S. (1926): An attempted explanation of some hysterical stigmata. In: *Further Contributions to the Theory and Technique of Psychoanalysis.* Hogarth Press, London.
92. Domhoff, G. W. (1969): But why did they sit on the king's right in the first place? *Psychoanal. Rev.,* 56:586–596.
93. Varni, J. G., Doerr, H. O., and Franklin, J. R. (1971): Bilateral differences in skin resistance and vasomotor activity. *Psychophysiology,* 8:390–400.
94. Hoff, E. C., Kell, J. F., and Carroll, M. N.: (1963): Effects of cortical stimulation and lesions on cardiovascular function. *Physiol. Rev.,* 43:68–114.
95. Wang, S. C. (1964): *Neural Control of Sweating.* University of Wisconsin Press, Madison.
96. Holloway, F. A., and Parsons, O. A. (1969): Unilateral brain damage and bilateral skin conductance levels in humans. *Psychophysiology,* 6:138–148.
97. DeGeest, H., Levy, M. N., Zieske, H., and Lipman, R. I. (1965): Depression of ventricular contractility by stimulation of the vagus nerves. *Circ. Res.,* 17:222–234.
98. Randall, W. C., McNally, H., Cowan, J., Caliguiri, L., and Rohse, W. G. (1957): Functional analysis of cardioaugmentor and cardioaccelerator pathways in the dog. *Am. J. Physiol.,* 191:213–217.
99. Chai, C. V., and Wang, S. C. (1962): Localization of central cardiovascular control mechanisms in the lower brain stem of the cat. *Am. J. Physiol.,* 202:25–42.
100. Cohen, B. D., Berent, S., and Silverman, A. J. (1973): Field-dependence and lateralization of function in the human brain. *Arch. Gen. Psychiatry,* 28:165–167.
101. Cohen, R. A. (1969): Conceptual styles, culture conflict and nonverbal tests of intelligence. *Am. Anthropologist,* 71:828–856.
102. Bogen, J. E., DeZure, R., TenHouton, W. D., and Marsh, J. F. (1972): The other side of the brain IV. The A/P ratio. *Bull. Los Angeles Neurol. Soc.,* 37:49–61.
103. Lee, D. (1950): Codifications of reality: Lineal and nonlineal. *Psychosom. Med.,* 12:89–97.

104. Humphrey, M. E., and Zangwill, O. L. (1951): Cessation of dreaming after brain injury. *J. Neurol. Neurosurg. Psychiat.*, 14:322–325.
105. Austin, M. D. (1971): Dream recall and the bias of intellectual ability. *Nature*, 231:59.
106. Alajouanine, T., and Lhermitte, F. (1957): Des agnosies electives. *Encephale*, 46:505.
107. Gainotti, G. (1969): Reactions "catastrophiques" et manifestations d'indifférence au cours des atteintes cerebrales. *Neuropsychologia*, 7:195–204.
108. Gainotti, G. (1972): Emotional behavior and hemispheric side of the lesion. *Cortex*, 8:41–55.
109. Critchley, M. (1957): Observations on anosodiaphoria. *Encephale*, 46:540–546.
110. Weinstein, E. A., and Kahn, R. L. (1955): *Denial of Illness. Symbolic and Physiological Aspects*. Charles C Thomas, Springfield, Ill.
111. Critchley, M. (1953): *The Parietal Lobes*. Arnold, London.
112. Sprague, J. M. (1966): Visual, acoustic, and somesthetic deficits in the cat after cortical and midbrain lesions. In *The Thalamus*, edited by D. P. Purpura and M. Yohr, pp. 391–417. Columbia University Press, New York.
113. Terzian, H., and Cecotto, C. (1959): Determinazione e studio della dominanza emisferica mediante iniezione intra carotide di amytal sodico nell'uomo Part I (modification cliniche) *Boll. Soc. Ital. Biol. Sper.*, 35:1623–1626.
114. Terzian, H. (1964): Behavioural and EEG effects of intracarotid sodium amytal injections, *Acta Neurochir.*, 12:230–240.
115. Wada, J., and Rasmussen, T. (1960): Intracarotid injection of sodium amytal for the lateralization of cerebral speech dominance. *J. Neurosurg.*, 17:226–282.
116. Alema, G., Rosadini, G., and Rossi, G. F. (1961): Psychic reactions associated with intracarotid amytal injection and relation to brain damage. *Excerpta Medica Int. Cong. Series*, 37:154–155.
117. Rossi, G. F., and Rosadini, G. R. (1967): Experimental analysis of cerebral dominance in man. In *Brain Mechanisms Underlying Speech and Language*, edited by D. H. Millikan and F. L. Darley. Grune and Stratton, New York.
118. Milner, B. (1967): See discussion in Rossi, G. F., Rosadini, G. R.: Experimental analysis of cerebral dominance in man. In: *Brain Mechanisms Underlying Speech and Language*, edited by D. H. Millikan and F. L. Darley, p. 177. Grune and Stratton, New York.
119. Hommes, O. R., and Panhuysen, L. H. H. M. (1970): Bilateral intracarotid amytal injection. *Psychiatr. Neurol. Neurochir.*, 73:447–459.
120. Hommes, O. R., and Panhuysen, L. H. H. M. (1971): Depression and cerebral dominance. *Psychiatr. Neurol. Neurochir.*, 74:259–270.
121. Halliday, A. M., Davison, K., Brown, M. W., and Kreeger, L. C. (1968): Comparison of effects on depression and memory of bilateral ECT and unilateral ECT to the dominant and nondominant hemisphere. *Br. J. Psychiat.*, 114:997–1012.
122. Cronin, D., Bodley, P., Potts, L., Mather, M.D., Gardner, R. K., and Tobin, J. C. (1970): Unilateral and bilateral ECT: A study of memory disturbance and relief from depression. *J. Neurol. Neurosurg. Psychiatry*, 33:705–713.
123. Costello, C. G., Belton, G. P., Abra, J. C., and Dunn, B. E. (1970): The amnesic and therapeutic effects of bilateral and unilateral ECT. *Br. J. Psychiatry*, 116:69–78.
124. Fleminger, J. J., Del Horne, D. J., Nair, N. P. V., and Nott, P. N. (1970): Differential effect of unilateral and bilateral ECT. *Am. J. Psychiatry*, 127:430–436.
125. Sutherland, E. M., Oliver, J., and Knight, D. (1969): EEG memory and confusion in dominant and non-dominant and bi-temporal ECT. *Br. J. Psychiatry*, 115:1059–1064.
126. Zinkin, S., and Birtchnell, J. (1968): Unilateral electroconvulsive therapy: Its effects on memory and its therapeutic efficacy. *Br. J. Psychiatry*, 114:973–988.
127. d'Elia, G. (1970): Comparison of electroconvulsive therapy with unilateral and bilateral stimulation. *Acta Psychiatr. Scand. Suppl.* 215:30–43.
128. Lancaster, N. R., Steinert, R., and Frost, I. (1958): Unilateral electroconvulsive therapy. *J. Ment. Sci.*, 104:221–227.
129. Impastasto, D. J., and Karliner, W. (1966): Control of memory impairment in

ECT by unilateral stimulation of the non-dominant hemisphere. *Dis. Nerv. Syst.* 27:182–188.

130. Bidder, T. G., Strain, J. J., and Brunschwig, L. (1970): Bilateral and unilateral ECT: Follow-up study and critique. *Am. J. Psychiatry,* 127:737–745.

131. Abrams, R., Fink, M., and Dornbush, R. L. (1972): Unilateral and bilateral electroconvulsive therapy. *Arch. Gen. Psychiatry,* 27:88–91.

132. Ottosson, J. O. editor (1960): Experimental studies of the mode of action of electroconvulsive therapy. *Acta Psychiat. Scand. Suppl.* 145:35.

133. Costello, C. G., and Belton, G. P. (1970): Depression: Treatment. In: *Symptoms of Psychopathology,* edited by C. G. Costello, pp. 201–215. Wiley, New York.

134. McAndrew, J., Berkey, B., and Mathews, C. (1967): Effects of dominant and nondominant unilateral ECT as compared to bilateral ECT. *Am. J. Psychiatry,* 124:483–490.

135. Silverman, A. J. (1974): Perception, personality, and brain lateralization. Presented at *Proceedings of the Fifth World Congress of Psychiatry, Mexico City, 1971.*

136. Silverman, A. J. (1969): Some psychophysiological aspects of stress responsivity. *Aust. N.Z. J. Psychiatry,* 3(3A):216–221.

137. Adevai, G., Silverman, A. J., and McGough, W. E. (1968): Perceptual correlates of the Rod and Frame Test. *Percept. Motor Skills,* 26:1055–1064.

138. Silverman, A. J., Adevai, G., and McGough, W. E. (1966): Some relationships between handedness and perception. *J. Psychosom. Res.,* 10:151–158.

Biological Foundations of Psychiatry,
edited by R. G. Grenell and S. Gabay.
Raven Press, New York © 1976.

Sensory and Perceptive Factors in Emotional Functions of the Triune Brain

Paul D. MacLean

Laboratory of Brain Evolution and Behavior, National Institute of Mental Health, Bethesda, Maryland 20014

In the world of literature and the fine arts there are countless illustrations of the importance that introspective human beings place on the role of sensation and perception in the generation of emotional feelings. Add to this what has been written on the subject in such fields as religion, philosophy, psychology, and medicine, and the amount of information would choke the output of an ordinary computer. Imagine, however, a computer search in which the three words "sensation," "perception," and "emotion" were tied to brain function. Suddenly the outflow of substantive references would be reduced to a mere trickle!

But even this mere trickle would be more than we could cope with in the limits of this chapter. If, for example, we were to examine "first causes," we would need to analyze the extensive literature on receptors, as well as to review the effects of sensory deprivation of whatever origin on emotional experience and expression. I will therefore set arbitrary limits on the ground to be covered and deal mainly with the unanswered question of how sensory and perceptive mechanisms exert their influence on forebrain structures believed to be involved in emotion. In attempting an orderly approach to this problem, I shall deal successively with the three main evolutionary formations of the forebrain. Somewhat like an archaeological dig, I shall begin at the surface with the most recent formation and proceed towards the most ancient. For reasons to be explained, I shall focus particular attention on the limbic system which phylogenetically represents an inheritance from lower mammals. Then in conclusion, I shall call attention to some seldom asked questions that are possibly relevant to functions of the major counterpart of the reptilian forebrain in mammals.

In constructing a piece of writing we use words both as building materials and tools for thought. Because of the lack of unanimity about the meanings of psychological terms employed in this paper, it will be worthwhile to read the fine print of the following "contract" regarding the use of certain key words such as sensation, perceptions, and emotions.

I. DEFINITIONS[1]

It is the element of subjectivity that most clearly distinguishes psychological from other functions of the brain (MacLean, 1960). Even so-called unconscious processes probably require the existence of the subjective state. The case of sleep presents no exception because introspection reveals that a feeling of subjectivity is pervasive in dreaming. Subjectivity refers to the awareness associated with various forms of psychological information. A philosopher such as Kant might have called it an *a priori* "form of consciousness." To paraphrase Spencer (1896), objective psychology begins with subjective psychology. In addition to what we vaguely recognize as awareness or consciousness, introspection reveals five main classes of psychological information that will be here considered under the provisional categories of sensations, perceptions, propensions, emotions, and intellections. All these elements of the psyche are of themselves no more than information. As Wiener (1948) stated more succinctly than Berkeley and Hume, "Information is information, not matter or energy." At the same time, it is empirically established that there can be no communication of information without the intermediary of what we recognize as *behaving entities*. The statement of this invariance might be considered as a law of communication.

Information itself is regarded as orderliness, or in other words, the order that emerges from a background of disorder. The greater the ratio of order to disorder, the greater is the amount of information. In this respect immaterial information lends itself to a quantification. (In information theory the word "information" is used in the strict sense to refer to a numerical quantity that is the measure of uncertainty in a communications system. In the present context it is used in the broad sense to refer to anything meaningful.)

The derivation and communication of information in animals depends upon behaving entities of the nervous system. Although introspection *per se* can give no clue as to the workings of these behaving entities (see MacKay, 1970)

---

[1] This section is based on previously published material (MacLean, 1960, 1969*b*, 1970) and a book in preparation.

it is, as already stated, the first step in making an investigation. How shall we define sensations and perceptions? As a beginning, we may say that sensation represents the raw feelings which, under normal circumstances, depend upon the initiation of impulses resulting from activation of intero- and exteroceptors. In Sherringtonian terms, sensations fall into two broad classes of interoceptions and exteroceptions. They are distinguished in terms of quality (modality) and intensity. Individually, or in combination, sensations become more informative as they are appreciated in terms of time and space. In such transformation they are introspectively recognized as perceptions.

Sensing and perceiving, vis-à-vis mentation

With exception of certain pathological conditions, it is characteristic of sensations and perceptions that they depend on incoming signals to the brain from specific afferent systems and cease to exist after the termination of such activity. Contrast this situation with what applies to the three other main classes of psychological information, namely, propensions, emotions, intellections. The latter are distinguished from sensations and perceptions by their capacity to occur "after-the-fact." The unexplained process that makes this possible is referred to as mentation. In terms of a behaving nervous system, one might say that mentation involves self-regenerating neural replica of events either as they first occurred or in some rearrangement. How the original ordering of the events is preserved (i.e., memorized) or reordered (i.e., imagined or conceived) remains a mystery.

Of the three psychological terms in the title of this paper we have yet to consider the definition of emotions. It is usual to speak of both the expressive and subjective aspects of emotion. I will use the word "affect" to refer to the subjective state. Only we as individuals can experience affect. The existence of affects in another individual must be inferred through some form of verbal or nonverbal behavior. In the sense that originally inspired its use by Descartes (1967), the word "emotion" is an appropriate designation for such behavior.

The affects differ from other forms of psychological information by being imbued with a "physical" quality that is either agreeable or disagreeable. There are no neutral affects because emotionally speaking, it is impossible to feel unemotionally. As illustrated in Fig. 1, the agreeable and disagreeable affects can be subdivided into three main categories, which I have labeled basic, specific, and general.

The basic and specific affects are first-order affects insofar as they are immediately dependent, respectively, on interoceptions and exteroceptions. The

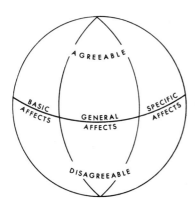

FIG. 1. A scheme for viewing the world of affects. From MacLean (1970).

basic affects derive from interoceptions signaling different kinds of internal states associated with basic bodily needs—namely, the needs for food, water, air, sexual outlet, sleep, and those associated with various emunctories. The specific affects apply to exteroceptions and perceptions immediately generated by activity in a specific sensory system. Some are unlearned, while others are conditioned. The latter include aesthetic affects identified with agreeable and disagreeable aspects of music and various art forms. Examples of unlearned specific affects are ones associated with repugnant odors, startling sounds, and intense flashes of light.

The general affects are second-order insofar as they originally derive from the first-order affects, but which through mentational processes mentioned above may persist or recur "after-the-fact." I call them general affects because they may apply to feelings aroused by other individuals, situations, or things. All the general affects may be considered from the standpoint of self-preservation and the preservation of the species. Those general affects that are informative of threats to the self or the species are disagreeable in nature, whereas those that signal the removal of threats and the gratification of needs are agreeable.

Exclusive of verbal behavior, there are six main types of animal and human behavior that we identify in varying degree with affective experience and emotional expression. These behaviors are recognized as (1) searching, (2) aggressive, (3) protective, (4) dejected, (5) gratulant, and (6) caressive. Corresponding words that would be broadly descriptive of the associated affective states are desire, anger, fear, sorrow, joy, and affection. Symbolic language and the introspective process make it possible to identify many variations of these are obsessive-compulsive, repititious, ritualistic, superstitious, deceptive, states must be based largely on these six general types of behavior.

There are several behaviors that, at first, might not seem to fit these categories, but turn out to be amenable to such classification. Primary among these are obsessive-compulsive, repetitious, ritualistic, superstitious, deceptive, and imitative behaviors.

II. EVOLUTIONARY CONSIDERATIONS: THE TRIUNE BRAIN

Given these psychological and behavioral definitions, we next consider how the three main evolutionary formations of the forebrain participate in the sensory and perceptive aspects of emotional processes. In its evolution the primate forebrain expands along the lines of three basic patterns that may be characterized as reptilian, paleomammalian, and neomammalian (Fig. 2). There results a remarkable linkage of three cerebrotypes which are radically different in chemistry and structure and which in an evolutionary sense are eons apart. There exists, so to speak, a hierarchy of three-brains-in-one, or what I call, for short, a *triune* brain (MacLean, 1970, 1973c). It is inferred that each cerebrotype has its own special kind of intelligence, its own special memory, its own sense of time and space, and its own motor and other functions. Although the three brain types are extensively interconnected and functionally dependent, there is evidence that each is capable of operating somewhat independently.

The major counterpart of the reptilian forebrain in mammals includes the corpus striatum (caudate + putamen), globus pallidus, and peripallidal struc-

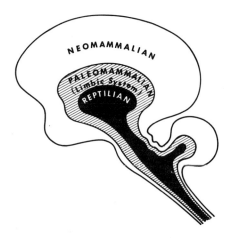

FIG. 2. In evolution the human brain expands in hierarchic fashion along the lines of three basic patterns referred to in the diagram as reptilian, paleomammalian, and neomammalian. As indicated in parentheses, the limbic system conforms to the paleomammalian pattern. Since the limbic system has been shown to play an important role in emotional behavior, the present paper gives particular attention to the question of how it is influenced by sensory and perceptive mechanisms. From MacLean (1967).

tures.[2] The paleomammalian brain is represented by the limbic system, a designation that I suggested in 1952. Most of the phylogenetically old cortex is contained in the limbic lobe which surrounds the brainstem (Fig. 3) and conforms somewhat like a mold to the corpus striatum (see Fig. 2 in MacLean, 1972a). The neomammalian brain is represented by the rapidly evolv-

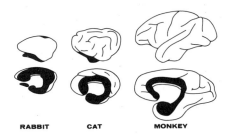

RABBIT CAT MONKEY

FIG. 3. The limbic lobe, which was so named by Broca because it surrounds the brainstem, contains most of the phylogenetically old cortex. Indicated by the shading, it is found as a common denominator in the brains of all mammals. The neocortex which undergoes great expansion relatively late in evolution is shown in white. After MacLean (1954).

ing neocortex and structures of the brainstem with which it is primarily connected.

III. ROLE OF THE NEOMAMMALIAN BRAIN

It has long been recognized from clinical observations that specific areas of the neocortex are respectively related to the somatic, auditory, and visual systems, and that these cortical areas are essential for normal sensation and perception. The evolutionary ascendancy of these systems indicates that the neocortex is primarily oriented towards the external environment. As I have commented elsewhere, ". . . the signals to which these three systems are

---

[2] "Peripallidal structures" applies to the variously named structures closely associated with the globus pallidus, including the substantia innominata, basal nucleus of Meynert, nucleus of the ansa peduncularis, and entopeduncular nucleus.

receptive are the only ones that lend themselves to electronic amplification and radiotransmission. Smells, tastes, and interoceptions have no such avenue for communication (MacLean, 1972b). Anatomical and electrophysiological studies have demonstrated that an orderly projection exists between receptors and thalamus and between thalamus and neocortex, resulting in a "point-to-point," topographical relationship. The evoked potential technique has made it possible to subdivide the somatic, auditory, and visual areas into a number of subareas, with the recognition thus far of the first, second, and third visual areas; the first, second, and third auditory areas; and the first, second, and supplementary somatosensory areas.

With encephalization, it is evident that in spite of the many redundancies of the nervous system, the neocortex becomes more and more crucial for sensation and perception, and that indeed there is hierarchical ordering within the neocortex itself. Higher primates, for example, are for all intents and purposes blind without the primary striate cortex. This is the extreme opposite of what Snyder and Diamond (1968) have recently observed in the tree shrew, an animal that is presumed to represent an antecedent of primates. "With a complete removal of the geniculo-striate system," they report, "tree shrews retain form and pattern vision as well as the capacity to localize visual objects in space." Even after removal of all the known visual areas of the neocortex, these animals are capable of differentiating between horizontal and vertical stripes.

The work of Diamond and his colleagues has also added to the accumulating knowledge of the anatomical course of other than the classical sensory pathways to the neocortex (Harting, Hall, Diamond, and Martin, 1973). They have demonstrated a collicular-pulvinar-temporal pathway that presumably accounts for sparing of visual function in the tree shrew after ablation of the striate cortex (Snyder and Diamond, 1968). I shall refer to this pathway again when discussing limbic connections.

Electrophysiological studies have identified a number of functional properties of the neocortical sensory areas that are presumed to be involved in the perception of form. The "inhibitory surround" detected in testing receptive fields of cells in the somatosensory (Mountcastle, Davies, and Berman, 1957) and visual areas (Hubel and Wiesel, 1962), for example, is believed to be of fundamental importance in this respect. Studies of individual cells of the visual system have revealed units that respond specifically to edges, contrast, orientation, directional movement, color, etc. The findings have tended to generate a magical jargon in which reference is made to "sophisticated neurons" that are "edge detectors," "motion detectors," and the like, somewhat as though they possessed subjective properties of Leibnitz's monads, and were especially constituted to recognize only one or two types of stimuli, when in actuality it is the neural network to which they belong that accounts for the selective response. Curiously enough, as Michael (1969), points out, the retinas of such animals as the frog, ground squirrel, and rabbit have the capacity for discriminative functions that take place only in the visual cortex of higher mammals—specifically the detection of edges, orientation, and direction of movement.

In neurophysiological studies of mechanisms of perception it is usually implicit that the primary goal is to learn how animals achieve the recognition of well-defined patterns, as though this aspect of perception was what mattered most to the organism. As yet, little consideration has been given to a fundamental question of the opposite sort—namely, what is it that makes an animal reactive to environmental apparitions, including ill-defined partial representations of an object or animal, that are conducive to propensive and emotional behavior, serving also, in ethological terms, as "releasers" of specific forms of behavior? Of the many examples, one of the best known is that of infants responding to crude, partial representations of the human face. I shall return to this question in discussing the limbic system and the major mammalian counterpart of the reptilian forebrain.

During neurosurgical procedures it has been learned that crude sensations may result from stimulation of the somatic, auditory, and visual cortex (see Penfield and Jasper, 1954). In attempting to locate epileptogenic foci, Penfield has found that in some individuals brain stimulation of the so-called association areas of the temporo-occipital cortex may induce auditory and visual illusions or hallucinations (Penfield and Perot, 1963).

But neither clinical nor experimental observations have made it possible to trace the neural circuitry by which verbal or nonverbal information derived through the visual, auditory, and somatic systems generates affective states. Of the *specific* affects, pain has received foremost attention. In their analysis of disturbances associated with thalamic lesions, Head and Holmes (1920) noted that sometimes simple tones, like various somatic stimuli, aggravated the sense of pain on the affected side of the body. In addition, they described a curious situation that is somewhat the reverse of the one we are considering. No one seems to have recognized, they pointed out, that states of emotion may evoke different sensations on different sides of the body. "One of our patients," they continued, "was unable to go to his place of worship because he 'could not stand the hymns on his affected side.' " Cases of this kind led them to infer that the optic thalamus was the well-spring of emotion.

IV. PROLEGOMENON TO THE CONSIDERATION OF THE LIMBIC AND REPTILIAN FORMATIONS

Von Economo (1931) singled out more ventral loci as being of primary consequence in emotional experience. In his monograph *Encephalitis Lethargica* he concluded that the tegmentum, the basal and posterior walls of the third ventricle, and the region of the aqueduct were the "favorite target" of the disease. He emphasized the relevance of these findings to the observation that among the persisting symptoms "the difficulty of arousing emotion . . .

is above all a primary defect." He pointed out that some patients may feel hungry, but take no pleasure in eating, or recognize the sensation of cold without experiencing the usual feeling of cold. In general, they may complain that they "feel like a spent volcano."

It is to be noted that the structures particularly mentioned by Von Economo lie in the region fed by the perforating vessels of the interpeduncular fossa (see Mettler, 1955). Thanks to recent investigations it is known that there are dopamine-containing neurons in this region that innervate the corpus striatum, including the so-called olfactory striatum. In view of the profound influence of these ascending systems on spontaneous behavior of animals, we may wonder in retrospect to what extent the emotional blunting emphasized by Von Economo was due to the destruction of dopamine-containing cells of the substantia nigra, as well as those of the network spanning the interpeduncular fossa (groups A9 and A10 of Dahlström and Fuxe, 1964). Let me give two unpublished illustrations: We have found that destruction by 6-hydroxydopamine of these cell groups in the squirrel monkey results first in catalepsy followed by a picture of parkinsonism. The cataleptic signs can be detected before the monkey fully recovers from anesthesia. In retrospect, it would appear that the catalepsy that Ingram, Barris, and Ranson (1936) observed in cats following lesions between the mammillary bodies and the third nerve may have resulted from damage of these cell groups. The incapacity produced by lesions in this region is to be contrasted with the mobilizing effect of apomorphine which is believed to act on dopamine receptors. A comparative survey has revealed that in such diverse species as the parrot, turkey, opossum, and squirrel monkey apomorphine induces aimless, increased activity. The turkey, for example, will run aimlessly in and out of the flock for 3 to 4 hr. The two opposing conditions that have been described would support other kinds of evidence that the ascending dopaminergic systems exert an "energizing" influence on an animal's behavior.

In extrapolating from animal experiments by Ranson (1939) and others, one might go further than Von Economo and say that the main avenues for the expression of the basic personality pass through the ventral diencephalon, with the lateral and the medial forebrain bundles, respectively, being two major fiber systems leading to and from striatal and limbic structures. The lateral forebrain bundle includes the ansa and fasciculus lenticularis, as well as the nigrostriatal and striatonigral pathways. The ansa lenticularis sweeps out of the rostromedial part of the globus pallidus like the swish of a mare's tail, with both compact and diffuse components coursing through the dorsolateral part of the hypothalamus and becoming partly entangled with the medial forebrain bundle. It is curious in rereading the literature to find how investigators have either discounted or overlooked the significance of the compact and widely diffuse portions of the *ansa,* as well as the fasciculus lenticularis. This may be in part due to Ranson's conclusion that these striatal connections probably did not play an important part in the emotional changes observed in rhesus monkeys with bilateral lesions of the lateral hypothalamus (Ranson, 1939). Yet at the same time he pointed out that lesions of the ansa resulted in complete disappearance of the neurons in the medial segment of the globus pallidus. Parenthetically, it should be noted that the ansa is not simply a pallidofugal pathway. It is now evident that like the medial forebrain bundle, it contains ascending fibers (Carpenter and Peter, 1972). Jacobowitz and I (*unpublished data*), in experimental material on the squirrel monkey, have found that it contains ascending dopamine fibers, some of which run through the hypothalamus just lateral to the fornix.

Experimental findings in animals attest to the fundamental role of the lenticular pathways in the expression of an animal's "character." In connection with investigations of brain mechanisms of species-typical behavior of the squirrel monkey (see below), I have had occasion to produce large bilateral lesions in the ventral diencephalon involving the central ansal system and part of the medial forebrain bundle. As the result of careful nursing, a number of monkeys have survived the acute postoperative period. Although there is a recovery of locomotion and an ability for self-feeding, the striking thing about these monkeys is the complete lack of what one might call their animality. They have, so to speak, a zombie-like behavior which is distressing to observe.

V. THE LIMBIC SYSTEM

With this background we turn next to the limbic system which represents an inheritance from lower mammals. The best evidence of the role of the limbic system in emotional behavior is derived from clinical observations. Neuronal discharges in or near the limbic cortex of the temporal lobe may trigger a broad spectrum of vivid, affective feelings. The *basic* and *general* affects are usually of the kind associated with threats to self-preservation (MacLean, 1958). More rarely, there may be affects of an agreeable or ecstatic nature, possibly reflecting a spread of the seizure to other subdivisions of the limbic system.

The *basic* affects include those of hunger, thirst, nausea, and feelings associated with the emunctories. *Specific* affects include unpleasant tastes and odors and somatic sensations such as pain, tingling, etc. (see also below). Among the *general* affects are feelings of fear, terror, sadness, wanting to be alone, familiarity, unfamiliarity, and (very rarely) anger. The feeling of fear is commonly referred to the epigastric region and may give the impression of rising in the chest to the throat. As I have emphasized elsewhere (MacLean, 1952), the *general* affects are usually "free-floating" insofar as they are not identified with any particular person or situation. One of the more common affective experiences is the so-called déjà vu. Significantly, as Penfield and Erickson (1941) have noted, the patient may experience *only the feeling* that accompanies the act of remembering. A similar situation applies to auras conveying eureka-type feelings expressed by such words as "This is it, the absolute truth," "This is what the world is all about" (MacLean, 1970, 1973b). Ironically, it would seem that the ancient limbic system provides free-floating, strong affective feelings of conviction that we attach to revelations and beliefs, regardless of whether they are true or false.

Case histories of limbic epilepsy also indicate (1) that the limbic system is basic for affective feelings of the reality of the self and of the environment and (2) that ictal disruptions of its functions may result in changes of mood, distortions of perception, feelings of depersonalization, hallucinations and paranoid delusions (MacLean, 1973c).

The affective aspects of one's experiences—as illustrated by the déjà vu—seem to be an important requisite for memory (MacLean, 1969a). One of the consequences of limbic seizures is the amnesia that is temporally related to the termination of the aura and the onset and duration of the automatism. Sometimes the automatism involves activities that almost certainly require a functioning neocortex.

Feelings triggered by epileptogenic foci may involve any one of the sensory systems. There may be olfactory, gustatory, visceral, and genital sensations; sounds may seem unusually loud or faint; parts of the body may seem swollen to large proportions; there may be the condition of micropsia or macropsia in which objects seem unusually small or large.

Sensations, perceptions, affect!—there is no clinical entity other than limbic epilepsy that combines these three psychological aspects of our topic in its symptomatology. What is the neural basis for these and other manifestations that have been summarized?

In the "visceral brain" paper of 1949, I elaborated upon the Papez theory of emotion (Papez, 1937) by suggesting that impulses from all the intero- and exteroceptive systems find their way to the hippocampus via the hippocampal gyrus. The hypothetical pathways were schematized in Fig. 3 of that paper. The hippocampal formation was visualized as a mechanism that combined information of internal and external origin into affective feelings that found further elaboration and expression through connections with the amygdala, septum, basal ganglia, hypothalamus, and the principle reentry circuit to the limbic lobe that has become known as "the Papez circuit."

Prior to discussing the question of inputs to the limbic cortex, two other important considerations require mention. First, the pathological studies of Sano and Malamud (1953) and of Margerison and Corsellis (1966) have revealed that Ammon's horn sclerosis is, in Malamud's words (1966), the "common denominator" in cases of psychomotor epilepsy. Since the sclerosis often extends to other medial temporal structures, Falconer, Serafetinides, and Corsellis (1964) prefer to use the term "medial temporal sclerosis." That such sclerosis or other medial temporal lesions are responsible for epileptogenic foci is strongly supported by two series of 100 cases of epilepsy in which Falconer (1970) resected the offending temporal lobe in one block, a procedure that not only affords removal of all or most of the damaged tissue but also allows complete pathological examination.

Second, it is a remarkable fact that seizure discharges originating in or near the limbic cortex have a tendency to spread in and be largely confined to the limbic system. It is probable that the hippocampus is almost always involved, with the discharge either originating in it or spreading to it from related structures. Simultaneous recordings from the neocortex may show little change during such seizures except for a generalized desynchronization. For such reasons I have referred to the potential "schizophysiology" (MacLean, 1954) of limbic and neocortical systems and suggested that this situation may partly account for conflicts between what we affectively "feel" and what we "know."

Except for olfaction with its representation in the piriform lobe, and the less certain evidence of the representation of gustatory and visceral sensation in the limbic part of the insula, it has not been at all clear how various sensory and perceptive phenomena are generated by limbic discharges. There is experimental evidence that limbic seizures do not appreciably change the bioelectrical activity of the primary sensory areas of the neocortex. Acoustic stimuli, for example, continue to be effective in evoking potentials in the auditory area during propagating hippocampal seizures (Flynn, MacLean, and Kim, 1961; Prichard and Glaser, 1966).

In the 1949 paper mentioned above, I hypothesized that somatic, auditory, and visual information was channeled to the hippocampal gyrus by transcortical connections from the primary receiving areas. Subsequently, Pribram and I reported strychnine neuronographic findings in the cat (MacLean and Pribram, 1953) and monkey (Pribram and MacLean, 1953) that would be compatible with this hypothesis. Three years ago, Jones and Powell (1970) described an experimental anatomical study in the macaque which not only revealed the possibility of stepwise cortical connections from these areas to the hippocampal gyrus, but also to the limbic cortex of the anterior cingulate gyrus and posterior orbital area (see also recent anatomical study by Van Hoesen, Pandya, and Butters, 1972).

After a brief recapitulation of earlier electrophysiological findings, I shall summarize a series of microelectrode studies that indicate on the basis of response latencies, that visual, auditory, somatic, and visceral information reaches respective parts of the limbic lobe by rather direct subcortical pathways. At the same time, I will mention supporting anatomical evidence.

In a study by MacLean, Horwitz, and Robinson (1952) we found that gustatory and noxious somatic stimulation resulted in rhythmically recurring olfactory-like potentials in the piriform area. Sometimes rhythmic potentials appeared in the hippocampus following olfactory or gustatory stimulation. In pursuing this lead, Green and Arduini (1954) showed that various forms of sensory stimulation evoked rhythmic theta activity in the hippocampus of unanesthetized animals. Such effects were observed in macrosmatic animals but not in primates, and were regarded as nonspecific in nature.

In continuing the investigation of limbic inputs we have employed microelectrode recording of evoked unit responses in chronically prepared, awake, sitting squirrel monkeys. Such experimentation avoids the depressant effects of anesthesia on neural transmission and, in contradistinction to the technique for recording evoked slow potentials with macroelectrodes, makes it possible to be sure of the locus of the neural response. Thus far we have tested more than 7,500 cerebral units, of which about 2,500 (33%) were located in the limbic cortex. We have explored all of the cortex of the limbic lobe except for the posterior orbital and piriform areas. I shall now summarize briefly our published findings on the results of visual, auditory, and somatic stimulation.

A. Visual Stimulation

Virtually all photically responsive units were located in the posterior hippocampal gyrus (see Fig. 4), the parahippocampal cortex of the lingual gyrus,

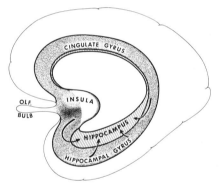

FIG. 4. Shaded areas show main subdivisions of the limbic lobe referred to in the review of microelectrode findings on inputs from intero- and exteroceptive systems. The insular cortex overlying the claustrum is limbic by definition because it forms part of the phylogenetically old cortex surrounding the brainstem. OLF bulb = olfactory bulb. From MacLean (1970).

and the retrosplenial cortex near its junction with the striate cortex (MacLean, Yokota, and Kinnard, 1968). The conditions of the experiment made it impractical to plot receptive fields and to do more than to test with moving patterns. The regularity and character of the photic responses, as well as the latency values, were suggestive of a subcortical, rather than transcortical, pathway. Evidence in support of this inference was obtained in a neuroanatomical study in which improved techniques for demonstrating fine fibers were used to trace degeneration from lesions in the lateral geniculate body and pulvinar (MacLean and Creswell, 1970). Lesions in the ventrolateral part of the lateral geniculate nucleus resulted in degeneration in that part of the optic radiations known as Meyer's loop which makes a temporal detour and enters the core of the posterior hippocampal gyrus. Some fibers could be traced to the photically responsive limbic cortex and adjoining neocortical areas. A coarser type of degeneration was seen in the posterior hippocampal gyrus and contiguous areas following lesions of the inferior pulvinar. The pulvinar projections are contained in a band of fibers just lateral to the optic radiations. These observations will recall the discussion (see section titled "Role of the Neomammalian Brain") of recently described connections between the superior colliculus and the inferior pulvinar.

About half the cells in the posterior hippocampal gyrus gave a sustained on-response to ocular illumination, raising the question of their possible role in states of wakefulness, alerting, and attention, or in the regulation of neuroendocrine functions affected by diurnal and seasonal changes in light.

Some cells in the retrosplenial cortex responded only to stimulation of the contralateral eye, suggesting that they may receive their innervation from the primitive temporal monocular crescent, the part of our retina through which we become aware of objects moving in from the side or rear. As witness the blinders used for horses, unexpected movements in the peripheral visual field may induce startle and alarm. I recall a patient with psychomotor epilepsy whose aura began with a feeling of fear that someone was standing behind him. If he turned to see who it was, the feeling became intensified, and he might have a generalized convulsion. He learned that by resisting the impulse to turn, he could usually prevent a generalized seizure. Horowitz, Adams, and Rutkin (1968) have reported clinical cases in which stimulation with electrodes presumably in "posterior hippocampal areas" was more apt to result in visual imagery than stimulation at other sites in the temporal lobe.

The insular cortex overlying the claustrum (Fig. 4) is by definition limbic because it forms part of the phylogenetically old cortex surrounding the brainstem. We encountered a few units in the limbic cortex of the insula that responded with a brisk discharge to an approaching object. This finding recalls observations by Penfield and Jasper (1954) that discharges in the parainsular region may result in macropsia, a condition in which objects appear to become larger.

B. Somatic and Auditory Stimulation

Responses to somatic and to auditory stimulation were elicited only in the limbic cortex of the insula (Sudakov, MacLean, Reeves, and Marino, 1971). The receptive fields of the somatic units were usually large and bilateral. Units responding to auditory stimulation were located somewhat more caudally. There were two main types, one of which discharged with short latencies ranging from 7 to 15 msec. Latencies of this order suggest the possibility of direct connections from the medial geniculate body. As discussed in the original paper, both anterograde and retrograde degeneration studies indicate that the insular cortex overlying the claustrum receives projections from the medial geniculate body. The anatomical evidence is conflicting in regard to somatic projections.

C. Gustatory Stimulation

While exploring the insula we also tested the responsiveness of units to gustatory stimulation. Responsive units were located anteriorly in the same region from which Benjamin and Burton (1968) recorded evoked potentials upon stimulation of the chorda tympani in the squirrel monkey. Other units in this same region were activated by mechanical stimulation of the oral cavity, including the pharynx.

D. Vagal Stimulation

Somewhat surprisingly, units of the cingulate cortex (see Fig. 4) are virtually unresponsive to visual, auditory, and somatic stimulation (Bachman and MacLean, 1971). In a further attempt to discover the nature of inputs to the cingulate cortex we have investigated the possibility of visceral projections by testing the effects of vagal volleys on unit activity. These experiments have been performed on awake, sitting squirrel monkeys previously prepared with electrodes chronically implanted on the cervical vagus or at the site where the vagus enters the jugular foramen (Bachman, Katz, and MacLean, 1972b). Of more than 300 units thus far tested a little more than 20% have been responsive, with the ratio of initially excited to initially inhibited units being about 2 to 3. Most of the responsive units have been located in the middle portion of the gyrus. The response latencies of the excited units have been as short as 15 msec, suggesting a fairly direct pathway. In a parallel study we have attempted to mimic natural stimulation of visceral receptors by injecting micro-amounts of 5-hydroxytryptamine (serotonin) through an indwelling catheter in the superior vena cava (Bachman, Katz, and MacLean, 1972a). Of 82 tested units in the supracallosal cingulate cortex, 18% were affected, with two-thirds showing an increased firing rate and one-third a decrease. These units were also located in the midportion of the gyrus. The anatomical studies of Morest (1961) suggest the possibility of an ascending pathway from the nucleus solitarius to the dorsal tegmental nucleus of Gudden, from which impulses might ascend via the mammillary peduncle system to the anterior ventral nucleus of the thalamus and the cingulate cortex. The findings in histofluorescence studies (e.g., Fuxe, 1965; Jacobowitz and Kostrzewa, 1971; Olson and Fuxe, 1972) are not incompatible with the interesting possibility of an ascending norepinephrine system from the nucleus solitarius. The anterior ventral nucleus of the thalamus has numerous fine norepinephrine terminals, and such terminals are also found in the cingulate gyrus. In a comparative histofluorescence study, including the pygmy marmoset and squirrel monkey, Jacobowitz and I (*unpublished data*) have found that the organizational pattern of all of the recognized aminergic systems have been preserved with remarkable consistency in the evolution of primates.

Among other limbic areas we hope to explore in the monkey for vagal responses are the posterior orbital and anterior insular areas which correspond to a region in the cat from which a number of investigators recorded changes in spontaneous activity (Bailey and Bremer, 1938) or evoked potentials (Dell and Olson, 1951a,b; Korn, Wendt, and Albe-Fessard, 1966) with vagal stimulation.

E. Sensory Integration

In prefacing the question of sensory integration I would like to emphasize that in our own experiments no hypothalamic units responded to photic and somatic stimulation, and only a few were affected by auditory stimulation (Poletti, Kinnard, and MacLean, 1973). This would suggest that sensory information affecting the hypothalamus is first integrated and processed in related structures such as the limbic cortex.

In our initial studies in monkeys anesthetized with alpha-chloralose we found a few limbic cortical units that showed convergence of sensory inputs. But it is remarkable that in the awake, sitting monkey all responsive units appear to be modality specific, indicating a high degree of selectivity. This raises the additional question as to how information reaching the limbic cortex from the intero- and exteroceptive systems is integrated and processed. Or metaphorically stated, where do the "viewers" reside in the limbic system? One likely place is the entorhinal cortex of the hippocampal gyrus which receives connections from the frontotemporal cortex (posterior orbital, anterior insular, piriform, and temporal polar areas) and from the caudally lying parahippocampal cortex (Fig. 4). The entorhinal cortex forms an extensive area in man. From the entorhinal area information would be fed forward through the perforant and alveolar pathways to the hippocampus (Fig. 4). The anterior hippocampus also receives connections from the fronto-temporal region, and there are afferent connections to the posterior hippocampus from the cingulate gyrus via the cingulum, as well as from the lamina medullaris superficialis. These latter pathways might transmit information of vagal origin (see above). In the hippocampus the Schaffer collateral system would provide one means of interrelating information from the various sensory modalities.

The septum, which receives connections from the hypothalamus, is another presumed source of interoceptive information reaching the hippocampus. The septal projections are believed to terminate in the stratum oriens, possibly on the basal dendrites of the hippocampal pyramids, whereas the perforant pathway terminates on the apical dendrites. In an intracellular study of hippocampal neurons in the awake, sitting monkey we found that septal stimuli elicited excitatory postsynaptic potentials (EPSP) associated with neuronal discharge, whereas the stimulation of the olfactory bulb generated EPSPs but never spikes (Yokota, Reeves, and MacLean, 1970). In terms of classical conditioning, impulses from these respective exteroceptive inputs might be compared to unconditional and conditional stimuli. Brazier (1964) has reported photically evoked slow potentials in the hippocampus of patients undergoing diagnostic tests for epilepsy.

F. Limbic Outputs

It is beyond the scope of this paper to deal with output mechanisms of the limbic system, but a few salient points deserve mention. Microelectrode studies have shown that fornix volleys or hippocampal afterdischarges inhibit unit responses in the caudal intralaminar region to potentially noxious stimuli of the fifth nerve (Yokota and MacLean, 1968). In a recent paper we have reported that hippocampal volleys elicit responses in a large proportion of units in *certain* structures of the basal forebrain, preoptic region, and hypothalamus (Poletti et al., 1973). In each case, more than 80% of the responsive units showed initial excitation. Hippocampal afterdischarges also more commonly excited than inhibited units. Following afterdischarges, units showed changes in their firing patterns that lasted from 1 to 11 min. These latter findings may help to explain the prolonged "rebound" behavioral and autonomic changes seen following hippocampal afterdischarges, including agitated states on the one hand and enhanced pleasure and sexual reactions on the other.

As seemed evident from the electrophysiological findings, a parallel neuroanatomical study showed for the first time in a primate that the fornix projects to the medial preoptic area and to the perifornical region (Poletti et al., 1973). The work of Hess and Brügger (1943) implicated the perifornical region (the so-called intermediate zone of Hess) in the expression of angry behavior. The medial preoptic area has become of increasing interest not only because of its participation in the control of gonadotropic activity and genital function, but also because of its role in sexual differentiation in certain macrosmatic animals.

A few fibers could also be traced to the tuberal region where the electrophysiological study had shown a cellular response to hippocampal volleys. In view of this and other findings, attention should be called to the accumulating evidence that hippocampal stimulation, depending on the physiological state at the time, may have a facilitatory or inhibitory effect with respect to adrenocorticotropic hormone release, cardiovascular reflexes, and visceral responsiveness (see Poletti et al., 1973, for references). The results of our own microelectrode studies would indicate that in the awake, sitting monkey there is leeway for attributing a range of inhibitory, excitatory, and modulating functions to the hippocampus.

Poletti, Sujatanond, and Sweet (1972) have since shown that following section of the fornix, hippocampal volleys were still effective in eliciting unit responses in the structures examined in the preceding study, but with a longer latency. It seems probable that the impulses are transmitted via the amygdala, which represents one of the major avenues for projections from the fronto-temporal division of the limbic system.

Clinically, as well as experimentally in animals, the hippocampal formation has been implicated in dreaming and other manifestations of REM sleep. This is a matter relevant to our topic because of the strong affective component of dreaming. The subject has recently attracted additional interest because aminergic systems have been implicated in mechanisms of sleep (see Jouvet, 1972, for review). As we reported, the cellular parts of the hippocampus, as well as its closely associated nuclei, the amygdala and the septum, contain relatively large amounts of serotonin (Paasonen, MacLean, and Giarman, 1957), and the work of Fuxe (1965) has demonstrated the presence of norepinephrine terminals in the radiate layer.

In summary, the work that has been reviewed suggests mechanisms by which information of intero- and exteroceptive systems can interact in the hippocampal formation and influence hypothalamic and other brainstem structures involved in emotional behavior.

VI. STRIATAL COMPLEX

There remains, in conclusion, the question of the role of the striatal complex in sensory and perceptive aspects of emotional behavior. Here we are obliged to sound even greater depths of ignorance than in the case of the neo-mammalian and limbic formations. Evidence has accumulated in recent years that most parts of the neocortex and limbic cortex project to the corpus striatum. The observed degeneration, however, appears to be rather scant. From an evolutionary point of view, it would appear to be of special significance that the limbic lobe conforms to the corpus striatum somewhat like a mold. The seemingly obligatory relationship between the two is reflected by the way the head of the caudate is drawn out into a long tail that is enfolded by the temporal part of the limbic lobe.

In addition to reciprocal connections with the substantia nigra, the corpus striatum (caudate + putamen) projects to the globus pallidus which in turn establishes connections with the ventral part of the thalamus and other structures of the brainstem. Nauta and Mehler (1966) have failed to find evidence of connections of the so-called pallidohypothalamic tract with the ventromedial nucleus or other parts of the hypothalamus. The peripallidal portion of the substantia innominata, however, appears to project to the caudolateral part of the hypothalamus. Albe-Fessard, Rocha-Miranda, and Oswaldo-Cruz (1960) have reported that heterogenous afferents converge on individual neurons of the caudate nucleus of the cat. There are, however, no clear indications as to the course of ascending pathways.

Various authorities have pointed out that despite 150 years of experimentation, remarkably little has been learned about the functions of the striatal complex. The finding that large bilateral lesions of the corpus striatum or globus pallidus in mammals may result in no apparent motor deficit is evidence against the traditional clinical view that these structures subserve purely motor functions. Perhaps because of a major interest in learning, memory, perception, and related problems, there has been a failure to ask the right questions. At our field laboratory we are investigating the role of the striatal complex in natural forms of behavior, testing the hypothesis that it is basic for species-typical, genetically constituted forms of behavior such as selecting a homesite, establishing and defending territory, hunting, homing, mating, forming social hierarchies, selecting leaders, and so forth. We also hope that this work will shed light on neural mechanisms underlying compulsive, repetitious, ritualistic, deceptive, and imitative forms of behavior. The comparative approach to this work is strengthened now that developments in neurochemistry (particularly the Koelle stain for cholinesterase and the histofluorescence technique of Falck and Hillarp) have made it possible to identify corresponding structures in the striatal complex of reptiles, birds, and mammals.

In a study involving lesions in various parts of the brain in more than 90 squirrel monkeys, I have obtained evidence that the striatal complex is essential for the expression of the species-typical display behavior of this species, as well as the associated imitative factors (MacLean, 1972a, 1973a).

It is relevant to mechanisms of imitation that partial representations have the capacity to trigger replicative forms of behavior. In the case of the squirrel monkey the reflection of a single eye may be enough to elicit a full display (MacLean, 1964). In reptiles and lower forms, dummies or even parts of dummies are sufficient to elicit courtship and aggressive display, as well as other patterns of behavior. In the case of domestic mammals, partial dummies are used as incitements for the purpose of collecting semen for artificial insemination. Shadowy forms or partial representations are notorious for their capacity to evoke fearful and paranoid reactions in animals and man.

As I mentioned in the introduction, workers in psychophysics seem to be interested in perceptual illusions only insofar as they help to analyze mechanisms by which subjects derive perfect images of objects regardless of size. In future neuroethological work, it is evident that more attention must be given to neural mechanisms that account for complex behavioral responses to phantoms and partial representations. As might be illustrated by several examples, the problem applies not only to the visual system, but also to other sensory systems.

VII. SUMMARY

In evolution, the primate forebrain has evolved and expanded along the lines of three basic patterns characterized as reptilian, paleomammalian, and neomammalian. Radically different in structure and chemistry, the three evolutionary formations comprise, so to speak, a *triune* brain. This paper focuses on the question of how sensory and perceptive mechanisms exert their influence on forebrain structures believed to be involved in the experience and expression of emotion. Particular attention is given to recent experimental findings on inputs to the limbic system which represents an inheritance from lower mammals and which has been shown to play an important role in emotional behavior.

REFERENCES

Albe-Fessard, D., Rocha-Miranda, C. E., and Oswaldo-Cruz, E. (1960): Activités évoquées dans le noyau caudé du chat en réponse à des types divers d'afférences. II. Étude microphysiologique. *Electroencephalogr. Clin. Neurophysiol.*, 12:649–661.

Bachman, D. S., Katz, H. M., and MacLean, P. D. (1972a): Effect of intravenous injections of 5-hydroxytryptamine (serotonin) on unit activity of cingulate cortex of awake squirrel monkeys. *Fed. Proc.*, 31:303 (Abst.).

Bachman, D. S., Katz, H. M., and MacLean, P. D. (1972b): Vagal influence on units of cingulate cortex in the awake, sitting squirrel monkey. *Electroencephalogr. Clin. Neurophysiol.*, 33:350–351.

Bachman, D. S., and MacLean, P. D. (1971): Unit analysis of inputs to cingulate cortex in awake, sitting squirrel monkeys. I. Exteroceptive systems. *Int. J. Neurosci.*, 2:109–113.

Bailey, P., and Bremer, F. (1938): A sensory cortical representation of the vagus nerve. *J. Neurophysiol.*, 1:405–412.

Benjamin, R. M., and Burton, H. (1968): Projection of taste nerve afferents to anterior opercular-insular cortex in squirrel monkey (Saimiri sciureus). *Brain Res.*, 7:221–231.

Brazier, M. A. B. (1964); Evoked responses recorded from the depths of the human brain. *Ann. N.Y. Acad. Sci.*, 112:33–59.

Carpenter, M. B., and Peter, P. (1972): Nigrostriatal and nigrothalamic fibers in the rhesus monkey. *J. Comp. Neurol.*, 144:93–116.

Dahlström, A., and Fuxe, K. (1964): Evidence for the existence of monoamine-containing neurons in the central nervous system. I. Demonstration of monoamines in the cell bodies of brain stem neurons. *Acta Physiol. Scand.*, 62:5–55.

Dell, P., and Olson, R. (1951a): Projections thalamiques, corticales et cérébelleuses des afférences viscérales vagales. *C.R. Soc. Biol. (Paris)*, 145:1084–1088.

Dell, P., and Olson, R. (1951b): Projections "secondaires" mésencéphaliques, diencéphaliques et amygdaliennes des afférences viscérales vagales. *C.R. Soc. Biol. (Paris)*, 145:1088–1091.

Descartes, R. (1967): *The Philosophical Works of Descartes*, Vols. 1 and 2, translated into English by E. S. Haldane and G. R. T. Ross. Cambridge University Press, Cambridge.

Falconer, M. A. (1970): Historical review: The pathological substrate of temporal lobe epilepsy. *Guys Hosp. Rep.*, 119:47–60.

Falconer, M. A., Serafetinides, E. A., and Corsellis, J. A. N. (1964): Etiology and pathogenesis of temporal lobe epilepsy. *Arch. Neurol.*, 10:233–248.

Flynn, J. P., MacLean, P. D., and Kim, C. (1961): Effects of hippocampal afterdischarges on conditioned responses. In: *Electrical Stimulation of the Brain*, edited by D. E. Sheer, pp. 382–386. University of Texas Press, Austin.

Fuxe, K. (1965): Evidence for the existence of monoamine neurons in the central nervous system. IV. Distribution of monoamine nerve terminals in the central nervous system. *Acta Physiol. Scand.*, 64(Suppl. 247):37–84.

Green, J. D., and Arduini, A. A. (1954): Hippocampal electrical activity in arousal. *J. Neurophysiol.*, 17:533–557.

Harting, J. K., Hall, W. C., Diamond, I. T., and Martin, G. F. (1973): Anterograde degeneration study of the superior colliculus in *Tupaia glis:* Evidence for a subdivision between superficial and deep layers. *J. Comp. Neurol.*, 148:361–386.

Head, H., and Holmes, G. (1920): Part IV. The brain. Sensory disturbances from cerebral lesions. Chapt. 2. Sensory disturbances associated with certain lesions of the optic thalamus. In: *Studies in Neurology*, edited by H. Head. Vol. 2:55–569. Oxford University Press, London.

Hess, W. R., and Brügger, M. (1943): Der Miktions und der Defäkationsakt als Erfolg zentraler Reizung. *Helv. Physiol. Acta*, 1:511–532.

Horowitz, M. J., Adams, J. E., and Rutkin, B. B. (1968): Visual imagery and brain stimulation. *Arch. Gen. Psychiatry*, 19:469–486.

Hubel, D. H., and Wiesel, T. N. (1962): Receptive fields, binocular interaction and functional architecture in the cat's visual cortex. *J. Physiol. (Lond.)*, 160:106–154.

Ingram, W. R., Barris, R. W., and Ranson, S. W. (1936): Catalepsy: An experimental study. *Arch. Neurol. Psychiatry*, 35:1175–1197.

Jacobowitz, D., and Kostrzewa, R. (1971): Selective action of 6-hydroxydopa on noradrenergic terminals: Mapping of preterminal axons of the brain. *Life Sci.* 10:1329–1342.

Jones, E. G., and Powell, T. P. S. (1970): An anatomical study of converging sensory pathways within the cerebral cortex of the monkey. *Brain*, 93:793–820.

Jouvet, M. (1972): Veille, sommeil et reve: Le discours biologique. *Rev. Méd.*, 16: 1003–1063.

Korn, H., Wendt, R., and Albe-Fessard, D. (1966): Somatic projection to the orbital cortex of the cat. *Electroencephalogr. Clin. Neurophysiol.*, 21:209–226.

MacKay, D. M. (1970): Perception and brain function. In: *The Neurosciences*, edited by F. O. Schmitt, pp. 303–316. The Rockefeller University Press, New York.

MacLean, P. D. (1949): Psychosomatic disease and the "visceral brain." Recent developments bearing on the Papez theory of emotion. *Psychosom. Med.*, 11:338–353.

MacLean, P. D. (1952): Some psychiatric implications of physiological studies on frontotemporal portion of limbic system (visceral brain). *Electroencephalogr. Clin. Neurophysiol.*, 4:407–418.

MacLean, P. D. (1954): The limbic system and its hippocampal formation. Studies in animals and their possible application to man. *J. Neurosurg.*, 11:29–44.

MacLean, P. D. (1958): Contrasting functions of limbic and neocortical systems of the brain and their relevance to psychophysiological aspects of medicine. *Am. J. Med.*, 25:611–626.

MacLean, P. D. (1960): Psychosomatics. *Handbook of Physiology*. In: *Neurophysiology III*, pp. 1723–1744. American Physiological Society, Washington, D.C.

MacLean, P. D. (1964): Mirror display in the squirrel monkey, Saimiri sciureus. *Science*, 146:940–952.

MacLean, P. D. (1967): The brain in relation to empathy and medical education, *J. Nerv. Ment. Dis.*, 144:374–382.

MacLean, P. D. (1969a): The internal-external bonds of the memory process. *J. Nerv. Ment. Dis.*, 149:40–47.

MacLean, P. D. (1969b): The hypothalamus and emotional behavior. In: *The Hypothalamus*, edited by W. Haymaker, E. Anderson, and W. J. H. Nauta, pp. 659–678. Charles C Thomas, Springfield.

MacLean, P. D. (1970): The triune brain, emotion, and scientific bias. In: *The Neurosciences Second Study Program*, edited by F. O. Schmitt, pp. 336–349. The Rockefeller University Press, New York.

MacLean, P. D. (1972a): Cerebral evolution and emotional processes: New findings on the striatal complex. *Ann. N.Y. Acad. Sci.*, 193:137–149.

MacLean, P. D. (1972b): Implications of microelectrode findings on exteroceptive inputs to the limbic cortex. In: *Limbic System Mechanisms and Autonomic Function*, edited by C. H. Hockman, pp. 115–136. Charles C Thomas, Springfield.

MacLean, P. D. (1973a): Effects of pallidal lesions on species-typical display behavior of squirrel monkey. *Fed. Proc.*, 32:384 (Abst.).

MacLean, P. D. (1973b): The brain's generation gap: Some human implications. *Zygon J. Religion Sci.*, 8:113–127.

MacLean, P. D. (1973c): A triune concept of the brain and behaviour; Lecture I. Man's reptilian and limbic inheritance; Lecture II. Man's limbic brain and the psychoses: Lecture III. New trends in man's evolution. In: *The Hincks Memorial Lectures*, edited by T. Boag, and D. Campbell. University of Toronto Press, Toronto.

MacLean, P. D., and Creswell, G. (1970): Anatomical connections of visual system with limbic cortex of monkey. *J. Comp. Neurol.*, 138:265–278.

MacLean, P. D., Horwitz, N. H., and Robinson, F. (1952): Olfactory-like responses in pyriform area to nonolfactory stimulation. *Yale J. Biol. Med.*, 25:159–172.

MacLean, P. D., and Pribram, K. H. (1953): Neuronographic analysis of medial and basal cerebral cortex. I. Cat. *J. Neurophysiol.*, 16:312–323.

MacLean, P. D., Yokota, T., and Kinnard, M. A. (1968): Photically sustained on-responses of units in posterior hippocampal gyrus of awake monkey. *J. Neurophysiol.*, 31:870–883.

Malamud, N. (1966): The epileptogenic focus in temporal lobe epilepsy from a pathological standpoint. *Arch. Neurol.*, 14:190–195.

Margerison, J. H., and Corsellis, J. A. N. (1966): Epilepsy and the temporal lobes: A clinical, electroencephalographic and neuropathological study of the brain in epilepsy, with particular reference to the temporal lobes. *Brain*, 89:499–530.

Mettler, F. A. (1955): Perceptual capacity, function of the corpus striatum, and schizophrenia. *Psychiatr. Q.*, 29:89–111.

Michael, C. R. (1969): Retinal processing of visual images. *Sci. Am.*, 220:104–114.

Morest, D. K. (1961): Connexions of dorsal tegmental nucleus in rat and rabbit. *J. Anat.*, 95:1–18.

Mountcastle, V. B., Davies, P. W., and Berman, A. L. (1957): Response properties of neurons of cat's somatic sensory cortex to peripheral stimuli. *J. Neurophysiol.*, 20:374–407.

Myers, R. E. (1963): Projections of the superior colliculus in monkey. *Anat. Rec.*, 145:264 (Abst.).

Nauta, W. J. H., and Mehler, W. R. (1966): Projections of the lentiform nucleus in the monkey. *Brain Res.*, 1:3–42.

Olson, L., and Fuxe, K. (1972): Further mapping out of central noradrenaline neuron systems: Projections of the 'subcoeruleus' area. *Brain Res.*, 43:289–295.

Paasonen, M. K., MacLean, P. D., and Giarman, N. J. (1957): 5-Hydroxytryptamine (serotonin, enteramine) content of structures of the limbic system. *J. Neurochem.*, 1:326–333.

Papez, J. W. (1937): A proposed mechanism of emotion. *Arch. Neurol. Psychiatry*, 38:725–743.

Penfield, W., and Erickson, T. C. (1941): *Epilepsy and Cerebral Localization*, Charles C Thomas, Springfield.

Penfield, W., and Jasper, H. (1954): *Epilepsy and the Functional Anatomy of the Human Brain*. Little, Brown and Company, Boston.

Penfield, W., and Perot, P. (1963): The brain's record of auditory and visual experience. A final summary and discussion. *Brain*, 86:596–696.

Poletti, C. E., Kinnard, M. A., and MacLean, P. D. (1973): Hippocampal influence on unit activity of hypothalamus, preoptic region, and basal forebrain in awake, sitting squirrel monkeys. *J. Neurophysiol.*, 36:308–324.

Poletti, C. E., Sujatanond, M., and Sweet, W. H. (1972): Hypothalamic, preoptic, and basal forebrain unit responses to hippocampal stimulation in awake sitting squirrel monkeys with fornix lesions. *Fed. Proc.*, 31:404 (Abst.).

Pribram, K. H., and MacLean, P. D. (1953): Neuronographic analysis of medial and basal cerebral cortex. II. Monkey. *J. Neurophysiol.*, 16:324–340.

Prichard, J. W., and Glaser, G. H. (1966): Cortical sensory evoked potentials during limbic seizures. *Electroencephalogr. Clin. Neurophysiol.*, 21:180–184.

Ranson, S. W. (1939): Somnolence caused by hypothalamic lesions in the monkey. *Arch. Neurol. Psychiatry*, 41:1–23.

Sano, K., and Malamud, N. (1953): Clinical significance of sclerosis of the cornu ammonis. Ictal "psychic phenomena." *Arch. Neurol. Psychiatry*, 70:40–53.

Snyder, M., and Diamond, I. T. (1968): The organization and function of the visual cortex in the tree shrew. *Brain Behav. Evol.*, 1:244–288.

Spencer, H. (1896): *Principles of Psychology*, 2 vols. D. Appleton and Company, New York.

Sudakov, K., MacLean, P. D., Reeves, A. G., and Marino, R. (1971): Unit study of exteroceptive inputs to claustrocortex in awake, sitting, squirrel monkey. *Brain Res.,* 28:19–34.

Van Hoesen, G. W., Pandya, D. N., and Butters, N. (1972): Cortical afferents to the entorhinal cortex of the rhesus monkey. *Science,* 175:1471–1473.

Von Economo, C. (1931): *Encephalitis Lethargica. Its Sequelae and Treatment,* translated by K. O. Newman. Oxford University Press, London.

Wiener, N. (1948): *Cybernetics, or Control and Communication in the Animal and the Machine.* Wiley, New York.

Yokota, T., and MacLean, P. D. (1968): Fornix and fifth-nerve interaction on thalamic units in awake, sitting squirrel monkeys. *J. Neurophysiol.,* 31:358–370.

Yokota, T., Reeves, A. G., and MacLean, P. D. (1970): Differential effects of septal and olfactory volleys on intracellular responses of hippocampal neurons in awake, sitting monkeys. *J. Neurophysiol.,* 33:96–107.

N.B. This article originally appeared in Levi, L., editor (1975): *Emotions—Their Parameters and Measurement,* pp. 71–92. Raven Press, New York.

Biological Foundations of Psychiatry,
edited by R. G. Grenell and S. Gabay.
Raven Press, New York © 1976.

Evoked Potentials in Man

Charles Shagass

Temple University, Department of Psychiatry and Eastern Pennsylvania Psychiatric Institute,
Philadelphia, Pennsylvania 19104

I. INTRODUCTION

Two main kinds of brain electrical activity can be recorded from the surface of the human scalp, the spontaneous rhythms of the electroencephalogram (EEG) and potentials related to definable events. The best-known type of event-related potential (ERP) (Vaughan, 1969) is the sensory response evoked by an external stimulus. EEG recordings may be obtained in a relatively direct manner by amplifying and displaying the activity picked up by electrodes placed on the scalp, but most ERP activity can be displayed only after application of special averaging methods to the EEG. This is because the ERP activity is generally embedded in EEG activity of greater amplitude than the ERP.

Historically sensory evoked potentials and the EEG were discovered at the same time by Richard Caton (1875). Caton apparently began his experiments to determine whether the negative variation that DuBois-Reymond had found in nerves could be shown in the brain following stimulation of sensory receptors. In other words he was looking for an evoked potential in the brain. He put one recording electrode on the exposed cerebral cortex of an animal and the other on a cut surface and, using the light from a lamp as a stimulus, observed changes in potential. Simultaneously he found that, when both electrodes were on cut brain, there were incessant oscillations of current in the absence of stimulation; this was the EEG. Hans Berger (1929) discovered that the EEG can be recorded through the unopened human skull. The development of electroencephalography from the middle 1930s on was quite rapid, and the method has found significant clinical applications mainly in the study of neurologic disorders, such as the epilepsies and intracranial lesions.

The evoked potentials discovered by Caton provided a useful research tool for neurophysiologists who could place electrodes directly on or into the brain substance. However, because in scalp recordings they are almost totally obscured by the larger spontaneous EEG rhythms, exploration of evoked-potential phenomena in man awaited the development of special techniques. Dawson (1947) was the first to report a method for detecting cerebral action potentials evoked by nerve stimulation from human scalp recordings. He assumed that the evoked responses would occur at a fixed time after application of a stimulus and be relatively uniform in wave shape, whereas the timing of the EEG rhythms would be random with respect to the stimulus. Dawson displayed EEG traces on a cathode ray oscilloscope and superimposed a number of these tracings on a single photographic record; by this method he demonstrated that certain EEG events are time-coherent to the stimulus and can thus be distinguished from the background rhythms. Subsequently Dawson (1951, 1954) devised an instrument for automatic summation to detect small evoked potentials.

Several evoked-response summation or averaging instruments were developed during the 1950s; these were essentially custom-made for individual laboratories. In the early 1960s, commercially manufactured special purpose digital computers for averaging were introduced, giving investigators easy access to effective equipment. Soon thereafter evoked-response recording achieved widespread utilization as a research method.

This chapter deals with the main ERP phenomena, techniques for recording them, and methodologic problems encountered in applying ERP methods within the context of psychologic and psychiatric research. The material presented also includes a brief survey of results obtained in psychiatrically relevant ERP investigations.

II. METHODOLOGY

A. Averaging: Concepts and Limitations

The terms averaging and summation are often used interchangeably to denote the method used to extract average evoked responses from the EEG. Many of the commonly used averaging instruments yield the sum of the group of observations or the sum plus a constant, so that summation would be a more accurate term than averaging. However, for most purposes there are no essential differences between sum and mean.

The summation principle for extraction of small signals from larger noise is illustrated in Fig. 1. The desired signal is represented by wave C, which is ⅛ the peak-to-peak amplitude of sine waves A and B, shown completely out of phase with one another. The middle portion of Fig. 1 depicts waves A and C and waves B and C summed; the nature of C would be difficult to ascertain from the summed waves. The right-hand portion of Fig. 1 indicates what happens when the two wave forms in the middle of the figure are added together;

A and B sum to a horizontal line, forming the background against which the summed C waves are clearly visible.

If the evoked response is viewed as the signal and the EEG as random noise, averaging should improve the signal-to-noise ratio to an extent proportional to the square root of the number of observations added. This means that the gain in accuracy with only 16 observations is already half that obtained with 64. However, because the background EEG is rarely truly random, the square root law probably does not apply fully to the usual averaging situation. Walter (1964) has argued that this departure probably reduces the number of samples required. The decision as to how many samples will be averaged is usually empiric; one must compromise among the needs for a reliable, noise-free measurement, minimal time expenditure, and the least possible changes in the subject during the averaging sequence.

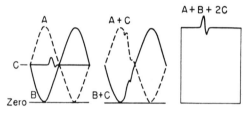

FIG. 1. Summation principle for extraction of small signals from larger noise. Signal of interest is wave C. A and B are sine waves completely out of phase with one another. (Middle) C is superimposed on both A and B, and is hard to distinguish. (Right) summation of waves in the middle figure; A and B add to a horizontal line, and C is clearly apparent. From Shagass (1972).

It is important to realize that there may be both random and systematic changes during an averaging sequence. Several consecutive averages may differ considerably, whereas such variations would not be suspected in a single average of all the samples. This brings the representativeness of the average into question. If only amplitude varies but wave shape and timing remain constant, the average may be satisfactorily representative for many purposes. However, when the time of occurrence (latency) of peaks fluctuates, the average can be quite unrepresentative. Variations of latency during the averaging sequence may lead to apparent reduction in amplitude of an average response; large latency fluctuations of a single wave could look like more than one wave in the average. Whenever possible, it is desirable to employ procedures that may indicate the sources of variation in the average response, e.g., averaging subsamples to determine whether latencies were constant.

B. Psychologic Issues in Averaging

From the standpoint of psychologically oriented experimentation, the averaging method involves some special problems. The usual assumption in averaging is that the repeated stimuli in a sequence have identical properties. Although this may be true from a physical standpoint, repetition of stimuli may alter the subject in a variety of ways, such as fatigue, boredom, inattentiveness, and habituation. When meaningful stimuli such as verbal sounds or pictures are used, their attention-getting qualities may change as the averaging sequence progresses. Investigators in the field of attention have devised a number of ingenious techniques for imparting to some stimuli greater attention value than others. Nevertheless the problems of equating stimuli psychologically both within and between subjects have probably never been adequately resolved. This means that some degree of doubt surrounds important attributes of the stimulus, just as it does the representativeness of the average evoked response.

Sutton (1969) has discussed the problems connected with the psychologic properties of the stimulus within the concept of subject options. In the commonly used recording situation, which involves a passive subject who has been instructed to be as relaxed as possible while remaining awake, subject options are maximal. The subject can do whatever he wishes as long as he remains relaxed and awake; his mental activity is essentially uncontrolled. Some workers have attempted to control the attentive state of the subject, and simultaneously to reduce artifact due to muscle activity, by having the subject monitor his own EEG on a cathode ray oscilloscope (CRO) screen. The most precise monitoring of the state of the subject may be obtained when specific objectively measurable voluntary responses are demanded from him, such as discrimination responses to particular stimuli.

C. Recording Procedures and Instrumentation

Electrodes. Many kinds of electrodes may be used with satisfactory results. The main consideration is that they be stably attached, with a low resistance (5 kohm or less) between two unpolarized electrodes. A lead to ground the subject is required in addition to those used for recording. Head locations for recording electrodes have not been standardized for evoked-potential work, although many workers have adopted the international 10–20 system developed for EEG recording (Jasper, 1958). Both bipolar (scalp-to-scalp) and unipolar (scalp-to-reference) derivations are employed. Unipolar recordings are more desirable from a theoretic point of view. Favorite locations for reference electrodes are one ear lobe or the two linked together, the mastoid, the bridge of the nose, the chin, and the zygoma. Some of these locations are not electrically inactive. Possibly the least active reference that has been proposed is noncephalic (Lehtonen and Koivikko, 1971); it links leads placed over the right sternoclavicular joint and the spine of the seventh cervical vertebra; a variable potentiometer is adjusted to greatly minimize the residual electrocardiogram (EKG). Although this noncephalic reference has a number of advantages, it usually records considerably more artifact than a reference on the ear. In turn recordings employing ear references generally contain more biologic artifacts than bipolar recordings. However, bipolar recordings are difficult to interpret; when both electrodes are over active areas, the signals picked up from each of these areas cannot be ascertained and potential gradients cannot be plotted. Figure 2 illustrates the difficulty of interpretation that may result from bipolar recordings.

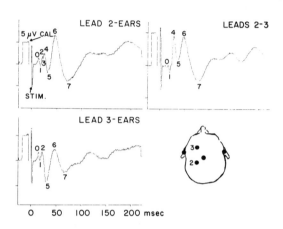

FIG. 2. Average responses to median nerve shock (768 sweeps) recorded from monopolar and bipolar derivations. Reference for monopolar recording, two ears linked together through a 22 kΩ resistor. Relative positivity at electrode 2 in bipolar and scalp leads in monopolar gives upward deflection. Peaks are numbered sequentially according to scheme used in our laboratory. Note difficulty of determining nature of activity at individual electrodes from bipolar derivation.

General instrumentation needs. The essential equipment required for recording averaged evoked responses consists of a stimulating device, an amplifying system with the appropriate frequency and gain characteristics, an averaging device, a synchronizing or trigger signal to start the averager, and a device for displaying the average. Many instruments are available for each of these functions. In practice the system may be considerably extended by adding extra timing devices, preset counters, calibration sources, instrumentation tape recorders, etc.

Averaging instruments. Commencing with Dawson's summator, many different devices have been used to accomplish averaging. These can be grouped into two categories: analog and digital. The storage elements of analog devices have included capacitor-integrators, photographic transparencies, electronic storage tubes and magnetic tape; their advantages and disadvantages have been discussed elsewhere (Shagass, 1972). Given sufficient memory, digital averagers generally provide better resolution and accuracy than analog devices. Both special- and general-purpose digital computers are used for averaging. There are now many makes of special-purpose digital averagers, most of which will also perform a few other functions, such as accumulating interval histograms. The obvious advantage of the small laboratory general-purpose computer is that it can be programmed to perform many functions in addition to averaging; these have great value for quantification of evoked-response data.

Additional devices for recording. Preset counters are used to standardize the number of sweeps entered into an average, and circuits are arranged to stop the stimulator when the desired count is obtained. Timing devices serve various purposes: to initiate and sometimes terminate stimuli, to start the action of the averager and to control the speed of some of the display devices. Complex stimulus sequences may require fairly elaborate timing circuits; these have become relatively inexpensive since the advent of integrated circuits. Random presentation of stimuli is often desirable and can be accomplished by means of a random-interval generator placed in the timing circuit.

Satisfactory amplitude calibration is important. In our laboratory we have used Emde's (1964) low-level calibrator for many years. With this, or a similar device, the calibration signal can be inserted in series with the recording electrodes and treated essentially like the evoked response. However, if the noise level is high, due either to unaveraged EEG or other biologic artifacts, the low-level calibration signal may be obscured.

The amplifiers used in the recording system must amplify the EEG to the voltage level optimal for the averager. The available range of upper and lower frequency cutoffs should provide minimal distortion of any desired signal. However, to record very slow potential changes, such as the contingent negative variation (CNV), special amplifiers may be needed; these should have either a long time constant (several seconds) or be direct-coupled (dc). At the other extreme, a very high upper frequency cutoff is needed for recording nerve action potentials or the very rapid early events of the auditory response (Jewett, Romano, and Williston, 1970). The frequency characteristics of instrumentation tape recorders must also conform to the nature of the signal of interest. Evoked responses are commonly displayed on paper, employing an XY plotter or some other ink-writing device, although some workers photograph the face of the CRO tube.

D. Stimulators and Stimulus Problems

In addition to the difficulties encountered in equating stimuli psychologically between and within subjects, there are some major problems in making stimuli physically equivalent. Although the stimulus energy may be standardized at source, significant variations can be introduced as stimuli are applied to receptors. The difficulties are perhaps greatest in the sphere of vision, because of pupillary mobility and eye movements. Regan (1972) has provided a detailed and sophisticated discussion of the factors that require control, particularly in the visual modality.

Many studies of visual evoked responses (VER) have been performed with very brief, bright flash stimuli, such as generated by the stroboscopic type of photic stimulator. With very brief flashes, only the response to the onset of the flash is observed, but when flashes exceed a 25-msec duration, there is an off response, so that the total response represents a combination of on and off components (Efron, 1964). On and off components also occur with prolonged somatosensory and auditory stimuli.

Commercially built stimulators are available to generate relatively simple punctate stimuli such as brief flashes of light, clicks, or shocks to the skin over a peripheral nerve. To increase the uniformity of the visual stimulus field, some workers have projected the light flash from behind the subject onto the concave surface of a large reflecting perimeter. Sine-wave modulated light has been used to generate a visual stimulus of a steady-state nature (Regan, 1972); the effect of modulation is to produce changing intensity of light, even though mean brightness and consequently light adaptation remain constant. The depth of modulation governs the strength of stimulation.

Patterned visual stimuli and pictures are commonly generated by means of slide projectors, often equipped with a tachistoscopic exposure device; special precautions may be needed to eliminate accompanying sounds. Some workers have employed digital logic circuits to generate pattern displays on CRO tubes for visual stimulation; these ordinarily are noiseless. There has been much recent interest in the responses to pattern reversal stimuli; the favorite procedure is to reverse the black and white squares in a checkerboard pattern. Checkerboard reversal is used in an evoked response test that may be of value in the diagnosis of multiple sclerosis (Halliday, 1973).

Clicks and tone pips, applied either through loudspeakers or through earphones, have been favorite auditory stimuli. Although such auditory stimuli have been used in many studies, these have often been conducted in a poorly controlled acoustic environment. More frequently investigators have attempted to eliminate extraneous noise by masking. Complex auditory stimuli, such as voice sounds, are usually placed on magnetic tape.

Somatosensory responses (SER) are most frequently evoked by percutaneous electrical stimulation of a peripheral nerve. Tactile stimuli have been generated by attaching a blunt pin or a stylus to a solenoid or a loudspeaker, releasing a puff of air by means of a valve, or pulsing one or more vibrators. Since the position of stimulating electrodes may vary in relation to the stimulated nerve tissue, it has been customary to relate stimulus strength to the subject's sensory threshold. The threshold is usually determined by increasing stimulus strength from an imperceptibly low level to the intensity at which it is first sensed; intensity is then diminished from a clearly sensed level to the point at which it is no longer perceived. The mean of the ascending and descending determinations is taken as the threshold. The strength of the stimulus is expressed as volts or milliamperes above threshold. Because variations in subject impedance can produce marked differences in the actual electrical energy delivered to a nerve, it is desirable to use either a constant-current or constant-voltage stimulator. The consistency of evoked-response amplitudes with these two types of stimulator appears to be about the same (Schwartz, Emde, and Shagass, 1964). A stimulus isolation unit is placed at the output of the electrical stimulator to reduce stimulus escape.

In general, the first evidence of an evoked potential is obtained with stimulus intensities that correspond to sensory threshold. However, there is evidence that this relation may hold true only for recordings made from the scalp or the dura, but not directly from the pial surface of the brain (Libet, Alberts, Wright, and Feinstein, 1967).

E. Quantification Problems

Amplitude and latency. Effective research use of evoked-response data, particularly in a behavioral context, usually requires quantitative treatment of the results. Quantification would be relatively easy if a response could be assumed to reflect a single kind of neural event. However, most investigators believe that the response curve reflects several types of activity, with differing temporal and possibly spatial characteristics. This view is suggested by complex wave forms; it has given rise to the concept of different components, usually defined by latency and polarity of visible maxima and minima in the curve (peaks). Figure 3 illustrates one of the commonly accepted models of how the evoked response is constituted. Figure 3A shows a series of positive and negative events, each with its own time course, but also overlapping in time. Thus, waves *a* and *c* of the graph are negative events separated in time, whereas *b* and *d* are positive events that overlap. Figure 3B shows the curve obtained by summing events *a, b, c,* and *d*. The negativity assumed to occur at *c* is not reflected as actual negativity in the curve. Also the positivity associated with *b* and the peak negativity of *c* are apparently displaced in

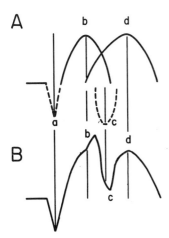

FIG. 3. The component model of a compound evoked response. (A) four assumed components; (B) algebraic summation of the components. Vertical lines show that peaks b and c are displaced to the right. Also negativity of c is not apparent in the synthesized response. From Shagass (1972).

time, so that the latency measurements of these peaks would not accurately depict these maxima. Figure 3 shows that only those individual events that do not overlap in time with others can be accurately depicted and measured in the evoked-response record. With the exception of the very earliest events, it follows that amplitude and latency measurements based on visible response peaks are probably inaccurate estimates.

The timing (latency) of peaks presents no serious quantification problems if the point to be measured is identified. Amplitude measurement may present difficulties if one wishes to measure the positivity or negativity from an isoelectric line. This is because the estimate of the zero level may be inaccurate due to baseline drift. Measurement between peaks is more accurate, but may reflect a mixture of activities. Measurements based on visual inspection can be done on a graph or with computer assistance by means of cursor programs. In our recent studies, we have found that amplitudes can be depicted quite accurately by automatically obtained computer measurements; the response is divided into several time epochs containing events of interest, and then the average deviation of the activity around the mean of the epoch is computed. This average deviation measure correlates at the 0.9 level with hand measurements of peak-to-peak excursions in the same portion of the response. In contrast we have had little success in attempts to obtain latency measures by automatic methods; only the latency of the earliest negative peak was determined reliably (Shagass, Overton, and Straumanis, 1972a).

Fourier analysis. A number of workers have applied Fourier analysis to evoked potential wave forms. Amplitude measurement of some components could then conceivably be achieved by determining the power within specified frequency ranges. Although the method is elegant, certain precautions must be observed in applying Fourier analysis to evoked-response data. Edge effects can be rather pronounced unless special steps are taken to round off the beginning and end of the signal so as not to produce an artifactually sharp rise and fall. Baseline drifts in the signal will also produce an artifactual ramp, resulting in inflated power at the slow frequency end of the spectrum. Before applying Fourier analysis to our data, we customarily determine the best least-squares fit to the available data points and then rotate the signal so that the mean slope is zero; this eliminates the ramp.

Fourier analysis may be used to fractionate evoked-response signals by frequency; this has the possibility of achieving relatively simple wave forms for quantification. Although this could theoretically be done with hardware filters, such instruments introduce a delay varying with the frequency band and produce artifactual effects due to oscillation of the filters when excited by a fast transient. Digital filtering, based on Fourier analysis with a general purpose computer, avoids these difficulties; the signal that has been Fourier analyzed can be reconstituted within specified frequency bands. We have employed this technique to show differing effects of drugs on the fast and slow frequency components of somatosensory responses (Shagass, 1974a).

The problem of noise. Noise, caused by biologic artifacts, such as muscle activity, can invalidate quantification procedures. Arithmetic smoothing of the signal may be used to reduce such noise, but smoothing will also introduce distortion, particularly in sharply rising components. The only real solution to the noise problem is at the recording level, i.e., to avoid recording when noise is present. This can be achieved by techniques for managing the subject or with difficult subjects, such as psychiatric patients, by use of an artifact-suppressing device. The artifact suppressor can be arranged to halt the stimuli and the recording when the EEG exceeds an arbitrary amplitude level within a given frequency range.

Variability. In addition to measurements of amplitude and frequency, investigators have been interested in quantifying the degree of similarity between two wave shapes, either in whole or in part. A favorite procedure for this purpose has been to compute the product-moment correlation coefficient between the temporally corresponding successive data points of two average responses (Callaway, Jones, and Layne, 1965). Although there are some theoretic objections to the use of correlation coefficients in this way, the procedure has proved practical. For statistical analysis, the correlation coefficients are converted to Z values, which are normally distributed. Callaway and Halliday (1973) have described several additional procedures for assessing variability.

Measurement of interactions. In studies aimed at determining the interactions between two or more stimuli employing either the same or different sensory modalities, it is a problem to visualize the effects of the later stimuli by themselves when the responses overlap in time. A common example occurs in the measurement of recovery functions; here two stimuli of the same modality are applied, and the interval between them is varied from one averaging sequence to another. To solve this problem, we have employed a device for automatic subtraction; single and paired stimuli are both presented, either alternately or in pseudorandom order, and the response to the single stimuli is entered alone into one averager channel and in inverse polarity into a second channel, which also accumulates the response to paired stimuli (Schwartz and Shagass, 1964). The automatic subtraction procedure thus yields a reasonable estimate of the response to the second stimulus alone, which can be compared with that to a single stimulus obtained in the same averaging sequence. The subtraction procedure can be applied to any number of stimuli in a sequence, e.g., to visualize the response to the tenth stimulus in a train, trains of ten and nine are used, and the nine responses are subtracted from the ten.

F. Biologic Contaminants

Activity originating outside of the brain can be time-coherent with a stimulus and may be difficult to distinguish from brain potentials. Important sources of extracerebral ERPs are the muscles of the head and neck (electromyogram, EMG); the structures of the orbit, particularly effects resulting from large retino-corneal potential changes, which can be recorded in the electrooculogram (EOG); movements of the tongue; and, should the stimulus fall consistently in a particular part of the cardiac cycle, the EKG. Bickford and his colleagues have drawn attention to the existence of microreflexes associated with sensory stimuli, and have shown that these EMG events can be mistaken for brain potentials (Bickford, Jacobson, and Cody, 1964; Cracco and Bickford, 1968). In our own experience, sustained or episodic muscle tension tends mainly to obscure evoked responses, rather than to generate consistent artifactual deflections; however, the problem needs to be constantly borne in mind. The EOG contamination of evoked responses can be quite serious, particularly with visual stimulation, and it is desirable to monitor EOG potentials by placing electrodes close to the eye, so as to determine to what extent the scalp-recorded responses resemble the EOG.

G. Subject Factors

A number of subject factors must be taken into account in evoked-response studies aimed at comparing populations. Age and sex are perhaps the most important and have been described elsewhere in some detail (Shagass, 1972, chap. 4). Evoked responses are generally of higher amplitude during infancy or childhood, and reach their lowest amplitude between the ages of 20 and 40 years, after which amplitude once again increases. The latencies of evoked response peaks are prolonged early in life, decrease as maturation progresses, and tend to increase in later years. Sex differences are most pronounced in latency measures, which tend to be shorter in females for both VER and SER. The shorter SER latency in females is attributable to the shorter average conduction pathway. There is evidence that, although sex differences in SER amplitudes are minimal in normal subjects, females tend to have much larger amplitudes than males in the presence of mental illness (Shagass, Straumanis, and Overton, 1972b). This means that the experimental design should make possible a test of the sex by group interaction. Handedness is another factor that may influence certain kinds of VER (Eason, Groves, White, and Oden, 1967).

Less permanent subject factors may exert profound effects on evoked responses. There are numerous drug effects, and a variety of endocrine influences have been demonstrated (Shagass, 1972). It is important to bear in mind that some commonly used agents, often not thought of as drugs can exert significant effects. These include tobacco (Hall, Rappaport, Hopkins, and Griffin, 1973); alcohol (Lewis, Dustman, and Beck, 1970); and marijuana (Lewis, Dustman, Peters, Straight, and Beck, 1973). There is always a need to attempt control of fluctuations in attentiveness and level of awareness.

Evoked-response amplitudes may also differ according to time of day

(Heninger, McDonald, Goff, and Sollberger, 1969), so that recording hours should be standardized or counterbalanced.

III. CHARACTERISTICS OF BRAIN ERPs

Vaughan (1969) has divided brain ERPs into four types: (1) sensory evoked potentials; (2) motor potentials; (3) long latency potentials related to complex psychologic variables; (4) steady potential shifts. In describing the various kinds of ERPs in this section, it should be emphasized that many factors influence the actual appearance of ERPs, and that any one type of ERP may vary greatly from subject to subject and with different parameters of stimulation in the same subject.

A. SER

Examples of SER to median nerve stimulation recorded with unipolar and bipolar lead derivations are shown in Fig. 2. In unipolar recordings, a small, but clearly visible, positive deflection is generally the earliest event in the response; its latency is 13 to 17 msec (Cracco, 1972). This initial event, sometimes called peak 0, is recorded at virtually the same amplitude from electrodes placed over wide regions of the brain (Goff, Matsumiya, Allison, and Goff, 1969), although it does display some potential gradient and contralateral predominance (Cracco, 1972). It may reflect activity originating in the central depths of the brain, perhaps at the prethalamic level. The succeeding deflections within about 100 msec after the stimulus, commencing with peak 1, tend to be localized to the hemisphere contralateral to the stimulated wrist, whereas the slow waves occurring after 100 msec again tend to be rather widely distributed over the head.

Scalp-recorded SER resemble in shape responses recorded simultaneously with electrodes on the dura or on the surface of the brain (Jasper, Lende, and Rasmussen, 1960; Giblin, 1964; Domino, Matsuoka, Waltz, and Cooper, 1965). Their cerebral origin thus seems well established. Attempts have been made to relate SER components to specific neurophysiologic events. Goff, Rosner, and Allison (1962) suggested that the initial SER component, mainly negative at approximately 18 to 20 msec, represents potentials in presynaptic thalamocortical fibers of the primary somatosensory projection pathway. The succeeding positive peak (25 to 30 msec) was interpreted as the corresponding postsynaptic potential. The next positive component (peak latency near 50 msec) was considered to reflect extra-lemniscal activity, perhaps mediated by the reticular formation. Later peaks were taken to indicate nonspecific mechanisms. However, subsequent evidence suggests that later response components may also originate in specific pathways (Domino, et al., 1965; Liberson, 1966; Tsumoto, Hirose, Nonaka, and Takahashi, 1973).

Responses to tactile stimuli tend to be somewhat simpler in wave shape and of slightly longer latency than those to electrocutaneous stimulation (Nakanishi, Takita, and Toyokura, 1973; Halliday and Mason, 1964). This may be related to the fact that nerve stimulation excites several types of fibers in a compound nerve, with an increase in wave-shape complexity. There is evidence that the SER evoked by peripheral nerve stimulation is largely dependent upon activity of fibers mediating proprioception (Halliday and Wakefield, 1963).

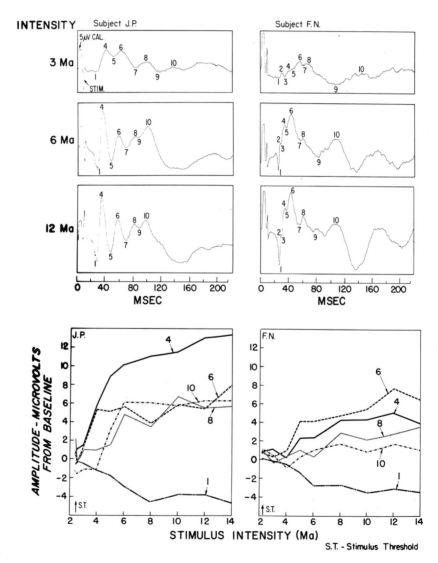

FIG. 4. Variations in amplitude as a function of intensity for different somatosensory response peaks in two subjects. Curves for peak 1 are drawn to reflect negativity. From Shagass (1972).

The wave shape of the SER, for a given individual, tends to be quite consistent over time (Shagass and Schwartz, 1961). The latency of the initial peak is largely determined by the length of the conduction pathway; the distance between the point of stimulation of the median nerve at the wrist and the seventh cervical spine correlates by approximately 0.8 with SER peak 1 latency (Straumanis, Shagass, and Overton, 1973a). When stimuli are near threshold strength, latencies tend to be longer than with intense stimuli. With stimuli near threshold, amplitudes are generally low; they tend to increase with greater stimulus strength, but the intensity-response relations are not linear, the usual curve tending to reach an asymptote. Figure 4 shows intensity-response curves for several SER peaks, numbered according to a sequential scheme used in our laboratory.

Lee and White (1974) have recently demonstrated that active voluntary movements increase the amplitude and prolong the latency of the negative SER peak at 120 msec, whereas they slightly decrease the amplitudes of peaks between 50 and 100 msec. Passive movement did not produce these changes. The finding is relevant to any studies that may involve voluntary responding by the stimulated limb.

The normal SER amplitude recovery function for the initial negative-positive component, with relatively high-intensity stimuli, generally follows a triphasic pattern in the first 200 msec (Shagass and Schwartz, 1962a). Although this pattern is far from regular when many intervals are tested in a given subject, there is usually some full recovery with intervals less than 20 msec, i.e., the R2:R1 ratio equals or exceeds 1.0 at one or more intervals. This initial recovery phase is followed by a variable-duration phase of diminished responsiveness, usually observed with interstimulus intervals between 20 and 40 msec. In the third phase, the R2:R1 ratios vary near 1.0. The time course of latency recovery generally differs from that of amplitude recovery; the curves tend to be monotonic with a slight prolongation of R2, in comparison with R1, from the shortest interstimulus intervals to between 20 and 40 msec (Shagass, 1968a). Amplitude recovery of tactile SER takes place within 64 msec (Nakanishi, et al., 1973).

B. Auditory Evoked Responses

Picton, Hillyard, Krausz, and Galambos (1974) have recently described the full range of auditory evoked response (AER) components, some 15 in all. These can be divided into three latency ranges (Fig. 5). With low frequency cutoff set at 10 Hz, and summing 500 to 2,000 sweeps, the very early AER events first described by Jewett et al. (1970) can easily be shown, as in Fig. 5A. It appears likely that the earliest event may reflect activity in the auditory nerve, and that this is followed by activity picked up from the cochlear nucleus. We have found that these early AER events are unchanged during sleep, but that prolongation of latency and diminution of amplitude take place over several hours of stimulation, apparently due to

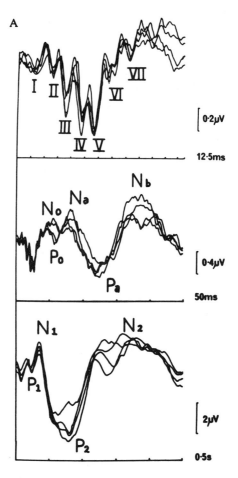

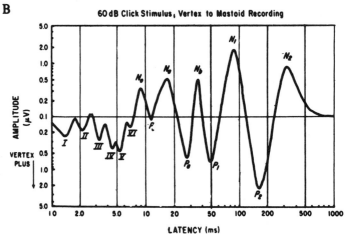

FIG. 5. Identification of the auditory evoked potential components for one subject. (A) Auditory evoked potentials to 60 dBSL clicks presented monaurally at a rate of 1/sec. Each tracing represents the average of 1,024 responses from vertex-mastoid electrodes. Averaging was done using three separate time bases. (B) Diagrammatic representation of the auditory evoked potential components plotted on logarithmic scales. Mean data from eight subjects. From Picton, Hillyard, Krausz, and Galambos (1974).

fatigue (Amadeo and Shagass, 1973*a*). Although the events up to 7 msec latency are highly regular, those from 7 to 50 msec latency vary considerably, and may often be of muscle origin. Commencing at about 50 msec, the AER to clicks and tone pips tend to have fairly regular characteristics. A positive peak (P1), with a latency of about 50 msec, is followed by negative (N1, latency from 80 to 105 msec), positive (P2, latency from 160 to 200 msec), and negative (N2, latency about 250 to 300 msec) peaks. A late positive peak (P3, latency from 300 to 500 msec) is highly dependent upon psychologic conditions.

The latencies of the early AER components vary in relation to intensity of stimulus, being greater with weaker stimuli. Except with intensities very near threshold, when they may be significantly prolonged, the later (P1 to N2) components do not vary with stimulus intensity (Davis, Mast, Yoshie, and Zerlin, 1966). With tone pips, latency is apparently also not a function of stimulus frequency between 300 and 4800 Hz. AER recovery functions tend to be prolonged so that to obtain maximal amplitude the intervals between stimuli must be over 6 sec and probably at least 10 sec. With tones delivered every 2 sec, the amplitude of the vertex P2 component drops rapidly during the first two stimuli, but remains steady when the interval is 10 sec or more (Ritter, Vaughan, and Costa, 1968). However, when sounds are presented at the rate of 25/sec, N1-P2 amplitude is greater than at 5/sec, suggesting that the 25/sec sound is treated as continuous (Butler, 1973). Tones of different frequency can be presented close together without the same amplitude decrement found with tones of the same frequency; this suggests frequency-specific organization of the auditory cortex (Butler, 1972).

AER wave shape is quite consistent for a given individual. Although one would expect the AER to be of greater amplitude on the side contralateral to the ear stimulated, this is difficult to demonstrate; the distribution of the N1-P2 components is essentially the same with monaural and binaural stimuli. Maximal amplitudes are in frontocentral regions.

Since language functions in right-handed persons are generally considered to be localized in the left hemisphere, attempts have been made to use AER to provide electrical indicators of this hemispheric functional specialization. Morrell and Salamy (1971) averaged auditory responses evoked by such stimuli and found that the amplitude of the N1 component (100 msec) was consistently larger in the left temporoparietal derivation than the right. Unfortunately a recent attempt to replicate his work in our laboratory was unsuccessful. Matsumiya, Tagliasco, Lombroso, and Goodglass (1972) recorded AERs to speech- and sound-effect stimuli. In some subjects wave amplitudes (N1) differed in magnitude as a function of the speech or non-speech character of the stimuli. Their results, however, indicated that the meaningfulness of the auditory stimuli to the subject was more relevant to the occurrence of the interhemispheric asymmetry than the mere use of verbal versus nonverbal materials. Wood, Goff, and Day (1971) demonstrated evoked response differences in the left hemisphere, not present in the right, when a linguistic distinction was made from auditory stimuli.

C. VER

Responses to flash. Cigánek (1961) provided the classic description of the VER to light flash, designating the series of peaks by successive numerals. He found the onset of the response to take place at about 28 msec, and the initial peak was negative with a mean latency about 40 msec. Mean latencies of waves II to VII were, respectively, 53, 73, 94, 114, 135, and 190 msec. Following the initial complex of the major peaks in Cigánek's scheme, a rhythmic after-discharge may be recorded. This after-discharge, which has been termed ringing by Walter (1962), is most frequently seen when the lids are closed. Figure 6 shows an example of VERs to flash; the

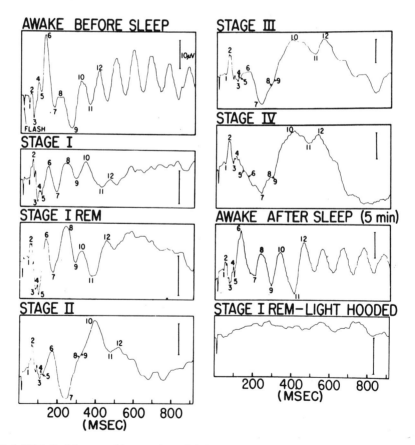

FIG. 6. VER to flash for one subject, awake and during various stages of sleep. After-rhythm disappears from stage I on. VER for stages I and I REM are very similar. From Shagass (1972).

waking records demonstrate the after-rhythm. Cigánek distinguished two major constituents among the waves preceding the after-rhythm. He considered waves I to III to be the primary response, and the portion following wave III to be the secondary response. There is, however, considerable reason to doubt that even the earliest three waves of Cigánek's response originate in the primary visual area. It seems likely that the only true visual response is the very early positive event described by Cobb and Dawson (1960), which has a latency of 20 to 25 msec and is of very low amplitude (1 to 1.5 μV).

The early components of the VER appear to originate in the occipital region; Cobb and Dawson's (1960) early wave reversed in phase between 3 and 6 cm above the inion. Vaughan (1969) found that both early and late components were maximally recorded from electrodes overlying the occiput. The later wave also showed a secondary maximum in the central region, suggesting that the central and occipital components were not the same and probably represented two distinct generators.

Although the response to flash may have quite a different appearance in different subjects, the degree of stability for a given subject under similar conditions seems to be great. Dustman and Beck (1963) found correlations approaching 0.9 between corresponding data points in responses recorded at intervals of 1 week or more.

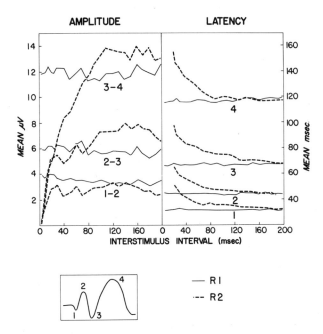

FIG. 7. Mean amplitude (left) and latency (right) recovery curves of visual responses for 60 subjects. Measurements are peak-to-peak for amplitude.—R1,– – –R2. From Shagass (1972).

Cobb and Dawson (1960) reported that light flashes of reduced brightness gave responses of smaller amplitude and more prolonged latency. This intensity-response function appears to hold in a general way (Diamond, 1964; Shagass, Schwartz, and Krishnamoorti, 1965). However, it is possible to demonstrate inversions in the intensity-response curve in many subjects, and this has been used as the basis for an evoked response test of augmenting-reducing by Buchsbaum and Silverman (1968).

The recovery functions of VERs to flash have been studied by a number of workers. Different components appear to have different recovery functions. Figure 7 shows average amplitude and latency recovery curves obtained in our laboratory (Shagass and Schwartz, 1965a).

Stimuli other than flash. With sine-wave-modulated light, the response tends to be roughly sinusoidal and resembles that elicited by intermittent flashes of light (photic driving). Spehlmann (1965) demonstrated that responses to patterned light differed considerably in shape from those obtained with unpatterned visual stimuli. The dominant feature was a positive late wave with a latency of 180 to 250 msec, which was localized in the occipital region. The critical factor, according to Spehlmann, was the density of contrast borders between black and white lines of the stimulus pattern. In Spehlmann's study the checkerboard pattern was flashed. With checkerboard reversal stimuli, the checkerboard is constantly present, but the locations of the black and white squares are reversed to constitute the stimulus. It is noteworthy that patterned stimulus fields can evoke potentials with amplitudes that are as large, or larger, than those elicited by unpatterned stimuli, even when light energy may be 10,000 times less with the patterned stimulus.

The main component (100 to 120 msec) of VER to the appearance of pattern is opposite in polarity and usually of larger amplitude than the major event in VER to disappearances of pattern (Mackay and Jeffreys, 1971). The pattern appearance VER contains a positive major component at the inion, whereas the disappearance VER contains a negative peak. According to Regan (1972), pattern reversal VERs are more closely related to pattern disappearance than to pattern appearance. The size of the checks appears to be a significant variable affecting VER amplitude. Eason, White, and Bartlett (1970), using flashed checks, found the greatest amplitude of the 90 to 100 msec wave to occur with checks of 10-min subtense for upper-field stimulation, whereas 40-min checks gave the greatest amplitudes for the lower field. Halliday and Michael (1970) found that the 100 msec peak in the pattern reversal VER showed consistent and systematic changes with variation in position of the stimulus in the visual field. With upper-field stimuli the peak was surface-negative, whereas with lower-field stimuli it was surface-positive. Furthermore, when the octants of the visual field stimulated were adjacent to the vertical meridian, amplitude was greater than when they were adjacent to the horizontal meridian. Michael and Halliday

(1971) reported a further analysis of these responses, which led them to suggest that the upper-field responses arise from the inverted neurons on the under surface of the occipital lobe; these are sufficiently near to be picked up by an ear reference electrode. On the other hand, they considered the lower field responses to arise from the neurons on the upper convexity. Regan (1972) gives a comprehensive treatment of the factors influencing pattern VERs.

Variations in VER associated with different patterns of dots and colors have been demonstrated (Shipley, Jones, and Fry, 1965; Clynes, Kohn, and Gradijan, 1967; Beatty and Uttal, 1968).

Responses to olfactory and gustatory stimuli. Allison and Goff (1967) used 1- to 200-msec pulses of odorized air at 6-sec intervals to produce olfactory evoked responses. These consisted mainly of a 450- to 500-msec latency positive wave, largest in the vertex region although widely distributed. Different odors gave responses of different latencies. More recently Smith, Allison, Goff, and Principato (1971) reported evidence indicating that their olfactory responses were probably caused by trigeminal stimulation. Electrical stimulation of the tongue gives rise to taste sensations and a compound evoked response with peaks as early as 45 msec, and continuing to over 400 msec (Plattig, 1968). Peak latencies decreased as stimulus intensity was made greater.

D. Motor Potentials

Brain potential correlates of movement in man were first described by Bates (1951). He found a cortical potential starting 20 to 40 msec after the onset of contraction. Kornhüber and Deecke (1965) described a "readiness potential," which was enhanced by the "intentional engagement" of the subject. Gilden, Vaughan, and Costa (1966) demonstrated the existence of additional aspects of cortical potentials associated with voluntary movement. Figure 8 illustrates the motor potential associated with dorsiflection of

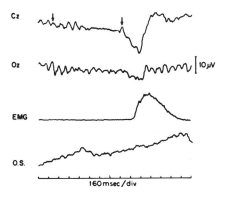

FIG. 8. Summated EEG and EMG potentials associated with dorsiflection of the left foot. The onset of the contraction is preceded by a slow negative shift, beginning at the point indicated by the left arrow, and also by a positive-negative deflection indicated by the second arrow. Scalp negativity gives a downward deflection. EMG recorded from anterior tibial muscle. OS, activity from electrode below left eye. From Gilden, Vaughan, and Costa (1966).

the foot. There are four main components: (1) starting about 1 sec prior to onset of EMG evidence of muscular contraction, a slow negative shift of the baseline; (2) approximately 50 to 150 msec prior to contraction, a small positive deflection; (3) a larger negative wave, which develops a peak amplitude of 10 to 15 μV during the rising phase of the summated EMG; (4) approximately 50 to 150 msec after the start of contraction, a large 20 to 30 μV positive wave. The topography of the motor potential appears to show maximal amplitude over the Rolandic cortex and is somewhat similar to that of the late component of the SER (Vaughan, Costa, and Ritter, 1968). Recently Gerbrandt, Goff, and Smith (1973) have challenged the interpretation that the motor potential reflects events generated primarily in motor cortex. They assign other interpretations to the different components of the motor potential, including the idea that the second negativity may be a polarity reversal of the positive component of the SER.

E. Long-Latency Potentials

A long-latency component, usually occurring from 300 to 500 msec after the stimulus, commonly designated the P300 or P3 wave, appears to be related more to complex psychologic variables than to the physical attributes of the stimulus. It is not modality specific and is recorded optimally near the vertex. Sutton, Braren, and Zubin (1965) described the P3 wave as a correlate of stimulus uncertainty. It is of higher amplitude when the nature of the forthcoming stimulus is least certain and may also be elicited by the absence of an expected stimulus (Sutton, Teuting, Zubin, and John, 1967). Ritter and Vaughan (1969) concluded that the P3 wave reflects a shift of attention associated with the orienting response. Although Sutton (1969) has emphasized the great importance of careful attention to the details of instructions to the subject for P3 recording, recent evidence suggests that the P3 wave can be elicited in a relatively unstructured situation (Roth and Cannon, 1972).

F. CNV and Other Steady Potential Shifts

The early slow negativity in the motor potential and in the readiness potential represent slow potential shifts. However, the slow potential that has received the most investigative attention is the CNV. The CNV, also called the expectancy (E) wave, was described by Walter, Cooper, Aldridge, McCallum, and Winter (1964). In a paradigm similar to that used for measuring reaction time, an alerting or warning signal precedes the delivery of an imperative signal to which the subject must make some kind of response, such as a button press. The interval between stimuli is usually 1 to 2 sec; the CNV develops during this interval, and a minimum interval of 0.5 sec is needed to permit its adequate development. The experiment often contains a control

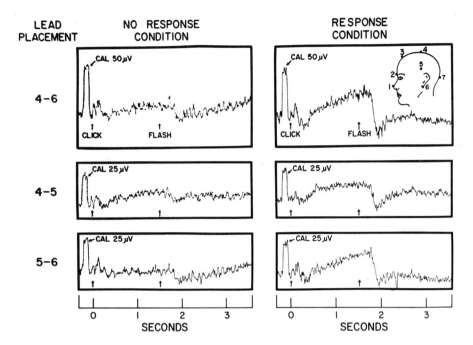

FIG. 9. Contingent negative variation. Average of 20 responses. In response condition (right) a click in the right ear signifies button press after the succeeding flash. In no response condition (left) left click signifies button not to be pressed. Upward deflection indicates relative negativity in upper electrode. Note the slow potential shift in response condition. From Shagass (1972).

condition in which a similar signal, without the same significance for respond-ing, is administered. Figure 9 shows the records obtained in an experiment in which a warning click in the right ear signified that the response button was to be pressed after a succeeding flash, whereas a click in the left ear did not have this meaning. With the response condition, a slow potential deviation, negative to vertex, may be observed commencing about 200 msec after the stimulus. The CNV continues to rise until there has been a response to the imperative stimulus, at which time there is a precipitous shift back toward the baseline or positivity. In the test of Fig. 9, the no-response condition did not elicit a CNV. CNV may also be demonstrated without requiring a motor response, as when the subject anticipates seeing a picture or is instructed to think a word (Cohen, 1969).

Although there is little doubt that the CNV phenomenon is real, it is easily contaminated by a number of events recordable at the same electrodes, and which have the same general appearance. Perhaps the most important of these are the EOG, associated with eye movements and eye blinks, and scalp electrodermal responses (GSR). GSR is particularly prominent at the mastoid area, which happens to have been a favorite of CNV workers for the location of the reference lead; the ear lobe is relatively free of GSR

(Picton and Hillyard, 1972). Various means of correcting the CNV for EOG activity have been proposed (Walter, 1967; Hillyard, 1969b), but none are wholly satisfactory. A satisfactory technique would require corrections based on accurate knowledge of both the eye movement and eye blink potential fields and separate determination of both kinds of activity, since these are not identical. McCallum and Cummins (1973) have reported that, in the absence of neurologic lesions, the CNV is generally symmetrically distributed. Although they found some asymmetry, they attributed this to asymmetrical EOG contamination. The greatest CNV amplitude was found in the coronal plane with a peak near the vertex.

IV. ERP AND IMPAIRED AWARENESS

A. Sleep

Sensory evoked responses show remarkable variations during sleep. Figures 10 and 6, respectively, give examples of changes found in recordings of SER and VER. In general all peak latencies become prolonged, and the degree of prolongation increases from drowsiness through stage I, stage REM, etc., with the greatest change in stage IV sleep (Shagass and Trusty, 1966). The composite evoked response graphs in Fig. 10 illustrate the tendency for increase in the amplitude of responses, particularly during deep sleep. When the subject is wakened, the latencies of the peaks do not return immediately to those of the presleep waking state. The delayed restoration of peak latencies is associated with subjective reports of grogginess (Shagass and Trusty, 1966; Saier, Régis, Mano, and Gastaut, 1968). Studies of AER during sleep similarly show tendencies for increased latency and amplitude, particularly in stages III and IV (Weitzman and Kremen, 1965; Picton et al., 1974).

As indicated in Figs. 6 and 10, the most dramatic changes with sleep take place in the later components. The rhythmic after-rhythm in the VER disappears entirely in drowsiness or early sleep; it reappears on awakening. In the SER Goff, Allison, Shapiro, and Rosner (1966) found that components 4 and 5 in their schemes were markedly reduced during drowsiness and stage REM, but commencing in stage II, and becoming most prominent in stages III and IV, they observed very late potentials in the form of two negative-positive sequences. The latest of these occurred 700 msec or more after the stimulus. These very late responses, which were of considerable amplitude during deep sleep, appear to resemble those found with AER and VER (Kooi, Bagchi, and Jordan, 1964). Most workers have considered these large, late sleep waves in evoked responses as having some identity with the K-complex described by Loomis, Harvey, and Hobart (1938) for the sleep EEG.

Whereas latency prolongations have been found consistently during

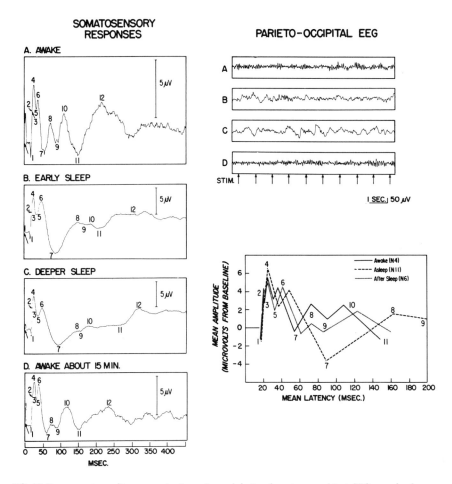

FIG. 10. Responses to median nerve shock awake and during sleep in one subject. EEG samples from corresponding averaging sequence. Note marked changes in components numbered from 5 on during sleep. Composite mean evoked response on lower right shows that amplitude of early components increased during sleep, and that latencies became prolonged.

sleep, amplitude results have been more variable. Although we found a statistically significant increase in the amplitude of the initial SER components (Shagass and Trusty, 1966), this did not happen in some subjects. Nevertheless the observation that amplitude of the initial components may be increased in many subjects during sleep is of some importance; it suggests that latency does not become more variable, and that afferent input to the cortex is not reduced during sleep. In a recent study of SER recovery functions during sleep, we found a variable tendency for amplitude recovery to be diminished, whereas latency recovery showed a consistent and unexpected early speeding; also amplitude variability was decreased, particularly during the later stages of sleep (Amadeo and Shagass, 1973b; and *unpublished observations*). Figure 11 shows the mean latency recovery data for a group of subjects. It will be noted that the latency of R2 was actually less than that of R1 with intervals from 3 to 20 msec, but that between 50 and 140 msec R2 latency tended to become greater than that of R1. The results in Fig. 11 suggest that, for a period of about 20 msec, the volley generated by the first stimulus of the pair counteracts the inhibitory mechanism associated with prolongation of latency during sleep.

The results from human evoked response studies are nearly unanimous in indicating that responses obtained during the REM phase of sleep resemble those of waking more than they do those obtained during slow-wave sleep. Although investigators of sleep in animals consider the REM phase to be

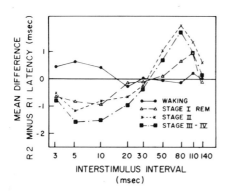

FIG. 11. Mean SER latency recovery for 12 subjects, expressed as mean difference between peak 1 R2 and R1 latencies during waking and three sleep stages. Logarithmic scale used for interstimulus intervals on abscissa. From Amadeo and Shagass (1973b).

the deepest stage of sleep, this view seems inconsistent with the results of evoked response studies in man.

B. Delirium

The disorder of sensorium designated as delirium involves impairment of orientation, a blunting or loss of critical faculty, and incoherent thought content. The acute and chronic brain syndromes may be regarded as deliria.

SER and VER changes associated with acute delirium have been investigated by administering ethylisobutrazine (Ditran®, Lakeside Laboratories) (Brown, Shagass, and Schwartz, 1965). This agent produces a relatively stereotyped reaction, characterized usually by gross signs of acute brain syndrome, such as disorientation, with subsequent amnesia for most of the experience. The later components of SER and VER show changes resembling those found in sleep (Figs. 6 and 10). In contrast to the effects on later components, the earlier portions of the responses appear to be speeded by ethylisobutrazine.

SER and flash VER have been studied in elderly patients with arteriosclerotic brain syndromes, all of whom were disoriented (Straumanis, Shagass, and Schwartz, 1965). Compared with healthy controls of the same age and sex, the amplitude of the first VER positive peak (latency about 45 msec) was greater in the patients, and the latencies of peaks from 120 msec on were significantly prolonged. The patients also showed significantly less VER after-rhythm; this agrees with Cohn's (1964) observations. The SER results revealed that, whereas there were no significant sex differences in the matched control group, the amplitudes in female brain syndrome patients were greater than those of the controls, and the amplitudes of the male patients were lower than normal. Levy, Isaacs, and Behrman (1971) have reported a significant prolongation of the negative SER peak at 40 msec in a small group of patients with senile dementia.

In studies of AER variability, Malerstein and Callaway (1969) found that patients with Korsakoff's syndrome showed greater than normal variability and gave results similar to those found in schizophrenic patients. They obtained similar results in patients with senile psychosis.

C. Coma

Bergamasco, Bergamini, Mombelli, and Mutani (1966) studied VER in patients with posttraumatic coma, unaccompanied by clinical signs of localized lesions. When the EEG was predominantly occupied by 2 to 3 cycles/sec activity, VER was markedly altered. The latency was increased to about 100 msec and the response was greatly simplified, consisting of only two or three waves. There was no after-rhythm. Responses were present only between the occiput and vertex, but not between the vertex and a frontal lead. Responses tended to spread frontally, to become more complex and with shorter latencies as the patient improved from coma. Lille, Lerique, Pottier, Scherrer, and Thieffry (1968) obtained similar results in SER, AER, and VER recorded from comatose children; they considered loss of waveform complexity the characteristic most related to depth of coma.

Recently Dolce and Sannita (1973) used a CNV paradigm, with click preceding flash by 900 msec, to record from two patients in deep coma. With 120 and 150 paired stimuli, they observed negative shifts between the click and flash, which resembled the CNV and were considered not to arise from extracerebral sources. These observations suggest that CNV may be based on more basic neural mechanisms than generally supposed, since it appears to be elicitable in states of severely impaired consciousness.

V. ERP AND PHENOMENA OF ATTENTION

A. Habituation

Habituation is recognized by diminution of response size with repetitive stimulation. In contrast to fatigue, habituation is reversed if novelty is introduced, or if a stimulus sequence is briefly interrupted (Perry and Childers, 1969). Habituation may take place within a single averaging sequence or between sequences. The mechanisms underlying habituation can be peripheral, central, or both. Bergamini, Bergamasco, Mombelli, and Gandiglio (1965) demonstrated that VER habituation occurs in 10 min when the pupils are mobile, but that there is no habituation when the pupils are fixed; they also reported absence of habituation in subjects with congenital absence of the iris. On the other hand, habituation of the VER has been shown by other workers who have kept pupil size constant (Perry and Copenhaver, 1965). Habituation has also been reported for AER and SER.

B. Directed Attention

Many techniques have been employed to direct attention to particular stimuli, such as telling the subject to count them, to concentrate on stimuli with certain qualities and to disregard others, to respond to some stimuli by pressing a key, etc. Some workers have found VER and AER to be augmented when the subject counted repetitive stimuli (Garcia-Austt, 1963; Garcia-Austt, Bogacz, and Vanzulli, 1964; Williams, Morlock, Morlock, and Lubin, 1964; Gross, Begleiter, Tobin, and Kissin, 1965). However, such augmentation of amplitude does not always occur with counting (Spong, Haider, and Lindsley, 1965).

Evoked-response correlates of attention have been more consistent in experimental paradigms that required differential attending to one of two or more stimuli. For example Satterfield (1965) presented clicks and shocks alternately and asked the subject to attend to one or another stimulus; he obtained large differences as a function of the direction of attention. A component peaking at about 150 msec in vertex electrodes was markedly augmented when the stimulus was the focus of attention. In contrast the initial components of the responses were not affected by the instructions. Similar results, i.e., augmentation of a later component, when the stimulus was attended to, have been obtained by many other workers (Chapman and Bragdon, 1964; Satterfield and Cheatum, 1964; Chapman, 1965; Spong et al., 1965; Shevrin and Rennick, 1967; Picton, Hillyard, Galambos, and Schiff, 1971). For the AER, Picton and Hillyard (1974) have clearly demonstrated that the components augmented with differential attention are N1 and P2. Eason, Harter, and White (1969) used low-intensity visual stimuli, presented in randomized order, to show selective attention effects; their study met the criticisms of earlier work raised by Näätänen (1967), but also supported Näätänen's contention that many of the previous results could have reflected arousal more than selective attention.

In the reaction time experiment, it seems reasonable to interpret that attentiveness is greater with faster than with slower responses. Several investigators have shown faster reaction times to flash to be associated with greater VER amplitude (Dustman and Beck, 1965; Donchin and Lindsley, 1966; Morrell and Morrell, 1966; Shagass, Straumanis, and Overton, 1972b). It is important to note that this is strictly a within-subject relationship, i.e., for a given subject, faster reaction times are associated with greater amplitudes of VER components after 100 msec. The average VER amplitudes and reaction times are not usually correlated across subjects.

C. Hypnosis and Suggestion

Studies of hypnosis, which may be considered a special attentive state, have given variable results. Several investigations, employing one or two subjects, demonstrated increase or decrease of amplitude upon the suggestion of higher or lower stimulus intensity (Hernández-Peón and Donoso, 1959; Clynes, Kohn, and Lifshitz, 1964; Guerrero-Figueroa and Heath, 1964). In contrast, more investigators employing groups of subjects failed to demonstrate changes with hypnotic suggestion, e.g., Halliday and Mason (1964) found no reduction in SER in subjects who reported little or no perception of the stimulus during hypnotic anesthesia. AER to click did not change during attempts to induce hypnotic deafness, but complete deafness was not reported by the subjects. Other workers have failed to show VER to flash with hypnotic suggestions of stimulus brightness and dimness (Beck and Barolin, 1965; Beck, Dustman, and Beier, 1966).

A more positive experiment reported by Levy (1973) offers the possibility that, with careful attention to stimulus conditions, evoked-potential correlates of the hypnotic state may be demonstrated. Levy compared the SER, obtained by stimulating the affected and unaffected limbs, of nine patients with hysteric anesthesia. Using skin, rather than nerve, stimulation, he was able to show significantly reduced amplitude in SER from the affected area. He likewise showed reduced amplitude with nerve stimulation when stimulus intensity was near threshold, rather than at the usual supramaximal level.

D. Distraction

A number of studies have shown that responses were smaller when the subject's attention was directed away from the stimulus, by requiring the performance of mental activity, such as arithmetic, during stimulation (Garcia-Austt et al., 1964; Cigánek, 1967; Shevrin and Rennick, 1967). In contrast Eason, Aiken, White, and Lichtenstein (1964) found VER amplitude augmented during mental arithmetic and other mental effort. Shagass, Overton, Bartolucci, and Straumanis (1971) found no SER differences when the responses were recorded at rest with the eyes shut and while the subject was watching television. Thus, the effects of distraction upon evoked-response amplitude seem variable.

E. Long-Latency Potentials

The **P3** phenomenon has received varying psychologic interpretations (Sutton, 1969). However, it seems difficult to conceptualize any of these interpretations, such as stimulus uncertainty, task relevance, or orienting, without considering them involved in some way with attentive activity. Ritter and Vaughan (1969) concluded that the P3 appears to be a correlate

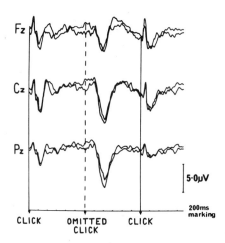

FIG. 12. Evoked potentials to omitted stimuli for one subject. Clicks were presented regularly every 1.1 sec and occasionally a click was omitted; the subject was asked to count the number of omissions. The averaging computer was triggered by the click immediately preceding the omission. Evoked potentials are shown for three different scalp positions. Each tracing represents the average of 64 responses. From Picton and Hillyard (1974).

of central processes for cognitive evaluation of stimulus significance. Picton and Hillyard (1974) demonstrated large P3 waves peaking at about 450 msec when responses to an occasional fainter auditory stimulus were averaged. The P3 component was distributed more posteriorly on the scalp than the earlier N1-P2 components. Picton and Hillyard were also able to show a P3 response in the absence of an immediate stimulus, when the subject was asked to detect and count the number of omitted stimuli occurring irregularly in an averaging sequence. The latency, shape, and scalp distribution of the P3 to an omitted stimulus were similar to the P3 parameters found with actual signals. Figure 12 illustrates the P3 to omitted signals.

F. CNV

The psychologic correlates of CNV have been variously designated as expectancy, decision, motivation, volition, preparatory set, conation, and arousal. One state accompanying all of these is heightened attentiveness (Tecce, 1971).

McCallum and Walter (1968) showed that the amplitude of CNV was greater during trials in which subjects reported themselves to be concentrating than when they were not concentrating. Conversely these authors and Tecce and Sheff (1969) showed that the introduction of distracting stimuli between the alerting and imperative stimuli, tends to reduce CNV amplitude. Low and McSherry (1968) found that CNV was greater when the subject was required to press harder on a lever. There is some evidence that CNV may be greater when reaction times are faster (Hillyard, 1969a), but this relationship has been disputed by Näätänen (1973).

Although there is much evidence that CNV amplitude is greater with attention and lower with distraction (Dargent and Dongier, 1969; McCallum, 1973), it should be borne in mind that many of the CNV data reported in the literature may have been contaminated by EOG and GSR. Consequently, although the CNV relationships to attentive activity are probably valid, the weight of evidence may not be as massive as appears.

G. ERP and EEG

It should be clear that, although the validity of individual findings can be questioned, a large body of data supports the conclusion that cerebral ERPs change when consciousness is either impaired or heightened. As is the case with the EEG, the area of consciousness appears to be the sphere of psychologic functioning most intimately correlated with ERP events. ERP and EEG events are not, however, simply duplicate indicators of the same central processes. A review of the evidence (Shagass, 1972, Chap. 7) indicates that, although EEG and ERP may be significantly correlated with one another, the correlations are frequently low, and vary considerably with such factors as lead placement. In many instances, EEG and ERP can be considered to be relatively independent indicators of brain activity, and should both be recorded to obtain a more comprehensive picture than either can give alone.

VI. EVOKED RESPONSES, INTELLIGENCE, AND PERSONALITY

A. Intelligence

The first to report evoked response correlates of intelligence were Chalke and Ertl (1965). They found that the latencies of VER recorded from bipolar leads placed over the left motor area were longer in less intelligent subjects. They interpreted their results to indicate that central processing time, as reflected in VER latency, was slowed in individuals of low IQ. Ertl and Schafer (1969) obtained similar findings in subsequent studies, although the correlation coefficients for a large sample, composed of over 500 grade school students, were rather low, the greatest being −0.35. Similarly low, but significant, correlations between VER latencies and measures of intellectual ability have been reported by Shucard and Horn (1972) and Callaway (1973). Shucard and Horn noted that the correlations between VER latency and IQ were greater under conditions of low arousal, which favored less attention to stimuli. Butler and Engel (1969) found that neonatal VER latency correlated with mental test scores obtained at the age of 8 months to the level of −0.33, and to a slightly lesser degree with fine and gross motor performance measures. Several workers have also reported that VER frequency measures, yielded by Fourier analysis, correlated with IQ (Osborne, 1969; Weinberg, 1969; Bennett, 1972).

In contrast to the foregoing findings indicative of significant correlations between VER latency and intelligence, two major studies, involving about 1,000 children, have failed to demonstrate such relationships (Engel and Fay, 1972; Engel and Henderson, 1973).

Few significant correlations between evoked response amplitude and intelligence have been reported. Rhodes, Dustman, and Beck (1969) found that bright children with average IQs of 130 had larger amplitudes of a late component from 100 to 125 msec in the VER than dull children with an average IQ of 79. The same workers found that amplitudes of VER recorded from central areas were greater on the right than on the left in bright but not in dull children. Callaway (1973) also reported that evoked-response asymmetry was correlated with intelligence when the subjects were passive, but not when they were required to perform a task.

In a recent review of evoked-response correlations with measures of intelligence, Straumanis and Shagass (1975) concluded that there was a general consensus for longer VER latency to be associated with low IQ, and for larger right than left VER responses in the central areas to be demonstrated in subjects with higher intelligence.

B. Mental Retardation

Chalke and Ertl's first study (1965) included some mental retardates, who had prolonged VER latencies. Bigum, Dustman, and Beck (1970) compared normal and mongoloid children and found that the late VER peak latencies were greater than in normals. Marcus (1970) found longer VER latencies in phenylketonuric retardates, and Galbraith, Gliddon, and Busk (1970) obtained similar results in severely retarded subjects.

Prolonged AER latencies have been reported in retarded subjects by Hogan and Graham (1967), Nodar and Graham (1968), and Shimizu (1970). On the other hand, several investigators have failed to find AER latency differences between retardate and normal groups; among these, the largest sample studied was that of Taguchi, Goodman, and Brummitt (1970).

Prolonged SER latencies in mongolism have been reported by Bigum et al. (1970), and Straumanis, et al. (1973a).

The amplitude of the late (180 to 200 msec) VER component was found to be greater than normal in mongoloid children by Bigum et al. (1970); these investigators also observed that mongoloids lacked the VER hemisphere asymmetry they found in normals. Findings of high VER amplitude in both mongoloids and bright children (Rhodes, et al., 1969) seem paradoxical; there might be a special factor in the mongoloids. Barnet and Lodge (1967) reported larger amplitudes of click AER in mongoloid infants than in normals, and similar, although smaller, differences have been found in young adult mongoloids (Straumanis, Shagass, and Overton, 1973b). Bigum et al. (1970) observed that mongoloid children had a late SER component of greater than normal amplitude. Greater SER amplitudes in both mongoloids and idiopathic retardates of young adult age were found by Straumanis et al. (1973a).

The available data suggest that evoked response characteristics tend to be deviant from normal in severe mental retardation. More data are required before it can be established whether the deviations relate to specific etiologic factors or represent extreme cases of the less striking correlations with IQ found in the general population.

C. Personality

Shagass and Schwartz (1965b) reported that SER amplitudes in a normal population were correlated with the extraversion (E) score on the Maudsley Personality Inventory (MPI). The correlation was age dependent; in subjects aged 15 to 19, above median E was accompanied by high amplitude of components in the first 50 msec; in contrast, in subjects aged 40 years or more, above median E was associated with low amplitudes. High and low E subjects did not differ in the age range from 20 to 39. However, the SER results, with respect to E in the adolescent age range, were not confirmed in a more recent study (Häseth, Shagass, and Straumanis, 1969).

Shagass and Canter (1972) correlated scores obtained from the Minnesota Multiphasic Personality Inventory (MMPI) and SER characteristics in a large group of psychiatric patients. They interpreted their results to indicate that greater amplitude and slower latency recovery were obtained in patients with MMPI evidence of less dysphoria, less introversion, and better ego strength. Since controls showed greater amplitude and slower latency recovery than patients, these results seemed to indicate that, within a patient population, the SER relationships were probably associated with the degree of psychopathology rather than with specific personality characteristics.

Petrie (1967) has introduced the concept of a personality factor, known as augmenting-reducing, which is based on the idea that stimuli are handled in a characteristic style by individuals. Reducers have higher pain thresholds than augmenters. Buchsbaum and Silverman (1968) developed an evoked-response test that correlated well with Petrie's behavioral test of augmenting-reducing, based on kinesthetic figural after-affects (KFA). In the evoked-response test, four intensities of light are used. Measurements are made of the amplitude of a vertex-recorded VER component, positive at about 90 msec and negative at about 140 msec. The slope of the curve relating these amplitudes to stimulus intensity tends to be much steeper in augmenters and may be negative in reducers. Figure 13 shows examples of such responses, recorded in a recent study in our laboratory. Spilker and Callaway (1969) have used different modulation depths of sine-wave-modulated light as the stimuli for another evoked-response test of augmenting-reducing, which correlates with KFA scores. We found that the results given by the flash and sine-wave-modulated light tests of agumenting-reducing were poorly correlated with one another (Soskis and Shagass, 1974). Although problems with pupillary mobility and ocular fixation could influence the results, our findings showed these to be generally unimportant with the flash method. Furthermore our data showed a significant positive correlation between the

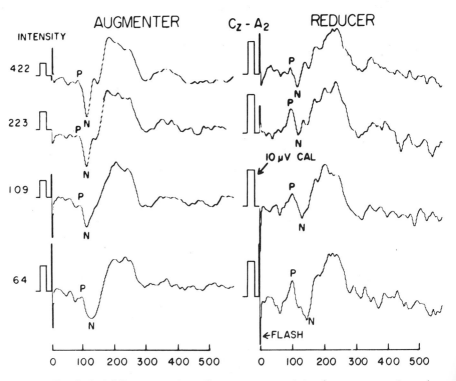

FIG. 13. VER to flash of different intensities to illustrate extreme variations between augmenting and reducing tendencies in two subjects. Positivity at Cz gives upward deflection. The event of interest is between P and N. Augmenter has greatest amplitude with highest intensity, whereas reducer has greatest amplitude with lowest intensity of flash. From Soskis and Shagass (1974).

MPI extraversion score and an augmenting tendency in the VER intensity-response curve.

The rod-and-frame test of field dependence-independence has been employed in many investigations of personality. SER initial component amplitudes were found to be greater in field-dependent psychiatric patients (Shagass and Canter, 1972). Field-dependent subjects also showed greater amplitude recovery for several SER peaks. These results were interpreted as suggesting reduced inhibitory activity in field-dependent subjects.

It seems likely that ERP methods will be used to an increasing extent in personality studies. The flash augmenting-reducing test has already found favor with many investigators (Silverman, 1972). Perceptually based dimensions of personality would seem to be logical psychologic variables to relate to ERP characteristics.

VII. FUNCTIONAL PSYCHIATRIC DISORDERS

A. Evoked Responses to Unpaired Stimuli

SER amplitude, in the first 100 msec, was found to be greater in psychiatric patients than in controls in studies employing several intensities to derive intensity-response functions (Shagass and Schwartz, 1963a; Shagass, 1973a), although no differences were found in a study using only a single, high-intensity stimulus (Shagass, 1968a). Lower than normal AER amplitudes have been found in several studies of schizophrenic patients (Jones and Callaway, 1970; Saletu, Itil, and Saletu, 1971a; Cohen, 1973), but not in depressed patients (Satterfield, 1972). It may be noted that the SER measurements showing patient-control differences were based on early components, whereas the AER differences were in later peaks. VER amplitudes were greater and latencies shorter in a heterogeneous group of psychiatric patients than in controls (Shagass and Schwartz, 1965a); amplitudes were greater in nonpsychotics, whereas schizophrenics had faster latencies for the initial positive peak of the response. Significantly less rhythmic VER after-activity was also found in the schizophrenics. On the other hand, two groups of investigators reported that a patient population composed mainly of schizophrenics did not differ significantly from normals in VER amplitude or latency (Speck, Dim, and Mercer, 1966; Floris, Morocutti, Amabile, Bernardi, Rizzo, and Vasconetto, 1967).

Unfortunately VER studies in schizophrenic patients have nearly all been carried out without fixation of the pupil. Control over this factor is important, as is indicated by the differing results in schizophrenics obtained by Rodin and his co-workers, according to whether or not the pupils were immobilized; significant differences observed with mobile pupils disappeared when they were fixed (Rodin, Zacharopoulos, Beckett and Frohman, 1964; Rodin, Grisell, and Gottlieb, 1968).

The augmenting-reducing test employing flash has been used in several studies of psychiatric populations (Silverman, 1972). Blacker, Jones, Stone, and Pfefferbaum (1968) found that chronic LSD users tended to be reducers. Borge, Buchsbaum, Goodwin, Murphy, and Silverman (1971) found significant differences between bipolar manic-depressive patients (both manic and depressive episodes) and unipolar (depressive episodes only) depressed patients; the bipolars were augmenters, and the unipolars were reducers.

With the possible exception of the AER, the results with simple evoked-response measurements in psychiatric disorders have tended to be somewhat variable.

B. Evoked Response Variability

Callaway et al. (1965) used the correlation method to measure waveshape similarity in responses to two tones of different frequency. They later reported that the different tone frequencies were not required, and that the essential measure was one of variability (Jones and Callaway, 1970). Variability was found to be significantly greater in schizophrenics than in normal controls. Saletu et al. (1971a) also obtained evidence of greater AER variability in schizophrenics, particularly those with thought disorders. Lifshitz (1969) found greater VER variability in schizophrenics than in normals. Greater spatial variability in VER was demonstrated by Rodin et al. (1968).

The foregoing evidence of greater AER and VER variability in schizophrenic disorders is based on measurements heavily influenced by the events occurring between 100 and 500 msec after the stimulus. In our own studies of SER variability, we analyzed the response for epochs from 15 to 100 msec and 100 to 200 msec after the stimulus. Our data indicated that variability of SER to single median nerve shocks during the first 100 msec was *less* in chronic schizophrenic patients than in most other subjects (Shagass, 1973a,b). On the other hand, variability from 100 to 200 msec tended to be greater in the chronic schizophrenic patients. Our variability data are thus not at variance with those of other workers, but do indicate that the fluctuation in modulating influences, which may be responsible for degree of variability, is not the same at differing times after the stimulus.

Additional analysis of the results within our heterogeneous schizophrenic population showed that the variability measures did not differ from normal in patients who were high in clinical depression ratings, but low in ratings of psychotic symptoms, such as bizarreness, hallucinations, unusual thought content, etc. On the other hand, reduced variability in the first 100 msec, and increased variability in the second 100 msec of the SER were found in patients who are rated low on depression, but very high on psychoticism (Shagass, Soskis, Straumanis, and Overton, 1974b).

C. Evoked Response Recovery Functions

In several studies of SER recovery functions, we found that, with intervals from 2.5 to 20 msec, degree of amplitude recovery of the initial negative-positive SER component was significantly less than normal in a variety of psychiatric disorders (Shagass and Schwartz, 1962a, 1963b; Shagass, 1968a). The deviant groups were schizophrenias, psychotic depressions, and personality disorders. On the other hand, the recovery values of patients with neuroses characterized by anxiety and depression (dysthymic) were either similar to those of the normal controls, or intermediate between those of controls and other patients. Measurements of later peaks (from 35 to 120 msec) appeared to add little to the discriminations given by the initial negative-positive SER component. In contrast to amplitude recovery, latency recovery was greater, or more rapid, in the patient groups (Shagass, 1968a). This suggests that latency and amplitude recovery may be mediated and influenced by different mechanisms.

In recent years we have studied large groups of psychiatric patients and controls with a modification of the recovery function procedure. Instead of using paired stimuli of equal intensity, with various interstimulus intervals, the modified procedure maintains a constant interstimulus interval of 10 msec. However, the intensity of the conditioning stimuli is varied, whereas that of the test stimulus is kept constant. Also, in addition to a single conditioning stimulus, trains of nine conditioning stimuli are applied. The four SER yielded by the procedure are illustrated in Fig. 14. These include average responses to single stimuli of test (R1T) and conditioning (R1C) intensity, as well as responses to the second stimulus in a pair (R2), and to the tenth stimulus in a train of ten (R10). The idea of varying conditioning-stimulus intensity arose from the observation that test response amplitude tends to be inversely related to conditioning-stimulus intensity. It appeared, therefore, that by using both weak and strong conditioning stimuli, it might be possible to measure the extent of both inhibitory and facilitatory cortical reaction tendencies in one experiment. In addition to measures of recovery, the procedure provides intensity-response curves, based on the averaged responses to single conditioning stimuli of differing intensity.

The results obtained with the modified recovery function procedure have been somewhat disappointing in relation to its original purpose (Shagass, 1973a; Shagass, Overton, and Straumanis, 1974a). The only significant trend in the recovery measures suggested that the dynamic range of responsiveness was restricted in certain kinds of male patients, particularly chronic schizophrenics and patients with a history of drug-related psychotic reaction (Shagass, 1974a). More interesting results were obtained with the amplitude and variability measures based on responses to single stimuli. Among schizophrenic patients those with low depression and high psychoticism ratings had

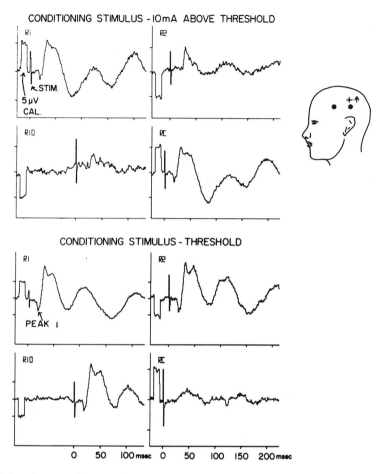

FIG. 14. Sample tracings from one subject obtained in modified SER recovery function procedure. (Upper) Both conditioning and test stimulus intensities were 10 mA above threshold. (Lower) Conditioning stimuli at threshold. R1 and RC each represent averages to 50 single stimuli of test and conditioning intensity. R2 is response to the second stimulus of a pair. R10 is the response to the 10th stimulus of the train. Interstimulus interval, 10 msec. R2 and R10 are of small amplitude with conditioning stimulus 10 mA above threshold, and are greater than R1T with conditioning stimulus of threshold intensity. From Shagass (1972).

higher amplitudes and less variability in the first 100 msec of the SER, whereas the reverse was true in patients with high depression and low psychoticism ratings (Shagass et al., 1974b). Also high amplitudes and low variability characterized chronic schizophrenics, whereas the acute and latent subtypes were rather similar to normal.

VER recovery functions have been investigated by several workers. In our own study, only delayed latency recovery of the initial VER peak, negative at about 30 msec, was found in psychiatric patients; this occurred particularly in nonpsychotic patients (Shagass and Schwartz, 1965a). More positive results with VER amplitude recovery were obtained by Speck et al. (1966), who showed that psychiatric patients, most of whom were schizophrenic, had less than normal recovery. Heninger and Speck (1966) retested some of these patients after treatment, and related the changes in recovery ratio to clinical improvement; they found a number of significant relationships, among which improvement in hallucinations had the highest correlation with an increase in the recovery ratio. Another group of workers headed by Floris also found VER recovery function reduced from normal in schizophrenics; they did not find differences between normals and patients with psychotic depressions, but showed that epileptics had greater than normal recovery (Floris, Morocutti, Amabile, Bernardi, and Rizzo, 1968,1969). Ishikawa (1968), in a study of VER recovery functions in schizophrenics, found differences mainly between patients with hallucinations and those without; recovery was significantly later in the hallucinating patients.

AER recovery functions were compared in depressed patients and controls by Satterfield (1972). He found that the distribution of recovery ratios was wider in the patient group. Comparing the patients with extreme high and low recovery values, those with low recovery, but not those with high recovery, had a history of depressive illness in first-degree relatives. Family history of mental illness showed few correlations with results from the modified SER recovery function procedure (Shagass et al., 1974b).

It will be evident that consistent significant discriminations between clinical psychiatric groups have been obtained more frequently with variability and recovery function measures than with the characteristics of simple evoked responses. This is probably because nonfunctional anatomic factors exert less influence on the variability and recovery measures. Although the degree of diagnostic specificity of the discriminations has been rather low, the evidence that symptom patterns within a diagnostic group may be related to evoked-response measurements is encouraging.

D. P3 Waves

Roth and Cannon (1972) used a test of passive attention, involving frequent and infrequent clicks and tones, to compare schizophrenic patients with controls. In response to the infrequent auditory stimuli, the P3 waves in the AER were demonstrated in the control subjects, but not in the schizophrenics. P3 amplitude decreased systematically over the 10-min period of recording in the controls. The results suggest either that the schizophrenics were not attending to the infrequent auditory stimuli, or that, if they were in a sustained hyperattentive state, habituation of their P3 response had occurred before the experiment commenced. The passive attention paradigm deserves further investigation in a psychiatric context.

E. CNV and Other Slow Potentials

Walter (1966) noted that the CNV was absent, or appeared only occasionally, in autistic children. McCallum and Walter (1968) reported that neurotics had smaller CNVs than normals, but that the differences became accentuated when distraction was introduced, the neurotics showing a much greater reduction of amplitude. Walter found that patients with psychopathic disturbances of an antisocial type were virtually incapable of producing more than a trace of CNV, and he noted greater variability of CNV in patients with schizoid features. Schizophrenic patients tended to show small CNVs, similar to those in anxious patients, but with greater variability. Low amplitude CNVs have been found in affective psychoses by Small and Small (1972). McCallum (1973) reported the results of an experiment in which schizophrenic patients were subdivided according to the presence of Schneider first-rank symptoms and also compared with a normal control group. CNV amplitude was lower and distraction effects greater in the Schneider-positive subgroup than in the controls and the Schneider-negative subgroup.

It will be recalled that the slow negative rise in the CNV is resolved by precipitous descent to baseline once the response to the imperative stimulus is made. Timsit, Koninckx, Dargent, Fontaine, and Dongier (1969) found that this return to baseline was delayed in psychiatric patients. Whereas the negativity following the imperative stimulus lasted less than 1.5 sec in 91% of normals and 66% of neurotics, the duration was greater than 1.5 sec in 93% of psychotics. The greatest prolongations of negativity were found in acute schizophrenic patients and the finding was stable after more than a 15-day interval. The results of CNV studies in a large series of psychiatric patients, summarized by Timsit-Berthier (1973), again showed a high incidence of prolonged negativity among psychotics. Among psychoneurotics, the negativity was prolonged more frequently in hysteric than in obsessional patients. The differences between the psychotic and neurotic groups were present before drug treatment.

Timsit-Berthier (1973) also described the results obtained by recording long-latency potentials in response to imperative stimuli alone and motor potentials obtained by asking the subject to press a button repetitively. Among several variations in the form of the long-latency potential following a sensory stimulus, a prolonged negative deflection, lasting more than 300 msec, occurred most often in the psychotic patients. Timsit-Berthier also classified motor potentials into a variety of types, according to the presence or absence of the readiness potential, and persistent negativity after the button press. The readiness potential appeared in only 23% of 80 psychotics, compared to 85% of controls and 71% of neurotics. In contrast a persistent negativity following button press was found in 77% of psychotics, 15% of controls, and 29% of neurotics. Dongier, Dubrovsky, and Garcia-Rill (1974), in a study well controlled for EOG and GSR artifact, have recently reported similar slow-potential significant discriminations between psychiatric patients and normals.

The neurophysiologic significance of the prolonged after-negativity found in severely ill psychiatric patients is not understood. The results suggest that motor activity in many psychotics may be associated with synchronized depolarization of cortical neurons to a degree seldom found in normals.

VIII. EFFECTS OF DRUGS AND TREATMENTS

ERP changes produced by psychiatric drugs and treatments have been the subject of several reviews by the author (Shagass, 1968b,1972,1974b). Some of the main findings will be described briefly here.

From a psychiatric viewpoint, concomitant study of the effects of drugs on evoked responses and clinical symptoms offers the possibility of shedding some light on neurophysiologic changes associated with alterations in psychopathology. The methodologic difficulty in such investigations is to discriminate between those electrophysiologic effects of drugs that may underlie amelioration of psychopathology and those that are unrelated. Two important kinds of unspecific drug effects result from the changes in alertness produced by most psychoactive agents and from generalized electrophysiologic changes, or tissue effects. An example of a tissue effect is the augmented negativity in somatosensory responses at about 35 msec latency, which we have observed with agents as diverse as barbiturates, amphetamines, phenothiazines, LSD, and even electroconvulsive therapy (ECT) (Shagass, Schwartz, and Amadeo, 1962).

A. ECT

In serial studies of SER recovery functions in patients with psychotic depressive states, most of the patients studied were treated with ECT (Shagass and Schwartz, 1962b). The early peak of recovery, i.e., with interstimulus intervals up to 20 msec, which was reduced from normal in the patients before treatment, increased progressively toward normal levels as the patients' clinical condition improved.

B. Barbiturates, Minor Tranquilizers, Alcohol, and Marijuana

Hypnotic doses of secobarbital increased VER amplitude in association with sleep (Corssen and Domino, 1964). However, intravenous amobarbital did not change the amplitude of the initial SER component in doses insufficient to produce sleep (Shagass et al., 1962). The newer minor tranquilizers, i.e., diazepam, chlordiazepoxide, and oxazepam tend to produce amplitude reduction and latency prolongation in both VER and SER (Dolce and Kaemmerer, 1967; Saletu, Saletu, and Itil, 1972a). VER appears to be unaffected by meprobamate in doses of 800 to 1200 mg (Prieto, Villar, and Bachini, 1965).

Alcohol reduces amplitude of AER, SER, and VER when given in sufficiently high amounts (Gross, Begleiter, Tobin, and Kissin, 1966; Lewis et al., 1970). Δ^9-tetrahydrocannibal (THC) in adequate dose increases VER and SER latencies, with little change in amplitude (Lewis et al., 1973). However, Rodin, Domino, and Porzak (1970) found no significant evoked-response changes after marijuana smokers had obtained a social high; probably the dose of THC was insufficient.

C. Excitants and Antidepressants

Pentamethylenetetrazol (Metrazol®), a convulsant, tends to increase VER amplitude, and to shorten the VER recovery cycle (Bergamasco, 1966). The effects of amphetamines have been inconsistent. For example, intravenous methamphetamine did not affect the initial SER component in patients (Shagass et al., 1962), whereas single doses of dextroamphetamine produced SER latency decreases in nonpatients (Saletu, Saletu, Itil, and Coffin, 1972b). The latter workers found some differences between the effects of dextroamphetamine and methylphenidate.

Some of the psychotic depressive patients for whom serial SER recovery functions were obtained in our serial study were treated with drugs; imipramine and tranylcypromine tended to normalize the recovery function (Shagass and Schwartz, 1962b). In a recent study, employing the modified recovery function procedure, we found that amitryptyline reduced SER amplitude (Shagass, Straumanis, and Overton, 1973). The amplitude of the entire SER for 200 msec was diminished, and the effect was seen both in responses to single test stimuli and those preceded by conditioning stimuli or trains of stimuli. An analysis with digital filtering showed that the amplitude reduction was almost entirely in the 4 to 28 Hz portion of the response. In contrast to the tendency for imipramine and amitryptyline to reduce SER amplitude in severely depressed patients, similar effects were not observed in normals (Shagass et al., 1962).

D. Major Tranquilizers

As suggested above for the antidepressants, there is also some evidence to indicate that the major antipsychotic agents may produce different evoked response effects in patients than in nonpatients. Fluphenazine and thiothixene reduce the amplitude of the initial SER component in schizophrenics (Saletu, Saletu, Itil, and Hsu, 1971b; Saletu, Saletu, Itil, and Jones, 1971c); on the other hand, 50 mg of chlorpromazine, given in a single dose to nonpatient volunteers, tended to produce amplitude increase (Saletu et al., 1972a). These workers did find that the amplitudes of later components tended to decrease in all subjects with major tranquilizers, and latencies, particularly of the later SER peaks, tended to become prolonged.

In our long-term studies of SER and VER characteristics in psychiatric patients, we have made repeated attempts to demonstrate consistent effects of phenothiazines by comparing the results between patients who had not received drugs for some time with those of patients who were receiving drugs. Such comparisons have yielded largely negative results. One of the main reasons may be the great variability in the effects of drugs on SER. This variability may be of clinical significance in predicting drug responsiveness. Saletu and his co-workers demonstrated pretreatment differences in SER of patients who did and did not show favorable clinical response to various major antipsychotic drugs (Saletu et al., 1971*b,c;* Saletu, Saletu, Itil, and Marasa, 1971*d*). Furthermore the drugs had little effect on the measurements of those who did not respond clinically, but altered SER of those who did respond. We have obtained some results with the modified recovery function procedure that seem to be of a similar nature (Shagass, 1973*c*). An important observation in Saletu's studies is that there may be a rather prolonged rebound effect after major antipsychotic drugs are stopped and replaced by placebo.

Silverman (1972) has reviewed evidence suggesting that phenothiazines tend to reduce augmentation in the flash VER test of augmenting-reducing. AER variability, as measured in the Callaway two-tone procedure, has been found to be diminished after effective phenothiazine therapy (Jones, Blacker, Callaway, and Layne, 1965). VER recovery functions in schizophrenics apparently tend to normalize with phenothiazine therapy (Heninger and Speck, 1966).

E. Lithium

Heninger (1969) reported that lithium carbonate increased the amplitude of the initial negative-positive SER component. We have recently confirmed and extended Heninger's findings by means of the modified SER recovery function procedure (Shagass et al., 1973). Figure 15 shows tracings of three subjects before and during lithium therapy; there is an evident increase in amplitude of the initial component. Figure 16 shows the mean curves for modified recovery function measurements for fourteen patients before and during lithium therapy. The curves are based on computer measurements of the activity from 15 to 30 msec after the stimulus. The increased amplitudes in responses to single stimuli (R1T) are clearly demonstrated. With conditioning stimuli of highest intensity (10 mA above threshold), the amplitudes of both R2 and R10 were at about the same level as before treatment. However, when the conditioning stimuli were of threshold intensity, both R2 and R10 amplitude were considerably greater than before drug administration. The increased R2 and R10 amplitudes, with threshold conditioning stimuli, indicate

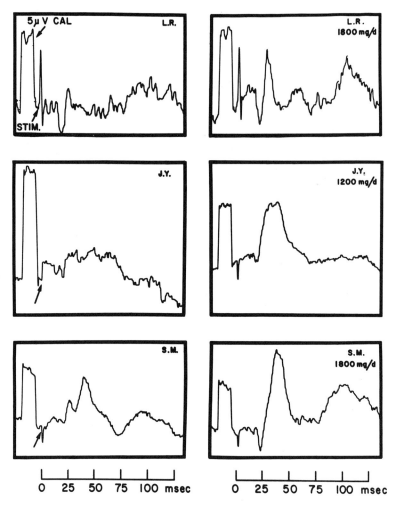

FIG. 15. SER of three patients before (left) and during (right) lithium carbonate therapy. From Shagass (1972).

relative facilitation. Since R1T amplitude was increased, the lack of change in R2 and R10, with conditioning stimuli 10 mA above threshold, suggests a relative decrease or inhibition. It thus appears that lithium may increase both inhibitory and facilitatory response tendencies; this may be described as augmentation of the dynamic range of cerebral responsiveness. Digital filtering of the R1T responses in our data indicated that the amplitude augmentation produced by lithium occurred mainly in the frequency band from 32 to 500 Hz; this contrasts with the effects of amitryptyline, which appear mainly in the slower frequency band from 4 to 28 Hz.

Borge et al. (1971) have measured augmenting-reducing with a flash

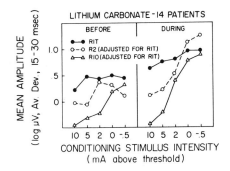

FIG. 16. Effects of lithium on modified somato-sensory recovery test. Mean results for 14 patients before and during treatment. Note generally increased amplitude of R1T, and marked increase of R2 and R10 amplitude with conditioning stimulus intensities near threshold. From Shagass, Straumanis, and Overton (1973).

stimulus in unipolar and bipolar manic depressive patients. They found that lithium treatment decreased augmentation in both groups, i.e., the intensity-response function was reduced. Although the VER effects of lithium seem opposite to the SER findings, it should be noted that the measurements were based on early SER and later VER components.

IX. CONCLUSION

ERP recording offers investigators the possibility of examining several aspects of brain activity directly in the intact subject, who is capable of reporting his experiences. The large volume of research reports published since the technique was introduced shows that behavioral scientists have recognized the exciting implications of the method for research in their field. The reader will, however, have noted that the information yielded by ERP data may be difficult to interpret in terms of specific neurophysiologic events and that the methodologic problems and constraints are formidable. Clearly productive research in this field requires a high level of methodologic sophistication. However, it is hoped that the material presented has also shown that the difficulties inherent in ERP methods have not prevented them from contributing significantly to many areas of psychologic and psychiatric research.

One of the great sources of difficulty in ERP research may be an important asset, namely the variations in response produced by even minor changes in experimental conditions. With the application of investigative ingenuity in tracking down the reasons for such variations, it seems probable that new kinds of ERP will be discovered and that there will be more precise specification of the external events and internal states that determine ERP characteristics. As computer methods develop, we can also expect more sophisticated techniques for quantifying and reducing ERP data. One area of ERP research obviously in need of further development concerns the spatial distribution of ERP events; not only are more topographic studies required in relation to behavioral criteria, but new methods to express the findings in a readily understandable form are also needed.

The application of ERP methods to psychiatric research has to be regarded as being in a very early stage of development. To date, ERP methods have yielded positive findings with respect to phenomena of consciousness, intellectual functioning, personality, psychiatric diagnosis, and the effects of psychoactive drugs. However encouraging these results may be, they have so far led to few significant new insights into basic neurophysiologic processes underlying psychopathology. Clearly, a long road lies ahead. This will probably involve two lines of research effort. In one line it will be necessary for psychiatric investigators to discover closer and more convincing ERP correlates of well-defined psychopathologic states or processes than have so far been demonstrated. In the other line, which is interdependent with the first, it is essential that the neurophysiologic mechanisms underlying ERP-clinical correlations become the subject of focused animal experimentation. Without the focus provided by a strong clinical correlation, much animal research on the neurophysiology of behavior may be of remote psychiatric relevance. Without focused animal research, the neurophysiologic significance of correlations between ERP and psychopathology will remain speculative. A productive pathophysiology of mental illness requires work at both levels.

ACKNOWLEDGMENT

This research was supported in part by U.S. Public Health Service Grant MH 12507.

REFERENCES

Allison, T., and Goff, W. R. (1967): Human cerebral evoked responses to odorous stimuli. *Electroencephalogr. Clin. Neurophysiol.*, 23:558–560.

Amadeo, M., and Shagass, C. (1973a): Brief latency click-evoked potentials during waking and sleep in man. *Psychophysiology*, 10:244–250.

Amadeo, M., and Shagass, C. (1973b): Evoked response latency recovery cycles: Changes during sleep in man. *Life Sci.*, 12:241–248.

Barnet, A. B., and Lodge, A. (1967): Click evoked EEG responses in normal and developmentally retarded infants. *Nature,* 214:252–255.

Bates, J. A. V. (1951): Electrical activity of the cortex accompanying movement. *J. Physiol.* (Lond.), 113:240–257.

Beatty, J., and Uttal, W. R. (1968): The effects of grouping visual stimuli on the cortical evoked potential. *Percept. Psychophys.,* 4:214–216.

Beck, E., and Barolin, G. S. (1965): Effect of hypnotic suggestions on evoked potentials. *J. Nerv. Ment. Dis.,* 140:154–161.

Beck, E. C., Dustman, R. E., and Beier, E. G. (1966): Hypnotic suggestions and visually evoked potentials. *Electroencephalogr. Clin. Neurophysiol.*, 20:397–400.

Bennett, W. F. (1972): The Fourier transform of evoked responses. *Nature,* 239:407–408.

Bergamasco, G. (1966): Study of the modification of cortical response in man induced by drugs acting on the CNS. *Sist. Nerv.,* 18:155–164.

Bergamasco, B., Bergamini, L., Mombelli, A. M., and Mutani, R. (1966): Longitudinal study of visual evoked potentials in subjects in post-traumatic coma. *Schweiz. Arch. Neurol. Neurochir. Psychiatr.,* 97:1–10.

Bergamini, L., Bergamasco, B., Mombelli, A. M., and Gandiglio, B. (1965): Visual evoked potentials in subjects with congenital aniridia. *Electroencephalogr. Clin. Neurophysiol.,* 19:394–397.

Berger, H. (1929): Über das Elektrenkephalogramm des Menschen. *Arch. Psychiatr.,* 87:527–570.

Bickford, R. G., Jacobson, J. L., and Cody, D. T. (1964): Nature of average evoked potentials to sound and other stimuli in man. *Ann. N. Y. Acad. Sci.,* 112:204–223.

Bigum, H. B., Dustman, R. E., and Beck, E. C. (1970): Visual and somatosensory evoked responses from mongoloid and normal children. *Electroencephalogr. Clin. Neurophysiol.,* 28:576–586.

Blacker, K. H., Jones, R. T., Stone, G. C., and Pfefferbaum, D. (1968): Chronic users of LSD: The "acidheads." *Am. J. Psychiatry,* 125:341–351.

Borge, G. F., Buchsbaum, M., Goodwin, F., Murphy, D., and Silverman, J. (1971): Neuropsychological correlates of affective disorders. *Arch. Gen. Psychiatry,* 24:501–504.

Brown, J. C. N., Shagass, C., and Schwartz, M. (1965): Cerebral evoked potential changes associated with the Ditran delirium and its reversal in man. In: *Recent Advances in Biological Psychiatry, Vol. VII,* edited by J. Wortis, pp. 223–234, Plenum Press, New York.

Buchsbaum, M., and Silverman, J. (1968): Stimulus intensity control and the cortical evoked response. *Psychosom. Med.,* 30:12–22.

Butler, R. A. (1972): Frequency specificity of the auditory evoked response to simultaneously and successively presented stimuli. *Electroencephalogr. Clin. Neurophysiol.,* 33:277–282.

Butler, R. A. (1973): The cumulative effects of different stimulus repetition rates on the auditory evoked responses in man. *Electroencephalogr. Clin. Neurophysiol.,* 35:337–345.

Butler, V. B., and Engel, R. (1969): Mental and motor scores at 8 months in relation to neonatal photic responses. *Dev. Med. Child Neurol.,* 11:72–82.

Callaway, E. (1973): Correlations between averaged evoked potentials and measures of intelligence. *Arch. Gen. Psychiatry,* 29:553–558.

Callaway, E., and Halliday, R. A. (1973): Evoked potential variability: Effects of age, amplitude and methods of assessment. *Electroencephalogr. Clin. Neurophysiol.,* 34:125–133.

Callaway, E., Jones, R. T., and Layne, R. S. (1965): Evoked responses and segmental set of schizophrenia. *Arch. Gen. Psychiatry,* 12:83–89.

Caton, R. (1875): The electric currents of the brain. *Br. Med. J.,* 2:278.

Chalke, F. C. R., and Ertl, J. (1965): Evoked potentials and intelligence. *Life Sci.,* 4:1319–1322.

Chapman, R. M. (1965): Evoked responses to relevant and irrelevant visual stimuli while problem solving. *Proceedings of the American Psychiatric Association, 73rd Annual Convention,* pp. 177–178. American Psychiatric Assoc., Washington, D.C.

Chapman, R. M., and Bragdon, H. R. (1964): Evoked responses to numerical visual stimuli while problem solving. *Nature,* 203:1155–1157.

Cigánek, L. (1961): *Die Electroencephalographische Lichtreizantwort Der Menschlichen Hirnrinde.* Bratislavia: Slowakischen Akademie Der Wissenschaften.

Cigánek, L. (1967): The effects of attention and distraction on the visual evoked potential in man: A preliminary report. *Electroencephalogr. Clin. Neurophysiol.,* Supplement 26:70–73.

Clynes, M., Kohn, M., and Gradijan, J. (1967): Computer recognition of the brain's visual perception through learning the brain's physiologic language. *Institute of Electrical and Electronic Engineers International Convention Record,* Part 9, pp. 125–142.

Clynes, M., Kohn, M., and Lifshitz, K. (1964): Dynamics and spatial behavior of light evoked potentials, their modification under hypnosis, and on-line correlation in relation to rhythmic components. *Ann. N. Y. Acad. Sci.,* 112:468–509.

Cobb, W. A., and Dawson, G. D. (1960): The latency and form in man of the occipital potentials evoked by bright flashes. *J. Physiol.,* 152:108–121.

Cohen, J. (1969): Very slow brain potentials relating to expectancy: the CNV. In: *Average Evoked Potentials: Methods, Results and Evaluations,* edited by E. Donchin and D. B. Lindsley, pp. 143–163. NASA, Washington, D.C.

Cohen, R. (1973): The influence of task-irrelevant stimulus variations on the reliability of auditory evoked responses in schizophrenia. In: *Human Neurophysiology, Psychology, Psychiatry: Average Evoked Responses and Their Conditioning in Normal Subjects and Psychiatric Patients,* edited by A. Fessard and G. Lelord, pp. 373–388. Inserm, Paris.

Cohn, R. (1964): Rhythmic after-activity in visual evoked responses. *Ann. N. Y. Acad. Sci.,* 112:281–291.

Corssen, G., and Domino, E. F. (1964): Visually evoked responses in man: A method for measuring cerebral effects of preanesthetic medications. *Anesthesiology,* 25:330–341.

Cracco, R. Q. (1972): The initial positive potential of the human scalp-recorded somatosensory evoked response. *Electroencephalogr. Clin. Neurophysiol.,* 32:623–629.

Cracco, R. Q., and Bickford, R. G. (1968): Somatomotor and somatosensory evoked responses. Median nerve stimulation in man. *Arch. Neurol.,* 18:52–68.

Dargent, J., and Dongier, M. (1969): *Variation Contingentes Négatives.* University of Liège Press, Liège.

Davis, H., Mast, T., Yoshie, N., and Zerlin, S. (1966): The slow response of the human cortex to auditory stimuli: Recovery process. *Electroencephalogr. Clin. Neurophysiol.,* 21:105–113.

Dawson, G. D. (1947): Cerebral responses to electrical stimulation of peripheral nerve in man. *J. Neurol. Neurosurg. Psychiatry,* 10:134–140.

Dawson, G. D. (1951): A summation technique for detecting small signals in a large irregular background. *J. Physiol.,* 115:2P–3P.

Dawson, G. D. (1954): A summation technique for the detection of small evoked potentials. *Electroencephalogr. Clin. Neurophysiol.,* 6:65–84.

Diamond, S. P. (1964): Input-output relations. *Ann. N. Y. Acad. Sci.,* 112:160–171.

Dolce, G., and Kaemmerer, E. (1967): Effect of the Benzodiazepin adumbran on the resting and sleep EEG, and on the visual evoked potential in adult man, *Med. Welt,* 67:510–514.

Dolce, G., and Sannita, W. (1973): A CNV-like negative shift in deep coma. *Electroencephalogr. Clin. Neurophysiol.,* 34:647–650.

Domino, E. F., Matsuoka, S., Waltz, J., and Cooper, I. S. (1965): Effects of cryogenic thalamic lesions on the somesthetic evoked response in man. *Electroencephalogr. Clin. Neurophysiol.,* 19:127–138.

Donchin, E., and Lindsley, D. B. (1966): Averaged evoked potentials and reaction times to visual stimuli. *Electroencephalogr. Clin. Neurophysiol.,* 20:217–223.

Dongier, M., Dubrovsky, B., and Garcia-Rill, E. (1973): Slow cerebral potentials in psychiatry. *Can. Psychiat. Ass. J.,* 19:177–183.

Dustman, R. E., and Beck, E. C. (1963): Long-term stability of visually evoked potentials in man. *Science,* 142:1480–1481.

Dustman, R. E., and Beck, E. C. (1965): Phase of alpha brain waves, reaction time and visually evoked potentials. *Electroencephalogr. Clin. Neurophysiol.,* 18:433–440.

Eason, R. G., Aiken, L. R., White, C. T., and Lichtenstein, M. (1964): Activation and behavior. II. Visually evoked cortical potentials in man as indicants of activation level. *Percept. Mot. Skills,* 19:875–895.

Eason, R. G., Groves, P., White, C. T., and Oden, D. (1967): Evoked cortical potentials: Relation to visual field and handedness. *Science,* 156:1643–1646.

Eason, R. G., Harter, M. R., and White, C. T. (1969): *Physiol. Behav.,* 4:283–289.

Eason, R. G., White, C. T., and Bartlett, N. (1970): Effects of checkerboard pattern stimulations on evoked cortical responses in relation to check size and visual field. *Psychonomic Sci.,* 2:113–115.

Efron, R. (1964): Artificial synthesis of evoked responses to light flash. *Ann. N. Y. Acad. Sci.,* 112:292–304.

Emde, J. (1964): A time locked low level calibrator. *Electroencephalogr. Clin. Neurophysiol.,* 16:616–618.

Engel, R., and Fay, W. (1972): Visual evoked responses at birth, verbal scores at three years, and IQ of four years. *Dev. Med. Child Neurol.,* 14:283–289.

Engel, R., and Henderson, N. B. (1973): Visual evoked responses and IQ scores at school age. *Dev. Med. Child Neurol.,* 15:136–145.

Ertl, J. P., and Schafer, E. W. P. (1969): Brain response correlates of psychometric intelligence. *Nature,* 223:421–422.

Floris, V., Morocutti, C., Amabile, G., Bernardi, G., and Rizzo, P. A. (1968): Recovery cycle of visual evoked potentials in normal, schizophrenic and neurotic patients. In: *Computers and Electronic Devices in Psychiatry,* edited by N. S. Kline and E. Laska, pp. 194–205, Grune and Stratton, New York.

Floris, V., Morocutti, C., Amabile, G., Bernardi, G., and Rizzo, P. A. (1969): Cerebral reactivity in psychiatric and epileptic patients. *Electroencephalogr. Clin. Neurophysiol.,* 27:680.

Floris, V., Morocutti, C., Amabile, G., Bernardi, G., Rizzo, P. A., and Vasconetto, C. (1967): Recovery cycle of visual evoked potentials in normal and schizophrenic subjects. *Electroencephalogr. Clin. Neurophysiol.,* Supplement 26:74–81.

Galbraith, G. C., Gliddon, J. B., and Busk, J. (1970): Visual evoked responses in mentally retarded and nonretarded subjects. *Am. J. Ment. Defic.,* 75:341–348.

Garcia-Austt, E. (1963): Influence of the state of awareness upon sensory evoked potentials. *Electroencephalogr. Clin. Neurophysiol.,* Supplement 24:76–89.

Garcia-Austt, E., Bogacz, J., and Vanzulli, A. (1964): Effects of attention and inattention upon visual evoked response. *Electroencephalogr. Clin. Neurophysiol.,* 17:136–143.

Gerbrandt, L. K., Goff, W. R., and Smith, D. B. (1973): Distribution of the human average movement potential. *Electroencephalogr. Clin. Neurophysiol.,* 34:461–474.

Giblin, D. R. (1964): Somatosensory evoked potentials in healthy subjects and in patients with lesions of the nervous system. *Ann. N. Y. Acad. Sci.,* 112:93–142.

Gilden, L., Vaughan, H. G., and Costa, L. D. (1966): Summated human EEG potentials with voluntary movement. *Electroencephalogr. Clin. Neurophysiol.,* 20:433–438.

Goff, W. R., Allison, R., Shapiro, A., and Rosner, B. S. (1966): Cerebral somatosensory responses evoked during sleep in man. *Electroencephalogr. Clin. Neurophysiol.,* 21:1–9.

Goff, W. R., Matsumiya, T., Allison, T., and Goff, G. D. (1969): Cross-modality comparisons of averaged evoked potentials. In: *Average Evoked Potentials—Methods, Results, and Evaluations,* edited by E. Donchin and D. Lindsley, pp. 95–141. NASA, Washington, D.C.

Goff, W. R., Rosner, B. S., and Allison, R. (1962): Distribution of cerebral somatosensory evoked responses in normal man. *Electroencephalogr. Clin. Neurophysiol.,* 14:697–713.

Gross, M. M., Begleiter, H., Tobin, M., and Kissin, B. (1965): Auditory evoked response comparison during counting clicks and reading. *Electroencephalogr. Clin. Neurophysiol.* 18:451–454.

Gross, M. M., Begleiter, H., Tobin, M., and Kissin, B. (1966): Changes in auditory evoked response induced by alcohol. *J. Nerv. Ment. Dis.,* 143:152–156.

Guerrero-Figueroa, R., and Heath, R. G. (1964): Evoked responses and changes during attentive factors in man. *Arch. Neurol.,* 10:74–84.

Hall, R. A., Rappaport, M., Hopkins, H. K., and Griffin, R. (1973): Tobacco and evoked potentials. *Science,* 180:212–214.

Halliday, A. M. (1973): Evoked responses in organic and functional sensory loss. In: *Human Neurophysiology, Psychology, Psychiatry: Average Evoked Responses and Their Conditioning in Normal Subjects and Psychiatric Patients,* edited by A. Fessard and G. Lelord, pp. 189–211. Inserm, Paris.

Halliday, A. M., and Mason, A. A. (1964): The effect of hypnotic anesthesia on cortical responses. *J. Neurol. Neurosurg. Psychiatry,* 27:300–312.

Halliday, A. M., and Michael, W. F. (1970): Changes in pattern-evoked responses in man associated with the vertical and horizontal meridians of the visual field. *J. Physiol.* (Lond.), 208:499–513.

Halliday, A. M., and Wakefield, G. S. (1963): Cerebral evoked potentials in patients with dissociated sensory loss. *J. Neurol. Neurosurg. Psychiatry,* 26:211–219.

Häseth, K., Shagass, C., and Straumanis, J. J. (1969): Perceptual and personality correlates of EEG and evoked response measures. *Biol. Psychiatry,* 1:49–60.

Heninger, G. (1969): Lithium effects on cerebral cortical function in manic depressive patients. *Electroencephalogr. Clin. Neurophysiol.,* 27:670.

Heninger, G., McDonald, R. K., Goff, W. R., and Sollberger, A. (1969): Diurnal variations in the cerebral evoked response and EEG: Relations to 17-hydroxycortico-steroid levels. *Arch. Neurol.,* 21:330–337.

Heninger, G., and Speck, L. (1966): Visual evoked responses and mental status of schizophrenics. *Arch. Gen. Psychiatry,* 15:419–426.

Hernández-Peón, R., and Donoso, M. (1959): Influence of attention and suggestion upon subcortical evoked electrical activity in the human brain. In: *First International Congress on Neurological Sciences, Vol. 3,* edited by L. van Bogaert and J. Rader-mecker, pp. 385–396. Pergamon Press, New York.

Hillyard, S. A. (1969a): Relationships between the contingent negative variation (CNV) and reaction time. *Physiol. Behav.,* 4:351–358.

Hillyard, S. A. (1969b): The CNV and the vertex evoked potential during signal detection: A preliminary report. In: *Average Evoked Potentials—Methods, Results, and Evaluations,* edited by E. Donchin and D. Lindsley, pp. 349–353. NASA, Washington, D.C.

Hogan, D. D., and Graham, J. T. (1967): The use of summing computer for analyzing auditory evoked responses of mentally retarded adults. *J. Auditory Res.,* 7:1–13.

Ishikawa, K. (1968): Studies on the visual evoked responses to paired light flashes in schizophrenics. *Kurume Med. J.,* 15:153–167.

Jasper, H. H. (1958): The ten twenty electrode system of the International Federa-tion. *Electroencephalogr. Clin. Neurophysiol.,* 10:371–375.

Jasper, H. H., Lende, R., and Rasmussen, T. (1960): Evoked potentials from the ex-posed somatosensory cortex in man. *J. Nerv. Ment. Dis.,* 130:526–537.

Jewett, D. L., Romano, M. N., and Williston, J. S. (1970): Human auditory evoked potentials: Possible brain stem components detected on the scalp. *Science,* 167:1517–1518.

Jones, R. T., Blacker, K. H., Callaway, E., and Layne, R. S. (1965): The auditory evoked response as a diagnostic and prognostic measure in schizophrenia. *Am. J. Psychiatry,* 122:33–41.

Jones, R. T., and Callaway, E. (1970): Auditory evoked responses in schizophrenia: A reassessment. *Biol. Psychiatry,* 2:291–298.

Kooi, K. A., Bagchi, B. K., and Jordan, R. N. (1964): Observations on photically evoked occipital and vertex waves during sleep in man. *Ann. N. Y. Acad. Sci.,* 112:270–280.

Kornhüber, H. H., and Deecke, L. (1965): Cerebral potential changes in voluntary and passive movements in man: Readiness potential and reafferent potential. *Pfleügers Arch.,* 284:1–17.

Lee, R. G., and White, D. G. (1974): Modification of the human somatosensory evoked response during voluntary movement. *Electroencephalogr. Clin. Neurophysiol.,* 36:53–62.

Lehtonen, J. B., and Koivikko, M. J. (1971): The use of a non-cephalic reference electrode in recording cerebral evoked potentials in man. *Electroencephalogr. Clin. Neurophysiol.,* 31:154–156.

Levy, R. (1973): The averaged evoked response (A.E.R.) in psychiatric patients with perceptual disturbances. In: *Psychiatry,* edited by R. de la Fuente and M. N. Weisman. Excerpta Medica, Amsterdam.

Levy, R., Isaacs, A., and Behrman, J. (1971): Neurophysiological correlates of senile dementia: II. The somatosensory evoked response. *Psychol. Med.,* 1:159–165.

Lewis, E. G., Dustman, R. E., and Beck, E. C. (1970): The effects of alcohol on visual and somatosensory evoked responses. *Electroencephalogr. Clin. Neurophysiol.,* 28:202–205.

Lewis, E. G., Dustman, R. E., Peters, B. A., Straight, R. C., and Beck, E. C. (1973): The effects of varying doses of Δ^9-tetrahydrocannabinol on the human visual and somatosensory evoked response. *Electroencephalogr. Clin. Neurophysiol.,* 35:347–354.

Liberson, W. T. (1966): Study of evoked potentials in aphasics. *Am. J. Phys. Med.,* 45:135–142.

Libet, B., Alberts, W. W., Wright, E. W., and Feinstein, B. (1967): Responses of human somatosensory cortex to stimuli for conscious sensation. *Science*, 158:1597–1600.

Lifshitz, K. (1969): An examination of evoked potentials as indicators of information processing in normal and schizophrenic subjects. In: *Average Evoked Potentials—Methods, Results, and Evaluations*, edited by E. Donchin and D. B. Lindsley, pp. 357–362. NASA, Washington, D.C.

Lille, F., Lerique, A., Pottier, M., Scherrer, J., and Thieffry, S. (1968): Cortical evoked responses during coma in children. *Presse Med.*, 76:1411–1414.

Loomis, A. L., Harvey, E. N., and Hobart, G. (1938): Distribution of disturbance patterns in the human electroencephalogram, with special reference to sleep. *J. Neurophysiol.*, 1:413–430.

Low, M. D., and McSherry, J. W. (1968): Further observations of psychological factors involved in CNV genesis. *Electroencephalogr. Clin. Neurophysiol.*, 25:203–207.

Mackay, D. M., and Jeffreys, D. A. (1971): Visual evoked potentials and visual perception in man. In: *Central Processing of Visual Information, Handbook of Sensory Physiology*, edited by R. Jung. Springer Verlag, New York.

Malerstein, A. J., and Callaway, E. (1969): Two-tone average evoked response in Korsakoff patients. *J. Psychiatr. Res.*, 6:253–260.

Marcus, M. M. (1970): Visual evoked responses to patterns in normals and mental retardates. *Clin. Res.*, 18:206.

Matsumiya, Y., Tagliasco, V., Lombroso, C. T., and Goodglass, H. (1972): Auditory evoked response: Meaningfulness of stimuli and interhemispheric asymmetry. *Science*, 175:790–792.

McCallum, W. C. (1973): Some psychological, psychiatric and neurologic aspects of the CNV. In: *Human Neurophysiology, Psychology, Psychiatry: Average Evoked Responses and Their Conditioning in Normal Subjects and Psychiatric Patients*, edited by A. Fessard and G. Lelord, pp. 295–324. Inserm, Paris.

McCallum, W. C., and Cummins, B. (1973): The effects of brain lesions on the contingent negative variation in neurosurgical patients. *Electroencephalogr. Clin. Neurophysiol.*, 35:449–456.

McCallum, W. C., and Walter, W. G. (1968): The effects of attention and distraction on the contingent negative variation in normal and neurotic subjects. *Electroencephalogr. Clin. Neurophysiol.*, 25:319–329.

Michael, W. F., and Halliday, A. M. (1971): Differences between the occipital distribution of upper and lower field pattern-evoked responses in man. *Brain Res.*, 32:311–324.

Morrell, L. K., and Morrell, F. (1966): Evoked potentials and reaction times: A study of intra-individual variability. *Electroencephalogr. Clin. Neurophysiol.*, 20:567–575.

Morrell, L. K., and Salamy, J. G. (1971): Hemispheric asymmetry of electrocortical responses to speech stimuli. *Science*, 174:164–166.

Näätänen, R. (1967): Selective attention and evoked potentials. *Ann. Acad. Sci. Fenn.* [*Med.*], 151:1–226.

Näätänen, R. (1973): On what is the contingent negative variation (CNV) contingent in reaction-time experiments? In: *Human Neurophysiology. Psychology, Psychiatry: Average Evoked Responses and Their Conditioning in Normal Subjects and Psychiatric Patients*, edited by A. Fessard and G. Lelord, pp. 121–174. Inserm, Paris.

Nakanishi, T., Takita, K., and Toyokura, Y. (1973): Somatosensory evoked responses to tactile tap in man. *Electroencephalogr. Clin. Neurophysiol.*, 34:1–6.

Nodar, R. H., and Graham, J. T. (1968): An investigation of auditory evoked responses of mentally retarded adults during sleep. *Electroencephalogr. Clin. Neurophysiol.*, 25:73–76.

Osborne, R. T. (1969): Psychometric correlates of the visual evoked potential. *Acta Psychol.* (Amst.), 29:303–308.

Perry, N. W., and Copenhaver, R. M. (1965): Differential cortical habituation with stimulation of central and peripheral retina. *Percept. Mot. Skills*, 20:1209–1213.

Perry, N. S., and Childers, D. G. (1969): *The Human Visual Evoked Response. Method and Theory*. Charles C Thomas, Springfield.

Petrie, A. (1967): *Individuality in Pain and Suffering*. University of Chicago Press, Chicago.

Picton, T. W., and Hillyard, S. A. (1972): Cephalic skin potentials in electroencephalography. *Electroencephalogr. Clin. Neurophysiol.,* 33:419–424.
Picton, T. W., and Hillyard, S. A. (1974): Human auditory evoked potentials. II. Effects of attention. *Electroencephalogr. Clin. Neurophysiol.,* 36:191–199.
Picton, T. W., Hillyard, S. A., Galambos, R., and Schiff, M. (1971): Human auditory attention: A central or peripheral process? *Science,* 173:351–353.
Picton, T. W., Hillyard, S. A., Krausz, H. I., and Galambos, R. (1974): Human auditory evoked potentials. Evaluation of components. *Electroencephalogr. Clin. Neurophysiol.,* 36:179–190.
Plattig, K. H. (1968): Über den electrischen Geschmack. *Z. Biol.,* 116:162–211.
Prieto, S., Villar, J. I., and Bachini, O. (1965): Influencias farmacologicas sobre la respuesta visual provocada en el hombre. *Acta Neurol. Lat. Am.,* 11:295–296.
Regan, D. (1972): *Evoked Potentials in Psychology, Sensory Physiology and Clinical Medicine.* Chapman and Hall, Ltd., London.
Rhodes, L. E., Dustman, R. E., and Beck, E. C. (1969): The visual evoked response: A comparison of bright and dull children. *Electroencephalogr. Clin. Neurophysiol.,* 27:364–372.
Ritter, W., and Vaughan, H. G. (1969): Average evoked responses in vigilance and discrimination: A reassessment. *Science,* 164:326–328.
Ritter, W., Vaughan, H. G., and Costa, L. D. (1968): Orienting and habituation to auditory stimuli: A study of short term changes in average evoked responses. *Electroencephalogr. Clin. Neurophysiol.,* 25:550–556.
Rodin, E., Domino, E. F., and Porzak, J. P. (1970): The marihuana-induced "social high." *JAMA,* 213:1300–1302.
Rodin, E., Grisell, J., and Gottlieb, J. (1968): Some electrographic differences between chronic schizophrenic patients and normal subjects. In: *Recent Advances in Biological Psychiatry,* edited by J. Wortis, pp. 194–204. Plenum Press, New York.
Rodin, E., Zacharopoulos, G., Beckett, P., and Frohman, C. (1964): Characteristics of visually evoked responses in normal subjects and schizophrenic patients. *Electroencephalogr. Clin. Neurophysiol.,* 17:458.
Roth, W. T., and Cannon, E. H. (1972): Some features of the auditory evoked response in schizophrenics. *Arch. Gen. Psych.,* 27:466–471.
Saier, J., Régis, H., Mano, T., and Gastaut, H. (1968): Potentiels évoqués visuels et somesthésiques pendant le sommeil de l'homme. *Brain Res.,* 10:431–440.
Saletu, B., Itil, T., and Saletu, M. (1971a): Auditory evoked response, EEG, and thought process in schizophrenics. *Am J. Psychiatry,* 128:336–344.
Saletu, B., Saletu, M., and Itil, T. (1972a): Effect of minor and major tranquilizers on somatosensory evoked potentials. *Psychopharmacologia,* 24:347–358.
Saletu, B., Saletu, M., Itil, T., and Coffin, C. (1972b): Effect of stimulatory drugs on the somatosensory evoked potential in man. *Pharmakopsychiatrie,* 5:129–136.
Saletu, B., Saletu, M., Itil, T., and Hsu, W. (1971b): Changes in somatosensory evoked potentials during fluphenazine treatment. *Pharmakopsychiatr. Neuropsychopharmakol.,* 4:158–168.
Saletu, B., Saletu, M., Itil, T., and Jones, J. (1971c): Somatosensory evoked potential changes during thiothixene treatment in schizophrenic patients. *Psychopharmacologia,* 20:242–252.
Saletu, B., Saletu, M., Itil, T., and Marasa, J. (1971d): Somatosensory evoked potential changes during haloperidol treatment of chronic schizophrenics. *Biol. Psychiatry,* 3:299–307.
Satterfield, J. H. (1965): Evoked cortical response enhancement and attention in man. A study of responses to auditory and shock stimuli. *Electroencephalogr. Clin. Neurophysiol.,* 19:470–475.
Satterfield, J. H. (1972): Auditory evoked cortical response studies in depressed patients and normal control subjects. In: *Recent Advances in the Psychobiology of the Depressive Illnesses,* edited by T. A. Williams, M. M. Katz and J. A. Shield, Jr., pp. 87–98. U.S. Government Printing Office, DHEW Publication No. (HSM) 70–9053, Washington, D.C.
Satterfield, J. H., and Cheatum, D. (1964): Evoked cortical potential correlates of attention in human subjects. *Electroencephalogr. Clin. Neurophysiol.,* 17:456.

Schwartz, M., Emde, J., and Shagass, C. (1964): Comparison of constant current and constant voltage stimulators for scalp-recorded somatosensory responses. *Electroencephalogr. Clin. Neurophysiol.,* 17:81–83.

Schwartz, M., and Shagass, C. (1964): Recovery functions of human somatosensory and visual evoked potentials. *Ann. N.Y. Acad. Sci.,* 112:510–525.

Shagass, C. (1968a): Averaged somatosensory evoked responses in various psychiatric disorders. In: *Recent Advances in Biological Psychiatry,* edited by J. Wortis, pp. 205–219. Plenum Press, New York.

Shagass, C. (1968b): Pharmacology of evoked potentials in man. In: *Psychopharmacology: A Review of Progress 1957–1967,* edited by D. H. Efron, J. O. Cole, J. Levine, and J. R. Wittenborn, pp. 483–492. Public Health Service Publication No. 1836, Washington, D.C.

Shagass, C. (1972): *Evoked Brain Potentials in Psychiatry.* Plenum Press, New York.

Shagass, C. (1973a): Evoked response studies of central excitability in psychiatric disorders. In: *Human Neurophysiology, Psychology, Psychiatry: Average Evoked Responses and Their Conditioning in Normal Subjects and Psychiatric Patients,* edited by A. Fessard and G. Lelord, pp. 223–252. Inserm, Paris.

Shagass, C. (1973b): Evoked potential studies of the dynamic range of cortical responsiveness in psychiatric patients. In: *Psychiatry,* edited by R. de la Fuente and M. N. Weisman, pp. 771–781. Excerpta Medica, Amsterdam.

Shagass, C. (1973c): Evoked potential studies in patients with mental disorders. In: *Chemical Modulation of Brain Function,* edited by H. C. Sabelli, pp. 313–326. Raven Press, New York.

Shagass, C. (1974a): Evoked potentials in psychopathology and psychiatric treatment. Presented at the 7th Annual Symposium on Behavior and Brain Electrical Activity, Houston, Texas.

Shagass, C. (1974b): Effects of psychotropic drugs on human evoked potentials. In: *Psychotropic Drugs and the Human EEG,* edited by T. Itil. Karger, Basel. pp. 238–257.

Shagass, C., and Canter, A. (1972): Cerebral evoked responses and personality. In: *Biological Bases of Individual Behavior,* edited by V. D. Nebylitsyn, pp. 111–127. Academic Press, New York.

Shagass, C., Overton, D. A., Bartolucci, G., and Straumanis, J. J. (1971): Effect of attention modification by television viewing on somatosensory evoked responses and recovery functions. *J. Nerv. Ment. Dis.,* 152:53–72.

Shagass, C., Overton, D. A., and Straumanis, J. J. (1972a): Sex differences in somatosensory evoked responses related to psychiatric illness. *Biol. Psychiatry,* 5:295–309.

Shagass, C., Overton, D. A., and Straumanis, J. J. (1974a): Evoked potential studies in schizophrenia. In: *Biological Mechanisms of Schizophrenia and Schizophrenia-like Psychoses,* edited by H. Mitsuda and T. Fukuda, Igaku-Shoin Ltd., Tokyo. pp. 214–234.

Shagass, C., and Schwartz, M. (1961): Evoked cortical potentials and sensation in man. *J. Neuropsychiatry,* 2:262–270.

Shagass, C., and Schwartz, M. (1962a): Excitability of the cerebral cortex in psychiatric disorder. In: *Physiological Correlates of Psychological Disorder,* edited by R. Roessler and N. S. Greenfield, pp. 45–60. University of Wisconsin Press, Madison.

Shagass, C., and Schwartz, M. (1962b): Cerebral cortical reactivity in psychotic depressions. *Arch. Gen. Psychiatry,* 6:235–242.

Shagass, C., and Schwartz, M. (1963a): Cerebral responsiveness in psychiatric patients, *Arch. Gen. Psychiatry,* 8:177–189.

Shagass, C., and Schwartz, M. (1963b): Psychiatric correlates of evoked cerebral cortical potentials. *Am. J. Psychiatry,* 119:1055–1061.

Shagass, C., and Schwartz, M. (1965a): Visual cerebral evoked response characteristics in a psychiatric population. *Am. J. Psychiatry,* 121:979–987.

Shagass, C., and Schwartz, M. (1965b): Age, personality and somatosensory evoked responses. *Science,* 148:1359–1361.

Shagass, C., Schwartz, M., and Amadeo, M. (1962): Some drug effects on evoked cerebral potentials in man. *J. Neuropsychiatry,* 3:S49–S58.

Shagass, C., Schwartz, M., and Krishnamoorti, S. R. (1965): Some psychologic correlates of cerebral responses evoked by light flash. *J. Psychosom. Res.,* 9:223–231.

252   EVOKED POTENTIALS IN MAN

Shagass, C., Soskis, D. A., Straumanis, J. J., and Overton, D. A. (1974b): Symptom patterns related to somatosensory evoked response differences within a schizophrenic population. *Biol. Psychiatry,* 9:25–43.

Shagass, C., Straumanis, J. J., and Overton, D. A. (1972b): Electrophysiological recordings in the reaction time experiment: Exploratory studies for possible psychiatric research application. *Biol. Psychiatry,* 5:271–287.

Shagass, C., Straumanis, J. J., and Overton, D. A. (1973): Effects of lithium and amitryptyline therapy on somatosensory evoked response "excitability" measurements. *Psychopharmacologia,* 29:185–196.

Shagass, C., and Trusty, D. (1966): Somatosensory and visual cerebral evoked response changes during sleep. In: *Recent Advances in Biological Psychiatry,* edited by J. Wortis, pp. 321–334. Plenum Press, New York.

Shevrin, H., and Rennick, P. (1967): Cortical response to a tactile stimulus during attention, mental arithmetic and free associations. *Psychophysiology,* 3:381–388.

Shimizu, H. (1970): AER in the severely retarded. *Excerpta Medica Int. Congr. Sess.,* 206:530–534.

Shipley, T., Jones, R. W., and Fry, A. (1965): Evoked visual potentials and human color vision. *Science,* 150:1162–1164.

Shucard, D. W., and Horn, J. L. (1972): Evoked cortical potentials and measurement of human abilities. *J. Comp. Physiol. Psychol.,* 78:59–68.

Silverman, J. (1972): Stimulus intensity modulation and psychological Dis-Ease. *Psychopharmacologia,* 24:42–80.

Small, J. G., and Small, I. F. (1972): Expectancy wave in affective psychoses. In: *Recent Advances in the Psychobiology of the Depressive Illnesses,* edited by T. A. Williams, M. M. Katz, and J. A. Shield, Jr., pp. 109–118. U.S. Government Printing Office, DHEW Publication No. (HSM) 70–9053, Washington, D.C.

Smith, D. B., Allison, T., Goff, W. R., and Principato, J. J. (1971): Human odorant evoked responses: Effects of trigeminal or olfactor deficit. *Electroencephalogr. Clin. Neurophysiol.,* 30:313–317.

Soskis, D. A., and Shagass, C. (1974): Evoked potential tests of augmenting-reducing. *Psychophysiology,* 11:175–190.

Speck, L. B., Dim, B., and Mercer, M. (1966): Visual evoked responses of psychiatric patients. *Arch. Gen. Psychiatry,* 15:59–63.

Spehlmann, R. (1965): The averaged electrical responses to diffuse and to patterned light in the human. *Electroencephalogr. Clin. Neurophysiol.,* 19:560–569.

Spilker, B., and Callaway, E. (1969): "Augmenting" and "reducing" in averaged visual evoked responses to sine wave light. *Psychophysiology,* 6:49–57.

Spong, P., Haider, M., and Lindsley, D. B. (1965): Selective attentiveness and cortical evoked responses to visual and auditory stimuli. *Science,* 148:395–397.

Straumanis, J. J., and Shagass, C. (1975): Relationship of cerebral evoked responses to "normal" intelligence and mental retardation. In: *Studies on Childhood—Psychiatric and Psychological Problems,* edited by D. V. Siva Sankar. PJD Publications, Ltd., Westbury, N.Y.

Straumanis, J. J., Shagass, C., and Overton, D. A. (1973a): Somatosensory evoked responses in Down syndrome. *Arch. Gen. Psychiatry,* 29:544–549.

Straumanis, J. J., Shagass, C., and Overton, D. A. (1973b): Auditory evoked responses in young adults with Down's syndrome and idiopathic mental retardation. *Biol. Psychiatry,* 6:75–79.

Straumanis, J. J., Shagass, C., and Schwartz, M. (1965): Visually evoked cerebral response changes associated with chronic brain syndrome and aging. *J. Gerontol.,* 20:498–506.

Sutton, S. (1969): The specification of psychological variables in an average evoked potential experiment. In: *Average Evoked Potentials—Methods, Results, and Evaluations,* edited by E. Donchin and D. Lindsley, pp. 237–297. NASA, Washington, D.C.

Sutton, S., Braren, M., and Zubin, J. (1965): Evoked-potential correlates of stimulus uncertainty. *Science,* 150:1187–1188.

Sutton, S., Teuting, P., Zubin, J., and John, E. R. (1967): Information delivery and the sensory evoked potential. *Science,* 155:1436–1439.

Taguchi, K., Goodman, W. S., and Brummitt, W. M. (1970): Evoked response audiometry in mentally retarded children. *Acta Otolaryngol.* (Stockh), 70:190–196.

Tecce, J. J. (1971): Attention and evoked potentials in man. In: *Attention: Contemporary Theory and Analysis,* edited by D. I. Mostofsky, pp. 331–365, Appleton-Century-Crofts, New York.

Tecce, J. J., and Scheff, N. M. (1969): Attention reduction and suppressed direct-current potentials in the human brain. *Science,* 164:331–333.

Timsit, M., Koninckx, N., Dargent, J., Fontaine, O., and Dongier, M. (1969): Étude de la durée des VCN chez un groupe de sujets normaux un groupe de névrosés et un groupe de psychotiques. In: *Variations Contingentes Négatives,* edited by J. Dargent and M. Dongier, pp. 206–214. University of Liège Press, Liège.

Timsit-Berthier, M. (1973): CNV, slow potentials and motor potential studies in normal subjects and psychiatric patients. In: *Human Neurophysiology, Psychology, Psychiatry: Average Evoked Responses and Their Conditioning in Normal Subjects and Psychiatric Patients,* edited by A. Fessard and G. Lelord, pp. 327–366. Inserm, Paris.

Tsumoto, T., Hirose, N., Nonaka, S., and Takahashi, M. (1973): Cerebrovascular disease: Changes in somatosensory evoked potentials associated with unilateral lesions. *Electroencephalogr. Clin. Neurophysiol.,* 35:463–473.

Vaughan, H. G. (1969): The relationship of brain activity to scalp recordings of event-related potentials. In: *Average Evoked Potentials—Methods, Results and Evaluations,* edited by E. Donchin and D. B. Lindsley, pp. 45–75, NASA, Washington, D.C.

Vaughan, H. G., Costa, L. D., and Ritter, W. (1968): Topography of the human motor potential. *Electroencephalogr. Clin. Neurophysiol.,* 25:1–10.

Walter, W. G. (1962): Spontaneous oscillatory systems and alternations in stability. In: *Neural Physiopathology,* edited by R. G. Grenell, pp. 222–257. Hoeber, New York.

Walter, W. G. (1964): The convergence and interaction of visual, auditory, and tactile responses in human nonspecific cortex. *Ann. N.Y. Acad. Sci.,* 112:320–361.

Walter, W. G. (1966): Electrophysiologic contributions to psychiatric therapy. In: *Current Psychiatric Therapies, Vol. VI,* pp. 13–25. Grune and Stratton, New York.

Walter, W. G. (1967): Slow potential changes in the human brain associated with expectancy, decision and intention. *Electroencephalogr. Clin. Neurophysiol.,* Supplement 26:123–130.

Walter, W. G., Cooper, R., Aldridge, V. J., McCallum, W. C., and Winter, A. L. (1964): Contingent negative variation: An electric sign of sensorimotor association and expectancy in the human brain. *Nature,* 203:380–384.

Weinberg, H. (1969): Correlation of frequency spectra of averaged visual evoked potentials with verbal intelligence. *Nature,* 224:813–815.

Weitzman, E. D., and Kremen, H. (1965): Auditory evoked responses during different stages of sleep in man. *Electroencephalogr. Clin. Neurophysiol.,* 18:65–70.

Williams, H. L., Morlock, H. C., Morlock, J. V., and Lubin, A. (1964): Auditory evoked responses and the EEG stages of sleep. *Ann. N.Y. Acad. Sci.,* 112:172–181.

Wood, C. C., Goff, W. R., and Day, R. S. (1971): Auditory evoked potentials during speech perception. *Science,* 173:1248–1251.

Biological Foundations of Psychiatry,
edited by R. G. Grenell and S. Gabay.
Raven Press, New York © 1976.

Emotion and Sensory Perception: Human and Animal Studies

Robert G. Heath

Department of Psychiatry and Neurology, Tulane University School of Medicine,
New Orleans, Louisiana 70112

I. INTRODUCTION AND BACKGROUND

For the past 25 years, a program for treatment of patients with intractable behavioral and neurologic disorders has been under way in the Tulane Department of Psychiatry and Neurology. The techniques that have been used have permitted recording of activity from deep and surface brain sites of conscious human subjects while simultaneously collecting introspective data in the form of their verbal reports. With these methods correlations have been established between brain function and certain behavioral alterations, particularly those that are characteristic of the psychotic. Our findings from these studies in patients, backed and augmented by extensive studies in animals, suggested heretofore unidentified brain pathways that we were later able to demonstrate by anatomic methods.

It is widely believed that no correlation is possible between localized brain pathology and psychotic behavior, either organic or functional. In the organic psychoses, varied lesions have been described at many different brain sites and of various etiologic origins. Although cellular lesions have been histopathologically identified at widely disparate sites, correlations between the site of the cytopathologic lesion and signs and symptoms have been inconsistent. In some psychoses (schizophrenia and manic depressive illness), no cellular pathology has been disclosed, and by default these disorders have been termed functional (Kolb, 1968). In categorizing disorders of behavior, the traditional concept paradoxically prevails that cellular abnormality demonstrable under the light microscope must underlie clinical signs and symptoms for the pathogenesis to be considered organic or physical, whereas certain other states (dyskinesia and many types of epilepsy) are usually considered organic neurologic disorders despite absence of demonstrable cellular pathology. New procedures are obviously required to study sites of pathology in the brains of persons with psychosis and ultimately to delineate the nature of the functional pathologic problem. In our investigations, we have used the traditional two-step neurologic approach: first, localization of the physiologic change causing the signs and symptoms and then identification of the pathologic process causing it. The information obtained by this approach provides the basis for development of specific treatment.

The psychotic state—a disorder of thinking, feeling, and perceiving—is a mental disease. Man is the only species capable of reporting his thoughts and feelings, thereby providing access to mental function, a necessary source of data for correlation of aberrant mental function with brain disturbances. It is these data that provide the most specific leads for applying physiologic methods to study of the brain. For psychiatrists to have so widely resisted use of physiologic techniques is therefore as incongruous as the almost universal rejection of psychodynamic data by brain-behavior physiologists and neurologists.

In the Tulane laboratories, use of depth electrode techniques for treating psychiatric and neurologic disorders of patients (augmented always by extensive studies in experimental animals) has yielded data that have permitted us to move toward localization of pathologic sites underlying psychotic behavior (Heath and the Tulane Department of Psychiatry and Neurology, 1954; Heath, 1964a,b; Heath, 1966). By implantation of electrodes into predetermined specific brain sites of patients capable of reporting thoughts and feelings, long-term observations of functional changes have been made while simultaneously monitoring mental activity of the fully conscious subjects (Heath and Gallant, 1964; Heath, Cox, and Lustick, 1974). The data gathered by these methods, together with information from animal experiments suggested by the human data, have enabled us to demonstrate a consistent correlation between brain function and psychotic signs and symptoms. The septal region of the brain, as we defined it in the early 1950s, has invariably shown aberrant electrical activity, in the form of spikes and slow-waves, during psychotic episodes, regardless of cause (Heath, 1954; Heath and Mickle, 1960). Summarized here are the observations we have made during 25 years of investigations. Up until now the only published report of independent studies in which the researchers used our techniques was confirmatory (UCLA Conference, 1969).

The data reported herein substantiate an anatomic localization in the brain for the syndrome of psychotic behavior. To validate these findings in psychotic patients, we conducted control studies of nervous system activity in nonpsychotic, conscious human subjects and in animals. During the course of these studies, data were also collected that have identified brain pathways for emotional expression. It became evident that the anatomic basis for the relation between brain structures for emotional expression and levels of awareness, on the one hand, and brain nuclei for sensory perception on the other, were pathophysiologic components of the psychotic state.

Schizophrenia is probably the most common cause of psychosis. Some features of the psychotic state are constant. Other features differ with the underlying etiology. Gross impairment of feelings and emotional expression, a fluctuating level of (sometimes profound reduction in) psychologic awareness, and disturbances in sensory perception are characteristic of the psychotic syndrome. The altered emotionality is manifest by defective integration of pleasurable feelings, often associated with excessively painful (emergency) emotional behavior (Rado, Buchenholz, Dunton, Karlen, and Senescu, 1956). Characteristic of lowered thought level are weakened ego defenses. Normally hidden unconscious thought processes, manifested in gross disorders of thought (delusions), become conscious reality. Correspondingly fuzzy is self-image. Distorted bodily image and hallucinations (auditory more often than visual) usually reflect the disturbances in perception. Resembling mild parietal cortical dysfunction, altered perception of stereognosis is also frequent.

In using the objective components of the psychotic state to construct bridges between activity of the mind and of the brain, we have tried to identify brain sites and pathways where activity correlates with emotional expression and levels of awareness, and to determine, by physiologic and anatomic studies, which brain sites involved in sensory perception are interrelated with those sites. In addition to allowing greater precision in physiologic treatment, such data also provide a foundation for development of specific pharmacologic therapy.

II. BRAIN MECHANISMS—POSTULATES

Observations of the limited desirable effects of frontal lobe operation (including cingulectomy) in treating psychotic schizophrenic patients led to our earliest studies (*Selective Partial Ablation of the Frontal Cortex,* 1949). The surgical intervention indeed seemed effective in altering emotions associated with memory. Furthermore it was somewhat beneficial in the treatment of patients handicapped by painful affect caused by anticipatory thoughts (the intractable obsessive-compulsive, borderline psychotic patient) or by intractable depression, with associated feelings of rejection, anguish, gloom, despair, and suicidal ideation. On the other hand, it failed to correct the defective mechanism of emotional expression of the psychotic (impaired pleasure or anhedonic, flat affect) or the impaired level of awareness, suggesting that the brain mechanism for these phenomena was principally elsewhere than in the cortex.

On the basis of extensive animal studies in our laboratory, a certain rostral medial forebrain site seemed to be the principal neural site for emotional expression and level of awareness (Heath, 1954). In animals destruction of this site, which we called the septal region, reduced awareness and profoundly impaired emotional expression. In contrast electrical stimulation of the region heightened awareness and induced what appeared to be a pleasurable state (Heath and the Tulane Department of Psychiatry and Neurology, 1954). When stimulation techniques were later applied to patients (beginning in 1950), their subjective reports confirmed the impressions from the animal studies that septal-region stimulation elicited pleasurable feelings (Heath and Mickle, 1960; Heath, 1964a,b; Heath, John, and Fontana, 1968).

Impaired affect (specifically, the inability to integrate pleasure) and reduced awareness are acknowledged clinical features of psychotic behavior. We therefore postulated that function of the septal region of the psychotic was impaired, either by direct cellular damage (organic psychoses with septal lesions) or functionally (physiologic aberration caused by local chemical changes), in the absence of cellular damage (functional psychoses and organic psychoses with cellular pathology elsewhere in the brain). We speculated that the pathologic behavior of patients with organic psychoses who had lesions elsewhere than in the septal region might be caused by changes in the function of that region as a consequence of the effect of lesions at distal, but connected, brain sites. A further and critical assumption was also made that pathologic activity, in the absence of cellular damage at a given brain site, would induce essentially the same effects as a destructive lesion (R. G. Heath and J. W. Harper, *in preparation*).

III. IMPLANTATION OF DEEP AND SURFACE ELECTRODES

The therapeutic rationale for investigating these postulates in patients was based on studies in animals. Our findings in animals prepared with electrodes implanted into the brains suggested that faulty emotional responsivity might be corrected by activation of an impaired septal region. Specifically the animal data indicated that stimulation of this seemingly vital region of patients should activate pleasure responsivity and elevate the level of psychologic awareness. We therefore adapted our procedures to patients with reasonable confidence that some psychotic disorders could be treated more effectively by them than by existing modes of therapy. In selecting patients for these procedures over the years, rigid criteria have been applied. Failure of the patient to respond to all conventional forms of treatment have been the foremost consideration.

Certain ground rules were established to assure meaningful correlation of brain activity with behavior. For example, because recordings from a single brain site were of little value in identifying sites of origin of brain changes responsible for clinical phenomena, electrodes were implanted into numerous deep and surface brain sites. Such multiple implantations also permitted evaluation of nonspecific effects from the trauma of implantation and allowed localization of recording abnormalities. All parts of the brain are richly interconnected. Unless activity from numerous sites is viewed simultaneously, it is impossible to localize the site from which aberrant activity originates. Altered activity at one site, as well as clinical signs and symptoms, can originate either from a cellular lesion at that site or from propagation of abnormal activity at a distal site. Likewise one could not be certain that focal recordings around the electrode induced symptoms; clinical effects might just as well have been the result of propagated distal effects from focally damaged cells. Recordings from a single site often proved misleading in localization of brain lesions. For example epileptic foci localized by electroencephalographic (EEG) recordings and extirpated surgically as treatment for seizures sometimes proved to be mirror or distal reflections of the primary focus.

Behavior continually fluctuates. In order to correlate brain activity and behavior, it was also necessary to leave the electrodes in exact position for long periods. We therefore developed techniques that permitted long-term study and treatment with electrical stimulation for months and in a few patients for as long as 2 to 3 years (Heath, John, and Fontana, 1968). Chemical stimulation also became possible when a cannula was developed that could be accurately implanted and fixed into position to remain as long as the electrodes (Heath and Founds, 1960). It was so constructed that it could be used repeatedly for introduction of putative synaptic transmitter chemicals (Heath and deBalbian Verster, 1961). Although primarily therapeutic, these procedures also permitted collection of data concerning brain activity in association with widely variable behavior, during normal psychologic fluctuations (sleep, wakefulness), as well as during changes occurring with psychotic behavior.

Most of our early patients, particularly those in the first reported group of 26 studied between 1950 and 1952, were schizophrenic (Heath and the Tulane Department of Psychiatry and Neurology, 1954). For meaningful evaluation of the data from schizophrenic patients, it was necessary to also gather comparative data from nonpsychotic subjects suffering from other previously intractable illnesses that might be alleviated by our procedures. Increasing numbers of patients who participated in our studies over the years have therefore had diseases other than schizophrenia. In fact our last schizophrenic patient was operated on in 1962, the effects of electrical and chemical stimulation having proved to be not much better justification for invasive techniques than the effects of the antipsychotic drugs, which were then coming into wide use. Furthermore the focus of our studies of schizophrenia had shifted more to identification of the nature of the basic pathologic processes affecting the brain to produce the consistent recording changes.[1] Our continuing studies in human subjects with other intractable illnesses than schizophrenia, many without notable behavioral pathology, were prompted by the need to characterize the impaired emotional responsivity of the schizophrenic patient by acquiring comparative data that could be obtained only from such patients.

IV. BRAIN ACTIVITY CORRELATED WITH SPECIFIC EMOTION

As data from human subjects have continued to accumulate, it has become possible to identify those brain sites and pathways in man that are associated with specific emotional states, such as pleasurable emotion and adversive emotion. Our findings do not agree with textbook presentations based on animal studies. To elucidate relations between perception and emotion, extensions of these studies have also shown the physical substrate for emotion to be different from that formerly described.

Our findings indicate that sites and pathways for pleasurable emotional expression include the septal region and the medial forebrain bundle to and including the interpeduncular nuclei in the mesencephalon. On the other hand, sites for adversive emotional expression have been shown to be the hippocampi, and parts of the amygdalae, periaqueductal sites in the mesencephalon, and sites in the medial hypothalamus near the third ventricle. Activity of other brain sites into which electrodes were implanted could not be related to either pleasurable or painful emotional states.

Our demarcation of the pleasure system of the brain is substantiated by data demonstrating how it is activated:

1. Profound pleasure was induced with passive electrical stimulation of sites in the pleasure system (Heath, 1964b). Moreover, when a patient was given the opportunity to selectively self-stimulate various deep-brain regions, he repeatedly and exclusively chose to stimulate these sites (Heath, 1963, 1964b).

2. A similar response was induced with introduction of putative synaptic chemical transmitter agents (acetylcholine being most effective) directly into this pleasure system (Heath, 1964b).

3. Similar activation of the septal region and occasionally of other directly connected sites, as evidenced by EEGs, occurred with feelings of pleasure, spontaneous or induced by an action (notably, sexual orgasm), or

---

[1] Some of the refocusing has involved approaches centered in isolation of taraxein (Heath, Martens, Leach, Cohen, and Angel, 1957; Heath, 1959; Heath, Guschwan, and Coffey, 1970). But it was the data from our depth electrode studies in patients, indicating a physiologic abnormality in recordings from the septal region in association with psychotic behavior, that provided the appropriate assay (the rhesus monkey with similarly implanted electrodes) for these other approaches.

by association through psychiatric interview (Heath and Gallant, 1964; Heath, 1972a). Bursts of slow, high-amplitude activity characterized the septal recordings when the pleasurable state was one of relaxation (behavior induced by pleasant memories) (Heath and Gallant, 1964; Heath, Cox, and Lustick, 1974). On the other hand, electrical activity of the septal region was characterized by faster frequencies of high-amplitude and sharp spiking, often coupled with a slow wave (resembling activity we have recorded throughout the brain during an epileptic seizure) when pleasure was intense and explosive, such as that of the sexual orgasm. Spindling recordings were obtained from the same sites, of similar frequency and amplitude as those recorded during adversive states, when patients were alerted by anticipation of pleasure (Heath, 1964b; Heath and Gallant, 1964).

4. Similar activation of the pleasure system, as reflected in the patient's EEGs, occurred with administration of certain pleasure-inducing agents (Heath, 1972b).

Further substantiation of this pleasure system of the brain is the fact that human ability to experience pleasure is reduced if function of the system is impaired by the following:

1. The psychotic state with associated abnormal recordings (spikes and slow-waves) from the septal region (Fig. 1);

2. Administration of some psychotomimetics or of taraxein (Heath, Leach, and Byers, 1963; Heath, 1966). When given to monkeys, these agents have consistently induced septal spiking (Fig. 2);

3. Induction of spiking in the septal region by electrical stimulation of remote brain sites that, by direct connection, influence the septal region (Heath, 1963).

Several methods also established correlations between adversive emotional responses and brain activity:

1. When feelings of rage and fear were displayed by a patient, whether spontaneous or activated by psychiatric interview, high-amplitude fast spindling (12 to 14/sec) spontaneously appeared, focal in the hippocampus or amygdala (Heath and Gallant, 1964). In a recent patient in whom electrodes had also been implanted into the cerebellum and cingulate gyrus because animal data had indicated their direct connections to deep temporal lobe nuclei, similar activity was recorded from these regions concomitant with her display of emergency emotion.

2. When epileptic patients had aura characterized by intense fear or rageful outbursts, focal epileptiform activity invariably appeared in these same nuclear sites (hippocampus or amygdala) deep in the temporal lobe, presumably a consequence of the basic pathology in epilepsy (Heath, 1964b, 1971).

3. An emergency state dominated by fear or rage was induced by electri-

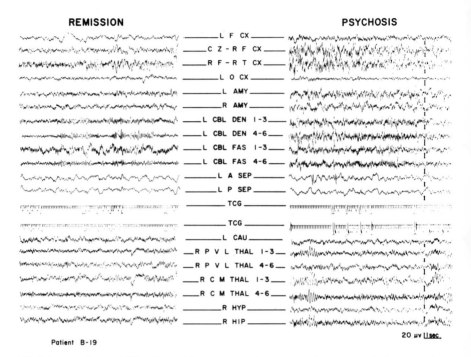

Patient B-19

FIG. 1. Deep and cortical EEGs obtained from a patient during states of remission and of psychosis. Note sharp spike in anterior septal leads, appearing also in cerebellar leads. LF Cx, left frontal cortex; CZ-RF Cx, central zone to right frontal cortex; RF-RT Cx, right frontal to right temporal cortex; L O Cx, left occipital cortex; L Amy, left amygdala; R Amy, right amygdala; L Cbl Den, left cerebellar dentate; L Cbl Fas, left cerebellar fastigius; L A Sep, left anterior septal region; L P Sep, left posterior septal region; TCG, time code generator; L Cau, left caudate nucleus; R P V L Thal, right posterior ventral lateral thalamus; R C M Thal, right central median thalamus; R Hyp, right hypothalamus; R Hip, right hippocampus.

cal stimulation to the hippocampus, to many sites within the amygdala, and to numerous medial hypothalamic and mesencephalic periaqueductal sites. Patients always abstained when they were given the opportunity to self-stimulate in this system; indeed, they inactivated the self-stimulation device (Heath, 1963, 1964b).

4. Epileptiform activity and associated emergency emotion was induced with introduction of levarterenol into the hippocampus (Heath, 1964b).

These correlations of activity at specific brain sites with painful emotion have been consistent. In several instances, however, similar changes have occurred at these same sites during other kinds of strong emotional arousal, sometimes anticipatory of pleasure rather than being adversive. These observations suggest that the cerebellar-cingulate-hippocampal-amygdala spindling may be a correlate of intense arousal of emotion, not necessarily painful.

Each system of the brain (pleasure and pain) is seemingly capable of overwhelming or inhibiting the other. Activation of the pleasure system by

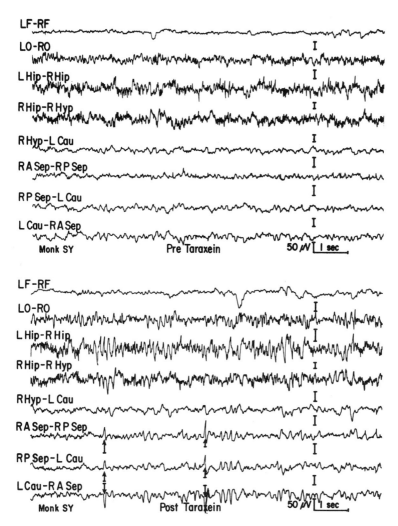

FIG. 2. Deep and cortical EEGs obtained from a rhesus monkey before and after intravenous administration of taraxein.

electrical stimulation or by administration of drugs eliminates signs and symptoms of emotional or physical pain, or both, and obliterates changes in recordings associated with the painful state. Similarly activation of brain sites for adversive emotional response replaces pleasurable feelings with painful feelings, and obliterates recording correlates of the pleasure state.

It is clinically assumed that a deficient pleasure mechanism in patients with schizophrenia and some borderline states causes an unpleasant or painful emotional state. In studies in our large series of schizophrenic patients, a physiologic correlate for this state has now been demonstrated. Furthermore, in both schizophrenic and nonschizophrenic patients, inordinate emergency emotion (adversive emotion) has been shown to correlate with excessive activity of deep temporal lobe nuclei and related brain sites.

V. ANATOMIC–PHYSIOLOGIC RELATION OF PERCEPTION AND EMOTION

The importance of sensory input has long been recognized in regard to emotion (Cannon, 1927; James and Lange, 1922). Emotion can be induced by memory experiences, as well as by sensory stimuli. The intensity of the emotional response is usually determined by the person's interpretation of the sensory stimulus against the background of memory experiences. The effector mechanism for emotionality is therefore activated both through sensory receptor mechanisms and from higher neural centers. Those brain sites where function relates to qualitatively specific emotional states have been demarcated by the correlative studies described herein. Neural pathways between cortical sites and these subcortical sites for specific emotions have been described by other researchers (Akert and Hummel, 1968; Nauta, 1958; Papez, 1937; Zanchetti, 1967). The focus of this discussion will be on those subcortical sites at which activity has been correlated with emotion.

There is abundant clinical evidence of the effect of sensory stimuli on emotion and reciprocally the effect of an emotional state on perception. An obvious relation similarly exists among level of awareness (alertness), emotional state, and sensory receptivity. There is also extensive documentation of interrelations of impaired emotionality with the altered level of awareness of the psychotic state and perception. On the other hand, there is sparse evidence of the anatomic-physiologic tie-in of structures involved in perception with those involved in emotion and levels of awareness. In our laboratories data from recent studies indicate that these systems, usually considered separate, are so functionally interrelated as to constitute one system.

The consistent clinical observations in our reporting patients have pointed the way for our physiologic studies in animals. These in turn have provided direction for anatomic studies. And additional studies in human subjects, prompted by the findings in animals, have substantiated some of the observations of the structural-functional interrelation between sensory phenomena and emotion. Whereas sensory stimuli can alter a person's feeling-emotional state toward heightened pleasure or intensified adversion, attention for incoming sensory stimuli is selectively altered by a person's emotional state. The influence of sensory stimuli is evident in our everday life. Movement stimulation can be very pleasant: children like to be picked up, rocked, and swung; merry-go-round and roller coaster rides are fun; deep muscle massage and various forms of vibration can be exceedingly pleasant; physical exercise, particularly that of contact sports, is exhilarating. Other sensory stimuli, such as the warm temperature of a bath, can induce relaxation and a feeling of well-being. The emotional effects of sound range widely, from the calming effects of Beethoven's works to the exhilaration of John Phillip Sousa's marches, from the restful lapping of water against a shore to the wild pounding rains of a tropic storm, from dulcet murmurs to piercing screams. A wide range of visual, olfactory, and tactile stimuli similarly affect a person's emotional state. Reciprocally acumen for specific sensory stimuli is influenced by one's prevailing emotional state. An agitated person responds differently to sights, sounds, and somatosensory stimuli from one who is in a tranquil state. Emotional state, level of awareness, and sensory perception are seemingly interrelated phenomena: a change in one affects the others.

The interrelations of these phenomena are perhaps more evident during psychotic states. Changes in sensory perception and levels of awareness invariably occur with disturbances in feeling and emotional expression of the psychotic person (Bleuler, 1950; Kolb, 1968). Furthermore certain programmed manipulation of one of these basic phenomena can predictably alter the others. Sensory isolation or prolonged sleep deprivation (altering level of awareness) have been shown to induce transient psychotic behavior in human subjects (Lilly, 1956). Permanent basic behavioral features of the psychotic state develop in primates raised in isolation and thereby deprived of certain sensory stimuli (Harlow and Harlow, 1962; Heath, 1972c). Deprivation of somato-sensory stimuli, particularly of the kinesthetic-vestibular type, is proving to be the primary cause for the syndrome.

Our initial investigations of anatomic relationships between sensory systems and brain sites for emotional response were prompted by our findings in the isolation-raised primates. Recording abnormalities from brain sites where activity was correlated with emotionality were similar in these seriously disturbed monkeys to those we had obtained from the same brain sites of psychotic patients (Heath, 1972c). In the monkeys, however, because sensory deprivation, particularly of proprioceptive and somatosensory stimuli, had induced the emotional disturbance, we had also implanted electrodes into the somatosensory thalamus and into deep cerebellar nuclei known to be part of the vestibular proprioceptive system. Gross abnormalities were also recorded from the implanted sensory relay nuclei of these monkeys when recordings from the septal region and hippocampus were abnormal. Furthermore computer analyses, showing frequent and almost simultaneous spiking in sensory relay nuclei and in sites for emotional expression, offered the first suggestion of direct connections between these sites, that is, an anatomic substrate for the relationship suggested by clinical observations.

The anatomic and physiologic studies in animals that were prompted by these findings revealed a number of heretofore undescribed neural connections between brain sites involved in emotional expression and sensory relay nuclei. The clinical leads were thus substantiated. The functional interrelations among these sites were shown by additional studies in monkeys and cats (Heath, 1972d,e; Heath and Harper, 1974). When these findings were applied to a few patients in our depth electrode series, the recording changes from related brain sites coupled with the reporting of the patients confirmed that the functional physiologic relation among these interconnected brain sites are indeed basic to emotional expression in man as well as in the animals (Heath, 1972*a,b*).

VI. DEMONSTRATION WITH EVOKED POTENTIALS

The evoked potential technique was applied to cats and monkeys in which bipolar electrodes had been chronically implanted into specific brain sites. It consisted in the delivery of a brief stimulus to one nuclear site under study, while recordings were obtained from other sites suspected of being interconnected. An indication of the kind of pathway that was involved, that is, the degree to which it was myelinated and whether or not the connection was direct (monosynaptic) or indirect (polysynaptic), was provided by the delay time from stimulus to onset of response (speed of conduction). The results of these studies have been reported (Heath, 1972*d;* Harper and Heath, 1973, 1974; Heath and Harper, 1974). Important to the present thesis were the following demonstrations of:

1. monosynaptic connections within nuclear sites involved in emotional expression, that is, among the hippocampus, amygdala, and septal region;

2. direct monosynaptic connections within pertinent sensory relay nuclei: the posterior ventral lateral nucleus of the thalamus for somato-sensory sensation, the fastigial nuclei of the cerebellum for proprioception, the medial geniculate bodies for audition, and the lateral geniculate bodies for vision; and

3. direct back-and-forth monosynaptic connections between these sensory relay nuclei and the sites for emotional expression, both for pleasurable and adversive states. Figure 3 illustrates the evoked potential technique for demonstrating these anatomic connections. A richly interconnected network demonstrating an integral relation between brain sites for emotional expression and those for sensory perception was thus established physiologically in animals.

VII. ANATOMIC VERIFICATION

Using anatomic techniques, most of the pathways demonstrated by evoked potential techniques have now been verified (Harper and Heath, 1973, 1974; Heath and Harper, 1974, *in preparation*). A lesion-producing electrode was implanted stereotaxically into a selected nuclear site of monkeys and cats, and fulgerating, continuous, unidirectional current was applied at two sites within the nucleus. The animals were killed on different days after the surgical procedure, and the brains were fixed, sectioned, and stained. With

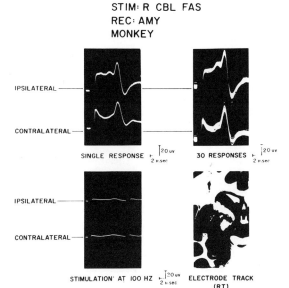

STIM: R CBL FAS
REC: AMY
MONKEY

IPSILATERAL

CONTRALATERAL

SINGLE RESPONSE 20 uv / 2 μ sec   30 RESPONSES 20 uv / 2 μ sec

IPSILATERAL

CONTRALATERAL

STIMULATION AT 100 HZ 20 uv / 2 μ sec   ELECTRODE TRACK
(RT)

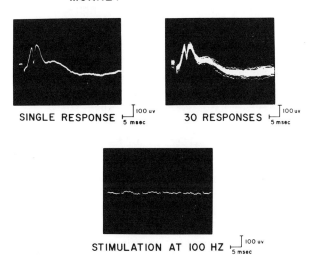

STIM: R A SEP
REC: R MED GEN
MONKEY

SINGLE RESPONSE 100 uv / 5 msec   30 RESPONSES 100 uv / 5 msec

STIMULATION AT 100 HZ 100 uv / 5 msec

FIG. 3. Evoked potentials demonstrating direct (indicated by short latency) connections between sensory relay nuclei and some sites in the pathways for emotional expression. The response is validated by the fact that high-frequency stimulation eliminates it and, furthermore, that it is consistent, as shown by the 30 superimposed responses. The anatomic site shows the site of the recording electrode.

these procedures, monosynaptic (direct) connections from the fastigial nucleus to the somatosensory thalamus, to the medial and lateral geniculates, and to the septal region, hippocampus, and amygdala were verified. Many other ascending and descending connections between sites for emotional expression and the sensory relay nuclei that were demonstrated by use of evoked potentials were also substantiated by this technique.

VIII. MIRROR FOCUS STUDIES

The functional interrelations among these directly connected brain sites has also been shown by a technique involving stereotaxic implantation of cobalt into a selected brain site. In cats and monkeys prepared with deep and surface electrodes and implanted with the irritant, a primary epileptiform focus developed at the implantation site and was later propagated over efferent pathways to activate secondary epileptiform activity in nuclei directly connected with the primary site (Heath, 1972d).

For example a primary epileptiform focus induced in the septal region, on one side, by cobalt implantation induced secondary epileptiform activity in the postero ventral lateral thalamus and in the fastigial nucleus of the cerebellum. By this demonstration, one can see how function of the septal region, involved in pleasurable emotion, can alter function of the cerebellum, which is involved in movement and proprioception. The reverse relation between these nuclei has also been demonstrated. The primary epileptiform discharge from the fastigial nucleus of the cerebellum, induced by cobalt implantation there, spread to encompass the septal region, hippocampus, and amygdala, and then involved the temporal cortex, this activity coinciding with onset of a generalized epileptic seizure.

Functional relations have also been shown between nuclear sites for emotional expression and those for perception of sensory stimuli by use of this technique, lending additional support to findings of other studies which indicated integral functional relations among these sites.

IX. CONFIRMATORY FINDINGS IN PATIENTS

To assist in diagnosis and treatment, we have implanted electrodes into some sensory relay nuclei of a few intractably ill patients. Profound changes in electrical activity were recorded from the septal region and part of the amygdala, anatomic sites where activity has been correlated consistently with feelings of pleasure, in one patient in our depth electrode series when he was having an orgasmic climax (Heath, 1972a). Intermittent high-amplitude spindle bursts were recorded not only in the hippocampus and amygdala at frequencies of 10 to 14 cycles/sec (typical of recordings we had obtained previously in other patients in our series) in association with intense emergency emotion of another patient, but also in deep cerebellar structures for proprioception and in the cingulate gyrus when the patient reported profound anxiety (Heath, Cox, and Lustick, 1974). Only one patient in our series has had electrodes in the medial geniculate body, the auditory relay station. Only occasionally was activity in the geniculate of this patient, an epileptic with an occasional aura of auditory hallucinations, unusual. Pertinent to this discussion was an occasion when the patient was drowsy, but not asleep. Delta activity of high amplitude was first recorded in the pleasure site of the brain, the septal region. It then spread to involve the medial geniculate body (Fig. 4). In response to questioning by the interviewing psychiatrist, the patient reported erotic fantasies associated with recall of provocative music.

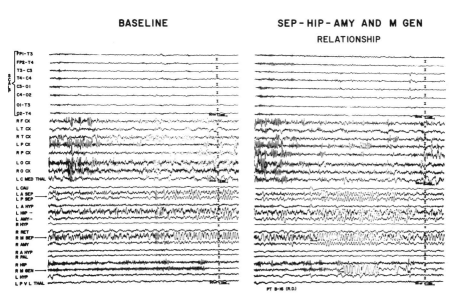

FIG. 4. Deep, cortical, and scalp EEGs obtained from a patient who had electrodes implanted into the medial geniculate.

In our experimental animals, we not only demonstrated direct connections among nuclei for emotional expression and among those for sensory perception, but also direct connections between the two groups of nuclei. A functional relation among these sites was also shown. The few studies in patients demonstrated that physiologic relations between these key sites did indeed correlate with the subjective phenomenon of emotion. Taken together these findings provide evidence that sensory relay nuclei and the rostral septal region, along with the deep temporal nuclei (more commonly identified with emotion) are functionally related and are involved in the substrate for emotional expression.

X. SUMMARY

Our studies in patients with deep and surface electrodes have permitted the identification of an anatomic substrate for emotion and awareness. Precise anatomic studies were subsequently carried out in animals. The pathways that we have demonstrated are different from those based solely on animal experiments. Furthermore, the approaches that we used have led to demonstration of previously undisclosed anatomic connections, which provide a physical substrate for the clinically observed relation between perception and emotionality.

REFERENCES

Akert, K. and Hummel, P. (1968): *The Limbic System—Anatomy and Physiology.* Roche Laboratories, Nutley, N.J.

Bleuler, E. (1950): *Dementia Praecox or The Group of Schizophrenias.* International Universities Press, New York.

Cannon, W. B. (1927): The James-Lange theory of emotions: A critical examination and an alternative theory. *Am. J. Psychol.,* 39:106–124.

Harlow, H. F., and Harlow, M. (1962): Social deprivation in monkeys. *Sci. Am.,* 207:137–146.

Harper, J. W., and Heath, R. G. (1973): Anatomic connections of the fastigial nucleus to the rostral forebrain in the cat. *Exp. Neurol.,* 39:285–292.

Harper, J. W., and Heath, R. G. (1974): Ascending projections of the cerebellar fastigial nuclei: Connections to the ectosylvian gyrus. *Exp. Neurol.,* 42:241–247.

Heath, R. G., and the Tulane University Department of Psychiatry and Neurology (1954): *Studies in Schizophrenia.* Harvard University Press, Cambridge, Mass.

Heath, R. G. (1954): Definition of the septal region. In: *Studies in Schizophrenia,* edited by R. G. Heath and the Tulane University Department of Psychiatry and Neurology, pp. 3–5. Harvard University Press, Cambridge, Mass.

Heath, R. G., Martens, S., Leach, B. E., Cohen, M., and Angel, C. A. (1957): Effect on behavior in humans with the administration of taraxein. *Am. J. Psychiatry,* 114: 14–24.

Heath, R. G. (1959): Physiological and biochemical studies in schizophrenia with particular emphasis on mind-brain relationships. *Int. Rev. Neurobiol.,* 1:299–331.

Heath, R. G., and Founds, W. L. (1960): A perfusion cannula for intracerebral microinjections. *Electroencephalogr. Clin. Neurophysiol.,* 12:930–932.

Heath, R. G. and Mickle, W. A. (1960): Evaluation of seven years experience with depth electrode studies in human patients. In: *Electrical Studies on the Unanesthetized Brain,* edited by E. R. Ramey and D. S. O'Doherty, pp. 214–247. Paul B. Hoeber, New York.

Heath, R. G., and deBalbian Verster, F. (1961): Effects of chemical stimulation on discrete brain areas. *Am. J. Psychiatry,* 117:980–990.

Heath, R. G. (1963): Electrical self-stimulation of the brain in man. *Am. J. Psychiatry,* 120:571–577.

Heath, R. G., Leach, B. E. and Byers, L. W. (1963): Taraxein: Mode of action. In: *Serological Fractions in Schizophrenia,* edited by R. G. Heath, pp. 107–125. Hoeber Medical Division, Harper & Row. New York.

Heath, R. G. (1964a): Developments toward new physiologic treatments in psychiatry. *J. Neuropsychiatry,* 5:318–331.

Heath, R. G. (1964b): Pleasure response of human subjects to direct stimulation of the brain: Physiologic and psychodynamic considerations. In: *The Role of Pleasure in Behavior,* edited by R. G. Heath, pp. 219–243. Hoeber Medical Division, Harper & Row, New York.

Heath, R. G., and Gallant, D. M. (1964): Activity of the human brain during emotional thought. In: *The Role of Pleasure in Behavior,* edited by R. G. Heath, pp. 83–106. Hoeber Medical Division, Harper & Row, New York.

Heath, R. G. (1966): Schizophrenia: Biochemical and physiologic aberrations. *Int. J. Neuropsychiatry,* 2:597–610.

Heath, R. G., John, S. B., and Fontana, C. J. (1968): The pleasure response: Studies by stereotaxic technics in patients. In: *Computers and Electronic Devices in Psychiatry,* edited by N. Kline and E. Laska, pp. 178–189. Grune & Stratton, New York.

Heath, R. G., Guschwan, A. F., and Coffey, J. W. (1970): Relation of taraxein to schizophrenia. *Dis. Nerv. Syst.,* 31:391–395.

Heath, R. G. (1971): Depth recording and stimulation studies in patients. In: *The Surgical Control of Behavior, A Symposium,* edited by A. Winter, pp. 21–37. Charles C Thomas, Springfield, Ill.

Heath, R. G. (1972a): Pleasure and brain activity in man: Deep and surface electroencephalograms during orgasm. *J. Nerv. Ment. Dis.,* 154:3–18.

Heath, R. G. (1972b): Marihuana: Effects on deep and surface electroencephalograms of man. *Arch. Gen. Psychiatry,* 26:577–584.

Heath, R. G. (1972c): Electroencephalographic studies in isolation-raised monkeys with behavioral impairment. *Dis. Nerv. Syst.,* 33:157–163.

Heath, R. G. (1972d): Physiologic basis of emotional expression: Evoked potential and mirror focus studies in rhesus monkeys. *Biol. Psychiatry,* 5:15–31.

Heath, R. G. (1972e): Fastigial nucleus connections to the septal region in monkey and cat: A demonstration with evoked potentials of a bilateral pathway. *Biol. Psychiatry,* 6:193–196.

Heath, R. G., and Harper, J. W. (1974): Ascending projections of the cerebellar fastigial nucleus to the hippocampus, amygdala, and other temporal lobe sites: Evoked potential and histological studies in monkeys and cats. *Exp. Neurol.,* 45:268–287.

Heath, R. G., Cox, A. W., and Lustick, L. S. (1974): Brain activity during emotional states. *Am. J. Psychiatry,* 131:858–862.

James, W., and Lange, G. C. (1922): *The Emotions.* Williams and Wilkins, Baltimore.

Kolb, L. C. (1968): *Noyes' Modern Clinical Psychiatry.* Saunders, Philadelphia.

Lilly, J. C. (1956): Mental effects of reduction of ordinary levels of physical stimuli on intact, healthy persons. *Psychiatr. Res. Rep., No. 5,* pp. 1–28. American Psychiatric Association.

Nauta, W. J. H. (1958): Hippocampal projections related neural pathways to the midbrain in the cat. *Brain,* 81:319–340.

Papez, J. W. A. (1937): A proposed mechanism of emotion. *Arch. Neurol. Psychiatry,* 38:725–743.

Rado, S., Buchenholz, B., Dunton, H., Karlen, S. H., and Senescu, R. (1956): Schizotypal organization. Preliminary report on a clinical study of schizophrenia. In: *Changing Concepts of Psychoanalytic Medicine,* edited by S. Rado and G. E. Daniels, pp. 225–235. Grune & Stratton, New York.

Selective Partial Ablation of the Frontal Cortex (1949): Edited by F. A. Mettler. Hoeber, Harper & Bros., New York.

UCLA Conference (1969): Clinical Neurophysiology: Newer diagnostic and therapeutic methods in neurological disease and behavior disorders. *Ann. Intern. Med.,* 71:619–645.

Zanchetti, A. (1967). Subcortical and cortical mechanisms in arousal and emotional behavior. In: *The Neurosciences,* edited by G. C. Quarton, T. Melnechuk, and F. O. Schmitt, pp. 602–614. Rockefeller University Press, New York.

Biological Foundations of Psychiatry,
edited by R. G. Grenell and S. Gabay.
Raven Press, New York © 1976.

Neural Basis of Threat and Attack

John P. Flynn

Department of Psychiatry, Yale University School of Medicine, New Haven, Connecticut 06508

I. INTRODUCTION

This chapter deals with threat and attack because these phenomena are the ones that experimenters have actually observed. Threat is largely of the defensive kind, and attack itself may show up in different ways. The term "defensive" is used to distinguish this form of threat from offensive threat, about whose neural basis very little is known, although it has been observed to occur naturally (Leyhausen, 1956).

Hess and Brugger (1943) described defensive threat and attack of a cat in this way: "There is an initial growl, which changes into hissing, snarling and spitting. The tail becomes thick and bushy as the hair on it rises. The hair on the spine also rises, and the back is sometimes arched. Pupils are dilated. The animal often shifts from defense to attack, usually against the nearest person. This can be so intense that the cat sinks its claws into the cloth that the experimenter holds for protection." This description shares common features with the description given by Woodworth and Sherrington (1904), by Cannon and Britton (1925), and by Ranson (1936–1937), and most of the investigators dealing with threat and attack. The response is not purely defensive, but a mixture of defense and attack. The classical studies of rage and anger have regularly focussed on the defensive threat display. For the most part, the observations on attack were incidental.

The study of the interaction of two or more animals, whether of the same or different species was not common among experimenters dealing with the neural basis of threat and attack. One of the early studies of this sort was that of Brody and Rosvold (1952), who dealt with the effects of frontal lobotomy on dominance in a colony of rhesus monkeys. Another early example is the work of Karli (1956–1957), who investigated the killing of mice by rats.

When attack itself is studied, the threat component may be minimal. Experienced rats kill mice by biting the spinal cord, and cats attacking rats behave in a similar fashion (Leyhausen, 1956; Adamec, 1974). Attack with little or no display associated with it was elicited in cats by stimulation of the hypothalamus (Wasman and Flynn, 1962). Similar behavior was elicited in the opossum (Roberts, Steinberg, and Means, 1967) and in rats (Panksepp, 1970; Woodworth, 1970).

The quiet form of attack is often thought by observers to be predation, and essentially based on hunger. While it is true that rats, for example, that attack mice often eat them (Paul, 1972), it is also true that killing takes place without eating being associated with it. Satiated rats will still kill (Karli, 1956–1957), and even if they have no opportunity to eat, rats will kill mice (Myer and White, 1965).

In the case of attack elicited by stimulation of the brain, again some of it seems to be associated with eating, because at some sites from which attack is elicited, eating can be elicited at lower intensities (Hutchinson and Renfrew, 1966). Equally so, there are other sites not associated with eating (Flynn, Vanegas, Foote, and Edwards, 1970), and killing is not followed by eating if stimulation is continued. Therefore, it seems that while the two may be related, killing is a discrete kind of behavior even if it is of a quiet form.

We propose in this chapter to deal with the mechanisms of defensive threat and the attack associated with it, as well as with quiet attack. In the first section the capabilities of animals with truncated brains will be examined. In the second section the activities of animals with either limited lesions or whose behavior is elicited by stimulation of the brain will be considered. In the third section an attempt will be made to specify how the behavior is brought about.

II. BEHAVIOR OF ANIMALS WITH TRUNCATED BRAINS

Bard and Macht (1958) observed two cats in which the medulla and the greater part of the pons and the caudal two-thirds of the midbrain remained. The rostral fourth of the pons, the entire tegmentum of the midbrain, and the rostral third of the tectum had been removed. These animals could not walk; but, when they were shocked, they made running movements, growled, extended their claws, their hair stood on end, and their breathing and heart rates quickened. Two additional cats in which the brains were truncated dorsally at the level of the rostral part of the superior colliculi and ventrally at the exit of the third nerve, similarly growled, extended their claws, gave evidence of piloerection, and increased heart rate and breathing. Over and above this, these animals hissed and attempted to right themselves, two activities not observed in the previous animals. Two other cats in which the brains were sectioned dorsally at the rostral border of the superior colliculi and ventrally just behind the mamillary bodies were able to walk and turn their heads, growled, hissed, showed piloerection, and pupillary dilatation. Even though this constitutes a demonstration of a threat display, there is no evidence of attack. In a cat in which a small area of mesencephalon was added to the brains just described, striking and biting were seen. These cats without hypothalamus but with relatively complete midbrain, were capable of demonstrating elements of threat in combination, and they also were capable of striking and biting, but these last two activities were ineffective and not directed. Rats with similar lesions are more capable than cats and show evidence of being able to direct their bites towards the area pinched (Woods, 1964).

The stimuli that were required in order to elicit these various behaviors were for the most part of sufficient intensity as to be noxious, and in fact one of the first studies, that of Woodworth and Sherrington (1904), used this form of threat to delineate the pathways mediating pain. The description of the response that is given by Woodworth and Sherrington is along the same lines as those used by Hess and Brugger (1943): that is, opening of the mouth, retraction of the lips and tongue, snapping of the jaws, opening of the eyelids, dilatation of the pupils, and vocalization that was angry in tone. It was Sherrington's interpretation that these reactions were indicative of resentment and defense. The stimuli used by Woodworth and Sherrington were shocks applied to nerves mediating impulses from the viscera alone, from muscles alone, as well as nerves mediating stimuli applied to the skin. The importance of the visceral and muscular stimuli is worthy of note, because they suggest that internal states can give rise to displays of threat.

The region of the junction of the midbrain and the thalamus is of importance, not only because it brings in the instruments for attack, namely striking and biting, but also because the character of the stimuli required to elicit a threat display is changed. Whereas for the most part noxious stimuli were required, the effective stimuli need no longer be noxious. When this junction is reached, movements of the leg or the insertion of a rectal thermometer become sufficient to elicit the display. This change was noted by Carli, Malliani, and Zanchetti (1965) as well as by Bard (1928). If large parts of the subthalamus and centrum medianum were spared, light stimuli such as touching the skin were effective in eliciting struggle, lashing of the tail, pupillary dilatation, and biting, as well as respiratory and blood pressure changes. If only small parts of these structures were spared, relatively weak noxious stimuli in contrast to the strong noxious stimuli were effective. Up to this point the reactions that have been described were initiated by the experimenter and not by the animal.

If the posterior hypothalamus is added to the more caudal structures, then there is a marked change in the animal's behavior. The cat, if tied to an animal board, will initiate the full threat display, including lashing of the tail, arching of the back, thrusting and jerking of the restrained limbs, display of the claws and striking, snarling and attempts to bite, as well as erection of the hair, dilatation of the pupils, and changes in heart rate. The spontaneous behavior was observed by Bard (1928) and also by Carli et al. (1965) if the intersection went from the rostral portion of the superior colliculi to the region between the middle of the tuber cinereum and the optic chiasm. Carli et al. attempted to specify more closely what structures in the posterior hypothalamus gave rise to this initiation of behavior, and they found that it was only the combined destruction of the caudal parts that was not compatible with its appearance. Individual parts could still be destroyed, and self-initiated behavior would remain. Even if a cat is not tied to a board, but is unrestrained, it will initiate walking (Hinsey, 1939). The trauma associated with the operations was not responsible for the activities observed, since the same behaviors were seen in a long-surviving cat (Bard and Rioch, 1937) and dog (Bard, 1934) with essentially the same sections of the brain. Inclusion of the thalamus leaves the animals still extremely responsive to light stimulation (Bard and Rioch, 1937). In the rat the inclusion of the thalamus leads to continuation of vocalization after the stimulation is removed (Carroll and Lim, 1960).

Animals with hypothalamus intact and cortex removed are much more likely to display threat in response to light stimuli than are normal animals. This heightened responsiveness is the decorticate rage that has been described since the time of Goltz (1892). The responsiveness decreases somewhat and returns closer to the normal state when the striatum is present (Wang and Akert, 1962). With the striatum intact, the animals respond as they would prior to operation. However, if the limbic system is left intact, together with the more caudal parts of the brain, there is an extreme lack of responsiveness (Bard and Mountcastle, 1948). Even the most painful stimuli, which prior to operation were effective in eliciting growling, hissing, spitting, striking, biting, tail lashing, pupillary dilatation, and piloerection, no longer produced these responses in cats in which the limbic system is intact. Removal of a portion of the telencephalic limbic system, however, renders them again responsive (Bard and Mountcastle, 1948; Rothfield and Harman, 1954).

In summary, a display can be seen in animals in which a large portion of the midbrain tegmentum is destroyed. The display has more components as more of the midbrain is left intact; however, noxious stimuli for the most part are required to elicit display. At the junction of the midbrain and thalamus, less noxious stimuli become effective, and the instruments of attack, striking, and biting, are seen. If the posterior hypothalamus is present, stimuli that are ordinarily not noxious, such as light-tactile stimuli, become effective in eliciting a display, and the animal also initiates some of these behaviors itself. This heightened responsiveness remains as thalamus is added to the hypothalamus and caudal portions of the brain, returning to normal levels when striatum is present, and an extreme placidity intervenes when limbic system is intact but the neocortex removed. In the absence of neocortex there does not appear to be either a well-directed attack, nor is the attack directed against clearly differentiated objects.

III. LOCALIZED LESIONS AND ELICITATION OF BEHAVIOR BY ELECTRICAL STIMULATION

A. Medulla, Pons, and Midbrain

1. *Defensive Threat and Attack*

The actual regions of the brainstem that mediate threat and attack can be determined somewhat more precisely by observations on animals in which the lesions are limited or in which behavior can be elicited by stimulation of specified sites.

Electrical stimulation of a narrow strip about 2.5 mm from the midline in the region of the pons and medulla elicits in conscious animals running or clawing, extension of the claws, pupillary dilatation, piloerection, and, occasionally, growling. The response to medullary stimulation is neither as well integrated nor as vigorous as the response to stimulation of the hypothalamus or midbrain (Coote, Hilton, and Zbrozyna, 1973). This finding is in accord with the data presented earlier, indicating a relatively incomplete reflex mechanism located at the level of the pons and medulla. A fragmentary form of threat behavior has also been elicited from stimulation in the pontine tegmentum, usually only one or two components being elicited from a single site (Berntson, 1972).

Studies of vocalization, accompanied by threat displays, indicate the presence of a more complete integrating mechanism, located in the midbrain. The displays elicited by electrical stimulation consisted of facial expressions such as opening of the mouth, dilation of the nostrils, retraction of the angle of the mouth, elevation of the upper lip, exposing the teeth, and giving the face a snarling expression. Less commonly, the forehead was wrinkled and the ears retracted and flattened against the side of the head. The region from which vocalization accompanied by these facial expressions was elicited was the central gray around the aqueduct and dorsal and lateral tegmentum, leading to an area medial to the brachium of the inferior colliculus and lateral lemniscus (Magoun, Atlas, Ingersoll, and Ranson, 1936–1937). The region of the central gray matter around the aqueduct was stimulated in conscious animals, and the behavior was much more complete (Hunsperger, 1956).

When stimulation begins, a relaxed cat lying on a test table opens its eyelids, the pupils dilate, the cat gets up, its breathing becomes faster and deeper, the hair on the back and tail rises, the cat arches its back, the ears are pulled back, the corner of the mouth is retracted, and with the mouth open wide and the upper lip raised, the cat hisses. The hissing may be preceded by growling. The animal was not immediately quieted after stimulation stopped. Some of the changes persisted. The importance of the central gray matter around the aqueduct was further established by showing that animals that would respond in a similar fashion when stimulated at the hypothalamus no longer did so when the central gray matter was destroyed (Hunsperger, 1956). With destruction of the central gray matter, cats no longer responded to threatening dogs, and if the lesion was made somewhat larger than it was in Hunsperger's experiments, the abolition of the hypothalamic response could also be made permanent (Skultety, 1963).

The importance of the lateral tegmental area, which had been implicated in the studies on vocalization, is shown by the fact that when it is destroyed, the behavior of cats is markedly altered. With relatively small lesions in this region, Glusman, Won, Burdock, and Ransohoff (1962) changed so-called savage cats into docile ones. In addition, cats with lesions in the lateral and ventral tegmentum, when bitten or dragged by another cat, did not struggle, vocalize, or attempt to escape or fight back (Randall, 1964). These lesions were relatively large in the region of the inferior colliculus and rostral pons. Similar large but more rostral lesions in the lateral tegmentum of the midbrain resulted in a great reduction of both the somatic and the autonomic signs of affective behavior (Sprague, Levitt, Robson, Liu, Stellar, and Chambers, 1963). An exception to the disappearance of defensive threat and attack following destruction of the lateral tegmentum was noted by Skultety (1965), who made rostral lateral tegmental lesions and found that stimulation of the hypothalamus still elicited a threat display but eliminated attack in some animals.

In general, these experiments confirm the importance of the central gray matter and the lateral tegmentum of the midbrain in the mediation of defensive threat and attack. Hunsperger (1956) maintained that these mechanisms were sufficient in and of themselves to mediate this form of behavior. He destroyed an area in the hypothalamus from which he could elicit the behavior, and he still managed to elicit it on stimulation of the central gray matter. These conclusions were strengthened by the finding that animals in which the hypothalamus had all its neural connections severed from the rest of the brain were still capable of showing a full threat display and also attack (Ellison and Flynn, 1968).

In summary, partial mechanisms for the mediation of defensive threat were found in the medulla and pons. These mechanisms, however, do not seem capable of delivering a full expression of the behavior, whereas those in the midbrain, particularly its anterior portions, do. When the parts of the nervous

system other than the hypothalamus are intact, a well-directed attack, together with a threatening display, can be seen.

2. Quiet Attack

From the data in the first section it would appear that the instruments of
attack are integrated into the picture of defensive threat at the level of the
rostral end of the mesencephalon. Since quiet attack is not detectable in
terms of the threat display, little could be learned from the animals with
brains truncated below this level, the first indications being given by the
appearance of striking and biting.

In intact cats, stimulation in the central portion of the pontine tegmentum
just ventral to the central gray matter elicits biting attack accompanied by
kicking of the attack object (Berntson, 1973). The attack was not only
directed at rats, but it was of a discriminate character with the cats preferring
rats over other similar-sized objects. There are two other regions caudal to
the midbrain from which quiet attack can be elicited, although it seems to be
somewhat fragmentary; the rostral portion of the fastigial nucleus of the
cerebellum (Reis, Doba, and Nathan, 1973) and the region of the nucleus
of the superior cerebellar peduncle.

A site in the midbrain ventral to the central gray, when destroyed, eliminates the spontaneous attack of rats upon mice (Chaurand, Schmitt, and
Karli, 1973). Lesions whose field of overlap in various cats was located just
ventral to the central gray and slightly lateral to the midline eliminated or
markedly elevated thresholds for biting attack elicited by hypothalamic stimulation. The effect lasted in some instances for longer than 92 days (Berntson,
1972). Quiet attack can be elicited from this region (Sheard and Flynn,
1967).

There is another indication of the involvement of the midline region in
quiet attack. However, the attack elicited here is dependent upon the rat's
coming into the cat's visual field and on the distance that separates the rat
from the cat. The cat initiates movement only when the rat comes into view.
The area from which this form of attack is elicited along the midline region
is located in the dorsal portions of the rostral central gray matter of the midbrain. This is a region where fibers located at attack sites in the thalamus
terminate (Bandler and Flynn, 1974).

Quiet attack can also be achieved by stimulation in the midbrain reticular
formation (Sheard and Flynn, 1967). It can also be elicited by electrical
stimulation in the ventral tegmental area of Tsai (Bandler, Chi, and Flynn,
1972). The pathways of fibers which are located at quiet attack sites in the
hypothalamus terminate in the ventral tegmental area of Tsai (Chi and
Flynn, 1971a,b). Lesions at this point again block the attack elicited by
stimulation of the hypothalamus (Proshansky, Bandler, and Flynn, 1974).
The elicitation of attack at the area of termination and then blocking of the

attack elicited at a more rostral site such as the hypothalamus or the thalamus have been used as criteria for the determination of the neural pathways involved in attack. The pathways that are involved in quiet attack run in the medial forebrain bundle. These three criteria have been met both in the case of the ventral tegmental area of Tsai and in the case of the attack sites located in the dorsal portion of the central gray area (Bandler and Flynn, 1974). How these three regions in the midbrain are interconnected, if they are, is still not clear; but it is possible that the midline area and the area in the ventral tegmentum may be connected by fibers associated with the medial forebrain bundle or others directly within the midbrain reticular formation. Since quiet attack can be elicited by electrical stimulation of the midbrain in cats in which the hypothalamus has been isolated from the rest of the brain, there is clearly an adequate mechanism for quiet attack located in the midbrain or more caudal part of the brainstem.

Cats with lesions in intracollicular tegmentum, lateral tectum, and some medial regions persisted while awake in performing one of three prey behaviors: approaching prey, carrying prey, or attempting to get at prey. In addition, these animals showed enhancement of reflex biting. Touching the lips with any object would elicit the bite (Randall, 1964). However, none of these animals actually killed and ate mice or rats.

A similar kind of response, both with and without killing, was seen in cats in which there were again large lateral tegmental lesions (Sprague et al., 1963). These effects were noted for long periods of time. A facilitation of attack but of a temporary nature, for 11 days or less, was noted in a number of cats (Berntson, 1972). The common area of the lesions was again lateral tegmentum. The large size of the lesions leaves the precise area poorly defined.

B. Hypothalamus

1. Defensive Threat and Attack

Stimulation of the hypothalamus in cats (Hess, 1928; Kabat, Anson, Magoun, and Ranson, 1935; Hess and Brugger, 1943), in rats (Panksepp and Trowill, 1969), and in monkeys (Robinson, Alexander, and Bowne, 1969) can bring about threatening and attack behavior. The behavior that was elicited in the cats stimulated by Hess and Brugger (1943) has been described at the beginning of this chapter. Similar descriptions were provided by Ranson (1939) and his associates (Kabat et al., 1935). In both cases the investigators interpreted the display as a defensive one corresponding to what is seen when a cat is confronted with a dog and seeks safety in defense. The areas within the hypothalamus from which this behavior can be elicited are extensive.

The active area is dorsal and rostral to the ventromedial nucleus of the hypothalamus and can also be found in ventral portions of the ventromedial nucleus; it goes rostral to the medial preoptic area and in the perifornical region of the hypothalamus. Attempts have been made to determine the critical region on the basis of the smallest intensity of current required to elicit the behavior and on the basis of the completeness of the response. Such maps still yield moderately extensive areas. Hess was of the opinion that the regions caudal to the hypothalamus were essentially secondary integrating centers, but this is difficult to reconcile with the persistence of threat and attack following destruction of areas from which attack is elicited in the hypothalamus (Hunsperger, 1956) or following isolation of the hypothalamus from the rest of the brain (Ellison and Flynn, 1968). Hess was also clearly aware of the importance of the attack directed against the experimenter, and the implication that, since it was directed in this fashion, the sense organs and cortex were involved.

Evidence must be sought for the directed character of the behavior. Threat display by itself is insufficient, although occasionally it can be demonstrated that an animal fixes his gaze on the experimenter and follows his actions; in this way there is evidence of sensory motor coordination. The mere appearance of a threat is not sufficient since cats are found in which there is no evidence of there being a sensory motor coordination. Masserman (1938) observed cats in which there was little evidence of sensory involvement. Hunsperger (1956) recognized that the hypothalamus gave rise to attack more frequently than did the central gray matter and that at times solely threat was present (Flynn et al., 1970). This has been confirmed, there being a large area in the region of the central gray from which a threat can be elicited, but a very small region from which a threat and attack is elicited. As a further cautionary note, it might be stated that at times stimulated cats will bite more or less indiscriminately at any object near them. This must be recognized, too, as being different from the discriminate form of attack that can be regularly elicited (Levison and Flynn, 1965).

The stimulation associated with the elicitation of defensive threat and attack is frequently aversive. Animals trained to avoid a shock will perform a similar learned response to stimulation of the brain that elicits defensive threat and attack. However, some forms of defensive threat do not share this quality (Adams and Flynn, 1966). It is clear that aversive stimulation can bring about defensive threat and attack. The experiments on animals in which the brain was truncated at the rostral part of the midbrain were for the most part done with noxious stimuli. Fighting can be induced in a confined space between rats by shocking their feet, and monkeys stimulated at sites within the brain that coincide with pathways known to carry pain will respond by fighting (Plotnik, Mir, and Delgado, 1971). However, Nakao (1958) had several animals show little or no reluctance to enter the cage in which they were stimulated, whereas other animals showing flight were clearly reluctant to do so. It has also been found that aversive stimulation alone would not suffice to bring about threat and attack. So, the two are probably interlinked, but the threat behavior is possible in the absence of noxious stimuli much as it is in the case of the decorticate animal. Fighting between two rats induced by electrical stimulation of the paws is increased following lesions of the medial portion of the hypothalamus. When the lesions were at this site, the increase in fighting was associated with an increased responsiveness to noxious stimulation (Turner, Sechzer, and Liebelt, 1967); but such an increase in responsiveness to noxious stimulation per se did not bring with it an increase in fighting when the lesions were at other sites within the brain.

Glusman (1974), who made lesions in the ventromedial nucleus of the hypothalamus of cats and subsequently found that they became more savage, thought that an increased sensitivity to pain might account for their increased responsiveness; however, after operation the cats became more tolerant of higher levels of electrical stimulation applied to the skin. In the case of monkeys attack is accompanied by threat, but in at least a few instances it has been demonstrated that the stimulation was not aversive and that the animal would in fact stimulate itself at sites from which attack was elicited (Robinson et al., 1969).

A lesion can be made in the hypothalamus of cats which produces an animal whose behavior is similar to that of the thalamic and hypothalamic cats described in the earlier section in terms of their greatly heightened responsiveness to relatively innocuous stimulation. These animals, however, differ from the decorticate cats in that they show behavior that is both well directed and discrete, and it can be initiated by visual stimuli as well as by tactile stimuli. Wheatley (1944) selected 42 cats from several hundred on the basis of their friendliness and failure to become aggressive even when subjected to noxious stimuli. The cats were stimulated daily for several weeks before being operated on. Lesions were made in the hypothalamus and observations were made over periods ranging from several weeks to more than a year after operation. Some of the cats became savage immediately. Others did not do so until several weeks after operation. The savage animals displayed pupillary dilatation, piloerection, angry vocalization, spitting, lashing of the tail, arching of the back, defecation, and urination. They would attack the experimenter in a vicious aggressive manner, biting and clawing when attempts were made to pet them. Of the 18 cats that had demonstrated this behavior, all but one had lesions completely destroying the ventromedial nucleus on both sides of the brain. Similarly, those cats which did not respond to petting threatened the observer, but did not manifest all the elements listed above; all had lesions in this same structure, although some were incomplete. The cats that were unchanged had no or slight injury to the ventromedial nucleus. The lesions in the so-called savage cats were not restricted to the ventromedial nucleus; they included the fornix and the pallido-hypothalamic fibers. The lesions may have cut off the influences from the hippocampus, amygdala, and septal region which were presumably responsible for the placid cats described earlier. The animal would thus be left as reactive as a decorticate cat but have the benefits of neocortex in being well directed and discriminate.

There are two additional aspects of the hypothalamus which deserve to be noted. They gain credence in light of the phenomena which appear when the posterior hypothalamus is left joined to the more caudal brainstem. These are the lower thresholds for the elicitation of the threat display and the initiation of activity by the cat itself. Ranson (1939) found in monkeys that animals were somnolent if lesions were made in the hypothalamus lateral to the mamillary bodies and extended throughout this region; but he noted that (1) these same animals, even when they were awake, would not initiate behavior, and (2) their emotional activity was extremely limited. The same deficiency has been noted in cats in which the whole hypothalamus was destroyed or was isolated from the rest of the brain (Bard, 1928). Even though one knows that one of the main routes, the medial forebrain bundle, passes through this region into and out of the hypothalamus, and it would be reasonable to attribute the deficits noted by Ranson to such pathways, the loss of initiative and the absence of emotional responsiveness cannot be associated with destruction of the more rostral parts of the hypothalamus. Therefore, one is forced on the basis of the evidence to think of this region lateral to the mamillary bodies as having an important part in the initiation of behavior and in emotional responsiveness. This deserves stress because one of the most important aspects of motivated acts is that they are not always subject to control by external stimuli and at times appear in the absence of identifiable stimuli.

2. Quiet Attack

Rats that attack mice will stop doing so after lesions in the lateral hypothalamus. At the same time these animals stop eating. Both functions are ultimately recovered, and the animals begin to kill mice before they begin to eat (Karli and Vergnes, 1964). There is also a temporary loss of territorial fighting in rats in which the rat fought against an intruder placed in a large "home cage," made up of six levels with connecting ramps. Fighting that was induced in rats by shocking them through the feet in a confined space was not altered by this lesion; whereas, they were, as stated earlier, more likely to fight if the lesion were in the ventromedial hypothalamus. This last change, however, is only temporary (Adams, 1971).

Quiet attack has been elicited in cats by stimulation of the hypothalamus. Either rats or cats were attacked (Wasman and Flynn, 1962). It is similarly observed in the opossum, and again the attack is directed to rats and to both young and adult opossums, provided the adults' mouths are bound closed so that they cannot attack back (Roberts et al., 1967). This attack upon members of the same species occurs naturally in rats that attack mice in that they will also attack rat pups, although they are less likely to do so if the pups are at a weanling stage (Paul, 1972).

The sites from which quiet attack can be elicited lie in an area dorsomedial and ventrolateral to the area from which defensive threat and attack can be elicited. A similar distribution is found in the opossum and in the rat, although in the opossum the sites giving rise to the complete influence have been more accurately defined.

The sites from which quiet attack can be elicited are also sites at which rats will stimulate themselves. In fact, some animals will stimulate themselves with trains of pulses of sufficient length to elicit attack from the rat on a mouse (Panksepp, 1970).

C. Thalamus

1. Defensive Threat and Attack

In the region of the thalamus just medial to the medial geniculate body and to some extent within the magnocellular part of that same body fibers associated with the main sensory systems, such as the medial lemniscus and the spinothalamic and trigeminothalamic tracts, pass. Lesions in this area eliminate the savage behavior (Kaelber, Mitchell, and Way, 1965) that Wheatley (1944) was able to bring about by lesions in the ventromedial nucleus in the hypothalamus. The 10 cats in which the behavior was eliminated had complete destruction of this area bilaterally. In the five animals in which the behavior was unaltered, the destruction was incomplete. The destruction of the main sensory thalamic nuclei in two animals would not alter this behavior, although attack can be elicited in monkeys after stimulation of this area (Plotnik, Mir, and Delgado, 1971). Attack subsequent to stimulation in this area has also been observed in cats (MacDonnell and Flynn, 1968).

From some portions of the thalamus a response that has been called fearlike has been elicited. The response, however, consists of hissing, opening of the mouth, showing the teeth, flattening of the ears, as well as attempts to bite and scratch any obstacle placed in the way of the animal if it attempted to escape (Delgado, Roberts, and Miller, 1954). Sham rage was reported on stimulation of nucleus reuniens and from nucleus anterior dorsalis (Hunter and Jasper, 1949).

Lesions in the dorsal medial nuclei of the thalamus of cats, that had been shocked regularly when they approached food, changed these animals from being relatively inactive to being hostile and attacking others. This change, however, was not noted in animals that had not been subjected to this preoperative kind of treatment (Pechtel, Masserman, Schreiner, and Levitt, 1955). However, in an earlier publication by some of the same authors

(Schreiner, Rioch, Pechtel, and Masserman, 1952), it was stated that lesions of the nucleus medialis dorsalis which either destroyed them or spared their lateral aspects with minimum destruction of adjacent thalamic structures gave rise to pronounced behavioral change in normal animals, which in some animals lasted for as long as 12 months. The animals showed retraction of the ears, pupillary dilatation, piloerection, low growling, as well as spitting. When they were approached in their cages, similar responses were made to other cats.

2. Quiet Attack

A quiet form of attack has been released by stimulation of sites in the thalamus. Most of these sites are in nucleus centralis medialis or nucleus reuniens or in medial portions of the medialis dorsalis (MacDonnell and Flynn, 1964). There are a few sites in the anterior portion of the thalamus. On being stimulated, the cat approaches a rat and bites its neck. Pupillary dilatation and moderate piloerection are also observed, but vocalization and other marked signs of affect were not seen. There is a striking difference between attack elicited from the thalamus and the attack elicited from the hypothalamus. The cat that has been stimulated in the thalamus often sits quietly until the rat comes into view, at which time the cat approaches and bites the rat. If the cat is blindfolded, it does not approach, whereas a hypothalamic cat, even if blindfolded, locates and bites a rat, provided the cage space is limited. The attack elicited from the midline thalamus is not dependent upon the integrity of the hypothalamic outflow, since the major components of the attack continued on stimulation of the thalamus if the lesions were made in the posterior hypothalamus (MacDonnell and Flynn, 1968). There is a direct pathway back to the dorsal portion of the anterior central gray matter (Bandler and Flynn, 1974). This pathway was seen after making lesions at sites from which attack was elicited in the thalamus, then staining the brains of these animals to reveal the degeneration resulting from the lesion at the attack site; the degenerating fibers projected to the area indicated and to confirm that these fibers were in fact related to attack, attack was elicited at the sites of termination. Furthermore, lesions in the area of termination blocked the effects of stimulating the more rostral thalamic sites.

There are sites in the thalamus from which suppression of both defensive threat and attack as well as the quiet attack can be effected. The suppression is not in the nature of altering the threshold for the elicitation of attack from the hypothalamus, but rather more in the nature of the induction of a response different from the attack itself. The animal, for example, would retreat into a corner and then simply remain unmoved. Many of the sites from which suppression was elicited lie in the anterior thalamus, although some go back through the somewhat more lateral portions of nucleus medialis dorsalis, even back into centrum medianum. Eclancher and Karli (1971) found that out of 22 rats that did not kill mice spontaneously, 15 did so after lesions of nucleus medialis dorsalis.

D. Limbic System

1. Septal Region

Brady and Nauta (1953) found that rats in which lesions were made in the septal region showed gross dramatic changes within 2 hr after operation. The animals showed a striking alertness, and their eyes followed the movements of an observer approaching the cage. An ordinary stimulus produced a marked startle reaction. Rapidly approaching objects were attacked with vigorous biting, and attempts to handle the animal were responded to with fierce attacks on the experimenter. When placed in a group cage, five or six septal animals would fight continuously and vigorously for extended periods of time. None of these phenomena was noted in either the operated or unoperated control animals. Differences between the experimental and the control animals gradually disappeared over a matter of approximately 10 days. In mice this effect lasts somewhat longer (Slotnick and McMullen, 1972), but no such increase in emotionality is noted in hamsters (Sodetz, Matalka, and Bunnell, 1967). Cats with these lesions, instead of becoming more difficult to handle, become more tractable (Glendenning, 1972). Rats in which the septal area is destroyed fight more if fighting is induced by shocks to the feet (Blanchard and Blanchard, 1968; Eichelman, 1971; Miczek and Grossman, 1972), and this form of fighting, which is due to noxious stimuli, would seem comparable to the defensive threat if for no other reason than similarity in the type of stimuli used. It was also found that when the septal region was stimulated concurrently with stimulation of the hypothalamus that induced hissing and escape in cats, these two forms of behavior occurred more quickly (Siegel and Skog, 1970).

When rats kill mice, they usually do so by positioning the mouse with the forepaws so as to be able to bite the cervical region of the spine, and these movements are executed without any great display. If the lesions were made in the septal region of rats that previously did not kill mice, they began to do so, but the way in which they killed them was quite different and much more like the kind of attack associated with defensive threat. The septal rat reacts strongly to the introduction of the mouse, immediately follows it and attempts to bite it regardless of the position of the mouse, and the biting is not directed towards any specific region of the mouse's body. The rat continues to bite the severely lacerated body of the dead mouse. Again, like the other behaviors, this form of attack disappeared within 10 days (Miczek and Grossman, 1972).

2. Quiet Attacks

Rats will fight in a chamber to which they had been accustomed to go to obtain food. The encounter is brought about by two rats attempting at the same time to reach the food chamber through a tube which is large enough for only one rat to run. In this situation the one rat manifests its dominance over the other either by taking a blocking position, turning sideways towards the other rat, biting the other rat, or forcing the other rat into a position in which its ventral surface is exposed. If the dominant animal of such a pair has his septal area destroyed, he loses his dominance and becomes submissive to the previously submissive animal. Again this effect is transitory (Miczek and Grossman, 1972).

Mice will fight when placed in a chamber, actually biting one another. If the two mice have been exposed to one another on repeated trials, one animal usually emerges as dominant, and the submissive animal either runs away after disengaging from a fight or adopts a submissive posture exposing its ventral surface. Following lesions of the septal area, the dominant mice regularly lost to their sham-operated partners. Previously dominant animals ran away and failed to fight back with their opponents (Slotnick and McMullen, 1972). Quiet attack elicited by stimulation of the hypothalamus of cats is slowed down by concurrent stimulation of the septal region (Siegel and Skog, 1970).

E. Amygdala

The observation that stimulation of the amygdala elicits defensive threat in cats and other species constitutes the most direct link between the amygdala and defensive threat behavior. Growling, hissing, retraction of the ears, pawing with claws extended, and other customary signs of defensive threat are elicited on stimulation (Ursin and Kaada, 1960). The behavior differs from that elicited from the stimulation of the hypothalamus in that the response of the amygdala builds up gradually in contrast to the regular elicitation obtainable from the hypothalamus. In addition, the response always outlasts the period of stimulation (Zbrozyna, 1972). In the descriptions provided by various authors there is a lack of information about directed attack. Fernandez DeMolina and Hunsperger (1959) assign attack to the hypothalamically elicited behavior but not to the similar behavior elicited from stimulation of the amygdala. Ursin and Kaada (1960) speak as though the animal were directing its attention to an imaginary object. Shealey and Peele (1957) state directly that the rage was not directed to any particular person or object.

There are features of this behavior that suggest that it may be triggered from the amygdala, but actually not organized there. The amygdala, like the hippocampus, is highly susceptible to epileptic-like electrical afterdischarges, and some of the aspects of the results of stimulation are akin to what is seen during seizure activity associated with the amygdala. Twitching of the face ipsilateral to the site of stimulation is frequently reported and this itself is a concomitant of afterdischarge. Furthermore, the very fact that the effects of stimulation outlast the stimulus is itself an indication that additional neural activity is involved. Direct evidence of this hypothesis is provided by Naquet (1954). In our own experiments only once was the response seen in the absence of afterdischarges. The electrical activity of the amygdala was constantly monitored in this study (Egger and Flynn, 1963). In this instance the electrode was situated very close to the stria terminalis which could serve as a pathway for driving the hypothalamus.

Studies in which lesions have been made in the amygdala provide better evidence for modulation of the hypothalamic and basic brainstem structures by the amygdala. Klüver and Bucy (1939) had observed a taming of rhesus monkeys following large lesions of the temporal lobe including the amygdala, uncus and part of the hippocampus. Bard and Mountcastle (1948), on the other hand, had, after producing amygdaloid lesions in cats, observed an increase in aggressive behavior, and subsequently Schreiner and Kling (1953) observed in cats a taming following lesions of the same structure. Although many experiments have been carried out, and most are in support of Kluver and Bucy's and Schreiner and Kling's results, nonetheless, contradictions remain.

An explanation is frequently sought in terms of differential influences of various parts of the amygdala. The bulk of the data is consistent with this interpretation. However, the strongest demonstration that there are differential activities of this sort comes from the work of Fonberg (1973), who found that lesions in the dorsal medial portion of the amygdala produced aphagia and subsequently hypophagia with partial recovery occurring later. The second operation destroyed the lateral part of the amygdaloid complex, reversed the initial syndrome and produced hyperphagia, a generalized arousal and an increase in body weight. Many other experiments, as have been indicated, are in support of this duality of the functions of the amygdala. The specific localization, however, is still in need of clarification.

There is no evidence that quiet attack itself can be elicited from the amygdala, although stimulation of the amygdala in the absence of afterdischarges can at certain sites retard attack elicited by stimulation of the hypothalamus, and at other sites facilitate it (Egger and Flynn, 1963). In general, it has been found that such facilitating and inhibiting areas are located in major parts of the limbic system (Siegel and Flynn, 1968; Siegel and Skog, 1970; Siegel and Chabora, 1971).

IV. NEURAL MECHANISMS

Although it is clearly not possible at the present time to provide an adequate account of threat and attack in terms of neural mechanisms, some suggestions emerge from a consideration of the data.

Defensive threat and attack require the integrity of the midbrain mechanisms and those of the neocortex involved in directing and selecting a suitable target of attack.

Defensive threat itself can be mediated by the structures just caudal to the mesodiencephalic junction. Even though the defensive threat is elicited most readily by noxious stimuli, the display itself is quite complete, including vocalizations, facial expressions, and autonomic activities. In addition, the two main instruments of attack, striking and biting, are present when the rostral sections include the junction between the midbrain and thalamus. Furthermore, the intensity of the stimuli required is reduced by the presence of the junction. The animal, however, is still largely a reflex preparation, activated primarily by somatic stimuli including visceral and muscular stimuli. Even when the forebrain, aside from the hypothalamus, is left joined to the midbrain and lower brainstem, the cat lacks spontaneity, and is strongly dependent upon the application of external stimuli. The external stimuli, however, in such an animal may well be visual as well as somatic.

Self-initiated behavior appears when the posterior hypothalamus is joined to lower brainstem. Even though the activity is dependent upon the external environment, the timing and duration of the activity can be set by the animal itself as well as by the experimenter. This is a major feature of motivated behavior.

A second feature of motivated acts is that they are directed towards some object. The neocortex seems to be required for effective attack directed at a suitable object detected by means of distance receptors, such as vision and audition. The specific parts of neocortex required are undetermined. Even though decerebrate cats turn their heads to the flank that is being pinched, and thus demonstrate partial localization of the object, and decorticate cats can strike out and attempt to bite other cats which brush against them, a discriminate attack upon a distant object is not seen in animals lacking neocortex. This deficiency in animals lacking neocortex may appear to be simply due to a lack of adequate sensory mechanisms. The presence of adequate sensory mechanisms is undoubtedly necessary, but their simple presence does not appear to be sufficient. There is evidence that the sensory and motor systems must be biased in certain specific ways.

The major reason for believing that the simple presence of an adequate sensory system is insufficient to account for directed behavior comes from experiments on attack elicited by stimulation of the hypothalamus. The force of the argument against a simple presence and in favor of a bias being established comes from the fact that the side of the animal contralateral to the site stimulated is much more effective in mediating the behavior than the side ipsilateral to the stimulating site, and furthermore, that the inadequacy of the ipsilateral side is not due to disruption of it.

For example, during stimulation of an attack site in the hypothalamus, a mouse was presented to the contralateral eye and to the ipsilateral eye. The cat lunged towards the mouse. The frequency of the cat's lunge towards the mouse was much greater when the mouse was presented to the contralateral eye than it was when presented to the ipsilateral eye (Bandler and Flynn, 1971). If this result were due to some sort of disruption of the ipsilateral visual system, one would expect the disruption to be increased when the intensity of stimulation was raised. Instead, with increasing intensity of stimulation the ipsilateral eye became more effective. Comparable results have been demonstrated for a number of actions which in combination constitute the terminal aspects of attack (Flynn, Edwards, and Bandler, 1971).

The inadequacy of an intact sensory system to the task is further supported by the finding that there is sensory neglect on the ipsilateral side in rats with lesions in the hypothalamus (Marshall and Teitelbaum, 1974) and in the amygdala (Turner, 1973).

Thus far, the essential mechanisms for integrating the elements of defensive threat and for imposing certain patterns on the sensory and motor systems including those of neocortex have been discussed. These are regarded as residing in the midbrain. They are not simply secondary coordinating systems as Hess and Brugger (1943) maintained, because they can function adequately in the absence of hypothalamus. A region at the junction of the mesencephalon and diencephalon lowers the intensity of the stimuli needed to elicit a reflex response in decerebrate cats. This area should be considered separately from the posterior hypothalamus, since it is effective while the decerebrate animal is still primarily a reflex preparation.

The posterior hypothalamus appears not only to be a critical region for the initiation of behavior by the animal itself, but also is an adequate mechanism for the integration of threat and attack. It may further have a role in the regulation of emotional reactivity.

Destruction of the ventromedial nucleus greatly increases the probability of threat and attack behavior. Although in rats destruction of this area is associated with greater sensitivity to pain, in cats there seems to be greater tolerance of electric shock (Glusman and Fields, cited in Glusman, 1974).

Since this heightened responsiveness is also present in animals in which the thalamus in part is present but not the striatum or the entire limbic system or neocortex, one is tempted to look upon the ventromedial nucleus as having an inadequate input to maintain normal responsivity. With the striatum present, the animals retain their preoperative responsiveness. With the addition of the limbic system the animal without neocortex is remarkably placid, so much so that the net effect of its influences when freed of neocortex is predominantly to damp responsiveness. This occurs despite there being good evidence of duality of functioning within many structures of the limbic system, damping activities on the one hand and enhancing them on the other. Injury to different parts of the limbic system in neodecorticate animals returns them to the status of thalamic animals.

The amygdala may well have a role in assessing the importance of sensory stimuli, since lesions there lead to sensory neglect, and single-unit studies reveal some cells that respond to relevant stimuli (O'Keefe and Bouma, 1969; Jacobs and McGinty, 1972). The experiments of Klüver and Bucy (1939), in which the lesions embraced much more than the amygdala, demonstrated that the monkeys suffered from a visual agnosia.

The importance of neocortex for the visual discriminate attack has already been stressed. In the case of threat and attack elicited by electrical stimulation of the hypothalamus or midbrain, there appear to be regions which not only bring about direct motor responses, but which also dispose sensory and motor systems to act in highly specific ways, so that if an adequate object for attack is found, these state-dependent or patterned reflexes come into play, and are the components of the overt behavior (Flynn, 1972).

Naturally occurring behavior is assumed to be mediated by similar mechanisms, with natural stimuli bringing the patterning or integrating mechanisms into a state where overt behavior is elicited. The natural stimuli can be provided by proprioceptors and interoceptors thus initiating behavior, and these can be combined with external stimuli to increase activity in these mechanisms. On the other hand, external noxious stimuli can induce the behavior, and it is probably reinforced by internal changes. Finally, the role of learning is clear in experiments in which attack follows the delaying or withholding of a reward. Patterning similar to that induced by stimulation of the brain presumably occurs in response to these various sorts of natural stimuli.

ACKNOWLEDGMENTS

The preparation of this manuscript was supported by U.S. Public Health Service grant nos. 2-R01-MH-08936 and 5-K05-MH-25466.

REFERENCES

Adamec, R. (1974): Neural correlates of long-term changes in predatory behavior in the cat. Doctoral Thesis, McGill University, Montreal.

Adams, D. B. (1971): Defence and territorial behavior dissociated by hypothalamic lesions in the rat. *Nature (Lond.)*, 232:573–574.

Adams, D., and Flynn, J. P. (1966): Transfer of an escape response from tail shock to brain-stimulated attack behavior. *J. Exp. Anal. Behav.*, 14:399–405.

Bandler, R. J., Chi, C. C., and Flynn, J. P. (1972): Biting attack elicited by stimulation of the ventral midbrain tegmentum of cats. *Science*, 177:364–366.

Bandler, R. J., and Flynn, J. P. (1971): Visual patterned reflex present during hypothalamically elicited attack. *Science*, 171:703–706.

Bandler, R. J., and Flynn, J. P. (1974): Neural pathways from thalamus associated with regulation of aggressive behavior. *Science;* 183:96–99.

Bard, P. (1928): A diencephalic mechanism for the expression of rage with special reference to the sympathetic nervous system. *Am. J. Physiol.*, 84:490–513.

Bard, P. (1934): On emotional expression after decortication with some remarks on certain theoretical views. *Psychol. Rev.*, 41:309–329.

Bard, P., and Macht, M. B. (1958): The behavior of chronically decerebrate cats. In: *Neurological Basis of Behavior*, edited by G. E. W. Wolstenholme and C. M. O'Connor. J. and A. Churchill, Ltd., London.

Bard, P., and Mountcastle, V. B. (1948): Some forebrain mechanisms involved in expression of rage with special reference to suppression of angry behavior. In: *The Frontal Lobes,* edited by J. F. Fulton. Williams and Wilkins Co., Baltimore.

Bard, P., and Rioch, D. McK. (1937): A study of 4 cats deprived of neocortex and additional portions of the prebrain. *Bull. Johns Hopkins Hosp.,* 60:73–147.

Berntson, G. G. (1972): Blockade and release of hypothalamically and naturally elicited aggressive behaviors in cats following midbrain lesions. *J. Comp. Physiol. Psychol.,* 81:541–554.

Berntson, G. G. (1973): Attack, grooming and threat elicited by stimulation of the pontine tegmentum in cats. *Physiol. Behav.,* 11:81–87.

Blanchard, R. J., and Blanchard, D. C. (1968): Limbic lesions and reflexive fighting. *J. Comp. Physiol. Psychol.,* 68:603–605.

Brady, J. V., and Nauta, W. J. H. (1953): Subcortical mechanisms in emotional behavior: Affective changes following septal forebrain lesions in the albino rat. *J. Comp. Physiol. Psychol.,* 46:339–346.

Brody, E. B., and Rosvold, H. E. (1952): Influence of prefrontal lobotomy on social interaction in a monkey group. *Psychosom. Med.,* 16:406–415.

Cannon, W. B., and Britton, S. W. (1925): Studies on the conditions of activity in endocrine glands: XV. Pseudaffective medulliadrenal secretion. *Am. J. Physiol.,* 72:283–294.

Carli, G., Malliani, A., and Zanchetti, A. (1965): Lesioni selettive di varie strutture ipotalamiche E comportamento spontaneo E provacato de falsa rabbia del gatto decorticato acuto. *Boll. Soc. Ital. Biol. Sper.,* 42:291–294.

Carroll, M. N., and Lim, R. K. S. (1960): Observations on the neuropharmacology of morphine and morphinelike analgesia. *Arch. Int. Pharmacodyn. Ther.,* 125:383–403.

Chaurand, J. P., Schmitt, P. and Karli, P. (1973): Effets de lesions du tegmentum ventral du mesencephale sur le comportement d'agression Rat-Souris. *Physiol. Behavior,* 10:507–515.

Chi, C. C., and Flynn, J. P. (1971a): Neural pathways associated wtih hypothalamically elicited attack. *Science,* 171:817–818.

Chi, C. C., and Flynn, J. P. (1971b): Neuroanatomic projections related to biting attack elicited from hypothalamus in cats. *Brain Res.,* 35:49–66.

Coote, J. H., Hilton, S. M., and Zbrozyna, A. W. (1973): The pontomedullary area integrating the defense reaction in the cat and its influence on muscle blood flow. *J. Physiol. (Lond.),* 229:257–274.

Delgado, J. M. R., Roberts, W. W., and Miller, N. E. (1954): Learning motivated by electrical stimulation of the brain. *Am. J. Physiol.,* 179:587–593.

Eclancher, F., and Karli, P. (1971): Comportement d'agression interspecifique et comportement alimentaire du rat: Effets de lesions des noyaux ventromédians de l'hypothalamus. *Brain Res.,* 26:71–79.

Egger, M. D., and Flynn, J. P. (1963): Effects of electrical stimulation of the amygdala on hypothalamically elicited attack behavior in cats. *J. Neurophysiol.,* 26:705–720.

Eichelman, B. S. (1971): Effect of subcortical lesions on shock-induced aggression in the rat. *J. Comp. Physiol. Psychol.,* 74:331–339.

Ellison, G. D., and Flynn, J. P. (1968): Organized aggressive behavior in cats after surgical isolation of the hypothalamus. *Arch. Ital. Biol.,* 106:1–20.

Fernandez De Molina, A., and Hunsperger, R. W. (1959): Central representation of affective reactions in forebrain and brain stem: Electrical stimulation of amygdala, stria terminalis and adjacent structures. *J. Physiol. (Lond.),* 145:251–265.

Flynn, J. P. (1972): Patterning mechanisms, patterned reflexes and attack behavior in cats. In: *Nebraska Symposium on Motivation,* edited by J. K. Cole and D. D. Jensen. University of Nebraska Press, Lincoln.

Flynn, J. P., Edwards, S. B., and Bandler, R. J. (1971): Changes in sensory and motor systems during centrally elicited attack. *Behav. Sci.,* 16:1–19.

Flynn, J. P., Vanegas, H., Foote, W., and Edwards, S. (1970): Neural mechanisms involved in a cat's attack on a rat. In: *The Neural Control of Behavior,* edited by R. Whalen. Academic Press, New York.

Fonberg, E. (1973): The normalizing effect of lateral amygdalar lesions upon the dorsomedial amygdalar syndrome in dogs. *Acta Neurobiol. Exp.* 33:449–466.

Glendenning, K. K. (1972): Effects of septal and amygdaloid lesions on social behavior of the cat. *J. Comp. Physiol. Psychol.,* 80:199–207.

Glusman, M. (1974): The hypothalamic "savage" syndrome. In: *Aggression,* edited by S. H. Frazier. The Williams and Wilkins Co., Baltimore.

Glusman, M., Won, W., Burdock, E. I., and Ransohoff, J. (1962): Effects of midbrain lesions on "savage" behavior induced by hypothalamic lesions in the cat. *Trans. Am. Neurol. Assoc.,* 216–218.

Goltz, F. (1892): Der Hund ohne Grosshirn. *Pflugers Arch. Ges. Physiol.* Menschen Tiere, 51:570–614.

Hess, W. R. (1928): Stammanglien reizzversuch. 10. Tagung der Deutschen Physiologischen Gesellschaft in Frankfurt. *Berl. Ges. Physiol.* 42:554.

Hess, W. R., and Brugger, M. (1943): Das subkortikale Zentrum der affektiven Abwehrreaktion. *Helv. Physiol. Pharmacol. Acta,* 1:33–52.

Hinsey, J. C. (1939): The hypothalamus and somatic responses. *Proceedings of the Association for Research in Nervous and Mental Diseases,* 20:657–685.

Hunsperger, R. W. (1956): Affektreakionen auf elektrische Reizung in Hirnstamm der Katze. *Helv. Physiol. Pharmacol. Acta,* 14:70–92.

Hunter, J., and Jasper, H. H. (1949): Effects of thalamic stimulation in unanaesthetized animals. *Electroencephalogr. Clin. Neurophysiol.,* 1:305–324.

Hutchinson, R. R., and Renfrew, J. W. (1966): Stalking attack and eating behaviors elicited from the same sites in the hypothalamus. *J. Comp. Physiol. Psychol.,* 61:360–367.

Jacobs, B. L., and McGinty, D. J. (1972): Participation of the amygdala in complex stimulus recognition and behavioral inhibition. Evidence from unit studies. *Brain Res.,* 36:431–436.

Kabat, H., Anson, B. J., Magoun, H. W., and Ranson, S. W. (1935): Stimulation of the hypothalamus with special reference to its effect on gastro-intestinal motility. *Am. J. Physiol.,* 112:214–226.

Kaelber, W. W., Mitchell, C. L., and Way, J. S. (1965): Some sensory influences on savage behavior in cats. *Am. J. Physiol.,* 209:866–870.

Karli, P. (1956–1957): The Norway rat's killing response to the white mouse: An experimental analysis. *Behaviour,* 10:81–103.

Karli, P., and Vergnes, M. (1964): Dissociation experimentale du comportement d' agression interspecifique rat-souris et du comportement alimentaire. *C. R. Soc. Biol.,* 158:650–653.

Klüver, H., and Bucy, P. C. (1939): Preliminary analysis of functions of the temporal lobes in monkeys. *Arch. Neurol. Psychiatry,* 42:979–1000.

Levison, P. K., and Flynn, J. P. (1965): The objects attacked by cats during stimulation of the hypothalamus. *Anim. Behav.,* 13:217–220.

Leyhausen, P. (1956): *Verhaltensstudien an Katzen.* Paul Parey, Berlin.

MacDonnell, M., and Flynn, J. P. (1964): Attack elicited by stimulation of the thalamus in cats. *Science,* 144:1249–1250.

MacDonnell, M. F., and Flynn, J. P. (1968): Attack elicited by stimulation of the thalamus and adjacent structures of cats. *Behaviour,* 31:185–202.

Magoun, H. W., Atlas, D., Ingersoll, E. H., and Ranson, S. W. (1936–1937): Associated facial, vocal and respiratory components of emotional expression: An experimental study. *J. Neurol. Psychopathol.,* 17:241–255.

Marshall, J. F., and Teitelbaum, P. (1974): Further analysis of sensory inattention following lateral hypothalamic damage in rats. *J. Comp. Physiol. Psychol.,* 86:375–395.

Masserman, J. H. (1938): Destruction of the hypothalamus in cats. Effects on activity of the central nervous system and its reaction to sodium amytal. *Arch. Neurol. Psychiatry,* 39:1250–1271.

Miczek, K. A., and Grossman, S. P. (1972): Effects of septal lesions on inter- and intra-species aggression in rats. *J. Comp. Physiol. Psychol.,* 79:37–45.

Myer, J. S., and White, R. J. (1965): Aggressive motivation in the rat. *Anim. Behav.,* 13:430–433.

Nakao, H. (1958): Emotional behavior produced by hypothalamic stimulation. *Am J. Physiol.,* 104:411–418.

Naquet, R. (1954): Effects of stimulation of the rhinencephalon in the waking cat. *Electroencephalgr. Clin. Neurophysiol.,* 6:711–712.

O'Keefe, J., and Bouma, H. (1969): Complex sensory properties of certain amygdala units in the freely moving cat. *Exp. Neurol.,* 23:384–398.

Panksepp, J. (1970): Aggression elicited by electrical stimulation of the hypothalamus in albino rat. *Physiol. Behav.,* 6:321–329.

Panksepp, J., and Trowill, J. (1969): Electrically induced affective attack from the hypothalamus of the albino rat. *Psychonomic Sci.,* 16:118–119.

Paul, L. (1972): Predatory attack by rats, its relationship to feeding and type of prey. *J. Comp. Physiol. Psychol.,* 78:69–76.

Pechtel, C., Masserman, J. H., Schreiner, L., and Levitt, M. (1955): Differential effects of lesions of the mediodorsal nuclei of the thalamus on normal and neurotic behavior in the cat. *J. Nerv. Ment. Dis.,* 121:26–33.

Plotnik, R., Mir, D., and Delgado, J. M. R. (1971): Aggression, noxiousness and brain stimulation in unrestrained rhesus monkeys. In: *The Physiology of Aggression and Defeat,* edited by J. P. Scott and B. E. Eleftheriou. Plenum Press, New York.

Proshansky, E., Bandler, R. J., and Flynn, J. P. (1974): Elimination of hypothalamically elicited biting attack by unilateral lesion of the ventral midbrain tegmentum of cats. *Brain Res.,* 77:309–313.

Randall, W. L. (1964): The behavior of cats with lesions in the caudal midbrain region. *Behaviour,* 23:107–139.

Ranson, S. (1936–1937): Some functions of the hypothalamus. *Harvey Lect.,* 32:93–121.

Ranson, S. W. (1939): Somnolence caused by hypothalamic lesions in the monkey. *Arch. Neurol. Psychiatry,* 41:1–23.

Reis, D. J., Doba, N., and Nathan, M. A. (1973): Predatory attack grooming and consummatory behaviors evoked by electrical stimulation of cat cerebellar nuclei. *Science,* 82:845–847.

Roberts, W. W., Steinberg, M. L., and Means, L. W. (1967): Hypothalamic mechanisms for sexual, aggressive and other motivational behaviors in the opossum, *Didelphis Virginiana. J. Comp. Physiol. Psychol.,* 64:1–15.

Robinson, B. W., Alexander, M., and Bowne, G. (1969): Dominance reversal resulting from aggressive responses evoked by brain telestimulation. *Physiol. Behav.,* 4:749–752.

Rothfield, L., and Harman, P. J. (1954): On the relation of the hippocampal-fornix system to the control of rage responses in cats. *J. Comp. Neurol.,* 101:265–281.

Schreiner, L., and Kling, A. (1953): Behavioral changes following rhinencephalic injury in cat. *J. Neurophysiol.,* 16:643–659.

Schreiner, L., Rioch, D. McK., Pechtel, C., and Masserman, J. H. (1952): Behavioral changes following thalamic injury in cat. *J. Neurophysiol.* 16:234–246.

Shealy, C. N., and Peele, T. L. (1957): Studies on amygdaloid nucleus of cat. *J. Neurophysiol.,* 20:121–139.

Sheard, M., and Flynn, J. P. (1967): Facilitation of attack by stimulation of the midbrain of cats. *Brain Res.,* 27:165–182.

Siegel, A., and Chabora, J. (1971): Effects of electrical stimulation of the cingulate gyrus upon attack behavior elicited from the hypothalamus in the cat. *Brain Res.,* 32:169–177.

Siegel, A., and Flynn, J. P. (1968): Differential effects of electrical stimulation and lesions of the hippocampus and adjacent regions upon attack behavior in cats. *Brain Res.,* 7:252–267.

Siegel, A., and Skog, D. (1970): Effects of electrical stimulation of the septum upon attack behavior elicited from the hypothalamus in the cat. *Brain Res.,* 23:371–380.

Skultety, F. M. (1963): Stimulation of periaqueductal gray and hypothalamus. *Arch. Neurol.,* 8:608–620.

Skultety, M. (1965): The effects of lateral midbrain lesions on evoked behavioral responses. *Neurology,* 15:438–443.

Slotnick, B. M., and McMullen, M. F. (1972): Intraspecific fighting in albino mice with septal forebrain lesions. *Physiol. Behav.,* 8:333–337.

Sodetz, F. J., Matalka, E. S., and Bunnell, B. N. (1967): Septal ablation and affective behavior in the golden hamster. *Psychonomic Sci.,* 7:189–190.

Sprague, J. M., Levitt, M., Robson, K., Liu, C. N., Stellar, E., and Chambers, W. W. (1963): A neuroanatomical and behavioral analysis of the syndromes resulting from midbrain lemniscal and reticular lesions in the cat. *Arch. Ital. Biol.*, 101:225–294.

Turner, B. H. (1973): Sensorimotor syndrome produced by lesions of the amygdala and lateral hypothalamus. *J. Comp. Physiol. Psychol.*, 82:34–47.

Turner, S. G., Sechzer, J. A., and Liebelt, R. A. (1967): Sensitivity to electrical shock after ventromedial hypothalamic lesions. *Exp. Neurol.*, 19:236–244.

Ursin, H., and Kaada, B. R. (1960): Functional localization within the amygdaloid complex in the cat. *Electroencephalogr. Clin. Neurophysiol.*, 12:1–20.

Wang, G. K., and Akert, K. (1962): Behavior and reflexes of chronic striatal cats. *Arch. Ital. Biol.*, 100:48–85.

Wasman, M., and Flynn, J. P. (1962): Directed attack elicited from hypothalamus. *Arch. Neurol.*, 6:220–227.

Wheatley, M. D. (1944): The hypothalamus and affective behavior in cats: A study of the effects of experimental lesions with anatomic connections. *Arch. Neurol. Psychiatry*, 52:296–316.

Woods, J. W. (1964): Behavior of chronic decerebrate rats. *J. Neurophysiol.*, 27:635–644.

Woodworth, C. (1970): Attack elicited in rats by electrical stimulation of the lateral hypothalamus. *Physiol. Behav.*, 6:345–353.

Woodworth, R. S., and Sherrington, C. S. (1904): A pseudaffective reflex and its spinal path. *J. Physiol. (Lond.)*, 31:234–243.

Zbrozyna, A. W. (1972): The organization of the defence reaction elicited from amygdala and its connections. In: *The Neurobiology of the Amygdala,* edited by B. E. Eleftheriou. Plenum Press, New York.

Biological Foundations of Psychiatry,
edited by R. G. Grenell and S. Gabay.
Raven Press, New York © 1976.

Hunger and Thirst

J. A. Deutsch and *H. S. Koopmans

*Department of Psychology, University of California, San Diego, La Jolla, California 92037, and
Department of Psychology, Columbia University, New York, New York 10027

I. INTRODUCTION

In this chapter we review the physiological bases of hunger and thirst, paying special attention to the events that bring about the onset and offset of eating and drinking. An animal is able to regulate his intake of food and water in a surprisingly accurate manner. Accordingly, we shall focus our attention on the investigation of the mechanisms which enable such regulation to take place.

II. THE INITIATING PHYSIOLOGICAL CHANGES IN THIRST

There are two general changes which can lead to drinking. The body may either have too little water in it altogether, or the tonicity of the body fluids may be too high. The first type, which is due to a diminution of the total amount of body fluid, is called volemic thirst. The second type, called osmotic thirst, appears to be the more common cause of drinking. When an animal is osmotically thirsty, it prefers to drink a fluid which has a much lower tonicity like water or hypotonic saline. The animal is thereby capable of diluting the body fluids. Let us deal first with osmotic thirst.

Osmotic thirst may arise when there is no decrease in the total body volume of water. For instance, injection of hypertonic saline will give rise to strong thirst. However, osmotic thirst is not merely a reaction to the hypertonicity of the whole body system. It is caused by the withdrawal of water from inside the body cells, and into the extracellular space. This is shown clearly by Gilman (1937) who produced equal increases of osmotic pressure in dogs by injecting either urea or sodium chloride. Drinking was greater after saline injections than after urea injections. This is because urea passes easily through cell membranes, whereas sodium chloride does not. Therefore, after injecting urea there would be very little alteration in the osmotic pressure gradient between the intra- and extracellular fluid compartments. In contrast, there is a large change in the gradient after an injection of sodium chloride. The sodium chloride withdraws water from inside the cells into the extracellular fluid until the osmotic pressure inside and outside the cell is more nearly equal. This cellular dehydration causes thirst.

Turning now to volemic thirst, it has been found that blood loss in rats induces drinking (Fitzsimmons, 1961). However, the onset of drinking as a result of bleeding is quite delayed as compared to the case of thirst induced by injection of sodium chloride. In the case of sodium chloride, the onset of drinking is almost immediate. However, the onset of drinking as a result of bleeding is delayed by at least a half hour. This suggests that volemic thirst has first to be translated into biochemical changes at the peripheral level before it has an effect on central neural mechanisms which in turn translate it into drinking behavior. When fluid volume of the vascular fluid inside the animal is decreased, there is a reduction in the local blood flow in the kidney. When such a reduction occurs, the kidney releases renin and renin acts on a substance in the blood to produce angiotensin. Injections of angiotensin into the central nervous system produces drinking. When rats are given a choice between water and isotonic saline when they suffer from volemic thirst, they prefer isotonic saline (Smith and Stricker, 1969). Isotonic saline is a better replacement for blood than water.

III. THE INITIATING CHANGE IN HUNGER

In contrast to the case of thirst, the nature of initiating change in hunger remains obscure. However, although there is no firm evidence about the change itself, there are some theories that have been proposed. The three most prominent theories are the thermostatic theory of Brobeck, the glucostatic theory of Mayer, and the lipostatic theory of Kennedy. The thermostatic theory (Brobeck, 1948) proposed that animals start eating to prevent hypothermia and stop eating to prevent hyperthermia. Body temperature rises after the ingestion of food, but the amount of rise differs depending on the food constituents. This tendency to produce the rise in temperature is called the specific dynamic action of food. Supporting this theory is the fact that eating is reduced by subjecting the animal to high temperatures, and increased by exposing the animal to low temperatures. However, Kennedy (1953) points out that the fat diet has a low specific dynamic action, lower than protein, whereas fat is more satiating than protein. Therefore, on the thermostatic theory animals fed on a fat diet should become obese but this is not the case. Moreover, direct measurements show that there is no change in brain temperature following the injection of liquid diet into the stomach (Koopmans, *unpublished observation*). Apparently, the increase in brain temperature following the ingestion of solid food is caused by the activity of feeding. The second theory, called the glucostatic theory (Mayer, 1953), proposes that hunger occurs when glucose is unavailable for metabolic purposes, and satiation supervenes when glucose is made available. A proposed measure of such availability is the arteriovenous (A-V) glucose difference. The tissues are not taking up any glucose en route between the arteries and the veins when there is no difference between the arterial and venous glucose content. The available glucose is therefore zero. If, on the other hand, there is a large A-V difference, this must be due to the fact that glucose is being taken up by the tissues. Correlations between A-V glucose differences and hunger have been measured by Stunkard, Van Itallie, and Reis (1955). On the other hand, a number of studies have shown that injection of glucose into the bloodstream does not affect satiety (Yin and Tsai, 1973). Koopmans (*unpublished doctoral dissertation*) has demonstrated A-V differences in rats that remain hungry. Although the glucostatic theory may be wrong, it does seem that some aspect of glucose metabolism is important in the initiation of hunger. 2-Deoxy-*d*-glucose is a specific inhibitor of glucose utilization inside the cell. Injection of 2-deoxy-*d*-glucose increases the food intake in a number of different species. Novin, Vanderweele, and Rezek (1972) have shown that 2-deoxy-*d*-glucose can produce feeding by affecting glucoreceptors in the liver. 2-Deoxy-*d*-glucose injected into the rabbit's portal vein produces relatively quick initiation of large meals. The effect appears to be mediated by the vagus nerve since vagotomy reduces the increase in feeding to the level found when 2-deoxy-*d*-glucose is injected systemically (Smith and Epstein, 1970; Houpt and Hance, 1971).

The third theory is the lipostatic theory of Kennedy (1953). He suggested that an animal is in some way able to monitor the overall fat stored in its body, perhaps through alterations in blood content as its fat depots enlarge. Although there is little direct evidence to support this theory, it is attractive because some explanation must be given for the fact that an animal is capable of long-term regulation of its weight in a very accurate manner, and this would be difficult to explain on the thermostatic and glucostatic theories alone. For instance, it has been shown that rats which have been artifically fattened lose weight quickly and soon reach their previous size when they are allowed to eat without any interference.

IV. THE LOCUS OF ACTION OF THE CHANGES
INITIATING THIRST AND HUNGER

It was once a popular view that changes occurring in hunger and thirst acted first on peripheral tissue and that the changes occurring in peripheral tissue were then relayed by neural pathways to the central nervous system. However, the notion that hunger contractions lead to hunger or that dryness of the throat leads to thirst have now been discredited. (For a review, see Deutsch and Deutsch, 1973.) In the case of hunger, we are not sure what the initiating changes are. Therefore, it is difficult to know where they act. From the experiments with 2-deoxy-d-glucose (summarized above; Novin et al., 1972) the locus of action could be the liver. It seems as if the physiological changes initiating osmotic thirst act directly on circumscribed sites in the central nervous system. For instance, microinjections of amounts of sodium chloride, too small to produce any behavioral change when injected peripherally, cause vigorous drinking when injected into the hypothalamus of laboratory animals. Such manipulations produce the normal desire or drive for water rather than some automatic and specialized act of drinking. An injection of small quantities of sodium chloride (Miller, 1961) caused cats to form a learned response of working for water, and an injection of distilled water reduced responding in a previously thirsty cat. Similarly, Herberg (1962) showed that when rats were given a minute injection of hypertonic saline into the lateral ventricle, they almost immediately learned to rush to the spout of a water bottle for a drink. These results show that there are structures in the hypothalamus highly sensitive to changes in osmotic pressure, and that these structures are connected to other neural structures which produce the behavioral onset and maintenance of drinking. Electrical stimulation of some loci in the hypothalamus can also cause drinking, and lesions of such loci produce animals which do not regulate their fluid intake and simply refuse to drink water. However, such animals are perfectly capable of the act of drinking, as is shown by the fact that they will drink nutrient fluids such as broth quite freely. A third type of supporting evidence is provided by chemical stimulation of areas in the hypothalamus. For instance, minute injections of carbachol, a cholinomimetic, into the preoptic area of the hypothalamus have been shown by Quartermain and Miller (1966) to produce drinking in rats. However, if the rats so injected are not given immediate access to water, they remain thirsty even if access to water is delayed up to at least 60 min. Such carbachol-induced thirst persists only if drinking is not allowed to occur. This suggests that carbachol-induced thirst is satiated in a similar way to normal thirst. Pharmacologically induced drinking also produces thirst drive as normally conceived. Rats learn, remember, and extinguish in the same way under cholinergic brain stimulation when running through a maze for a reward of water and when they are deprived (Khavari and Russell, 1966). Drinking in rats is also produced by implants of carbachol in the septal region and nucleus of the thalamus, the cingulate gyrus, and the lateral hypothalamus (Fisher and Coury, 1962). However, it is not clear whether such pharmacological stimulation is not in fact due to spread of drug through the nervous system through vascular or ventricular systems, and this has in fact been shown to be the case at least in some instances by

Routtenberg (1965). It should be borne in mind that stimulation of drinking by pharmacological or electrical means does not show the locus of the initiating change in thirst. Stimulation with small amounts of hypertonic saline solution forms better evidence though it is not entirely certain that a solution acts on the center which actually translates hypertonicity of the body fluids into neural activity. There is a chance that such hypertonic fluid stimulates pathways or neural systems that are relatively nonspecific and that simply carry messages from a center which is sensitive to body fluid hypertonicity. The same argument can of course be made when we consider the effect of electrical stimulation. In the case of electrical stimulation we have no guarantee at all that we are activating the center which is sensitive to body fluid osmotic pressure. It is equally likely in such a case that simply stimulating systems that carry information from such a center to other neural structures initiates drinking activity. In fact, there is good evidence that many of the electrodes which stimulate drinking are actually stimulating axonal systems. Hu (1973) and Hawkins (1974) have obtained results which strongly suggest that the electrode which produces drinking and eating upon having an electrical stimulus pass through it is stimulating the axonal processes of neurons rather than the cell bodies themselves.

Stimulation by pulse pairs produces behavior that indicates the presence of refractory periods typical of axons. The behavioral results are not consistent with the supposition that cell bodies are being stimulated. Therefore, we have to conclude that electrical stimulation at a locus which produces a given type of behavior does not necessarily produce it by stimulating the cells which initiate that type of behavior in the central nervous system, but can often stimulate tissue which simply acts as a conduit for a message that travels from one locus to another. Somewhat more convincing evidence about the locus of initiation of the change which leads to drinking has been obtained by Novin and Durham (1969). The activity of single cells and DC changes in the supraoptic nucleus of the hypothalamus was recorded. When hypertonic solutions were injected through the carotid artery excitation was observed in many of the cells in that nucleus. Other cells, however, showed inhibition. A negative shift in DC potential was also seen. When this area was isolated from the rest of the brain by cutting around it, this DC shift was not abolished. From this evidence, Novin and Durham conclude that this DC shift is a generator potential (such as is present in sense receptors) and that it is this change in potential which is translated into action potentials, and that these action potentials then signal thirst to the rest of the central nervous system.

An effort has recently been made to identify the neural locus of volemic as distinct from osmotic thirst. For instance, Blass (1968) completely destroyed the front portion of the rat's brain. Such destruction included the olfactory lobes and the frontal portion of the cortex and also some of the septal nuclei, caudate nucleus, globus pallidus, and preoptic area. When rats with such a lesion are injected with polyethylene glycol, intravascular volume is reduced but cellular dehydration does not occur. Such a reduction of intracellular volume in these rats produces the same reaction in the latency of drinking and in the total amount drunk as occurs in nonlesioned rats. However, when osmotic thirst was induced by the injection of a hypertonic sodium chloride solution there was a large difference between the lesioned rats and normal controls. The lesioned rats took much longer to begin drinking and drank much less in total volume. Further, in another experiment (Blass and Hanson, 1970) it was demonstrated that the exaggerated thirst after lesions of the septal nuclei (first described by Harvey and Hunt in 1965) is a disorder of the regulatory mechanism for hypovolemic thirst. When osmotic thirst was produced by an injection of a sodium chloride solution, septally lesioned animals increased their drinking in the same way as nonlesioned controls. When, however, polyethylene glycol was injected (and this reduces intravascular volume, thus producing volemic thirst) the lesioned rats drank much more than the controls in response to this manipulation. Lesions in the rat's hypothalamus abolished thirst in response to a decrease in intravascular fluid volume, and this suggests that at least some of the neural pathways associated with such volemic regulations pass through this part of the hypothalamus (Wolf and Stricker, 1967). As we saw above, volemic thirst is signalled by angiotensin.

Simpson and Routtenberg (1973) questioned the importance of the hypothalamus in initiating angiotensin-produced thirst. They had previously located the carbachol-stimulating action of thirst in the subfornical organ, a small tissue present on the roof of the third ventricle. By applying very low doses of angiotensin to the subfornical organ, they elicited drinking in water-sated rats. When the subfornical organ was destroyed, injections of angiotensin in various hypothalamic structures were without effect. The study explained how a polypeptide-like angiotensin which crosses the blood-brain barrier slowly could affect drinking behavior. The subfornical organ lies outside the blood-brain barrier and requires very small doses to produce drinking. It seems that the central nervous receptors for both osmotic and volemic thirst lie in the subfornical organ.

V. HUNGER

While various manipulations of the central nervous system have shown that drinking can be provoked by small changes in central nervous structures, no one has been able to demonstrate that a sensory area (a transducer) that controls eating is actually located in the central nervous system. This is due to the fact that we do not know what the physical state is that an animal responds to behaviorally when it eats. In the case of osmotic thirst, it seems likely that the transducer which translates hypertonicity of extracellular fluids exists somewhere in the central nervous system because we can inject very tiny amounts of hypertonic solution into the central nervous system loci to produce thirst. As is stated above, we do not as yet know what the physiological state is which produces hunger. Therefore we cannot be sure that such physiological states actually act directly on the nervous system or on some peripheral receptor. The three types of intervention which have been successful in producing changes in food intake are lesion experiments, electrical stimulation experiments, and pharmacological stimulation of the nervous system tissue. Let us begin with the evidence from lesions. It has been found by Anand and his co-workers (Anand, 1951; Anand and Brobeck, 1951; Anand, Ova, and Shoenberg, 1961) that bilateral extirpation of the lateral region of the hypothalamus produces aphagia. An animal with such lesion will not eat even though it is wasting away in the midst of a plentiful food supply. Williams and Teitelbaum (1959) also found that animals with this lesion had an aversion to drinking. A normal rat can be taught to hydrate itself by pumping water directly into its own stomach. Epstein (1960) found that rats with lateral hypothalamic lesions did not learn this procedure even though their learning ability was unimpaired. It is therefore possible that an animal may not eat simply because it will not drink, for if it is in a state of osmotic imbalance it will not get hungry. That the effects of lateral hypothalamic lesions is complicated is suggested by an experiment reported by Devenport and Balagura (1971). Rats that recovered from lateral hypothalamic lesions, although incompletely, and which maintained their weight voluntarily at 70% of normal, displayed greatly enhanced food-motivated behavior. In spite of the fact that they eat much less than normal animals, such animals begin eating almost five times as fast as normal controls after a 21 hr fast in both a novel and familiar environment. They also show much faster learning than normals in a Y-maze for a food reward after undergoing a 36 hr period of deprivation.

A second method of modifying activity in the central nervous system is to stimulate the central nervous tissue. If the lateral hypothalamic area is stimulated electrically, eating is produced in a satiated animal almost instantaneously. When the electrical stimulation starts, the animal begins to eat. The animal also stops eating as soon as the electrical stimulation is switched off. Wyrwicka, Dobrzecka, and Tarnecki (1959) have shown that such electrical stimulation in an animal does not simply produce some automatic act of eating, but will also motivate food-seeking habits which were previously learned when the animal was hungry. Similarly, Coons, Levak, and Miller (1965) have shown that it is possible to teach animals to press a lever in order to obtain food to satiate a craving produced by the electrical stimulation of the lateral hypothalamus. It seems then that lateral hypothalamic stimulation produces what one would want to call the state of hunger rather than simply isolated acts of feeding. However, there are cases in which electrical stimulation of the central nervous system does produce acts of eating rather than a state of hunger in the animal. For instance, Harwood and Vowles

(1966) stimulated the forebrain of the ringdove through an implanted electrode. The stimulation brought about pecking and eating directed at food and not toward nonnutritious objects such as feces or grit. However, such stimulation did not evoke the performance of habits to obtain food which had been previously learned by the ringdoves under food deprivation. The second interesting point is that such forebrain stimulation did not increase the rate of pecking to obtain a food reward on a schedule which gives only intermittent reward. Ringdoves, whose hunger is increased by food deprivation, speed up their rate of key pecking when only a certain proportion of responses are rewarded. Forebrain stimulation of the ringdove therefore seems to elicit no real hunger but only certain isolated components of feeding behavior. Returning again to the mammal, eating has been evoked by the stimulation of other central nervous system loci besides the lateral hypothalamus. Experimenting with rhesus monkeys, Robinson and Mishkin (1962) found that in a small percentage of the animals, they were able to induce eating by the stimulation of such areas as the anterior cingulate gyrus and the midline thalamus. Further, Wyrwicka and Doty (1966) evoked feeding from electrical stimulation from the fibers in the globus pallidus passing to the lateral hypothalamus. From the lateral hypothalamus such fibers then travel to the ventrolateral boundary of the central gray. Feeding could be elicited by electrical stimulation from parts of all these structures.

A third type of manipulation which has produced eating by stimulation of the central nervous system tissue is pharmacological. Grossman (1960) injected minute amounts of carbachol into the lateral hypothalamus through an implanted hypodermic needle and was able to produce drinking. When he injected epinephrine or norepinephrine, he would produce an increase in eating. Miller (1965) confirmed the notion that an adrenergic system is involved in eating where the cholinergic system is involved in drinking by the use of other pharmacological agents. However, the significance of these findings must be carefully assessed. Simpson and Routtenberg (1973) have been able to show that these effects of increased eating or drinking do not occur if the subfornical organ is removed.

VI. THE REGULATORY SYSTEM IN HUNGER AND THIRST

Eating and drinking are homeostatic functions. During eating or drinking the organism maintains certain parameters of the body's functioning within certain limits. For instance, it is evident that by eating the animal maintains a certain body weight not deviating from such a weight over a long time to any significant extent in the vast majority of cases. Similarly, by drinking, the animal maintains the tonicity of the bodily fluids within very close tolerance due to the functioning of osmotic thirst. We may therefore inquire about the general nature of the regulatory mechanism present in hunger and thirst. Such inquiry is not a mere academic pasttime, nor is it a classification just for the sake of it. It is a useful inquiry, because if we can determine the type of regulatory mechanism that is present, we can then begin to look for the actual physical counterpart to the abstract scheme that we know must be operating to produce the type of behavior present.

One of the earliest ideas about the type of homeostatic mechanism in hunger and thirst was that suggested by C. L. Hull. He assumed that when drive—of which hunger and thirst are instances—acts on an organism the physiological state generates stimuli which in turn evokes relevant responses, e.g., drinking in response to the stimuli of thirst. As such responses continue to be made, they will, in time, reverse the change that provoked them with the consequence that the organism stops eating or drinking, whichever the case may be. One of the salient predictions from this model is that eating or drinking should continue while the afferent stimuli generated by the drive state continues. Such a regulatory mechanism is, in fact, possible. It is a mechanism that is employed in simple regulatory devices such as thermostats. In the case of the thermostat, when the temperature of the environment falls below a certain point, this somehow switches on a heater. As the heater increases temperature around the thermometer, the thermometer falls and the heater is switched off. It is obvious that in this case we only have to look for the initiating change and the detector transducer which signals this change. However, it seems that in the case of the animal the system employed to regulate eating or drinking is somewhat more complicated. Common observation would suggest that we stop eating or drinking long before physiological change, which initiates eating or drinking, has been reversed. Processes of digestion, for instance, take quite a while and whatever it is that sets eating in motion cannot have been reversed by the time the animal stops eating. [Although it is true that the bulk of the food eaten is not completely digested for many hours, some food gets absorbed from the intestines minutes after feeding has begun. This is true of a rat eating lab chow (Steffens, 1969). Because the intestines have a self-regulating feedback loop, through intestinal hormones, the amount of food eaten is measured by the rate of absorption, and that could be monitored immediately after feeding.]

However, more sophisticated evidence about the mechanism can be obtained by actual experiments on laboratory animals. Let us begin with the case of thirst. One method of finding out whether animals stop drinking before the deficit which instigated their drinking is replenished is to compare the time an animal normally takes to drink with the time it takes for the physiological initiating change to be reversed. Such a reversal of the initiating change can be most directly assessed by placing water directly into the animal's stomach. This is the preload technique. At various time intervals after the water has been placed into the animal's stomach, water is offered to the animal to drink. If the time it takes to stop drinking after a preload is longer than the time the animal normally spends in drinking, we can conclude that drinking, when there has been no preload and the animal drinks normally, is not due to the absorption of water by the system. It has been shown by Bellows (1939) that a dog can drink just over 10% of its body weight in 4 min, and that it takes 15 min after a preload of about 8% of body weight placed in the dog's stomach before drinking is suppressed. This would indicate that drinking stops long before the initiating physiological change is reversed.

However, not all experimenters have obtained this same result, e.g., Towbin (1949). It seems likely in Towbin's experiment that the more rapid suppression of drinking was caused by sensations of discomfort induced by too rapid an injection of water into the stomach. He obtained similar results of immediate inhibition of drinking by injecting air into the stomach or by inflating a balloon in the stomach. Unfortunately, when substances are placed in the stomach and satiation is assessed, we may be dealing with a loss of appetite rather than true satiation. That this is sometimes the case has been shown in an excellent experiment by Miller and Kessen (1954). In their experiment, rats were given the choice between two goal boxes of a T-maze. A balloon was inflated in their stomach in one goal box. Although this apparently satiated them in the sense that they were less ready to eat food, they nevertheless learned to avoid the goal box in which the balloon was inflated in their stomachs. These results demonstrate clearly that an apparent satiation can actually be caused by discomfort or nausea.

Another method for assessing whether the reversal of osmotic thirst is the factor that shuts off drinking is to use a preparation in which drinking can occur without its normal physiological consequences. Such a preparation involves the use of an esophageal fistula. In this preparation the esophagus is transected before it reaches the stomach and its two cut ends are externalized. With this preparation, water taken in by mouth emerges through the upper opening in the esophagus and fails to reach the stomach. The problem with such a preparation is to decide how much the dog would have drunk normally. All researchers seem to agree that drinking in such an animal does stop. However, the extent of drinking is variously estimated. Some, such as Towbin (1949), estimate that there is overdrinking up to 250% when the esophagus is transected. Others, such as Adolph (1941), conclude that the amount drunk under such conditions is almost equal or identical to the physiological deficit. Whatever the upshot of the controversy, it does seem that drinking stops in spite of no change in the initiating deficit which led to drinking in the first instance.

Another way of trying to assess the effect of drinking on reversal of physiological state to avoid some of the problems associated with preloads or esophageal fistulae has been devised by Deutsch and Blumen (1962). A tube was implanted in the animal's stomach and as the animal was given water to drink, an amount of hypertonic saline proportional to its drinking was pumped into the animal's stomach such that as the animal was drinking, concentrated salt water was pumped into the rat's stomach, producing an isotonic water load. In this way, while the animal drank water normally, the normal physiological consequences of drinking water could not be produced; it could be assumed that the initiating deficit of thirst had not been reversed by the ingestion of water. Under such circumstances, it was found that the animal would stop drinking normally in the way that a normal animal stops drinking. In fact, it was possible to test the animal with such a stomach tube under conditions in which hypertonic saline was being pumped into its stomach simultaneously to drinking, and under conditions in which no such injections were taking place so that comparison was possible in the very same animal. Under these circumstances, it emerges that even though the deficit that initiates drinking is not reversed, drinking stops at the same time as when such a deficit is being reversed. However, drinking soon recurs because the physiological deficit is not reversed. The inhibition of drinking that results simply from the ingestion of water through the mouth tends to suppress drinking in the absense of the reversal of the initiating change only for approximately 10 to 15 min. After that, the animal will resume drinking. It appears, then, that factors arising from the act of drinking itself (presumably from the taste and other sensations arising from the swallowing of water) do have an inhibiting effect on the tendency to drink even though the change which initiated the drinking is still present. Let us now look at the evidence for hunger.

Experiments similar to those described above have been carried out in the study of hunger. But here the results have been different. Food placed directly in the stomach (Kohn, 1951; Berkun, Kessen, and Miller, 1952) produced almost immediate satiation even though precautions were taken to prevent discomfort or nausea. Kohn (1951) measured the rate of responding in a Skinner box in response to hunger. Stomach injections of food depressed the rate of lever pressing in this apparatus. Berkun et al. (1952) measured the amount of food actually eaten by rats after food had been placed in the stomach. There was a decrease in eating. It is unlikely that the digestion of the bulk of the inserted food had taken place to a significant extent in the time allowed. Carrying this line of research further, Smith and Duffy (1955) attempted to discover what the factors were that led to a suppression of eating through direct injection into the stomach. They found that sheer bulk had no effect on the rate of responding in a Skinner box. This showed that both the stimulation by bulk and the method of injection did not affect food intake. However, when different amounts of nutrients were placed in the stomach, they found that the rate of lever pressing did decline quite swiftly after injection of the nutrient bulk. They also found that when the bulk was nutrient the depressive effect on the rate of lever pressing was approximately linear with respect to quantity. In view of this evidence, it can be strongly argued that the satiation of eating is not caused by reversal of the change that acts on the central nervous system, because digestion of the total food mass occurs more slowly than can be expected from the above experiment.

Experiments have also been carried out with the technique of esophageal fistulation. Most researchers have found that their animals overeat extensively. Hull, Livingston, Rouse, and Barker (1951) used a 10-kg dog in a study carefully controlled for psychological factors. They found that when the dog was allowed to eat freely with open esophageal fistula, he ate 8 kg of food before stopping for 5 min. Such cessation of eating was probably not due to normal satiation but to sheer exhaustion. It is stated that the dog showed violent, nervous shaking when he finally stopped eating. In contrast with the case of thirst, the effect of swallowing food when it does not reach the stomach does not seem to be strong enough to make the dog stop eating. This finding, of course, is quite consistent with the notion that eating would continue until digestion of the food took place which is in accordance with Hull's simple model. However, such a model is contradicted by the finding that placing food in the stomach inhibits eating before digestion can take place. Using this type of evidence, it has been suggested by Deutsch (1953 and 1960) and Stellar (1954) that satiation in hunger and thirst is normally produced by afferent messages due to sensations produced by eating and drinking, and it is thought that these messages inhibit centers which are sensitive to the initiating change so that initiating change can no longer produce the activity which started eating or drinking. This theory would assume that the afferent activity generated in drinking originates in taste receptors in the mouth and perhaps in other receptors which are stimulated simultaneously when the act of swallowing takes place. On the other hand, in hunger it would be assumed that such afferent messages originate not in the mouth or throat but only in the stomach or the upper intestinal tract. The theory therefore assumes that the amount eaten or drunk will not simply be a function of the amount of excitation of the initiating central structure by the physiological factors typical of hunger or thirst, but also a function of the amount of signal fed back produced by the quality and quantity of water or food ingested. Given a certain level of excitation in the centers sensitive to physiological changes in hunger and thirst, the greater the amount of specific afferent stimulation per unit of time, the more quickly these centers will be rendered temporarily unexcitable. On the other hand, given a fixed amount of afferent stimulation per unit of time, the greater the excitement of the centers generated by the physiological changes, the longer the activity will last because it will take a longer time for such centers to be desensitized.

As was described previously, messages from the mouth and throat play a substantial role in producing a cessation of drinking. It seems plausible to believe that satiation of thirst is produced initially by some combination of taste and proprioceptive messages which occur when the animal drinks. A possible glimpse of how such messages operate can be gained from considering the phenomenon of the overdrinking of hypotonic saline. It has been known for a long time that hypotonic saline is drunk in large quantity when the animal is thirsty. This overdrinking of saline increases with the concentration of the saline solution up to the point where this solution is isotonic and such overdrinking occurs even when water is freely available at the same time as the saline (Nelson, 1947; Bare, 1949; Young, 1949; Randoin, Causeret, and Gabrel-Szymanski, 1950). Of course, hypotonic saline is less efficient in reversing the hypertonicity of the extracellular fluids which leads to osmotic thirst. However, it is unlikely that it is the postingestional qualities of such hypotonic saline that cause its overdrinking. Stellar and McCleary (1952) and Mook (1963) found that hypertonic saline was drunk to a greater extent than water using animals with esophageal fistulae (so that the ingested fluid did not reach the stomach). Hence, it appears that there is some afferent signal that controls overdrinking. It is possible, of course, that the animal prefers the taste of saline to that of water. The factor of preference is known to operate when the animal drinks sweet solutions. However, such a factor of preference seems unlikely to operate in the case in hypotonic saline. Deutsch and Jones (1959 and 1960) placed rats in a T-maze so that when they were thirsty they had to choose between equal volumes of water and hypotonic saline. Had there been a true preference for the taste of hypotonic saline, the rats should have learned to run to the hypotonic saline. If, on the other hand, it appeared to the rats that the hypotonic saline was less satiating, and therefore less thirst quenching, they should have learned to seek out the water. The rats learned to run to the water. Furthermore, they would not run to either the water or the hypotonic saline when they were not made thirsty. This finding supports the view that saline was overdrunk because it is less satiating to a thirsty animal.

These findings are interesting because a great deal is known about the effects of hypotonic saline on the taste receptors of the rat. Zotterman (1956) made electrophysiological recordings from the chorda tympani nerve, which conveys afferent signals from the taste buds. He found that the same nerve fibers in the rat as well as the human are affected when a hypertonic solution of sodium chloride is placed on the tongue and when water is placed on the tongue. The difference is that when hypertonic saline is placed on the tongue the nerve fibers increase their rate of firing. When water is placed on the tongue, these same nerve fibers decrease their rate of firing from an intermediate rate of spontaneous discharge. Zotterman was able to show that the degree of reduction of firing of spontaneous discharge was a function of the tonicity of the sodium chloride hypotonic solution. When the fluid placed on the tongue was distilled water, the suppression of spontaneous firing in this pathway was almost complete. When the fluid was a hypotonic solution of sodium chloride of some intermediate value, then the suppression of firing from the spontaneous level was also intermediate. When the solution placed on the tongue was a hypertonic solution of sodium chloride, then the rate of firing in the neural pathway increased over the spontaneous rate. When an animal drinks water, we would therefore expect the total amount of afferent activity to be depressed while the animal tastes the water. When the animal drinks saline, on the other hand, if such saline is hypotonic, we would expect the activity in certain neural pathways to be depressed to an intermediate extent. If we assume that certain peripheral signals act to depress the excitability of centers in the nervous system responsive to osmotic imbalance, we would then have to suppose that a more complete depression of activity in the nerve fibers responsive to salt and water produces a larger depressive effect on such centers. This larger depressive effect would lead to a swifter suppression of the activity in the osmotically sensitive centers when the animal was tasting water. When the animal was tasting hypotonic saline, the depressive fact of the afferent message would not be as large. Therefore, it would take a longer time to depress the sensitivity of the thirst centers to a point at which the animal would stop experiencing thirst. Although the facts cited so far support the notion that gustatory afferent messages produce at least short-term satiation of thirst, there are, however, discrepant findings in this area. The notion that animals overdrink hypotonic saline because it produces fewer afferent messages per unit of time, and so is less satiating to thirst, has been challenged by Chiang and Wilson (1963). When a rat was given a choice between a bottle containing saline and a bottle containing water, the rat would drink more frequently from the saline bottle than from the water bottle. This result would not be predicted from the hypothesis that hypotonic saline produces fewer afferent messages. This hypothesis would predict a random and equal choice of the two models, although we would expect longer drinking bouts on the saline bottle simply because the fluid in such a bottle is supposedly less satiating. However, it is actually quite difficult to define what constitutes a drinking bout in an *ad libitum* situation. It is quite possible that rats pause during drinking and that the frequency of such pausing may be somewhat independent of the fluid being drunk. If this were the case, then a longer time spent in drinking from the saline bottle would of necessity be divided into a larger number of segments which could then give the appearance of a greater frequency of choice of the saline bottle.

Studies on this phenomenon of saline drinking are complicated by the fact that rats can have a craving for salt if a sodium chloride deficiency exists in their diet, or if their rate of excretion of sodium chloride is abnormally high. That such problems can confound the issue has been shown by Deutsch and Wiener (1969). That saline drinking due to salt deficiency and the overdrinking of hypotonic saline when there is no discernible deficiency have different neural substrates has been shown by Wolf (1964). He showed that lesions in the dorsal section of the lateral hypothalamus will abolish an increase of salt intake in response to treatments producing such increases in normal animals. However, such lesioned animals show the same pattern of overdrinking of hypotonic saline as normal, nondeprived controls. From this anatomical dissociation it seems plausible to assume that normal overdrinking of hypotonic saline and salt craving due to salt deficiency are two different phenomena produced by different mechanisms.

Whereas it seems that it is neural messages from the mouth and the throat which cause a satiation of thirst, we will recall that in the case of hunger the messages causing satiation seem instead to arise in the stomach or the upper gastrointestinal tract. It is not presently known whether such messages from the stomach are hormonal in nature or whether they are neurally mediated. In spite of the relative paucity of evidence, there has been a great deal of speculation about their nature. Stunkard et al. (1955) have suggested that glucagon, a protein secreted by the alpha cells in the pancreas, may contribute to hunger satiety. A number of hormones from the gastrointestinal tract have been suggested as possible satiety signals. Schally, Redding, Lucien, and Meyer (1967) injected hungry mice with enterogastrone and found an inhibition of feeding. However, they never controlled for possible anorexia caused by the injection of impure chemical extracts. In a similar study, Koopmans, Deutsch, and Branson (1972) injected cholecystokinin, a hormone that provokes the flow of digestive enzymes from the pancreas and liver, and found an inhibition of feeding. However, when thirsty mice were given the same dose of cholecystokinin, they failed to drink. Under normal circumstances, cholecystokinin should not reduce thirst because animals tend to drink immediately after a meal at the time when endogenous cholecystokinin has been released into the bloodstream. The cholecystokinin injection probably caused a general malaise in these mice. The satiating effectiveness of cholecystokinin remains controversial. Glick, Thomas, and Mayer (1971) found no effect of intravenous injections of cholecystokinin on food intake in rats, while, in a more recent study, Gibbs, Young, and Smith (1973) demonstrated a reduction in food intake for intraperitoneally injected hormone. Further behavioral experiments are needed to settle this controversy.

There is as yet no convincing evidence that hunger satiety signals are carried in the blood. The argument that a humoral signal causes satiety has usually been made by excluding other alternatives. Grossman, Cumming, and Ivy (1947) and Harris, Ivy, and Searle (1947) demonstrated that cutting all nerves leading to a dog's stomach produced no change in their feeding habits once surgical recovery had occurred. In fact, denervated dogs increased their food intake when injected with insulin and decreased their food intake when given amphetamines. This evidence shows that denervated dogs continue to eat normally at various levels of hunger and suggests that the stomach nerves do not mediate satiety. A series of studies directly showing the involvement of blood signals was done by Davis, Cambell, Gallagher, and Zurakov (1971); Davis, Gallagher, and Ladove (1967); and Davis, Gallagher, Ladove, and Turavsky (1969). They transfused the blood between a pair of rats when one was hungry and the other was fully satiated. Two cubic centimeters of blood were withdrawn through a chronic intravenous cannula from both rats simultaneously. Then the blood from each rat was injected into the other. This procedure was repeated until 26 cc of blood was crossed between two rats. Immediately after the transfusion each rat was given access to food. In the first experiment, one rat of the pair was kept on an unrestricted diet and the other was kept without food for 23½ hr each day. Transfusion between the two animals was made 30 min before the food-deprived animal was fed each day. The deprived rat ate 50% of his normal food intake, suggesting that the transferred blood contained a factor which produces satiety. The reduction of food intake does not seem to be due to some nonspecific effect of the transfusion technique. When blood was transferred between hungry rats, no decrease in feeding occurred. The transferred blood signal seems to have reduced feeding in a hungry rat, but its relative lack in the *al lib.* rat did not increase feeding.

In a second experiment Davis kept both rats without food for 23½ hr each day. The donor member of the pair was given food 30 min before transfusion so that it was satiated before its blood was withdrawn. The recipient of this freshly satiated blood did not show a significant reduction in intake. This could be interpreted to show that 30 min after feeding, the humoral state which initiates eating has not been reversed by the process of digestion. Therefore when the blood of a freshly satiated donor is used, it does not prevent feeding in a hungry rat. Apparently, blood transferred from a recently satiated rat has no effect on hunger, while blood transferred from a rat fed for a few hours does reduce feeding.

Davis's experiment on freshly satiated rats implies that the signals which normally turn off hunger are not transferred from donor to recipient. There are two possible reasons for this. First, the signals may not be humoral. They may normally travel through the nerves of animals with intact peripheral nervous systems. Second, such signals are humoral but they have a rapid turnover rate in the animal. The signal would be quickly destroyed after it was transferred to the recipient rat. Intestinal hormones have a half-life of only a few minutes and would disappear almost immediately from the recipients' blood. A single shot transfusion would not produce the same blood level of these hormones in donor and recipient rat.

A recent experiment by Koopmans (*unpublished doctoral dissertation*) has greatly reduced the number of humoral substances that could produce hunger satiety. Koopmans crossed a 12 inch segment of the intestines of two parabiotic rats. In this surgical preparation, the food that one rat ate arrived in his own stomach, traveled through 2 inches of his own intestines and then crossed into the intestines of his parabiotic partner. It traveled through 12 inches of the partner's intestines and then returned to the intestines of the rat that fed. The food was about equally absorbed in the two rats.

In the experiment itself, one rat was fed first. This rat lacked possible satiety signals arising in his lower duodenum and jejunum. Such signals would include food absorbed from this segment and hormones released by it. Despite this lack, the rat ate a normal meal: it did not overeat. The second rat of each pair was fed 30 or 60 min after the first. Radioactive absorption studies showed that glucose and amino acids were equally absorbed in the two rats. Despite the presence of food in its intestines and the absorption of this food, the second rat ate a meal of normal size. Apparently, food absorbed from the intestines and hormones released by it do not produce hunger satiety. These observations should apply to the hormone cholecystokinin, since it is known to be present in the lower duodenum and jejunum.

In a further experiment (*unpublished doctoral dissertation*), Koopmans tested the importance of absorbed food in the long-term regulation of hunger. Only one rat of each intestines-crossed pair was allowed to eat. The food that this rat ate was distributed about equally between the two rats. Thus, the feeding rat lost about half his food. Had the ingested food been important in determining the level of the rat's hunger, the feeding rat should have increased its food intake. The rat did not do so for 5 days. Thus, food loss at the level of the small intestines produces no immediate increase in feeding. If the food is diluted with an equal volume of water before being fed to the rat, the animal doubles his food intake in 1 day. The experiment suggests that regulation of the quantity of food eaten originates in the stomach or first segment of the duodenum.

The results of Koopmans's study are supported by the reports of patients receiving intravenous injections while in the hospital. Jordan, Hamilton, MacFayden, and Dudrick (1974) found that patients receiving a more than adequate number of calories from the injection of glucose and amino acids remained hungry. When these patients were allowed to eat, they ate only small meals. The small size of their meals, however, is not surprising, since most of the patients were in the hospital for gastrointestinal ailments. The interesting finding is that sick patients remained hungry while given more than adequate caloric infusions.

The experiment by Koopmans (*unpublished doctoral dissertation*) contradicts the glucostatic theory of hunger regulation. Direct measurements showed a decrease in blood glucose level at the same time that glucose was being continuously absorbed. An A-V glucose difference must have been present at a time when the unfed rat was still hungry. The experiment also adds further evidence against the thermostatic theory. Any heat generated by the absorbed food failed to reduce food intake.

Whatever the nature of the message which produces hunger satiation, we may ask where in the central nervous system such a message has its effect. Lesions showing startling effects on satiation of eating have in fact been discovered. Animals with destruction of the ventromedial nuclei of the hypothalamus appeared to overeat grossly and this leads to the speculation that the message which produces a satiation of eating is in some way closely connected with such loci. While a great deal of work has been done utilizing this lesion and the view that the ventromedial nucleus of the hypothalamus is linked to feeding activity has become quite commonly accepted, it has lately been shown that the relevant lesion is not that of the ventromedial nucleus of the hypothalamus itself but of the ventral adrenergic pathway which is a somewhat inconspicuous tract which is found close to the ventro-medial nucleus (Gold, 1973). This ventral adrenergic bundle appears to originate in or close to the nucleus solitarius of the medulla, a nucleus which is also important as a way station in the gustatory pathway (Ahlskog and Hoebel, 1973). While we now know from the work of these authors that the anatomical identification of the overeating syndrome was incorrect, the be-havioral consequences which occur as a result of the lesion in the region of the ventromedial nucleus are still of great interest. When the animal awakes from the anesthesia after the lesion is first made, it begins to eat ravenously. It overeats until some high level of obesity is reached. At this point the animal's eating behavior, while much more continuous than that of a normal animal, ceases to be ravenous. For instance, if the task of obtaining food is at all strenuous or the food somewhat unpalatable, the rat with such a lesion will actually tend to be more easily discouraged from obtaining or ingesting food than the normal rat. However, under conditions of normal availability of food, the hyperphagic rat will eat the larger meal (Teitelbaum and Camp-bell, 1958). If, however, animals with ventromedial lesions are force fed so that their weight becomes larger than that which they would normally attain, they will actually lose weight when they are allowed to regulate their own food intake and will stabilize again in weight at their previous level of obesity. A possible explanation of this type of deficit is that the satiety message which is generated by some of the consequences of eating is no longer as efficient in stopping eating as it is in the normal animal.

VII. QUALITATIVE ASPECTS OF FOOD SELECTION

So far we have addressed ourselves to the question of the regulation of the amount of food which is eaten or drunk. We have considered what gives rise to the act of feeding or drinking and what stops these two activities. Now we will consider some other aspects of hunger and thirst, mainly why it is that the animal accepts certain substances when it is hungry and certain fluids when it is thirsty. There is evidence that these certain species have an un-learned attraction to certain visual shapes. For instance, Tinbergen and Perdeck (1950) showed that newly hatched herring gull chicks peck at objects resembling the beak of an adult herring gull. This responsiveness to stimuli which emanate from the adult beak is probably innate because re-sponses can be evoked most effectively by exaggerated copies of the adult beak. Rheingold and Hess (1957) found that there were certain visual properties to which domestic chicks were attracted when they were thirsty. It was found that substances which resembled water were more attractive to the chick when it was thirsty. It was noted that most of the chicks attempted to drink mercury, a substance which seemed to evoke more drinking responses than water. Such tests were made without any previous experience on the part of the chicks with water. Fantz (1957) performed a similar experiment on food preferences in domestic chicks. He found that chicks attempted to peck at objects which were round rather than objects which were angular. Therefore, it seems clear that when a chick hatches, it already has various predispositions to ingest objects with certain definite visual qualities. Similarly, it seems likely that there are certain qualities which are aversive to animals and many such aversions are probably unlearned. Such aversions are abolished following bilateral amygdalectomy. It seems that after amygdalectomy, monkeys and some other animals become tractable and tame (although exceptions have been noted), sexually indiscriminate, and eat objects such as feces. Amygdalectomized monkeys will ingest such foods as meat or fish which they normally reject (Pribram and Bagshaw, 1953).

There are also cases in which food preferences are learned rather than innate. It is known that animals, when given a selection of a large number of foods, will generally select a healthful and beneficial diet. Some of this ability, as has been noted above, is probably due to factors which are unlearned. A striking example of unlearned appetite which can be demonstrated in adult animals is that of the appetite for sodium chloride. It is possible by various manipulations to induce a severe salt deficiency in adult animals: animals that up to that point had not been differentially rewarded for the ingestion of salt and who had not ingested salt as a separate item of their diet. Epstein and Stellar (1955) showed that when animals were first allowed to drink salt after being rendered highly salt deficient, they would consume a large amount of salt solution immediately. The results of Epstein and Stellar were further confirmed by Rodgers (1967). Not all appetites in response to deficiency are unlearned. It has been shown by Rozin (1967) and Booth and Simson (1971) that there seems to be a learned aversion to a standard diet which is deficient in some necessary dietary component such as a vitamin. For instance, thiamine-deficient rats would show preference for any new diet over the standard thiamine-deficient diet (Rodgers and Rozin, 1966). It was also shown that rats kept for a time on a thiamine-deficient diet continued to avoid this deficient diet even after they had been permitted to recover (Rozin, 1967). Holman's (1968) work suggests that long-term associations can be formed by rats between stimuli and their beneficial aftereffects. This is to be suspected from much of the primary work on the learning of animals to select vitamins which are needed. Scott and Verney (1947) showed that an appetite for the B complex vitamins is acquired. Animals deficient in the B complex would learn to ingest food injected with anise instead of plain food if the food flavored with anise contained the needed vitamin. If the vitamin was left out of the diet flavored with anise, but added to the plain food instead, the rats preferred to eat the plain food. In order to learn that a substance is beneficial, the animal must associate the taste of the substance with a beneficial aftereffect which only occurs at least 15 min after the animal has tasted the substance. Such learning was first demonstrated by Scott and Verney in 1947. Just as animals can learn to ingest beneficial substance or substances for which they have a deficit, they can also learn to avoid substances if their ingestion is followed by harmful consequences. It is not yet clear what such consequences have to be in order to produce avoidance. Many substances which one would not expect to produce nausea or even malaise seem to produce such conditioned aversion in the case of the rat. For instance, it has been shown that morphine and amphetamine can produce such an aversion. If the ingestion of a substance is followed by some aversive event such as X-irradiation, the rat will show an aversion to the taste which preceded this irradiation.

REFERENCES

Adolph, E. F. (1941): The internal environment and behavior: III. Water content. *Am. J. Psychiatry,* 97:1365–1373.

Ahlskog, J. E., and Hoebel, B. G. (1973): Overeating and obesity from damage to a noradrenergic system in the brain. *Science,* 182:166–169.

Anand, B. K. (1951): Nervous regulation of food intake. *Physiol. Rev.,* 41:677–708.

Anand, B. K., and Brobeck, J. R. (1951): Hypothalamic control of food intake in rats and cats. *Yale J. Biol. Med.,* 24:123–140.

Anand, B. K., Ova, S., and Shoenberg, K. (1961): Hypothalamic control of food intake in cats and monkeys. *J. Physiol. (Lond.),* 127:143–152.

Bare, J. K. (1949): The specific hunger for sodium chloride in normal and adrenalectomized white rats. *J. Comp. Physiol. Psychol.,* 42:242–253.

Bellows, R. T. (1939): Time factors in water drinking dogs. *Am. J. Physiol.,* 125:87–97.

Berkun, M. M., Kessen, M. L., and Miller, N. E. (1952): Hunger reducing effects of food by mouth, measured by a consumatory response. *J. Comp. Physiol. Psychol.,* 45:550–554.

Blass, E. M. (1968): Separation of cellular from extracellular controls of drinking in rats by frontal brain damage. *Science,* 162:1501–1503.

Blass, E. M., and Hanson, D. G. (1970): Primary hyderdipsia in the rat following septal lesions. *J. Comp. Physiol. Psychol.,* 70:87–93.

Booth, D. A., and Simson, P. C. (1971): Food preferences acquired by association with variations in amino acid nutrition. *J. Exp. Psychol.,* 23:135–145.

Brobeck, J. R. (1948): Food intake as a mechanism of temperature regulations. *Yale J. Biol. Med.,* 20:545–552.

Chiang, H. M., and Wilson, W. A. (1963): Some tests of the diluted-water hypothesis of saline consumption in rats. *J. Comp. Physiol. Psychol.,* 56:660–665.

Coons, E. E., Levak, M., and Miller, N. E. (1965): Lateral hypothalamus: Learning of food-seeking response motivated by electrical stimulation. *Science,* 150:1320–1321.

Davis, J. D., Cambell, C. S., Gallagher, R. J., and Zurakov, M. A. (1971): Disappearance of a humoral satiety factor during food deprivation. *J. Comp. Physiol. Psychol.,* 75:476–482.

Davis, J. D., Gallagher, R. J., and Ladove, R. (1967): Food intake controlled by a blood factor. *Science,* 156:1247–1248.

Davis, J. D., Gallagher, R. J., Ladove, R. F., and Turavsky, A. J. (1969): Inhibition of food intake by a humoral factor. *J. Comp. Physiol. Psychol.,* 67:407–414.

Deutsch, J. A. (1953): A new type of behaviour theory. *Br. J. Psychol.,* 44:304–317.

Deutsch, J. A. (1960): *The Structural Basis of Behavior.* University of Chicago Press, Chicago.

Deutsch, J. A., and Blumen, H. L. (1962): Counter-injection: A new technique for the analysis of drinking. *Nature (Lond.),* 196:196–197.

Deutsch, J. A., and Deutsch, D. (1973): *Physiological Psychology* (2nd ed.), Dorsey Press, Homewood, Illinois.

Deutsch, J. A., and Jones, A. D. (1959): The water-salt receptor and preferences in the rat. *Nature (Lond.)*: 183:1412.

Deutsch, J. A., and Jones, A. D. (1960): Diluted water: An explanation of the rat's preference for saline. *J. Comp. Physiol. Psychol.*, 53:122–127.

Deutsch, J. A., and Wiener, N. I. (1969): *J. Comp. Physiol. Psychol.*, 69:179–184.

Devenport, L. D., and Balagura, S. (1971): Lateral hypothalamus: Reevaluation of function in motivated feeding behavior. *Science*, 172:744–746.

Epstein, A. N. (1960): Water intake without the act of drinking. *Science*, 131:497–498.

Epstein, A. N., and Stellar, E. (1955): The control of salt preference in the adrenalectomized rat. *J. Comp. Physiol. Psychol.*, 48:167–172.

Fantz, R. L. (1957): Form preferences in newly hatched chicks. *J. Comp. Physiol. Psychol.*, 50:422–430.

Fisher, A. E., and Coury, J. N. (1962): Cholinergic tracing of a central neural circuit underlying the thirst drive. *Science*, 137:691–693.

Fitzsimmons, J. T. (1961): Drinking by nephrectomized rats injected with various substances. *J. Physiol. (Lond.)*, 155:563–579.

Gibbs, J., Young, R. C., and Smith, G. P. (1973): Cholecystokinin decreases food intake in rats. *J. Comp. Physiol. Psychol.*, 56:645–659.

Gilman, A. (1937): The relation between blood osmotic pressure, fluid distribution and voluntary water intake. *Am. J. Physiol.*, 120:323–328.

Glick, Z., Thomas, D. W., and Mayer, J. (1971): Absence of effect of injections of the intestinal hormones secretin and cholecystokinin-pancreozymin upon feeding behavior. *Physiol. Behav.*, 6:5–8.

Gold, R. M. (1973): Hypothalamic obesity: The myth of the ventromedial hypothalamus. *Science*, 182:488–490.

Grossman, M. I., Cumming, C. M., and Ivy, A. C. (1947): The effect of insulin on food intake after bagotomy and sympathectomy. *Am. J. Physiol.*, 149:100–102.

Grossman, S. P. (1960): Eating or drinking elicited by direct adrenergic or cholinergic stimulation of the hypothalamus. *Science*, 132:301–332.

Harris, S. C., Ivy, A. C., and Searle, L. M. (1947): The mechanism of amphetamine induced loss of weight. *J. Am. Med. Assoc.* 134:1468–1475.

Harvey, J. A., and Hunt, H. F. (1965): Effect of septal lesions on thirst in the rat as indicated by water consumption and operant responding for water reward. *J. Comp. Physiol. Psychol.*, 59:49–56.

Harwood, D., and Vowles, D. M. (1966): Forebrain stimulation and feeding behavior in the ring dove (*Streptopelia risoria*), *J. Comp. Physiol. Psychol.*, 62:388–396.

Hawkins, R. D. (1974): Behavioral measurement of the neural refractory periods for stimulus-bound eating and self-stimulation in the rat. *J. Comp. Physiol. Psychol.*, 86:942–948.

Herberg, L. J. (1962): Physiological drives investigated by means of injection into the cerebral ventricles of the rat. *J. Exp. Psychol.*, 14:8–14.

Holman, G. L. (1968): Intragastric reinforcement effect. *J. Comp. Physiol. Psychol.*, 69:432–441.

Houpt, T. R., and Hance, H. E. (1971): Stimulation of food intake in the rabbit and rat by inhibition of glucose metabolism with 2-doxy-D-glucose. *J. Comp. Physiol. Psychol.*, 76:395–400.

Hu, J. W. (1973): Refractory period of hypothalamic thirst pathway in the rat. *J. Comp. Physiol. Psychol.*, 85:463–468.

Hull, C. L., Livingston, J. R., Rouse, R. O., and Barker, A. N. (1951): Time, sham, and esophageal feeding as reinforcements. *J. Comp. Physiol. Psychol.*, 44:236–245.

Jordan, H. A., Hamilton, M., MacFayden, B. V., and Dudrick, S. J. (1974): Hunger and satiety in humans during parenteral hyperalimentation. *Psychosom. Med.*, 36:144–155.

Kennedy, G. C. (1953): The role of depot fat in the hypothalamic control of food intake in the rat. *Proc. Soc. Ser. B.*, 140:578–592.

Khavari, K. A., and Russell, R. W. (1966): Acquisition, retention and extinction under conditions of water deprivation and of central cholinergic stimulation. *J. Comp. Physiol. Psychol.*, 61:339–345.

Kohn, M. (1951): Satiation of hunger from food injected directly into the stomach versus food ingested by mouth. *J. Comp. Physiol. Psychol.*, 44:412–422.

Koopmans, H. S., Deutsch, J. A., and Branson, P. J. (1972): The effect of cholecystokinin-pancreozymin on hunger and thirst in mice. *Behav. Biol.*, 7:441–444.

Mayer, J. (1953): Glucostatic mechanism of regulation of food intake. *N. Engl. J. Med.*, 249:13–16.

Miller, N. E. (1961): Learning and performance motivated by direct stimulation of the brain. In: *Electrical Stimulation of the Brain*, edited by D. E. Sheer, pp. 387–397. University of Texas Press, Austin.

Miller, N. E. (1965): Chemical coding of behavior in the brain: *Science*, 148:328–338.

Miller, N. E., and Kessen, M. L. (1954): Is distention of the stomach by a balloon rewarding or punishing? *Am. Psychol.*, 9:430–431.

Mook, D. G. (1963): Oral and postingestinal determinants of the intake of various solutions in rats with esophageal fistulas. *J. Comp. Physiol. Psychol.*, 56:645–659.

Nelson, D. (1947): Do rats select more sodium than they need? *Fed. Proc.*, 6:169.

Novin, D., and Durham, R. (1969): Unit and DC potential studies of the supraoptic nucleus. *Ann. N.Y. Acad. Sci.*, 157(2):740–753.

Novin, D., Vanderweele, D. A., and Rezek, M. (1972): Infusion of 2-deoxy-*d*-glucose into the hepatic-portal system causes eating: Evidence for peripheral glucoreceptors. *Science*, 181:858–860.

Pribram, K. H., and Bagshaw, M. (1953): Further analysis of the temporal lobe syndrome utilizing fronto-temporal ablations. *J. Comp. Neurol.*, 99:347–375.

Quartermain, D., and Miller, N. E. (1966): Sensory feedback in time response elicited by carbachol in preoptic area of rat. *J. Comp. Physiol. Psychol.*, 62:350–353.

Randoin, L., Causeret, J., and Gabrel-Szymanski, M. (1950): Comportement du jeune rat normal auquel on donne le choix entre de l'eau pure et une solution peu concentrée de chorure de sodium. *J. Physiol. (Paris)*, 42:447–450.

Rheingold, H. I., and Hess, E. H. (1957): The chicks preference for some visual properties of water. *J. Comp. Physiol. Psychol.*, 50:417–421.

Robinson, S. W., and Mishkin, M. (1962): Alimentary responses evoked from forebrain structures in *Macaca mulatta*. *Science*, 136:260–261.

Rodgers, W., and Rozin, P. (1966): Novel food preferences in thiamine deficient rats. *J. Comp. Physiol. Psychol.*, 61:1–4.

Rodgers, W. L. (1967): Specificity of specific hungers. *J. Comp. Physiol. Psychol.*, 64:49–58.

Routtenberg, A. (1965): The effects of chemical stimulation in the dorsal midbrain tegmentum on self-stimulation in hypothalamus and septal area. *Psychonomic Sci.*, 3:41.

Rozin, P. (1967): Specific aversions as a component of specific hungers. *J. Comp. Physiol. Psychol.*, 63:429–433.

Schally, A. V., Redding, T. W., Lucien, H. W., and Meyer, J. (1967): Enterogastrone inhibits eating in fasted mice. *Science*, 157:211.

Scott, E. M., and Verney, E. L. (1947): Selfselection and diet. VI. The nature of appetites for B vitamins. *J. Nutr.*, 34:471–480.

Simpson, J. B., and Routtenberg, A. (1973): Subfornical organ: Site of drinking elicited by angiotensin II. *Science*, 181:1172–1175.

Smith, D. F., and Stricker, E. M. (1969): The influence of need on the rat's preference for dilute NaCl solutions. *Physiol. Behav.*, 4:407–410.

Smith, G. P., and Epstein, A. N. (1970): Increased feeding in response to decreased glucose utilization in the rat and monkey. *Am. J. Physiol.*, 217:1083–1087.

Smith, M., and Duffy, M. (1955): The effects of intragastric injection of various substances on subsequent bar-pressing. *J. Comp. Physiol. Psychol.*, 48:387–391.

Steffens, A. B. (1969): Rapid absorption of glucose in the intestinal tract of the rat after ingestion of a meal. *Physiol. Behav.*, 4:829–833.

Stellar, E. (1954): The physiology of motivation. *Psychol. Rev.*, 61:5–22.

Stellar, E., and McCleary, R. A. (1952): Food preferences as a function of the method of measurement. *Am. Psychol.*, 7:256.

Stunkard, A. J., Van Itallie, T. B., and Reis, B. B. (1955): The mechanism of satiety: Effect of glucagon on gastric hunger contractions in man. *Proc. Soc. Exp. Biol. Med.*, 89:258–261.

Teitelbaum, P., and Campbell, B. A. (1958): Ingestion patterns in hyperphagic and normal rats. *J. Comp. Physiol. Psychol.*, 51:135–141.

Tinbergen, N., and Perdeck, A. C. (1950): On the stimulus situation releasing the begging response in the newly hatched herring gull chick (*Larus argentatus* pont.), *Behaviour*, 3:1–39.

Towbin, E. J. (1949): Gastric distension as a factor in the satiation of thirst in esophagustomized dogs. *Am. J. Physiol.*, 159:533–541.

Williams, D. R., and Teitelbaum, P. (1959): Some observations on the starvation resulting from lateral hypothalamic lesions. *J. Comp. Physiol. Psychol.*, 52:458–465.

Wolf, G. (1964): Effect of dorsolateral hypothalamic lesions on sodium appetite elicited by desoxycorticosterone and by acute hyponatremia. *J. Comp. Physiol. Psychol.*, 58:396–403.

Wolf, G., and Stricker, E. M. (1967): Sodium appetite elicited by lypovolemia in adrenalectomized rats: Reevaluation of the reservoir hypothesis. *J. Comp. Physiol. Psychol.*, 63:252–257.

Wyrwicka, W., Dobrzecka, C., and Tarnecki, R. (1959): On the instrumental conditioned reaction evoked by electrical stimulation of the hypothalamus. *Science*, 130:336–337.

Wyricka, W., and Doty, R. W. (1966): Feeding induced in cats by electrical stimulation of the brain stem. *Exp. Brain Res.*, 1:152–160.

Yin, T. H., and Tsai, C. T. (1973): Effects of glucose on feeding in relation to routes of entry in rats. *J. Comp. Physiol. Psychol.*, 85:258–264.

Young, P. T. (1949): Studies of food preference, appetite and dietary habit. IX. Palatability versus appetite as determinants of the critical concentrations of sucrose and sodium chloride. *Compr. Psychiatry*. Monograph No. 5. 19:45–74.

Zotterman, Y. (1956): Species differences in the water taste. *Acta Physiol. Scand.*, 37:60–70.

Biological Foundations of Psychiatry,
Raven Press, New York © *1976.*

Behavioral Studies of Hypothalamic Functions: Drives and Reinforcements

James Olds

Division of Biology, Beckman Laboratories 216–76,
California Institute of Technology, Pasadena, California 91125

I. INTRODUCTION

The rewarding effects of electric stimulation applied in some parts of the brain are well known. The electric shocks are pursued as if they were the positive goals of active drives, or as if they were of such a hedonically appetizing character that no drive was needed to provoke pursuit behavior. The brain centers involved are to a large degree the same as those shown by other stimulation and lesion experiments to be involved in the control of drive behaviors. They are also the same as or heavily interdigitated with the main hormone control centers of the brain. Pharmacological experiments show that reward, drive, and hormone systems are controlled by drugs that appear to have their main influence on a special neurochemical messenger system, the catecholamine system. The catecholamines involved are two specialized "transmitters"—norepinephrine and dopamine—which convey neuronal messages to smooth muscles, glands, and other neurons.

Neuroanatomical evidence shows that fibers containing catecholamines pervade the critical brain areas and course through them to targets in many other parts of the brain. Because the catecholamine systems pervade the hormone systems in the same areas where reward systems pervade drive systems, it is tempting to suppose the pair of chemical messengers underlies the pair of behavior processes. Because the catecholamine transmitters are slower than other well-known transmitters, and hormones are slower still, it is possible to imagine a chain from fast neuronal processes, through slower catecholamine events, to still slower neurohormonal states which would then possibly exert an influence back on the fast processes. If this were a reward-drive cycle, it would be involved in determining priorities and stabilizing behavioral directions. Studies of the brain reward systems, related drive systems, catecholamine fibers that pervade them, coresident hormone systems, and large neurons that make up the main dramatis personae in the critical brain centers are brought together here with a view to moving toward a clarification of some of the mechanisms.

II. ELECTRIC STIMULATION

A. Reward

Psychologists have long identified "positive reinforcements" (i.e., rewards) by their effects on behavior. The behavior involved is easy to describe: The rewarding stimulus causes the animal to come back for more. It is more difficult to formulate a definition that is scientifically precise. Usually rewards used in animal experiments cause repetition of behaviors which immediately precede them. However, it is possible to conceive a reward which, being sought only once a day, would not have any important effect on the frequency of a normal antecedent behavior. In such a case the reward is often defined in terms of some obstruction the animal crosses or some other "cost" the animal "pays" to get it. In the end, obstruction-crossing, and cost-paying are behaviors chosen for their prior infrequency. Their frequency therefore *is* increased by infrequently sought rewards. Thus we are back again to defining reward in terms of changed frequencies or repetition rates of normal behaviors or of originally infrequent behaviors. Following Skinner's (1938) terminology, behaviors that can be controlled in this way are called operant behaviors; they are distinguished from reflex behaviors, whose incidence cannot be modified by manipulation of consequences. Operant behaviors, because they can be modified by manipulation of outcomes or effects, are said to obey the "law of effect."

"Negative reinforcements" (i.e., punishments) are similarly identified by their effects on behavior. On the operant side there is (1) failure to repeat punished responses, and (2) repetition of responses which terminate the punishment. On the reflex side there is (3) general activation of the animal during application of the punishing stimulus, and (4) some set of aversive or withdrawal reflexes.

Thus in relation to operant behavior, the application of a rewarding stimulus and the termination of a punishing one have similar effects; both cause repetition of the preceding operant responses. This similarity has led many psychologists to postulate a single hypothetical mechanism for appetitive and aversive behaviors (Miller, 1957).

In experiments used to demonstrate positive reinforcement, the animal, usually deprived of food, water, or sexual stimulation, is placed in a situation where a certain response previously decided on by the experimenter leads to the stimulus that has been withheld. The response initially exists in the animal's repertory, but it occurs rarely. The experiment is begun by placing the animal in the apparatus and waiting until the response occurs at first by "accident." Immediately thereafter the previously withheld stimulus is presented either mechanically or by the experimenter. As a consequence of this correlation between response and stimulus, either at once or after several repetitions, the response becomes more frequent.

In experiments used to demonstrate the effects of negative reinforcement, the animal is not deprived; instead, a noxious stimulus is presented repeatedly or in a steady train. As in the positive reinforcement experiment, a response rare at the outset is selected by the experimenter as the response whose frequency is to be augmented. When the response occurs, the experimenter or the apparatus terminates the train of noxious stimulation for some period of time. After one or several repetitions of this correlation between response and cessation of noxious stimulation, an obvious change in response frequency occurs, the response becoming more frequent while the animal is subjected to the noxious stimulation.

B. Rewarding Stimulation of the Brain

A new window on the brain was opened in 1953 when a rat fortuitously evidenced a neural rewarding effect by returning to the place in an open field

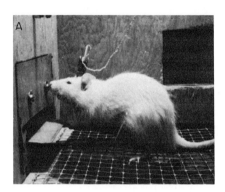

FIG. 1. A and B: Rat pedal-pressing to stimulate itself in the lateral hypothalamus. C: X-ray film showing wires penetrating the brain and screws holding plaque to the skull.

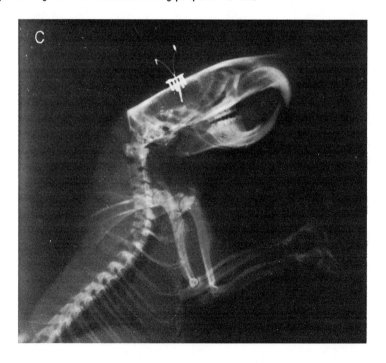

where it had been when an electric stimulus was applied to the brain via chronically implanted electrodes (Olds, 1955). The ensuing studies provided not only a neural substrate as a focal point for further study of a key psychological concept (i.e., the "law of effect") but also a stable preparation, and thereby a method of studying many brain-behavior relationships. On the basis of accomplishments to date, the method bodes well in its own way to prove as fruitful as other well-known landmarks in the behavioral sciences, e.g., Skinner's method for studying operant behavior or Lashley's method for studying discrimination and choice on a jumping stand.

The initial observation led to studies which showed that electrical excitation in a restricted region of the central nervous system caused rats to work steadily at arbitrarily assigned tasks (Fig. 1) in order to obtain the electric stimulus (Olds and Milner, 1954). The behavior was called "self-stimulation" by Brady (1960), and this designation is widely used. The behavior was easily reproducible from animal to animal; it was sustained during extended periods of testing; and it was not accompanied by any other obvious pathological signs. It seemed possible, therefore, to view this self-stimulation behavior in terms of an artificial activation of the brain's normal positive reinforcement mechanism.

Since that time similar effects have been obtained in many vertebrates from fish to primates (Olds, 1962). There is evidence from therapeutic procedures that human brains do not differ from those of other vertebrates in this regard (Bishop, Elder, and Heath, 1963). Most of the experiments on brain reward behavior, however, were carried out on rats. The goal of the experiments was to determine what parts of the brain were involved, if the rewarding effects were valid and general rather than being limited to irrelevant features of the testing situation, and how these "brain rewards" matched ordinary ones (and which kinds of ordinary ones they might match). The overriding goal, of course, was to look at brain function in the hope that these experiments would clarify the brain mechanisms of reward.

My strategy in the next subsection is to answer a set of questions that are regularly asked about the brain areas and the behaviors involved. I believe that this direct question and answer format is the clearest way to present this part of the material.

C. Reward and Drive Behaviors Caused by Electric Stimulation of the Brain

1. *What parts of the brain were involved?* The answer in the form of a list starting from the front includes: (1) olfactory bulbs; (2) primary olfactory centers such as the prepyriform cortex; (3) secondary olfactory centers (septal area, amygdala, and pyriform cortex); (4) tertiary olfactory centers (e.g., cingulate cortex and hippocampus); (5) *main subcortical area related to this olfactory system, i.e., hypothalamus;* (6) a part of the thalamus which is also tied into the olfactory system, i.e., the anterior thalamus; (7)

certain parts of the midbrain which have strong fiber connections with the hypothalamus and with olfactory systems of the telencephalon; (8) a set of fibers (possibly dopamine secretors) connecting two main subcortex motor centers; and (9) a set of fibers (possibly norepinephrine secretors) originating near the gustatory centers of the medulla and projecting to near the hypothalamus and elsewhere (Olds, 1956*a;* Olds and Peretz, 1960; Olds, Travis, and Schwing, 1960; Olds and Olds, 1963; Wurtz and Olds, 1963; Valenstein and Campbell, 1966; Wetzel, 1968; Routtenberg and Malsbury, 1969; Phillips and Mogenson, 1969; Routtenberg, 1971; Crow, 1971, 1972*b;* Crow, Spear, and Arbuthnott, 1972; Ritter and Stein, 1973; Routtenberg and Sloan, 1974; German and Bowden, 1974).

The neuroanatomical systems seemed to form a single topographical continuum. The system originating in the medulla, the one originating in the extrapyramidal motor system, and the one related to the olfactory bulb could nevertheless be quite different; and other grounds suggested that even more different systems might be involved. It was not clear, therefore, whether there were several systems or one. Planting a probe in a given area did not give assurance that the effect of stimulation would be rewarding. There were different probabilities for different locations ranging from near certainty for some specifiable locations in or near the hypothalamus (Olds and Olds, 1963) to near 20% or 30% for the cingulate cortex and the hippocampus (Olds, 1956*a;* Ursin, Ursin, and Olds, 1966). In the last two areas it was even suspected that the stimulation was not actually rewarding but that some special artifact gave the appearance but not the substance of reward (e.g., hippocampal seizures might cause repetitive behavior giving the illusion of reward behavior). However, I believe this suspicion to be false.

There were also reports of self-stimulation from points that appeared originally to be totally outside the system. These were questioned at first but are now treated as valid. The brain areas involved included the neocortex (Routtenberg and Sloan, 1974; G. Ball, *private communication*), the cerebellum (J. Lilly, *private communication*), and the midline system of the thalamus (Cooper and Taylor, 1967). In the neocortex the best results were achieved with probes in those parts that were on the boundaries of the pyriform, cingulate, and hippocampal regions (Routtenberg and Sloan, 1974).

When probes were planted in the midline thalamus, reports of negative, positive, and no reinforcement were sufficiently stable in different experiments to suggest that slight differences in method or location would move marginal areas into or out of the set of "brain reward areas." The probe size, stimulating parameters, or behavior used for testing could make large differences. One possibility I entertain seriously is that there may be no areas of the brain where the reward effect is completeley absent. Nevertheless, there were clear differences in the brain. In some central locations the phenomenon was stable and strong through any modification of methods. At the other extreme there were areas where most methods failed to demonstrate any sign of reward, and those that succeeded showed an extremely weak effect. The lateral hypothalamus was at the center of the class where the effect was stable and strong (Olds and Olds, 1963). Most parts of the neocortex lay at the other extreme (Olds, 1956a).

2. *Were there any fiber systems that pervaded all the reward areas and thus might be candidates for "reward neurons?"* The descending fibers from the olfactory bulb and olfactory centers in and near the cortex, the ascending amine fiber systems from medulla, midbrain, and hypothalamus, and the large path neurons of the medial forebrain bundle were alternate candidates for the "reward neuron" status. The lower fifth of the brain hangs together (see Fig. 2). Its parts are interconnected by large numbers of fibers. Its connections to the rest of the brain are by comparison sparse, although by no means absent (Crosby, Humphrey, and Lauer, 1962). It is made up of the lower part of the neocortex and all parts of the paleocortex (including central parts that surround the ventricles). In the system also are the olfactory bulbs. All parts are tied bidirectionally to the hypothalamus which lies at the center and coordinates the actions of the diverse structures (Haymaker, Anderson, and Nauta, 1969). The hypothalamus is a subcortical collection of cell groups which works in consort with two other similar sets, two outposts of the hypothalamus. These are the septal area up front and the amygdala at the sides. The system is like a wheel—the cortex and paleocortex comprising the tire, and the hypothalamus with its outposts the hub and spokes. Just as the hypothalamus lies at the central base of the paleocortical system, the pituitary lies at the central base of the hypothalamus.

Anatomists divide the hypothalamus into 12 to 20 parts, but this number may be reduced for convenience. This is partly because the behavioral studies have been relatively gross and partly because the maps of behavioral functions have not followed either the fine or the coarse divisions drawn by the anatomists.

The following subdivisions of hypothalamus are appropriate to begin with. First there are medial and lateral sectors. The lateral sector is a tube that runs the full length. A fiber pathway, the medial forebrain bundle (Fig. 3A), runs through the tube occupying 30% to 50% of its cross section. Eight or 10 different olfactory forebrain structures project bundles downward into this pathway. Several different areas in the midbrain, pons, and medulla project bundles upward into it. Many of these ascending fibers carry one of the three monoamine neurotransmitters: norepinephrine, dopamine, or serotonin. These are specialized chemicals which form a bridge and a compromise between neuronal and endocrine functions. Beside and between the fiber pathways, the tube is populated by cell bodies (Fig. 3B). The most prominent family of cell bodies has dendrites, like the spokes of a wheel, spread as if to monitor all the bundles in the tube, plus another set of bundles which forms a partial shell around it (Millhouse, 1969). In the surrounding shell there is a great concourse of sensory and motor systems: (1) the three main

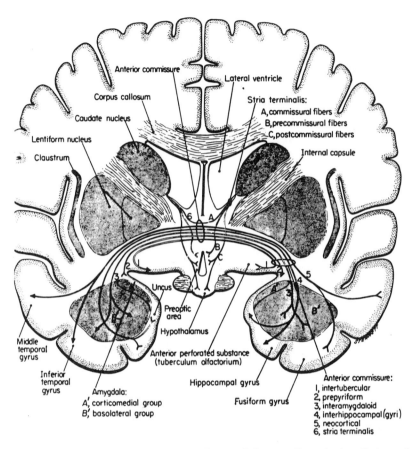

FIG. 2. The lower fifth of the brain hangs together. This is well shown on this section from the human brain (Crosby et al., 1962). At bottom center is the hypothalamus. Above that, in ascending order are: (1) between the lateral ventricles, the preoptic area; (2) the anterior commissure, which connects the basal cortical and paleocortical systems of the two sides; (3) the septum pellucidum (in rats this area contains the septal nuclei; in humans those nuclei are just in front of the septum pellucidum); (4) the corpus callosum, which is not part of the "lower fifth," but just above that is the "cingulate gyrus" (central cortex, which is closely connected to the septal nuclei and to the other systems of the lower fifth). On the sides, the middle temporal gyrus, inferior temporal gyrus, and fusiform gyrus are the parts of the neocortex closely tied into this motivational system; the hippocampal gyrus begins the olfactory or paleocortex (closely tied to the cingulate cortex on top). Following the line of the hippocampal gyrus we come to the uncus and the olfactory tubercle, and this brings us back to the hypothalamus. The gray areas marked A′ and B′ are the two main parts of the amygdala; the lentiform and caudate nuclei are two parts of the extrapyramidal system (these are sometimes called the striatum). Sometimes the amygdala and the striatum are grouped together and called the basal ganglia (often the thalamus, which does not appear here, is also included in the term "basal ganglia"). The stria terminalis is a strange, looping pathway from the amygdala to the preoptic area and hypothalamus; it is shown coming through the septal region, but its origin in amygdala is not shown.

motor pathways (from cortex, extrapyramidal motor systems, and cerebellum); (2) special sensory fibers from olfactory and gustatory receptors (Scott and Pfaffman, 1967; Norgren and Leonard, 1973); (3) side paths from the other sensory systems (Findlay, 1972); (4) a bundle of fibers from the "arousal" system; and (4) a special bundle from the computer-like

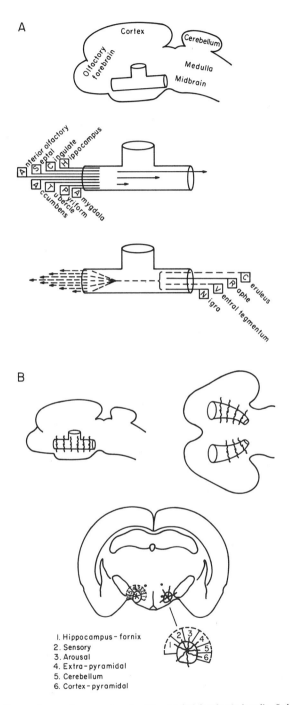

FIG. 3. A: Descending and ascending components of the medial forebrain bundle. B: Wheel-like neurons (i.e., the path neurons) spread to monitor the medial forebrain bundle and the shell of ascending and descending pathways that surrounds it. In the shell the fiber systems are identified by the functional systems which they are related to.

hippocampus of the paleocortex. The spokes of the wheel-like neurons penetrate into these and must therefore receive afferents from many if not all.

The medial sector of the hypothalamus has three main subsets: anterior, middle, and posterior. These subsets are even more heavily populated with cells than their lateral neighbor. They also contain a system of "tubules," (Bleier, 1972) from the blood and possibly also from the cerebrospinal fluid. These may carry hormones from the body and possibly from the hypothalamus itself or other parts of the brain (Knigge, Scott, and Weindl, 1972). The medial sector contains some cells very like the wheel-like neurons of the lateral sector. The medial and lateral families of large neurons interdigitate

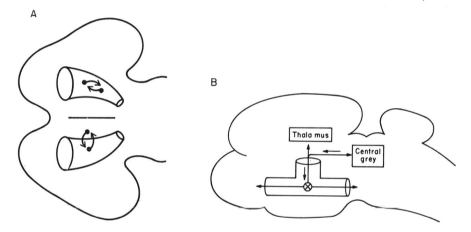

FIG. 4. A: Communication of path neurons with one another and with their medial neighbors. B: Outputs from medial and lateral hypothalamic neurons. Wheel-like neurons project four ways.

their dendrites in a border region along the medial edge of the medial forebrain bundle, and they project to one another (Millhouse, 1969) (Fig. 4A). Neuronal input-output systems for both the medial and lateral sectors run (1) through the medial forebrain bundle to the olfactory forebrain structures and to the several midbrain and lower structures; (2) across the medial forebrain bundle toward the amygdala and the extrapyramidal motor system; (3) up toward the thalamus; and (4) toward the "central gray" (Fig. 4B). From both of the last two, the messages are relayed through "nonspecific" pathways to cortex and probably also to outgoing motor centers.

Many bidirectional pathways appear to be common between medial and lateral sectors. The main differences seem to be the hormonal message systems (which have more access to the medial sector) and the shell of fiber systems (which appear to have more effect on the dendrites of the lateral wheel-like neurons). This puts the medial set in a position to monitor the hormonal actions and the lateral set to monitor the activities of the brain.

3. *Were all the "reward areas" similar in respect to brain reward behavior?*

By no means. For many of the questions that follow there were different answers for different areas.

4. *Were seizures associated with brain rewards?* When probes were planted in the anterior thalamus, the septal area, the anterior hypothalamus, and in telencephalic locations, seizures were often produced by stimulations near the reward thresholds (Porter, Conrad, and Brady, 1959). Stimulations in hippocampus seemed to be rewarding only so long as they induced periodic seizures. Stimulations in the amygdala appeared quite the opposite; as soon as the stimulus caused a seizure it ceased to be rewarding for a period of 24 hr or so. With probes in the ventral tegmental area (just in back of the hypothalamus), however, there were no seizures associated with brain reward behavior. Very high self-stimulation rates were achieved with very low currents, and even very high currents gave no recordable seizure activity (Bogacz, St. Laurent, and Olds, 1965). I conclude that seizures, insofar as they match or add to the effect of brain rewards, may be rewarding; but seizures are not necessary to produce the phenomenon (unless it be argued that the momentary and local effect of the brain stimulus is itself a seizure).

5. *Did animals press pedals at different rates to stimulate different parts of the brain?* Yes. There appeared to be a continuum spreading from central areas in lateral posterior hypothalamus and ventral tegmentum where rates were high. In a second tier, including parts of anterior hypothalamus and parts of pons and medulla, rates were somewhat lower although still quite high. When probes were planted in the medial hypothalamus, the rates were often lower; although stable high rates occurred in the case of some medial probes. When probes were placed in cingulate cortex or hippocampus, rates were very low (but still far above chance levels). The septal area, amygdala, and pyriform cortex fell between anterior hypothalamus and cingulate cortex, both anatomically and in self-stimulation rates (Olds, 1956a; Olds et al., 1960; Olds and Olds, 1963; Wurtz and Olds, 1963; Routtenberg and Malsbury, 1969; Routtenberg, 1971; Atrens and von Vietinghoff-Riesch, 1972).

6. *Did animals run mazes as well as press pedals?* With probes in some places they did not run mazes at all or did so very poorly. When probes were placed elsewhere, however, they learned mazes with ease (Fig. 5). The best locations for maze behavior did not correlate perfectly with the best locations for high pedal rates. Animals with septal area probes had low rates and poor maze performance (so this correlation was good). Those with medial hypothalamus probes had lower rates than if probes were in the lateral hypothalamus; but medial stimulation supported equal maze or runway behavior (Olds, 1956b; Newman, 1961; Spear, 1962; Wetzel, 1963; Scott, 1967).

7. *Did the brain reward impart its rewarding properties to objects with which it was associated?* To some degree associating a signal with a brain reward caused it to become rewarding; but learned reward experiments of this kind did not work as readily with brain rewards as with ordinary re-

wards. In one experiment rats were presented with two pedals. One activated a brief tone signal; the other did not. At the outset animals pressed the two pedals about equally but showed a slight preference for the one that did not cause a tone. The tone was then paired with a brain reward (with no pedals available). When retested with pedals after this "training," the rats pressed the tone pedal more frequently than the other (Stein, 1958). This showed that the tone had acquired some of the rewarding property. In a second try this experiment did not work (Mogensen, 1965), but in a third case the experiment was repeated successfully (Knott and Clayton, 1966). Other experiments of different detail have also been successful in showng that signals

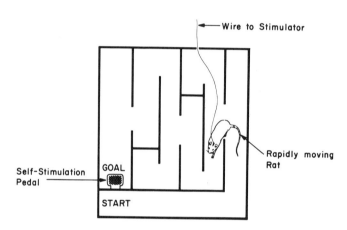

FIG. 5. Rats with probes positioned near the preoptic area sector of the medial forebrain bundle ran this maze well, eliminating errors from trial to trial and from day to day. On the first runs of the third and fourth days (each being 23 hr after the last previous stimulation), behavior was rapid and nearly errorless, indicating that it did not require immediate prior stimulation to sustain it.

associated with brain rewards became rewarding (Trowill and Hynek, 1970; Wald and Trowill, *in press*).

8. *How much work would animals do for brain rewards?* In "ratio" experiments, tests were made for the number of pedal responses a rat would make for just one brain reward. The number was smaller than would have been guessed from the very rapid pedal rates that occurred if each pedal response was rewarded (Sidman, Brady, Boren, Conrad, and Schulman, 1955; Brady, 1960; Brodie, Moreno, Malis, and Boren, 1960; Keesey and Goldstein, 1968). Rats working for food would pedal 50 to 100 times for a single reward. Rats working for brain reward were usually stopped if the ratio was raised to 20:1 or 30:1. There were individual differences, some animals doing much more work for a brain stimulus than others. The difference was thought to be due mainly to probe locations, but no anatomical mapping differentiated those sites which sustained high ratios from those that did not. Certain methods could be used to increase the ratios. The first

was to make each "reward" a multiple one. For example, a repeated train of stimulations was applied as the brain reward (Brown and Trowill, 1970), or the animal could be rewarded by presenting it with a second pedal (automatically introduced into the cage after a ratio of responses on the first pedal) with which it could stimulate its brain several times (Pliskoff, Wright, and Hawkins, 1965). In a different kind of experiment with a puzzling outcome a signal coming just before the brain reward greatly augmented the number of pedal responses the animal would make for a single reward, up to ratios of 200:1 in one instance (Cantor, 1971). The animal thus gave many responses for one brain reward as long as there was some way to anticipate its exact time of application (as if the rat needed to prepare for it).

Several arguments have been made to explain the discrepancy between the very high rates on one for one pedal schedules and the poor behavior on some schedules that required several responses for one reward. One explanation was that the multiple reinforcement of a 100% schedule might contain a reinforcement that was more than the sum of the individual trains. In other words, 10 reinforcements in rapid succession would be reinforcing even though each one alone would not be positive at all. This would match the observation that hungry or thirsty animals often refuse to work for very small amounts of food or water. A second argument was that the brain stimulus triggered both a reward and a "drive," and the drive provoked by the first stimulus in a set was required to make the next one be pursued. Both of these arguments are probably true for some cases, especially the first one. They clearly did not account for all cases, as when a single reinforcement preceded by a signal was rewarding, but without the signal it was not. There were other puzzling cases of a similar nature. In some experiments animals avoided the same temporal pattern of stimulation as they self-administered (Steiner, Beer, and Shaffer, 1969). Animals were first allowed to pedal-press for brain reward. The sequence of self-administration was recorded and an exactly similar sequence applied later by a programming device. Animals were then permitted to escape from this by performing an operant response. This they did at a rate which was substantially above the chance level. The predictability of the stimulus when self-administered apparently made it rewarding; its unpredictability during program administration apparently made it aversive.

9. *How long would the animal keep working after the brain reward was stopped?* Brain-rewarded behavior usually subsided rapidly when the brain stimulus was withdrawn. Hungry animals working for food kept trying longer, but the brain-rewarded behavior matched that of rats motivated by the incentive of highly appetizing foods rather than by deprivation (Gibson, Reid, Sakai, and Porter, 1965). In these cases, when the reward was withdrawn, the animal turned readily to other pursuits. The rapid subsidence of brain reward behavior has been used as an argument for the view that the

animal needs a drive caused by one brain stimulus to sustain the motivation for a second one (Deutsch and Howarth, 1963). Extinction was said to occur rapidly because this drive component dropped rapidly after stimulation. One main truth in this formulation is that all behavior which depends heavily on incentive and very little on drive loses motivation rapidly when the incentive is withdrawn. If the concept of drive is expanded to lump together the drive caused by deprivation and that caused by signaling or titillating with an appetizing incentive, the "drive decay" view becomes true (by definition). However, brain reward behavior did not require some electrical activation of an artificial deprivation state to start it. This was shown by the fact that the extinguished behavior could be started by a signal which promised brain reward just as well as by a brain reward stimulus itself. Moreover, extinction could be prolonged by a variety of procedures. One was to arrange the training so the animal became used to periodic withdrawal and return of rewards (Herberg, 1963b).

Clarifying this problem further, subsidence of the behavior in "extinction" experiments was shown to depend on inhibition emanating from the higher brain centers rather than on a subsidence of stimulated drive emanating from lower centers (Huston and Borbely, 1974); this was demonstrated by destroying the higher centers. Almost all of the "higher centers," including cortex, hippocampus, striatum, amygdala, and septum, were removed bilaterally. The lesioned animals then learned to perform gross behaviors such as sitting, climbing, or moving the tail in return for stimulation in the lateral hypothalamus. In the cases where the response was discrete and clearly observable, it did not appear to subside at all after withdrawal of the brain stimulus. This remarkable absence of extinction was observed as long as 2 weeks after training. The paradox of rapid subsidence of behavior in normal animals and long-lasting behavior after lesions is best interpreted in terms of a special inhibition emanating from the higher centers. A mechanism for conservation of effort might bring behaviors to a halt by some inhibitory process when drive or incentive was withdrawn.

10. *Did animals accept pain in order to get brain rewards?* This depended on where the brain probes were placed and on the amount of electric current used. With probes in some hypothalamic locations animals crossed an electrified grid (Fig. 6), which gave 0.5-mA shocks to the feet, to get to a pedal where currents approximately half that large were delivered to the brain (Olds and Sinclair, 1957; Olds, 1958c). The 0.5-mA shocks to the feet were more than five times as large as shocks which stopped hungry animals (deprived for 24 hr) on the path to food. Making a similar point was the fact that these animals with rewarding lateral hypothalamus probes and high currents were also quite undistractable and looked compulsive in their brain-rewarded behaviors. With smaller "reward" currents or other probe locations, however, it was quite easy to stop animals by imposing a foot shock on the path to brain reward. Such animals were easy to disturb and

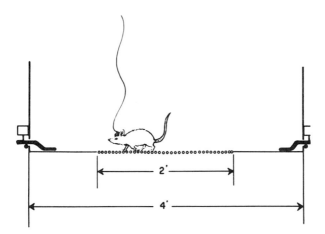

FIG. 6. Obstruction box. Pedal responses were rewarded with brain shocks. After every three of these the rat was required to cross a foot-shock grid to get more.

would self-stimulate only when distracting events were absent from the environment.

11. *Would animals give up food and starve to get rewarding brain stimulations?* This did happen with some probes and some stimulation levels, but it was quite unusual (Routtenberg and Lindy, 1965; Spies, 1965; Miliaressis and Cardo, 1973). When probes were planted in some parts of the hypothalamus and in some parts of the ventral tegmental area, with the currents set at several times threshold, animals gave up eating to devote themselves to brain reward behavior. In one experiment the animals were first trained to get food by pedal-pressing in a Skinner box (one 45-mg pellet for each pedal response). The Skinner box feeding time was limited to about 45 min/day. (Actually the amount of time was determined to be that required to maintain body weight at a steady level; the animals did not gain weight.) Then a second pedal whose depression yielded a rewarding brain shock was introduced. For some animals this was fatal or nearly so. They split their time between brain reward and food on the first 2 or 3 days, thus losing weight. After this they gave up food altogether and died if they were not rescued by termination of the experiment. In a different experiment, deprived rats consistently chose the arm of a T-maze equipped for self-stimulation in preference to the one with a feeding mechanism.

12. *How was the rewarding brain stimulation related to aversive factors?* In most areas where brain rewarding effects could be obtained, the same electric stimulation was shown to have aversive effects as well (Fig. 7) in experiments where the animal could reduce or interrupt an ongoing brain stimulus series by some measurable behavior (Bower and Miller, 1958; Roberts, 1958; Kent and Grossman, 1969; Steiner et al., 1969; Steiner, Bodnar, Ackerman, and Ellman, 1973). Either longer trains had aversive ef-

fects, or the selfsame train appeared to be positive when the animal was allowed to generate a series of trains by its own behavior, and negative when it later responded to reduce or interrupt a "replay" of that same series of trains programmed now from a tape recorder (Steiner et al., 1969). With probes in the lateral hypothalamus when animals were given free control over stimulus duration, they did not turn the stimulus on and leave it on. Instead, they stopped the stimulus after brief trains (often approximately 0.5 sec). If probes were planted in parts of the medial hypothalamus animals would sometimes take much longer trains (Atrens and von Vietinghoff-

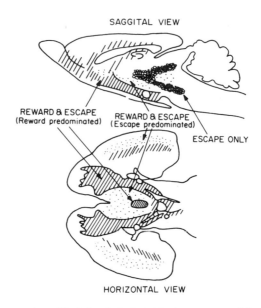

FIG. 7. Reward-escape overlaps. Stimulation in single-hatched areas was mainly rewarding. In stippled areas it was mainly aversive. In both it was mixed. In scrambled areas there was escape only.

Riesch, 1972). If probes were planted in some parts of the cingulate cortex, longer trains were also taken (*unpublished observations*). With probes in some places (e.g., on the boundaries between the tectum and the tegmental reticular formation) electric stimulation of the brain was mainly aversive (Delgado, Roberts, and Miller, 1954; Olds and Olds, 1963), and there was no appreciable tendency for animals to turn the stimulus on at all.

A surprising finding about most of the areas where both positive and negative effects could be demonstrated was that the self-selected train duration was not usually optimal in other tests. Animals self-selected short trains if allowed to control the duration by pressing a pedal to start and releasing it to stop. However, if they were forced to do much work for a single train, trains longer than the self-selected ones turned out to be optimal (Keesey, 1964; Hodos, 1965).

Between brain rewards and aversive stimulations, there were different interactions. Some rewarding brain stimulation counteracted aversive stimulation so that if a negative stimulus was applied within the 0.25-sec period just after the brain stimulus it had no influence at all (Cox and Valenstein, 1965; Valenstein, 1965). In quite different tests some reinforcing brain stimulation (in hypothalamus) augmented aversive behavior (Olds and Olds, 1963), whereas other rewarding brain stimulation (in septal area) suppressed the same escape behavior (Routtenberg and Olds, 1963).

13. *Was rewarding brain stimulation arousing or quieting?* The answer depends on the probe location. When stimulation was applied near the septal area it arrested overt behavior (Olds, 1956b). In these cases it also had parasympathetic effects, lowering the heart rate, blood pressure, and respiratory rate (Malmo, 1961). It slowed or halted escape behavior (Routtenberg and Olds, 1963). It sometimes even slowed the avid brain reward behavior that could be simultaneously provoked by stimulating a hypothalamus electrode (Keesey and Powley, 1968). When stimulation was applied in lateral hypothalamus it had quite the opposite effect (Perez-Cruet, Black, and Brady, 1963; Perez-Cruet, McIntire, and Pliskoff, 1965). It excited the animal and caused much overt locomotor activity and sympathetic peripheral effects, raising respiratory rate and blood pressure. In this case it also increased aversive behavior (Olds and Olds, 1962; Stein, 1965).

14. *When stimulated in brain reward centers, what did humans feel?* If it was in the telencephalic centers, there were some reports of great reduction of pain or even hedonic experiences that seemed to be related to basic drives such as sex. If it was in hypothalamus there were no clear reports of positive affect in spite of behavioral signs of reward (patients manipulated switches to stimulate probes that were most likely in the hypothalamus). The actual location of probes in human studies was poorly determined (Fig. 8). These tests were carried out during therapeutic procedures or during medical researches aimed at developing therapeutic procedures; the patients were ill with major diseases, and all other therapeutic efforts had failed (Heath, 1954, 1964; Bishop, Elder, and Heath, 1964; Sem-Jacobsen, 1968; Delgado, 1969; Mark and Ervin, 1970).

15. *What was the relation, if any, to drug addiction?* Some addictive drugs (e.g., cocaine, amphetamine, and apomorphine) appeared to have strong relations to the brain reward behavior itself and to the neurochemical systems thought to underlie it (Stein, 1964a,b, 1966; Crow, 1970; Broekkamp and van Rossum, 1974). These drugs promoted the brain reward behaviors and most likely activated some of the same synaptic mechanisms as the brain reward stimulations. Other addictive drugs (e.g., morphine) did not have known relations to the underlying neurochemical systems and did not promote the behavior. There were signs, however, that morphine might affect the same neurons as the rewarding brain stimulus (Kerr, Triplett, and Beeler, 1974). Animals "addicted" to morphine had neurons "turned on"

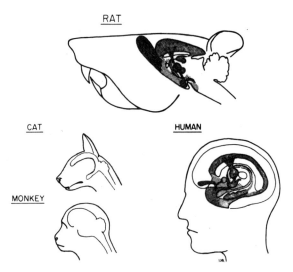

FIG. 8. Reward maps in different animals. The most detailed map is the one for rats (Olds and Olds, 1963). The ones for cats (Wilkenson and Peele, 1963) and monkeys (Bursten and Delgado, 1958) are in less detail, and the pictures presented here involve some speculative additions based on analogies. The human map (Bishop et al., 1963) is based on even less data and more speculation.

during the active high drive condition evidenced by withdrawal symptoms; these neurons were turned off by morphine administration. In other experiments neurons recorded from the same areas fired actively during periods intervening between self-administered brain shocks but were turned off by the brain shocks themselves. A similarity of function between brain reward and morphine was shown by experiments in which the rewarding brain stimulation exhibited pain-reducing properties (Rose, 1974). Quite different studies showed a regional distribution of an "opiate receptor" in the brain that seemed to parallel the reward map to some degree (Kuhar, Pert, and Snyder, 1973). Therefore although the evidence is fragmentary, it is fair to suppose that a strong connection may be established between self-stimulation and drug-induced behaviors.

16. *Was there a period of addiction or incubation involved in brain reward behaviors?* The answer is yes and no (but mainly no). Brain stimulation often appeared to be rewarding when first applied. I have observed several times in my own laboratory, however, that there was an improvement in brain reward behavior that accumulated for 2 or 3 weeks. It first suggested a growing addiction, but this interpretation was wrong. This was shown by the fact that the improvement occurred regardless of whether the animals were stimulated (*unpublished observations*). In other words, if the first stimulations were delayed for several weeks, the improvement had already occurred by that time. The animals performed better than controls that had received implants more recently. Furthermore, when tests were started this

late there was no further improvement. Thus the improvement occurred even without practice and without stimulation. It appeared at first as if it depended entirely on recovery from the effects of surgery. It now appears equally likely that it depends on some proliferation of nerve fibers which is surprisingly triggered by surgery; this proliferation required a period of growth to develop fully (Pickel, Segal, and Bloom, 1974b). Thus although there was a period of improvement in the brain-rewarding effects after probes were planted, there did not appear to be any addiction to the brain stimulation necessary to make it rewarding. Anecdotal observations from almost all "brain reward laboratories" tell of some animals pressing the pedal avidly within a minute or two of their first experience.

17. *Was there satiation of brain reward behavior?* The behavior often continued at high rates for substanial periods. If animals were permitted continuous access for hours or days, however, there were usually long pauses while eating, drinking, and sleeping occurred (Olds, 1958b; Valenstein and Beer, 1964). With probes in some locations the animals pedal-pressed at a slow but very steady pace when permitted only an hour of this behavior daily. When there was a shift to "continuous access," however, behavior gradually dropped to a new and much lower level. After this there were periodic rises and falls. In most cases of slow or moderate self-stimulation rates, diurnal rhythms (sometimes mixed with faster rhythms) could be detected (Terman and Terman, 1970). When the behavior rates were maintained at higher levels by higher stimulating currents or by probes in locations yielding higher rates, the diurnal rhythms were not clear, but there were still periodic pauses in self-stimulation which permitted eating, drinking, sleeping, and so forth (Annau, Heffner, and Koob, 1974). When high currents were administered via probes planted in parts of the hypothalamus, the animals pressed continuously at very high rates after being switched to continuous access schedules showing no important decrement in rate for approximately 24 to 48 hr, but they did not continue indefinitely. In one case a rat averaged 30 responses per minute for 20 days (Valenstein and Beer, 1964).

18. *Did animals need a "priming" stimulus to start the behavior?* In other words, was some brain stimulation necessary in a trained animal to create an incentive or drive which then motivated further behavior? With some probe locations this "priming" was clearly necessary; in other cases it was not necessary but very helpful; and in still other cases it caused only moderate improvement in performance (Reid, Hunsicker, Lindsay, Gallistel, and Kent, 1973). Thus in some cases animals performed as if no incentive were needed other than being placed in a permissive environment, which triggered behavior toward the brain stimulus. In other cases where priming was more effective, it was interesting that the priming could often be obtained by stimulating a probe different from the one used for reward (Gallistel, 1969b). When two brain reward probes were planted in the same animal, one might be best for priming and the other for rewarding. In this case behavior was

optimized by priming with one of the two and rewarding with the other. Furthermore, the rewardingness of a brain stimulus could be considerably enhanced by a different procedure which did not involve brain stimulation at all (Cantor and LoLordo, 1970, 1972). If a normal sensory signal preceded (and thus allowed the animal to anticipate) the brain stimulus by a brief time interval (a fraction of a second or so), this greatly improved the animal's response. The animal preferred signaled to unsignaled brain stimulation in almost all cases. This procedure could even convert a stimulus treated as aversive into one that was positive. This made it seem that one important effect of priming was to "tell" the animal of the availability of brain reward so it could correctly anticipate the outcome of the next behavioral response. It was generally assumed that probe location made the main difference in the need for priming. Priming was necessary (or at least very helpful) with probes in some locations, whereas with probes elsewhere it was not necessary (although priming always causes some improvement in the rate of approach). The anatomical locations that require priming have not yet been differentiated from those that do not; therefore the possibility of individual differences must still be entertained. The most likely answer is that two closely concurrent fiber streams exist, priming being required in one and not the other.

19. *Was an internal drive state required as a precondition for brain reward behaviors?* The first answer is that no deprivation measures were required to cause brain reward behavior. However, the necessity of priming as a prerequisite for brain reward behavior in some cases was possibly an indication that in these cases a drive was needed and that it was supplied as an aftereffect of the same brain stimulation which was rewarding. The rapid approach of other animals to brain pedals after 24 hr with no stimulation and with no deprivation suggested that at least in these cases no drive was required (Scott, 1967; Kornblith and Olds, 1968; Kent and Grossman, 1969).

20. *Did drive manipulations modify brain reward behavior?* Even though drives were unnecessary to provoke brain reward behavior, operations to increase drive often improved performance or caused thresholds to fall (Brady, Boren, Conrad, and Sidman, 1957); and sometimes (but rarely) they had just the opposite effect (Olds, 1958a). Food and water deprivation usually caused brain reward thresholds to fall and pedal rates to improve (Brady et al., 1957). However, because these drives made the animals more active, it was difficult to differentiate between the specific and the nonspecific effects of drive. The behavior had a positive feedback character because more pedal behavior (dependent variable) caused more reinforcement (independent variable); or to put it more bluntly, more effect resulted in more of the cause. That there was some specificity was indicated by the fact that deprivation sometimes had the opposite effect. In one experiment animals were maintained on a feeding schedule and tests were made during deprived and sated conditions (Olds, 1958a). Some pedal rates were improved during satiation, and others during hunger. In the same experiment animals (males in this

case) were castrated and tests were continued for several weeks after castration. Then androgen replacement therapy was used. Some animals were slowed by castration and improved by replacement, whereas others were improved by castration and slowed by replacement therapy. There was a negative correlation between the effect of food and sex drives; in cases where castration improved performance, so did hunger. In cases where testosterone administration improved performance, hunger was inimical to some degree. In other words, most probes responded positively to either hunger or testosterone but not to both. The difference was assumed to be a result of differing probe location, but because there was only one probe per animal the differences could have been individual ones. Individual differences, however, were ruled out in an experiment comparing the effects of hunger and thirst (Gallistel and Beagley, 1971). Given the choice between stimulating one of two different probes, animals chose one of the two when thirsty and the other when hungry. In a different experiment, female rats were used and the self-stimulation rate was observed to covary with the normal estrous cycle (Prescott, 1966). The probe in this case was in the lateral posterior hypothalamus, a location which showed covariation with androgens in males (Olds, 1958a).

In some experiments it was shown that the condition of excessive food satiety caused by loading the stomach caused a decrement in self-stimulation behavior (Hoebel, 1968). In this experiment food was injected by means of a tube, which probably caused excessive distention of the stomach. Therefore the "loaded condition" was different from the behaviorally "full" condition of the other experiment. There have been no reports of improved brain reward behavior caused by this procedure, but only a limited range of probe location was reported. In a different kind of experiment, self-stimulation by probes in a region of the midbrain was motivated by a fear-producing stimulus [apparently indicating that in this case the brain stimulus was not as much rewarding as "soothing" (Deutsch and Howarth, 1962)].

21. *Did some brain stimulations cause drive states or drive behaviors?* The answer is yes. Brain stimulation in certain areas often caused one drive or another depending partly on the location of the probe and partly on other factors that are not fully clarified (Hess, 1954; Miller, 1960; Morgane, 1961; Herberg, 1963a; Coons, 1964; Mogenson and Stevenson, 1966). Saying the brain stimulation caused a drive means that if the drive object was present the stimulation caused consummatory behavior, and if the object was absent the stimulation caused instrumental behavior. Often this involved some work to get to or at the drive object. Such behaviors were often obtained with probes placed between the medial and lateral hypothalamus (Fig. 9). They were also produced with stimulation in other parts of the hypothalamus or farther afield, but the area between medial and lateral is thought to be most effective. If probes were placed in the anterior part of this longitudinal region, temperature-adjusting and sex responses were most likely to appear

(*unpublished observations*). If probes were planted in the anterior part of a middle region, food and water responses appeared but water responses were more likely. In the posterior part of the same middle region, food and water responses were still evoked but food responses were more likely (Valenstein, Cox, and Kakolewski, 1970). Probes placed more posteriorly were somewhat more likely to produce sexual behaviors (Herberg, 1963*a*). Because the latter were also sometimes obtained with anteriorly placed probes and because there was much overlap, the idea of localized drive centers was rejected. The idea of an undifferentiated system was also rejected because there was an array of regions from anterior to posterior hypothalamus where

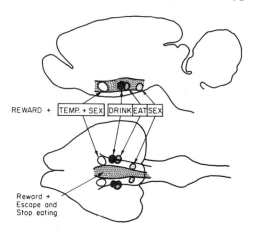

FIG. 9. Array of lateral hypothalamic regions where electrical stimulation causes instrumental and consummatory behaviors related to temperature, drinking, eating, and sex as most likely. The effects are heavily overlapped, but the most likely effect depends on the location of the stimulus.

temperature, drinking, eating, and sex responses, respectively, were most likely.

Probes placed in a very small medial nucleus near the midline cause oxytocin release and so milk ejection. This can be considered a reproductive drive behavior. The site of stimulation was the paraventricular nucleus of the hypothalamus. Its boundaries were clearly defined and the effects of stimulating this region were well documented. Oxytocin is a fast-acting blood-borne hormone which causes milk ejection through the teats and other reproductive responses in a reflex fashion. Stimulation of the paraventricular nuclei evoked milk ejection in animals with thoracic spinal transections or spinal anesthesia. In estrogenized lactating rabbits, the milk ejection responses were accompanied by augmented uterine contractions (Cross, 1966).

In other experiments the anterior hypothalamus was stimulated thermally, causing temperature drive behaviors (Corbit, 1969, 1970; Adair, Casby, and Stolwijk, 1970; Murgatroyd and Hardy, 1970). When a thermal probe was used to heat or cool the area, it aroused compensatory temperature adjustments. When the area was heated, the animal sought cool stimulation; when it was cooled, the animal performed behaviors to warm the environment.

The "drive centers" defined by electric stimulation were by no means focused. There was no way to place a probe so that a drive effect could be guaranteed on this basis alone. In the best area the ratio of hits was below 100% (possibly as low as one-half or one-third). However, there were focal points where these (rather high) probabilities were achieved. As the probe

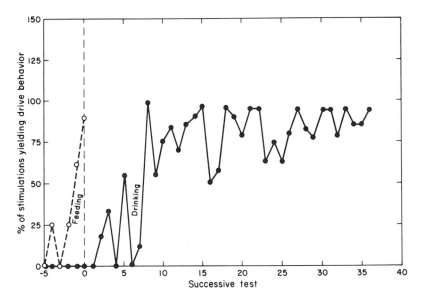

FIG. 10. Valenstein effect. Stimulation caused little drive behavior in early tests, but later it caused eating when both food and water were available. After repeated application of stimulus trains with only water available, the stimulus gradually came to evoke drinking.

was moved away from the focus the likelihood of stimulating a drive declined but stayed considerably above zero through all the various parts of the hypothalamus and the related telencephalic and midbrain structures.

22. *Were the drive behaviors evoked by electric stimulation stable?* No. If it was first determined that a given hypothalamic probe could be used for stimulation of a drive behavior, it was usually possible to modify the drive effects of the stimulus by a rather simple kind of "training" procedure (Fig. 10) (Valenstein, Cox, and Kakolewski, 1968; Valenstein, 1973b). Suppose the probe evoked eating. If the animal was repeatedly stimulated with interrupted trains (e.g., 1 min on, 5 min off) in the presence of a different drive object, the stimulus eventually appeared to evoke the drive appropriate to the new object. In the end, the rat sometimes still ate during stimulation if given a choice; but in other cases it preferred the new drive object. Because

the stimulus did not originally provoke any behavior toward the second drive object, there was evidence of a change in the drive behavior even when the animal preferred to eat. It is sometimes argued that the original eating response to the brain stimulus might itself have been learned in a similar fashion at the beginning of the tests. This had led to serious question of whether the stimulated effect is appropriately called a drive effect at all. Mapping the most likely areas for the different drives into different parts of the hypothalamus, however, was scarcely compatible with the view that all drive effects were learned.

23. *Did some brain stimulations stop specific drive behaviors in the way that satiety stops feeding?* This was a difficult question to answer because aversive stimulation brought many behaviors to a halt without having any specific relation to the drives involved (Krasne, 1962). There were, however, some stimulations that appeared to halt eating behavior in a more specific fashion. The stimulation seemed specific because of special food behaviors that occurred during a poststimulatory "rebound," i.e., during the period just after the stimulation was terminated. The stimulations that had this effect were in the medial hypothalamus, but the exact locations are unknown or in dispute. Possibly the anterior part of the ventromedial nucleus and the adjacent posterior part of the anterior nucleus, or some pathways in this general area were involved (Wyrwicka and Dobrzecka, 1960; Olds, Allan, and Briese, 1971). When stimulation was applied in these areas in some animals or with some probes it caused hungry animals to stop feeding during the stimulus and the sated animals to begin eating at (or shortly after) the offset of the stimulus. In other words, the electric stimulus caused feeding of a hungry animal to stop, and its offset caused a sated animal to begin eating. Because many brain-stimulated behaviors are replaced by opposed behaviors during a brief period just after cessation of the stimulus, the concept of "rebound" is used. The brain is considered to be replete with "opponent process" systems; electric stimulation is thought to fatigue the stimulated member of an opponent pair, weakening it; and this is supposed to result in a rebound of the opposite character as soon as the stimulus stops. Because of this view, the locations where stimulation stopped eating and rebound evoked it were thought to be more specifically related to this drive system than those locations where stimulation stopped all behaviors without specific rebound effects. The latter stimuli with only general effects were thought to be aversive or inhibitory. The stimuli with specific rebound effects were viewed as possibly activating "satiety" mechanisms. There have been no extensive research programs on "satiety-like" mechanisms for drives other than hunger.

24. *Did the brain "centers" for drives or satiety overlap with those for reward?* In most areas where electric stimulation caused drive behaviors such as eating, drinking, or sex responses, the brain stimulus also provoked brain reward behaviors (Hoebel and Teitelbaum, 1962; Margules and Olds, 1962;

Caggiula and Hoebel, 1966; Mogenson and Stevenson, 1966). This was particularly true of the areas in middle and posterior hypothalamus between the medial and lateral areas, and in the lateral area. Stimulation in these areas also produced aversive reactions, but the balance was tipped toward reward. The aversive behaviors were high in threshold and low in rate (and sometimes required that the trains be lengthened). The appetitive behaviors were low in threshold and high in rate. Thus even though there was some *a priori* view that "reward" and "satiety" might be correlated, there was evidence for a correlation of brain reward and brain drive centers. Brain reward behavior, however, was also provoked in other parts of the hypothalamus where drive behaviors were not (or at least where drive effects have not yet been documented). Reward behaviors were also provoked by electric stimulations in the medial hypothalamic centers, e.g., the ventromedial nucleus (Atrens and von Vietinghoff-Riesch, 1972). This was previously thought of as an area where stimulation halted eating (based on experiments with goats mainly). Stimulation here often did not stop eating in the rat. Still there were other parts of the hypothalamus whose stimulation both halted eating and caused rebound eating. Stimulation at least at some of these locations was rewarding. This might suggest a correlation of brain reward centers with both "drive" and "satiety" centers, which points to the obvious fact that related functions such as reward, drive, and satiety need to interdigitate their mechanisms if they were to interact conjointly to control behavior. Most of the medial hypothalamic nuclei (e.g., ventromedial, dorsomedial, or anterior nucleus) were controversial as members of the "brain reward map." This was because, even though both positive and negative reinforcements were represented, the scale in many medial centers was tipped to the negative. Aversive thresholds were low, and aversive behavior rates high. Self-stimulation thresholds were higher than those in lateral hypothalamus, and rates were lower. It was the slow rates which were especially notable. Nevertheless, there was some reason to believe that stimulation of some medial centers might be better for rewarding maze behaviors and possibly less likely to require priming to elicit reward behavior than stimulation in lateral centers. Moreover, one of the few locations in the brain where there was almost pure positive behavior (rapid behavior to start the stimulus and almost no behavior to shut it off) was the midline, periventricular nucleus of the posterior hypothalamus (Atrens and von Vietinghoff-Riesch, 1972).

That a stimulus should at the same time cause consummatory responses and be pursued as a goal seemed in good accord. Thus the sex, eating, and drinking behaviors caused during a stimulus fitted with the strong goal-directed behaviors aimed at self-stimulation; both effects might derive from a single neuronal mechanism. However, because the stimulus usually also caused instrumental behavior (sometimes hard work) in pursuit of food or water, this made it seem that the stimulus might have a driving or goading character, which might imply a negative state. Therefore it was better to assume that the brain stimulus was affecting a mixed set of elements, both drive and reward ones. It seemed fair to suppose that the different elements were associated in the hypothalamus so they could interact in the control of behavior.

25. *Was the rewarding effect of stimulating the "feeding center" increased by hunger?* The term "feeding center" is used to refer to those locations where electric stimulation caused food-directed behavior. When "reward" probes were planted in areas where eating was also induced, there were paradoxical effects. When animals were "oversatiated" by loading the stomach, reward behavior was reduced (Hoebel, 1968); but when in different experiments the animals were deprived of food for 1 or 2 days, this also curtailed and eventually stopped behavior rewarded by "feeding center" stimulation (*unpublished observation;* Fig. 11). The same animal continued to pedal-press and even increased response rates when the reward was delivered to a different probe, one where sex drive behavior was evoked. Thus the responses augmented during extreme starvation were not the ones rewarded by stimulations of the "feeding center."

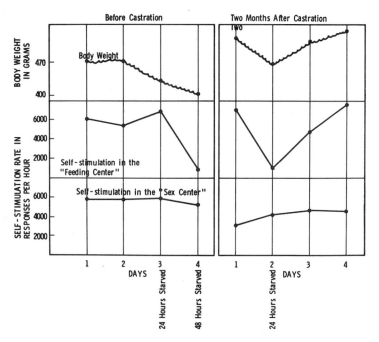

FIG. 11. Self-stimulation in feeding and sex-related areas during food-deprivation and after castration. One probe was said to be in the feeding center because its stimulation caused eating, and the other in the sex center because its stimulation caused ejaculation of motile sperm. The two probes were in the same animal, and during tests alternate 2-min periods were devoted first to one and then to the other probe. Starvation often caused slowing of pedal behavior when the food-related probe was being stimulated, but it did not slow self-stimulation of the sex probe.

26. *Did the animal give up food in order to get "feeding center" stimula-lation?* No. Animals gave up food as was previously described for some rewarding brain stimulations (Routtenberg and Lindy, 1965; Spies, 1965; Miliaressis and Cardo, 1973), but those which evoked feeding behavior in pretests usually failed in the "self-starvation" tests (*unpublished observations*). In these cases as the animals got hungrier, the brain reward pedal responses became scarcer and the animal gradually returned to eating. Other brain stimulations in hypothalamus and in the ventral tegmental area, however, did cause animals to renounce food and run the danger of starvation. Because the stimulations did not cause eating, however, they would be viewed as being outside of the "feeding center."

27. *Could brain rewards be added to normal rewards?* Yes. In some experiments olfactory bulb stimulation was used as the reward (Phillips and Mogenson, 1969). This was enhanced by simultaneous administration of odors shown to be positive, and curtailed by odors shown to be negative (Phillips, 1970). In other experiments brain stimulation that evoked both drinking and reward behavior was used (Mendelson, 1967; Mogenson and Morgan, 1967). In these cases currents below the "reward threshold" evoked self-stimulation if water was available but not if it was absent. The animals in these cases would self-stimulate and then drink and continue this cycle of self-administered stimulation alternating (or running concurrently) with normal consummatory behavior. Similar results were also produced with feeding center stimulation and food reward (Coons and Cruce, 1968; Poschel, 1968). Although these experiments and others like them gave the appearance of additivity between the brain reward and peripheral ones, other interpretations (not greatly different) were possible. In the case of the positive odor, it is not clear if this would have been facilitating to any ongoing behavior (and the aversive odor might have slowed behavior generally). In the case of the water behavior, the subthreshold current might have been rewarding by itself, but the simultaneously evoked drive might have been aversive in the absence of water. However, self-stimulation could go on in the presence of water to assuage the induced thirst.

28. *Was the "drive" effect the same as the "priming effect?* No. The animal primed by a prior brain stimulus sought further brain stimulations (Gallistel, 1973), but it did not eat or seek food during this poststimulatory period (Cox, Kakolewski, and Valenstein, 1969). If the probe was in a "drive center" as was quite common, the animal sought the drive object avidly during the duration of the stimulus and switched its attention abruptly away from the drive object during the period when the stimulus was turned off (*unpublished observation*). In the aftereffect of stimulation there was a strong behavior directed toward more stimulation. The drive for food (or another drive object) had disappeared immediately at the offset. Thus the impulse to self-stimulate that decayed gradually after the stimulus was not the same as the drive activated during the stimulus. Furthermore, priming

was effective at many sites where there was no sign of any drive being aroused. (Valenstein et al., 1970).

29. *Was the reward effect the same as the priming effect?* In some cases the two could be separated. In one set of experiments a start box connected to a goal box by a simple runway or alley was used. A stimulus applied in the start box was used for priming. A stimulus in the goal box was used for reward. In this test some probes yielded better priming and others better reward [so the animal with two probes gave the best behavior if primed with one and stimulated with the other (Gallistel, 1969b)]. Moreover, it was possible to show that the stimulus parameters most effective for priming were different from those most effective for rewarding. Interesting experiments on this have been done with pulse pairs (Deutsch, 1964; Gallistel, Rolls, and Greene, 1969). A repetition rate of pulses (R) was chosen such that R was below threshold but $2R$ was above it. Then pulse pairs were used instead of single pulses and were applied at the repetition rate R. When separation of the two pulses in a pair was sufficient, the effective rate was $2R$; but when the separation was too small, the second pulse became ineffective and the effective rate was R. An abrupt behavior change was expected to occur at the transition, and it was supposed to be possible to test for this. To some degree this expectation was fulfilled. With this method it was possible to determine for a stimulated effect the "cutoff point" at which the second pulse changed from effective to ineffective. This was taken to be a measure of the "refractory period" or some such parameter of the underlying neuronal elements. If two stimulated phenomena had the same cutoff point, it indicated similar underlying neurons. These were, of course, not necessarily identical; many neurons in the brain have similar refractory periods so, even at best, the method was not very strong. If two stimulated phenomena had different cutoff points, it indicated different underlying elements. Brain reward and brain stimulated "drives" had the same cutoff point, 0.6 msec (Rolls, 1973). The priming effect had a different one, 0.8 msec (Gallistel, Rolls, and Greene, 1969). Since this was also the cutoff point for a set of simultaneously stimulated neurons thought to be involved in "arousal," it was considered possible that priming and arousal might have something in common (Rolls, 1971a). Even a differentiation of two effects by this method, however, did not imply two totally different mechanisms; it is possible to imagine several ways in which a partly common mechanism would be differentiated. Suppose, for example, that stimulation was applied to an axon. It would fire the axon and its terminals in the forward direction and the soma-dendrite input mechanism in a backward direction. Now imagine that the axon could be fired at a high rate but the soma-dendrite mechanism could not. The second pulse in a pair might then be effective for the axons but ineffective for the dendrite. What difference could this make? One answer is that the axon alone might support continued brain reward within a bout of behavior, but sustained interest or renewed behavior after several

minutes of waiting might require a short-term memory. This might neces-
sitate activating the dendrites during the initial reward period in order to
cause connections to form between them and other coactive sensory traces.

30. *Were the rewarding effects of a brain stimulus simple or a compound?*
If priming were an essential component of the reward stimulus then the
answer would be: compound. The animal would need to be primed by one
effect of the stimulus and rewarded by a different one. The two fiber sets
implied by the pulse pair experiments might suggest this kind of complexity.
The fact that animals run mazes without priming puts a dent in this supposition, but there are other possibilities that need to be considered. The
drive might not be needed during the pursuit behavior but only during the
consummatory endpoint. Some experiments (Mendelson, 1966) appeared
to show that the animal would run a maze without a drive if the drive was
supplied along with the reward at the end of the maze. In this experiment
probes in a drive center were used to present the "drive" (electrical drive) in
the goal box. It is not clear to me that the "drive" stimulus was not itself
an added reward, but other experiments have pointed in the same direction.
Reward may therefore be complex in much the same way pain is supposed to
be. One theory of pain is that it always depends on a pattern of stimulation
(Melzak and Wall, 1965). Nonintense stimulation of the skin surrounding a
point stimulus may suppress pain, while punctate stimulation, which appears
to make up but a small part of the larger stimulus, is painful. This has led to
a theory that pain is not simple. It requires one kind of stimulation un-
counteracted by another kind. There seems reason why rewarding stimulation
might also be compound. The notion that a drive and a reward need to go
together to make reinforcement fits with food behavior. Almost any food
can be made aversive if the animal is pretreated with sufficient excess of it.
It seems possible, therefore, that a brain stimulus might activate more than
one component of the pattern of neural events required to "key" the reward
lock. At least it seems likely that a combination of neuronal processes might
be required to trigger the reward process.

If the effect were complex, the complexity might be on the afferent side of
the "reward neurons," and thus the brain reward stimulus might still be
simple. In other words, a hunger plus a gustatory signal would need to be
conjoined to cause normal activation of a reward neuron, but the activated
reward neuron would not require further complementary conditions.

31. *Was there any indication of a common denominator such as the term
"pleasure" implies?* The fact that stimulation in the lateral hypothalamus
could be "converted" from drive to drive by training procedures (Valenstein
et al., 1970) suggested that the main import of the stimulus might be its
common denominator properties. It is equally likely, however, that the
stimulus affected several drives which could be further sensitized by their
appropriate targets. It seems possible that the stimulus caused rather specific
drives, which then became pathologically channeled toward false goals by

the regular association between the brain drive stimulus and the particular goal object. If there were a common denominator, its stimulation might be purely positive. That purely positive reinforcement caused by brain stimulation was rare mitigated the likelihood of such a system. However, this might be explained by arguing that positive and negative common denominator neurons were mixed (so as to act reciprocally). In such a case stimulation would be ambivalent even though the actual neurons involved were not. In any event the question of whether there is some common denominator of positive reinforcement (or possibly even a common denominator between positive and negative reinforcement) (Olds and Olds, 1962, 1964; Stein, 1964c, 1965) is unanswered. It deserves further study.

32. *Was there a focal center where lesions abolished reward behavior?* The answer was not clear, but probably there was not. Lesions of specific telencephalic areas such as the septal area or the amygdaloid complex had small effects if any on brain reward behavior evoked by hypothalamic stimulation (Ward, 1960, 1961). Lesions along the main path to the hypothalamus failed to stop olfactory bulb self-stimulation (Valenstein and Campbell, 1966), although there were alternate pathways (Routtenberg and Sloan, 1974). Procaine applied in the hypothalamus stopped olfactory bulb-evoked reward behavior (Nakajima and Iwasaki, 1973). Lesions anteriorly placed in the hypothalamus did not stop pedal behavior reinforced by more posterior stimulation (Olds and Olds, 1969). These anterior lesions did, however, block maze behavior reinforced by the same stimulus (Olds and Hogberg, 1964). This seemed to indicate that a path from hypothalamus to cortex might be necessary if the behavior to be reinforced were so complex that it needed the "higher centers." Pointing in this same direction were experiments in which all of the brain anterior and dorsal to the thalamus was removed (Fig. 12) (Huston and Borbely, 1974), including neocortex, paleocortex, and basal ganglia. Many behaviors did not occur at all in these animals. The animals were "rewarded" with brain stimulation for performing rather simple behaviors, and the frequency of these was substantially and appropriately modified by brain reward. Thus the telencephalon was dispensable as far as the reinforcing effects of brain stimulation were concerned even though complex behaviors could not be trained by reinforcement without it. The most interesting feature of the animals without telencephalons was that there was no extinction of the reinforced behaviors. Withdrawal of the reinforcing stimulus did not cause the behavior to disappear or its frequency to be reduced. The only way the behavior could be stopped was by changing the stimulus contingencies so as to reward the animal for doing incompatible things. Thus the upper part of the brain was required for complicated performances and for extinction of even simple ones.

Even though electrical stimulation in the middle part of the medial forebrain bundle was still reinforcing after anterior hypothalamic lesions in the same bundle, still there was some reduction in rates (Fig. 13) (Boyd and

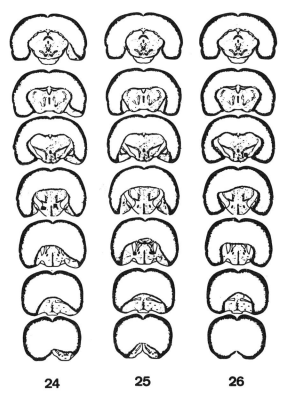

24   25   26

FIG. 12. Large telencephalic lesions in three brains that failed to block self-stimulation but did block its extinction. (From Huston and Borbely, 1974.)

Gardner, 1967; Olds and Olds, 1969). Sometimes this was quite pronounced; but usually after several weeks for recovery, the rates came back up to approximately two-thirds of original levels. Lesions placed above the hypothalamus on pathways up to the thalamus had similar effects, reducing the rates at first but permitting substantial recovery. Posterior lesions placed on the medial forebrain bundle path toward the midbrain were the most effective, but even in these cases there was usually substantial recovery (up to 50% of former levels or even higher several weeks after surgery). These experiments appeared to imply that lesions in all three zones might have abolished the behavior altogether, but no such experiments were reported.

Damage to the locus coeruleus, which is the origin of the main norepinephrine path to telencephalon, caused similar (or possibly even more severe) damage to brain reward behavior (M. E. Olds, *private communication;* L. J. Ellman, *private communication*). Also poisons applied in the ventricles which damaged all the forebrain catecholamine pathways were extremely effective in blocking brain reward behavior (M. E. Olds, *private communication*).

33. *What were the best parameters for the electric stimulus?* Often it did not seem to matter. Sine wave trains of alternating current and square wave trains of pulses were used. Negative pulses were more effective than positive ones—as is generally the case with electrical stimulation of nerve or muscle (Wetzel, Howell, and Bearie, 1969). Increases in frequency added to the effectiveness of a train. As this occurred when the duration was fixed, it appeared to indicate only that more stimulations were more effective than fewer (Ward, 1959; Keesey, 1962). When frequencies became too high, however, the effectiveness did not increase further; it appeared likely that alternate pulses were rendered ineffective by the refractory periods of the cells involved. In square wave studies, lengthening the duration of the pulses was not so effective a way of adding to the amount of stimulation as was augmenting the frequency or the peak amplitude. It took approximately two

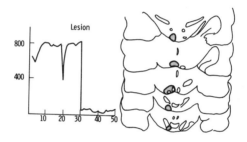

FIG. 13. Lesion in the medial forebrain bundle that caused a nearly complete cessation of self-stimulation via a nearby probe placed on the same side anterior to the lesions. Pedal rate in responses per test are on the ordinate. Successive days of testing are on the abscissa (Boyd and Gardner, 1967).

or three times as much charge added by lengthening the pulses to get the same increase in self-stimulation rate as by increasing the amplitude. Thus to get the most behavior for the least charge, very brief pulses were by far the most effective. However, the mixed nature of the response often observed with short pulses of very large amplitude suggested that the cost of this procedure was to stimulate a very broad swath of brain tissue and thus a loss of stimulus localization (*unpublished observations*). As opposed to increasing the duration of the pulses, which was relatively ineffective, doubling the frequency often had quite the same effect as doubling the amplitude. This seemed to indicate that doubling the number of stimuli applied to a small area or doubling the area had quite similar effects.

The probe size and stimulus parameters interacted; and the larger the probe, the larger the minimum effective amplitude (*unpublished observations*). This was logically attributable to the fact that current density rather than current *per se* was the effective stimulus. Thus with probes of approximately 60 μ diameter, sine wave currents of about 5 μA (rms) were sometimes effective stimuli. With probes of 400 μ diameter, currents under 200 μA were never effective.

The "size" of the stimulus was best varied by increasing the frequency, amplitude, or duration. Frequency was rarely the method chosen because it became confused in the region between 500 and 2,000 Hz (as indicated above). Increases in the amplitude of the stimulus caused three kinds of change depending on the location of the probe. One was a steady increase in rate of pedal-pressing for each increase in current level up to a ceiling, with no decline in rates at very high stimulus levels (Olds et al., 1960). A second was an increase up to a point with later decrease on further addition of current (Reynolds, 1958; Keesey, 1962). A third was an "undulation"— small increases augmented pedal rates, further increases would bring them down, still further increases in current would cause rates to go higher again (Olds, et al., 1960). These three effects were interpreted in terms of the layered or homogeneous composition of the stimulated area. If the area surrounding the tip was relatively homogeneous, more stimulation caused more effect. If there was a border between a positive reinforcement area and a counteracting area, small currents could be positive and larger currents would engage the countersystem. If a positive reinforcement area was transected by a narrow pathway of counteracting elements, the undulating curves would be explained.

When "trials to criterion" in a maze or discrimination problem were used as the measure of learning rate, animals learned just as fast to low-intensity as to high-intensity stimuli, even though they ran much faster to the high-intensity ones (Keesey, 1966). Theories about possible confusion from high-intensity signals were introduced as a possible explanation. Although this seems likely, it is surprising that things would be so well balanced between rising reinforcement and rising confusion that there would be neither improvement nor decline in learning rate as the intensity was increased. A second possibility was that the learning rate itself had some sort of asymptote. This did not appear to be the answer either, as animals learned faster if food reward was used.

The effect of train duration on brain reward behavior turned out to be complicated. At the long end of the continuum I have observed animals to self-administer trains in the cingulate cortex that lasted 5 to 15 min. At the other extreme, in search of a minimum effective train, I once used a single pulse of 2.4 msec duration; it served as a reward for a skilled rat with a hypothalamic probe. The animal had a pedal rate of two to four per second, and it was likely the self-administered train rather than the individual pulses that sustained the behavior.

Different brain locations had different optimal stimulus durations (*unpublished observations*); different electric current intensities also had different optimal durations. To support self-stimulation, septal area probes required longer trains than those in the hypothalamus; and in either location, weaker stimulations needed to be longer than strong ones.

As indicated above in the discussion of aversive countereffects, animals self-selected trains that were shorter than those shown to be maximally effective in other situations (Keesey, 1964). This led to the conclusion that even though several short trains were more rewarding than a long one, a long one was still more rewarding than a single short one. Support for the view that a repeatedly interrupted train should be more rewarding than the same amount of stimulation applied continuously came from experiments showing that the onset of the train was probably more rewarding than its continuation (Poschel, 1963; Deutsch and Albertson, 1974). Other experiments supported the complementary view, however, that aversive side effects apparently built up over time (Bower and Miller, 1958). Most likely adaptation to both continued trains and aversive countereffects were involved.

One interesting argument was that the added effectiveness of long trains came not from added reward value but from added priming power. An experiment aimed to demonstrate this seemed to show that trains of approximately 0.3 sec (64 pulses at 200/sec) were maximally rewarding, but that the priming power was augmented by increasing the number of 0.3-sec trains to 10 or more delivered at 1/sec (Gallistel, 1969a). The cutoff of the rewarding effect at 0.3 msec ran counter to the common sense notion that more rewards are more rewarding than fewer (even for rats). From my experience with experiments of this kind, I would not expect this finding to hold up under several changed conditions. With less intense stimulation, I would expect to see a considerable lengthening of the 0.3-sec period during which added stimulation had added reward value. Similarly, with other probe locations I would also expect a substantial lengthening of this period. Furthermore, by using another mode of testing that would eliminate the priming altogether, having one trial an hour or one trial a day, I would expect a much longer series of rewards to be much more effective than a 0.3-sec train. Thus I have come to three tentative conclusions regarding the problems and controversies related to extending the duration of the stimulus trains. First, with some probe locations the onset of the train may be more rewarding than its continuation; but with other locations the opposite might be true. Second, in some cases there may be aversive effects that are slow in onset and that attenuate the rewarding effects of extended trains. Third, the argument that extending trains beyond 0.3 sec adds to "priming" but not to "reward'" may be true only for a limited set of conditions.

34. *Could one guess either by the animals' responses or by the nature of the stimuli that these would be rewarding?* In some cases, as already indicated, this might be possible. For example, when the stimulus produced a consummatory sex (Herberg, 1963a) or food (Coons, 1964) behavior, this might be guessed to be rewarding. However, when the stimulus caused the animal to brave a painful foot shock on the way to food it would not be guessed that the stimulus itself was rewarding. In a different (and possibly unrelated) kind of experiment, a cold animal pressed a pedal to heat the hypothalamus (Corbit, 1973). To me this seemed the only case where it was

obvious that the animal was pressing a pedal to counteract the brain effects of a drive.

35. *Were there any relations of brain reward to sleep?* Yes, some rewarding brain stimulations put animals to sleep, although this was not usual (Angyan, 1974). The more usual rewarding stimulations (which did not put animals to sleep) were related by experiments to paradoxical sleep (Steiner and Ellman, 1972). This is the kind of sleep with rapid eye movements, twitches, and an awake-looking EEG that is thought to be related to dreams in humans. Mammals normally devote a certain proportion of their sleep time to this kind of sleep. If they are deprived of paradoxical sleep by special experimental procedures, they later make up for the loss by spending a larger part of the sleep in this state. The deprivation also causes a moderate increase in feeding, sexual behavior, and brain reward behavior. Animals deprived of paradoxical sleep but permitted to self-stimulate are interesting. The brain reward behavior seems to compensate for the shortage of paradoxical sleep so that such animals do not spend sleep time making up the loss.

Other reports indicate daily rhythms in self-stimulation behavior (Olds, 1958b; Terman and Terman, 1970). These suggest a relation of the behavior to sleep and waking cycles. Besides these more or less direct (but poorly understood) connections to sleep and paradoxical sleep, there is a pharmacological connection that is discussed in more detail later. A neuronal messenger substance, serotonin, which is possibly involved as a "sleep hormone," opposes brain reward behavior under some circumstances and promotes it under others (possibly probe location makes the main difference). From the evidence, therefore, I would guess that some brain reward behavior is related to the main sleep system, but most is not. That which is not, however, may have an important relation to paradoxical sleep, because such sleep may be tied into the brain's drive-reward system.

D. Summary

Brain reward behavior occurred when fibers of the olfactory brain and the brain's catecholamine sytems were stimulated. The main point of intersection of these two systems was in the hypothalamus; at least this was the area where the greatest concentrations of these two kinds of fibers were located. All parts of the hypothalamus yielded reward behavior, but in the lateral parts (which handle most of the input-output messages) positive effects were most unambiguous. An in-between area (between medial and lateral hypothalamus) yielded very ambiguous effects, including aversive and drive components. That is, the animal escaped from these stimulations as well as approaching them, and the stimulations also caused instrumental and consummatory responses in pursuit of normal rewards. Some very medial areas of hypothalamus near the ventricle yielded predominantly positive effects like the far lateral areas. Even in the predominantly positive areas, negative countereffects were detected by careful analytical methods. In the mixed in-between areas of reward-aversive-and-drive effects, there was a vague map with temperature, drinking, eating, and sex behaviors arrayed from front to back. However, these behaviors could be changed to some degree from one to the other by a simple "training" procedure (i.e., stimulating the animal in the presence of the to-be-pursued goal object). Self-starting behavior that required no drive and no priming was evoked with some probes, and these were also the best for motivating complicated maze behaviors. In other cases the behavior appeared to need priming (prior brain stimulation) to get it going.

Four problems arising from the brain stimulation studies were: (1) What neurons caused the rewarding effects? (2) Why did training cause drive behaviors to change? (3) What caused the aversive countereffects (or the responding to interrupt stimulus trains) in the predominantly positive areas? (4) What made the difference between stimulations which required priming and those that did not?

III. LESIONS

A wide range of hypothalamic lesions and pathologies affect drive and reinforcement behaviors. The lesion methods have been sharpened by the use of quite small knife cuts to sever fibers. With these cuts and with electrolytic methods, some lesions caused obesity and others a loss of eating and drinking behaviors. In other experiments male sex behavior, female sex behavior, and temperature regulation were impaired or abolished. The cuts and lesions severed input-output paths from widely dispersed areas. Therefore the brain structures involved in the various effects are still unknown. Nevertheless, the studies have been extensive, particularly in relation to obesity and starvation, and the character of these effects has been clarified to some degree.

Experiments aimed at finding specific sites where tissue damage caused these effects were done mostly with rats. There is some indication that in this regard rats may be only a rough model for other mammals. There are differences even between male and female rats. Nevertheless, the rat work is taken as giving some idea of the locus and character of the effects for the "general mammal."

A. Overeating and Obesity Caused by Hypothalamic Damage

It has been known for a long time that lesions at the base of the brain cause animals and humans to become obese. The difficulty was originally ascribed to the pituitary and to a fault in the metabolic system under its control. Later research opposed this view to some degree, although still later research caused a partial revival. The opposed researchers showed (1) that the lesions did not have to affect the pituitary to be effective (Hetherington and Ranson, 1942a,b); and (2) that overeating was more important than faulty utilization of food as the most obvious culprit (Brobeck, Tepperman, and Long, 1943). Both overeating and the excessive laying down of fat deposits are now supposed to be twin (and somewhat independent) culprits (Bernardis, Chlouverakis, Schnatz, and Frohman, 1974). Research emphasis, at least, makes overeating a main one.

The anatomical focus of this effect has not been pinpointed with certainty even in the rat. Large lesions (which destroyed 2 or 3 mm^3 of the 8 mm^3 of hypothalamic tissue) placed in many different parts of the hypothalamus caused animals to become obese. There were some large lesions that did not have the effect, and likely a small minority that had the opposite effect, but the majority were effective in causing hypothalamic obesity (Hetherington, 1944). Smaller lesions of about 1 mm^3 were used to further localize the critical tissues. When these were placed bilaterally, there turned out to be a large number of different locations in the medial hypothalamus and in the midlateral parts of the hypothalamus where lesions caused obesity to some degree. Almost two-thirds of the points tested in a map of the hypothalamus yielded these effects (Anand and Brobeck, 1951).

From these studies the focus was thought to be the ventromedial nucleus, which is a very prominent member of the medial group of hypothalamic nuclei. It is almost at the bottom of the hypothalamus and about halfway from the front to the back. It is because of this central location in relation to the effective lesions that it has been accepted as a focus. It has seemed possible to many that, instead of the ventromedial nucleus, some set of fibers easily damaged by lesions in this general vicinity might be an alternate candidate for the focus.

Other experiments added some weight to the view that a fiber bundle was mainly involved. These demonstrated that the effect could be achieved without destroying neuron cell bodies. It was only necessary to make a knife cut between the medial and lateral sectors of the hypothalamus (Albert and Storlien, 1969; Gold, 1970). If these knife cuts were placed in anterior or posterior sectors they failed, but if placed in a middle sector they appeared to have quite similar effects to the medial lesions (Paxinos and Bindra, 1972). Because this seemed a likely method to destroy important input or output pathways of the ventromedial nucleus, it did not by itself upset the generally accepted view that the ventromedial nucleus was the focus. However, one set of knife-cut studies was a little surprising. Instead of cutting between medial and lateral, the cut was made in the heart of the ventromedial nucleus, cutting it in two, or even along its medial edge. This left either one-half of the nucleus or most of it still attached to the lateral area. Still it caused the full measure of obesity (Sclafani, Berner, and Maul,

1973). This made it seem that something still more medially placed than the ventromedial nucleus might be involved—possibly the special cells along the wall of the ventricle, or transport systems coming from the ventricle or from the blood. Substantial (but milder) obesity was also caused when the knife-cut lesions were placed some distance out into the lateral hypothalamus (Sclafani et al., 1973). Thus it appeared that a connecting system traversing a rather long distance between the ventricular wall and the wheel-shaped neurons of the lateral hypothalamus might be involved. Although these studies caused some doubt about ventromedial hypothalamic involvement, they did not cause any revolution. It was still some medial part of the middle hypothalamus that seemed to be involved.

A much newer method of selectively poisoning a pathway that is more tangentially related to this part of the hypothalamus has, however, led to second thoughts (Ahlskog and Hoebel, 1972). These experiments are discussed later. Although they suggest that there may be no tightly bounded satiety center in this part of the hypothalamus, they do not eliminate this region as a candidate for some specially important role in the effect.

What kind of effect is involved? To find out if it was really a fault in metabolism, rats with these lesions were prevented from overeating (Brobeck et al., 1943). Their diet was matched to that of an unlesioned group to see if they would become obese on the same diet. They did not. This indicated that the lesions did not by themselves cause the rats to become obese and that they did cause overeating. The experiments might be thought to show that the lesions did not by themselves modify the proportion of food that got converted to fat deposits. This is mistaken. Dieted (nonobese) animals with these lesions had a disproportionate amount of their weight in fat (Bernardis et al., 1974). The excessive fat was produced by an over-rapid conversion of glucose to fat. This by itself would cause overeating. The generally accepted view, however, is that even if there is a more direct effect on fat stores there is also an independent effect on eating.

What kind of overeating was it? The picture is clouded to some degree. As the animals recovered from anesthesia during the hours after electrolytic surgery, they appeared at first to have a very high hunger drive. They ate ravenously (Brobeck et al., 1943). Animals almost choked to death trying to get more food into their mouths. I do not know how long this voracious feeding lasted. My impression is that it disappeared in a day or two, after which the animal settled into a long "dynamic" period which lasted for several months. During this time there was regular day-to-day overeating. If food was available around the clock, the animals spent a great deal of time eating. It was not that meals lasted too long but rather that they started too soon. A normal rat waits between meals for a period determined by the previous meal size; the lesioned rats started eating again too soon (Le Magnen, Devos, Gaudilliere, Louis-Sylvestre, and Tallon, 1973). Thus their body weight rose. The rate of weight gain was substantially above that of normal controls (Brobeck et al., 1943). When the animals reached a weight of two or three times that of controls after a month or two, the weight gain leveled off and eating slowed. The animals became "static" obese animals. The word "static" was used because the weight gain was stabilized. Because the dynamic phase of weight gain terminated in this static condition, it became attractive to suppose that one effect of the lesion was to cause something like a thermostat to be reset at a new and much higher level.

Fitting with this interpretation of a changed level of "regulation" was evidence that the animal would "defend" the new high level against experimental manipulations which caused body weight to go temporarily higher or lower than the new "set point" (Hoebel and Teitelbaum, 1966).

The voracious behavior immediately after the lesion, the overeating which came during the longer later period, and the high stabilized weight in the third period could all be taken to indicate a heightened hunger drive. Several experiments appeared to counter this supposition. Obese animals, when briefly deprived of food, were much less tolerant of quinine-adulterated foods than normal animals (Teitelbaum, 1955). Moreover, after they had become "static," these animals gave up sooner if work was required for food (Miller, Bailey, and Stevenson, 1950). In other experiments normal and lesioned rats were given foods mixed with a non-nutritive ingredient. At some mixture levels, normal rats made up the nutritional deficit by eating more. Obese rats, apparently responding to the worse taste, often ate less (Teitelbaum, 1955). Because of the failure to tolerate unappetizing foods, to work for food, and to compensate for nutritional deficiencies, the view arose that there was a lowering of the hunger drive side by side with the resetting upward of the "hungerstat." However, in many experiments animals with the obesity-causing lesions were kept nonobese by limited diet; in these cases there were good indications of heightened rather than lowered hunger drive (Kent and Peters, 1973; Singh, 1973; Wampler, 1973). Moreover, these lesioned but nonobese rats were induced by hunger to accept nonpalatable (quinine-adulterated) foods much as normal rats were (Franklin and Herberg, 1974). Thus modification of the hungerstat upward was accompanied by increased drive, which could be demonstrated if animals were not allowed to overeat. While the cause of the overeating may have been the over-rapid conversion of blood glucose to fats (which thus required eating to replenish the blood glucose), the main symptom was that the animals did not wait a normal interval between meals.

Besides augmenting the food drive, these lesions also increased the level of a less-focused drive that might be called "irritability." The animals became excessively reactive to all the signals of their world, and showed a mixture of fear and aggression in circumstances where this seemed inappropriate. This was first observed in cats (Wheatley, 1944). Thus animals with medial lesions appeared to be both hungrier and more irritable. While the two effects could have been related, it is hard to guess whether they were.

B. Starvation Caused by Hypothalamic Damage

Damage in a small set of lateral hypothalamic locations caused an opposite pathology (Anand and Brobeck, 1951). The animals refrained from eating and drinking; they starved to death unless remedial steps were taken. Tubing a liquid diet into the stomach kept them alive. This was first observed incidentally in experiments on hypothalamic obesity, and it was amply verified in later experiments. Lesions had this effect if they removed the lateral half of the lateral hypothalamus at the level of the middle sector. Milder effects having similar initial appearance were caused by just lowering a lesion probe into the area and then withdrawing it—without passing the electric current usually used to make a lesion (Morrison and Mayer, 1957). Complete effects could also be induced by knife cuts that severed the lateral hypothalamus from other still more laterally placed structures (Grossman, 1971; Grossman and Grossman, 1971; Sclafani et al., 1973). Among these still more laterally placed structures, two parts of the extrapyramidal system (globus pallidus and substantia nigra) have attracted the most attention, although connections of the lateral areas to other basal ganglia (including the caudate nucleus and the amygdala) or even to the neocortex could not be ruled out as the ones whose cutting caused the effect.

A comparison of obesity and starvation-inducing knife cuts was interesting. In different experiments bilateral cuts extending from the top to the bottom of the hypothalamus were made at different distances from the midline (in the rat the hypothalamus extends just over 2 mm from the midline). Cuts 0.5 mm from the midline (shaving the edge of the third ventricle, which occupies the medial-most 0.25 mm) caused obesity; cuts 1 mm from the midline between medial and lateral hypothalamus had the same effect. Cuts 1.5 mm lateral in the middle part of the lateral area were ambiguous. There were initial undereating reactions followed by overeating of appetizing foods. In some cases there was simultaneous undereating of unappetizing foods and overeating of normal or positive ones (Sclafani et al., 1973). Cuts 2.2 mm from the midline at the lateral edge of the lateral area caused the full syndrome: undereating and starvation; this was the maximum point. Cuts 0.3 mm more lateral caused much milder undereating. Thus medial and lateral cuts had opposed effects (Grossman and Grossman, 1971). The medial effect extended so close to the midline as to suggest involvement of the ventricular wall. Cuts quite close together in the 1.5-mm region had radically different effects; and the lateral effect dropped off sharply at the lateral edge (even though lesions at 2.2 and 2.5 mm severed many of the same pathways).

What fibers would be severed by the 2.2-mm cut and spared by the 2.5-mm cut? One group was those connecting the substantia nigra and caudate nucleus of the extrapyramidal system (Oltmans and Harvey, 1972). This made it interesting that "poisoning" the ascending "dopamine" fibers in this bundle caused many of the effects of lateral hypothalamic lesions, i.e., loss of instrumental and consummatory responses, particularly those related to eating (Ungerstedt, 1971b). These were different fibers from the set whose poisoning caused obesity, but like them they did not really involve the hypothalamus as their main origin or target. Because this dopamine bundle is one important member of the catecholamine neuron systems and because they may be a set of drive or reward fibers, they are discussed again later in a special section on the catecholamines.

What behaviors and controls were lost with these lesions, knife cuts, and poisonings? The answer is multifold. First, temporarily after the lesion there was a general loss of appetitive behavior and possibly a loss of all instrumental behavior. The behaviors temporarily blocked included eating and drinking (Teitelbaum and Epstein, 1962), male sex responses (Hitt, Hendricks, Ginsberg, and Lewis, 1970; Hitt, Bryon, and Modianos, 1973; Modianos, Flexman, and Hitt, 1973), behavioral thermoregulation (Satinoff and Shan, 1971), and even operant escape and avoidance behaviors (Balinska, Romaniuk, and Wyrwicka, 1964; Appel, Sheard, and Freedman, 1968; Coscina and Balagura, 1970; Schwartz and Teitelbaum, 1974). Furthermore, there was a pronounced sensorimotor defect that also made feeding and other operant behaviors difficult (Marshall and Teitelbaum, 1974). During the same temporary period there was a pronounced aversive reaction to food and water when placed in the mouth (Teitelbaum and Epstein, 1962). Animals responded with manifestations of distaste or disgust. The food was not swallowed but wiped from the mouth with the paws and there were other signs that food or water in the mouth was aversive. Because of this aversion it was not sufficient to place liquid diet in the mouth, for the animal rejected it. Some additional method was required to get the nutrients into the stomach. However, even when the lesions were sufficient to cause death by starvation, time and appropriate remedial procedures could bring about considerable recovery (Fig. 14). This was prompted first by tubing liquid diets. After several days of tube feeding, animals began to accept highly palatable foods by mouth. At first these needed to be supplemented by tube feeding. After another period of time, several days to several weeks, animals would keep themselves alive eating palatable foods if they were provided. Still, they needed water tubed into the stomach, or liquid diets that served to hydrate the animals by normal means. At some time after this they would eat regular food and drink enough water during eating to stave off dehydration. The loss of voluntary or instrumental behavior and the changed affective reactions to food were thus relatively short-lasting.

There were other more specific deficits that did not repair with time. One was a failure to respond to internal water shortages by drinking; a second was a failure to respond to internal glucose shortages by eating; possibly also there was a failure to respond to similar sodium shortages appropriately (Epstein, 1971). Recovered animals would drink to relieve dryness of the mouth and this could keep them alive; but they did not drink on the basis of dehydration of cells or body fluids. Thus if the animals were offered water separately when there was no food to cause the mouth to become dry, they would not drink, and if water was available only at these times they would die of dehydration. Similarly, they ate in response to many factors, but when glucose in the blood (glucose available to the brain) was sharply reduced by insulin, they did not meet this deficit by eating (as normal rats do). When sodium shortages were induced by special procedures, animals with similar but possibly not identical lesions failed to meet the challenge as normal rats do (Wolf, 1964). Thus there were specific sources of ingestion behavior that were inoperative; all could have involved brain cells that failed to detect local shortages in the brain itself.

Besides these, there was also a change in the "hungerstat" settings so the

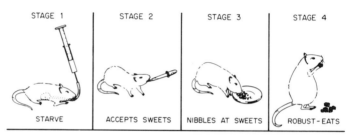

| STAGE 1 | STAGE 2 | STAGE 3 | STAGE 4 |
| STARVE | ACCEPTS SWEETS | NIBBLES AT SWEETS | ROBUST - EATS |

FIG. 14. Successive stages of recovery from lateral hypothalamic damage (Teitelbaum and Epstein, 1962).

animal regulated its body weight at a new and unnaturally low level (Powley and Keesey, 1970). If body weight was artificially lowered by experimental manipulations before the brain damage, there was sometimes no initial period of food rejection (even though similar lateral lesions always caused this initial failure to eat in animals that were not prestarved).

Thus lateral lesions damaged several mechanisms involved in normal food and water ingestion: (1) instrumental behavior; (2) hedonic properties of food; (3) specific remedial responses to water, glucose, and possibly NaCl deficits; and (4) the target level for body weight. The loss of instrumental behavior and the modification of hedonic properties was temporary; the animal recovered from these in several days. The loss of responses to cellular water, glucose, and NaCl deficits lasted; but animals eating normal diets on the basis of taste and other factors, and drinking on the basis of dryness of the mouth, compensated adequately for these lasting defects. Thus to the unsophisticated observer, the animals appeared completely recovered after a month or two had passed from the time of the lesioning.

Because medial and lateral lesions caused opposite changes in body weight targets (setting them higher and lower, respectively), the question of how the two would interact was interesting. In one set of experiments medial lesions were made at first, causing obesity; lateral ones were made later, and these caused starvation as they would have done if they had been made alone (Anand and Brobeck, 1951). This led to the view that the lateral mechanism was needed for eating; and the medical sector did nothing by itself but only acted on the lateral sector as a brake when energy stores became excessive.

Other cases involving more complete medial lesions changed the picture, turning it half-way about, by showing that the medial sector might act by itself, countering eating by some other path not directed to the lateral sector (Ellison, Sorenson, and Jacobs, 1970). These showed that aversive reactions to food depended on the medial area even when there was no lateral sector for it to act upon. Lateral lesions alone caused cessation of feeding and ejection of food from the mouth as if it were aversive. Medial plus lateral disconnections caused cessation of feeding, but food placed in the mouth was not ejected; there was no aversive reaction in this case. Thus the aversive reaction exhibited in animals without lateral areas depended in some way on the medial area. Hence it had some action even after the lateral area was gone.

These data at first suggested a dual control. Some mechanism passing through the lateral hypothalamus (e.g., the nigrostriatal system) might promote instrumental and consummatory reactions of a positive character directed toward the goals of the basic drives. Some mechanism passing through the medial hypothalamus might mediate aversive reactions toward food during periods when hormonal, metabolic, or visceral conditions made positive reactions inappropriate. Other studies suggested that there were at least two other controls that also acted against the positive reactions. These were revealed by lesions in the caudate nucleus and the amygdala.

Lesions in the caudate nucleus, when reasonably complete, caused positive instrumental reactions to be aimed at inappropriate (nonsense) targets. In cats, lesions which removed all of the caudate nucleus turned many stimuli into targets or "magnets." The animal behaved as if imprinted on things put before it, and would endlessly follow a tin can, a ball of string, or an experimenter's hand (Villablanca, 1974). They did not, however, eat these things or even mouth them as if trying to eat them. This looked like a release phenomenon and made it reasonable to guess that the caudate nucleus in normal behavior checked positive instrumental reactions when targets were inappropriate. The caudate nucleus exchanges messages with substantia nigra through the nigrostriatal system. Neuropharmacological experiments suggest that the two may be reciprocal inhibitors. Because the lateral lesions which damaged the substantia nigra end of the same system caused a deficiency of positive reactions and the caudate lesions caused excesses of these, it was tempting to imagine an opponent process mechanism with the substantia nigra end promoting and the caudate end opposing positive instrumental actions toward things. Other lesion studies pointed to the amygdala as still another opponent.

The amygdala exchanges messages with the hypothalamus through two well-known fiber systems, the stria terminalis and a larger system of smaller fibers. It is known to have both excitor and inhibitor actions on medial centers of the hypothalamus (Murphy and Renaud, 1969); its actions on lateral systems are not well documented, and it has no known action on the substantia nigra. Lesions in the amygdala caused consummatory reactions to inappropriate objects. Rats with these lesions failed to avoid novel foods—which were treated as dangerous by unlesioned animals (Rolls, E. T., and Rolls, B. J., 1973). They also consumed foods previously associated with poisoning that are also avoided by normal rats (Rolls and Rolls, 1973). Aside from these rather subtle defects, there was also an immediately obvious set of abnormal behaviors. Animals with these lesions repeatedly commenced consummatory responses with inappropriate objects; both feeding and sex responses were frequently misdirected (Klüver and Bucy, 1937). There was also a loss of aversive reactions to dangerous objects. The facet

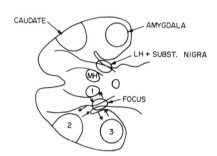

FIG. 15. Positive focus and its three opponents as indicated by lesions. Focus = lateral hypothalamus (LH) and substantia nigra; here lesions cause a temporary loss of appetitive behavior. Its three opponents are: (1) medial hypothalamus (MH), (2) caudate, and (3) amygdala.

of this behavior that marked it off from that caused by the other lesions was the repeated misdirection of consummatory reactions. These animals actually tried to eat inedible things and often tried to mate with inappropriate (even inanimate) objects.

The medial hypothalamus, caudate nucleus, and amygdala thus appeared to comprise three separate sources opposing positive reactions. The medial hypothalamus opposed positive reactions to food during periods when the visceral state said no; the caudate nucleus opposed positive reactions of an instrumental character directed at nonsense objects; and the amygdala opposed positive reactions of a consummatory character directed at inappropriate objects. At the hypothalamic level these three counterinfluences appeared to be acting against a single mechanism that promoted instrumental and consummatory reactions of a positive nature, a mechanism that could be destroyed or damaged by lesions in the lateral area, particularly if these damaged the substantia nigra end of the nigrostriatal bundle. While this would suggest three negative influences acting against a single positive one (Fig. 15), the course of recovery from lateral hypothalamic lesions suggested that the lateral hypothalamic area might have one or more allies working on its positive side.

What other structures might be on the positive side? Experiments on the course of recovery from lateral hypothalamic lesions suggested the cortex itself. Cortex manipulations could dramatically modify the course of recovery. The normal course of recovery (which progressed from loss of all instrumental behavior, through eating palatable foods but needing water tubed into the stomach, to eating more or less normally and looking robust) took approximately 4 to 8 weeks (Teitelbaum and Epstein, 1962). After this, newly learned adaptive mechanisms, or redundant ones that recovered after the first traumatic period, served to make the animals appear normal in spite of losing important controls.

These backup mechanisms ("learned," "recovered," or "unwrapped") were more precarious than would be guessed from watching the recovered behavior; and they depended in some unexplained way on the cortex (Teitelbaum, 1971). Their borderline character and their relation to the cortex were demonstrated by experiments involving a bizarre cortical manipulation that has had a vogue because of its supposed "temporary" character. The manipulation is to apply excessive potassium to an area of the cortical surface. This causes waves of unnatural electrical activity to sweep slowly and repeatedly across the cortex for a period lasting several hours. Neuronal activity is silenced by this "spreading depression." As a consequence, temporary feeding aberrations occurred even in normal animals; but in the rats recovered after lateral hypothalamic lesions, these "temporary" cortical depressions had much more enduring effects. The hard-won recovery that had taken 1 to 2 months to accomplish was set back almost to its beginnings. It required the full range of therapeutic procedures and time to be reinstated. This is, so far as I know, the only reported behavioral effect of spreading depression that outlasts the electrocortical phenomenon and then lasts not just for hours but for days, weeks, and likely even months. This new and puzzling finding does not, of course, answer the question of how recovery occurs, but it does tell that recovery is precarious when it is complete and that it depends in some way on relations of hypothalamus and cortex.

To me this seems to fit the idea that the cortex itself may be one main partner of the hypothalamus in the emotional control of behavior. If the hypothalamus is putting together an "affective package" (i.e., a set of signals making some things taste good and some bad), it seems likely that the cortex is a prime source of data for these computations, and a prime target for the emotional message after it has been computed.

The reacquisition of positive food responses after hypothalamic lesions and the connection of this to the cortex may be related to another set of findings. Experience in the normal animal has a profound influence on the "taste" of food (insofar as this term may be defined by behavioral reactions).

Interestingly, both the hypothalamus and its outposts toward the cortex are needed for these effects of experience on taste.

C. Experience and the Taste of Food

Observational studies on humans and other animals and experiments with rats all indicate that food does not "carry its flavor on its sleeve." The hedonic character of the taste changes after experience; i.e., the taste of things is rarely determinate at first encounter. Furthermore, after many encounters, things that have "tasted good" for a substantial period can change and begin to "taste bad." The reason for this instability in the taste of things appears to be twofold. The first is that tastes are rarely positive when they are new (Rolls and Rolls, 1973). The second is that foods closely correlated with illness (at least with certain types of sickness) are changed to negative (Fig. 16) (Garcia and Ervin, 1968).

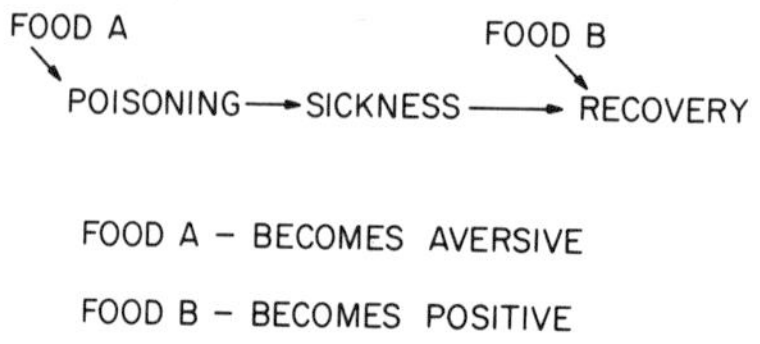

FOOD A   FOOD B

POISONING ⟶ SICKNESS ⟶ RECOVERY

FIG. 16. Garcia effect.

FOOD A – BECOMES AVERSIVE

FOOD B – BECOMES POSITIVE

This does not mean that experience can make "anything" taste good; but experience is an important component in this determination. By itself this of course comes as no great surprise. What is interesting is the repeatable set of details surrounding the behavioral mechanisms that produce these effects in rats. From the present point of view, it is even more interesting to observe the way these mechanisms interact with the hypothalamic mechanisms we have been discussing.

The function of these mechanisms is to make dangerous foods taste bad. There is both a distrust of novel foods and a negative reaction to poisons. This mode of speaking does scant justice to the way the "intrinsic" taste of things seems to be modified. When a rat first encounters a food with a novel taste, it nibbles and then responds with surprise and apparent distaste (Rolls and Rolls, 1973). The food is then treated as negative for a period of time (amounting, I believe, to several days). After this the food is responded to as good, middle, or bad, depending on its other characteristics; but in the beginning the food is treated as if it had a bad taste until (1) it is tested in small amounts, and (2) a time has passed.

The other side of this coin is that if the animal gets sick during this waiting period, the food ends up tasting bad (Garcia and Ervin, 1968). Furthermore, if the food has been acceptable and has been treated as hedonically positive, one sickness can cause a 180° reversal of this evaluation even if this occurs after its ingestion.

There are two features of this acquired negative reaction to food which are quite surprising to psychologists who have studied other kinds of "learning." One is that it works especially with taste stimuli. In most learning experiments it does not much matter whether the conditioned stimulus is an auditory, visual, or somatic signal. If any one of these is paired with shock, the animal learns to fear it. In the taste experiments, it is not the way the food looks or its tactual qualities, but only the gustatory and olfactory properties that make up its "taste" that become aversive when the animal gets sick. The animal does not learn to avoid the places where he ate the meal or the sounds that accompanied the meal, but only to avoid foods that taste that way. Moreover, after training, the animal does not respond to the taste as if it were a signal of impending danger but rather as if it were intrinsically negative, distasteful, and disgusting.

The second interesting character different from what would be expected by the psychologist of normal learning is the time scale involved. The time between eating and getting sick can be several hours. Even though this long time intervenes, the animal can learn in just one trial. In Pavlov's experiment, if the bell and the food were separated by an hour or so, one would not call that an association of these two stimuli, but rather a dissociation. I do not believe any other circumstance is known where an animal or a human being woud learn to associate things separated by such long periods of time.

Both the restriction of this taste aversion learning to gustatory signals and the association of stimuli separated by hours from one another make this a special phenomenon. The learning mechanisms involved in most rat learning experiments are likely not involved here at all.

Perhaps it is even wrong to speak of learning. This is perhaps the basic way a drive like hunger gets converted into a set of well-targeted homing reactions so that the animal starting with ill-defined drives ends up with particular object pursuit patterns.

Damage to the lateral hypothalamus (Roth, Schwartz, and Teitelbaum, 1973) or to the amygdala (Rolls and Rolls, 1973) modified this set of mechanisms for establishing the hedonic quality of food. Lateral hypothalamic lesions created animals that first responded to everything with distaste, and later could not learn to respond with appropriate distaste after poisoning. On the contrary, amygdala lesions from the beginning caused a failure of several different distaste reactions—based on novelty, inappropriate objects, or poisoning. This left the possibility that amygdala was a home of distaste reactions, and lateral hypothalamus one of its suppressors or opponents. It is not quite this simple, however, because the loss of learned distaste reactions after lateral hypothalamic lesions suggested that in one way or another this "distaste-suppressing" region was necessary in distaste learning. The amygdala at least could be considered a home of negative definitions of inappropriate objects.

D. Other Drives

The effects of hypothalamic lesions were not restricted to feeding behavior, although this was by far the best studied. The lateral lesions which caused temporary loss of positive and instrumental reactions toward food at the same time caused the loss of other positive and instrumental reactions. Those directed to get water (Teitelbaum and Epstein, 1962), to correct the temperature of the environment (Satinoff and Shan, 1971), or to avoid danger (Balinska, 1968) were all absent during this period. The reactions involved in male sexual behavior were also gone (Hitt et al., 1970). It seems likely, therefore, that the whole repertory of operant, instrumental, or voluntary behavior was abolished, at least temporarily. Moreover, the permanent damage to defenses against glucose shortage were matched by permanent losses of defenses against water and sodium shortages (Epstein, 1971). Lateral hypothalamic damage, at least in the middle or posterior part, had a broad spectrum of effects, and no single drive was the common denominator.

The medial lesions that caused overeating caused a concomitant increase in irritability, aggression, and in some cases drinking. These lesions also caused a moderate decline in sexual behavior (Paxinos and Bindra, 1973). The multidrive effects weighed against the argument for specific drive centers anatomically differentiated. Some facets of the data, however, weighed against a total lack of specificity. First, some of the different effects could be caused separately. Sometimes even though the experimenter could not give rules for separating the effects, he often observed one of the results without the other (Satinoff and Shan, 1971). Second, the different effects had different optimum loci. The best knife cuts to cause obesity and irritability were those just lateral to the anterior part of the ventromedial nucleus and the posterior part of the anterior hypothalamic area (Paxinos and Bindra, 1972). The best area for drinking excesses (diabetes insipidus) was more ventral and possibly more lateral (Sclafani et al., 1973). Other neurons at the "source" of one part of the drinking deficiency were discovered in the front part of the lateral hypothalamus (i.e., the lateral preoptic area). These were not related to feeding and were related to only one of the causes of drinking (Epstein, 1971).

Sexual behavior was maximally affected by lesions in the anterior hypothalamic complex (Lisk, 1968; Singer, 1968; Hitt et al., 1973), lesions which also abolished automatic temperature regulatory behaviors (Hamilton and Brobeck, 1964; Anderson, Gale, Hökfelt, and Larsson, 1965). Medial lesions in one anterior hypothalamic area caused impairment of female sex behavior; and those in another area, which stands just one step farther forward, caused impairment of male sex behavior (Singer, 1968). The latter was also damaged by lesions in two neighboring regions (i.e., the olfactory tubercle, which is still farther forward, and the nearby part of the lateral hypothalamus). Anterior lateral lesions impaired male sex behavior without having general effects against instrumental behavior such as were caused by more posterior lesions in the medial forebrain bundle (Hitt, Bryon, and Modianos, 1973). As can be deduced from earlier statements, posterior medial forebrain bundle lesions also damaged or abolished male sex behavior, but in this case it was a general effect (Paxinos and Bindra, 1973).

Automatic mechanisms of temperature regulation were maximally impaired by about the same medial preoptic lesions that had maximum negative influence on male sex behavior (Anderson et al., 1965). It is interesting that operant behaviors to regulate the temperature of the environment survived these lesions (Satinoff and Rutstein, 1970). As I said earlier, these depended on the integrity of the lateral hypothalamic pathway, as did other instrumental and operant behaviors. The separation of the two kinds of mechanism seems to indicate that although some steps of the temperature control process may be housed in the "preoptic temperature center," there must also be some temperature driven system that survives lesions in this area. Interestingly, the anterior lesions that interfered with automatic temperature regulation had main side effects related to eating and drinking (Hamilton, 1963; Hamilton and Brobeck, 1964). Warm temperatures normally depress food intake, and cold temperatures usually raise it; after the anterior lesions, however, they no longer did. These lesions also caused a failure to drink similar to that which occurred after lateral hypothalamic lesions; the animals drank in response to a dry mouth but did not drink on the basis of dehydration alone (Epstein, 1971). Similar (but not of course the same) lesions in dog and goat caused an even greater loss of drinking behavior (Anderson and McCann, 1956; Anderson, Gale, and Sundsten, 1964).

The lesion studies thus suggested a way to divide the hypothalamus into clusters (Fig. 17) with different behavior control functions. From this point of view, the hypothalamus was divided into three medial clusters: an anterior one related to temperature and sex mechanisms; a middle one related to feeding, drinking, irritability, and aggression; and a posterior sector with no set of well-demonstrated drive relations. The anterior and middle clusters were each shown to have special relations to adjacent lateral areas (in the sense that the medial and lateral lesions had effects related to the same general cluster of drive behaviors). Each medial sector apparently needed the adjacent parts and all the more posterior parts of the medial forebrain bundle. The geometry suggested that critical input-output fiber systems between the medial clusters and lower brain levels arched bidirectionally through the medial forebrain bundle. Thus posterior, middle, and anterior lateral lesions all damaged sex behavior, whereas only middle and posterior lesions damaged eating behavior. The integrity of the lateral hypothalamic pathway needed to be preserved between the posterior boundary of the diencephalon and the particular cluster in order to preserve the drive behavior involved.

Besides having relations to different drives, the anterior and middle clusters differed in another way. The middle seemed to be a "stop" part of a start-stop system related to feeding; the anterior cluster seemed to be only part (or the focal part) of a start-and-go system related to other drives. The anterior cluster, particularly in its relation to sex behavior, had but one side to its picture. Lateral or medial sector lesions could damage the drive by causing

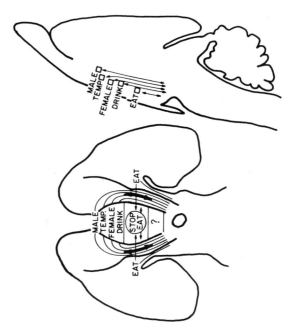

FIG. 17. Drive clusters in the hypothalamus suggested by lesions studies.

a behavioral deficit, but there was no way to cause an excessive performance of sex behaviors. The drives of the middle sector, however, were subject to both excess and deficit pathologies. At least eating illustrated this bidirectionality. It is possible that the character of the drive had something to do with whether it had bidirectional "centers" and whether it was centered in the anterior or middle cluster. Sex and temperature "drives" are stimulus-aroused to a large degree. Food and water drives are often aroused by internal deficit states. Possibly the drives that depend on internal conditions need both start and stop mechanisms, and are accordingly tied to the middle cluster, whereas the stimulus-aroused drives need only start and go mechanisms and are therefore tied to the anterior cluster.

Why were clusters placed medially? Hormone-transport mechanisms near the ventricle might be "the reason." The main blood-borne messengers related to food drives are thought to be those which stop or attenuate feeding. The ones in the sex system, on the contrary, facilitate or trigger sex behavior. This makes it possibly appropriate that the stop part of the food start-stop system should be placed medially to receive the chemical "stop" message; by the same token the start part of the sex drive mechanism might also be appropriately placed in a medial area.

IV. CATECHOLAMINES AND OTHER NEUROTRANSMITTERS

A. Clinical, Anatomical, and Biochemical Studies Relating Amines to Behavior

The best known neurotransmitter, acetylcholine, has important relations to the hypothalamus, as have other less well-known transmitters such as gamma-aminobutyric acid (GABA). Of paramount importance in the hypothalamus, however, are the amine transmitters. These include norepinephrine, dopamine, and serotonin. The behavioral and autonomic controls exercised by the "visceral brain" and the hormone systems appear inextricably linked to the amine transmitter systems. Therefore these receive major attention here.

The amine transmitter systems are different from that of acetylcholine. Their action time is much slower in onset and more enduring (Bloom, 1974). Acetylcholine transmitter action starts in less than a millisecond, and its action is complete in several milliseconds. Norepinephrine starts in hundreds of milliseconds, and its action endures for seconds. Norepinephrine can be carried in the blood like a hormone. There its half-life of approximately 1 min is in almost the same order of magnitude as that of some hormones. The amines thus form a bridge between the faster neurotransmitters and the slower hormones. The long time constants are of interest because drives and rewards involve processes that need to be stabilized for periods of seconds, minutes, or hours, and drive cycles extend even to days.

The study of the brain amines was greatly stimulated by the discovery of a family of drugs useful in schizophrenia. Actually there were three families: the rauwolfia alkaloids (best exemplified in reserpine), the phenothiazines (of which chlorpromazine is the most important), and the butyrophenones (Shepherd, Lader, and Rodknight, 1968). The latter two families are in wide use. Their main action is to block norepinephrine and dopamine receptors in the brain (Snyder, 1974). Reserpine causes all the amines to be discharged from their storage sites (synaptic vesicles), making a temporary surfeit of unbound amine, but this is oxidized and in the end there is a substantial depletion (Bruecke, Hornykiewicz, and Sigg, 1969). These drugs focused the quest for an understanding of schizophrenia on the amines and provided a set of tools for the manipulation of amines in the brain.

The counteraction of agitated psychotic behavior by drugs which blocked the action of catecholamines was matched by antidepressive actions of drugs synergistically related to the amines (Loomer, Saunders, and Kline, 1957).

Of these, amphetamine was most interesting and best studied, even though it has a poor antidepressant record (Stein, 1964*a,b*). It is interesting because of its direct positive actions on general activity levels, its special actions on drive behaviors, and its well-documented synergism with the catecholamine transmitters (Snyder, 1974). Other chemicals which counteract the degrading enzyme showed much more clinical promise (Bruecke et al., 1969). These "monoamine oxidase inhibitors" were effective antidepressant drugs, but they had side effects that curtailed their use.

Catecholamines were thus apparently implicated in schizophrenia and depression. Anticatechol drugs were effective in the former; proacting drugs were active in the latter. This made the study of brain catecholamines a matter of considerable interest.

Scientific study of the brain's amine systems was greatly facilitated by discovery of a neuroanatomical method. The method of Falck and Hillarp (Falck, Hillarp, Thieme, and Thorpe, 1962) made it possible to stain these systems so they could be clearly seen in the brain and to some degree even separated from one another. This is something that has not been possible to such a degree for any other transmitter system. The organization and arrangement of the amine systems that emerged from using this method were quite unexpected.

The cell bodies occur in small clusters in lower parts of the brain and the axons are broadcast from these to supply endings in the whole brain (Fuxe, 1965; Ungerstedt, 1971*c;* Lindvall and Björklund, 1974). In the rat, which is best studied, this focalization of cell bodies and broadcast of axons is carried to an extreme degree (Fig. 18), but even in higher animals it occurs to a considerable extent (Nobin and Björklund, 1973). The norepinephrine fibers start farthest back and go farthest forward. These fibers have their origin in the medulla and the midbrain. The axons of the norepinephrine system point down to the cord, up to the cerebellum, forward to the midbrain, and to all of the forebrain. Ascending fibers are grouped into at least two bundles. The dorsal bundle converges in the lateral hypothalamus or just above it and then diverges to thalamus, paleocortex, and neocortex. The ventral bundle converges on the hypothalamus and ends there, comprising a main source of neural control over hormonal function. There are other norepinephrine bundles, but these two are the best described.

The serotonin fibers start farther forward in the midbrain (the best-known system of these comes from a medial nucleus, the raphe). They converge on the lateral hypothalamus and then diverge. It is not clear whether they innervate paleocortex or neocortex to as great a degree as the norepinephrine fibers do.

The dopamine fibers start still farther forward—at the boundary of midbrain and diencephalon, in ventral "limbic" midbrain areas, in substantia nigra, and in medial hypothalamus. The bundles from ventral midbrain and substantia nigra converge on the lateral hypothalamus and then run well-

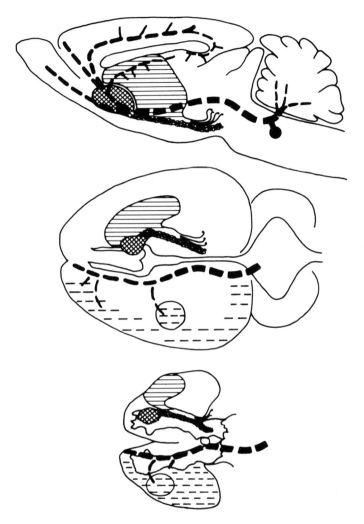

FIG. 18. Three catecholamine systems. The dorsal norepinephrine bundle (dashes) starts in the locus coeruleus at the boundary of the medulla and runs to cerebellum, hippocampus, and cortex. The meso-limbic dopamine system (scrambled lines and cross-hatching) starts in the ventral midbrain and runs to lower parts of the paleocortical-olfactory system. The nigrostriatal dopamine system (straight lines and single hatching) starts in the substantia nigra and runs to the caudate nucleus. One or both of the last two may run beyond their known targets because dopamine is found in the cortex. The raphe serotonin system is not shown; it starts between the source of the dorsal bundle and that of the dopamine systems and runs much of its course near the norepinephrine system.

known (and relatively short) courses to olfactory tubercle and caudate nucleus, respectively (both of these are just in front of the hypothalamus). They probably also go beyond because dopamine is found in cortex along with norepinephrine.

Thus it is something like a set of Chinese boxes: norepinephrine starting first and going farthest, serotonin starting next and stopping sooner, dopamine starting last and stopping first. All three systems of fibers are very concentrated in parts of the lateral hypothalamus (in or near the medial forebrain bundle). There they leave many endings, and from there they emerge to send their widely broadcast axons. Why they come together before diverging (which is unusual) is not clear. The most surprising thing, however, is the small number of cells, and the small size of the clusters in relation to the extremely wide ramification of these long, minute, and multiple dividing axons. Each of the neurons involved, if it functions like an ordinary neuron, exerts from an area deep in the brain an influence on other neurons distributed throughout the whole brain.

The small size of the axons had caused them to be more or less invisible to older neuroanatomical methods. The amine pathways therefore are long point-to-point fibers that had never been "seen" before. It is the only known case of a relatively small cluster of neurons sending axons to more or less all other parts of the brain.

Chemical and neurophysiological studies show the amines to have seven or eight special properties. First, two of them (dopamine and norepinephrine) have a common substrate, tyrosine (de la Torre, 1972); moreover, one (dopamine) is the normal precursor of the other (norepinephrine). Second, these differ from acetylcholine in the mode of inactivation. The acetylcholine messages are limited in time by degradation. This takes the form of hydrolysis under the influence of an enzyme, acetylcholinesterase (Krnjevic, 1974). Acetylocholine supplies are then replenished by acetylating choline under the control of a different enzyme, cholinacetylase. The amines were originally thought to be inactivated by degradation (oxidation in this case). Excessive supplies are degraded by this process under the influence of the monoamine oxidase enzyme, but this is not the route of inactivation. When amines are secreted by nerve terminals the messages are limited in time by reuptake of the amine back into nerve terminals where it is thought to be repackaged into vesicles for reuse [or oxidized if supplies are excessive (Iversen, 1967)]. Reuptake apparently also allows these neurons to replenish their stores from "free" amines in the interstitial fluid, possibly permitting them to borrow excesses from their neighbors. Third, monoamine oxidase provides a negative feedback mechanism to limit the brain supplies of the catecholamines so that the brain contents remain within narrow limits. Fourth, all three of the amines convey their message by causing a second messenger to be released inside the target cell; this is cyclic adenosine monophosphate (AMP) (Siggins, Hoffer, and Bloom, 1969). This second messenger is a common step between the amines and the peptide hormones. All use it to activate their targets. Fifth, the amines usually have inhibitory effects when piped directly into the nervous system (Phillis, 1970). Sixth, the same amine when circulating in the brain's vascular system often appears to excite the animal and to cause acceleration of the same neurons that are suppressed by direct chemical stimulation. Seventh, a "blood-brain" barrier separates the amines in the bloodstream from the brain amines. Eighth, as already mentioned, the onset and offset of the effect is slow when these are compared with the onset of acetylcholine.

Thus a considerable list of properties fits the catecholamines for special functions (Fig. 19): (1) the common substrate (tyrosine) between dopamine and norepinephrine, and the precursor role of dopamine to norepinephrine; (2) the reuptake mechanism which apparently permits the monoamine terminals to compete for scarce supplies; (3) the monoamine oxidase which provides a negative feedback on available supplies (a preplanned scarcity); (4) the "second messenger" cyclic AMP, which forms a common step in the action of catecholamine and peptide hormones (some of which may also be central nervous system transmitters); (5) the deceleratory or inhibitory modulation; (6) the sometimes opposed action of the same chemicals when they circulate as hormones; (7) the blood-brain barrier to separate circulating from brain amines; and (8) the slow onset and long duration of action. Although it is by no means clear what special functions they mediate, their properties would fit them for controlling behavioral priorities. This is because

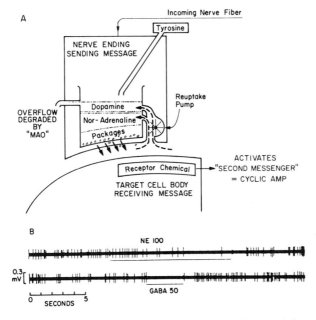

FIG. 19. Special properties of catecholamine systems. A: Nerve endings. Tyrosine is the common substrate of dopamine and norepinephrine (Nor-Adrenaline), and dopamine is the direct precursor of norepinephrine (other endings use dopamine without converting it to norepinephrine). Whichever catecholamine is used is packaged in inactive "capsules" or packages. These are released from endings and the substance released from them by the incoming nerve message. They act on a receptor chemical in the target cell, and this in turn acts through a second messenger (cyclic AMP), which is a common denominator between functions of amine transmitters and peptide hormones. After use, the catecholamine is recovered by the reuptake pump for reuse. Monoamine oxidase (MAO) forms a negative feedback system to keep supplies in a brain area at a relatively constant level. B: Iontophoretic application of catecholamine on neurons causes inhibitory actions with slow onset and long duration (Segal and Bloom, 1974a). NE, norepinephrine.

the repeating theme is competition for an "artificially" limited resource, and all the time constants involved are in the order of magnitude of behavioral episodes rather than of neurophysiological events.

B. Catecholamine Depressor Drugs and Brain Reward

The chemicals which depress the actions of the amine systems, particularly the catecholamines, fall into three classes (Bowman, Rand, and West, 1968). First there are chemicals which act as if they blocked the receptor mechanism so the chemical message carried by the amine would not be received. These include chlorpromazine itself, as well as haloperidol, which is its equal in counteracting psychotic agitation (Snyder, 1974). Both of these most likely have other actions, but blocking amine receptors is thought to be the main one. These drugs blocked electrically stimulated reward behavior in low doses (chlorpromazine, 2 mg/kg; Olds, Killam, and Bach y Rita, 1956). At these doses the animals appeared behaviorally alert; there was no obvious soporific effect. The counteraction of brain reward behavior in these cases was not as informative as it might seem. This is because a number of other behaviors were simultaneously suppressed or mitigated in much the same way (Chance and Silverman, 1964; Cook, 1964). Feeding, drinking, and sexual behavior were curtailed if work was required for these goals; however, patients treated by these drugs sometimes became obese (Lewis, 1965). The deficit was not even limited to positive responses. Behaviors motivated to avoid noxious stimulation before it happened were depressed by the same doses that depressed self-stimulation (Cook, 1964). However, in some cases escape behaviors that occurred after the noxious stimulation was applied survived (Olds, Hogberg, and Olds, 1964). This at least proved that behavioral capability still existed. Chlorpromazine and haloperidol thus abolished or at least curtailed a variety of behaviors with foresightful or anticipatory character. These were behaviors that would be considered voluntary or purposeful if they were performed by humans. If there was a general loss of voluntary or purposive behavior, this at first would suggest that the loss of brain reward behavior was not by itself surprising or interesting. On second thought, however, one might argue that the brain reward system evidenced in self-stimulation experiments forms the brain's substrate of purposive behavior; and thus it might still be the specific target of these drugs. Many studies make this supposition appealing (even though it is still unproved).

Another family of drugs is made up of those that block the peripheral actions of the catecholamines. The "alpha blockers" usually counter exciter actions, and the "beta blockers" usually counter inhibitory ones (Lewis, 1965). Neither of these blocks either self-stimulation or psychotic agitation when applied systemically. However, this was to be expected because they do not cross the blood-brain barrier. The alpha blockers do bring self-stimulation to a halt if applied in the ventricles of the brain (Wise, Berger, and Stein, 1973). The relative lack of vogue of these drugs in psychiatry and brain research probably derives from their failure to cross the blood-brain barrier. It is interesting and a little surprising that although most of the brain actions of the amines are supposed to be inhibitor actions, self-stimulation and many other central actions are blocked by the drug that usually blocks exciter action in the periphery.

Besides the blockers, the next main class of amine action depressors is the inhibitors of synthesis. Alpha-methyl-*p*-tyrosine blocks the conversion of tyrosine to dopamine, thereby blocking the normal route of formation for both catecholamines (Cooper, Bloom, and Roth, 1974). The conversion of tyrosine to dopamine is called the "rate-limiting step" because there is a scarcity of the enzyme that causes the transformation. This scarcity is possibly used by the organism as part of a feedback mechanism to maintain a relatively stable level of these two amines in the brain. As far as I know, the synthesis blockers have no fame as psychoactive drugs. (I do not know why.) They are effective in blocking brain reward behavior (at least alpha-methyl-*p*-tyrosine is) (Poschel and Ninteman, 1966; Black and Cooper, 1970; Gibson, McGeer, and McGeer, 1970; Cooper, Black, and Paolino, 1971). Disulfiram and diethyldithiocarbamate are drugs which block the formation of norepinephrine from dopamine. For some reason they make the animal quite sick. They also block brain reward behavior but incompletely (Wise and Stein, 1969; Roll, 1970).

The third class of amine depressors is the depleters. These act by releasing amines from stores. The released amines are soon degraded by oxidation. This is the process blocked by the monoamine oxidase inhibitors. The releasers have mixed effects (Stein, 1966). The two drugs best known as releasers are reserpine and tetrabenazine. They were mainly negative with respect to brain reward behavior. There was, however, a brief initial period of behavior acceleration when tetrabenazine was used; this lasted only a few minutes. It was followed by a suppression that lasted for hours. Reserpine caused a much longer-lasting depression of behavior and caused the animal to respond to drugs and other things in a strange way for an even longer period, days to weeks (Olds et al., 1956). Reserpine was originally the favored drug for use against psychotic agitation. Eventually it gave way to chlorpromazine (Lewis, 1965). I would guess that long-lasting side effects were the main problem, but I am not sure. So far as I know, tetrabenazine is not used for treatment of disease. The main effect of both drugs on brain reward behavior was to depress it.

However, this effect could be temporarily reversed (Stein, 1966). Both drugs had a strong initial positive effect if used in combination with a monoamine oxidase inhibitor. The latter prevented degradation of the freed amnes, keeping them unbound but undegraded. So long as it lasted, this appeared to have a very positive effect on brain reward behavior. If the amines packaged and ready in vesicles inside of nerve terminals were required to make brain stimulation rewarding, then getting them out of the vesicles should have damaged rather than improved this effect. If the amines were already released, and if this was all there was to reward, then why was the animal still stimulating its brain? Several answers seemed possible. One was that the freed amines were taken up into other fibers and re-released by stimulation (but if the drug prevented the packaged pool from existing, this did not fit). Another was that the animal—being confused as the noncontingent "drug-reward" gradually replaced the contingent electrical reward—was unable to learn that the link between responding and reward had been broken, and thus perseverated in what had now become a "superstitious response." A third was that the free amines brought receptors to near threshold; and brain stimulation, causing still further amine secretion, pushed them over. The "superstitious" explanation was not wholly unlikely; after extinction, free rewards sometimes cause rewarded behaviors to recur. However, I think another possibility must also be seriously entertained: that the amines are only part of the story, and possibly released amines plus stimulation of other brain fibers are required for reward.

C. Catecholamine Synergists and Brain Reward

The positive relation of the brain catecholamines to brain reward behavior was further attested to by studies of drugs that augmented or promoted the actions of the amines. Clinically these counteracted psychotic depression, and in animal studies they promoted brain reward behaviors. However, the case was far from completely clear. There are several classes of proacting drugs.

The first class is the "releasers." The activating releasers include amphetamine, relatives of amphetamine, and alpha-methyl-*m*-tyrosine. All had direct positive actions on brain reward behavior (Stein, 1964*a,b;* 1966; Crow, 1970). These drugs release catecholamines from their binding sites, much as the "depleters" do, making them free and therefore active (Trendelenberg, 1959; Snyder, 1974). For some reason the released amines in this case are not as totally depleted and degraded as is the case when depleters such as reserpine are used. Thus these releasers act as if they were depleters plus monoamine oxidase inhibitors rolled into one. They probably also have other actions that add to the effect. Amphetamine, for example, mimics the action of the catecholamines to some degree, and also prevents reuptake, thus keeping the amines free; it may also be a monoamine oxidase inhibitor, albeit a poor one (Lewis, 1964; Snyder, 1974). Amphetamine is used clinically for temporary relief in depressed or somnolent conditions (Lewis, 1964), but its benefits are brief and there is a pronounced negative aftereffect (Goodman and Gilman, 1955).

Its positive effects on brain reward behavior are mixed and there is a troubling lack of specificity. In many kinds of behavior experiments amphetamine augments "slow" behaviors and depresses "fast" ones (Dews, 1958). Brain reward behavior is no exception to this rule.

Nevertheless, it seems possible that some special relation exists. One of the main signs pointing in this direction came from experiments in which undrugged rats did not at first show any brain reward behavior, even though the probes were correctly placed (Olds, 1972). In most experiments there were a number of animals that failed to stimulate their brains. In some cases this was due to gross misplacement of the brain probes, but in others the probes were not obviously misplaced. It was originally thought that small differences in location (too small to be analyzed) were of paramount importance. However, amphetamine treatment dispelled this view to some degree. When probes were in the right general area, amphetamine regularly caused brain reward behavior to occur even in cases where there had been no prior sign of it (Fig. 20). When probes were grossly misplaced, there was

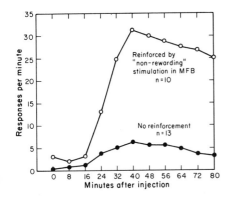

FIG. 20. Interaction of amphetamine with previously "unrewarding" hypothalamic stimulation (Olds, 1972). n, number. MFB, medial forebrain bundle.

no such effect. Animals started responding only when responses were followed by stimulations in the appropriate parts of the brain. Amphetamine has a reputation for enhancing previously learned behaviors (extinguished ones, for example) over other random behaviors, but this was not a previously learned behavior. Thus it looked as if some deficiency specially related to brain reward was compensated for by amphetamine. If so, then amphetamine might have a specific relation to brain reward behavior. Another argument pointing in the same direction was that the general effect of amphetamine on behavior had certain similarities to the effect of the rewarding brain stimulation.

The observation of so-called "stereotyped behavior" (Ellinwood, cited in Snyder, 1972) in amphetamine-treated animals (and humans) is well known. At certain descriptive levels this behavior would be indistinguishable from brain reward behavior itself. It is "a stereotyped compulsive behavior . . . the exact pattern varying with different species. . . . This includes a single activity performed continuously or a repertoire of a few sequences, which dominate behavior. This behavior is compulsive in the sense that it is seemingly nondistractable, driven, rapid, and repetitious in character." Moreover, such behavior appears to be purposeless since "it has no observable significance to the experimenters." Because rewarding brain stimulation and amphetamine both caused behaviors to become compulsive, there was further presumption of a special relation between them.

Further light on these problems was contributed by other relations of the amphetamine drugs. Besides releasing catecholamines, amphetamine is thought to imitate them to some degree. This is partly because it has a structural similarity with norepinephrine. Phenethylamine is a drug whose structure contains all the elements which norepinephrine and amphetamine have in common. If amphetamine gets some of its effect by these common structural properties, then phenethylamine should have the same effects. It had very little if any effect on brain reward behavior when used alone, but this was attributed to its rapid degradation by monoamine oxidase. When used with a monoamine oxidase inhibitor it had the same properties as amphetamine in promoting brain reward behavior (Stein, 1966). This suggested that amphetamine had some of its actions by imitating the catecholamines, and more specifically by imitating norepinephrine.

Another class of procatechol actions is the blocking of reuptake. The main method of stopping catecholamine action, as indicated previously, is by taking the amines back up into axon terminals where it is rebound or degraded. Drugs which block this action of the terminals cause free amines to remain in the interstitial fluid. Amphetamine has this as an additional mode of action. Cocaine, imipramine, and other drugs of its class also have this action (Iversen, 1967). These drugs are best known for their clinical value in treating psychotic depression. They did not act positively on brain reward behavior when used alone, but did potentiate the action of amphetamine (Stein, 1966). This appeared to indicate again that catecholamines in the extraneuronal space (outside of their packages and outside the nerve) promoted brain reward behavior.

Still another class of actions is to prevent degradation of the free amines by inhibiting the enzyme (monoamine oxidase) that promotes degradation. The drugs with this action (monoamine oxidase inhibitors) have important clinical value. Iproniazid and pargyline are members of this class. They have been important in the treatment of psychotic depression. They would be even more valuable if they did not have dangerous side effects (Lewis, 1965). They promote self-stimulation in some experiments when used alone (Poschel and Ninteman, 1964); and when used in combination with releasers, or "imitators," their positive effects are dependable and large (Stein, 1966).

It seems most interesting to consider seriously that both monoamine oxidase inhibitors and reuptake inhibitors support brain reward behavior (and counter depression). The inhibitors counter degradation and thus promote both the packaged pool ready for use in the axon terminals and the free pool (that might be acting as a free hormone-like substance in the interstitial fluid). If this were all the evidence, it would not be possible to guess which was more important. The reuptake blockers possibly resolve the issue. They sustain only the free pool. From this it might be inferred that amines outside the vesicle packages, and even outside the nerve terminals, are active in promoting brain reward behavior. Neither the enzyme inhibitors nor reuptake blockers had by themselves an unambiguous effect on brain reward behavior; but both promoted brain reward behavior when they were combined with something else to release the amines, freeing them from the terminals (e.g., amphetamine or reserpine), or something to substitute for the amines as a false transmitter (e.g., phenethylamine). Therefore it appeared that getting the catecholamines out of the nerve terminals and keeping them out promoted reward behavior (and countered psychotic depression).

Precursors of the amines that caused the brain stores to rise were also used as procatecholamine drugs. L-DOPA is a precursor that is turned to dopamine in the brain and can then be converted to norepinephrine. This route of dopamine production bypasses blockade of the step from tyrosine to dopamine. A different drug, which is sometimes called DOPS, is considered a precursor of norepinephrine but not of dopamine. L-DOPA is used directly in treatment of Parkinson's disease and has seemed to promote sex behavior as a side effect. I do not know whether these two compounds work on brain reward behavior by themselves. L-DOPA and DOPS both counteract the suppressive effects of alpha-methyl-*p*-tyrosine (which blocks the

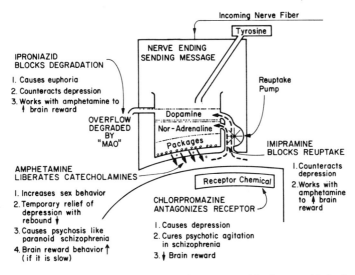

FIG. 21. Effect of catecholamine drugs on agitation, depression, and brain reward behavior. Releasers like amphetamine temporarily countered depressions in humans and augmented self-stimulation in rats. Drugs which blocked the degradation or reuptake of the liberated amines furthered the actions of amphetamine on self-stimulation and had quite good antidepressive qualities on their own in humans. Drugs which blocked the catecholamine receptors caused depressions but were very important in controlling psychotic agitation, particularly in schizophrenia. They generally stopped brain reward behavior and other purposive behaviors. Nor-Adrenaline, norepinephrine; MAO, monoamine oxidase.

formation of catecholamines by preventing conversion of tyrosine to dopamine). L-DOPA, which bypasses this blocade for both dopamine and
norepinephrine, is more effective than DOPS, which supposedly permits only
norepinephrine to be made (Stinus and Thierry, 1973).

The data on procatecholamine drugs thus showed all of them to support
brain reward behavior singly or in combination (Fig. 21). However, they
suggested a theory that leaves many questions unanswered: It was that free
amines outside the synaptic vesicles and even outside of the axon terminals
promote both self-stimulation behavior and relief from psychotic depressions.

D. Amine Pathways and Brain Reward

The study of the amine pathways has greatly added to the table of facts
and ideas relating brain reward, psychiatric drugs, and the amines. Using
the method of Falck and Hillarp (Falck et al., 1962), first Fuxe (1965),
then Ungerstedt (1971c), and finally Lindvall and Björklund (1974) mapped
the amine fiber pathways in the brain. These maps, which have successively
completed and corrected one another—and which have at times looked more
clear-cut than they do at present (Jacobowitz and Palkovits, 1974)—have
proved an important interlacing of the catecholamine and brain reward maps.
Even before these pathway maps were related to brain reward behavior, a
link of this phenomenon to catecholamine systems was championed on pharmacological grounds (Stein, 1964a). The maps therefore almost immediately raised the possibility that all the effects of stimulating lateral hypothalamus might be resulting from stimulation applied to one or several of
these bundles (Dresse, 1966; Stein, 1968; Crow and Arbuthnott, 1972).

A strong argument has been made in favor of the "dorsal norepinephrine
bundle" as one reward system (Crow et al., 1972; Ritter and Stein, 1973).
This originates at a site just below the cerebellum, a small cluster of cells,
most of them contained in a cell group named the locus coeruleus (Ungerstedt, 1971c). This sends norepinephrine-containing fibers into the cerebellum, the hippocampus, the neocortex, and likely to all other parts of the
forebrain. Even though the broadcast of these fibers covers almost the whole
brain, they are gathered together in tightly packed bundles (where special
effects from stimulating them might be expected) only in clearly demarcated
regions of passage, regions which include a dorsal part of the medial forebrain bundle. Besides the dorsal norepinephrine bundle, an equally strong
argument has added two dopamine bundles (Dresse, 1966; Routtenberg and
Malsbury, 1969; Crow, 1971; German and Bowden, 1974). One of these
originates in the ventral tegmental area and sends a focused bundle to the
olfactory tubercle and other ventral parts of the olfactory cortical system.
The other originates in the dorsal part of the substantia nigra and sends a
focused bundle to the caudate nucleus, which is a main part of the subcortical
motor system. Both collect heavily in the lateral hypothalamus, and both
probably send fibers beyond their targets in a more broadcast fashion. The

one norepinephrine bundle and the two dopamine bundles thus provided a common theme, matching much of the brain reward map. They also pointed the way to the discovery of new locations where electrical stimulation would cause brain reward behavior (Dresse, 1966; Crow et al., 1972; Farber, Steiner, and Ellmann, 1972; Ritter and Stein, 1973). Although not established as a fact, the view that these norepinephrine and dopamine elements widely broadcast in the brain make up important "reward systems" is a very strong hypothesis.

Mapping studies (Fig. 22) showed that electrical stimulation in or near the locus coeruleus itself caused brain reward behavior (Crow et al., 1972; Ritter and Stein, 1973). In this case there were some special characteristics.

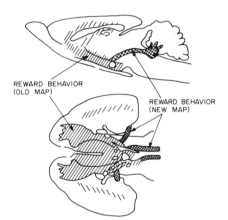

REWARD BEHAVIOR (OLD MAP)

REWARD BEHAVIOR (NEW MAP)

FIG. 22. New reward maps tracked self-stimulation to the origin of the dorsal norepinephrine bundle under the cerebellum, and to the substantia nigra at the front of the midbrain (Dresse, 1966; Routtenberg and Malsbury, 1969; Crow et al., 1972; Ritter and Stein, 1973).

The behavior was both slower, more regular, slightly less frenzied, and somewhat more difficult to train. Other stimulations along the course of the ascending "dorsal bundle" have also been shown to cause brain reward behavior (Crow, 1972a; Farber et al., 1972). In both the origins and the course, it is still possible that some other nearby close running systems might be at the root of the phenomena (Lindvall and Björklund, 1974), e.g., some visceral or gustatory afferent system. Still, because the effective sites do follow its course, the most likely hypothesis points to the dorsal norepinephrine bundle (Crow, 1972a; Ritter and Stein, 1973).

Other maps pointed with almost equal force to the centers where the two dopamine systems originate (Dresse, 1966; Routtenberg and Malsbury, 1969). Some argument was made in these cases that norepinephrine bundles might run to or through these areas and that the dopamine bundles might not be involved (Lindvall and Björklund, 1974). It seems somewhat more likely, however, that stimulation affecting dopamine bundles, even where they were separated from norepinephrine ones, also yielded brain reward behavior (German and Bowden, 1974).

Lesion studies (Fig. 23) showed that brain reward behavior in many cases could be abolished or depressed by lesions in the sources of the dorsal norepinephrine bundle (M. E. Olds, *private communication;* L. J. Ellman, *private communication*). This supported a catecholamine theory of brain reward. However, its force was mitigated to some degree by the ease with which these deficits could be repaired. Amphetamine "replacement therapy" served to make these animals behave as if there were no brain damage. The animals with locus coeruleus lesions behaved in much the same way as other animals that seemed to lack an innate predisposition to brain reward behavior (Olds, 1970). Both groups of animals responded to amphetamine application with responses that made them look in all ways like intact animals with no lack of disposition at all. If amphetamine substituted for free catecholamines, one wonders what fibers were being stimulated by these animals that made them press the pedal. The most likely answer would be that a few remaining nor-

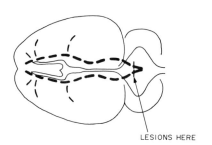

LESIONS HERE

FIG. 23. Lesions in the locus coeruleus at the source of the dorsal norepinephrine bundle abolished or weakened brain reward. This could often be restored to a considerable degree by administration of amphetamine (M. E. Olds, *private communication;* S. J. Ellman, *private communication*).

epinephrine fibers (or dopamine fibers) were potentiated by amphetamine so their effects would be sufficient to provoke behavior. The data still leave another possibility that cannot yet be entirely ruled out. This is that free norepinephrine (or amphetamine as a substitute) is a prerequisite to brain reward behavior, but that stimulation of some other fiber systems is also involved. That is, the combination of the two stimulations would be necessary, or stimulation of either one against a background of the other. The possibility that stimulation of two systems at the same time is necessary for brain reward has been raised many times by Deutsch and his followers (Deutsch, 1960; Gallistel, 1973).

Other, quite different lesion studies have added to a growing body of suggestive evidence correlating the norepinephrine fiber system with reward behavior. Substantial damage was done to that branch of the dorsal norepinephrine system entering the cerebellum. This produced a dramatic example of the previously documented finding that catecholamine neurons regrow and proliferate after damage to their axons in a way that may be an order of magnitude better than other neurons. When half the cerebellar projection of these neurons was cut, it caused a doubling of the catecholamine endings in cerebellum rather than the reduction that might seem the obvious outcome. At the same time, another branch of the dorsal norepinephrine system which supplies the hippocampus was studied. In the hippocampus, which is supplied by a different branch of the same dorsal norepinephrine system, there was an even larger (as much as sixfold) increase in norepinephrine endings (Pickel et al., 1974b). This seemed to imply a very large increase in all endings of the norepinephrine bundle when it was damaged anywhere. The change took 2 to 4 weeks to become complete.

It was the time course of the change that provided a surprisingly good match for a similarly timed improvement in self-stimulation behavior (Fig. 24). It has long been known (though not published except in symposium discussions) that self-stimulation behavior improves from the time

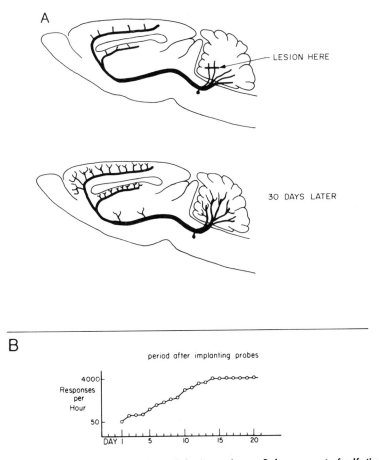

FIG. 24. A. Regrowth and proliferation of catecholamine pathways. B. Improvement of self-stimulation behavior caused over a 2- to 3-week period after damage to a part of the dorsal norepinephrine bundle (Olds, 1958d; Pickel et al., 1974b).

of implantation, and that this improvement continues for about 2 to 4 weeks from the date of surgery (Olds, 1958d). Because the improvement occurred, regardless of whether the animal was stimulated, it appeared to be a consequence of surgery. It was baffling because the results of surgery were thought to be over much sooner. Because probe implantation into a self-stimulation would damage a norepinephrine bundle if the norepinephrine theory of reward were correct, this suggests that the timed improvement might well be due to the regrowth and proliferation caused by this damage.

E. Poisoning the Catecholamine and Serotonin Pathways

The catecholamine view of brain reward and drive behavior was advanced by a special method to poison pathways selectively, either all at once or one at a time. For the catecholamine-containing neurons, the poisoning was done by applying 6-hydroxydopamine (6-HDA). When this was applied in the ventricles or in the cisterna magna together with a monoamine oxidase inhibitor, a large proportion of the catecholamine terminals in the forebrain was destroyed (Bloom, Algeri, Groppetti, Revuelta, and Costa, 1969; Burkard, Jalfre, and Blum, 1969; Uretsky and Iverson, 1970; Breese and Traylor, 1971). One way this could be assayed was by utilizing the fact that the catecholamine content of the forebrain was greatly depressed. For example, after pretreatment with pargylene (50 mg/kg), 200 μg 6-HDA in the ventricles of the rat caused more than 90% of the forebrain's dopamine and norepinephrine to be depleted (Stricker and Zigmond, 1974). Thus a method was provided to study the relation of these to reward and drive behaviors.

When this method was used, brain reward behavior was greatly reduced, abolished altogether in most cases (Breese, Howard, and Leahy, 1971; Antelman, Lippa, and Fisher, 1972). The brain reward behavior attenuated by this means could be restored either by the use of amphetamine or by ventricular application of norepinephrine (M. E. Olds, *private communication*). This provided another example of the apparent restoration of aminergic function by providing for free amines in the brain fluids even though a majority of the norepinephrine axonal systems was supposedly damaged. It must be supposed either that the epinephrine worked even without its fibers (in which case some other fibers must have been supporting the self-stimulation) or that cells undamaged by 6-HDA were sufficiently numerous to support brain reward behavior when replenished by exogenous amine, or that rapid regrowth and reuptake was the cause of the success of this kind of "replacement therapy."

Besides its relevance for brain reward theories, the method of amine pathway poisoning also had important implications tying other motivational behaviors to the catecholamine-containing neurons and axons (Fig. 25). When 6-HDA was applied to one of the special amine pathways, either at its source or along its course, the damage was restricted (Ungerstedt, 1970,

1971*b*). Much of the bundle (including many of its distant endings) together with many of the other neuronal structures near the injection site were damaged to some degree. Even though the chemical apparently damaged more than just the catecholamine elements, the method was still considered to have an important element of specificity (although this is not fully proved); at least different sites of application (i.e., application to different catecholamine bundles) caused different pathological conditions.

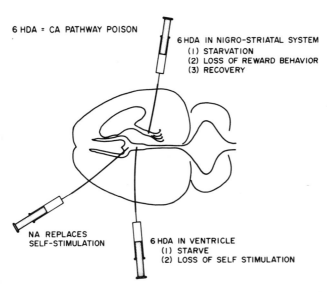

6 HDA = CA PATHWAY POISON

6 HDA IN NIGRO-STRIATAL SYSTEM
(1) STARVATION
(2) LOSS OF REWARD BEHAVIOR
(3) RECOVERY

NA REPLACES
SELF-STIMULATION

6 HDA IN VENTRICLE
(1) STARVE
(2) LOSS OF SELF STIMULATION

FIG. 25. 6-HDA poisoned the catecholamine (CA) pathways and affected motivated behavior. In the nigrostriatal pathway it caused the "lateral hypothalamic syndrome" (Ungerstedt, 1970, 1971b); in the ventricle it had much the same effect (Stricker and Zigmond, 1974) and also blocked self-stimulation (Breese et al., 1971). Self-stimulation blocked this way could often be restored by ventricular administration of norepinephrine (NA) (M. E. Olds, *private communication*).

When applied to the ventral norepinephrine bundle, the one that carries norepinephrine mainly toward the medial hypothalamus, 6-HDA caused many of the symptoms of the medial hypothalamic obesity syndrome (Ahlskog and Hoebel, 1973). Animals overate and became obese (Fig. 26).

When 6-HDA was applied to the nigrostriatal pathway—the one that carries dopamine mainly from the substantia nigra to the caudate nucleus of the extrapyramidal system—this caused what looked like "hypothalamic starvation." At first, animals refused food and ejected it from the mouth (Ungerstedt, 1971*a,b,c,* 1974*a,b*). They died of starvation if they were not force-fed. After recovery there was a lasting loss of response to dehydration and to cellular glucose deficits (Marshall and Teitelbaum, 1973). Like animals with lateral hypothalamic lesions, these animals retained or recovered their ability to modulate food intake in response to heat stress (Marshall and

Teitelbaum, 1973) and were sufficiently recovered to regulate body weight and to appear to be normal feeders and drinkers in spite of the loss of response to special hunger and thirst stimuli. Also like animals with lateral hypothalamic lesions, they lost the ability to generate new aversions to food when foods were correlated with later sickness. Furthermore, there was a pronounced sensorimotor defect that also made feeding (and other operant behavior) difficult; at least this appeared in the early stages. In all these

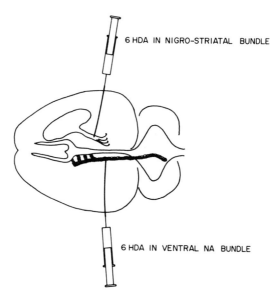

FIG. 26. Opposite effects of poisoning two catecholamine pathways. In the nigrostriatal pathway the lesions caused starvation and loss of voluntary behaviors; in the ventral norepinephrine (NA) bundle it caused overeating and obesity (Ahlskog and Hoebel, 1973).

respects, the pathology engendered by application of 6-HDA to the substantia nigra matched the pathology engendered by other lesions in or near the lateral hypothalamus. This was possibly not very surprising as there were lesions in or near the lateral hypothalamus caused by this method.

It was more surprising to find that many of the same symptoms could be produced by 6-HDA plus pargylene applied in the ventricles in a fashion that did very little obvious biological damage (Stricker and Zigmond, 1974). This caused temporary failure to eat and drink, and sensorimotor defects also occurred. After recovery there was a loss of responses to glucose deficiency and dehydration. However, in this case there was no loss of the ability to form new aversions when food was correlated with later sickness. Several things were surprising about this syndrome. First, because ventral bundle poisoning resulted in obesity, and nigrostriatal poisoning caused starvation, there was no way to guess in advance what the ventricular poison would do. If it poisoned the system closest to the ventricle, it should have caused obesity; instead it caused starvation. (The nigral pathway is the farthest from the ventricle.) This appeared to indicate a distant action of the chemical.

Another set of interesting findings came from studies in which pretreatments were used to direct the ventricular 6-HDA especially toward dopamine or norepinephrine systems (Stricker and Zigmond, 1974). If dopamine systems were mainly damaged there was a severe "lateral hypothalamic" syndrome, but all cases recovered. If norepinephrine was mainly damaged there was a much less severe syndrome and full recovery. If both systems were damaged in an exacerbated way (caused by pretreatment with a monoamine oxidase inhibitor) total failure of recovery occurred in about half the animals, although the others survived. In all cases, however, there was evidently permanent loss of response to glucose shortage and cellular dehydration. It was surprising that the "learning" of aversions based on sickness survived, apparently indicating that this did not depend on catecholamine systems. However, 6-HDA in the ventricles caused considerable impairment of another kind of aversive learning (Cooper, Breese, Howard, and Grant, 1972a). It was surprising that a type of aversive learning normally associated with the lateral hypothalamus syndrome was spared by ventricular 6-HDA, whereas a kind of aversive learning normally spared by lateral lesions was damaged.

Besides the effect on eating and drinking and avoidance learning, the ventricular 6-HDA augmented irritability and aggression (Nakamura and Thoenen, 1972; Coscina, Seggie, Godse, and Stancer, 1973). Moreover, 6-HDA poisoning of the dopamine pathway that travels from the ventral midbrain to the ventral aspects of the olfactory cortical system in cats caused some effects of lateral hypothalamic lesions, reducing eating and drinking to some degree but particularly in this case causing the sensorimotor aspects of the defect (Frigyesi, Ige, Iulo, and Schwartz, 1971). This was surprising because these would be thought to be related mainly to the nigrostriatal system.

In other experiments a different but similarly acting poison was applied in the ventricle to damage the serotonin fiber systems. The chemical in this case was 5,7-dihydroxytryptamine. It caused a major depletion of telencephalic serotonin levels. The main behavioral effect in this case was an increased irritability—as would be expected reasoning from other lesions causing similar depletion of serotonin (Ellison and Bresler, 1974).

F. Ventricular Injection

The amphetamine studies and studies with catecholamine precursors have been well supplemented by direct application of catecholamines in the lateral ventricles in such a way as to bypass the "blood-brain barrier" and make a direct test of some of the amine hypotheses (Wise and Stein, 1969).

When brain reward behavior was blocked by disulfiram, which prevented the conversion of dopamine to norepinephrine, the animals often became quite sick or sedated. For this or other more specific causes, brain reward behavior was suppressed or at least attenuated. Direct ventricular application of norepinephrine counteracted these effects to some degree, causing the behavior to return to near-normal rates. Ventricular application of dopamine and serotonin failed to have this effect. These experiments were criticized on the theory that "sedating effects" of the synthesis inhibitors might have

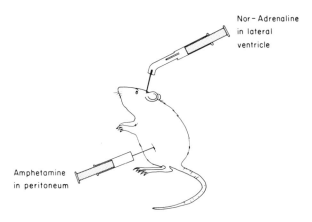

Nor-Adrenaline in lateral ventricle

Amphetamine in peritoneum

FIG. 27. Norepinephrine (Nor-Adrenaline) administered in the ventricles like amphetamine applied intra-peritoneally caused an improvement in self-stimulation behavior if rates were low to begin with (Wise et al., 1973).

been counteracted by the centrally administered norepinephrine, and this could have been a main source of the effect (Roll, 1970). Therefore further evidence was needed on centrally administered catecholamines.

In a later experiment aimed to answer this objection, norepinephrine was administered in the ventricles of animals with no antecedent treatment (Wise et al., 1973). In these experiments a well-trained animal was used. During a period when there was very slow brain reward behavior owing to a near-threshold brain reward stimulus, l-norepinephrine was administered in the ventricles. Locke's solution and d-norepinephrine (which is a relatively ineffective "isomer") were used for control. When 10 μg norepinephrine were administered in the ventricle, there was a prompt acceleration of brain reward behavior (Fig. 27). It appeared to commence within seconds of the chemical application in the ventricles. It reached a maximum about 24 min after application and was still present after 32 min. The rapid onset of the effect appeared to suggest some direct excitatory action of the drug on neural mechanisms along the ventricular wall—possibly, for example, an inhibitory action on the parts of the septal area that lie adjacent to the ventricle near the site of injection. Nevertheless, these experiments left little doubt that norepinephrine applied in the ventricle had a specific or nonspecific positive relation to brain reward behavior when applied in 5- or 10-μg quantities.

Saline and d-norepinephrine, used as control solutions, had minor excitatory effects. The l-norepinephrine was substantially more effective.

In these same experiments, serotonin was observed to have a negative effect on brain reward behavior when directly applied in 5- and 10-μg quantities. This agreed with data from other experiments in which p-chlorophenylalanine (PCPA; used to block serotonin production) caused augmentation in self-stimulation behavior, and 5-hydroxytryptophan (5-HTP; a precursor of serotonin) reduced it; but there was other opposed evidence to be discussed later. These experiments bolstered the view of Stein that brain reward behavior is both dependent on norepinephrine and countered by serotonin.

In other experiments of similar type, the positive action of exogenous norepinephrine applied in the ventricles was confirmed (Olds, 1974). Doses of 10, 20, 30, and 40 μg were applied in 2 to 7 μl of artificial cerebrospinal fluid. All doses augmented brain reward behavior under some conditions. The low (10 μg) dose was particularly effective. The largest effect was obtained when electrical stimulation was at or near threshold levels. Although this study confirmed the positive action of norepinephrine, it failed to confirm the negative actions of serotonin. Instead, like norepinephrine, serotonin had some positive effects at low doses, but the data were ambiguous. The effects with dopamine in the same experiment were even more equivocal; it may have had positive effects, but this was far from clear. The active isomer of norepinephrine is l-norepinephrine. In this experiment the inactive d-isomer was used as control. It also had some possible positive effects, but these were even less than those of serotonin or dopamine. In other experiments ventricular applications of d- and l-amphetamine were also made (M. E. Olds, *private communication*). In this case the d-isomer is more effective in norepinephrine systems. When 100 to 300 μg d-amphetamine was applied by this route, it had much the same effect as 1 to 3 mg/kg applied systemically; i.e., it augmented brain reward behavior, particularly when this was slow by virtue of threshold stimulus levels. In this case as peripherally d-amphetamine was far more effective than l-amphetamine. Thus while leaving some questions surrounding serotonin and dopamine, these studies confirmed the role of ventricular norepinephrine in promoting brain reward behavior. Norepinephrine and amphetamine applied centrally had much the same effects as amphetamine applied systemically.

Because the direct application findings were the most convincing evidence in favor of the catecholamine theories of brain reward behavior, it is important to keep the record straight by placing mitigating evidence alongside the positive facts. Detracting are several possibilities. One is that the amines applied in the ventricle suppress inhibitory systems along the ventricular wall. Norepinephrine at least has a mainly suppressive effect when applied directly in the brain. The septal area, caudate nucleus, hippocampus, and medial hypothalamus are all systems which line the ventricular wall, and all have substantial records as behavioral inhibitors. Thus norepinephrine could have its effect on brain reward behavior by suppressing these inhibitors. Second, the difference in findings between studies which show serotonin to be negative and those which show it to be positive in relation to brain reward behavior must be taken for now as evidence that small differences in method may reverse the main direction of these experiments. Finally, when telencephalic catecholamine systems have been greatly damaged by poisons, ventricular catecholamines still promote reward behavior. This leaves open the possibility that stimulation of noncatecholamine systems in some way is involved. As things stand, I do not see the mitigating evidence as sufficient to counteract the amine theory of brain reward. The theory, however, is nothing more than a good (but not yet compelling) hypothesis.

G. Direct Chemical Stimulation in Hypothalamus

Besides application in the ventricle, drugs and neurohumors have been applied in medial and lateral hypothalamus and similarly at other locations. The most dramatic effects were obtained with acetylcholine agonists (and angiotensin) on drinking. Carbamylcholine, which mimics some actions of acetylcholine but is much less easily inactivated, was used in most of these tests. When it was applied in small quantities in the hypothalamus, it caused animals to drink (Grossman, 1960). This at first caused the view that some "cholinergic drinking mechanism" was housed in the hypothalamus. Later studies showed that the chemical had similar effects when injected in many different brain regions (Fisher and Coury, 1962). Moreover, best effects were achieved in the "anterior hippocampal commissure," an area with no synapses—a place very near the ventricles and particularly near to one periventricular apparatus called the subfornical organ (Fisher, 1969). Later it was found that similar effects were induced by applying angiotensin, the hormone-like substance of the kidney which plays a role in hypovolemic drinking (Epstein, Fitzsimmons, and Rolls, 1970). While this substance had pronounced effects in the preoptic area (and possibly even activated the vasopressin-releasing neurosecretory cells in the supraoptic area) it has now been shown to cause drinking mainly by direct action on the subfornical organ (Simpson and Routtenberg, 1973). This is one of the "circumventricular organs" (specialized parts of the ventricular wall with neurosecretory activity, which may function as blood-brain "windows" for movement of messages both ways). While the action of angiotensin at this point very likely plays some role in drinking, the mechanism of action is unknown. It is now generally assumed that the actions of carbamylcholine and other acetylcholine agonists on drinking are also caused by action at the subfornical organ. At least it no longer seems likely that acetylcholine by itself is some sort of drinking hormone acting on a specially coded hypothalamic drive system.

Similar experiments with norepinephrine and feeding fared better. There was a relatively delimited set of locations where direct application of norepinephrine caused the satiated animal to eat (Booth, 1967). When these points were mapped, the results looked partly like a map of locations where electrical stimulation caused animals to eat, but also partly like a map of places where electrical stimulation caused animals to stop eating. Some of the locations were quite close to those areas where knife cuts, electrolytic lesions, or chemical blockers caused eating. This pointed to a possible depressive effect of the exogenous norepinephrine on a satiety mechanism (Coons and Quartermain, 1970). However, the chemical effects in areas where electrical stimulation caused eating pointed in the other direction. The case for norepinephrine as a special proeating hormone had many good arguments against it. First, amphetamine caused animals to undereat (Magour, Cooper, and Faehndrich, 1974); by this it would be guessed that catecholamines opposed eating. The same supposition was fostered by the obesity-inducing effects of chlorpromazine (Lewis, 1965). Furthermore, the 6-HDA experiments appeared to indicate a dopamine system (lateral) that promoted feeding and a norepinephrine (medial) system that suppressed it. Thus pharmacology and 6-HDA studies pointed to mixed actions of the catecholamines with norepinephrine as a mainly antifeeding substance.

In other experiments aimed at unraveling the problem further, alpha- and beta-norepinephrine receptors were blocked separately by appropriate drugs, and isoproterenol, which stimulates the beta receptor only, was also used (Margules, 1970a,b). The conclusion from these studies was that the alpha action of norepinephrine mediated the cessation of feeding caused by excessive stomach or vascular loads, and the beta action mediated cessation of feeding caused by aversive taste factors. These suppositions were in harmony with the negative action of amphetamine on food intake and the positive action of chlorpromazine. They also fit well with the later discovery that 6-HDA lesions of the ventral bundle caused overeating (Ahlskog and Hoebel, 1973). It was troubling nevertheless that smaller quantities of norepinephrine applied unilaterally in about the same region (perifornical area of medial forebrain bundle) should have had opposite effects (Leibowitz, 1974). One possibility was that amine fibers themselves were actually suppressed when amines were applied along their axonal course. Some other studies of quite a different nature seemed to make this a likely answer.

In experiments that occupied me for several years, unilateral applications of a variety of chemicals in the medial forebrain bundle were made (Olds, Yuwiler, Olds, and Yun, 1964). I became convinced that most direct chemical stimulation studies used far too much fluid. When I used even 0.1 μl of a control solution (neutral saline or artificial cerebrospinal fluid) animals would bar-press to "self-inject" these supposedly inert solutions. This led me to suppose a mechanical stimulating action of even these small amounts. When the quantities were reduced to 0.01 μl this action disappeared. In a series of studies, therefore, arrangements were made by a special system of devices (Fig. 28) to apply 0.003 μl after each pedal response. Under these conditions inert control solutions were not active, but "chelators" (i.e., substances which acted by withdrawing ionic calcium from brain fluids) caused a great deal of activity when applied in or near the medial forebrain bundle. Citrate, phosphate, pyrophosphate, ethylenediaminetetraacetate, bitartrate, and creatinine sulfate all had this kind of action, and it appeared that the threshold concentrations in each case agreed with the affinity for calcium. Thus it was fair to assume that these substances acted by withdraw-

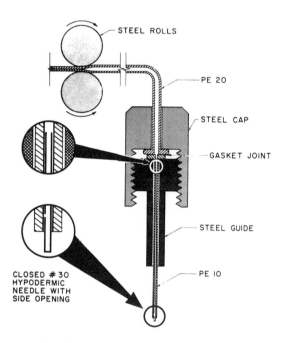

STEEL ROLLS

PE 20

STEEL CAP

GASKET JOINT

STEEL GUIDE

CLOSED #30
HYPODERMIC
NEEDLE WITH
SIDE OPENING

PE 10

FIG. 28. Device for automatic application of very small quantities of various neurohumors in the hypothalamus (Olds et al., 1964).

ing ionic calcium from the hypothalamic fluids. These experiments were originally arranged to test for rewarding effects of chemical injections, but they failed in this. Animals pressed pedals which caused injections of chemicals into the hypothalamus, but it turned out that the pedal responding was secondary to behavioral excitation caused by the applied chemicals. Special methods to dissociate the two kinds of effect (e.g., maze tests) that worked with electrical stimulations did not work with the chemical injections. The problem appeared to be that the chemical stimulation could not be brought under full control. The animals could inject a stimulating chemical, but there was no way for the experimenter to stop its action (to prevent negative aftereffects or to require the animals to press again to get "more"). However, the experiments did serve to divide chemicals (and mixtures) into those whose application in the hypothalamic reward areas caused activation (measured by pedal behavior) and those whose application had no effect. In one series of tests, the dose was kept constant at 3 nl of fluid per pedal response, and the concentrations of various chemicals were varied from 1 to 200 mmoles/liter. Acetylcholine, norepinephrine, epinephrine, and serotonin were used to determine if any of these would activate the hypothalamus. No activating effects were observed. These same substances were then applied again mixed with activating solutions of pyrophosphate. In mixtures all the supposed neurohumors suppressed the action of the "chelator." However, there were substantial differences in concentration required. Epinephrine and norepinephrine were effective in the smallest concentrations (12 mmoles/liter). These were followed by serotonin (75 mmoles/liter) and then GABA and acetylcholine (more than 150 mmoles/liter). Because the threshold for the acetylcholine effect was high, its negative action was possibly caused by excesses and depolarization block. The negative action of epinephrine and norepinephrine in much smaller quantities was more likely due to some direct "inhibitory" action. In view of the later discovery of positive actions of norepinephrine applied ventricularly and the many pharmacological indications of norepinephrine as a requisite for brain reward behavior, these negative actions (suppressive of all behavior) were surprising. To me the most likely explanation was that the directly applied norepinephrine had as its main action an unnatural inhibitory influence on the fibers of the medial forebrain bundle, this being just the opposite of the main excitatory action of electrical stimulation.

Later in the course of this same series of experiments, some positive actions related to transmitter and hormone systems were observed. Carbamylcholine and acetylcarnetine—both of which supposedly mimic acetylcholine action to some degree but are less vulnerable to the degrading action of cholinesterase—were found to cause brief episodes of behavioral activation when applied directly in medial forebrain bundle regions. These cholinergic substances were not as active as the chelators, however.

The most active substance used was testosterone sulfate (Olds, 1964). This substance was active in 3 mmole/liter quantities. Estrone sulfate and even cholesterol sulfate were tried as control substances; they appeared to have some positive action. These compounds were not stable, however, and so fair tests could not be made. The possibility remained, nevertheless, that steroid hormones might have general excitatory actions when applied along fiber bundles or, as would be even more interesting, special excitatory actions in the hypothalamus.

These studies did not answer the question I started with: a chemical code for reward in the brain. They did, however, make it clear that direct application of catecholamines in the brain (even when applied with careful attention to osmolarity, pH, and ultrasmall quantities with similarly small quanti-

ties of carrier solution) could yield outcomes strangely at odds with pharmacological evidence. Most likely, directly applied chemicals act in an un-
physiological fashion on passing fibers rather than acting on the appropriate
subsynaptic targets.

H. Dopamine

Is brain reward behavior supported mainly by norepinephrine or dopamine
pathways? Are both required or can either system sustain the behavior acting alone? Most evidence appears to point to the last possibility; but the issue
is still in doubt. Neuroanatomical data supported the view that dopamine
plays a role equally important as that of norepinephrine in brain reward
behavior. Electrical stimulation applied to the area compacta of the substantia nigra (the origina of the nigrostriatal pathway) and stimulation applied to the ventral tegmental area of Tsai (the origin of the mesolimbic
dopamine pathway) both caused high rates of brain reward behavior with
very low thresholds (Routtenberg and Malesbury, 1969). Of these, the
ventral tegmental area has passing norepinephrine fibers, but there is no
similar report yet for the substantia nigra. Furthermore, stimulation along
the lateral edges of the hypothalamus in an area mainly devoted to the
dopamine pathways caused intense brain reward behavior. These observations were best interpreted by assuming that the dopamine pathways, like
norepinephrine ones, marked brain regions where electrical stimulation was
rewarding. In a third dopamine system the cell bodies are medially placed
in the hypothalamus. This system is most likely involved in hypothalamic
regulation of hormone systems; its involvement in reward behavior is much
less clear. It is similar in this regard to the ventral norepinephrine system,
which is also involved in hormonal control. Of the two dopamine systems
that were implicated by the correlation of their brain maps with behavioral
reward maps, the mesolimbic system connects two poorly understood sectors
of the olfactory-visceral brain, and the nigrostriatal pathway makes up part
of the extrapyramidal motor system. The nigrostriatal system consists of the
substantia nigra, the caudate nucleus, and the pathway between. It is a bidirectional pathway that may carry inhibitory messages in both directions.
That is, the dopamine bundle from the substantia nigra is thought to have
mainly inhibitory actions in the caudate nucleus, and this is reciprocated by a
bundle containing a different inhibitory transmitter (GABA). Both paths
most likely have offshoots to the globus pallidus, which is another part of
the extrapyramidal motor system. Because lesions in the substantia nigra or
lesions cutting the pathway caused a temporary loss of purposive behavior,
and lesions in the caudate nucleus caused excessive behavior of a "targeted"
type, it was tempting to assume that this pair of opponents was a major force
in accelerating or decelerating behaviors of this type. The loss of operant behavior caused by poisoning the dopamine path and the positive reinforcement caused by its stimulation pointed to the substantia nigra as the positive

factor in the pair. The excesses of pursuit behavior caused by caudate lesions were matched by experiments in which caudate stimulation brought targeted behavior to a halt (Buchwald, Wyers, Lamprecht, and Heuser, 1961). Because pursuit reactions survived and were even exaggerated after caudate lesions, the substantia nigra might be considered the control center for these behaviors. However, if these behaviors recovered after substantia nigra influences were severed by lateral hypothalamic or 6-HDA lesions, this would indicate that there were other co-acting centers. Functions of this type have regularly turned out to be diffusely and redundantly localized. Attention should be turned to the globus pallidus, which is a target for offshoots of both ascending and descending aspects of the nigrostriatal pathway. It might be an integrator of the caudate and nigral effects. Even if this were true, however, there would probably be alternative stations where such integrations might also be carried out. The cortex (particularly frontal and motor cortex) and midline thalamus would come to my mind next because of their close ties to the extrapyramidal motor systems. The nearby amygdala and its "periamygdaloid cortex" also deserve candidacy because of their apparent involvement in the "motivationally meaningful" aspects of behavior (Klüver and Bucy, 1937; Olds, 1955; Weiskrantz, 1956; Schwartzbaum, 1965). For all of this, I believe that the caudate-substantia nigra "opponent system" (and possibly the globus pallidus between) may well turn out to be "first" among a set of "coequal" control systems for this kind of behavior.

Pharmacological studies point to dopamine as well as norepinephrine as having some special relation to brain reward. Amphetamine pointed in two directions: directly to norepinephrine in some cases and directly to dopamine in others (Taylor and Snyder, 1970, 1971; Svensson, 1971; Scheel-Kruger, 1972).

Studies appeared to show d-amphetamine 10 times more effective than l-amphetamine in relation to norepinephrine functions but the two equally effective on dopamine ones; but later studies blurred or reversed this (Taylor and Snyder, 1970, 1971; Snyder, *private communication*). Behaviorally, it was shown that the d-isomer was about 10 times as effective as the l-isomer in producing locomotor activity (or exploratory behavior). This was therefore assumed to represent a norepinephrine action of amphetamine, but d-amphetamine was only two times as effective as l-amphetamine in producing "stereotyped behavior." This was supposed to be to some degree (although not entirely) a dopamine action of amphetamine. Other experiments applied this method to brain reward behavior (Phillips and Fibiger, 1973). The d-isomer was seven to 10 times as effective as the l-isomer if probes were planted in the lateral hypothalamus, but the isomers were equally active if the brain reward probe was planted in the substantia nigra. This seemed to make the point that either of the two amines could play a major role depending on the probe location.

Other pharmacological experiments linking brain reward behavior and dopamine have been performed with apomorphine, which stimulates dopamine receptors (Andén, Rubenson, Fuxe, and Hökfelt, 1967; Ernst, 1967). Probes were planted in the "mesolimbic" dopamine system (at both ends), in the substantia nigra, in the lateral hypothalamus, and in the locus coeruleus of the dorsal norepinephrine system (Broekkamp and van Rossum, 1974). Apomorphine (0.2 mg/kg) consistently facilitated self-stimulation in some cases but inhibited it in others. This variability did not seem to be a function of the probe location; it appeared within each set of brain probes. The effect of the drug, however, was highly reproducible for individual animals (each of which had only one probe). Those animals that bar-pressed under the influence of the drug did not extinguish when the current was reduced to zero, indicating that pedal-pressing in this case had become a stereotyped behavior. The authors concluded that the apomorphine stimulation of the dopamine receptors was in this case just a different way to give the brain reward, and the question of whether an individual animal pedal-pressed depended on the chance contiguities that occurred at the onset of this rewarding condition.

An indirect link of dopamine and brain reward was also made by drugs which caused repetitive behaviors more directly. Drugs such as morphine, cocaine, and amphetamine (all of which have some reinforcing properties) were able to generate stereotyped behavior (Fog, 1969, 1970). The actual form of the behavior depended on the species and the behavioral situation (Randrup and Munkvad, 1970). In higher species with a complex behavioral repertoire the stereotyped behaviors differed from individual to individual. The stereotyped behavior of an individual, however, was reproducible during repeated injections (Ellinwood, 1971; Nymark, 1972; Rostrosen, Wallach, Angrist, and Gershon, 1972). One view was that the actual behavior that occurred depended on its chance occurrence at the onset of the drug action or on its previous reinforcement in a particular situation (Skinner, 1948; Ellinwood, 1971; Broekkamp and van Rossum, 1974). Due to the sustained performance of the behavior during the sustained reinforcing effect of the drug, this behavior was then thought to be repeated in a stereotyped and "superstitious" manner. By pharmacological and 6-HDA studies these stereotyped behaviors were linked to dopamine (as opposed to norepinephrine). For example, they were almost equally caused by d- or l-amphetamine (Taylor and Snyder, 1970, 1971), and they were modified by 6-HDA lesions and other lesions in the nigral or mesolimbic dopamine bundles (Randrup and Munkvad, 1970; Simpson and Iverson, 1971; McKenzie, 1972; Iverson, 1974; Neill, Boggan, and Grossman, 1974).

It is a similarity in character that relates this stereotyped behavior to brain reward (Ellinwood, cited in Snyder, 1972). Both often involved a compulsive repetition with the actual specification of what is to be repeated varying not only from species to species but from animal to animal. In rats amphetamine often induced sniffing or licking. In cats and chimps it was sometimes looking from side to side. In humans it was sometimes expressed as purposeless (paranoid) thought process (Angrist, Shopsin, and Gershon, 1971). It

could be a single activity performed repeatedly or a small repertoire of behavior so performed. It dominated behavior. It was nondistractable, driven,
rapid, and repetitious. It had no observable significance. The difference of
amphetamine-induced stereotypy from brain reward behavior is that it was
aimless, whereas we assumed there was an aim to get the brain reward. In
other words, self-stimulation was arranged so the compulsion inducer came
at the end of the behavior sequence. If we grant amphetamine as having
some rewarding side effects, these came before, during, and after the compulsive behavior. Thus self-stimulation makes sense in a way that amphetamine compulsions do not. Still, because there were situations where animals
sustained superstitious responses in the presence of sustained rewards, the
two kinds of behavior could be close relatives. This seemed particularly
likely when dopamine pathway were at the self-stimulation site.

I. Serotonin

5-Hydroxytryptamine (serotonin) is a close relative of the catecholamines. It occurs in the blood (where it is carried in platelets) and in the
stomach (where it has hormone-like actions involved in stomach motility).
It is distributed through the brain in uneven fashion, suggesting that it is a
transmitter in some systems (Lewis, 1965). It is stained by the fluorescence
method and this shows that most serotonin-containing cell bodies are located
in the midbrain along the midline; the axons of these traverse the medial
forebrain bundle and terminate in the paleocortex and other telancephalic
structures (Dahlström and Fuxe, 1964). Experiments point to a likely
involvement of serotonin as a neurohumor or neurotransmitter in a system
whose mainly inhibitory actions are involved in pain suppression (Tenen,
1967; Harvey and Lints, 1971) and sleep (Jouvet, 1974). Reserpine, the
best-known catecholamine depletor, is also a serotonin depletor (Lewis,
1965). Furthermore, serotonin is degraded by monoamine oxidase much as
the catecholamines. Thus the monoamine oxidase inhibitors favor serotonin
as well as the catecholamines (Lewis, 1965). The actions of serotonin
were thus at first hard to separate pharmacologically from those of the other
amines. Several methods are now available. PCPA prevents the formation of
serotonin in much the same way as alpha-methyl-*p*-tyrosine prevents the
formation of the catecholamines (Koe and Weissman, 1966); and 5-hydroxy-
tryptophan bypasses the PCPA block permitting a restoration of the serotonin
supplies (Harvey and Lints, 1971).

Proserotonin drugs have been known to antagonize brain reward behavior
(Bose, Bailey, Thea, and Pradhan, 1974); and antiserotonin drugs have increased pedal-pressing rates for brain rewards (Poschel and Ninteman,
1971). This has formed the basis for a mainstream conviction that serotonin
is a naturally occurring antibrain-reward compound—mediating the aversive
effects of negative things according to one view (Wise et al., 1973)—a view
supported by the fact that direct application of serotonin in the ventricles

can attenuate brain reward behavior (Wise et al., 1973). Nevertheless, there is a strong countercurrent of opinion suggesting that serotonin might be the mediator in one self-stimulation system while being an opponent force in another. This argument is that serotonin and the serotonin neurons are endogenous analgesic and soporific factors involved in sleep (Jouvet, 1974) and in the attenuation of pain (Tenen, 1967; Harvey and Lints, 1971; Yunger and Harvey, 1973). Such a system might simultaneously attenuate aversive and euphoric states. If self-stimulation of some catecholamine system induced a euphoric condition, serotonin agonists might attenuate this self-stimulation. If self-stimulation at some (possibly serotonergic) sites was mainly effective by inhibiting aversive conditions, serotonin agonists might well facilitate this behavior. The finding that some brain reward stimulation retards escape-avoidance responses (Routtenberg and Olds, 1963) would fit this view. The finding that some brain reward behavior is promoted by aversive drive (Deutsch and Howarth, 1962) also fits to some degree. The latter sites were in the dorsal midbrain in a location where they might well have had special effects on serotonin fiber systems. The finding that some self-stimulation behavior induces sleep (Angyan, 1974) also fits. Further support comes from pharmacological studies which show positive effects of serotonin agonists on self-stimulation (Poschel and Ninteman, 1968) and negative effects of serotonin antagonists (Stark, Boyd, and Fuller, 1964; Margules, 1969; Gibson et al., 1970; Stark, Fuller, Hartley, Schaffer, and Turk, 1970). In accord with the latter view, some recent studies have pointed to self-stimulation behavior induced by probes near the midbrain midline and thus possibly near or in serotonin cell or fiber systems. Indicating the possible independence of this behavior from catecholamines was the fact that it was highly resistant to ventricular 6-HDA (Olds, 1975). Correlated studies showed that other self-stimulation behavior which was slowed or halted by 6-HDA could be positively affected not only by ventricular application of norepinephrine but also by ventricular application of serotonin (Olds, 1974). This might indicate that the medial forebrain bundle brain probes involved were stimulating mixed fiber systems, getting some of their rewarding effects from catecholamine fibers and some from serotonin fibers. Thus evidence exists for serotonin's positive and negative relation to brain reward behavior. The negative evidence is still perhaps the strongest, but it is not yet strong enough to settle the issue.

J. Acetylcholine

Acetylcholine has two modes of action (Lewis, 1965). The faster action, exhibited at the neuromyal junction, is called a "nicotinic" action because the drug nicotine mimics this effect. This fast action is opposed by a number of drugs such as curare. The slower action is exhibited at the parasympathetic effectors (and in "slow postsynaptic potentials" elsewhere). It is called a "muscarinic" action because it is mimicked by the drug muscarine. It is also mimicked by pilocarpine. This slow action is opposed by a number of drugs such as scopolamine and atropine. Brain reward behavior is antagonized by pharmacological manipulations which increase or prolong the muscarinic actions in the central nervous system (Stark and Boyd, 1963). While there is a general muscarinic antagonism *vis-a-vis* operant behavior (Pfeiffer and Jenny, 1967), the same arguments which suggest a specifically positive role for amphetamine may be used to suggest that there is some special antagonism of muscarinic drugs and brain reward behavior. Physostigmine, which prevents the inactivation of acetylcholine in the brain, slows or stops self-stimulation. Atropine can counter this effect. Control studies with drugs which do not cross the blood-brain barrier show that it is the central not the peripheral actions of acetylcholine that are involved.

Nicotine, on the contrary, augments brain reward behavior (Olds and Domino, 1969; Newman, 1972), and this action can be countered by the antinicotinic drug mecamylamine. Because it has a generally positive action on operant behavior (Morrison, 1967), there is a question if this nicotinic effect is special to brain reward behavior; however, this question gets about the same answer given for muscarinic effects and amphetamine.

The interesting counterbalance of adrenergic and nicotinic agonists supporting operant behavior and muscarinic agonists opposing it with equal force may be an accident of the different numbers of synapses of different kinds involved in positive reinforcement. A more daring notion might point to "reward" neurons with a particular character. If there were adrenergic reward neurons in the brain, and if these were excited by nicotinic actions and countered by muscarinic ones, this would fit. It would make some sense of the fact that many maps of catecholamine cell bodies match with maps of acetylcholinesterase, which may indicate a sensitivity to acetylcholine of the neurons involved (Jacobowitz and Palkovits, 1974; Palkovits and Jacobowitz, (1974). It would also make reward systems somewhat like the sympathetic fibers exciting from the superior cervical ganglion. These are adrenergic. They are excited by nicotinic actions of acetylcholine and are both excited and suppressed by slower muscarinic actions. The suppression is mediated through a dopaminergic interneuron (Libet and Owman, 1974). It would be surprising if central reward neurons were very similar to peripheral sympathetic ones because naively one would associate sympathetic activity with aversive conditions. Nature, however, repeatedly makes do with mechanisms at hand and turns things to new uses.

V. SINGLE UNIT STUDIES

A. Units and Feeding

Neurons in the hypothalamic "feeding centers" often seemed ready to fire in any pattern hoped for by the investigator. Reciprocal inhibitory relations between the medial and lateral hypothalamus were observed in numerous experiments, but positive action of medial stimulation on lateral unit activity, and negative actions of lateral stimulations on lateral units, were also well documented.

In one set of studies medial unit spikes were accelerated and lateral ones decelerated by intravenous glucose infusions. In hungry animals ventromedial units first fired at a slower frequency than lateral ones; glucose infusion then reversed this (Anand, Chhina, Sharma, Dua, and Singh, 1964; Chhina, Anand, Singh, and Rao, 1971). In other experiments the spontaneous accelerations and decelerations of medial and lateral units were observed (Oomura, Oomura, Yamamoto, and Naka, 1967). Then ether and electrical stimulation were used to modify this activity. Each acceleration of medial activity was accompanied by a deceleration of lateral activity and vice versa. Furthermore, medial stimulation suppressed lateral activity, and lateral stimulation suppressed medial activity.

A harmonious view of medial-lateral opponent process emerged from these studies. It was rudely countered by experiments from other groups. Medial stimulation accelerated some lateral units and decelerated others; those accelerated were in larger numbers (Van Atta and Sutin, 1971). Lateral stimulation failed to inhibit medial units, although these could be decelerated by amygdaloid stimulation (Murphy and Renaud, 1969). Lateral stimulation suppressed the activity of the majority of nearby units in the same lateral area (Ito, 1972).

The reason for these widely divergent reports was apparently that different kinds of neurons resided in the same place and possibly were recorded selectively in different experiments. The diversity was shown by iontophoretic studies used to seek neurons activated by direct application of glucose through micropipettes (Oomura, Ono, Ooyama, and Wayner, 1969). In these, 0.4 M glucose was mixed with 0.4 M NaCl so that the NaCl would "transport" the glucose. Nearly half the units recorded from the ventromedial hypothalamus were accelerated and none decelerated by this method of glucose application. In the lateral area, approximately one-third were accelerated and a similar proportion slowed. No similar effects were observed in recordings from neurons in thalamus and cortex. The theory of a glucose receptor in the hypothalamus thus received some support. The findings, however, should be viewed with some caution because at least in one study glucose placed in the ventricle of the brain had no effect on eating (Epstein, 1960).

In other experiments neuronal activity in the hypothalamus was recorded before and during feeding behavior (Fig. 29) (Hamburg, 1971). Neurons of the "feeding" center were spontaneously active in hungry, food-seeking rats. This might signify a correlation of their activity with hunger drive; however, no test was made to determine if the activity would disappear at low drive levels. When hungry animals were given access to a dish of food they began eating, and at this time the neuron activity was considerably and abruptly decelerated. The animals could be induced to contend for food

FIG. 29. Silencing of lateral hypothalamic spikes during feeding (Hamburg, 1971). The two traces are recordings from the same probe. Spikes appeared at about 20/sec in trace 1, made while the animal was hungry and awaiting food. These spikes disappeared in trace 2, made while the animal was eating. The bursts in trace 2 are "chewing artifacts" not neuron action potentials. Traces are approximately 1 sec in duration.

while still eating by attempting to withdraw the food while the animal was chewing. The animal would struggle to retain the dish while continuing to eat. During these episodes of simultaneous instrumental and consummatory behavior the hypothalamic units began again to discharge at brisk rates. Thus the suppression was correlated with the cessation of instrumental activities rather than with the rewarding stimuli or the consumatory activity.

Further evidence for a correlation of this family of large lateral hypothalamic units with the preconsummatory phase of feeding behavior came from conditioning experiments. Units which yielded small responses or none at all to auditory signals prior to conditioning were markedly changed by a Pavlovian experiment in which the signal was correlated with food presentation 1 sec after each onset. After 10 or 20 trials of pairing, each auditory signal caused a substantial acceleration of many of these units (Linseman and Olds, 1973; Olds, 1973). The acceleration had a latency of approximately 40 msec (Fig. 30), indicating that it was a rather direct response (not fed

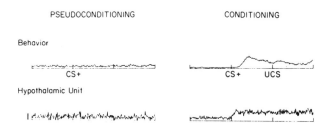

FIG. 30. Behavior and hypothalamic unit response before and after conditioning. The upper traces portray the average output of a detector attached to the head that measured head movements in arbitrary units. The lower traces represent the spike frequency of a lateral hypothalamic unit; the *vertical bar* (far left) represents a rate of 5 spikes/sec. The traces represent 3 sec. At the end of the first second a tone (CS+) was started which continued to the end. During conditioning a pellet dispenser (UCS) was triggered at the end of 2 sec. Prior to conditioning (pseudoconditioning) the tone caused very minor changes in the unit and behavior responses. After conditioning it caused a substantial behavior response with a 170 msec latency and a large unit response with a 20- to 40-msec latency (Linseman and Olds, 1973).

back from the newly learned behavior). Thus these supposed "drive" units were silenced during feeding behavior (when drive was still high) and were triggered into action by conditioned stimuli related to food. The fact that they were active during instrumental pursuit and accelerated by stimuli that heightened pursuit behavior suggested that they might be involved in controlling the instrumental phase of high drive behavior. The kinds of element that would be triggered during the instrumental but not the consummatory phases of drive behavior was not fully clarified.

B. Units and Drinking

Neurons that responded to water shortages and governed at least some compensatory responses were studied by Hayward and Vincent (1970). Neurons were recorded from the lateral preoptic area and the nearby suproptic nucleus, which contains vasopressin secreting cells. Thirst was triggered by piping hyperosmotic solutions into the carotid body. This activated a family of supposed osmodetectors in the preoptic area, and secondarily the vasopressin-containing neurons. Vasopressin acts through the kidney to preserve water. Both the osmodetectors and the vasopressin neurons were then slowed during drinking (Vincent, Arnauld, and Bioulac, 1972). The slowing was immediate, not waiting for digestive absorption of water to compensate for the deficit. The neurons were thus activated by drive inducing manipulations and slowed by rewarding ones.

Angiotensin is a hormone-like substance secreted from the kidney when the volume of body fluids is low. It acts on the brain to cause drinking. Direct application onto supraoptic neurons by iontophoresis caused them to fire (Nicoll and Barker, 1971). As the substance appeared to have its action on drinking at a different brain location (Simpson and Routtenberg, 1973), its action on the supraoptic nucleus might be to suppress water secretion.

C. Units and Reproductive Behavior

The mechanisms of reproduction involve many interactions of brain activity and hormone activity. Ovulation (bursting of the follicle and discharge of the egg) is caused by luteinizing hormone from the pituitary, and this in turn by a releasing factor from the brain. Because the causal chain passes through the brain and because ovulation is a clearly defined episode occurring during a critical period on the afternoon of the third day of the 4- or 5-day estrous cycle of the rat, it has been a target for studies aimed to unravel the interaction of brain and hormone activity. Neuronal activity during the critical period has been recorded in several laboratories. An accleration of activity occurred in a number of related brain centers: the amygdala, nucleus of the stria terminalis which links amygdala and hypothalamus, septal area, anterior hypothalamic-medial preoptic sex centers, and in deeper centers where the neurosecretory cells are thought to reside—the arcuate and ventromedial nuclei of the hypothalamus (Kawakami, Terasawa, and Ibuki, 1970). From these data it was thought that activity from the amygdala and septal area might converge on the preoptic area where it would start activity in trigger cells projecting to the neurosecretory cells in the arcuate region. Because much the same activity occurred even when hippocampal stimulation prevented ovulation (Gallo, Johnson, Goldman, Whitmoyer, and Sawyer, 1971) and because preoptic area stimulation both excited and inhibited neurons in the arcuate region (Haller and Barraclough, 1970), the hypothesis was treated with some caution but not abandoned. Some support for it came from experiments in which preoptic neurons were antidromically activated by stimulation in the arcuate region. These showed the fibers from the preoptic area to be slow-conducting, like neurosecretory neurons, but they were not generally thought to be neurosecretory neurons (Dyer and Cross, 1972).

Further tests were made by removing other brain influences first and hormonal factors second to find which of these activated the preoptic area neurons and if these neurons were themselves sufficient to trigger ovulation through the arcuate region. First, the preoptic-arcuate system was severed from the rest of the brain (Cross and Dyer, 1970a,b). Because preoptic neurons were accelerated during the critical period after this, the idea that other brain inputs were required to activate the preoptic area was eliminated. Ovariectomy stopped this neuronal activity (Cross and Dyer, 1972) showing that hormonal conditions were likely responsible for this (and that preoptic neurons might be hormone detectors). Surprisingly, the preoptic activity did not suffice to cause ovulation after the severing of other brain inputs (Cross and Dyer, 1971b), suggesting that some cofactor from other brain areas was required, possibly converging with preoptic axons at the arcuate level. Dopamine applied during the first hour after surgery compensated for the loss, suggesting a relation of the dopamine neuron system to the missing cofactor (Dyer, *unpublished observations,* cited in Cross, 1973).

Direct application of progesterone and estrogen intravenously caused biphasic and even triphasic effects on preoptic neuronal activity, but the main trend was for the gonadal hormones to suppress or slow these neurons (Lincoln, 1967; Alcaraz, Guzman-Flores, Salas, and Beyer, 1969; Chhina and Anand, 1969). Although this seemed at odds with the rise of activity during the critical period of ovulation (Dyer, Pritchett, and Cross, 1972), detailed study of the changes in hormone level resolved the difficulty (Brown-Grant, Exley, and Naftolin, 1970). Estrogens peaked prior to the critical period and fell rapidly, decreasing by half or more before the onset of this period. If estrogens suppressed preoptic neuron activity, this rapid decline could activate them by a release mechanism.

The interactions of brain and hormones in male sex behavior were less well studied. In this case the behavior is triggered by special signals from the female and by other arousing signals. These are synergistic with circulating male sex hormone, triggering its production, and profiting by the heightened levels which sensitize the animal to these signals. Unit activity recorded in the preoptic area became coupled to arousing signals and to the brain's arousal system when circulating androgens were present, and this correlation was attenuated by their absence (Pfaff and Gregory, 1971a,b). Fitting their supposed relevance to male sex behavior, these neurons were sometimes responsive to olfactory signals emanating from the estrous female. These and other scattered data did not provide a neuronal analysis of male sex behavior, but they did indicate the direction of current studies.

The best-studied units of a brain hormone system were the oxytocin neurosecretory cells. These are located in the paraventricular nucleus of the hypothalamus. They eject oxytocin into the blood, which causes milk ejection at the nipple (with several seconds required to transport the hormone from the brain to the teat). The hormone also causes other reproductive responses in male and female. The neurosecretory neurons have been monitored with microelectrodes. They were identified by antidromic stimulation from the neural lobe of the pituitary (Moss, Dyball, and Cross, 1972a). This electrical stimulation fired the paraventricular neurosecretory cells antidromically and at the same time caused milk ejection. When 50 pulses/sec was applied for approximately 15 sec, the ejection occurred at about the end of the train. In other tests the firing patterns of these neurons were correlated with milk ejection when it was caused by suckling (Lincoln and Wakerley, 1973). Milk ejection occurred periodically in lactating rats even when they were anesthetized if the pups were left nursing. The neurosecretory cells of the paraventricular nucleus anticipated and apparently caused these milk ejection episodes. They yielded explosive bursts firing at 50/sec for approximately 2 sec followed by 15 sec of total silence and then milk ejection (Fig. 31).

The hypothesis of a causal relation of the paraventricular events and the milk ejection was furthered by the fact that knife cuts separating these cells from the rest of the brain depressed their firing and reduced oxytocin secretions to zero (Dyball and Dyer, 1971). These neurons showed normal accelerations and decelerations of rate during the long intervals between milk ejections as if they were participating in normal neuronal processes at this time. Because 100 spikes per minute during these periods was not correlated with any sign of hormone secretion, but 100 spikes per 2 sec followed by 7 sec of silence was regularly followed by milk ejection, a special kind of neuronal activity correlated with neurosecretion seemed possible. Either a critical rate was needed to yield output, or a different pattern of neuronal activity was correlated with the neurosecretory message.

In other studies (Cross, Moss, and Urban, 1971; Moss, Urban, and Cross, 1972b) these cells were shown to be excited by acetylcholine and glutamate

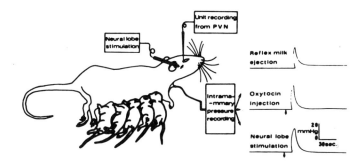

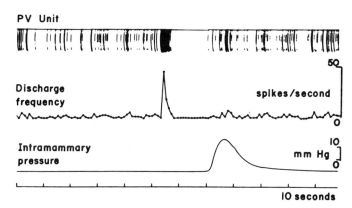

FIG. 31. Firing patterns of oxytocin neurosecretory cells correlated with milk ejection responses noted by Lincoln and Wakerly (1973) in the laboratory of Cross (Cross, 1973). Top: Intramammary pressure was similar during reflex milk ejection or during that caused by oxytocin injection or by stimulation of oxytocin axons in the neural lobe. Bottom: The tracings show (1) a digital portrayal of each unit spike, (2) a tracing indicating frequency of firing by its amplitude, and (3) the mammary response. When pups suckled there were periodic bursts of oxytocin neurons, followed by silence and then milk ejection. The burst and the silence may both have been required to cause the peptide secretion. PVN = paraventricular neurosecretory cells. (From Cross, 1973.)

as are many cells in the central nervous system. They were decelerated by norepinephrine and GABA, again in harmony with other neuronal populations. There was an interdigitated family of non-neurosecretory elements, however, that looked by several tests to be opponents or counterneurons. These were activated by surgical interventions that silenced their neurosecretory neighbors (Cross and Dyer, 1971a; Dyball and Dyer, 1971); they were also activated by norepinephrine and suppressed by acetylcholine (Moss et al., 1972b), which is most unusual for such a family of neurons. It seemed possible, therefore, that these counterelements might be reciprocal inhibitors of the neurosecretory neurons. Other experiments established the possibility (but far from proof) of positive feedback of neurosecretory elements on themselves (Moss et al., 1972*a*). These showed that the neuro-secretory cells were activated by iontophoretic application of oxytocin, the same peptide hormone which they produced, transported, and ejected.

D. Temperature

In temperature regulation there are two problems and two effector sys-tems. One is related to the temperature of the environment, the other to the internal or core temperature of the body. The animal normally adjusts core temperature by means of "vegetative" adjustments: shivering, perspiring, constricting or dilating vessels, and so forth. The animal usually adjusts environmental temperature by moving, although other "operant" responses may be used. Lesions in the preoptic area severely damaged the automatic adjusting system, but behavioral temperature adjustment still occurred. This means that both detectors and effectors sufficient to mediate the operant system survived.

The demonstrated brain responses to peripheral temperature detectors, however, were in the preoptic area. Units in the preoptic area of dogs re-sponded to environmental temperature changes before any central tempera-ture change had resulted (Witt and Wang, 1968). Besides these peripheral effects, local heating or cooling in the brain also excited or decelerated unit spikes recorded from some areas, including the preoptic, anterior hypo-thalamic, and even the posterior and tuberal area of the hypothalamus. Such experiments have been carried out in cats (Nakayama, Eisenman, and Hardy, 1961; Nakayama, Hammel, Hardy, and Eisenman, 1963), dogs (Hardy, Hellon, and Sutherland, 1964; Cunningham, Stolwijk, Murakami, and Hardy, 1967), and rabbits (Hellon, 1967; Cabanac, Stolwijk, and Hardy, 1968). Approximately 10% of the elements in the anterior hypothalamic and preoptic area region responded to local heating or cooling. The most common response was for these units to increase their rate of firing linearly during warming. However, there were units that responded only to cooling; and some responded to both warming and cooling. The temperature-sensitive units of the posterior hypothalamic areas were more apt to respond to cool-ing than those of the anterior and preoptic areas. In the preoptic area some of the temperature-sensitive units were also sensitive to environmental tempera-ture changes; others were specialized to central or peripheral changes (Hel-lon, 1970). Tests for effects of peripheral temperature changes on units outside the preoptic, anterior hypothalamic region have not been made.

E. Stress

The stress reaction initiated by pain or damage or negative stimulation causes a chain of hormonal events. The hypothalamic releasing factor (CRF) is the first member of the chain. Its only known action is on the pituitary to trigger adrenocorticotropic hormone (ACTH) release. ACTH or one of its fractional components probably acts back on the brain to trigger fear behavior (de Wied, 1974) and maybe even to curtail (Motta, Fraschini, and Martini, 1969) or enhance (Steiner et al., 1969) further ACTH secretion. ACTH also acts on the adrenal cortex to provoke secretion of a cortical steroid such as cortisol. The latter has numerous actions on the bodily stress mechanisms, and it also acts directly on the brain. It attenuates the fear reactions (which are promoted by ACTH) and inhibits ACTH secretion (de Wied, 1974). The possibility of direct brain actions of both ACTH and cortisol has been demonstrated by iontophoretic methods (Ruf and Steiner, 1967; Steiner et al., 1969). Several hundred units were recorded from hypothalamus and midbrain. Of these approximately 17% were suppressed by iontophoretic application of a cortisol substitute (dexamethasone-21-phosphate). Approximately 1% were accelerated, and the rest were unaffected. About half the cortisol-sensitive units were excited by acetylcholine and decelerated by norepinephrine. The most interesting outcome of these studies was from application of ACTH to some of the same cells. Four out of six cells tested (that were inhibited by the cortisol substitute) were excited by ACTH. These experiments therefore left the impression of either a special family of cells excited by ACTH and suppressed by cortisol, or of generally excitatory and inhibitory effects of these two substances.

Other evidence appeared to support the idea of a generally excitatory action of ACTH and of a generally decelerating role of cortisol. ACTH injections in rats under urethane anesthesia, for example, induced a rise in multiunit activity in the arcuate nucleus (Sawyer, Kawakami, Meyerson, Whitmoyer, and Lilley, 1968). ACTH also augmented firing activity of units widely scattered in the hypothalamus (Van Delft and Kitay, 1972). (However, there was no obvious diminution of activity caused by hypophysectomy, possibly because this caused a balanced loss of both ACTH and cortisol.) Adrenalectomy (depleting cortisol) increased the firing rate in anterior hypothalamus (Dafny and Feldman, 1970) but not in posterior hypothalamus (of rats under urethane). Aversive stimulation caused 80% of units in the posterior hypothalamus to respond with accelerations or decelerations. Adrenalectomy increased the ratio of excited to inhibited units. This made it tempting to suppose that the same stimulus could have both excitatory and inhibitory pathways to the same elements, and that cortisol could switch it from one to the other. Animals with hypothalamic islands in which most units fired fast were used in other experiments (Feldman and Sarne, 1970). In these, cortisol usually caused an initial reduction in firing frequency of most cells in the island. Although there was some counterevidence suggesting excitatory actions of cortisol, the consensus was that cortisol treatment had a general or specialized suppressive influence, and ACTH an effect in the excitatory direction.

F. Recordings and Brain Reward

The most common stimulation site in these experiments was the part of the lateral hypothalamus that contains the axons of the medial forebrain bundle. These axons come from many sources: several olfactory forebrain structures, several brainstem monoamine systems, local path neurons, medial hypothalamic neurons, and the brainstem sources of ascending periventricular and mammillary peduncle fibers. A single stimulus could well influence some elements from each of these fiber systems (and most likely there are others I have failed to mention). The stimulus would not only activate the soma-dendritic sources of these fibers (antidromically) but would influence the targets of these fibers (orthodromically) and the targets of fiber collaterals by an antidromic and then orthodromic route.

Although there are interesting arguments that brain reward behavior depends on simultaneous stimulation of a mixed set of fibers, even the proponents of such views would hardly argue that all the medial forebrain bundle axons participated in the causation of the reward behavior. It is the fact that more tracts are being stimulated than are needed for the effect that makes determination of neuronal correlates of brain reward a difficult and as yet unsolved puzzle.

The electrical brain reward stimulus has many direct and indirect influences. Effects may be considered as "nearly direct" if they have a fixed latency (of excitation or inhibition). Some of these effects are antidromic, others orthodromic. Effects may be considered indirect if there is instead a general excitation or suppression, without fixed latency.

Because of the diverse composition of a bundle it is clear that neither the direct nor the indirect effects can be taken *prima facie* as being related to the rewarding features of the stimulus. Ideally the search for the critical elements would be guided by the discovery of special neuronal activities correlated with peripheral rewards. The search for neuronal correlates of consummatory feeding behavior in an effort to discover these has not yet succeeded. The discovery of neuronal correlates of milk ejection could mark a positive case. However, it is not clear if stimulation of the paraventricular oxytocin cells is rewarding.

Several special methods have been tried to make direct identification of units correlated with brain reward. One method was to study the minimum interpulse (i.e., shock-shock) intervals for brain reward behavior and for units driven by the rewarding stimulus. In these experiments a train of shock pairs is applied (Deutsch, 1964). A set of parameters was chosen so that the second shock in each pair was required to maintain a suprathreshold stimulus train. Then the paired shocks were brought closer and closer together in time until the second shock became ineffective and the stimulus accordingly became subthreshold (ideally there was an abrupt drop in effectiveness at a fixed time interval). In this way, it was argued, the "refractory period" of the brain reward units could be discovered by behavioral tests. By this means it was determined that self-stimulation pedal behavior, in which the rewarding trains were rapidly repeated, did not stop until the intershock intervals were less than 0.6 msec; but runway behavior sequences, in which there was a longer time between rewarding trains, stopped when the intershock interval was less than 0.8 or 1.0 msec. Because stimulated feeding and drinking behaviors had the same 0.6-msec minimum interstimulus interval as the rapid pedal behavior (Rolls, 1973), it was likely that many different kinds of neurons had similar recovery times. In neurophysiological experiments, efforts were made to match these behaviorally determined minimum intershock times with the observed recovery times of units driven or accelerated by lateral hypothalamic stimulation (Rolls, 1971a, 1972, 1973). Some units recorded from the midbrain were observed to have recovery times of 0.8 or 1.0 msec; these were thought to be involved in an arousal mechanism but not in reward itself. The arousal mechanism was considered to be a prerequisite to brain reward behavior when longer intertrain intervals were involved. Neurons with 0.6 msec recovery times which were considered to be "reward" or "eating and drinking" neurons were recorded from the amygdala. All the reward neurons could not be in the amygdala as the behavior survived removal of the whole telencephalon (Huston and Borbely, 1974). However, this still might point to the olfactory forebrain as having some units that could be involved.

Another special method was to seek neurons that would be modified in opposite directions by rewarding and aversive brain stimulations on the view that such neurons might have a special relation to the underlying motive process (Keene, 1973). A family of neurons excited by aversive brain shocks and inhibited by rewarding ones was identified in the intralaminar system of the thalamus; and a second family accelerated by rewards and decelerated by punishments was observed with probes in the preoptic area.

A third method was to study the effects on local neurons of the medial forebrain bundle (Fig. 32) in the hope that these main target cells of the tracts in the bundle must be involved (Ito, 1972). Experiments showed that the nearest neurons to the brain reward were most often suppressed or inhibited, whereas more distant neurons (particularly those in the preoptic area) were more apt to be excited by the brain stimulation. Matching the rather surprising findings of Ito that lateral hypothalamic units were suppressed rather than excited by brain reward stimuli were data showing that these neurons were active during morphine withdrawal symptoms and were then suppressed by administration of morphine to addicted animals (Kerr et al., 1974).

Other studies of neurophysiological consequences of rewarding brain stimulation followed prior notions of where emotion mechanisms might lie (Ito and Olds, 1971). Neurons were driven in the cingulate cortex. Secondary effects were recorded in dorsal hippocampus where large neuronal

A

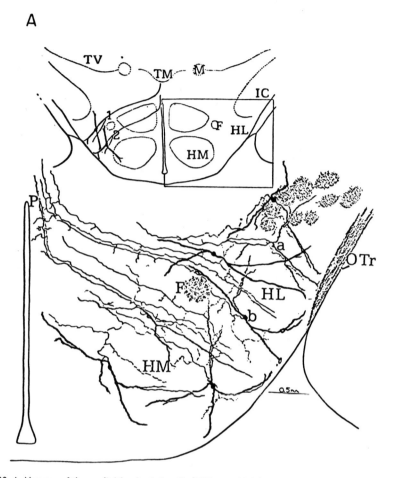

FIG. 32. A. Neurons of the medial forebrain bundle (Millhouse, 1969). 1 and 2, large neurons originating in medial forebrain bundle (MFB) path region and projecting into the periventricular system. TV, ventral thalamus. TM, medial thalamus. M, mammillothalamic tract. IC, internal capsule. F, fornix. HL, lateral hypothalamus. HM, medial hypothalamus. OTR, optic tract. a and b, path neurons showing the orientation of their dendrites in relation to descending fornix (F) and internal capsule (IC).

spikes, presumably from pyramidal cells, were regularly suppressed and smaller ones (most likely from a different population) were sometimes excited. Neurons were driven in midbrain locations, mainly in those areas whose stimulation did not itself yield rewarding effects (Routtenberg and Huang, 1968). Electrophysiological slow waves were recorded from various parts of the olfactory forebrain system that gives rise to the descending medial forebrain bundle (Porter et al., 1959). Because of the absence of any special evidence for the involvement of the recorded responses in rewarding effects, the question of brain activity requisite or sufficient for reward is still open, and the facts unknown. It is interesting, in view of the theories about the

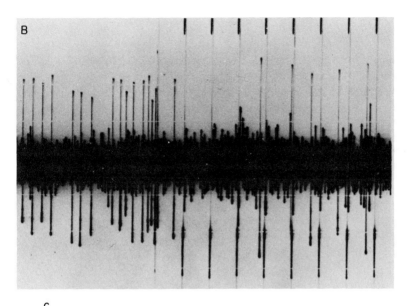

Experiment	Hours of withdrawal	Site of recording	Morphine			Naloxone		
			A	*B*	*C*	*A*	*B*	*C*
52	16	VMN	+	−	−	−	−	−
55	48	VMN	+	+	+	−	−	−
57	40	VMN	+	+	0	−	−	−
62	52	VMN	+	+	+	−	−	−
67	48	VMN	+	+	+	−	−	−
52	16	LHA	−	−	0	+	+	+
57	40	LHA	−	−	−	+	+	+
62	52	LHA	−	−	−	−	+	+
65	48	LHA	0	−	−	+	+	+

FIG. 32. B. Firing pattern of these units before and during self-stimulation (Ito, 1972). Full trace was 400 msec; large spikes (going off the figure) in the second half are artifacts of the self-administered brain shock. The other spikes are responses of medial forebrain bundle path neurons; these are greatly attenuated in their firing during the rewarding electrical shock train. C. Experimental results from Kerr et al. (1974) showing that the same neurons are activated during naloxone-induced "morphine drive" and quieted by "morphine reward." Interestingly, their medial neighbors are reciprocally affected. 0, unaffected. VMN, ventromedial nucleus of the hypothalamus; LHA, lateral hypothalamic area (region of the path neurons).

monoamines, that activity of the monoamine neurons of the locus coeruleus was correlated to some degree with waking and paradoxical sleep (Chu and Bloom, 1973) and with the consumption of natural reinforcers (German and Fetz, 1974).

Some attention was given to the monoamine question in experiments on the lateral hypothalamic and preoptic area unit responses, but the results were ambiguous. Tetrabenazine, which releases and then quickly depletes amine stores, suppressed self-stimulation and caused the "inhibitory" responses of nearby lateral hypothalamic units to disappear. Because the same drug suppressed the brain responses and behavior, it appeared that the inhibitory brain responses might be a necessary part of the brain reward effect (Olds and Ito, 1973*a*). However, chlorpromazine, which is supposed to act by blocking adrenergic receptors, also halted brain reward behavior. This drug did not diminish the inhibitory brain responses, but it did curtail the more anterior excitatory responses (Olds and Ito, 1973*b*). Thus both sets of responses were in question as correlates of self-stimulation. With tetrabenazine the anterior excitatory responses survived while self-stimulation was suppressed; with chlorpromazine the more posterior inhibitory responses survived while self-stimulation was suppressed. It might be that both sets of responses were required in order to elicit the behavior. Still, if the lateral hypothalamic responses were mediated by norepinephrine as might be supposed, it was surprising that they survived the treatment with chlorpromazine.

Is there a pattern emerging from these data? If there is, it points to a family of units located in the path of the medial forebrain bundle having quite the opposite character from what would be expected on the basis of the rewarding effects of stimulating this bundle. Neurons in this area were active during instrumental behavior but suppressed during consummatory behavior—if instrumental behavior was not occurring simultaneously (Hamburg, 1971). They are active in hungry animals and further accelerated by Pavlovian signals that promise rewards (Linseman and Olds, 1973). They are also active during the aversive drug withdrawal condition (Kerr et al., 1974), and are decelerated or turned off by rewarding brain stimulation and by morphine administration (Ito, 1972; Kerr et al., 1974). Therefore they may well be involved in the mediation of strivings. Their firing rates do not go up and down with the physiological drive state. That is, they stop responding in the still-hungry animal when it is given a dish of food, and they can be aroused by "learned" signals. They may well go up and down with the behavioral drive state. On this basis they would appear to be correlated partly with something called drive and partly with something psychologists have long referred to as learned drive.

VI. SUMMARY AND CONCLUSIONS

A. Stimulation Map

The reward map was made of locations where electrical stimulation caused mammals to come back for more. Rats, cats, and monkeys had much the same map. Humans pushed buttons to stimulate the same regions, although they often seemed confused as to why they were doing it. The map covered most of the hypothalamus and its satellites through the brain. In the hypothalamus it extended from far anterior to far posterior, from far lateral to midline. While probes placed in the hypothalamus often failed to cause reward behavior, there was no clear separation of anatomical locations. There were possibly individual differences between animals; at least there were some "uncooperative" rats that could be "cured" by a dose of amphetamine. A paradox was that the hypothalamus was also the home of aversive effects of electrical stimulation. If opposed aversive effects were not immediately obvious, they could usually be demonstrated by more careful analysis. Because the whole hypothalamus was covered by a reward map, and aversive countereffects were always in evidence, it might seem that the hypothalamus was homogeneous. It was not.

Rewarding effects of stimulation predominated in the far lateral parts and in some far medial ones. In these cases the animal was apparently at home with self-stimulation. No negative signs were seen during brain pedal behavior, and careful methods were required to reveal them. Aversive effects in these cases were evidenced only by the fact that continuously applied trains were interrupted periodically by the animal. This was possibly done only so that the stimulus might start again, the assumption being that onsets were more positive than the continuation of trains. An alternative was that these stimulations yielded unmixed rewards when applied in short doses, but had real aversive effects when the train endured too long. In any event there was a predominance of positive effects when stimulation was applied in far lateral and far medial areas.

In a large "in-between" area, there is an obvious mixture of positive and aversive effects. The animal pedal-pressed regularly and fast if closeted with an electrical stimulus; but if there was a way out, it was taken. There was no amount of stimulation in these areas that seemed just right. The animal behaved as if it could not stand it but could not resist it.

In this same middle area lay another paradox of the reward maps. Here the same electrical stimulus provoked both drives and rewards. The drives changed depending partly on the location of the stimulus. In anterior hypothalamus there were sex responses caused by stimulation and responses that adjusted the body temperature. In the anterior part of the middle hypothalamus there were both eating and drinking responses but the latter predominated. In the posterior part of the middle hypothalamus there were more eating and drinking responses, but here the eating responses predominated. In the posterior part of the hypothalamus sex responses were evoked again. Because there were many overlapping effects and sex responses were evoked in areas on both sides of the feeding and drinking areas, the idea of sharp localizations was rejected. However, because this in-between area could be mapped into four successive regions where stimulation caused temperature, drinking, eating, and sex responses, respectively, as the most likely responses, the idea of totally unlocalized drive systems was rejected. Obviously the truth lay somewhere in between.

One feature of the in-between answer was discovered; it was really quite surprising. The drive targets of these stimulations were found to be changeable by a simple training procedure. Animals were stimulated regularly in the presence of a drive object; after a while the stimulus began to evoke an appropriate drive state, i.e., one with the available drive object as its target. If probes were placed in a feeding point (where stimulation evoked feeding), and if 1 min trains of stimulation were applied every 5 min all night in the presence of water, the feeding point changed: In the morning it was a drinking point! This was called the Valenstein effect (Valenstein et al., 1968).

If drives were mapped into different areas of the brain to begin with, it seemed wrong that they could be modified by training. One possible answer to this puzzle is that a drive center might be predetermined by its sensitivity to visceral afferents or to particular hormones, but it still might need to be attached by learning to appropriate drive objects. The Valenstein effect might be evidence that electrical stimulation could pervert this normal learning mechanism. Assume that the stimulus was applied in a "hunger center" but that gradually the training artificially caused the animal to respond as if water were a hunger drive object. At present such a redirection of drives seem to me the most likely explanation of this surprising changeableness of the targets of the supposed drive centers.

To recapitulate the picture developed by the hypothalamic map of brain stimulation effects: there were far lateral and far medial areas where reward predominated, and in-between areas where aversive effects and drive effects were overlapped with reward.

This stimulation map matched the maps of several catecholamine neuronal systems. These are neurons containing the two specialized *slow* neurochemical transmitters: norepinephrine and dopamine. The far lateral and far medial areas contained *dopamine* neurons and the in-between areas contained *norepinephrine* neurons mixed with acetylcholine neurons. Acetylcholine is the more well-known *fast* chemical messenger. Thus all the reward

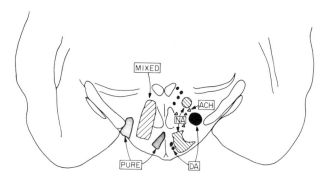

FIG. 33. Correlation of self-stimulation and neurotransmitter maps in the hypothalamus. Areas where stimulation effects were nearly "purely positive" (shaded), or mixed but predominantly positive (hatched). Chemical maps showing signs of the acetylcholine (ACH) transmitter system (triangles); norepinephrine (NA) axons or terminals (hatched); and dopamine (DA) neurons or pathways (black) (Jacobowitz and Palkovits, 1974).

areas were permeated by catecholamine slow-transmitter pathways. This led to a view that catecholamine neurons (or at least some of them) might be reward neurons (Stein, 1964a; Crow, 1972b). The intermixed aversive and drive effects might result from the intermixing of catecholamine and acetylcholine fibers in the in-between areas.

Thus the data suggested a dopamine system (or a pair of them) where reward predominated. Then another norepinephrine reward system mixed with an acetylcholine drive system (Fig. 33). This still left one question: What is the reason for the difference between dopamine neurons which characterized the more positive areas and the norepinephrine neurons which characterized the more mixed regions.

B. Lesion Map

Lesion studies divided the hypothalamus and its neighbors into a focus where lesions had one effect, and a set of three surrounding areas where different kinds of opposed effects were observed. The focus was the same far lateral hypothalamus region where stimulation had predominantly positive effects. It included the nearby substantia nigra where one dopamine bundle had its main origin. Lesions here caused a loss of positive drive-reward behaviors and other voluntary or instrumental performances (even ones aimed to avoid noxious stimulation). If the animal was kept alive for a few days there was a surprisingly good recovery. Animals died if not force-fed at first, but they recovered if kept alive by force-feeding (Teitelbaum and Epstein, 1962).

After recovery the animals were heavily dependent on the cortex for drive behavior (Teitelbaum and Cytawa, 1965). A damaging manipulation of cortex by application of potassium chloride in normals had a 4- to 8-hr effect (abolishing all instrumental behavior for that period). In recovered lateral hypothalamus animals it had a much more devastating effect, causing the full 3-week recovery to be needed once again. This dependence on the cortex showed that recovery was not really complete. There were other signs. After the lesions the animal never again responded to cellular water deficits by drinking. It drank to wet the mouth and for a number of reasons that would seem irrelevant (if they did not serve luckily for the animal to keep it alive). Similarly it did not respond to glucose deficits by eating, and it failed to respond appropriately to sodium deficits. However, with its repertoire of redundant hunger controllers or learned feeding behaviors, it got along; it ate well and looked robust. It was as if a learned cortex repertoire of drive behaviors recovered although a hypothalamic originator or starter of these was gone.

Fitting this view, a most important food learning mechanism was also gone. The animal did not learn well to exclude foods on the basis of poisoning or illness. Normal rats responded to foods that preceded illness as if they were aversive. This was called the Garcia effect (Garcia and Ervin, 1968). Similarly in normals there was a learning of special positive reactions of foods that were correlated with recovery from illness. These food-learning phenomena of Garcia matched the drive-target learning that occurred when Valenstein stimulated these areas. The Garcia effects were lost when these same areas were lesioned (Schwartz and Teitlebaum, 1974).

There were three areas surrounding the lateral hypothalamus substantia nigra region where lesions had opposed effects. (1) Medial or "between" hypothalamus lesions cause the opposite of starvation. The animals ate too often; i.e., meals began too early (as if no visceral or chemical trigger was needed). (2) Lesions in the caudate nucleus (i.e., the extrapyramidal area which is in a reciprocal inhibitory relation to substantia nigra) in cats caused nonsensical instrumental behavior directed at anything that moved (Villablanca, 1974). Instead of going toward nothing it went toward everything. (3) Lesions in amygdala caused consummatory behavior toward dangerous objects (or toward untested foods) or toward wrong objects, e.g., eating or mating with nonfood or nonsex objects (Klüver and Bucy, 1937; Rolls and Rolls, 1973a,b).

The fact that lesions in a central area stopped reward behaviors and lesions in three surrounding areas caused different kinds of excessive approach behaviors suggested a multiple opponent process system. A central positive region in the lateral hypothalamus and substantia nigra might inhibit and be inhibited by the three surrounding regions. In such a system a shifting balance of excitation and inhibition would determine acceleration or deceleration of approach behavior, and electrical stimulation along the communicating links might well have double effects.

Another kind of experiment connected the lesion studies to the catecholamine paths. A special method that caused poisoning of the dopamine pathway from the substantia nigra induced all or almost all of the loss of positive behavior that occurred with far lateral lesions (Ungerstedt, 1971b). The animal failed to eat and failed at other things. Similar poisoning applied to one of the norepinephrine pathways caused many of the effects of "in-between" or medial hypothalamic lesions; in this case the animals overate because they started meals too soon (Ahlskog and Hoebel, 1973). If both catecholamines were involved in reward, it was difficult to guess why lesions in the two would have such opposed effects.

One interesting supposition was offered by Crow (Crow, 1972b, 1973). The norepinephrine pathway might carry *drive-reducing satiety* messages, which would be rewarding. The dopamine pathway might carry *drive-inducing incentive* messages, which would also be rewarding. Rewards both start and stop things depending on whether they are incentive rewards or terminal consummatory rewards which bear the seeds of their own demise. Crow suggested that incentive rewards (e.g., the smell of food and maybe also learned rewards) used the dopamine pathways. Final rewards (e.g., the taste of food) would act through the norepinephrine pathways. Thus lesions in the two paths might block mechanisms to start and stop eating, respectively.

C. Catecholamine Maps

Catecholamine maps are neurochemical maps. They seemed to identify a set of brain reward neurons and the beginnings of an interpretation of the brain reward behavior and other reward processes. Small clumps of neurons from focal centers in the hindbrain, midbrain, and boundaries of the forebrain send axons broadcast through the brain. There are several clumps and several overlapping sets of broadcast fibers. The small origins and the widely diffusing fibers made these look like command centers that could send yes-no commands to the whole brain. All of them had amine-containing fibers; i.e., the transmitters they used were norepinephrine, dopamine, and serotonin.

The norepinephrine fibers started farthest back and went farthest forward. They ran from a crossroads of the brain in the medulla to all of its outposts, the cerebellum, thalamus, paleocortex, and neocortex. The serotonin fibers started in the middle of the midbrain and ran a less well-defined course to many parts of the forebrain. The dopamine fibers started in the front part of the midbrain and nearby parts of hypothalamus. They ran a shorter course, ending mainly in structures below the cortex, i.e., in the extrapyramidal motor systems (which may be the main control system for purposive instrumental behavior) and in some special but poorly understood lower centers of the olfactory brain. Most likely they did not all end here, for dopamine itself was found along with norepinephrine in many parts of the cortex.

For all amine fiber systems one property stood out; i.e., there was a very small source of origin and a very wide spread of influence. The norepinephrine, serotonin, and dopamine systems seemed almost like a small triumvirate: three little men deep in the brain making its command decisions.

Chemical and neurophysiological studies showed the amines to have special properties. First, two of them—dopamine and norepinephrine—have a common substrate, tyrosine. Moreover, one (dopamine) was the normal precursor of the other, norepinephrine. Second, these differed from other transmitters in the mode of inactivation. Other neurotransmitters were limited in time by degradation (destruction) of the transmitter. The catecholamines were originally thought to be inactivated in this way via oxidation. Excessive supplies were degraded by this process under the influence of the monoamine oxidase enzyme; but this was not the normal route of inactivation. When catecholamines were secreted by nerve terminals the messages were limited in time by reuptake of the amine via a pumping action back into the nerve terminals where the neurochemical was thought to be repackaged into vesicles for reuse (or oxidized if supplies were excessive). Reuptake apparently allowed these neurons to replenish their stores from "free" amines in the interstitial fluid, possibly permitting them to borrow or steal from their neighbors.

Third, the amines conveyed their message by causing a second messenger to be produced inside the target cell (this second messenger was cyclic AMP). This same second messenger was used to carry out the commands of the peptide hormones. It was possible to imagine it, therefore, as a common path that would demand both a hormone message and a simultaneous amine message to become active. Fourth, the amines had a mysterious exciter-inhibitor role. Drugs which stimulated their central actions often had excitatory influence on the animal. Yet direct application of amines onto neurons usually caused suppression of the neuronal spikes and slowing of activity. The catecholamines therefore might be stopping the normal action potentials but causing some special kind of activation. Fifth, the onset and offset of action was slow when compared with that of other transmitters.

Thus a considerable list of properties fitted the catecholamines for special functions: (1) the common substrate (tyrosine) between dopamine and norepinephrine, and the precursor role of dopamine to norepinephrine; (2) the reuptake mechanism, which apparently permitted the monoamine terminals to compete for scarce supplies; (3) the "second messenger" cyclic AMP, which formed a common step in the action of catecholamine and peptide hormones; (4) the deceleratory or inhibitory modulation, which nevertheless seemed to have excitatory consequences; (5) the slow onset and long duration of action; (6) the monoamine oxidases, which provided a negative feedback on available supplies (a planned scarcity—like the Federal Reserve Board).

While it was by no means clear what special function they mediated, their properties fit them for controlling behavioral priorities. This is because the repeating theme was competition for a limited resource, and the time constants involved were in the order of magnitude of behavioral episodes rather than of neurophysiological events.

Because their properties seemed to suit them for controlling behavioral priorities, it was interesting that experiments linked them to drive and reward systems in strong and intricate ways. These fibers pervaded the drive-reward systems in such a way as to match the drive-reward maps (German and Bowden, 1974). New maps based on the theory that these were reward neurons showed new rewarding locations tracking the norepinephrine pathway toward the medulla and the dopamine pathway toward the substantia nigra (Crow, 1971; Ritter and Stein, 1973). Drug studies indicated that catecholamine deficits stopped brain reward behaviors, and their excesses caused these behaviors to be augmented and thresholds to fall.

The broadcast fibers of these neurons formed networks or meshworks of terminals sufficiently diffuse to explain the relative lack of localization of the sites effective for drive and reward experiments. Where these fibers were concentrated, the stimulation effects were strong and had low thresholds; where they were less concentrated, the stimulation effects were weak and thresholds were higher.

There was still an enigma. Drugs which discharged amines from their terminals often augmented brain reward behavior. At first it seemed that the excess of amines caused by discharging amines *should* promote reward behavior; but second thought shows a problem. What was being electrically stimulated if the amines were already outside the fibers? A similar problem arose in some experiments in which the catecholamine fibers were cut. In these cases behavior could often be restored by amphetamine. Here it was as if the amines were important but the fibers were not. What was being stimulated if the amine fibers were cut? Three answers were given. Although not entirely satisfactory, these emphasize other remarkable properties of the amine systems. The first answer is that the excessive amines were pumped back into fibers or into other fibers and were quickly ready to be reused. This by itself was not very good because it did not tell us any advantage to freeing the amines in the first place. The second answer was more interesting. Amines may be pumped into some cortical and hypothalamic neurons which do not themselves manufacture them (Hökfelt and Fuxe, 1972). Thus it might be that amines carried to the cortex by catecholamine neurons would affect reward behavior mainly when ejected from these and taken up by cortex storage elements. This would still leave a problem. If the amines were already free, why did the animal self-stimulate their fibers? Maybe it was the cortex storage elements that were stimulated by some other afferent path in the hypothalamus or by antidromic stimulation of their descending axons. This would be somewhat unsatisfactory because these other fibers might just as well have been responsible for reward in the first place; at least it would remove the amine fibers from their role as the only reward neurons if other fibers in the medial forebrain bundle could play that role too. A better answer was that the self-stimulation behavior went on by some automatic and almost superstitious repetition compulsion, even though the animal was already fully rewarded by the free amines. This is not a bad answer. Amphetamine, which is one of the drugs used to free amines, often caused (in animals and humans) repetition of behavior in extinction or at other times when it was actually useless. Thus if the free amines were pumped into cortex neurons, and these were the ones correlated with the repetitious behavior, the behavior might continue even though the electrical stimulation no longer had a directly rewarding effect.

Another interesting question remains. Why did amphetamine help restore the behavior which was suppressed after catecholamine fibers were cut? The answer often given is that there was a rapid regrowth of catecholamine fibers. This was a special property of catecholamine fibers which seemed to add greatly to the likelihood that they were tied to both the stimulation and lesion effects. Amine fibers regrew and proliferated after cutting. They were not just like other fibers in this respect but were quite remarkable. By cutting a bundle from locus coeruleus to cerebellum in half, it was possible to double the number of its endings in the cerebellum, and to cause a whopping six fold increase of endings in the other leg of the same bundle far away in the hip-pocampus (Pickel, Segal, and Bloom, 1974). The recovery from lateral hypothalamic lesions seemed to be possibly explained by this kind of mecha-nism. It took approximately 3 to 4 weeks for the regrowth and proliferation of these endings to be completed, and it took about this time for recovery from lateral lesions to be completed. Brain self-stimulation also improved after probe implantation in what was originally a surprising course. From the time of implantation of probes until 3 weeks later the behavior improved. This is the time it would take the catecholamine fibers to proliferate after the damage caused by probe implantation. Other examples of improvement after damage exist. Placing a probe in such a way as to do excessive damage or implanting several probes sometimes yielded better brain reward in the end; or placing lesions in the brain reward system sometimes caused a sur-prising increase in brain reward behavior. These examples of recovery and even improvement after lesions fit the surprising property of the catecholamine fibers to regrow and proliferate.

In any event, the catecholamine system was corroborated by a number of studies with the drive-reward systems. The paths were the paths of reward. Poisoning the paths caused the same effects as the lesions. Regrowth in these paths was correlated with recovery in the lateral hypothalamic syn-drome and with recovery or improvement of self-stimulation. Drugs that modified catecholamines modified brain reward behavior (and normal reward behavior). Therefore catecholamine neurons could be reward neurons. If they were, how would a catecholamine reward system work?

D. Drive Connections

Because of the great convergence of catecholamine pathways on the hypo-thalamus before they diverge to the rest of the brain, an important clue to how they work might be found in the hypothalamus itself.

The most striking family of neurons in the catecholamine path through the hypothalamus was a family of large neurons with axons spread as if to monitor the ascending and descending messages in this path (Millhouse, 1969). The descending messages were from the paleocortex (the projection center for "rewards"?). The ascending messages were those from the locus coeruleus and substantia nigra (ascending messages about visceral and learned rewards?). To understand the large neurons better, we would like to have two questions answered. What do rewards do to them? What do drives do?

These questions were studied by recording neuron spikes during drive-reward behavior. The answer was surprising at first. These neurons were often turned off when animals ate (Hamburg, 1971). If they were rewarding neu-rons they should be turned on. It is not clear that they were turned off by the reward itself. Actually they were turned off when instrumental striving be-havior stopped, as the animal started to eat. If the animal was both eating and struggling at the same time, these neurons were turned on again. It was as if they were either turned on by information that striving was required and turned off by other information that the necessity was past, or they were correlates caused by the striving behavior.

That it was not just feedback from the behavior was demonstrated by Ito (1972), who showed that the brain reward signals also turned these neurons off, directly before any behavior was caused. The stimulus stopped them for several milliseconds. Thus two kinds of rewards turned them off: food and brain rewards.

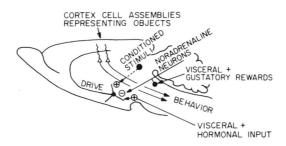

FIG. 34. "Drive reduction theory of reward." Norepinephrine (noradrenaline) neurons from the pons and medulla would be triggered by rewarding gustatory and visceral inputs. These would act to silence drive or learned drive neurons housed in or near the lateral hypothalamus (some of which might be dopamine neurons). Silencing drive neurons would cause them to become coupled to cortex cell assemblies active at the time. Excitatory inputs to drive neurons would come from visceral and hormonal factors and from conditioned stimuli.

What turns them on? I guessed they might become more active as the animal became more hungry, but it was hard to check this and to distinguish it from the general activity that built up as the animal got hungrier.

Two things, however, seemed to fit the notion that these might be drive (or learned drive) neurons. One was that they were turned on by a Pavlovian stimulus associated with reward (Linseman and Olds, 1973; Olds, 1973). It is well known that signals correlated with goals often trigger the correlated drives. Signals close to the goal also activated these neurons. Another set of experiments connected these neurons to the special drives of drug addiction. These neurons were turned on in addicted rats during withdrawal periods, and they were further activated by antimorphine drugs. On the other hand, they were quite abruptly quieted by morphine itself (Kerr et al., 1974). Once again they were on during drive but quieted by a reward.

These could therefore be the drive neurons, the ones involved in the Valenstein and Garcia effects. The catecholamine reward neurons might function to attenuate or silence them, thus causing a drive reduction kind of reward. By this action they might also attach or couple these neurons to correlated neuron firings in cortex (Fig. 34). Rearousal of the drive would then activate the attached set of cortex cell assemblies, causing the objects

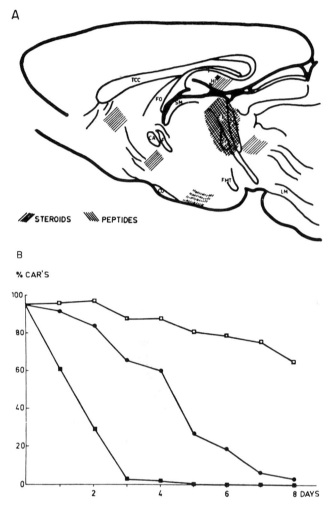

FIG. 35. Experiments of de Wied (1974). A. Regions of the brain where ACTH fractions caused "fear" reactions (cross-hatched) and where cortical steroids caused "bold" reactions (cross-hatched and single hatched). In much of the cross-hatch region electrical stimulation also caused negative reactions (Olds and Olds, 1963). TCC, truncus corporis callosum. HI, hippocampus. FO, fornix. SM, stria medullaris thalami. FR, fasciculus retroflexus. pf, nucleus parafascicularis. CA, commissura anterior. F, columna fornicis. FMT, fasciculus mamillothalamicus. CO, chiasma opticum. LM, lemniscus medialis. B. Persistence of conditioned avoidance reactions under the influence of an effective seven-peptide fragment of ACTH (*top trace*), and under control conditions (*middle trace*), and under the influence of a modified version of the seven-peptide fragment in which one of the peptides had been reversed from the L- to the D-stereoisomer (*bottom trace*). The effective fragment seemed to function as a "fear hormone" and the modified version had the opposite effect. (From de Wied, 1974.)

represented by them to become objects of pursuit. This might be a way for the Valenstein and Garcia effects to work.

Like any idea put together after the observations, this would need a good deal of testing. Still, it seemed a likely possibility that hypothalamic drive neurons were attenuated by catecholamine reward neurons.

E. The Hormones

A different idea about why the catecholamine neurons converged in the hypothalamus came from the brain hormone studies. These showed close interaction between the catecholamines and the hormones (Hökfelt and Fuxe, 1972).

Peptide hormones are generated by neurons in the brain, by other cells of the anterior pituitary, and similar cells in various organs. These peptide messengers are carried by the blood of the peripheral circulation and in special vascular systems such as the portal system. The portal system is a main window between the hormone systems of blood and the brain. Peptides are also carried by other fluids in the brain: in ventricles, specialized cells, and neurons. The effects of peptides are either directly on target glands or effectors, as in the milk ejection reflex, or on the pituitary where they trigger secondary control hormones; or their actions may be on the brain itself. It is the latter set of effects that needs to be further explored. Several findings pointed to direct brain actions.

One interesting set of observations pointed to a hormone of the stress system (ACTH) as having specialized subparts that acted as "fear hormones" directly on brain centers. ACTH is a 39-member peptide. A six- or seven-member fragment of it acted from blood to cause fear. In much smaller quantities it had this action if applied in a brain center where electrical stimulation caused aversive effects (Fig. 35A) (de Wied, 1974).

A still more surprising aspect of these ACTH studies was that by a slight change in the spelling of the peptide word (inversion of one member of the peptide chain) the effect could be reversed; i.e., it could be changed from acting like a fear hormone to acting like a security hormone (Fig. 35B). These researches pointed to the possibility that the drive mechanisms of the brain might be mainly peptide events, i.e., changes in the chemical state of the brain, changes which would bias neuronal processes.

This made it interesting that catecholamines were involved in controlling hormonal states (Ganong, 1974). Catecholamines blocked the ACTH system and promoted three other systems—thyroid, growth hormone, and sex. More detailed pictures of catecholamine actions showed that they modulate the various steps in sequential procedures such as sex and reproduction. The catecholamines seemed to help trigger hormone events, and then the hormone process seemed to carry the momentum over longer periods.

If hormones were actually the determining factors in brain states they would need to have widespread influence, and the question arose whether they might be broadcast in brain like the catecholamine fibers. Would they have special fiber systems? Some peptides have been mapped in brain, and the results looked a little like the catecholamine maps—at least one peptide (thyroid-releasing hormone) appeared in the medial and lateral feeding centers in significant amounts (Fig. 36) (Brownstein, Palkovits, Saavedra, Bassiri, and Utiger, 1974; Winokur and Utiger, 1974). That they might be transported was one thing. How they would be transported was possibly best indicated by studies of oxytocin (Cross, 1973). This substance is re-

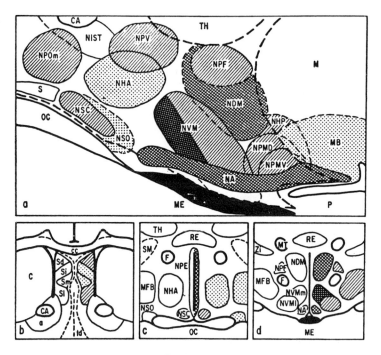

FIG. 36. Map of "thyroid-releasing hormone" (TRH), a three-member peptide chain in the hypothalamus and neighboring areas. Quantities of TRH range from 39 ng/mg protein (black) to less than 1 ng/mg (lightest stipple) with intermediate shades in between. The heaviest concentrations were in the median eminence (ME), medial part of the ventromedial nucleus (NVMm), the arcuate nucleus (NA), and the dorsomedial nucleus (NDM), respectively. Even the preoptic area (NPOm), medial forebrain bundle (MFB), and septal area (Sd, Si, Sm, SI) had appreciable amounts. Other studies (Winokur and Utiger, 1974) mapped smaller concentrations even farther afield. a: Parasagittal section through the rat hypothalamus. b–d: Frontal sections. b: Septal region. c: Anterior hypothalamus. d: Tuberal region. C, nucleus caudatus. CA, commissura anterior. CC, corpus callosum. F, fornix. M, mesencephalon. MB, mammillary body. ME, median eminence. MFB, medial forebrain bundle. MT, tractus mammillothalamicus. NHA, anterior hypothalamic nucleus. NHP, posterior hypothalamic nucleus. NIST, nucleus interstitialis striae terminalis. NPE, periventricular nucleus (hypothalamus). NPF, parafascicular nucleus (thalamus). NPMD, medial premammillary nucleus (hypothalamus). NPMV, ventral premammillary nucleus (hypothalamus). NPV, paraventricular nucleus (hypothalamus). NSC, suprachiasmatic nucleus. NSO, supraoptic nucleus. NVMi, ventromedial nucleus (hypothalamus), inferior part. OC, chiasma opticum. P, pituitary. RE, nucleus reuniens thalami. S, nucleus preopticus suprachiasmaticus. SM, stria medullaris. TH, thalamus. ZI, zona incerta. a, nucleus accumbens. td, nucleus tractus diagonalis. (From Brownstein et al., 1974.)

leased into the blood by neurons residing in the paraventricular nucleus of the hypothalamus. Its neurosecretory neurons have been studied carefully. The study of these cells was most important for showing that oxytocin cells had a type of activity during neurosecretion that was different from that observed normally. Between milk ejection episodes these neurons had fast and slow activity that looked normal. They appeared by accelerations and decelerations to be participating in normal neuronal processes. Approximately 15 sec prior to milk ejection, they raced at 50 spikes per second for approximately 2 sec and then became totally silent (Fig. 31) (Cross, 1973). The neurosecretion itself occurred approximately 7 sec after the burst. The burst of very fast activity and the period of silence might both have been involved. Why the rapid burst and the long silence appeared was not known. However, this picture suggested the possibility that the same cells might have two kinds of action, which would be represented by quite different recordings. The bursting and the silence might be involved in a peptide

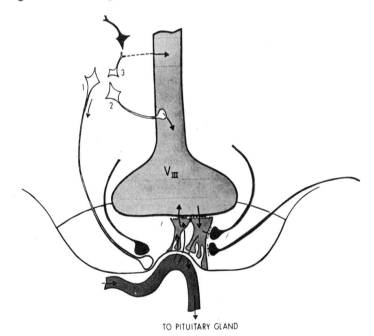

TO PITUITARY GLAND

FIG. 37. Schematic portrayal of the evidence and theory of Knigge (Knigge et al., 1971). The elements are (1) the portal vessel (to the pituitary gland), (2) the median eminence (in lightest grey); (3) the tanycytes (in dark grey) connecting it to (4) the third ventricle (V iii). The neurons in white numbered 1, 2, and 3 are dopaminergic; those in black are noradrenergic. Knigge's view is that the third ventricle and the ventricular system in general is a chemical pool collecting from production points in the brain and from the blood and acting on (1) sensors along the walls, (2) through the blood on the adenohypophysis, and (3) possibly through transport mechanisms that act farther afield in the brain. The tanycytes and the portal vessel (and other similar arrangements at other "circumventricular organs") act as two-way windows between the blood and the ventricular pool and thus between the blood and the brain. Dopaminergic and noradrenergic innervation may function in regulating tanycyte function.

neurosecretory mechanism that would be quite independent from the more normal neuronal messages.

Two other observations related the catecholamines to peptide hormones. One was that some nerve endings in the hormone parts of the brain appeared to have two kinds of neurochemical vesicles carried in the same endings. One kind was typical for catecholamines, and the other for neuropeptides (Hökfelt and Fuxe, 1972). Thus catecholamines and peptides might be co-occupants of the same fibers.

The other thing had to do with a set of tubules known as tanycytes, which linked the hormonal parts of the hypothalamus with the nearby blood supply (the portal system), and thence to the anterior pituitary. These were studied by Knigge et al. (1971). The system was thought to form a two-way window between hypothalamus (or the ventricle system) and the blood supply. Catecholamine neurons were observed ending on the tanycytes and Knigge says that "dopaminergic and noradrenergic innervation may function in regulating tanycyte function" (see Fig. 37).

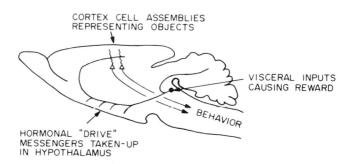

FIG. 38. Theory that catecholamine neurons might also be a peptide transport system. They would carry a reward message by one firing pattern that would release mainly catecholamines, and a drive message by a different firing pattern that would release mainly peptides. A rewarding input would couple these to active cell assemblies.

All of these things suggested that peptides could be carried in catecholamine neurons or transport systems controlled by them. It is well known that amino acids become incorporated into small proteins, which are moved rather rapidly along neurons. This transport mechanism studied by Ochs (1974) could move peptide hormones from hypothalamus throughout the brain in catecholamine fibers, and these might be released by special messages in the amine fibers.

The study of peptide hormones therefore suggests a second scenario to show how a catecholamine reward system might work (Fig. 38). What if the catecholamine neurons were both drive and reward neurons? The catecholamine transmitters would then be set off by normal action patterns, and they could carry the reward message. In addition there would be a peptide hormone carried by active transport mechanisms in the same neuron; this could be the drive message, which would be released by a different pattern of activity in the same fibers. This would resolve in a new way one paradox of reward, i.e., the question of why a reward attaches a drive to a goal or to a special instrumental behavior. If a burst of catecholamine neuronal activity caused the neurons involved to become connected or coupled to co-active cortex cell assemblies, this coupling might serve later as a method whereby a drive could have a selective action on that cell assembly because drive and reward would "come down the same pipe."

This of course is not a likely possibility as things stand. If peptide messengers in the brain become better understood, however, they might well be found to carry drive messages, and their interactions with catecholamine neurons will require careful study.

F. Summary

First, stimulation and lesion studies possibly showed that a broadcast set of catecholamine fibers were reward neurons. It may be stimulation of these that caused reward behavior, and cutting them that at least temporarily suspended it. Because there were different effects of stimulation and lesions in the paths of the two catecholamines, it was suggested that one of them, norepinephrine, might be more involved in those rewards that come toward the end of a consummatory process and which carry the seeds of satiety and the demise of the drive system. The other catecholamine, dopamine, might be involved in those rewards that come at the beginning of the consummatory process (or in the promising phases of the instrumental process) which were involved, in a positive feedback way, with initiating events.

A possible mechanism for involvement of these catecholamine neurons in drive-reward interactions was considered: The catecholamine axons inhibited a set of drive neurons in the lateral hypothalamus. From the experiments of Valenstein and Garcia it was supposed that these neurons were pre-wired to basic drives on the input side but had variable drive-object-targets learned on the basis of good and bad aftereffects of consummatory behaviors. This learning was supposed to be mediated by changing the connection of the drive neurons in the cortex.

A different possible mechanism was also considered: Catecholamine fibers were also transport fibers for peptide hormones picked up in hypothalamic stations. These would be carried through the brain and their release would produce the drive states. In this case the same fibers might carry two messages. A drive message would be carried by one pattern of activity that would release peptides. A reward message would be carried by a different pattern of activity that would release amines. In this case the problem of how a reward connects a drive to a set of behaviors or objects would be resolved in an easily conceptualized way. Connecting a reward fiber would consist in connecting a drive fiber.

REFERENCES

Adair, E. R., Casby, J. K., and Stolwijk, J. A. J. (1970): Behavioral temperature regulation in the squirrel monkey: Changes induced by shifts in hypothalamic temperature. *J. Comp. Physiol. Psychol.*, 72:17–27.

Ahlskog, J. E., and Hoebel, B. G. (1973): Overeating and obesity from damage to a noradrenergic system in the brain. *Science*, 182:166–169.

Albert, D. J., and Storlien, L. H. (1969): Hyperphagia in rats with cuts between the ventromedial and lateral hypothalamus. *Science*, 165:599–600.

Alcaraz, M., Guzman-Flores, C., Salas, M., and Beyer, C. (1969): Effect of estrogen on the responsivity of hypothalamic and mesencephalic neurons in the female cat. *Brain Res.*, 15:439–446.

Anand, B. K., and Brobeck, J. R. (1951): Hypothalamic control of food intake in rats and cats. *Yale J. Biol. Med.*, 24:123–140.

Anand, B. K., Chhina, G. S., Sharma, K. N., Dua, S., and Singh, B. (1964): Activity of single neurons in the hypothalamic feeding centers. *Am. J. Physiol.*, 207:1146–1154.

Andén, N.-E., Rubenson, A., Fuxe, K., and Hökfelt, T. (1967): Evidence for dopamine receptor stimulation by apomorphine. *J. Pharm. Pharmacol.*, 19:627–629.

Anderson, B., Gale, C. C., Hökfelt, B., and Larsson, B. (1965): Acute and chronic effects of preoptic lesions. *Acta Physiol. Scand.*, 65:45–60.

Anderson, B., Gale, C. C., and Sundsten, J. W. (1964): Preoptic influences on water intake. In: *Thirst in the Regulation of Body Water*, edited by M. J. Wayner, pp. 361–379. Macmillan (Pergamon), New York.

Anderson, B., and McCann, S. M. (1956): The effect of hypothalamic lesions on the water intake of the dog. *Acta Physiol. Scand.*, 35:312–320.

Angrist, B. M., Shopsin, B., and Gershon, S. (1971): The comparative psychotomimetic effects of stereoisomers of amphetamine. *Nature (Lond.)*, 234:152–154.

Angyan, L. (1974): Sleep induced by hypothalamic self-stimulation in cat. *Physiol. Behav.*, 12:697–701.

Annau, Z., Heffner, R., and Koob, G. F. (1974): Electrical self-stimulation of single and multiple loci: Long term observations. *Physiol. Behav.*, 13:281–290.

Antelman, S. M., Lippa, A. S., and Fisher, A. E. (1972): 6-Hydroxydopamine, noradrenergic reward, and schizophrenia. *Science*, 175:919–923.

Appel, J. B., Sheard, M. H., and Freedman, D. X. (1968): Behavioral effects of amine-depleting lesions in the medial forebrain bundle. *Community Behav. Biol. [A]*, 1:379–387.

Atrens, D. M., and von Vietinghoff-Riesch, F. (1972): The motivational properties of electrical self-stimulation of the medial and paraventricular hypothalamus. *Physiol. Behav.*, 9:229–235.

Balinska, H. (1968): The hypothalamic lesions: Effects on appetitive and aversive behaviors in rats. *Acta Biol. Exp.*, 28:47–56.

Balinska, H., Romaniuk, A., and Wyrwicka, W. (1964): Impairment of conditioned defensive reactions following lesions of the lateral hypothalamus in rabbits. *Acta Biol. Exp.*, 24:89–97.

Ball, G. G., and Adams, D. W. (1965): Intracranial stimulation as an avoidance or escape response. *Psychon. Sci.*, 39:39–40.

Bartholini, G., Pletscher, A., and Richards, J. (1970): 6-Hydroxydopamine-induced inhibition of brain catecholamine synthesis without ultrastructural damage. *Experientia*, 26:598–600.

Baumgarten, H. G., and Lachenmeyer, L. (1972): 5,7-Dihydroxytryptamine: Improvement in chemical lesioning of indoleamine neurons in the mammalian brain. *Z. Zellforsch. Mikrosk. Anat.*, 135:399–414.

Bernardis, L. L. (1970): Participation of the dorsomedial hypothalamic nucleus in the 'feeding center' and water intake circuitry of the weanling rat. *J. Neurovisc. Rel.*, 31:387–398.

Bernardis, L. L. (1972): Hypophagia, hypodipsia and hypoactivity following electrolytic lesions in the dorsomedial hypothalamic nuclei of mature rats of both sexes. *J. Neural Transm.*, 33:1–10.

Bernardis, L. L., Chlouverakis, C., Schnatz, J. D., and Frohman, L. A. (1974): Effect of dorsomedial hypothalamic lesions before and after placement of obesity-producing ventromedial hypothalamic lesions in the weanling male rat. *Brain Res.*, 69:67–75.

Bernardis, L. L., and Schnatz, J. D. (1971): Localization in the ventromedial hypothalamus of an area affecting plasma lipid levels. *J. Neurovisc. Rel.*, 23:90–99.

Bernardis, L. L., and Skelton, F. R. (1966): Growth and obesity following ventromedial hypothalamic lesions placed in female rats at four different ages. *Neuroendocrinology*, 1:265–275.

Bernardis, L. L., and Skelton, F. R. (1967): Growth and obesity in male rats after placement of ventromedial hypothalamic lesions at four different ages. *J. Endocrinol.*, 38:351–352.

Bishop, M. P., Elder, S. T., and Heath, R. G. (1963): Intracranial self-stimulation in man. *Science*, 140:394–396.

Bishop, M. P., Elder, T. S., and Heath, R. G. (1964): Attempted control of operant behavior in man with intracranial self-stimulation. In: *The Role of Pleasure in Behavior*, edited by R. G. Heath, pp. 55–81. Hoeber, New York.

Black, W. C., and Cooper, B. R. (1970): Reduction of electrically rewarded behavior by interference with monoamine synthesis. *Physiol. Behav.*, 5:1405–1409.

Bleier, R. (1972): Structural relationship of ependymal cells and their processes within the hypothalamus. In: *Brain-Endocrine Interaction, Median Eminance: Structure and Function. International Symposium on Brain-Endocrine Interaction Munich, 1971*, edited by K. M. Knigge, D. E. Scott, and A. Weindl, pp. 306–308. Karger, Basel.

Bloom, F. E. (1974): Dynamics of synaptic modulation: perspectives for the future. In: *The Neurosciences: Third Study Program*, edited by F. O. Schmitt and F. G. Worden, pp. 989–999. MIT Press, Cambridge, Massachusetts.

Bloom, F. E., Algeri, S., Groppetti, A., Revuelta, A., and Costa, E. (1969): Lesions of central norepinephrine terminals with 6-OH-dopamine: Biochemistry and fine structure. *Science*, 166:1284–1286.

Bogacz, J., St. Laurent, J., and Olds, J. (1965): Dissociation of self-stimulation and epileptiform activity. *Electroencephalogr. Clin. Neurophysiol.*, 19:75–87.

Booth, D. A. (1967): Localization of the adrenergic feeding system in the rat diencephalon. *Science*, 158:515–517.

Bose, S., Bailey, P. T., Thoa, N. B., and Pradhan, S. N. (1974): Effects of 5-hydroxytryptophane on self-stimulation in rats. *Psychopharmacologia*, 36:255–262.

Bower, G. H., and Miller, N. E. (1958): Rewarding and punishing effects from stimulating the same place in the rat's brain. *J. Comp. Physiol. Psychol.*, 51:669–674.

Bowman, W. C., Rand, M. J., and West, G. B. (1968): Sympathomimetics and drugs modifying their action. In: *Textbook of Pharmacology*, pp. 734–775. Blackwell Scientific Publications, Oxford.

Boyd, E. S., and Gardner, L. C. (1967): Effect of some brain lesions on intracranial self-stimulation in the rat. *Am. J. Physiol.*, 213:1044–1052.

Brady, J. V. (1960): Temporal and emotional effects related to intracranial electrical self-stimulation. In: *Electrical Studies on the Unanesthetized Brain*, edited by E. R. Ramey and D. S. O'Doherty. Hoeber, New York.

Brady, J. V., Boren, J. J., Conrad, D., and Sidman, M. (1957): The effect of food and water deprivation upon intracranial self-stimulation. *J. Comp. Physiol. Psychol.*, 50:134–137.

Breese, G. R., Howard, J. L., and Leahy, J. P. (1971): Effect of 6-hydroxydopamine on electrical self-stimulation of the brain. *Br. J. Pharmacol.*, 43:255–257.

Breese, G. R., and Traylor, T. D. (1971): Depletion of brain noradrenaline and dopamine by 6-hydroxydopamine. *Br. J. Pharmacol.*, 42:88–89.

Brobeck, J. R., Tepperman, J., and Long, C. N. H. (1943): Experimental hypothalamic hyperphagia in the albino rat. *Yale J. Biol. Med.*, 15:831–853.

Brodie, D. A., Moreno, O. M., Malis, J. L., and Boren, J. J. (1960): Rewarding properties of intracranial stimulation. *Science,* 131:929–930.

Broekkamp, C. L. E., and van Rossum, J. M. (1974): Effects of apomorphine on self-stimulation. *Psychopharmacologia,* 34:71–80.

Brown, S., and Trowill, J. A. (1970): Lever pressing performances for brain stimulation of FI and VI schedules in a single lever situation. *Psychol. Rep.,* 26:699–706.

Brown-Grant, K., Exley, D., and Naftolin, F. (1970): Peripheral plasma oestradiol and luteinizing hormone concentrations during the oestrus cycle of the rat. *J. Endocrinol.,* 48:295–296.

Brownstein, M. J., Palkovits, M., Saavedra, J. M., Bassiri, R. M., and Utiger, R. D. (1974): Thyrotropin-releasing hormone in specific nuclei of rat brain. *Science,* 185: 267–269.

Bruecke, F. T. V., Hornykiewicz, O., and Sigg, E. B. (1969): *The Pharmacology of Psychotherapeutic Drugs.* Springer-Verlag, New York.

Buchwald, N. A., Wyers, E. J., Lamprecht, C. W., and Heuser, G. (1961): The "caudate spindle." IV. A behavioral index of caudate-induced inhibition. *Electroencephalogr. Clin. Neurophysiol.,* 13:531–537.

Burkard, W. P., Jalfre, M., and Blum, J. (1969): Effects of 6-hydroxypopamine on behavior and cerebral amine content in rats. *Experientia,* 35:1295–1296.

Bursten, B., and Delgado, J. M. R. (1958): Positive reinforcement induced by intracranial stimulation in the monkey. *J. Comp. Physiol. Psychol.,* 51:6–10.

Cabanac, M., Stolwijk, J. A. J., and Hardy, J. D. (1968): Effect of temperature and pyrogens on single-unit activity in the rabbit's brain stem. *J. Appl. Physiol.,* 24:645–652.

Caggiula, A. R., and Hoebel, B. C. (1966): "Copulation-reward site" in the posterior hypothalamus. *Science,* 153:1284–1285.

Cantor, M. B. (1971): Signaled reinforcing brain stimulation establishes and maintains reliable schedule control. *Science,* 174:610–613.

Cantor, M. B., and LoLordo, V. M. (1970): Rats prefer signaled reinforcing brain stimulation to unsignaled ESB. *J. Comp. Physiol. Psychol.,* 71:183–191.

Cantor, M. B., and LoLordo, V. M. (1972): Reward value of brain stimulation is inversely related to uncertainty about its onset. *J. Comp. Physiol. Psychol.,* 79:259–270.

Chance, M. R. A., and Silverman, A. P. (1964): The structure of social behaviour and drug action. In: *Animal Behaviour and Drug Action,* edited by H. Steinberg, A. V. S. de Reuck, and J. Knight, pp. 65–79. Little Brown, Boston.

Chhina, G. S., and Anand, B. K. (1969): Responses of neurones in the hypothalamus and limbic system to genital stimulation in adult and immature monkeys. *Brain Res.,* 13:511–521.

Chhina, G. S., Anand, B. K., Singh, B., and Rao, P. S. (1971): Effect of glucose on hypothalamic feeding centers in deafferented animals. *Am. J. Physiol.,* 221:662–667.

Chu, N., and Bloom, F. E. (1973): Norepinephrine-containing neurons: Changes in spontaneous discharge patterns during sleeping and waking. *Science,* 179:908–910.

Cook, L. (1964): Effects of drugs on operant conditioning. In: *Animal Behaviour and Drug Action,* edited by H. Steinberg, A. V. S. de Reuck, and J. Knight, pp. 23–40. Little Brown, Boston.

Coons, E. E. (1964): Motivational correlates of eating elicited by electrical stimulation in the hypothalamic feeding area. Ph.D. thesis, Yale University.

Coons, E. E., and Cruce, J. A. F. (1968): Lateral hypothalamus: Food and current intensity in maintaining self-stimulation of hunger. *Science,* 159:1117–1119.

Coons, E. E., and Quartermain, D. (1970): Motivational depression associated with norepinephrine-induced eating from the hypothalamus: Resemblance to the ventromedial hyperphagic syndrome. *Physiol. Behav.,* 5:687–692.

Cooper, B. R., Black, W. C., and Paolino, R. M. (1971): Decreased forebrain and lateral hypothalamic reward after alpha-methyl-para-tyrosine. *Physiol. Behav.,* 6:425–429.

Cooper, B. R., Breese, G. R., Howard, J. L., and Grant, L. D. (1972a): Effect of central catecholamine alterations by 6-hydroxydopamine on shuttlebox avoidance acquisition. *Physiol. Behav.,* 9:727–731.

Cooper, J. R., Bloom, F. E., and Roth, R. H. (1974): *The Biochemical Basis of Neuropharmacology,* 2nd ed. Oxford University Press, New York.

Cooper, R. M., and Taylor, L. H. (1967): Thalamic reticular system and central grey: Self-stimulation. *Science,* 156:102–103.

Corbit, J. D. (1969): Behavioral regulation of hypothalamic temperature. *Science,* 166:256–258.

Corbit, J. D. (1970): Behavioral regulation of body temperature. In: *Physiological and Behavioral Temperature Regulation,* edited by J. D. Hardy, A. P. Gagge, and J. A. J. Stolwijk. Charles C Thomas, Springfield, Illinois.

Corbit, J. D. (1973): Voluntary control of hypothalamic temperature. *J. Comp. Physiol. Psychol.,* 83:394–411.

Coscina, D. V., and Balagura, S. (1970): Avoidance and escape behavior in rats with aphagia produced by basal diencephalic lesions. *Physiol. Behav.,* 5:651–657.

Coscina, D. V., Seggie, J., Godse, D. D., and Stancer, H. C. (1973): Induction of rage in rats by central injection of 6-hydroxydopamine. *Pharmacol. Biochem. Behav.,* 1:1–6.

Cox, V. C., Kakolewski, J. W., and Valenstein, E. S. (1969): Inhibition of eating and drinking following hypothalamic stimulation in the rat. *J. Comp. Physiol. Psychol.,* 68:530–535.

Cox, V. C., and Valenstein, E. S. (1965): Attenuation of aversive properties of peripheral shock by hypothalamic stimulation. *Science,* 149:323–325.

Crosby, E. C., Humphrey, T., and Lauer, E. W. (1962): *The Correlative Anatomy of the Nervous System.* Macmillan, New York.

Cross, B. A. (1966): The neural control of oxytocin secretion. In: *Neuroendocrinology, Vol. 1,* edited by L. Martini and W. F. Ganong, pp. 217–259. Academic Press, New York.

Cross, B. A. (1973): Unit responses in the hypothalamus. In: *Frontiers in Neuroendocrinology,* edited by W. F. Ganong and L. Martini, pp. 133–171. Oxford University Press, New York.

Cross, B. A., and Dyer, R. G. (1970a): Characterization of unit activity in hypothalamic islands with special reference to hormone effects. In: *The Hypothalamus,* edited by L. Martini, M. Motta, and F. Fraschini, pp. 115–122. Academic Press, New York.

Cross, B. A., and Dyer, R. G. (1970b): Effect of hypophysectomy on firing rates of hypothalamic neurons in diencephalic islands. *J. Endocrinol.,* 48:475–476.

Cross, B. A., and Dyer, R. G. (1971a): Unit activity in diencephalic islands: The effect of anesthetics. *J. Physiol. (Lond.),* 212:467–481.

Cross, B. A., and Dyer, R. G. (1971b): Cyclic changes in neurones of the anterior hypothalamus during the oestrus cycle, and the effects of anesthesia. In: *Steroid Hormones and Brain Function,* edited by R. Gorski and C. H. Sawyer, pp. 95–102. University of California Press, Los Angeles.

Cross, B. A., and Dyer, R. G. (1972): Ovarian modulation of unit activity in the anterior hypothalamus of the cyclic rat. *J. Physiol. (Lond.),* 222:25P.

Cross, B. A., Moss, R. L., and Urban, I. (1971): Effects of iontophoretic application of acetylcholine and noradrenaline to antidromically identified paraventricular neurones. *J. Physiol. (Lond.),* 214:30P (abstr.).

Crow, T. J. (1970): Enhancement by cocaine of intra-cranial self-stimulation in the rat. *Life Sci.,* 9:375–381.

Crow, T. J. (1971): The relation between electrical self-stimulation sites and catecholamine-containing neurones in the rat mesencephalon. *Experientia,* 27:662.

Crow, T. J. (1972a): A map of the rat mesencephalon for electrical self-stimulation. *Brain Res.,* 36:265–273.

Crow, T. J. (1972b): Catecholamine-containing neurones and electrical self-stimulation. 1. A review of some data. *Psychol. Med.,* 2:414–421.

Crow, T. J. (1973): Catecholamine-containing neurones and electrical self-stimulation. 2. A theoretical interpretation and some psychiatric implications. *Psychol. Med.,* 3:66–73.

Crow, T. J., and Arbuthnott, G. W. (1972): Function of catecholamine-containing neurons in mammalian central nervous system. *Nature (Lond.),* 238:245–246.

Crow, T. J., Spear, P. J., and Arbuthnott, G. W. (1972): Intracranial self-stimulation with electrodes in the region of the locus coeruleus. *Brain Res.,* 36:275–287.

Cunningham, D. J., Stolwijk, J. A. J., Murakami, N., and Hardy, J. D. (1967): Responses of neurons in the preoptic area to temperature, serotonin and epinephrine. *Am. J. Physiol.,* 213:1570–1581.

Dafny, N., and Feldman, S. (1970): Single cell activity in the hypothalamus in intact and adrenalectomized rats. *Physiol. Behav.,* 5:873–878.

Dahlström, A., and Fuxe, K. (1964): Evidence for the existence of monoamine-containing neurons in the central nervous system. *Acta Scand. [Suppl.],* 62(232):1–55.

de la Torre, J. C. (1972): *Dynamics of Brain Monoamines.* Plenum, New York.

Delgado, J. M. R. (1969): *Physical Control of the Mind.* Harper & Row, New York.

Delgado, J. M. R., Roberts, W. W., and Miller, N. E. (1954): Learning motivated by electrical stimulation of the brain. *Am. J. Physiol.,* 179:587–593.

Deutsch, J. A. (1960): *The Structural Basis of Behavior.* Chicago University Press, Chicago.

Deutsch, J. A. (1964): Behavioral measurement of the neural refractory period and its application to intracranial self-stimulation. *J. Comp. Physiol. Psychol.,* 58:1–9.

Deutsch, J. A., and Albertson, T. E. (1974): Refractory period and adaptation in prolonged brain reward. *Behav. Biol.,* 11:275–279.

Deutsch, J. A., and Howarth, C. I. (1962): Evocation by fear of a habit learned for electrical stimulation of the brain. *Science,* 136:1057–1058.

Deutsch, J. A., and Howarth, C. I. (1963): Some tests of a theory of intracranial self-stimulation. *Psychol. Rev.,* 70:444–460.

de Wied, D. (1974): Pituitary-adrenal system hormones and behavior. In: *The Neurosciences, Third Study Program,* edited by F. O. Schmitt and F. G. Worden, pp. 653–666. MIT Press, Cambridge, Massachusetts.

Dews, P. B. (1958): Studies on behavior. IV. Stimulant actions of methamphetamine. *J. Pharmacol. Exp. Ther.,* 122:137–147.

Dresse, A. (1966): Importance du système mesencephalo-telencephalique noradrenergique comme substratum anatomique du comportement d'autostimulation. *Life Sci.,* 5:1003–1014.

Dyball, R. E. J. (1971): Oxytocin and ADH secretion in relation to electrical activity in antidromically identified supraoptic and paraventricular units. *J. Physiol. (Lond.),* 214:245–256.

Dyball, R. E. J., and Dyer, R. G. (1971): Plasma oxytocin concentrations and paraventricular neurone activity in rats with diencephalic islands and intact brains. *J. Physiol. (Lond.),* 216:227–235.

Dyer, R. G., and Cross, B. A. (1972): Antidromic identification of units in the preoptic and anterior hypothalamic areas projecting directly to the ventromedial and arcuate nuclei. *Brain Res.,* 43:254–258.

Dyer, R. G., Pritchett, C. J., and Cross, B. A. (1972): Unit activity in the diencephalon of female rats during the oestrus cycle. *J. Endocrinol.,* 53:151–160.

Ellinwood, E. H., Jr. (1971): "Accidental conditioning" with chronic methamphetamine intoxication: Implications for a theory of drug habituation. *Psychopharmacologia,* 21:131–138.

Ellison, G. D., and Bresler, D. E. (1974): Tests of emotional behavior in rats following depletion of norepinephrine, or serotonin, or of both. *Psychopharmacologia,* 34:275–288.

Ellison, G. D., Sorenson, C. A., and Jacobs, B. L. (1970): Two feeding syndromes following surgical isolation of the hypothalamus in rats. *J. Comp. Physiol. Psychol.,* 70:173–188.

Epstein, A. N. (1960): Reciprocal changes in feeding behavior produced by intra-hypothalamic chemical injections. *Am. J. Physiol.,* 199:969–974.

Epstein, A. N. (1971): The lateral hypothalamic syndrome: Its implications for the physiological psychology of hunger and thirst. In: *Progress in Physiological Psychology, Vol. 4,* edited by E. Stellar and J. M. Sprague, pp. 263–317. Academic Press, New York.

Epstein, A. N., Fitzsimmons, J. T., and Rolls, B. J. (1970): Drinking induced by injection of angiotensin into the brain of the rat. *J. Physiol. (Lond.),* 210:454–474.

Ernst, A. M. (1967): Mode of action of apomorphine and dexamphetamine on gnawing compulsion in rats. *Psychopharmacologia,* 10:316–323.

Falck, B., Hillarp, N. A., Thieme, G., and Thorpe, H. (1962): Fluorescence of catecholamines and related compounds condensed with formaldehyde. *J. Histochem. Cytochem.,* 10:348–354.

Farber, J., Steiner, S., and Ellman, S. J. (1972): The pons as an electrical self-stimulation site. *Psychophysiology,* 9:105 (abstr.).

Feldman, S., and Sarne, Y. (1970): Effect of cortisol on single cell activity in hypothalamic islands. *Brain Res.,* 23:67–75.

Findlay, A. L. R. (1972): Hypothalamic inputs: methods, and five examples. *Prog. Brain Res.,* 38:163–190.

Fisher, A. E. (1969): The role of limbic structures in the central regulation of feeding and drinking behavior. *Ann. N.Y. Acad. Sci.,* 157:894–901.

Fisher, A., and Coury, J. N. (1962): Cholinergic tracing of a central neural circuit underlying the thirst drive. *Science,* 138:691–693.

Fog, R. (1969): Stereotyped and non-stereotyped behavior in rats induced by various stimulant drugs. *Psychopharmacologia,* 14:299–304.

Fog, R. (1970): Behavioral effects in rats of morphine and amphetamine and a combination of the two drugs. *Psychopharmacologia,* 16:305–312.

Fog, R. L., Randrup, A., and Pakkenberg, H. (1967): Aminergic mechanisms in corpus striatum and amphetamine-induced stereotyped behavior. *Psychopharmacologia,* 11:179–183.

Franklin, K. B. J., and Herberg, L. J. (1974): Ventromedial syndrome: The rat's "finickiness" results from the obesity, not from the lesions. *J. Comp. Physiol. Psychol.,* 87:410–414.

Frigyesi, T. L., Ige, A., Iulo, A., and Schwartz, R. (1971): Denigration and sensorimotor disability induced by ventral tegmental injection of 6-hydroxydopamine in the cat. *Exp. Neurol.,* 33:78–87.

Fuxe, K. (1965): Evidence for the existence of monoamine neurons in the central nervous system. IV. Distribution of monoamine nerve terminals in the central nervous system. *Acta Physiol. Scand. [Suppl. 247],* 64:37–85.

Gallistel, C. R. (1969a): The incentive of brain-stimulation reward. *J. Comp. Physiol. Psychol.,* 69:713–721.

Gallistel, C. R. (1969b): Failure of pretrial stimulation to affect reward electrode preference. *J. Comp. Physiol. Psychol.,* 69:722–729.

Gallistel, C. R. (1973): Self-stimulation: the neurophysiology of reward and motivation. In: *The Physiological Basis of Memory,* edited by J. A. Deutsch. Academic Press, New York.

Gallistel, C. R. and Beagley, G. (1971): Specificity of brain-stimulation reward in the rat. *J. Comp. Physiol. Psychol.,* 76:199–205.

Gallistel, C. R., Rolls, E. T., and Greene, D. (1969): Neuron function inferred from behavioral and electrophysiological estimates of refractory period. *Science,* 166:1028–1030.

Gallo, R. V., Johnson, J. H., Goldman, B. D., Whitmoyer, D. I., and Sawyer, C. H. (1971): Effects of electrochemical stimulation of the ventral hippocampus on hypothalamic electrical activity and pituitary gonadotropin secretion in female rats. *Endocrinology,* 89:704–713.

Ganong, W. F. (1974): Brain mechanisms regulating the secretion of the pituitary gland. In: *The Neurosciences, Third Study Program,* edited by F. O. Schmitt and F. G. Worden, pp. 549–563. MIT Press, Cambridge, Massachusetts.

Garcia, J., and Ervin, F. R. (1968): Gustatory-visceral and telereceptor-cutaneous conditioning—adaptation in internal and external milieus. *Community Behav. Biol. [A],* 1:389–415.

German, D. C., and Bowden, D. M. (1974): Catecholamine systems as the neural substrate for intracranial self-stimulation: A hypothesis. *Brain Res.,* 73:381–419.

German, D. C., and Fetz, E. E. (1974): Activity of locus ceruleus units responsive to stimulation at reinforcing sites in alert monkey. Fourth Annual Meeting of the Society of Neurosciences, St. Louis, p. 225.

Gibson, S., McGeer, E. G., and McGeer, P. L. (1970): Effect of selective inhibitors of tyrosine and tryptophan hydroxylases on self-stimulation in rats. *Exp. Neurol.,* 27:283–290.

Gibson, W. E., Reid, L. D., Sakai, M., and Porter, P. B. (1965): Intracranial reinforcement compared with sugar water reinforcement. *Science,* 148:1357–1359.

Gold, R. M. (1970): Hypothalamic hyperphagia without ventromedial damage. *Physiol. Behav.,* 5:23–25.

Goodman, L. S., and Gilman, A. (1955): *The Pharmacological Basis of Therapeutics,* 2nd ed. Macmillan, New York.

Grossman, S. P. (1960): Eating and drinking elicited by direct adrenergic or cholinergic stimulation of hypothalamus. *Science,* 132:301–302.

Grossman, S. P. (1971): Changes in food and water intake associated with an interruption of anterior or posterior fiber connections of the hypothalamus. *J. Comp. Physiol. Psychol.,* 75:23–31.

Grossman, S. P., and Grossman, L. (1971): Food and water intake in rats with parasagittal knife cuts medial or lateral to the lateral hypothalamus. *J. Comp. Physiol. Psychol.,* 74:148–156.

Haller, E. W., and Barraclough, C. A. (1970): Alternations in unit activity of hypothalamic ventromedial nuclei by stimuli which affect gonadotropic hormone secretion. *Exp. Neurol.,* 29:111–120.

Hamburg, M. D. (1971): Hypothalamic unit activity and eating behavior. *Am. J. Physiol.,* 220:980–985.

Hamilton, C. L. (1963): Interactions of food intake and temperature regulation in the rat. *J. Comp. Physiol. Psychol.,* 56:476–488.

Hamilton, C. L., and Brobeck, J. R. (1964): Food intake and temperature regulation in rats with rostral hypothalamic lesions. *Am. J. Physiol.,* 207:291–297.

Hardy, J. D., Hellon, R. F., and Sutherland, K. (1964): Temperature sensitive neurones in the dog's hypothalamus. *J. Physiol. (Lond.),* 175:242–253.

Harvey, J. A., and Lints, C. E. (1971): Lesions in the medial forebrain bundle: Relationship between pain sensitivity and telencephalic content of serotonin. *J. Comp. Physiol. Psychol.,* 74:28–36.

Haymaker, W., Anderson, E., and Nauta, W. J. H. (1969): *The Hypothalamus.* Charles C Thomas, Springfield, Illinois.

Heath, R. G. (1954): *Studies in Schizophrenia.* Harvard University Press, Cambridge, Massachusetts.

Heath, R. G. (1964): Pleasure responses of human subjects to direct stimulation of the brain: physiologic and psychodynamic considerations. In: *The Role of Pleasure in Human Behavior,* edited by R. G. Heath, pp. 219–243. Hoeber, New York.

Hellon, R. F. (1967): Thermal stimulation of hypothalamic neurones in unanesthetized rabbits. *J. Physiol. (Lond.),* 193:381–395.

Hellon, R. F. (1970): The stimulation of hypothalamic neurones by changes in ambient temperature. *Pfluegers Arch.,* 321:56–66.

Herberg, L. J. (1963a): Seminal ejaculation following positively reinforcing electrical stimulation of the rat hypothalamus. *J. Comp. Physiol. Psychol.,* 56:679–685.

Herberg, L. J. (1963b): Determinants of extinction in electrical self-stimulation. *J. Comp. Physiol. Psychol.,* 56:686–690.

Hess, W. R. (1954): *Diencephalon: Autonomic and Extrapyramidal Functions.* Grune & Stratton, New York.

Hetherington, A. W. (1944): Non-production of hypothalamic obesity in the rat by lesions rostral or dorsal to the ventro-medial hypothalamic nuclei. *J. Comp. Neurol.,* 80:33–45.

Hetherington, A. W., and Ranson, S. W. (1942a): The relation of various hypothalamic lesions to adiposity in the rat. *J. Comp. Neurol.,* 76:475–499.

Hetherington, A. W., and Ranson, S. W. (1942b): Effect of early hypophysectomy on hypothalamic obesity. *Endocrinology,* 31:30–34.

Hitt, J. C., Bryon, D. M., and Modianos, D. T. (1973): Effects of rostral medial forebrain bundle and olfactory tubercle lesions upon sexual behavior of male rats. *J. Comp. Physiol. Psychol.,* 82:30–36.

Hitt, J. C., Hendricks, S. E., Ginsberg, S. I., and Lewis, J. H. (1970): Disruption of male, but not female, sexual behavior in rats by medial forebrain bundle lesions. *J. Comp. Physiol. Psychol.,* 73:377–384.

Hodos, W. H. (1965): Motivational properties of long durations of rewarding brain stimulation. *J. Comp. Physiol. Psychol.,* 59:219–224.

Hoebel, B. G. (1968): Inhibition and disinhibition of self-stimulation and feeding: Hypothalamic control and post-ingestional factors. *J. Comp. Physiol. Psychol.,* 66:89–100.

Hoebel, B. G., and Teitelbaum, P. (1962): Hypothalamic control of feeding and self-stimulation. *Science,* 135:357–377.

Hoebel, B. G., and Teitelbaum, P. (1966): Weight regulation in normal and hypothalamic hyperphagic rats. *J. Comp. Physiol. Psychol.,* 61:189–193.

Hökfelt, T., and Fuxe, K. (1972): On the morphology and the neuroendocrine role of the hypothalamic catecholamine neurons. In: *Brain-Endocrine Interaction, Median Eminance: Structure and Function. International Symposium. on Brain-Endocrine Interaction, Munich, 1971,* edited by K. M. Knigge, D. E. Scott, and A. Weindl, pp. 181–223. Karger, Basel.

Hull, C. L. (1943): *Principles of Behavior.* Appleton-Century-Crofts, New York.

Huston, J. P., and Borbely, A. A. (1974): The thalamic rat: General behavior, operant learning with rewarding hypothalamic stimulation, and effects of amphetamine. *Physiol. Behav.,* 12:433–448.

Ito, M. (1972): Excitability of medial forebrain bundle neurons during self-stimulating behavior. *J. Neurophysiol.,* 35:652–664.

Ito, M., and Olds, J. (1971): Unit activity during self-stimulation behavior. *J. Neurophysiol.,* 34:263–273.

Iversen, L. L. (1967): *The Uptake and Storage of Noradrenaline in Sympathetic Nerves,* University Press, Cambridge, England.

Iverson, S. D. (1974): 6-Hydroxydopamine: A chemical lesion technique for studying the role of amine neurotransmitters in behavior. In: *The Neurosciences: Third Study Program,* edited by F. O. Schmitt and F. G. Worden, pp. 705–711. MIT Press, Cambridge, Massachusetts.

Jacobowitz, D. M., and Palkovits, M. (1974): Topographic atlas of catecholamine and acetylcholinesterase-containing neurons in the rat brain. I. Forebrain (telencephalon, diencephalon). *J. Comp. Neurol.,* 157:13–28.

Jouvet, M. (1974): Monoaminergic regulation of the sleep-waking cycle in the cat. In: *The Neurosciences, Third Study Program,* edited by F. O. Schmitt and F. G. Worden, pp. 49–508. MIT Press, Cambridge, Massachusetts.

Kawakami, E., Terasawa, E., and Ibuki, T. (1970): Changes in multiple unit activity of the brain during the estrous cycle. *Neuroendocrinology,* 6:30–48.

Keene, J. J. (1973): Reward-associated inhibition and pain-associated excitation lasting seconds in single intralaminar thalamic units. *Brain Res.,* 64:211–224.

Keesey, R. (1962): The relation between pulse frequency, intensity, and duration and the rate of responding for intracranial stimulation. *J. Comp. Physiol. Psychol.,* 55:671–678.

Keesey, R. E. (1964): Duration of stimulation and the reward properties of hypothalamic stimulation. *J. Comp. Physiol. Psychol.,* 58:201–207.

Keesey, R. E. (1966): Hypothalamic stimulation as a reinforcer of discrimination learning. *J. Comp. Physiol. Psychol.,* 62:231–236.

Keesey, R. E., and Goldstein, M. D. (1968): Use of progressive fixed-ratio procedures in the assessment of intracranial reinforcement. *J. Exp. Anal. Behav.,* 11:293–301.

Keesey, R. E., and Powley, T. L. (1968): Enhanced lateral hypothalamic reward sensitivity following septal lesions in the rat. *Physiol. Behav.,* 3:557–562.

Kent, E., and Grossman, S. P. (1969): Evidence for a conflict interpretation of anomalous effects of rewarding brain stimulation. *J. Comp. Physiol. Psychol.,* 69:381–390.

Kent, M. A., and Peters, R. H. (1973): Effects of ventromedial hypothalamic lesions on hunger-motivated behavior in rats. *J. Comp. Physiol. Psychol.,* 83:92–97.

Kerr, F. W., Triplett, J. N., and Beeler, G. W. (1974): Reciprocal (push-pull) effects of morphine on single units in the ventromedian and lateral hypothalamus and influences on other nuclei; with a comment on methadone effects during withdrawal from morphine. *Brain Res.*, 74:81–103.

Klüver, H., and Bucy, P. C. (1937): Psychic blindness and other symptoms following bilateral temporal lobectomy in rhesus monkey. *Am. J. Physiol.*, 119:352–353.

Knigge, K. M., Scott, D. E., and Weindl, A., editors. (1972): *Brain Endocrine Interactions.* Karger, Basel.

Knigge, K. M., Joseph, S. A., Scott, D. E., and Jacobs, J. J. (1971): Observations on the architecture of the arcuate-median eminence region after deafferentiation, with reference to the organization of hypothalamic RF-producing elements. In: *The Neuroendocrinology of Human Reproduction,* edited by H. C. Mack and A. I. Sherman, pp. 6–22. Charles C Thomas, Springfield, Ill.

Knott, P. D., and Clayton, K. N. (1966): Durable secondary reinforcement using brain stimulation as the primary reinforcer. *J. Comp. Physiol. Psychol.*, 61:151–153.

Koe, B. K., and Weissman, A. (1966): p-Chlorophenylalanine, a specific depletor or brain serotonin. *J. Pharmacol. Exp. Ther.*, 154:499–516.

Kornblith, C., and Olds, J. (1968): T-maze learning with one trial per day using brain stimulation reinforcement. *J. Comp. Physiol. Psychol.*, 66:488–491.

Krasne, F. B. (1962): General disruption resulting from electrical stimulation of the ventromedial hypothalamus. *Science,* 138:822–823.

Krenjevic, K. (1974): Chemical nature of synaptic transmission in vertebrates. *Physiol. Rev.*, 54:418–540.

Kuhar, M. J., Pert, C. B., and Snyder, S. H. (1973): Regional distribution of opiate receptor binding in monkey and human brain. *Nature (Lond.),* 245:447–450.

Leibowitz, S. F. (1974): Adrenergic receptor mechanisms in eating and drinking. In: *The Neurosciences, Third Study Program,* edited by F. O. Schmitt and F. G. Worden, pp. 713–720. MIT Press, Cambridge, Massachusetts.

Le Magnen, J., Devos, M., Gaudilliere, J-P., Louis-Sylvestre, J., and Tallon, S. (1973): Role of a lipostatic mechanism in regulation by feeding of energy balance in rats. *J. Comp. Physiol. Psychol.*, 84:1–23.

Lewis, J. J. (1964): *An Introduction to Pharmacology.* Williams & Wilkins, Baltimore.

Libet, B., and Owman, C. (1974): Concomitant changes in formaldehyde-induced fluorescence of dopamine interneurons and in slow inhibitory post-synaptic potentials of the rabbit superior cervical ganglion, induced by stimulation of the preganglionic nerve or by a muscarinic agent. *J. Physiol. (Lond.),* 237:635–662.

Lincoln, D. W. (1967): Unit activity in the hypothalamus, septum, and preoptic area of the rat: Characteristics of spontaneous activity and the effect of oestrogen. *J. Endocrinol.*, 37:127–189.

Lincoln, D. W., and Wakerley, J. B. (1972): Accelerated discharge of paraventricular neurosecretory cells correlated with reflex release of oxytocin during suckling. *J. Physiol. (Lond.),* 222:23–24 P.

Lindvall, O., and Björklund, A. (1974): The organization of the ascending catecholamine neuron systems in the rat brain as revealed by the glyoxylic acid fluorescence method. *Acta Physiol. Scand. [Suppl.* 412], 1974.

Linseman, M. A., and Olds, J. (1973): Activity changes in rat hypothalamus, preoptic area and striatum associated with Pavlovian conditioning. *J. Neurophysiol.*, 36: 1038–1050.

Lisk, R. D. (1968): Copulatory activity of the male rat following placement of preoptic-anterior hypothalamic lesions. *Exp. Brain Res.*, 5:306–313.

Loomer, H. P., Saunders, J. C., and Kline, N. S. (1957): A clinical and pharmacodynamic evaluation of iproniazid as a psychic energizer. *Psychiatr. Res. Rep. Am. Psychiatr. Assoc.*, 8:129–141.

Magour, S., Cooper, H., and Faehndrich, Ch. (1974): The effect of chronic treatment with d-amphetamine on food intake, body weight, locomotor activity and subcellular distribution of drug in rat brain. *Psychopharmacologia,* 34:45–54.

Malmo, R. B. (1961): Slowing of heart rate following septal self-stimulation in rats. *Science,* 133:1128–1130.

Margules, D. L. (1969): Noradrenergic synapses for the suppression of feeding behavior. *Life Sci.*, 8:693–704.

Margules, D. L. (1970a): Alpha-adrenergic receptors in hypothalamus for the suppression of feeding behavior by satiety. *J. Comp. Physiol. Psychol.*, 73:1–12.

Margules, D. L. (1970b): Beta-adrenergic receptors in the hypothalamus for learned and unlearned taste aversions. *J. Comp. Physiol. Psychol.*, 73:13–21.

Margules, D. L., and Olds, J. (1962): Identical "feeding" and "rewarding" systems in the lateral hypothalamus of rats. *Science*, 135:374–375.

Mark, V. H., and Ervin, F. R. (1970): *Violence and the Brain.* Harper & Row, New York.

Marshall, J. F., and Teitelbaum, P. (1973): A comparison of the eating in response to hypothermic and glucoprivic challenges after nigral 6-hydroxydopamine and lateral hypothalamic electrolytic lesions in rats. *Brain Res.*, 55:229–233.

Marshall, J. F., and Teitelbaum, P. (1974): Further analysis of sensory inattention following lateral hypothalamic damage in rats. *J. Comp. Physiol. Psychol.*, 86:375–395.

McKenzie, G. M. (1972): Role of the tuberculum olfactorium in stereotyped behavior induced by apomorphine in the rat. *Psychopharmacologia*, 23:212–220.

Melzak, R., and Wall, P. D. (1965): Pain mechanisms: A new theory. *Science*, 150:971–979.

Mendelson, J. (1966): Role of hunger in T-maze learning for food by rats. *J. Comp. Physiol. Psychol.*, 62:341–349.

Mendelson, J. (1967): Lateral hypothalamic stimulation in satiated rats: The rewarding effects of self-induced drinking. *Science*, 157:1077–1079.

Miliaressis, E., and Cardo, B. (1973): Self-stimulation versus food reinforcement: Comparative study of two different nervous structures, the lateral hypothalamus and the ventral tegmental area of the mesencephalon. *Brain Res.*, 57:75–83.

Miller, N. E. (1957): Experiments on motivation. *Science*, 126:1271–1278.

Miller, N. E. (1960): Motivational effects of brain stimulation and drugs. *Fed. Proc.*, 19:846–854.

Miller, N. E., Bailey, C. J., and Stevenson, J. A. F. (1950): Decreased "hunger" but increased food intake resulting from hypothalamic lesions. *Science*, 112:256–259.

Millhouse, O. E. (1969): A Golgi study of the descending medial forebrain bundle. *Brain Res.*, 15:341–363.

Modianos, D. T., Flexman, J. E. and Hitt, J. C. (1973): Rostral medial forebrain bundle lesions produce decrements in masculine, but not feminine sexual behavior in spayed female rats. *Behav. Biol.*, 8:629–636.

Mogenson, G. J. (1965): An attempt to establish secondary reinforcement with rewarding brain stimulation. *Psychol. Rep.*, 16:163–167.

Mogenson, G. J., and Morgan, C. W. (1967): Effects of induced drinking on self-stimulation of the lateral hypothalamus. *Exp. Brain Res.*, 3:111–116.

Mogenson, G. J., and Stevenson, J. A. F. (1966): Drinking and self-stimulation with electrical stimulation of the lateral hypothalamus. *Physiol. Behav.*, 1:251–254.

Morgane, P. J. (1961): Medial forebrain bundle and "feeding centers" of the hypothalamus. *J. Comp. Neurol.*, 117:1–26.

Morrison, C. F. (1967): Effects of nicotine on operant behavior of rats. *Int. J. Neuropharmacol.*, 6:229–240.

Morrison, S. D., and Mayer, J. (1957): Adipsia and aphagia in rats after lateral subthalamic lesions. *Am. J. Physiol.*, 191:248–254.

Moss, R. L., Dyball, R. E. J., and Cross, B. A. (1972a): Excitation of antidromically identified neurosecretory cells of the paraventricular nucleus by oxytocin applied iontophoretically, *Exp. Neurol.*, 34:95–102.

Moss, R. L., Urban, I., and Cross, B. A. (1972b): Microelectrophoresis of cholinergic and aminergic drugs on paraventricular neurons. *Am. J. Physiol.*, 223:310–318.

Motta, M., Fraschini, F., and Martini, L. (1969): "Short" feedback mechanisms in the control of anterior pituitary function. In: *Frontiers of Neuroendocrinology*, edited by W. F. Ganong and L. Martini, pp. 211–253. Oxford University Press, New York.

Murgatroyd, D., and Hardy, J. D. (1970): Central and peripheral temperatures in behavioral thermoregulation of the rat. In: *Physiological and Behavioral Temperature Regulation*, edited by J. D. Hardy, A. P. Gagge, and J. A. J. Stolwijk. Charles C Thomas, Springfield, Illinois.

Murphy, J. T., and Renaud, L. P. (1969): Mechanisms of inhibition in the ventro-medial nucleus of the hypothalamus. *J. Neurophysiol.,* 32:85–102.

Nakajima, S., and Iwasaki, T. (1973): Dependence of the anterior olfactory area self-stimulation upon the lateral hypothalamic area. *Physiol. Behav.,* 11:827–831.

Nakamura, K., and Thoenen, H. (1972): Increased irritability: A permanent behavior change induced in the rat by intraventricular administration of 6-hydroxydopamine. *Psychopharmacologia,* 24:359–372.

Nakayama, T., Eisenman, J. S., and Hardy, J. D. (1961): Single unit activity of anterior hypothalamus during local heating. *Science,* 134:560–561.

Nakayama, T., Hammel, H. T., Hardy, J. D., and Eisenman, J. S. (1963): Thermal stimulation of electrical activity of single units of the preoptic region. *Am. J. Physiol.,* 204:1122–1126.

Neill, D. B., Boggan, W. O., and Grossman, S. P. (1974): Behavioral effects of amphetamine in rats with lesions in the corpus striatum. *J. Comp. Physiol. Psychol.,* 86:1019–1030.

Newman, B. L. (1961): Behavioral effects of electrical self-stimulation of the septal area and related structures in the rat. *J. Comp. Physiol. Psychol.,* 54:340–346.

Newman, L. M. (1972): Effects of cholinergic agonists and antagonists on self-stimulation behavior in the rat. *J. Comp. Physiol. Psychol.,* 79:394–413.

Nicoll, R. A., and Barker, J. L. (1971): Excitation of supraoptic neurosecretory cells by angiotensin II. *Nature [New Biol.],* 233:172–174,

Nobin, A., and Björklund, A. (1973): Topography of the monoamine neuron system in the human brain as revealed in fetuses. *Acta Physiol. Scand. [Suppl.],* 388:1–40.

Norgren, R., and Leonard, C. M. (1973): Ascending central gustatory pathways. *J. Comp. Neurol.,* 150:217–238.

Nymark, M. (1972): Apomorphine provoked stereotypy in the dog. *Psychophar-macologia,* 26:361–368.

Ochs, S. (1974): Systems of material transport in nerve fibers (axoplasmic transport) related to nerve function and trophic control. *Ann. N.Y. Acad. Sci.,* 228:202–223.

Olds, J. (1955): Physiological mechanisms of reward. In: *Nebraska Symposium on Motivation,* edited by M. R. Jones, pp. 73–138. University of Nebraska Press, Lincoln.

Olds, J. (1956a): A preliminary mapping of electrical reinforcing effects in the rat brain. *J. Comp. Physiol. Psychol.,* 49:281–285.

Olds, (1956b): Runway and maze behavior controlled by basomedial forebrain stimula-tion in the rat. *J. Comp. Physiol. Psychol.,* 49:507–512.

Olds, J. (1958a): Effects of hunger and male sex hormone on self-stimulation of the brain. *J. Comp. Physiol. Psychol.,* 51:320–324.

Olds, J. (1958b): Satiation effects in self-stimulation of the brain. *J. Comp. Physiol. Psychol.,* 51:675–678.

Olds, J. (1958c): Self-stimulation of the brain. *Science,* 127:315–324.

Olds, J. (1958d): Discussion. In: *CIBA Foundation Symposium on the Neurological Basis of Behavior,* edited by G. E. W. Wolstenholme and C. M. O'Connor, p. 89. Churchill, London.

Olds, J. (1962): Hypothalamic substrates of reward. *Physiol. Rev.,* 42:554–604.

Olds, J. (1964): The induction and suppression of hypothalamic self-stimulation behavior by mirco-injection of endogenous substances at the self-stimulation site. *Proceedings of the Second International Congress on Endocrinology, London, August 1964.* Excerpta Medica International Congress Series No. 83, pp. 597–605. Excerpta Medica, Amsterdam.

Olds, J., Allan, W. S., and Briese, E. (1971): Differentiation of hypothalamic drive and reward centers. *Am. J. Physiol.,* 221:368–375.

Olds, J., Killam, K. F., and Bach y Rita, P. (1956): Self-stimulation of the brain used as a screening method for tranquilizing drugs. *Science,* 124:265–266.

Olds, J., and Milner, P. (1954): Positive reinforcement produced by electrical stimula-tion of septal area and other regions of rat brain. *J. Comp. Physiol. Psychol.,* 47:419–427.

Olds, J., and Olds, M. E. (1964): The mechanisms of voluntary behavior. In: *The Role of Pleasure in Behavior,* edited by R. G. Heath, pp. 23–53. Hoeber, New York.

Olds, J., and Peretz, B. (1960): A motivational analysis of the reticular activating system. *Electroencephalogr. Clin. Neurophysiol.*, 12:445–454.

Olds, J., and Sinclair, J. C. (1957): Self-stimulation in the obstruction box. *Am. Psychol.*, 12:464 (abstr.).

Olds, J., Travis, R. P., and Schwing, R. C. (1960): Topographic organization of hypothalamic self-stimulation functions. *J. Comp. Physiol. Psychol.*, 53:23–32.

Olds, J., Yuwiler, A., Olds, M. E., and Yun, C. (1964): Neurohumors in hypothalamic substrates of reward. *Am. J. Physiol.*, 207:242–254.

Olds, M. E. (1970): Comparative effects of amphetamine, scopolamine, chlordiazepoxide, and diphenylhydantoin on operant and extinction behavior with brain stimulation and food reward. *Neuropharmacology*, 9:519–532.

Olds, M. E. (1972): Comparative effects of amphetamine, scopolamine and chlordiazepoxide on self-stimulation behavior. *Rev. Can. Biol.*, 31:25–47.

Olds, M. E. (1973): Short-term changes in the firing pattern of hypothalamic neurons during Pavlovian conditioning. *Brain Res.*, 58:95–116.

Olds, M. E. (1974): Effect of intraventricular norepinephrine on neuron activity in the medial forebrain bundle during self-stimulation behavior. *Brain Res.*, 80:461–477.

Olds, M. E. (1975): Effects of intraventricular 6-hydroxydopamine and replacement therapy with norepinephrine, dopamine, and serotonin on self-stimulation in diencephalic and mesencephalic regions in the rat. *Brain Res. (in press)*.

Olds, M. E., and Domino, E. F. (1969): Comparison of muscarinic and nicotinic cholinergic agonists on self-stimulation behavior. *J. Pharmacol. Exp. Ther.*, 166:189–204a.

Olds, M. E., and Hogberg, D. (1964): Subcortical lesions and maze retention in the rat. *Exp. Neurol.*, 10:296–304.

Olds, M. E., Hogberg, D., and Olds, J. (1964): Tranquilizer action on thalamic and midbrain escape behavior. *Am. J. Physiol.*, 206:515–520.

Olds, M. E., and Ito, M. (1973a): Noradrenergic and cholinergic action on neuronal activity during self-stimulation behavior in the rat. *Neuropharmacology*, 12:525–539.

Olds, M. E., and Ito, M. (1973b): The effects of chlordiazepoxide, chlorpromazine and pentobarbital on neuronal excitability in the medial forebrain bundle during self-stimulation behavior. *Neuropharmacology*, 12:1117–1133.

Olds, M. E., and Olds, J. (1962): Approach-escape interactions in rat brain. *Am. J. Physiol*, 203:803–810.

Olds, M. E., and Olds, J. (1963): Approach-avoidance analysis of rat diencephalon. *J. Comp. Neurol.*, 120:259–295.

Olds, M. E., and Olds, J. (1969): Effects of lesions in medial forebrain bundle on self-stimulation behavior. *Am. J. Physiol.*, 217:1253–1254.

Oltmans, G. A., and Harvey, J. A. (1972): Lateral hypothalamic syndrome and brain catecholamine levels after lesions of the nigrostriatal bundle. *Physiol. Behav.*, 8:69–78.

Oomura, Y., Ono, T., Ooyama, H., and Wayner, M. J. (1969): Glucose and osmosensitive neurones of the rat hypothalamus. *Nature (Lond.)*, 222:282–284.

Oomura, Y., Oomura, H., Yamamoto, T., and Naka, F. (1967): Reciprocal relationship of the lateral and ventromedial hypothalamus in the regulation of food intake. *Physiol. Behav.*, 2:97–115.

Palkovits, M., and Jacobowitz, D. M. (1974): Topographic atlas of catecholamine and acetylcholinesterase-containing neurons in the rat brain. II. Hindbrain (mesencephalon, rhombencephalon). *J. Comp. Neurol.*, 157:29–42.

Paxinos, G., and Bindra, D. (1972): Hypothalamic knife cuts: Effects on eating, drinking, irritability, aggression, copulation in male rat. *J. Comp. Physiol. Psychol.*, 79:219–229.

Paxinos, G., and Bindra, D. (1973): Hypothalamic and midbrain neural pathways involved in eating, drinking, irritability, aggression and copulation in rats. *J. Comp. Physiol. Psychol.*, 82:1–14.

Perez-Cruet, J., Black, W. C., and Brady, J. V. (1963): Heart rate: Differential effects of hypothalamic and septal self-stimulation. *Science*, 140:1235–1236.

Perez-Cruet, J., McIntire, R. W., and Pliskoff, S. S. (1965): Blood pressure and heart rate changes in dogs during hypothalamic self-stimulation. *J. Comp. Physiol. Psychol.*, 60:373–381.

Pfaff, D. W., and Gregory, E. (1971a): Correlation between pre-optic area unit activity and the cortical electroencephalogram: Difference between normal and castrated male rats. *Electroencephalogr. Clin. Neurophysiol.,* 31:223–230.

Pfaff, D. W., and Gregory, E. (1971b): Olfactory coding in olfactory bulb and medial forebrain bundle of normal and castrate male rats. *J. Neurophysiol.,* 34:208–216.

Phillips, A. G. (1970): Enhancement and inhibition of olfactory bulb self-stimulation by odours. *Physiol. Behav.,* 5:1127–1131.

Phillips, A. G., and Fibiger, H. C. (1973): Dopamine and noradrenergic substrates of positive reinforcement: Differential effects of *d*- and *l*-amphetamine. *Science,* 179: 575–577.

Phillips, A. G., and Mogenson, G. J. (1969): Self-stimulation of the olfactory bulb. *Physiol. Behav.,* 4:195–197.

Phillis, J. W. (1970): *The Pharmacology of Synapses.* Pergamon Press, New York.

Pickel, V. M., Segal, M., and Bloom, F. E. (1974): Axonal proliferation following lesions of cerebellar peduncles: A combined fluorescence microscopic and radio-autographic study. *J. Comp. Neurol.,* 155:43–60.

Pliskoff, S. S., Wright, J. E., and Hawkins, T. D. (1965): Brain stimulation as a reinforcer: Intermittent schedules. *J. Exp. Anal. Behav.,* 8:75–88.

Porter, R. W., Conrad, D. G., and Brady, J. V. (1959): Some neural and behavioral correlates of electrical self-stimulation of the limbic system. *J. Exp. Anal. Behav.,* 2:43–55.

Poschel, B. P. H. (1963): Is centrally-elicited positive reinforcement associated with onset or termination of stimulation? *J. Comp. Physiol. Psychol.,* 56:604–607.

Poschel, B. P. H. (1968): Do biological reinforcers act via the self-stimulation areas of the brain? *Physiol. Behav.,* 3:53–60.

Poschel, B. P. H., and Ninteman, F. W. (1964): Excitatory (antidepressant) effects of monoamine oxidase inhibitors on the reward system of the brain. *Life Sci.,* 3:903–910.

Poschel, B. P. H., and Ninteman, F. W. (1966): Hypothalamic self-stimulation: Its suppression by blockade of norepinephrine biosynthesis and reinstatement by meta-amphetamine. *Life Sci.,* 5:11–16.

Poschel, B. P. H., and Ninteman, F. W. (1968): Excitatory effects of 5-HTP on intracranial self-stimulation following MAO blockade. *Life Sci.,* 7:317–323.

Poschel, B. P. H., and Ninteman, F. W. (1971): Intracranial reward and the forebrain's serotonergic mechanism: Studies employing para-chlorophenylalanine and para-chloroamphetamine. *Physiol. Behav.,* 7:39–46.

Powley, T. L., and Keesey, R. E. (1970): Relationship of body weight to the lateral hypothalamic feeding syndrome. *J. Comp. Physiol. Psychol.,* 70:25–36.

Prescott, R. G. W. (1966): Estrous cycle in the rat: Effects on self-stimulation behavior. *Science,* 152:796–797.

Randrup, A., and Munkvad, I. (1970): Biochemical, anatomical and psychological investigations of stereotyped behavior induced by amphetamines. In: *Amphetamines and Related Compounds,* edited by E. Costa and S. Garattini, pp. 695–713. Raven Press, New York.

Reid, L. D., Hunsicker, J. P., Lindsay, J. L., Gallistel, C. L., and Kent, E. W. (1973): Incidence and magnitude of the "priming effect" in self-stimulating rats. *J. Comp. Physiol. Psychol.,* 82:286–293.

Reynolds, R. W. (1958): The relationship between stimulation voltage and hypothalamic self-stimulation in the rat. *J. Comp. Physiol. Psychol.,* 51:193–198.

Ritter, S., and Stein, L. (1973): Self-stimulation of noradrenergic cell group (A6) in locus coeruleus of rats. *J. Comp. Physiol. Psychol.,* 85:443–452.

Roberts, W. W. (1958): Rapid escape learning without avoidance learning motivated by hypothalamic stimulation in cats. *J. Comp. Physiol. Psychol.,* 51:391–399.

Roll, S. K. (1970): Intracranial self-stimulation and wakefulness: Effects of manipulating ambient brain catecholamines. *Science,* 168:1370–1372.

Rolls, B. J., and Rolls, E. T. (1973a): Effects of lesions in the basolateral amygdala on fluid intake in the rat. *J. Comp. Physiol. Psychol.,* 83:240–247.

Rolls, E. T. (1971a): Contrasting effects of hypothalamic and nucleus accumbens septi self-stimulation on brain stem single unit activity and cortical arousal. *Brain Res.*, 31:275–285.

Rolls, E. T. (1972): Activation of amygdaloid neurons in reward, eating and drinking elicited by electrical stimulation of the brain. *Brain Res.*, 82:15–22.

Rolls, E. T. (1973): Refractory periods of neurons directly excited in stimulus-bound eating and drinking in the rat. *J. Comp. Physiol. Psychol.*, 82:15–22.

Rolls, E. T., and Rolls, B. J. (1973b): Altered food preferences after lesions in the basolateral region of the amygdala in the rat. *J. Comp. Physiol. Psychol.*, 83:248–259.

Rose, M. D. (1974): Pain reducing properties of rewarding electrical brain stimulation in the rat. *J. Comp. Physiol. Psychol.*, 87:607–617.

Rostrosen, J., Wallach, M. B., Angrist, B., and Gershon, S. (1972): Antagonism of apomorphine-induced stereotypy and emesis in dogs by thioridazine, haloperidol and pimozide. *Psychopharmacologia*, 26:185–194.

Roth, S. R., Schwartz, M., and Teitelbaum, P. (1973): Failure of recovered lateral hypothalamic rats to learn specific food aversions. *J. Comp. Physiol. Psychol.*, 83:184–197.

Routtenberg, A. (1971): Forebrain pathways of reward in Rattus norvegicus. *J. Comp. Physiol. Psychol.*, 75:200–276.

Routtenberg, A., and Huang, Y. H. (1968): Reticular formation and brainstem unitary activity: Effects of posterior hypothalamic and septal-limbic stimulation at reward loci. *Physiol. Behav.*, 3:611–617.

Routtenberg, A., and Lindy, J. (1965): Effects of the availability of rewarding septal and hypothalamic stimulation on bar pressing for food under conditions of deprivation. *J. Comp. Physiol. Psychol.*, 60:158–161.

Routtenberg, A., and Malsbury, C. (1969): Brainstem pathways of reward. *J. Comp. Physiol. Psychol.*, 68:22–30.

Routtenberg, A., and Olds, J. (1963): Attenuation of response to an aversive brain stimulus by concurrent rewarding septal stimulation. *Fed. Proc.*, 22:515 (abstr.).

Routtenberg, A., and Sloan, M. (1974): Self-stimulation in the frontal cortex of Rattus norvegicus. *Behav. Biol.*, 7:564–572.

Ruf, K., and Steiner, F. A. (1967): Steroid-sensitive single neurons in rat hypothalamus and midbrain: Identification by microelectrophoresis. *Science*, 156:667–669.

Satinoff, E., and Rutstein, J. (1970): Behavioral thermoregulation in rats with anterior hypothalamic lesions. *J. Comp. Physiol. Psychol.*, 71:77–82.

Satinoff, E., and Shan, S. Y. Y. (1971): Loss of behavioral thermoregulation after lateral hypothalamic lesions in rats. *J. Comp. Physiol. Psychol.*, 77:302–312.

Sawyer, C. H., Kawakami, M., Meyerson, B., Whitmoyer, D. I., and Lilley, J. J. (1968): ACTH, dexmethasone and asphyxia on electrical activity of the rat hypothalamus. *Brain Res.*, 10:213–226.

Scheel-Kruger, J. (1972): Behavioural and biochemical comparison of amphetamine derivatives, cocaine, benztropine and tricyclic anti-depressant drugs. *Eur. J. Pharmacol.*, 18:63–73.

Schwartz, M., and Teitelbaum, P. (1974): Dissociation between learning and remembering in rats with lesions in the lateral hypothalamus. *J. Comp. Physiol. Psychol.*, 87:384–398.

Schwartzbaum, J. S. (1965): Discrimination behavior after amygdalectomy in monkeys: Visual and somesthetic learning and perceptual capacity. *J. Comp. Physiol. Psychol.*, 60:314–319.

Sclafani, A., Berner, C. N., and Maul, G. (1973): Feeding and drinking pathways between medial and lateral hypothalamus in the rat. *J. Comp. Physiol. Psychol.*, 85:29–51.

Scott, J. W. (1967): Brain stimulation reinforcement with distributed practice: Effects of electrode locus, previous experience, and stimulus intensity. *J. Comp. Physiol. Psychol.*, 63:175–183.

Scott, J. W., and Pfaffman, C. (1967): Olfactory input to the hypothalamus: Electrophysiological evidence. *Science*, 158:1592–1594.

Segal, M., and Bloom, F. (1974): The action of norepinephrine in the rat hippocampus. I. Iontophoretic studies. *Brain Res.,* 72:79–97.

Sem-Jacobsen, C. W. (1968): *Depth-Electrographic Stimulation of the Human Brain and Behavior.* Charles C Thomas, Springfield, Illinois.

Shepherd, M., Lader, M., and Rodknight, R. (1968): *Clinical Psychopharmacology.* Lea & Febiger, Philadelphia.

Sidman, M., Brady, J. V., Boren, J. J., Conrad, D., and Schulman, A. (1955): Reward schedules and behavior maintained by intracranial self-stimulation. *Science,* 122:830–831.

Siggins, G. R., Hoffer, B. J., and Bloom, F. E. (1969): Cyclic adenosine monophosphate: Possible mediator for norepinephrine effects on cerebellar Purkinje cells. *Science,* 165:1018–1020.

Simpson, B. A., and Iverson, S. D. (1971): Effects of substantia nigra lesions on the locomotor and stereotyped responses to amphetamine. *Nature (Lond.),* 230:30–32.

Simpson, J. B., and Routtenberg, A. (1973): Subfornical organ: Site of drinking elicitation by angiotenson II. *Science,* 181:1172–1175.

Singer, J. J. (1968): Hypothalamic control of male and female sexual behavior in female rats. *J. Comp. Physiol. Psychol.,* 66:738–742.

Singh, D. (1973): Effects of preoperative training on food-motivated behavior of hypothalamic hyperphagic rats. *J. Comp. Physiol. Psychol.,* 84:38–46.

Skinner, B. F. (1938): *The Behavior of Organisms.* Appleton-Century-Crofts, New York.

Skinner, B. F. (1948): "Superstition" in the pigeon. *J. Exp. Psychol.,* 38:168–172.

Snyder, S. H. (1972): Catecholamines in the brain as mediators of amphetamine psychosis. *Arch. Gen. Psychiatry,* 27:169–179.

Snyder, S. H. (1974): Catecholamines as mediators of drug effects in schizophrenia. In: *The Neurosciences, Third Study Program,* edited by F. O. Schmitt and F. G. Worden, pp. 721–732. MIT Press, Cambridge, Massachusetts.

Spear, N. E. (1962): Comparison of the reinforcing effect of brain stimulation on Skinner box, runway, and maze performance. *J. Comp. Physiol. Psychol.,* 55:679–684.

Spies, G. (1965): Food versus intracranial self-stimulation reinforcement in food deprived rats. *J. Comp. Physiol. Psychol.,* 60:153–157.

Stark, P., and Boyd, E. S. (1963). Effects of cholinergic drugs on hypothalamic self-stimulation response rates of dogs. *Am. J. Physiol.,* 205:745–784.

Stark, P., Boyd, E. S., and Fuller, W. R. (1964): A possible role of serotonin in hypothalamic self-stimulation in dogs. *J. Pharmacol. Exp. Ther.,* 146:147–153.

Stark, P., Fuller, R. W., Hartley, L. W., Schaffer, R. J., and Turk, J. A. (1970): Dissociation of the effects of p-chlorophenylalanine on self-stimulation and on brain serotonin. *Life Sci.,* 9:41–48.

Stein, L. (1958): Secondary reinforcement established with subcortical stimulation. *Science,* 127:466–467.

Stein, L. (1964a): Amphetamine and neural reward mechanisms. In: *Ciba Foundation Symposium on Animal Behavior and Drug Action,* edited by H. Steinberg, A. V. S. de Reuck, and J. Knight, pp. 91–113. Churchill, London.

Stein, L. (1964b): Self-stimulation of the brain and the central stimulant action of amphetamine. *Fed. Proc.,* 23:836–850.

Stein, L. (1964c): Reciprocal action of reward and punishment mechanisms. In: *The Role of Pleasure in Behavior,* edited by R. G. Heath, pp. 113–119. Hoeber, New York.

Stein, L. (1965): Facilitation of avoidance behavior by positive brain stimulation. *J. Comp. Physiol. Psychol.,* 60:9–19.

Stein, L. (1966): Psychopharmacological aspects of mental depression. *Can. Psychiatr. Assoc. J.,* 11:34–49.

Stein, L. (1968): Chemistry of reward and punishment. In: *Psychopharmacology: A Review of Progress 1957–1967,* Public Health Service Publication No. 1836, edited by D. H. Efron, pp. 105–123. U.S. Government Printing Office, Washington, D.C.

Steiner, S. S., Beer, B., and Shaffer, M. M. (1969): Escape from self-produced rates of brain stimulation. *Science,* 163:90–91.

Steiner, S. S., Bodnar, R. J., Ackerman, R. F., and Ellman, S. J. (1973): Escape from rewarding brain stimulation of dorsal brainstem and hypothalamus. *Physiol. Behav.,* 11:589–591.

Steiner, S. S., and Ellman, S. J. (1972): Relation between REM sleep and intra-cranial self-stimulation. *Science,* 177:1122–1124.

Stinus, L., and Thierry, A.-M. (1973): Self-stimulation and catecholamines. II. Block-ade of self-stimulation by treatment with alpha-methylparatyrosine and the reinstate-ment by catecholamine precursor administration. *Brain Res.,* 64:189–198.

Stricker, E. M., and Zigmond, M. J. (1974): Effects on homeostasis of intraventricular injections of 6-hydroxydopamine in rats. *J. Comp. Physiol. Psychol.,* 86:973–994.

Svensson, T. H. (1971): Functional and biochemical effects of a d- and l-amphetamine on central catecholamine neurons. *Naunyn Schmiedebergs Arch. Pharmalcol.,* 271:170–180.

Taylor, K. M., and Snyder, S. H. (1970): Amphetamine: Differentiation by d- and l-isomers of animal behavior involving central norepinephrine or dopamine. *Science,* 168:1487–1489.

Taylor, K. M., and Snyder, S. H. (1971): Differential effects of *d-* and *l*-amphetamine on behavior and on catecholamine disposition in dopamine and norepinephrine con-taining neurons of rat brain. *Brain Res.,* 28:295–309.

Teitelbaum, P. (1955): Sensory control of hypothalamic hyperphagia. *J. Comp. Physiol. Psychol.,* 48:156–166.

Teitelbaum, P. (1971): The encephalization of hunger. In: *Progress in Physiological Psychology, Vol. 4,* edited by E. Stellar and J. H. Sprague, pp. 319–350. Academic Press, New York.

Teitelbaum, P., and Cytawa, J. (1965): Spreading depression and recovery from lateral hypothalamic damage. *Science,* 147:61–63.

Teitelbaum, P., and Epstein, A. N. (1962): The lateral hypothalamic syndrome: Re-covery of feeding and drinking after lateral hypothalamic lesions. *Psychol. Rev.,* 69:74–90.

Tenen, S. S. (1967): The effects of p-chlorophenylalanine, a serotonin depletor on avoidance acquisition, pain sensitivity, and related behavior in the rat. *Psychophar-macologia,* 10:204–219.

Terman, M., and Terman, J. S. (1970): Circadian rhythm of brain self-stimulation behavior. *Science,* 168:1242–1244.

Trendelenburg, U. (1959): The supersensitivity caused by cocaine. *J. Pharmacol. Exp. Ther.,* 125:55–65.

Trowill, J. A., and Hynek, K. (1970): Secondary reinforcement based on primary brain stimulation reward. *Psychol. Rep.,* 27:715–718.

Ungerstedt, U. (1970): Is interruption of the nigro-striatal system producing the "lateral hypothalamus syndrome?" *Acta Physiol. Scand.,* 80:35A–36A.

Ungerstedt, U. (1971a): Aphagia and adipsia after 6-hydroxydopamine induced de-generation of the nigro-striatal dopamine system. *Acta Physiol. Scand. [Suppl. 367],* 95–122.

Ungerstedt, U. (1971b): Postsynaptic supersensitivity after 6-hydroxydopamine induced degeneration of the nigro-striatal dopamine system. *Acta Physiol. Scand., [Suppl. 367],* 69–93.

Ungerstedt, U. (1971c): Stereotaxic mapping of the monoamine pathways in the rat brain. *Acta Physiol. Scand. [Suppl. 367],* 1–48.

Ungerstedt, U. (1974a): Brain dopamine neurons and behavior. In: *The Neurosciences, Third Study Program,* edited by F. O. Schmitt and F. G. Worden, pp. 695–704. MIT Press, Cambridge, Massachusetts.

Ungerstedt, U. (1974b): Functional dynamics of central monoamine pathways. In: *The Neurosciences, Third Study Program,* edited by F. O. Schmitt and F. G. Worden, pp. 979–988. MIT Press, Cambridge, Massachusetts.

Uretsky, N. J., and Iverson, L. L. (1970): Effects of 6-hydroxydopamine on cate-cholamine containing neurones in the rat brain. *J. Neurochem.,* 17:269–278.

Ursin, R., Ursin, H., and Olds, J. (1966): Self-stimulation of hippocampus in rats. *J. Comp. Physiol. Psychol.,* 61:353–359.

Valenstein, E. S. (1965): Independence of approach and escape reactions to electrical stimulation of the brain. *J. Comp. Physiol. Psychol.,* 60:20–30.

Valenstein, E. S. (1973*b*): Commentary. In: *Brain Stimulation and Motivation,* edited by E. S. Valenstein, pp. 162–172. Scott, Foresman, Glenview, Illinois.

Valenstein, E. S., and Beer, B. (1964): Continuous opportunity for reinforcing brain stimulation. *J. Exp. Anal. Behav.,* 7:183–184.

Valenstein, E. S., and Campbell, J. F. (1966): Medial forebrain bundle lateral hypothalamic area and reinforcing brain stimulation. *Am. J. Physiol.,* 210:270–274.

Valenstein, E. S., Cox, V. C., and Kakolewski, J. W. (1968): Modification of motivated behavior elicited by electrical stimulation of the hypothalamus. *Science,* 157:552–554.

Valenstein, E. S., Cox, V. C., and Kakolewski, J. W. (1970): Reexamination of the role of the hypothalamus in motivation. *Psychol. Rev.,* 77:16–31.

Van Atta, L., and Sutin, J. (1971): The response of single lateral hypothalamic neurons to ventromedial nucleus and limbic stimulation. *Physiol. Behav.,* 6:523–536.

Van Delft, A. M. L., and Kitay, J. I. (1972): Effect of ACTH on single unit activity in the diencephalon of intact and hypophysectomized rats. *Neuroendocrinology,* 9:188–196.

Villablanca, J. (1974): Presentation of films of kittens and cats with bilateral ablations of the caudate nuclei. Conference on Brain Mechanisms in Mental Retardation, Oxnard, California, January 1974. Jointly sponsored by NICHHD, NIH, and Mental Retardation Research Center, University of California, Los Angeles.

Vincent, J. D., Arnauld, E., and Bioulac, B. (1972): Activity of osmosensitive single cells in the hypothalamus of behaving monkey during drinking. *Brain Res.,* 44:371–384.

Vincent, J. D., and Hayward, J. N. (1970): Activity of single cells in osmoreceptor-supraoptic nuclear complex in the hypothalamus of the waking rhesus monkey. *Brain Res.,* 23:105–108.

Wampler, R. S. (1973): Increased motivation in rats with ventromedial hypothalamic lesions. *J. Comp. Physiol. Psychol.,* 84:268–274.

Ward, H. P. (1959): Stimulus factors in septal self-stimulation. *Am. J. Physiol.,* 196:779–782.

Ward, H. P. (1960): Basal tegmental self-stimulation after septal ablation in rats. *Arch. Neurol.,* 3:158–162.

Ward, H. P. (1961): Tegmental self-stimulation after amygdaloid ablation. *Arch. Neurol.,* 4:657–659.

Weiskrantz, L. (1956): Behavioral changes associated with ablation of the amygdaloid complex in monkeys. *J. Comp. Physiol. Psychol.,* 49:381–391.

Wetzel, M. C. (1963): Self-stimulation aftereffects and runway performance in the rat. *J. Comp. Physiol. Psychol.,* 56:673–678.

Wetzel, M. C. (1968): Self-stimulation anatomy: Data needs. *Brain Res.,* 10:287–296.

Wetzel, M. C., Howell, L. G., and Bearie, K. J. (1969): Experimental performance of steel and platinum electrodes with chronic monophasic stimulation of the brain. *J. Neurosurg.,* 31:658–669.

Wheatley, M. D. (1944): The hypothalamus and affective behavior in cats: A study of the effects of experimental lesions with anatomical correlations. *Arch. Neurol. Psychiatry,* 52:296–316.

Wilkinson, H. A., and Peele, T. L. (1962): Modification of intracranial self-stimulation by hunger satiety. *Am. J. Physiol.,* 203:537–540.

Winokur, A., and Utiger, R. D. (1974): Thyrotropin-releasing hormone: Regional distribution in rat brain. *Science,* 185:265–267.

Wise, C. D., Berger, B. D., and Stein, L. (1973): Evidence of alpha-noradrenergic reward receptors and serotonergic punishment receptors in the rat brain. *Biol. Psychiatry,* 6:3–21.

Wise, C. D., and Stein, L. (1969): Facilitation of brain self-stimulation by central administration of norepinephrine. *Science,* 163:299–301.

Wit, A., and Wang, S. C. (1968): Temperature-sensitive neurons in preoptic/anterior hypothalamic region: Effects of increasing ambient temperature. *Am. J. Physiol.,* 215:1151–1159.

Wolf, G. (1964): Effect of dorsolateral hypothalamic lesions on sodium appetite elicited by deoxycorticosterone and by acute hyponatremia. *J. Comp. Physiol Psychol.*, 58:396–402.

Wurtz, R. H., and Olds, J. (1963): Amygdaloid stimulation and operant reinforcement in the rat. *J. Comp. Physiol. Psychol.*, 56:941–949.

Wyrwicka, W., and Dobrzecka, C. (1960): Relationship between feeding and satiation centers of the hypothalamus. *Science,* 132:805–806.

Yunger, L. M., and Harvey, J. A. (1973): Effect of lesions in the medial forebrain bundle on three measures of pain sensitivity and noise-elicited startle. *J. Comp. Physiol. Psychol.*, 83:173–183.

Biological Foundations of Psychiatry,
edited by R. G. Grenell and S. Gabay.
Raven Press, New York © 1976.

Recent Advances in the Psychophysiology of Sleep and Their Psychiatric Significance

Ismet Karacan, A. Michael Anch, and Robert L. Williams

Sleep Laboratories, Department of Psychiatry, Baylor College of Medicine, Houston, Texas 77025
and Veterans Administration Hospital, Houston, Texas 77211

I. INTRODUCTION

The scientific study of the psychophysiology of sleep has been viewed as especially relevant to the concerns of psychiatry throughout much of its relatively short history. The field can be considered to have begun with Berger's (1929) construction of the electroencephalograph (EEG), and the subsequent use of the machine by Loomis, Harvey, and Hobart (1935) in the study of brain waves during sleep. There followed a relative hiatus in research activity (a notable exception being the study of depressed patients by Diaz-Guerrero, Gottlieb, and Knott in 1946), one lasting until 1953, when Aserinsky and Kleitman's discovery of rapid eye movement (REM) sleep, as monitored by the electrooculogram (EOG), launched a period of accelerating productivity which continues to this day. Aserinsky and Kleitman's work prompted this second birth for one major reason: in it and in other work shortly thereafter (Aserinsky and Kleitman, 1955; Dement and Kleitman, 1957b), it was determined that REM sleep is the state during which dreaming is reported most frequently.

It was precisely because this discovery provided a thoroughly respectable and, more important, scientific tool for the study of dreams that it generated so much excitement among both psychiatrists and researchers from other disciplines. In retrospect, we realize that the recognition of REM sleep as a distinctive state of consciousness had even more important implications for study of the nature and function of sleep, but at the time it was the implications for the study of dreams which captured the imagination and interest of many investigators and transformed them into those bleary-eyed scientists, sleep researchers.

Much of the research stimulated by the initial work on REM sleep and dreams reflected the belief that at last there existed a method for unravelling in an objective fashion some of the long-standing mysteries surrounding psychiatric illness. One question which soon received attention was whether the hallucinations of the schizophrenic are waking dreams. Another was the nature of the sleep disturbances of depressed patients and the significance of these disturbances to the affective disorder itself. Although research on these and other similar questions began with at least the implicit expectation of rapid and significant discoveries, it gradually became clear that in this area, as in many others, the research questions were far too complex for the attainment of any final answers within the near future. And, although there has accumulated a certain amount of important information concerning sleep and psychiatric illness, there are still only partial answers to many of the most intriguing questions in this area.

At present, the attitude among psychiatrically oriented sleep researchers reflects this reality. Work during the last 15 years has made it evident that an understanding of the sleep process itself can come only from a multidisciplinary approach to the problem. And an understanding of the aspects of sleep, or sleep disturbance, relevant to psychiatry must likewise result from contributions from many scientific disciplines. It is realized that progress in these areas will come very slowly.

In this chapter we survey the current knowledge derived from the study of sleep, with the objective of allowing the reader fully to appreciate what is known about sleep disorders associated with schizophrenia and depression. Elsewhere (Karacan, Salis, and Williams, 1973) we have reviewed data concerning a wide variety of sleep disorders, including primary insomnia, narcolepsy, and chronic hypersomnia. We restrict our discussion here to the data concerning the sleep disturbances characteristic of schizophrenia and depression because these conditions represent two of the major psychiatric disorders in which sleep disturbance is an important part of the clinical picture. Implicit in our organization of this material is the understanding that sleep is a state of the entire organism. As such, it has many interdependent manifestations—biochemical, electrophysiological, neuroendocrinological, electroencephalographic, physiological, and psychological. In order to set the stage, we first discuss sleep from the point of view of three distinct time perspectives—a typical night of sleep, typical daily variations in sleep-wakefulness, and typical lifetime changes in sleep patterns. It is obvious that our primary concern in this review is human sleep. The emphasis in this section is on the normal EEG-EOG aspects of sleep, reflecting the fact that presently the EEG-EOG is the most understood and reliable indicator of human sleep. From our standpoint, the EEG-EOG is the defining parameter of sleep in humans.

In the next section we discuss the neurophysiological and neurochemical manifestations of sleep. Because it is assumed that these manifestations are basic to the onset and maintenance of sleep, they are considered under the rubric of sleep mechanisms. The next section is concerned with the other major manifestations or correlates of sleep—psychological, physiological, and neuroendocrinological.

After this discussion of basic data, we briefly review several current theories of the function or functions of sleep. With this background, the reader is then in a position to evaluate the data we summarize on sleep and the psychiatric illnesses of schizophrenia and depression. Our last section is devoted to a brief consideration of the treatment of sleep disorders. Throughout this chapter our intention is to present a representative sample of the work done in each of these areas of research and thought.

II. CHARACTERISTICS OF SLEEP

A. Electroencephalographic, Circadian, and Ontogenetic Aspects

Sleep can be examined from at least three time perspectives—changes within a night of sleep, changes within the wider context of circadian and other biological rhythms, and changes throughout the natural lifetime. In this section we describe and discuss the highlights of normal sleep from these three perspectives.

1. A Normal Night of Sleep

A normal night of sleep consists of periodic oscillations among wakefulness and the five stages of EEG-EOG sleep. In their pioneering study, Loomis et al. (1935) described five types of activity characteristic of the sleep EEG (types A through E). The sleep EEG-EOG scoring system more recently elaborated by Dement and Kleitman (1957a) was based on that of Loomis and his associates, but was expanded to include criteria for scoring REM sleep. It, in turn, has provided the basis for most current scoring systems (Williams, Agnew, and Webb, 1964; Rechtschaffen and Kales, 1968; Agnew and Webb, 1972). In these systems, the six EEG-EOG stages are stages 0 or W through 4. Stage 0 is the awake state. Stage 1 sleep is characterized by a "flat" EEG (low amplitude and mixed frequency); stage 2 by 14 to 16 cps spindles and isolated large amplitude sharp waves known as K-complexes; and stages 3 and 4 by high voltage, slow frequency delta (1 to 4 cps) activity. Stage 1 sleep accompanied by REMs in EOG channels is defined as stage 1 REM sleep. Stage 1 without REMs and stages 2 through 4 are collectively called non-REM (NREM) sleep.

The progression through these six stages during a typical night of sleep is illustrated in Fig. 1. After a short period awake, the sleeper descends slowly through stages 1, 2, and 3 to stage 4 sleep, which is considered to be the deepest stage of sleep. This initial stage 4 episode is followed by the first REM period of the night, approximately 80 to 100 min after sleep onset. The interval from sleep onset through the first REM period is called the first sleep cycle. A brief awakening may interrupt sleep before the next sleep cycle begins. The remainder of the night consists of successive sleep cycles more or less similar to the first. However, during later sleep cycles the time spent in stages 3 and 4 may decrease and even be zero, while REM time may increase. An average of four or five of these 85 to 110-min sleep cycles occurs during a typical night of sleep in adults (Williams, Karacan, and Hursch, 1974).

Extensive study of healthy subjects has shown that under normal conditions a given individual displays a rather consistent sleep pattern on succes-

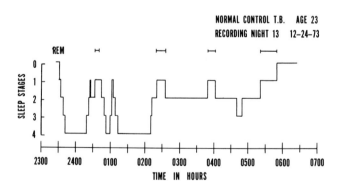

FIG. 1. Schematic diagram of a typical night of sleep in a healthy 23-year-old male. Stages 0–4 are indicated on the ordinate. REM periods are represented by the bars at the top of the figure. The abscissa represents clock time in hours.

sive nights. And, although there are differences in the sleep characteristics of normal individuals which depend on age, persons within the same general age range display roughly similar sleep patterns, all other things being equal (Williams et al., 1974). In most normal individuals, slow-wave sleep (stages 3 and 4) predominates during the first third of the night, whereas REM sleep predominates during the last third (Williams et al., 1964; Williams, Agnew, and Webb, 1966; Agnew, Webb, and Williams, 1967; Kohler, Coddington, and Agnew, 1968; Ross, Agnew, Williams, and Webb, 1968; Williams, Karacan, Hursch, and Davis, 1972a; Williams, Karacan, Thornby, and Salis, 1972b). However, in individuals of middle age or older, decreases in slow-wave sleep may result in a less striking concentration of REM during the last part of the night (Agnew et al., 1967; Williams et al., 1972b). Stages 1 REM and 4 sleep are considered to be particularly important aspects of sleep because normal subjects who are deprived of them by experimental means exhibit compensatory increases in these stages on recovery sleep nights (Dement, 1960; Agnew, Webb, and Williams, 1964). A number of early studies (Dement, 1960; Dement and Fisher, 1963; Sampson, 1966; Williams, Agnew, and Webb, 1967) suggested that deprivation of REM and stage 4 sleep produces certain psychological disturbances in normal subjects. However, these results have not been uniformly substantiated by other studies (Kales, Hoedemaker, Jacobson, and Lichtenstein, 1964; Dement, 1964a; 1966), and there remains some question as to their validity.

It has become a convention to describe EEG-EOG sleep patterns in terms of a number of standard parameters. Among these are time in bed (time from "lights out" to arising); sleep period time (time from sleep onset to final awakening); total sleep time (sleep period time less time awake); sleep latency (time from "lights out" to sleep onset); sleep efficiency (ratio of total sleep time to time in bed); number of awakenings; number of stages or stage shifts; average REM period length; average time between REM periods; number of REM periods; percentages of stages, computed in relation to either total sleep time or sleep period time; and latencies to each of the stages from sleep onset. It will be noticed that most of these parameters describe the total night of sleep in a static fashion, and only a few of them (REM period length, NREM time between REM periods) suggest the cyclical nature of sleep within the night. Many sleep researchers are presently attempting to devise descriptors of the dynamic aspects of a typical night of sleep.

In any case, given that normal values for each of these standard parameters exist, then one method of defining disturbed *EEG-EOG* sleep is in terms of significant deviations from the normal values. Unfortunately, very little work has been done by sleep researchers to determine whether disturbed EEG-EOG sleep bears any necessary relation to disturbed sleep as perceived by the individual sleeper. It is rather commonly assumed that disturbances such as gross deficiencies in REM or slow-wave sleep, or elevated numbers of awakenings or numbers of stage shifts, are responsible for complaints of disturbed sleep by patients. However, this relationship between objective EEG-EOG measures and subjective reports of sleep quality has not been well documented. Furthermore, although we have some evidence (Karacan, Thornby, Booth, Okawa, Salis, Anch, and Williams, 1975b) that normal sleepers can distinguish changes in such parameters as sleep latency and total sleep time, and that reports of increased restlessness may accompany increased EEG-EOG stage shifting and numbers of EEG-EOG awakenings, there are also data indicating that patients of various sorts cannot make these distinctions as reliably (Weiss, McPartland, and Kupfer, 1973). One possible explanation of these data is that in some patients, at least, there is a defect in the normal feedback system between what happens in the brain and what is perceived by the individual. Of course, it may also be that the parameters currently in use among sleep researchers simply are not clinically significant for some patients. In this case, only future research will uncover the parameters which are more relevant.

2. Sleep and Biological Rhythms

Examination of sleep from the point of view of biological rhythms, either circadian or ultradian, is helpful in appreciating sleep phenomena as aspects of the total functioning of the individual. It is obvious that sleep is one phase of the daily variation in level of arousal. Normal human adults generally spend two-thirds of their day at various levels of wakefulness and one-third at various levels of sleep. As data presented later will indicate, and as is known to every observer of human infants and animals of other species, this pattern of sleep-wakefulness is by no means universal. The human infant has a polyphasic sleep-wakefulness pattern, and only with maturation does the individual slowly acquire the monophasic pattern characteristic of the adult.

Data concerning the distribution of sleep stages within a normal night of sleep as well as those concerning the sleep stage characteristics of various daytime naps (Maron, Rechtschaffen, and Wolpert, 1964; Webb, Agnew, and Sternthal, 1966; Webb and Agnew, 1967; Karacan, Finley, Williams, and Hursch, 1970) indicate the existence of a circadian rhythm slightly different from, but conceivably closely related to, the one described above. Specifically, all these data indicate that REM sleep has a greater tendency to occur during early morning hours, while slow-wave sleep has a greater tendency to occur during late afternoon and evening hours. Thus, the REM phase of this rhythm can be roughly estimated to be between 2 or 3 A.M. and noon, while the slow-wave sleep phase is between noon and 2 or 3 A.M. Whether or not changes in the propensity for occurrence of these two types of sleep bear any relation to changes in mood or perceived level of arousal remains to be determined.

A rhythm which has stimulated some interesting speculation is that represented by the periodic occurrence of REM during sleep. Kleitman (1967; 1969) has suggested that there exists a "basic rest-activity cycle" throughout the day and night, and that during sleep REM represents the activity portion of this approximately 90 min ultradian rhythm. Attempts (Globus, 1966; Hartmann, 1968a; 1968c) to demonstrate the existence of comparable phases in EEG-EOG activity and behavior during wakefulness have not been numerous or uniformly convincing, but this view certainly emphasizes the intriguing periodicity of REM within sleep.

Up to this point we have discussed sleep and biological rhythms with respect primarily to sleep. However, the sleep rhythm does not occur in a vacuum. Instead, it, or perhaps specific aspects of it, are clearly concomitant with phase changes in a number of other important rhythms, and sleep appears to act as a synchronizer for many physiological functions. Characteristic changes in body temperature, neuroendocrine secretion, and cardiovascular activity (discussed in more detail later) are associated specifically with the sleeping state. This association is apparently quite strong, for changes in the pattern or timing of sleep (180 degree phase shifts, partial phase shifts, changes in the length of the "day") are accompanied by changes or disturbances in the pattern or timing of the other physiological rhythms (desynchronization) (Weitzman, Goldmacher, Kripke, MacGregor, Kream, and Hellman, 1968; Aschoff, 1969; Weitzman, Kripke, Goldmacher, McGregor, and Nogeire, 1970a). As much as 2 weeks may be required for the reestablishment of the normal relationship among these various rhythms (resynchronization) following the original change in the sleep rhythm. A shift back to the original sleep pattern is followed by a much more rapid resynchronization of the physiological rhythms.

There has been some speculation that a lack of synchrony among these various rhythms can produce physical and/or psychological malaise. For example, the discomfort and disorientation associated with the changes in sleeping and other habits required by rapid changes in time zone ("jet lag") may be related to desynchronization of the sleep-dependent and sleep-independent physiological rhythms. Although the recognition of the perspective of biological rhythms is relatively new among sleep researchers, it is clear that any discussion of disturbed sleep, with its implied assumption of deviation from established normal values, must consider it. Normal sleep cannot be defined only in terms of static descriptors. Biological rhythms, among other things, introduce a certain amount of variation into any normal physiological pattern (Sollberger, 1965). Thus, a full definition of normal sleep must include a description of the normal fluctuations in the sleep rhythm. Furthermore, the variations in normal sleep introduced by the functioning of biological rhythms are conceivably very large, and therefore should temper our view that there are easily determined, clear-cut distinctions between normal and abnormal states.

In addition to these warnings, it should be emphasized that early interpretations of results of total and selective sleep deprivation studies, and particularly the attempts to relate changes in psychological state to deprivation of specific sleep stages, completely neglected the fact that changes in EEG-EOG waveforms are only part of a complex of biological changes which characterize the sleeping state. The failure to consider the effect of total or selective sleep deprivation on the functioning of all the biological aspects of sleep resulted in rather simplistic ascriptions of great psychological importance to individual sleep stages. It may be that normal amounts and patterns of the states characterized by particular sleep EEG-EOG waveforms are critical for psychological health, but there is certainly no evidence that these activities are more important than other biological aspects of sleep.

3. Ontogenetic Changes in EEG-EOG Sleep Patterns

The longest time period over which the sleep rhythm can be considered to oscillate is from the birth or even conception of the individual until his death. The ideal method of plotting the changes in sleep over this time period would, of course, consist of monitoring selected individuals throughout their lifetimes. The unfeasibility of this longitudinal approach has dictated that data concerning ontogenetic changes in sleep patterns be derived from cross-sectional studies of groups of individuals of specified ages. A number of workers have performed such studies. A majority of this work has been concentrated on the sleep patterns of young infants [see Williams et al. (1974) for a recent review of this work], a topic which has little direct relevance to the concerns of this chapter. With the exception of early studies by Roffwarg, Muzio, and Dement (1966) and Feinberg and Carlson (1968), a more recent contribution by Jovanović (1971), and the series of papers from our Florida laboratory (Williams et al., 1964; 1966; Agnew et al., 1967; Kohler et al., 1968; Ross et al., 1968; Williams et al., 1972a; Williams et al., 1972b), very little direct study of variations in sleep patterns with age has been attempted. In an effort to correct this deficit, we decided several years ago to systematically study groups of males and females between the ages of 3 and 79. One of our additional goals was to include a number of subjects in each of the selected age ranges adequate to provide reliable normative ranges for the standard nighttime EEG-EOG sleep parameters. In this section, we briefly describe some of the highlights of our results. For further details, see Williams et al. (1974).

Our subjects were 237 physically and mentally healthy individuals. At least 10 males and 10 females (10 to 13) were studied for each of the following age ranges: 3 to 5, 6 to 9, 10 to 12, 13 to 15, 16 to 19, 20 to 29, 30 to 39, 40 to 49, 50 to 59, 60 to 69, and 70 to 79. For each sex and age group, subjects were selected so that their ages were evenly spread throughout the age range and so that the average age for the group was approximately in the middle of the age range. In the laboratory, all subjects retired at their normal bedtimes and arose at their normal rising times. On days preceding laboratory nights, taking of medications, drinking of alcoholic beverages, and daytime napping were prohibited. Females, if menstruating, slept during the follicular phase of their menstrual cycle. For each subject, data from 2 successive nights following an initial adaptation night were used in the analysis.

A U-shaped function best describes the relationship between total time in bed (TIB) and age: in both sexes, it is high in childhood, lower in early adulthood, and somewhat higher again in old age. The amount of time actually spent asleep, total sleep time (TST), is also high during childhood in both sexes, and decreases gradually until young adulthood, when it stabilizes at around 6½ hr for the remainder of the time until age 79. As consideration of the changes in TIB and TST would suggest, time spent awake during the night is fairly constant through early middle-age. In our subjects it represented an average of less than 2% of the sleep period time for all male groups between the ages of 3 and 39 and all female groups between 3 and 49. During and after middle age, it rapidly increased, and in older groups there was much greater variability between subjects for this parameter than in the younger groups. These data indicate that although most older individuals spend more time in bed than most young adults and middle-aged individuals, they also spend more time awake. For this reason, their TST remains fairly similar to that of younger adults.

In early childhood (3 to 5 years), REM sleep represents 30 to 33% of the sleep period. It gradually declines to a relatively stable 22 to 28% from young adulthood on, although our oldest groups (70 to 79) displayed a slight decrease to 18 to 19%. The percentage of stage 4 sleep is relatively constant at 16 to 20% between the ages of 3 and 19. Subsequently, it gradually declines with increasing age. This decline was more pronounced in our male subjects than in our female subjects: after age 30, average percent stage 4 was consistently lower in males than in females, and in the 70 to 79-year-old groups no men had stage 4 while half of the women exhibited at least small amounts.

Figure 2 summarizes some of these changes for our male subjects. It shows the average minutes of stage 0, REM sleep and NREM sleep for each of the 11 age groups. Females exhibited similar patterns of change.

In the context of this discussion of sleep and psychiatric illness, perhaps the most relevant point to be drawn from these ontogenetic data is that a characterization of sleep as disturbed must be based on comparisons of patients' sleep to that of normal, *age-matched* controls. For example, as is discussed in more detail later, the sleep of depressed patients is notable for the deficiency in stage 4 sleep. Clinically, it is recognized that depression is an affliction primarily of the middle-aged and elderly. As we have seen, many physically and mentally healthy individuals in their middle and later years

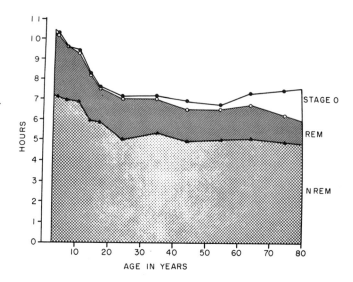

FIG. 2. Average total amount of nocturnal wakefulness (stage 0), REM, and NREM sleep for groups of healthy males between the ages of 3 and 79. See text for age-group ranges and numbers of subjects. (Reprinted by permission from Williams et al., 1974.)

also exhibit very little stage 4 sleep. Thus, unless it can be shown that the deficiency of stage 4 experienced by the depressed individual is significantly greater than that of a healthy individual of similar age, then the deficiency cannot be attributed to the disease state alone.

Another point worth noting is that quite often the EEG-EOG sleep patterns of young-adult or middle-aged individuals complaining of sleep disturbance resemble very closely those of the normal elderly. An experienced sleep EEG-EOG scorer might have great difficulty distinguishing the record of a 20-year-old depressed patient from that of an 80-year-old healthy subject. There would appear to be a common mechanism underlying the EEG-EOG manifestations of at least some disturbed sleep and the normal aging process characteristic of sleep.

B. Neurophysiological and Neurochemical Aspects: Sleep Mechanisms

A major interest of most sleep researchers is to define the basic brain mechanisms of sleep. Many researchers pursue this goal for its own intrinsic interest. However, the more clinically oriented researchers stress the importance of this information for a better understanding of sleep disturbances, because it is assumed that most sleep disturbances reflect a malfunction of normal sleep mechanisms. The traditional methods of neurophysiology (lesion and stimulation experiments) and the newer methods of neurochemistry (fluorescence microscopy and precursor loading) have begun to provide evidence of both the complexity and the specificity of the neural mechanisms controlling sleep. In this section we describe some of the current trends in these areas of research [Moruzzi (1972) and Jouvet (1972) have extensively reviewed this work recently].

1. Neurophysiological Mechanisms

One of the classic issues in sleep research has revolved around the question of whether sleep induction and maintenance mechanisms are active or passive in nature (Koella, 1973; Williams, Holloway, and Griffiths, 1973). Much early work was interpreted as indicating that sleep is a period of neural quiescence and is therefore a passive state. For example, the studies of Moruzzi and Magoun (1949) and Bremer (1954) suggested that sleep is induced and maintained by a passive shutdown in sensory systems, which is mediated by changes in the level of functioning of the reticular activating system. In Moruzzi's view (1964), sleep represents a deafferentation of the brain.

Although such a mechanism received logical support, other data indicated that an active process may also play a role in sleep induction and maintenance. For example, Hess (1933; 1944) demonstrated that electrical stimulation of various parts of the diencephalon, such as the thalamus and the massa intermedia, results in sleeping behavior in cats. This work quite clearly suggested that active inhibitory processes may underlie sleep. Studies by other investigators over the years have added weight to this view. Among other things, Jouvet (1962) found that total neodecortication of the cat is followed by a persistence and even an augmentation of the eye movements characteristic of REM sleep.

That sleep is primarily an active process receives additional support from the fact that there are electrophysiological and behavioral differences between NREM and REM sleep (Jouvet, 1961; 1963; Dement, 1971), and that two different neurophysiological systems regulate these two states. NREM sleep is primarily a cortical phenomenon, and results from cortical inhibition of the reticular activating system; for this reason it is known as telencephalic or "neo" sleep. By contrast, REM sleep appears to be actively induced and maintained by pontine mechanisms and is known as rhombencephalic sleep.

As sleep researchers have progressed in their descriptions of sleep, it has become necessary, as in so many other fields, to continually refine the descriptors of sleep in order to adequately reflect new data. Thus, the discovery of REM sleep necessitated the reconceptualization of the global state of sleep as consisting of two distinct types of sleep. As our knowledge has increased and our technology has advanced, we have been forced to make a further distinction, that between tonic and phasic events in the sleep EEG-EOG. Tonic events are those which persist throughout a given time period, providing the background characteristic of the state in question. Phasic events are short lasting, discrete events which occur only intermittently or periodically. K-complexes and 14-cps spindles are typical phasic events of NREM sleep. Phasic events of REM sleep are much more numerous, and include eye movements, cardiovascular and respiratory changes and irregularities, phasic dilations of the pupil, middle-ear muscle contractions, muscular twitches, episodes of penile tumescence, and bursts of monophasic sharp waves in pontine, geniculate, and occipital areas (PGO spike activity). The brain regions controlling tonic and phasic events would appear to be specialized anatomically and functionally. For example, tonic inhibition of muscle tone during REM sleep [measured by the electromyogram (EMG)] is suppressed by lesion of a small dorsal portion of the pontine tegmentum (Jouvet and Delorme, 1965), while medial and descending vestibular nuclei control the REMs, limb twitches, and cardiovascular irregularities characteristic of REM (Morrison and Pompeiano, 1965; Pompeiano and Morrison, 1965). PGO spikes appear to originate from a "pacemaker" located in the dorsolateral part of the pontine tegmentum (Jouvet, 1972).

If the brain activity reflected by the sleep EEG-EOG is complex, then that discovered by single unit recording is even more so. Some neurons fire faster during both REM and NREM sleep than during waking (Huttenlocher, 1961; Evarts, 1962; 1964; Bizzi, Pompeiano, and Somogyi, 1964). Within the same brain site, neurons may respond differentially during the transition between wakefulness and sleep and between NREM and REM sleep (Walsh and Cordeau, 1965; Parmeggiani and Franzini, 1970). Interactions among brain areas add to the complexity of the system. Thus, high-frequency stimulation of the nucleus of the solitary tract results in cortical EEG desynchronization, whereas low-frequency stimulation produces synchronization (Magnes, Morruzzi, and Pompeiano, 1961).

As this discussion should indicate, there is now sufficient evidence to conclude that sleep is the product of active brain processes, and that it is not simply the result of a massive neuronal shutdown. It is also clear that the activity mediating the state of sleep, as well as all its constituent states and events, is highly systematized and modulated. Future neurophysiological research can be expected to define more precisely the roles of the various brain systems in sleep events, as well as the interrelations among the systems.

2. Neurochemical Mechanisms

Although use of the methods of neurophysiology has produced significant advances in our understanding of sleep mechanisms, these methods can, in a sense, reveal only part of the story, since neuronal transmission is a chemical as well as an electrical process. Studies employing the methods of neurochemistry, some of which are still quite new, have begun to complete the story.

This research endeavor actually began early in this century when investigators such as Legendre and Piéron (1912) and Piéron (1913) presented data indicating the existence of a hypnogenic factor in cerebrospinal fluid. The search for such a factor, or a similar one in the blood, has continued to the present (Schnedorf and Ivy, 1939; Monnier, Koller, and Graber, 1963).

But the major concern of current research is the biogenic amines—substances such as serotonin, norepinephrine, dopamine, and epinephrine which are ascribed roles as neurotransmitters by most investigators. It now appears certain that the biogenic amines and acetylcholine all may play major roles in the induction and maintenance of sleep. This conclusion is derived from several types of studies. First, the use of fluorescence microscopy techniques has demonstrated that the areas shown by neurophysiological studies to be vital in the control and modulation of sleep are rich in biogenic amines (Dahlström and Fuxe, 1964; 1965; Jouvet, 1972). Most of the serotonin-containing cell bodies are located within the midline raphe nucleus of the medulla, pons, and lower midbrain. Norepinephrine-containing cell bodies are concentrated somewhat more laterally in the medullary and pontine reticular formation, and especially in the locus coeruleus complex. Dopamine-containing cell bodies are found predominantly in the substantia nigra. The terminals of all these neurons are distributed widely throughout the neocortex, hypothalamus, diencephalon, brainstem, and spinal cord.

Investigators have employed two different research strategies to explore directly the role of the biogenic amines in sleep. The first is the precursor-load strategy, and consists of administering the chemical precursor of the selected amine to the experimental subjects. It is necessitated by the fact that the amines themselves do not cross the blood-brain barrier, whereas the precursors do. The second strategy involves administration of substances which are known to interfere with one or more of the metabolic steps of the various transmitters, and is the neurochemical analogue of the lesion experiment in neurophysiology. Use of these techniques has increased greatly during the past several years and interesting data are fast accumulating. Interpretation of the results is made difficult at this stage, however, because results have often been inconsistent between studies. This is particularly the case when studies of humans are compared with those of lower animals. A further complication is the fact that many human studies have involved patients of one type or another, rather than normal subjects. In addition, it appears that results may be highly dependent on dose of drug administered, route and time of administration, and length of study [see Jouvet (1967; 1972) and Koella (1969; 1973) for recent reviews of this work].

Results from investigations of the role of serotonin in sleep provide a good example of the problems of interpretation in this area. Parachlorophenylalanine (PCPA) is a substance that blocks the synthesis of serotonin. Administration of typically high doses of PCPA to animals results in at least a temporary insomnia, characterized by reductions in both REM and NREM sleep. Only relatively low doses of PCPA have been administered to humans, and they have generally produced reductions in REM sleep and possibly compensatory increases in NREM sleep. The effects in both animals and humans can be temporarily reversed by administration of 5-hydroxytrypto-phan (5-HTP), the immediate precursor of serotonin. Administration to humans of various doses of L-tryptophan, the physiologic amino acid precursor of serotonin, has produced variable effects on REM sleep parameters, although there is a suggestion that relatively high doses increase REM time. This substance more consistently increases TST and NREM sleep. And finally, administration of 5-HTP alone has often produced an increase in REM time and a decrease in NREM sleep, but results from the several studies of this substance are particularly variable.

As many inconsistencies characterize work directed toward study of the catecholamines as serotonin, but there is enough evidence to suggest that adequate levels of catecholamines (norepinephrine and/or dopamine) are necessary for normal amounts of REM sleep, and that increases in catechol-amine levels probably reduce REM time, while decreases in catecholamine levels elevate REM time. No definitive conclusion about the role of catechol-amines in NREM sleep appears reasonable at this time.

Although there are data indicating that acetylcholine may play a role in the sleep of animals, very little work has been performed with human subjects. What work there is indicates that decreases in acetylcholine are accompanied by decreased REM time, and vice versa.

Jouvet (1972) has integrated data from animal studies into one of the most detailed explanations of the neurochemical control of sleep and wakefulness. In brief, he proposes that the onset of NREM sleep is controlled by the release of serotonin by certain serotonin-containing neurons whose cell bodies are located primarily in the anterior raphe system. Activity in different (posterior) serotonin-containing neurons in this system serves to "prime" REM sleep mechanisms by interaction with catecholamine-containing and acetylcholine-containing neurons located primarily in the locus coeruleus complex. Different portions of the locus coeruleus complex are postulated to constitute the "executive mechanisms" of the tonic and phasic aspects of REM sleep and the mechanisms of wakefulness. Dement, Zarcone, Ferguson, Cohen, Pivik, and Barchas (1969b) have emphasized a specific role for serotonin in confining PGO activity to the REM state. Hartmann (1973), in a more functional approach, has concentrated on the inverse relationship between catecholamine levels and amount of REM, and has proposed that through a feedback mechanism low levels of catecholamines trigger REM sleep.

These are only examples of the type of theorizing which now occupies certain sleep researchers. As we have felt compelled to caution repeatedly in this chapter, researchers in the various fields of sleep research, in spite of their enormous productivity, are only beginning to obtain faint glimmers of understanding of the phenomena of sleep. Because of the complexity of the events at the level at which they have chosen to make their observations, and because of the great number of variables which apparently play a role in determining sleep behavior at these levels, neurophysiologists and neurochemists have the most difficult tasks of all. We have seen that their results thus far are highly promising, but conclusions that can be drawn from the results are much less than definitive. Nevertheless, it seems certain that researchers in these areas will in the future provide insights into the nature of sleep which will significantly promote our understanding of observations from the other fields of sleep research.

C. Psychological, Physiological, and Neuroendocrinological Aspects

In spite of the fact that there is still much to learn about the regulation of sleep by the central nervous system, there is enough evidence now to indicate that the complexity of the sleep process is commensurate with the fact that sleep occupies a significant portion of the lives of most animals. It was probably an intuition of this complexity that led a number of researchers to investigate various other "systems" of the organism during sleep, in the belief that such an important process as sleep must surely involve more than the workings of the isolated nervous system. Moreover, in the absence of any definitive conclusions about the function of sleep, the wisest course in the exploration of sleep would seem to be one which progresses along a number of different avenues: premature restriction of the field of inquiry would inevitably hamper a full understanding of the process and its functions. In the present section we consider some of the data suggesting the participation and importance of the psychological, physiological, and neuroendocrinological systems in the sleep process.

1. Psychological Aspects of Sleep

Perhaps the aspect of sleep which has intrigued man the most throughout his recorded history is that unique psychological event, the dream. Although much thought and many words have been devoted to the dream down through the ages, the scientific investigation of dreaming can only be said to have begun with Freud's exploration of the dream and his assertions concerning its importance. As we mentioned earlier, the discovery of REM sleep and its association with dreaming brought the dream fully into the purview of the scientific method, and was to a great extent the sole inspiration for the onset of the furious activity which has characterized the field of sleep research since.

The fact that most dreaming does occur during REM sleep has now been validated many times, although the percentage of REM periods producing dream reports varies from study to study, as does the number of dream reports elicited during NREM sleep. Perusal of any of the recent treatises on sleep and dreams (e.g., Foulkes, 1966; Witkin and Lewis, 1967; Hartmann, 1970; Freemon, 1972) indicates that research on dreams and REM sleep has become increasingly more varied and sophisticated over the years. Investigators are examining such topics as the nature of the difference between REM and NREM mentation, the relationships between personality characteristics and dreaming and dream recall, changes in dream characteristics within a dream and during the entire night, the relationships between daytime events and dreams, the effects of the laboratory environment on dreams and dream recall, the nature of frightening dreams, and the relationship between reported dream events and various other measurable events occurring during sleep.

It is now known, for example, that there are two types of frightening dreams during sleep—the night terror (*pavor nocturnus* in children, incubus attacks in adults) and the dream anxiety attack (Jones, 1949; Gastaut and Broughton, 1965; Broughton, 1968; Fisher, Byrne, Edwards, and Kahn, 1970). The night terror is a slow-wave sleep arousal phenomenon and is characterized by reports of a single vivid scene occurring before awakening. The dream anxiety attack occurs during REM sleep and is generally more elaborate and less panic provoking than the night terror.

Investigation of the relationships between dream content and physiological events has provided some of the most intriguing data with respect to dreams. Thus, some studies (Roffwarg, Dement, Muzio, and Fisher, 1962) have indicated that the direction and number of eye movements may bear a close relation to the direction and degree of activity in the dream action. Other studies have failed to find such a relationship (Moskowitz and Berger, 1969; Jacobs, Feldman, and Bender, 1971), so this point has yet to be fully explained. More recently, interest has shifted to other of the phasic events during sleep. Dement et al. (1969b) believe that the human analogue of PGO spike activity is the "minimum neural substrate of dream images" in both REM and NREM sleep.

Two additional themes have characterized studies of the psychological aspects of sleep: (1) the psychological effects and/or benefits of sleep, and (2) the effects of psychological states and personality characteristics on sleep. Studies of total, partial, and selective sleep deprivation have provided the most evidence related to the first theme. These studies have been well reviewed by Kleitman (1963), Johnson (1969), and Webb (1969; 1972). Although such deprivation studies have yielded a long list of psychological functions affected adversely by sleep deprivation of one sort or another, a comment by Webb (1972) is indicative of the lack of satisfying results. He states (p. 336): "What impresses me so about (these data) is how hard you have to struggle to find something devastating about losing a lot of sleep."

Studies concerning the effect of psychological states on sleep are less plentiful than might be expected. There is evidence, however, that factors such as presleep stress (Lester, Burch, and Dossett, 1967) and social isolation (Adey, Kado, and Walter, 1967; Shurley, Pierce, Natani, and Brooks, 1970; Naitoh, Johnson, and Austin, 1971) may affect sleep patterns. Hartmann (1973) has presented data which he interprets as indicating that length of sleep is related to personality characteristics such as the tendency to "worry." Monroe (1967) and Elenewski[1] have shown that "poor sleepers" are generally high in depression and anxiety. In a later section we summarize data related to the effects of depression and schizophrenia on sleep.

2. Physiological Aspects of Sleep

Investigation of physiological and other body changes during sleep is a well-established endeavor, and much of the work in this area actually predates the current EEG-EOG era of sleep research [see recent reviews by Berger (1969), Johnson (1970), and Snyder and Scott (1972)]. The picture emerging from this study is indicative of the complex dynamics of the sleep process. For example, heart rate, arterial pressure, and respiration rate show a general decline during the period after sleep onset and then gradually increase as morning approaches (Richardson, Honour, Fenton, Stott, and Pickering, 1964; Snyder, Hobson, Morrison, and Goldfrank, 1964; Coccagna, Mantovani, Brignani, Manzini, and Lugaresi, 1971). In one study (Athanassiadis, Draper, Honour, and Cranston, 1969), the decline in systolic pressure during the first hour of sleep was found to range between 12 and 36 mm Hg, while the fall in diastolic pressure ranged between 11 and 29 mm Hg. Body temperature also reaches its nadir after the first few hours of sleep (Mellette, Hutt, Askovitz, and Horvath, 1951; Kleitman, 1963). In general, NREM sleep is associated with declines in all of these parameters, and arterial pressure reaches its lowest and most stable level during deep stage 4 sleep (Pickering, Sleight, and Smyth, 1967; Coccagna et al., 1971). By contrast, REM sleep is accompanied by general increases in mean values and in variability of parameters such as arterial pressure and heart and respiration rates (Aserinsky and Kleitman, 1953; Snyder, Hobson, and Goldfrank, 1963; Richardson et al., 1964; Shapiro, Goodenough, Biederman, and Sleser, 1964; Snyder et al., 1964; Burdick, Brinton, Goldstein, and Laszlo, 1970; Coccagna et al., 1971). Transient elevations in arterial pressure may reach 30 mm Hg during REM (Synder et al., 1963). Phasic dilation of the pupil also occurs during REM (Berlucchi, Moruzzi, Salvi, and Strata, 1964; Hodes, 1964), as does penile tumescence (Fisher, Gross,

---

[1] Elenewski, J. J. (1971): A study of insomnia: The relationship of psychopathology to sleep disturbance. Unpublished doctoral dissertation, University of Miami, Coral Gables, Florida.

and Zuch, 1965; Karacan, footnote 2; Karacan, Goodenough, Shapiro, and Starker, 1966; Karacan, 1969; 1970; Hursch, Karacan, and Williams, 1972; Karacan, Hursch, and Williams, 1972a; Karacan, Hursch, Williams, and Littell, 1972b; Karacan, Hursch, Williams, and Thornby, 1972c). Thus, in general, parasympathetic control predominates during NREM sleep, while sympathetic control is characteristic of REM sleep. This is only a general trend, however, since anomalies such as the occurrence of galvanic skin response storms during stage 4 sleep (Johnson and Lubin, 1966; Koella, 1967) disturb this simple characterization.

Decreases in spinal reflexes (Hodes and Dement, 1964) and in body motility (Cathala and Guillard, 1961; Rohmer, Schaff, Collard, and Kurtz, 1965) are associated with the progression into stage 4 sleep. Overall muscular tone, as well as chin EMG activity and spinal reflex activity, are at their lowest during REM sleep (Berger, 1961; Hodes and Dement, 1964; Jacobson, Kales, Lehmann, and Hoedemaker, 1964). Especially in animals, the drop in chin EMG activity is used as a reliable descriptor of the REM state (Jouvet and Jouvet, 1963; Pivik and Dement, 1970). On the other hand, gross and fine body movements and twitches are most frequent during REM sleep (Dement and Wolpert, 1958; Wolpert, 1960; Baldridge, Whitman, and Kramer, 1965). In cats, bursts of middle-ear muscle activity accompany eye movement bursts and the twitching of facial and limb muscles during REM (Dewson, Dement, and Simmons, 1965).

The REMs from which the REM state derives its name have been extensively described by Dement (1964b). As we have seen in the previous section, considerable attention has been given them in relation to dream content. Recently, Aserinsky (1969; 1973) has suggested that the density of REMs is a positive index of sleep satiety. As is discussed later, REM density has been described in detail in certain psychiatric patients. It should be clear from the foregoing, however, that the naming of REM sleep after the eye movements was, in a sense, premature. REM sleep is actually a unique state, characterized by a complex of physiological manifestations, only one of which is REM.

3. Neuroendocrinological Aspects of Sleep

Earlier we discussed the fact that sleep may act as a synchronizer of certain biological rhythms. Among the rhythms which have recently attracted the interest of sleep researchers are those related to hypothalamic-pituitary neuroendocrine function. In this section we summarize the current information concerning human growth hormone, adrenocorticotropic hormone (ACTH)-cortisol, luteinizing hormone, and prolactin.

---

[2] Karacan, I. (1965): The effect of exciting presleep events on dream reporting and penile erections during sleep. *Unpublished* doctoral dissertation, Downstate Medical Center, New York University, Brooklyn, New York.

It is now well established that a rise in plasma human growth hormone (GH) occurs shortly after sleep onset in children and adults (Takahashi, Kipnis, and Daughaday, 1968; Honda, Takahashi, Takahashi, Azumi, Irie, Sakuma, Tsushima, and Shizume, 1969; Parker, Sassin, Mace, Gotlin, and Rossman, 1969; Sassin, Parker, Mace, Gotlin, Johnson, and Rossman, 1969b; Underwood, Azumi, Voina, and Van Wyk, 1971). This activity is strictly sleep dependent, since delay or absence of sleep onset results in delay or absence of the GH rise (Sassin et al., 1969b). Sleep onset *per se* does not appear to precipitate the GH release (Karacan, Rosenbloom, Londono, Williams, and Salis, 1975a). Rather, this release is correlated in some manner with slow-wave sleep (Parker et al., 1969; Sassin et al., 1969b). Experimental suppression of slow-wave sleep dampens and/or delays the GH response but rarely abolishes it (Sassin, Parker, Johnson, Rossman, Mace, and Gotlin, 1969a; Karacan, Rosenbloom, Williams, Finley, and Hursch, 1971). The lack of a strict one-to-one relationship between the amount and timing of slow-wave sleep and GH release has led most investigators to conclude that nocturnal GH release is not solely dependent on or controlled by slow-wave sleep mechanisms. A satisfactory explanation of the release in terms of known metabolic functions of GH is not available (Lucke and Glick, 1971; Parker and Rossman, 1971); this suggests that the release serves some specifically sleep-related function. Of course the importance of GH in body growth and repair leads to interesting speculation about its function in relation to slow-wave sleep, which is considered by many to be the most restful stage of sleep.

The existence of a 24-hr circadian rhythm in ACTH-cortisol secretion is well established (Nichols and Tyler, 1967). Peak secretion occurs in the early morning hours, while the nadir in the rhythm occurs in the late evening (Weitzman, Schaumburg, and Fishbein, 1966; Carpenter and Bunney, 1971). Secretion is episodic, and the apparent peak results from a clustering of secretory episodes (Weitzman, Fukushima, Nogeire, Roffwarg, Gallagher, and Hellman, 1971). Since maximal secretion occurs shortly before morning awakening, an association between ACTH-cortisol secretion and REM sleep has been suggested (Hellman, Nakada, Curti, Weitzman, Kream, Roffwarg, Ellman, Fukushima, and Gallagher, 1970). In a series of studies, Weitzman and his associates (Weitzman et al., 1968; Weitzman et al., 1970a; Weitzman, Kripke, Kream, McGregor, and Hellman, 1970b) have shown that a shift of the sleep period from night to day (180 degree phase shift) results in a general disorganization of the ACTH-cortisol secretory pattern. As long as 3 weeks may be required for evidence of shift in this pattern to appear. When the sleep period is shifted back to the normal nighttime hours, the pattern returns to normal within a week.

Plasma prolactin is secreted episodically throughout sleep (Sassin, Frantz, Weitzman, and Kapen, 1972). The initial secretory episode occurs within the first 2 hr after sleep onset. Later episodes are characterized by progressively greater concentrations of prolactin, and peak concentrations occur between 5 and 7 A.M. Shortly after the morning awakening there is a rapid fall in concentration, and lowest daily concentrations occur between 10 A.M. and noon. During sleep there has been no detectable relationship between secretory episodes and any particular stage of sleep. The episodic release of prolactin appears to be sleep dependent, since a delay of sleep onset of up to 12 hr results in a corresponding delay in the pattern of prolactin secretory episodes (Sassin, Frantz, Kapen, and Weitzman, 1973).

In another series of studies, Weitzman and co-workers (Boyar, Finkelstein, Roffwarg, Kapen, Weitzman, and Hellman, 1972a; Boyar, Perlow, Hellman, Kapen, and Weitzman, 1972b; Kapen, Boyar, Hellman, and Weitzman, 1973a; Kapen, Boyar, Perlow, Hellman, and Weitzman, 1973b) have described the secretory patterns of luteinizing hormone in males and females of various ages. This hormone is also secreted episodically from 10 to 15 times per 24 hr. In prepubertal children (whose total concentrations are low) and adult men there are no apparent differences between waking and sleep secretory episodes. In pubertal boys and girls, however, total concentrations are greater during sleep than during wakefulness. In women examined during the follicular phase of the menstrual cycle (when basal concentrations are low relative to other phases of the cycle), concentrations are low during the first half of the night and high during the last half. Secretory episodes are superimposed on rising basal concentrations during the periovulatory phase of the menstrual cycle. Although Weitzman and his group have detected no consistent relationships between luteinizing hormone secretory episodes and a particular stage of sleep, Rubin, Kales, Adler, Fagan, and Odell (1972) found that in adult men concentrations were 14% higher during REM sleep than during NREM sleep.

We have summarized these data concerning the psychological, physiological, and neuroendocrinological aspects of sleep primarily in order to convey a picture of the activity and dynamics of the sleep process. It should be evident that sleep is not the state of quiescence envisioned by philosophers, poets, and scientists of old. Rather, sleep is characterized by continual changes in bodily functions, and there are periods during sleep when certain systems are as active as during wakefulness, and often more so. Given that this is the case, and given that most humans spend one-third of their lives asleep, there can be no doubt that physicians concerned with the total well-being of their patients have a duty to be equally as concerned with a patient's sleep and sleep problems as with his waking behavior and complaints.

III. FUNCTIONS OF SLEEP

In the preceding sections we sketched some of the more salient aspects of the current body of scientific knowledge about sleep. If nothing else is clear, it should be apparent that inquiry into the nature of sleep is proceeding in many different ways and at many different levels. Nevertheless, it is probably reasonable to state that the ultimate objective of most sleep researchers, whatever their approach, is the same—to understand the function of sleep, or why it is necessary for a living organism to spend a characteristic portion of its lifetime in a state outwardly resembling unconsciousness. The variety of approaches to the study of sleep implies that the answer to this question may be a very complex one. At this point, the strongest assertion we feel safe in making about the function of sleep is that there is probably no *one* function of sleep, but rather a complex of functions which contribute to the overall well-being of the organism and which quite possibly vary in relation to other factors such as health status and age. Thus, just as we would be reluctant to discuss *the* function of wakefulness, it would appear to be a gross oversimplification to seek to understand *the* function of sleep.

Since this is the case, it follows that any true and meaningful theory of the functions of sleep must integrate and reflect an astounding variety and quantity of information. In fact, today there is a noticeable absence of such true theorizing in the field of sleep research. Existing speculation has consistently concerned only a very circumscribed set of data and has more often than not directly reflected the theoretical and research interests and biases of the speculators. Although these speculations have frequently served the dual purposes of placing the selected data in a new perspective and generating further testable hypotheses, they cannot be considered to be formal theoretical systems unifying the entire area of sleep research. Hursch (1970) has presented a thoughtful discussion of this state of affairs in sleep research.

The lack of serious formal theorizing about the functions of sleep reflects two facts. First, it must be remembered that the modern era of sleep research began only 20 years ago, and quite appropriately the primary interest among sleep researchers has been to collect a sufficient amount of data to generate hypotheses which will lead to more systematic data collection. Second, there are differences of opinion among sleep researchers concerning the sufficiency of the present data base for formal theorizing. Some researchers believe that further data collection is necessary before any theories should be elaborated. Others believe that there are now enough data to begin the process of constructing theoretical systems. In the remainder of this section we summarize several of the current speculations concerning the functions of sleep, and conclude with a discussion of the recent attempt by Hartmann (1973) to provide a more general theory. Kleitman (1963) has reviewed many of the older theories of sleep function and Hartmann (1973) has provided a more recent review of the area.

Many current theories of the function of sleep fall into three general categories: phylogenetic, ontogenetic, and psychological. Snyder's (1966) suggestion that REM sleep has an arousal or "sentinal" function is an example of the phylogenetic approach. He postulates that REM sleep serves to arouse the organism periodically from the defenseless state in which it is an easy prey to predators. This emphasis on the survival value of REM sleep by Snyder derives logically from his own bias toward investigating sleep from the point of view of phylogeny. Hartmann (1973) has suggested that such a sentinal function would be better served by periodic brief and frank arousals during slow-wave sleep, and that evidence of a higher arousal threshold during REM sleep mitigates against Synder's hypothesis. However, we should note that Koella (1967) has concluded that arousal threshold depends upon the relevance of the stimulus to the individual: arousal thresholds for irrelevant stimuli (e.g., ambient environmental noise) are highest during REM sleep, but thresholds for relevant stimuli (e.g., a baby's cry to the mother) are lowest during REM.

An example of the ontogenetic approach is the hypothesis of Roffwarg et al. (1966). Study of the sleep characteristics of new-born infants led these investigators to suggest that REM sleep provides endogenous stimulation to the developing nervous system, especially during fetal life when exogenous stimulation is limited. However, the existence of a complete analogue of REM sleep in the fetus has yet to be demonstrated [see Williams et al. (1974) for a recent review of the literature]. Furthermore, this hypothesis does not satisfactorily explain why such large amounts of endogenous stimulation are required by the human adult throughout his lifetime. Thus, this speculation also quite clearly reflects the research bias of its proponents—the study of human neonatal sleep patterns.

There are a number of hypotheses concerning the psychological functions of sleep, and particularly of REM sleep. Among these are the suggestions that during REM sleep instinctual drives are released in a relatively benign situation (Fisher, 1965); that REM sleep serves selectively to destroy irrelevant information so that new information can be assimilated the next day (Newman and Evans, 1965); that sleep in general promotes the formation of engrams (Moruzzi, 1966) or that REM sleep promotes the consolidation of useful memories (Breger, 1967); that REM sleep especially facilitates the elaboration of new programs and even "metaprograms" (Dewan, 1970); and that REM sleep plays some role in intellectual functioning (Feinberg and Evarts, 1969). Many of these hypotheses reflect the tendency to derive analogies from the apparently more sophisticated area of current computer technology.

This brief list of some of the current hypotheses concerning the functions of sleep illustrates several of the points we made earlier: (1) most hypotheses are derived from a circumscribed set of data, (2) most directly reflect the research interests and biases of their proponents, and (3) most reflect the early interest of sleep researchers in REM sleep and the lack of interest in NREM sleep. None of these hypotheses has been generated by *all* of the current data about sleep, and in them there is a notable failure to incorporate information concerning the mechanisms and correlates of both REM and NREM sleep. Nor are data about the dynamic aspects of sleep within the night, within the circadian cycle, and over the lifetime given their due. The recent theorizing of Hartmann (1973) comes closest to meeting our criticisms. Hartmann suggests that NREM sleep, and specifically slow-wave sleep, is an anabolic phase of sleep during which protein and/or RNA macromolecules are synthesized. This anabolism serves both to restore products depleted during all the activities which produce "tiredness" (catabolism) and to provide macromolecules which are utilized during REM sleep. During REM sleep, systems related to "feedback-interactive self-guidance" (i.e., systems of focused attention, patterning, and homeostatic adaptation to environmental stimuli) are restored, by means of restoration of adequate conditions in catecholaminergic systems and their cortical endings.

This hypothesis incorporates much of the data neglected by earlier ones and serves the vital benefit of attempting to account for NREM sleep. Our own recent preliminary observations of sleep patterns in young-adult barbiturate addicts lend some support to the hypothesized anabolic role of slow-wave sleep. Such patients show a profound depression in stage 4 sleep even following gradual withdrawal of their drugs. It is well known clinically that these patients also have a tendency to develop persistent skin ulcerations. We suggest that the failure to heal may bear a direct relationship to the deficit in slow-wave sleep and all the other physiological deficits which presumably accompany it.

Hartmann's formulation is the most comprehensive to date and has the ability to generate future research, but it also can be faulted for neglecting certain areas of current knowledge. Although Hartmann does attempt to account for the dynamic morphology of a typical night sleep, he does not extend his view to dynamic changes over the circadian cycle and the entire lifetime. Since one of our own primary research interests over the last 10 years has been to describe systematically the ontogenetic changes and sex differences in sleep patterns, we are particularly sensitive to this deletion. In our studies (Williams et al., 1974), we have been impressed both with the rather drastic decline in stage 4 sleep which begins as early as the 30s and with the tendency for older men to exhibit less slow-wave sleep than comparably aged women. The fact that women typically live longer than men suggests that the maintenance of slow-wave sleep may bear some relation to length of life. To us, one of the most interesting current questions is whether the process reflected in the loss of stage 4 sleep is a normal aging process or a disease process. Put another way, we are asking whether the maintenance of stage 4 sleep at young-adult levels in older individuals would contribute to a longer life. An answer to such a question would, we believe, provide important new information about one of the functions of sleep in human and other animals. At this point, however, we must realize that all speculations about the functions of sleep are only speculations, and much physical and mental energy must be expended before any entirely acceptable and testable theoretical system will be available.

IV. DISORDERS OF SLEEP ASSOCIATED WITH SCHIZOPHRENIA AND DEPRESSION

The number of sleep disturbances to which humans are vulnerable is legion. In an effort to help systematize both our study of and thinking about these disorders, we recently (Karacan et al., 1973) proposed a classification scheme for sleep disorders; we chose to categorize the sleep disturbances accompanying schizophrenia and depression as secondary disorders. By this we mean that these sleep disturbances are symptoms of another chronic clinical complaint, and are clearly only one aspect of the total symptom complex. In this section we summarize the current information concerning these two secondary sleep disorders. Although other psychiatric disorders, such as anorexia nervosa (Crisp, Stonehill, and Fenton, 1971) and postpartum emotional disturbances (Karacan and Williams, 1970) are also accompanied by sleep disturbances, we will here limit our discussion to the two which have received the greatest attention from sleep researchers.

A. Schizophrenia

As we mentioned in our introduction, one of the first questions which attracted the interest of psychiatrically oriented sleep researchers was whether or not disturbances in the dreaming process might play a role in the development and maintenance of schizophrenia. This question was of course inspired by the apparent similarity between dreams and hallucinations. In particular, it was suggested (Fisher, 1965) that the schizophrenic's hallucinations might represent eruptions of REM events into waking life. However, investigations of this hypothesis have failed to support it conclusively. For example, the five actively ill schizophrenics studied by Rechtschaffen, Schulsinger, and Mednick (1964) displayed no consistent patterns of EEG, EOG, or EMG activity suggestive of the occurrence of REM sleep phenomena during wakefulness. Severe abnormalities of REM sleep during nighttime sleep have not been detected in either chronic adult schizophrenics (Dement, 1955; Caldwell and Domino, 1967) or schizophrenic or autistic children (Onheiber, White, DeMyer, and Ottinger, 1965; Ornitz, Ritvo, and Walter, 1965a; 1965b). Cross-sectional studies of "actively ill" or acute patients have revealed no significant abnormalities in REM time (Koresko, Snyder, and Feinberg, 1963; Feinberg, Koresko, Gottlieb, and Wender, 1964; Stern, Fram, Wyatt, Grinspoon, and Tursky, 1969), but some patients have exhibited abnormal REM latencies (Feinberg, Koresko, and Gottlieb, 1965; Stern et al., 1969). On the other hand, there are data indicating that the type of patient and/or the point of evolution of the patient's disease process may determine changes in REM sleep parameters. For example, Feinberg et al. (1964) found that short-term patients obtained less REM sleep than long-term patients, while Feinberg et al. (1965) reported that hallucinating patients exhibited greater eye-movement densities than nonhallucinating patients. Both Snyder (1969) and Kupfer, Wyatt, Scott, and Snyder (1970) have observed several patients throughout the course of an acute psychotic episode. These patients displayed changes in a number of sleep parameters, including those of REM sleep, which were associated with the waxing and waning phases of the psychotic episode. Feinberg and his associates (Feinberg et al., 1964; Feinberg et al., 1965) have failed to detect any REM abnormalities in several remitted patients.

From these data it can be concluded that schizophrenics do not suffer any consistent disturbances in REM sleep during the night, nor do they display detectable REM phenomena during wakefulness. It may be that the occasional changes in REM sleep that have been observed in schizophrenics reflect drug effects to some extent: varying amounts of control have been maintained over the drug status of the patients in these studies. Nevertheless, some data suggest that various subtypes of patients may exhibit more consistent changes in REM sleep parameters, and that such parameters may also change reliably during the course of a psychotic episode. Further research will be needed before these suggestions can be accepted as facts.

Even though the search for REM sleep abnormalities in schizophrenics has been less than fruitful when the conventional measures of REM are considered, study of these patients has revealed what appears to be a rather unique defect in REM sleep mechanisms. As we mentioned earlier, experimental deprivation of REM sleep in normal subjects is consistently followed by a compensatory rebound of REM on undisturbed recovery nights. By contrast, actively ill schizophrenics display little or no compensatory increase in REM sleep following experimental REM deprivation (Zarcone, Gulevich, Pivik, and Dement, 1968; Zarcone and Dement, 1969). Remitted patients exhibit normal (Vogel and Traub, 1968) or even exaggerated (Zarcone et al., 1968; Zarcone and Dement, 1969) amounts of REM sleep following such a procedure. This evidence may indicate that the neurophysiological and neurochemical mechanisms of REM sleep are affected by the schizophrenic process.

Dement and his colleagues (Dement, Ferguson, Cohen, and Barchas, 1969*a;* Dement et al., 1969*b;* Zarcone and Dement, 1969) have proposed an updated version of the REM intrusion hypothesis of schizophrenic symptoms. Drawing on data from various types of animal and human studies, they suggest that schizophrenic symptoms are related to a breakdown in serotoninergic mechanisms which serve to confine PGO spike activity to the REM state. Their argument is indeed elegant and intriguing, but, as they recognize, it rests on the as yet unvalidated assumption that there exists a human analogue of the PGO spike activity which has been observed in lower animals.

Although the early interest in exploring the REM sleep characteristics of schizophrenics resulted in a lack of study of other aspects of the EEG-EOG sleep of these patients, it has since been shown that schizophrenics typically exhibit lower than normal amounts of deep stage 4 sleep (Caldwell and Domino, 1967; Feinberg, Braun, Koresko, and Gottlieb, 1969). In fact, this abnormality appears to occur much more frequently in these patients than do REM sleep abnormalities. Furthermore, a study by Luby and Caldwell (1967) indicates that schizophrenics do not respond to sleep deprivation by increased amounts of stage 4 sleep on recovery nights. Thus, although schizophrenics do not appear to suffer from gross REM sleep abnormalities, evidence from deprivation studies suggests that they do suffer from basic disturbances of both REM sleep and slow-wave sleep mechanisms. The significance of these disturbances is still unknown, and researchers have yet to determine whether these disturbances are in any way unique to schizophrenia.

B. Depression

Clinicians are well aware that sleep disturbance is a primary complaint of many depressed patients, and this symptom often constitutes one of the criteria for diagnosing depression (Mayer-Gross, 1954). Although the distinction has not always been supported by laboratory studies, it is also widely believed that reactive depressives suffer from sleep onset insomnia, while endogenous depressives complain more of early morning awakening.

The clinical importance of sleep disturbance in depression led naturally to an interest in studying depressed patients in the sleep laboratory, and the pioneering study by Diaz-Guerrero et al. (1946) was certainly among the first studies of psychiatric patients in such a laboratory. Since their work, there has been an ever-increasing volume of sleep laboratory work devoted to study of depressed patients. In the remainder of this section we summarize data derived from the following types of studies: cross-sectional, follow-up, and longitudinal. We then briefly discuss several factors which have conceivably contributed to sometimes widely divergent findings concerning the sleep of depressed patients. Next we consider a number of miscellaneous findings from sleep laboratory studies which are directed toward a more detailed exploration of the complexity of the depressed patient's sleep disturbances. And last we survey several of the theoretical notions which have been advanced to explain the sleep disturbances in depression.

Diaz-Guerrero et al. (1946) reported that the sleep of their patients (manic-depressive, depressive type) was abnormally light and fragmented. Although there was great variability among the patients, there was a general tendency for patients, in comparison to normal subjects, to sleep a shorter length of time, take a longer time to fall asleep, experience earlier and/or more awakenings and more sleep stage shifts during the night, have greater amounts of wakefulness and light sleep, and obtain smaller amounts of deep sleep. The patients also seemed to exhibit more shifts from one EEG pattern to another within a scoring epoch.

It was about 20 years before depressed patients were again systematically studied in the sleep laboratory. In the interim, of course, Aserinsky and Kleitman (1953) had described REM sleep. Between 1963 and 1966, there appeared roughly one publication per year describing the sleep EEG-EOG characteristics of depressed patients. Beginning in 1966, work began to appear from the three laboratories (those of Mendels and Hawkins, Hartmann, and Snyder) which have become dominant in this specific research area. Perhaps the most important thing these workers have taught us thus far is that there is no single sleep pattern which is invariably characteristic of depressed patients. Nevertheless, it is also evident that disturbances of some EEG-EOG sleep parameters are more consistently characteristic of depressed patients than are others. The following two paragraphs represent a distillation of the most consistent results from the following reports: Diaz-Guerrero et al., 1946; Oswald, Berger, Jaramillo, Keddie, Olley, and Plunkett, 1963; Zung, Wilson, and Dodson, 1964; Gresham, Agnew, and Williams, 1965; Green and Stajduhar, 1966; Hartmann, 1968b; Lowy, Cleghorn, and McClure, 1971; Mendels and Hawkins, 1972; Snyder, 1972; Hajnšek, Dogan, Gubarev, Dürrigl, Stojanović, and Jovanović, 1973.

Most of the studies in which it has been directly measured indicate that the actual time spent asleep is reduced in depressed patients, but Hartmann (1968b), who studied manic-depressed patients in the depressed phase, found it to be normal or even slightly elevated. The reduced sleep time may frequently, but by no means always, be partially a function of increased sleep latency or time to fall asleep. More generally, it reflects increased minutes or percentage of wakefulness during the night. The number of awakenings is also generally elevated. Early morning awakening has been observed in some patients, but certainly not all. The number of shifts from one stage to another during the night has been elevated in some patients but essentially normal in many others.

The minutes and percentages of the various sleep stages have been studied in relative detail. Minutes of "drowsy" sleep, a stage scored by Mendels and Hawkins (1972) which is intermediate between waking and stage 1 sleep, were found to be increased in depressed patients, but there were no significant differences from controls in the minutes of stages 1, 2, and 3. The minutes of stage 4 sleep are frequently variable compared to normal values, but are in general reduced. Minutes of stage "drowsy" and stage 1 are elevated when expressed as percentages of total sleep time and/or sleep period time. Percentage of stage 2 may be normal, elevated, or reduced. Similar findings pertain to percentage of stage 3 sleep. In most studies, percentage of stage 4 sleep has been found to be depressed, but some workers have reported elevated or normal values.

Although there have been inconsistencies concerning these characteristics of sleep patterns in depressed patients, most authors agree that the sleep of the patients is unusually tenuous, being confined to the lighter stages of sleep and frequently interrupted by awakening. On the other hand, the cross-sectional studies concerning the various characteristics of REM sleep have provided highly variable descriptions of this intriguing aspect of sleep.

Mendels and Hawkins (1972) and Snyder (1972) found the minutes of REM sleep to be quite variable from patient to patient, but generally reduced. On the other hand, Hartmann's (1968b) manic-depressive patients exhibited elevated REM times. When minutes of REM sleep are expressed as a percentage of actual sleep time, the mean values are typically normal or not significantly different from control values (Green and Stajduhar, 1966; Mendels and Hawkins, 1967a; Snyder, 1969). When they are expressed as a percentage of the time from sleep onset to the final awakening (i.e., sleep plus nocturnal wakefulness), they may be reduced (Mendels and Hawkins, 1967a; Hajnšek et al., 1973) or no different from control values (Gresham et al., 1965).

The latency to the first REM period (i.e., the time from sleep onset to the first REM period) has often been found to be reduced in depressed patients (Green and Stajduhar, 1966; Hartmann, 1968b; Snyder, 1972). This is especially evident in some patients who exhibit REM periods at the very onset of sleep (Snyder, 1972). In some cases, however, REM latency may be quite long, and this apparently occurs when a patient experiences very little REM during the night (Snyder, 1972; Hajnšek et al., 1973).

Several investigators have described other characteristics of REM sleep in their patients. For example, some have observed that the first REM period of the night may be unusually long (Hartmann, 1968b; Snyder, 1972), while the interval between successive REM periods may be unusually short (Snyder, 1972; Hajnšek et al., 1973). In one study, the number of REM periods was elevated (Green and Stajduhar, 1966). Snyder and his associates have noted an increase in the number of eye movements and ususually abrupt transitions between waking and REM sleep (Snyder, 1972). Normally, a period of NREM sleep separates wakefulness from REM sleep. And finally, those who have examined it have consistently found that the number of awakenings from REM sleep is elevated in depressed patients (Green and Stajduhar, 1966; Mendels and Hawkins, 1972; Snyder, 1972; Hajnšek et al., 1973).

Once it was clear that depressed patients do in fact display quantifiable sleep disturbances, several researchers logically extended their work to a consideration of whether or not these disturbances become less severe as the patients improve clinically. In general, such follow-up studies (Zung et al.,

1964; Gresham et al., 1965; Mendels and Hawkins, 1967*b;* Hawkins, 1972) indicate that many of the EEG-EOG sleep disturbances of depressed patients disappear as clinical improvement occurs and continues. However, not all disturbances, such as exaggerated wakefulness, completely disappear at short-term follow-up, and apparently stage 4 sleep may never return to normal levels.

Possibly the most striking aspect of results from cross-sectional studies of depressed patients is the great interpatient and interstudy variability characteristic of many of the sleep parameters. Shortly we discuss some of the possible sources of this variability. As work in this area continued, however, some investigators began to suspect that much of the variability may be due to one factor—the changing clinical status of the individual patient, and a number of them undertook systematic longitudinal studies in an effort to isolate those points or phases in the natural history of the illness which are associated with consistent sleep pattern changes. Such studies (Green and Stajduhar, 1966; Hartmann, 1968*b;* Lowy et al., 1971; Mendels and Hawkins, 1971*b;* Snyder, 1972) indicate that most patients exhibit lower sleep times and amounts of stage 4 sleep during the most serious phases of illness. Improvements in sleep patterns accompany or even precede noticeable clinical improvement, although in many cases stage 4 sleep has never completely returned to normal levels during the study. The variability in REM sleep parameters noted in the cross-sectional studies is accentuated in the longitudinal studies, for the REM sleep characteristics of an individual patient may vary considerably from night to night. Nevertheless, the evidence suggests to several investigators (Mendels and Hawkins, 1971*b;* Snyder, 1972) that during the height of their illness many depressed patients exhibit the signs of prior or continuing REM deprivation. These signs include erratically reduced amounts of REM sleep and latencies to REM onset, as well as elevated frequencies of eye movements during REM sleep. The generally higher amounts of REM sleep during the period of clinical improvement also support this hypothesis. Whether this interpretation is correct or not remains to be determined. But at the very least, the highly variable nature of all the parameters of REM sleep during the whole clinical course implies that REM sleep disturbance is a crucial aspect of depression.

These longitudinal studies suggest that intrapatient variability plays a significant role in the variation of some parameters of EEG-EOG sleep in depressed patients. However, a number of other factors may also be important in this respect. First, in many studies several different types of patients have been included in the patient sample. Evidence of real differences in sleep patterns among types of depressives (Hartmann, 1968*b;* Mendels and Hawkins, 1968; Snyder, 1969; Hauri and Hawkins, 1973) suggests that this practice may have increased the variability in the results. Second, there is some indication (Mendels and Hawkins, 1968; Snyder, 1968) that differences in the severity of illness of study patients could contribute to differ-

ences in observed sleep patterns. And third, it must be borne in mind that
many of the patients used in these studies have been medicated in some
way, and their recorded sleep patterns may well have reflected, at least to
some degree, the well-documented ability of psychotropic and many other
agents to modify EEG-EOG sleep patterns.

As the interest in studying depressed patients in the sleep laboratory has
grown, a number of seemingly unrelated but potentially meaningful characteristics of such patients have been described. Thus, although shortened and
fragmented sleep is one of the most consistently documented sleep disturbances in depressed patients, there have also been both systematic (Kupfer,
Himmelhoch, Swartzburg, Anderson, Byck, and Detre, 1972) and less formal
(Hartmann, 1968b; Lowy et al., 1971; Hawkins, 1972; Hauri and Hawkins,
1973) descriptions of hypersomnia in some patients. Several sleep EEG-
EOG abnormalities have been described (Green and Stajduhar, 1966; Hawkins, Mendels, Scott, Bensch, and Teachey, 1967; Mendels and Hawkins,
1967a; Hawkins, 1972; Hauri and Hawkins, 1973). Snyder (1972) has
drawn attention to the unusually intense eye movement activity characteristic
of patients in certain phases of their clinical course. Hauri and Hawkins
(1971) and Kupfer and Heninger (1972) have demonstrated a negative relationship between amount of eye movement activity and rated degree of
depression, while Kupfer and Foster (1972) have presented data suggesting
a negative relationship between REM latency and rated severity of depression. Vogel and his associates (Vogel, Traub, Ben-Horin, and Meyers, 1968;
Vogel, Thompson, Thurmond, and Rivers, 1973) have been exploring their
interesting finding that experimental suppression of REM sleep in depressed
patients, and especially in endogenous depressives, is accompanied by decreased scores on various measures of depression. Using total sleep deprivation rather than REM deprivation, a number of European investigators are
conducting work along similar lines (Pflug and Tölle, 1971; 1973; Kretschmar and Peters, 1973). Although mania has been the subject of relatively little work in the sleep laboratory, it appears that manic patients have
both certain similarities to and differences from depressed patients in terms
of sleep disturbances (Hartmann, 1968b; Snyder, 1969; 1972; Mendels and
Hawkins, 1971a; Bunney, Goodwin, Murphy, House, and Gordon, 1972;
Jovanović, Dogan, Dürrigl, Gubarev, Hajnšek, Rogina, and Stojanović, 1973).

Speculation concerning the etiology of sleep disturbances in depression is
varied. Mendels and Hawkins (1967a) have proposed that depressed patients suffer from hyperactivity of central nervous system arousal mechanisms. This hyperactivity results in a tenuous balance between sleep and
arousal mechanisms during sleep and a general instability and lightness of
sleep. Drawing on additional neurophysiological data, Whybrow and Mendels
(1969) have recently expanded this formulation to encompass a variety of
data derived from study of both depressed and manic patients.

Snyder (1972) has concentrated on explaining the anomalies of REM sleep in depression. He argues that depressed patients have suffered, and perhaps continue to suffer, from REM deprivation, as indicated by shortened REM latencies and intervals between REM periods and increased frequencies of eye movements, as well as compensatory increases in REM time with clinical improvement. The deprivation may initially result from overall shortened sleep, but may also result from the tendency of depressed patients to awaken from REM sleep. According to Snyder, periodic increases in REM time in these patients are due to the fact that occasionally the pressure for REM sleep to occur overcomes all inhibiting factors.

Hartmann's (1968*b*) studies of manic-depressive patients have produced results somewhat at variance with most studies of unipolar depressives. To explain this, Hartmann has suggested that all depressives sustain an increased need or pressure for REM sleep. In manic-depressives, this is reflected by increased REM times, while in other types of depressives concomitant sleep disturbances prevent the increased need from being reflected in high REM times. In contrast to Snyder's view that the increased REM pressure is the result of prior REM deprivation, Hartmann believes that an increased need for REM sleep is inherent in depressive illness. He also argues that evidence concerning the role of catecholaminergic systems in REM sleep, depression, and mania support his view.

The proposition of Kaelbling (1971) is particularly intriguing. His major premises are that the rate of synthesis of catecholamines determines REM time, that availability of catecholamines at specific receptor sites determines mood, and that one function of REM sleep is to imbue factual memories with the prevailing emotional tone (if catecholamines are low, then that tone is depression). During depression, there is competition between mood-maintaining and REM sleep mechanisms for catecholamines (or presumably their precursor elements, since quite possibly the neural circuitry subserving REM sleep and mood is not identical). In this situation, the REM sleep that does occur helps to perpetuate the depression by imbuing factual memories with a depressive tone. But changes in REM sleep parameters are conceptualized as primarily reflecting the action of a homeostatic mechanism which is brought into play only when catecholamine levels are insufficient to serve both mood-elevating and REM sleep mechanisms. Antidepressants are believed to elevate functional catecholamine levels at the synaptic cleft; they also suppress REM sleep. To resolve this apparent paradox, Kaelbling suggests that one way in which antidepressant therapy might be effective is by conserving catecholamines and diverting them for REM sleep-sustaining functions (hence the REM suppression) to mood-elevating functions (hence the clinical improvement).

This proposal emphasizes the relationships among depression, REM sleep, and catecholamines, as does that of Hartmann (1968*b*). We have seen that various disturbances of REM sleep have been described for depressed patients, but that the great between-patient and within-patient variability in the conventional parameters of REM sleep has prevented the determination of any invariant relationships between REM sleep and mood. This may simply reflect the fact that measurement techniques for REM sleep phenomena and for mood are still very gross. Or it may reflect the homeostatic oscillations which Kaelbling postulates for REM sleep. A somewhat more promising relationship has been revealed by the studies of Hauri and Hawkins (1971) and Kupfer and Heninger (1972) showing a positive correlation between eye movement density (i.e., phasic event density) and positive mood. These findings bring to mind those of Dement and his co-workers (Dement et al., 1969*b*): in cats, a breakdown in the normal distribution of PGO spikes (phasic events) is accompanied by increases in drive-oriented behaviors (sexual, exploratory, eating, aggressive behaviors, etc.). It seems safe to assume some correspondence between the phasic eye movements and PGO spike activity. It could also be argued that there is at least a surface correspondence between mood and drive-oriented behavior (recall the loss of libido and appetite and restricted interests of the depressed patient). However, mention of these apparently parallel findings in the cat and the human complicates the matter. Although there is much evidence suggesting the importance of catecholamines in the occurrence of phasic REM events (Jouvet, 1972), Dement and his colleagues argue that serotonin, not catecholamines, plays a principal role in regulating *when* PGO spike activity occurs. Furthermore, we cannot neglect the fact that disturbances in slow-wave sleep are also prominent in depression, and that there is much evidence suggesting that slow-wave sleep depends primarily on serotoninergic mechanisms.

In our view, it would seem more profitable at this point not to underestimate the complexity of the nervous system mechanisms controlling both sleep and depression. Although emphasis on one or another of the amine systems may be required to give direction to a specific research program, the use of this strategy should not blind us to the fact that in all probability many interacting systems are involved in the production of the gross mood and sleep disturbances which have been documented in depression. To conclude, we would only note that much of the work in this area has been inspired by the question, "What sleep disturbances are symptomatic of depression?" In view of the foregoing, it would now seem more appropriate to consider both the mood and the sleep disturbances characteristic of the disease called depression as symptoms of a more basic disease process. If the question inspiring research were "What nervous system malfunction produces depression and the unique sleep disturbances of the depressed patient?" it might be easier to focus on the crucial variables in these rather debilitating complaints.

V. TREATMENT OF SLEEP DISORDERS

The process of determining an effective and safe treatment for a disease is evolutionary. The initial step can be made either by a chance observation that a particular treatment is beneficial or by a reasoned design of a treatment based on previous data. Obviously, the more that is known about the disease, the more successful the latter tactic will be. As experience with the treatment accumulates and as additional data concerning the disease are collected, refinements can be made in the treatment which render it even more effective.

Present knowledge about the treatment of sleep disorders is highly uneven and in general limited and rudimentary. This reflects to a certain extent the feeling, prevalent until quite recently, that sleep disturbance is usually only a symptom of some more basic psychological or physical disturbance, and that, in any case, no one ever dies from disturbed sleep. Convincing arguments against this view came only with the systematic study of sleep disturbances in the modern sleep laboratory. Nevertheless, the field is still so new that it has yet to fulfill its full potential with respect to the treatment of sleep disorders. Understandably, the initial years following the advent of present techniques were spent in collecting basic descriptions of the phenomena of EEG-EOG sleep under a variety of conditions. Only very recently have sleep researchers felt they had even the minimal understanding of sleep required for a serious consideration of sleep disorders and their treatment. Because of this, those who now seek definitive statements about the treatment of sleep disorders will be disappointed.

By far the most widely used method of treating sleep disturbance is the administration of drugs. Psychotherapy probably ranks second, at least for primary insomnia and the insomnias accompanying psychiatric disturbance. Recently, however, researchers have begun to explore the use of techniques such as relaxation therapy and biofeedback training. They have also begun a reassessment of cerebroelectrotherapy (CET), a treatment which is studied and used extensively in Eastern Europe and Russia. In this final section, we briefly survey human data concerning the effects of drugs on EEG-EOG sleep patterns. We consider a variety of drugs in addition to the hypnotics, in order to demonstrate the extreme sensitivity of sleep to pharmacological agents. We then discuss various nonpharmacological modes of treatment.

A. Effects of Drugs on EEG-EOG Sleep Patterns

Here we attempt only a brief statement of the most commonly observed effects on EEG-EOG sleep of the following classes of drugs: stimulants, hallucinogens, opiates, tranquilizers, antidepressants, barbiturates, and nonbarbiturate hypnotics. For more detailed information on the voluminous and often contradictory data in this area, the reader is referred to the following reviews: Oswald, 1968; 1969; 1970; Hartmann, 1969a; 1969b; Kales, Malmstrom, Scharf, and Rubin, 1969; Oswald, Evans, and Lewis, 1969; Zung, 1970; Freemon, 1972; Williams and Salamy, 1972; Kay, 1973.

Acute administration of most stimulants results in a suppression of REM sleep, and amphetamines have often been used by sleep researchers to achieve or facilitate experimental REM deprivation. Stimulants also appear to increase nocturnal wakefulness and decrease slow-wave sleep. Some evidence indicates that with chronic administration sleep may gradually normalize. Upon withdrawal of stimulants, there is frequently a compensatory increase in REM sleep ("REM rebound") and in TST. In our laboratory we have observed that acute doses of the natural stimulant coffee and of caffeine have many of the same effects as other stimulants, and that these effects are dose dependent (Karacan, 1975b). Stimulants are used primarily in the treatment of narcolepsy.

Of the hallucinogens, both lysergic acid diethylamide (LSD) and marijuana have been studied in the sleep laboratory. LSD produces an increase in REM sleep and heightened arousal as reflected by measures of body motility (Green, 1965; 1969; Muzio, Roffwarg, and Kaufman, 1966). Marijuana has been reported to affect both REM and stage 4 sleep (Barratt, Beaver, White, Blakeney, and Adams, 1972; Kales, Hanley, Rickles, Kanas, Baker, and Goring, 1972; Pivik, Zarcone, Dement, and Hollister, 1972; Bobon, Schulz, Mattke, and Simonova, 1973; Pranikoff, Karacan, Larson, Williams, Thornby, and Hursch, 1973), but it would appear that the effects observed depend on whether administration is acute or chronic and whether naive individuals or experienced users serve as subjects.

Opiates (morphine, heroin) and methadone appear to suppress REM and slow-wave sleep and generally to lighten sleep. These effects may completely or partially disappear with chronic administration, and there may be an increase in slow-wave delta bursts. There is suggestive evidence that withdrawal of opiates is accompanied by REM rebound and insomnia. Recovery of REM and slow-wave sleep following discontinuation of chronic methadone treatment may extend as long as 3 months.

Data concerning the minor tranquilizers as a class are highly variable. However, at least some or all of the substances studied, at the doses administered, have been found to decrease wakefulness, REM, and stage 4 sleep. Data concerning the major tranquilizers are even more difficult to interpret. Both chlorpromazine and reserpine have been reported to increase and to decrease REM sleep. Chlorpromazine appears to augment slow-wave sleep and may decrease wakefulness. Reserpine suppresses slow-wave sleep and has had variable effects on wakefulness.

The most consistently reported effect of antidepressants [tricyclics and monoamine oxidase (MAO) inhibitors] is suppression of REM sleep. The MAO inhibitors are capable of completely suppressing REM sleep, and discontinuation of the drug may or may not be accompanied by REM rebound and vivid dreams and nightmares (Wyatt, Kupfer, Scott, Robinson, and Snyder, 1969; Wyatt, Fram, Kupfer, and Snyder, 1971). Various effects of antidepressants on wakefulness and slow-wave sleep have been reported.

The barbiturates are, of course, in common use for the treatment of sleep disturbance. They, like the antidepressants, have consistently been found to reduce REM sleep, and this effect is dose dependent. The various barbiturates have differed in their reported effects on other EEG-EOG parameters: some apparently produce primary increases in the incidence of sleep spindles and slow-wave sleep, while others do not. Most of these drugs are effective in reducing nocturnal wakefulness. With chronic administration, there is apparently the development of tolerance to the REM-disturbing effects of barbiturates, but stage 4 sleep may be absent. In many studies, withdrawal of barbiturates has been accompanied by extended REM and slow-wave recovery and generally disturbed sleep, as well as reports of vivid dreams and nightmares. However, the evidence of a REM rebound following withdrawal of barbiturates has recently been questioned (Feinberg, Hibi, Cavness, and March, 1974).

Many of the nonbarbiturate hypnotics (including alcohol) have effects similar to the barbiturates, although there are apparent differences in the pattern of effects produced by the various members of this class of drugs. Most of them reduce REM sleep, at least with initial administration, and several also suppress slow-wave sleep. Although most of the nonbarbiturate hypnotics are initially effective in reducing nocturnal wakefulness, this effect, as well as the effects on some other EEG-EOG parameters, may be attenuated with chronic administration. Withdrawal of some of these drugs is accompanied by REM rebound and reports of vivid and frightening dreams.

From this very brief summary it is evident that most of the drugs used in the treatment of psychiatric and sleep disorders have effects on EEG-EOG sleep patterns. We emphasize to the reader that in order to make this point we have presented only simple generalizations derived from the vast amount of data currently available on this topic. By definition, a summary fails adequately to reflect inconsistencies in the data and specific aspects of the effects of the various different drugs. And if anything is true of data in this area, it is that there are inconsistencies and lacunae in the data.

As a result, at this time it is very difficult to describe with certainty the complete effect of any particular drug on sleep EEG-EOG patterns. This situation is at least partially due to several deficiencies in the data collection process. First, we now know that there are definite species differences in drug effects, and therefore data derived from study of lower animals may not be safely generalized to humans. In human studies, there has been little consistency in the selection of dose and time of administration of drug. Quite often various mixtures of patients have made up the subject samples, and this has prevented an assessment of drug effects independent of disease. By using patients of various sorts, some investigators have also introduced the confounding factor of concurrent medication during the study. As we have seen, withdrawal of many drugs is accompanied by at least short-term recovery effects in EEG-EOG sleep patterns. Too often, an insufficient time has been allowed between the withdrawal of the patients' usual medications and the administration of the study drug. As Freemon (1972) has documented, there has also been a failure to control for such carry-over or recovery effects in crossover studies of several drugs. Because of the expense of conducting sleep laboratory studies, much of the data results from study of only a few subjects. For the same reason, long-term studies of chronic drug effects and of withdrawal effects are sparse. Dose-response studies are virtually non-existent, as are attempts to determine equivalent doses of different drugs. This last point must be considered when evaluating claims of superior efficacy for one drug over another. In many studies, there has been no attempt to describe parameters other than those related to REM sleep. Thus, for very few drugs does there exist a validated description of the effects on *all* aspects of the EEG-EOG sleep pattern. And finally, as Freemon (1972) has discussed in detail, the use of a constant sleep length (in order to control for an exaggerated change in REM time due to changes in sleep length) and of double-blind drug administration procedures, and the analysis of data from portions of the night (in order to detect changes in the distribution of stages which may be obscured by total night values) have been far from standard procedures.

All of these factors contribute to the chaotic state of our knowledge about drug effects on sleep. In our opinion, sleep research will fail to make its full contribution in this area unless investigators adopt a more systematic and standardized methodology for the study of drugs, one which incorporates the principles of good pharmacological research and one which eliminates as many sources of confounding variation as possible.

In spite of the generally unsatisfactory state of our knowledge about the pharmacology of sleep, there are a number of treatment recommendations which can be made at this time. The first concerns the recent discovery by Guilleminault and his colleagues (Guilleminault, Eldridge, and Dement, 1973) that the primary cause of disturbed sleep in a certain percentage of insomniacs is the occurrence of repeated periods of apnea. In these patients, nocturnal restlessness results primarily from periodic arousals associated with the resumption of respiration. Since many barbiturates and other drugs depress respiration, it is highly advisable *not* to prescribe these medications for such patients. The drugs will in all probability not be effective, and they might even be life threatening. Chlorimipramine has been reported to be effective in the treatment of sleep apnea associated with the Pickwickian syndrome (Kumashiro, Sato, Hirata, Baba, and Otsuki, 1971; Schwartz and Rochemaure, 1973), and may benefit patients of this sort. Unfortunately, it may be difficult to identify patients with sleep apnea without a sleep laboratory evaluation which includes monitoring of respiratory patterns.

If hypnotics appear to be the treatment of choice for primary or secondary insomnia, we recommend use of one of the nonbarbiturate hypnotics, simply because their abuse potential seems to be somewhat smaller than that of the barbiturates. However, even patients given nonbarbiturate hypnotics should be monitored closely and continuously in order to prevent abuse of the drugs.

We have had success with a five-night on, two-night off schedule of hypnotic administration: it seems to retard the development of tolerance to the beneficial effects of the drug. Most patients are willing to tolerate discomfort on the off nights (usually weekends) when the reasons for this schedule are explained to them.

We would like to emphasize that in many cases a hypnotic may not be the most effective drug for alleviating primary or secondary insomnia. Quite often antidepressants or antianxiety agents relieve the sleep disturbance more effectively than hypnotics. The effectiveness of these agents of course depends on the complex of factors contributing to the particular patient's sleep disturbance.

A number of other sleep disorders can now be more or less effectively treated with drugs. For example, several of the slow-wave sleep arousal disturbances (pavor nocturnus and sleepwalking) may be alleviated at least partially by administration of diazepam (Fisher, Kahn, Edwards, and Davis, 1973; Saletu and Itil, 1973) or imipramine (Pesikoff and Davis, 1971). A combination of amphetamine or methylphenidate and a tricyclic antidepressant appears to reduce the sleep and other symptoms of narcoleptics (Parkes and Fenton, 1973; Zarcone, 1973; Guilleminault, Carskadon, and Dement, 1974). In study of several patients suffering from restless legs syndrome, a syndrome that has been described by Ekbom (1960), we have found the analgesic Percodan® to be effective in relieving the discomfort in the lower limbs which prevents the individual from sleeping. In our experience, hypnotics are ineffective in these patients. It should be noted, however, that addiction to Percodan is a potential problem, so only the smallest effective dose should be employed.

And finally, a number of sleep researchers have voiced warnings concerning the administration of REM-suppressing drugs to patients with cardiovascular disorders. It is known that heart rate and blood pressure increase and become more variable during REM sleep. If REM-suppressing drugs are administered to cardiovascular patients and are then discontinued, there is the danger that increased cardiovascular activity during the REM rebound may precipitate a cardiovascular crisis. For this reason, the management of sleep disturbances in cardiovascular patients presents very special problems and should be undertaken with extreme care and attention.

B. Nonpharmacological Modes of Treatment

Continuing study of and experience with psychotropic agents and sedative-hypnotics have revealed the great abuse potential of these drugs. As we have seen, the EEG-EOG sleep effects of many drugs are subject to the development of tolerance, and withdrawal of the drugs is often accompanied by disturbances of sleep and reports of nightmares. There has been much speculation that these factors contribute to the abuse potential of a drug. A desire to find alternative methods of treating sleep disorders which do not carry the risks of psychological or physical dependence has prompted current interest in extending and developing nonpharmacological methods of treatment.

Psychotherapy is, of course, a traditional method of treating primary and secondary insomnia. Successful treatment by psychotherapy is predicated on the fact that the patient's sleep disturbance has a psychological basis. Certainly psychological factors are primary in many patients, but without extensive physical and all-night EEG-EOG sleep evaluations it is unwise to assume that this is the case for any particular patient. Researchers are beginning to explore the uses of psychotherapy by investigating the efficacy of specific treatments for disturbances having a particular etiology. For example, Dr. L. E. Beutler in our laboratory is in the initial stages of a study designed to determine the effectiveness of implosive therapy in treating insomnia in which fear of death appears to be a major etiological factor. Several studies (Kahn, Baker, and Weiss, 1968; Hinkle and Lutker, 1972; Borkovec and Fowles, 1973) indicate that relaxation training may be beneficial for some insomniacs. Investigations along similar lines of other types of therapies may be expected to systematize the use of psychotherapy as a treatment of sleep disturbance and to increase its effectiveness.

CET involves the transcerebral application of a low-intensity electrical current. Although CET has been claimed to be effective in the treatment of a wide variety of conditions by Eastern European and Russian investigators, relatively little work has been done with it by American researchers. Wageneder and Schuy (1967; 1970) have edited two recent volumes concerning CET. There is some evidence (Rosenthal, 1972) that CET may be useful in the treatment of insomnia.

Current work on biofeedback training may have particular relevance to the treatment of sleep disturbances. As we have seen, the onset and maintenance of sleep is a complex process involving the interaction of many body systems, not the least of which is the autonomic nervous system. It may be that sleep onset is triggered by, among other things, the attainment of certain threshold values of autonomic nervous system function. We might speculate that certain insomniacs suffer from a narrowed range of such threshold values, and that this contributes to their difficulty in falling asleep. If the maintenance of sleep were also postulated to depend on the maintenance of autonomic function within a certain range, a similar defect might account for the inability of certain patients to sleep continuously throughout the night. There is growing evidence that biofeedback training techniques can provide some control over autonomic activity (Barber, DiCara, Kamiya, Miller, Shapiro, and Stoyva, 1971a; 1971b). Through application of such techniques it might be possible to train certain patients to induce more sleep-facilitating tone in their autonomic function. This area is largely unexplored, but would seem to be a promising one for future work.

The ideal treatment armamentarium for sleep disorders would be one which includes treatments which are designed and/or proven to be effective in correcting (i.e., *normalizing*) the sleep disorders for which they are intended. A first step in attaining this ideal is the development of an accurate description and classification of the disorders which must be treated. This step is far from being completed, as our discussion on disorders of sleep associated with schizophrenia and depression should indicate. However, there is enough information to suggest that no one treatment will benefit all patients with sleep disturbance. In all probability, future research will reveal that there are many very specific sleep disorders and that these specific disturbances require "tailor-made" therapies. Moreover, we can state categorically that no drug currently available meets the criterion of producing normal sleep. Many of them do appear to have at least short-term beneficial effects on nocturnal wakefulness, but these effects are invariably accompanied by distortions in the composition of sleep (percentages of stages, distribution of stages, etc.). Some investigators argue that these distortions should not constitute the basis for condemnation of a drug, since we now possess very little reliable evidence that lack of certain stages of sleep has deleterious effects on the individual's overall well being. In our opinion, this view fails to recognize the very primitive nature of our current knowledge about sleep and of our methods of investigating it. We prefer to assume that a normal night of sleep in a healthy individual has a certain configuration for a reason, and that with more systematic study and sophisticated methodologies we will be able to ascertain that reason. Although we are forced to make do with the drugs and other treatments which are currently available, we cannot fail to recognize that they are much less than satisfactory remedies for the variety of sleep disorders.

REFERENCES

Adey, W. R., Kado, R. T., and Walter, D. O. (1967): Computer analysis of EEG data from Gemini flight GT-7. *Aerosp. Med.*, 38:345–359.

Agnew, H. W., Jr., and Webb, W. B. (1972): Sleep stage scoring. Manuscript No. 293. Journal Supplement Abstracting Service, American Psychological Association.

Agnew, H. W., Jr., Webb, W. B., and Williams, R. L. (1964): The effects of stage four sleep deprivation. *Electroencephalogr. Clin. Neurophysiol.*, 17:68–70.

Agnew, H. W., Jr., Webb, W. B., and Williams, R. L. (1967): Sleep patterns in late middle age males: An EEG study. *Electroencephalogr. Clin. Neurophysiol.*, 23:168–171.

Aschoff, J. (1969): Desynchronization and resynchronization of human circadian rhythms. *Aerosp. Med.*, 40:844–849.

Aserinsky, E. (1969): The maximal capacity for sleep: Rapid eye movement density as an idex of sleep satiety. *Biol. Psychiatry*, 1:147–159.

Aserinsky, E. (1973): Relationship of rapid eye movement density to the prior accumulation of sleep and wakefulness. *Psychophysiology*, 10:545–558.

Aserinsky, E., and Kleitman, N. (1953): Regularly occurring periods of eye motility, and concomitant phenomena, during sleep. *Science*, 118:273–274.

Aserinsky, E., and Kleitman, N. (1955): Two types of ocular motility occurring in sleep. *J. Appl. Physiol.*, 8:1–10.

Athanassiadis, D., Draper, G. J., Honour, A. J., and Cranston, W. I. (1969): Variability of automatic blood pressure measurements over 24 hour periods. *Clin. Sci.,* 36:147–156.

Baldridge, B. J., Whitman, R. M., and Kramer, M. (1965): The concurrence of fine muscle activity and rapid eye movements during sleep. *Psychosom. Med.,* 27:19–26.

Barber, T., DiCara, L. V., Kamiya, J., Miller, N. E., Shapiro, D., and Stoyva, J., editors. (1971a): *Biofeedback and Self-Control 1970. An Aldine Annual on the Regulation of Bodily Processes and Consciousness.* Aldine-Atherton, Chicago.

Barber, T., DiCara, L. V., Kamiya, J., Miller, N. E., Shapiro, D., and Stoyva, J., editors. (1971b): *Biofeedback and Self-Control. An Aldine Reader on the Regulation of Bodily Processes and Consciousness.* Aldine-Atherton, Chicago.

Barratt, E., Beaver, W., White, R., Blakeney, P., and Adams, P. (1972): The effects of the chronic use of marijuana on sleep and perceptual-motor performance in humans. In: *Current Research in Marijuana,* edited by M. F. Lewis, pp. 163–193. Academic Press, New York.

Berger, H. (1929): Über das Elektroenkephalogramm des Menschen. *Arch. Psychiatr. Nervenkr.,* 87:527–570.

Berger, R. J. (1961): Tonus of extrinsic laryngeal muscles during sleep and dreaming. *Science,* 134:840.

Berger, R. J. (1969): Physiological characteristics of sleep. In: *Sleep. Physiology and Pathology. A Symposium,* edited by A. Kales, pp. 66–79. J. B. Lippincott Company, Philadelphia.

Berlucchi, G., Moruzzi, G., Salvi, G., and Strata, P. (1964): Pupil behavior and ocular movements during synchronized and desynchronized sleep. *Arch. Ital. Biol.,* 102:230–244.

Bizzi, E., Pompeiano, O., and Somogyi, I. (1964): Spontaneous activity of single vestibular neurons of unrestrained cats during sleep and wakefulness. *Arch. Ital. Biol.,* 102:308–330.

Bobon, D. P., Schulz, H., Mattke, D. J., and Simonova, O. (1973): Influence of synthetic Δ^8-tetrahydrocannabinol on all-night sleep EEG in man. In: *The Nature of Sleep. International Symposium, Würzburg, September 23–26, 1971,* edited by U. J. Jovanović, pp. 89–92. Gustav Fischer Verlag, Stuttgart.

Borkovec, T. D., and Fowles, D. C. (1973): Controlled investigation of the effects of progressive and hypnotic relaxation on insomnia. *J. Abnorm. Psychol.,* 82:153–158.

Boyar, R., Finkelstein, J., Roffwarg, H., Kapen, S., Weitzman, E., and Hellman, L. (1972a): Synchronization of augmented luteinizing hormone secretion with sleep during puberty. *N. Engl. J. Med.,* 287:582–586.

Boyar, R., Perlow, M., Hellman, L., Kapen, S., and Weitzman, E. (1972b): Twenty-four hour pattern of luteinizing hormone secretion in normal men with sleep stage recording. *J. Clin. Endocrinol. Metab.,* 35:73–81.

Breger, L. (1967): Function of dreams. *J. Abnorm. Psychol.,* Vol. 72. Monograph No. 641, pp. 1–28.

Bremer, F. (1954): The neurophysiological problem of sleep. In: *Brain Mechanisms and Consciousness,* edited by E. D. Adrian, F. Bremer, H. H. Jasper, and J. F. Delafresnaye, pp. 137–162. Charles C Thomas, Springfield, Illinois.

Broughton, R. J. (1968): Sleep disorders: Disorders of arousal? *Science,* 159:1070–1078.

Bunney, W. E., Jr., Goodwin, F. K., Murphy, D. L., House, K. M., and Gordon, E. K. (1972): The "switch process" in manic-depressive illness. II. Relationship to catecholamines, REM sleep, and drugs. *Arch. Gen. Psychiatry,* 27:304–309.

Burdick, J. A., Brinton, G., Goldstein, L., and Laszlo, M. (1970): Heart-rate variability in sleep and wakefulness. *Cardiology,* 55:79–83.

Caldwell, D. F., and Domino, E. F. (1967): Electroencephalographic and eye movement patterns during sleep in chronic schizophrenic patients. *Electroencephalogr. Clin. Neurophysiol.,* 22:414–420.

Carpenter, W. T., Jr., and Bunney, W. E., Jr. (1971): Behavioral effects of cortisol in man. *Semin. Psychiatry,* 3:421–434.

Cathala, H. P., and Guillard, A. (1961): La réactivité au cours du sommeil physiologique de l'homme. *Pathol. Biol.,* 9:1357–1375.

Coccagna, G., Mantovani, M., Brignani, F., Manzini, A., and Lugaresi, E. (1971): Arterial pressure changes during spontaneous sleep in man. *Electroencephalogr. Clin. Neurophysiol.*, 31:277–281.

Crisp, A. H., Stonehill, E., and Fenton, G. W. (1971): The relationship between sleep, nutrition and mood: A study of patients with anorexia nervosa. *Postgrad. Med. J.*, 47:207–213.

Dahlström, A., and Fuxe, K. (1964): Evidence for the existence of monoamine-containing neurons in the central nervous system. I. Demonstration of monoamines in the cell bodies of brain stem neurons. *Acta Physiol. Scand., Suppl. 232*, 62:5–55.

Dahlström, A., and Fuxe, K. (1965): Evidence for the existence of monoamine neurons in the central nervous system. II. Experimentally induced changes in the intraneuronal amine levels of bulbospinal neuron systems. *Acta Physiol. Scand., Suppl. 247*, 64:7–36.

Dement, W. (1955): Dream recall and eye movements during sleep in schizophrenics and normals. *J. Nerv. Ment. Dis.*, 122:263–269.

Dement, W. (1960): The effect of dream deprivation. *Science*, 131:1705–1707.

Dement, W. C. (1964a): Experimental dream studies. In: *Science and Psychoanalysis, Vol. 7: Development and Research*, edited by J. H. Masserman, pp. 129–184. Grune & Stratton, Inc., New York.

Dement, W. C. (1964b): Eye movements during sleep. In: *The Oculomotor System*, edited by M. B. Bender, pp. 366–416. Harper and Row, New York.

Dement, W. C. (1966): Psychophysiology of sleep and dreams. In: *American Handbook of Psychiatry, Vol. 3*, edited by S. Arieti, pp. 290–332. Basic Books, New York.

Dement, W. C. (1971): The nature and function of sleep. In: *Neuroelectric Research. Electroneuroprosthesis, Electroanesthesia and Nonconvulsive Electrotherapy*, edited by D. V. Reynolds and A. E. Sjoberg, pp. 171–204. Charles C Thomas, Springfield, Illinois.

Dement, W., Ferguson, J., Cohen, H., and Barchas, J. (1969a): Nonchemical methods and data using a biochemical model: The REM quanta. In: *Psychochemical Research in Man. Methods, Strategy, and Theory*, edited by A. J. Mandell and M. P. Mandell, pp. 275–325. Academic Press, New York.

Dement, W., and Fisher, C. (1963): Experimental interference with the sleep cycle. *Can. Psychiatr. Assoc. J.*, 8:400–405.

Dement, W., and Kleitman, N. (1957a): Cyclic variations in EEG during sleep and their relation to eye movements, body motility, and dreaming. *Electroencephalogr. Clin. Neurophysiol.*, 9:673–690.

Dement, W., and Kleitman, N. (1957b): The relation of eye movements during sleep to dream activity: An objective method for the study of dreaming. *J. Exp. Psychol.*, 53:339–346.

Dement, W., and Wolpert, E. A. (1958): The relation of eye movements, body motility, and external stimuli to dream content. *J. Exp. Psychol.*, 55:543–553.

Dement, W., Zarcone, V., Ferguson, J., Cohen, H., Pivik, T., and Barchas, J. 1969b): Some parallel findings in schizophrenic patients and serotonin-depleted cats. In: *Schizophrenia. Current Concepts and Research*, edited by D. V. Siva Sankar, pp. 776–811. PJD Publications Ltd., Hicksville, New York.

Dewan, E. M. (1970): The programing (P) hypothesis for REM sleep. In: *International Psychiatry Clinics, Vol. 7: Sleep and Dreaming*, edited by E. Hartmann, pp. 295–307. Little, Brown and Company, Boston.

Dewson, J. H., IV, Dement, W. C., and Simmons, F. B. (1965): Middle ear muscle activity in cats during sleep. *Exp. Neurol.*, 12:1–8.

Diaz-Guerrero, R., Gottlieb, J. S., and Knott, J. R. (1946): The sleep of patients with manic-depressive psychosis, depressive type. An electroencephalographic study. *Psychosom. Med.*, 8:399–404.

Ekbom, K. A. (1960): Restless legs syndrome. *Neurology (Minneap.)*, 10:868–873.

Evarts, E. V. (1962): Activity of neurons in visual cortex of the cat during sleep with low voltage fast EEG activity. *J. Neurophysiol.*, 25:812–816.

Evarts, E. V. (1964): Temporal patterns of discharge of pyramidal tract neurons during sleep and waking in the monkey. *J. Neurophysiol.*, 27:152–171.

Feinberg, I., Braun, M., Koresko, R. L., and Gottlieb, F. (1969): Stage 4 sleep in schizophrenia. *Arch. Gen. Psychiatry,* 21:262–266.

Feinberg, I., and Carlson, V. R. (1968): Sleep variables as a function of age in man. *Arch. Gen. Psychiatry,* 18:239–250.

Feinberg, I., and Evarts, E. V. (1969): Changing concepts of the function of sleep: Discovery of intense brain activity during sleep calls for revision of hypotheses as to its function. *Biol. Psychiatry,* 1:331–348.

Feinberg, I., Koresko, R. L., and Gottlieb, F. (1965): Further observations on electro-physiological sleep patterns in schizophrenia. *Compr. Psychiatry,* 6:21–24.

Feinberg, I., Koresko, R. L., Gottlieb, F., and Wender, P. H. (1964): Sleep electro-encephalographic and eye-movement patterns in schizophrenic patients. *Compr. Psychiatry,* 5:44–53.

Feinberg, I., Hibi, S., Cavness, C., and March, J. (1974): Absence of REM rebound after barbiturate withdrawal. *Science,* 185:534–535.

Fisher, C. (1965): Psychoanalytic implications of recent research on sleep and dreaming. Part I: Empirical findings. *J. Am. Psychoanal. Assoc.,* 13:197–270.

Fisher, C. Byrne, J., Edwards, A., and Kahn, E. (1970): A psychophysiological study of nightmares. *J. Am. Psychoanal. Assoc.,* 18:747–782.

Fisher, C., Gross, J., and Zuch, J. (1965): Cycle of penile erection synchronous with dreaming (REM) sleep. Preliminary report. *Arch. Gen. Psychiatry,* 12:29–45.

Fisher, C., Kahn, E., Edwards, A., and Davis, D. M. (1973): A psychophysiological study of nightmares and night terrors. The suppression of stage 4 night terrors with diazepam. *Arch. Gen. Psychiatry,* 28:252–259.

Foulkes, D. (1966): *The Psychology of Sleep.* Charles Scribner's Sons, New York.

Freemon, F. R. (1972): *Sleep Research. A Critical Review.* Charles C Thomas, Springfield, Illinois.

Gastaut, H., and Broughton, R. (1965): A clinical and polygraphic study of episodic phenomena during sleep. In: *Recent Advances in Biological Psychiatry, Vol. 7,* edited by J. Wortis, pp. 197–221. Plenum Press, New York.

Globus, G. G. (1966): Rapid eye movement cycle in real time. Implications for a theory of the D-state. *Arch. Gen. Psychiatry,* 15:654–659.

Green, W. J. (1965): The effect of LSD on the sleep-dream cycle. An exploratory study. *J. Nerv. Ment. Dis.,* 140:417–426.

Green, W. J. (1969): LSD and the sleep-dream cycle. *Exp. Med. Surg.,* 27:138–144.

Green, W. J., and Stajduhar, P. P. (1966): The effect of ECT on the sleep-dream cycle in a psychotic depression. *J. Nerv. Ment. Dis.,* 143:123–134.

Gresham, S. C., Agnew, H. W., Jr., and Williams, R. L. (1965): The sleep of depressed patients. An EEG and eye movement study. *Arch. Gen. Psychiatry,* 13:503–507.

Guilleminault, C., Carskadon, M., and Dement, W. C. (1974): On the treatment of rapid eye movement narcolepsy. *Arch. Neurol.,* 30:90–93.

Guilleminault, C., Eldridge, F. L., and Dement, W. C. (1973): Insomnia with sleep apnea: A new syndrome. *Science,* 181:856–858.

Hajnšek, F., Dogan, S., Gubarev, N., Dürrigl, V., Stojanović, V., and Jovanović, U. J. (1973): Some characteristics of sleep in depressed patients—a polygraphic study. In: *The Nature of Sleep. International Symposium, Würzburg, September 23–26, 1971,* edited by U. J. Jovanović, pp. 197–202. Gustav Fischer Verlag, Stuttgart.

Hartmann, E. (1968a): Dauerschlaf. A polygraphic study. *Arch. Gen. Psychiatry,* 18:99–111.

Hartmann, E. (1968b): Longitudinal studies of sleep and dream patterns in manic-depressive patients. *Arch. Gen. Psychiatry,* 19:312–329.

Hartmann, E. (1968c): The 90-minute sleep-dream cycle. *Arch. Gen. Psychiatry,* 18:280–286.

Hartmann, E. (1969a): Antidepressants and sleep. Clinical and theoretical implications. In: *Sleep. Physiology and Pathology. A Symposium,* edited by A. Kales, pp. 308–316. J. B. Lippincott Company, Philadelphia.

Hartmann, E. (1969b): Pharmacological studies of sleep and dreaming: Chemical and clinical relationships. *Biol. Psychiatry,* 1:243–258.

Hartmann, E., editor. (1970): *International Psychiatry Clinics, Vol. 7: Sleep and Dreaming.* Little, Brown and Company, Boston.

Hartmann, E. L. (1973): *The Functions of Sleep.* Yale University Press, New Haven.
Hauri, P., and Hawkins, D. R. (1971): Phasic REM, depression, and the relationship between sleeping and waking. *Arch. Gen. Psychiatry,* 25:56–63.
Hauri, P., and Hawkins, D. R. (1973): Individual differences in the sleep of depression. In: *The Nature of Sleep. International Symposium, Würzburg, September 23–26, 1971,* edited by U. J. Jovanović, pp. 193–197. Gustav Fischer Verlag, Stuttgart.
Hawkins, D. R. (1972): Sleep research and depression. In: *Recent Advances in the Psychobiology of the Depressive Illnesses. Proceedings of a Workshop Sponsored by the Clinical Research Branch, Division of Extramural Research Programs, National Institute of Mental Health.* D.H.E.W. Publication No. (HSM) 70–9053, edited by T. A. Williams, M. M. Katz, and J. A. Shield, Jr., pp. 141–146. U.S. Government Printing Office, Washington, D.C.
Hawkins, D. R., Mendels, J., Scott, J., Bensch, G., and Teachey, W. (1967): The psychophysiology of sleep in psychotic depression: A longitudinal study. *Psychosom. Med.,* 29:329–344.
Hellman, L., Nakada, F., Curti, J., Weitzman, E. D., Kream, J., Roffwarg, H., Ellman, S., Fukushima, D. K., and Gallagher, T. F. (1970): Cortisol is secreted episodically by normal man. *J. Clin. Endocrinol. Metab.,* 30:411–422.
Hess, W. R. (1933): Der Schlaf. *Klin. Wochenschr.,* 12:129–134.
Hess, W. R. (1944): Das Schlafsyndrom als Folge dienzephaler Reizung. *Helv. Physiol. Pharmacol. Acta,* 2:305–344.
Hinkle, J. E., and Lutker, E. R. (1972): Insomnia: A new approach. *Psychother. Theory Res. Pract.,* 9:236–237.
Hodes, R. (1964): Ocular phenomena in the two stages of sleep in the cat. *Exp. Neurol.,* 9:36–42.
Hodes, R., and Dement, W. C. (1964): Depression of electrically induced reflexes ("H-reflexes") in man during low voltage EEG "sleep." *Electroencephalogr. Clin. Neurophysiol.,* 17:617–629.
Honda, Y., Takahashi, K., Takahashi, S., Azumi, K., Irie, M., Sakuma, M., Tsushima, T., and Shizume, K. (1969): Growth hormone secretion during nocturnal sleep in normal subjects. *J. Clin. Endocrinol. Metab.,* 29:20–29.
Hursch, C. J. (1970): The scientific study of sleep and dreams. In: *International Psychiatry Clinics, Vol. 7: Sleep and Dreaming,* edited by E. Hartmann, pp. 387–402. Little, Brown and Company, Boston.
Hursch, C. J., Karacan, I., and Williams, R. L. (1972): Some characteristics of nocturnal penile tumescence in early middle-aged males. *Compr. Psychiatry,* 13:539–548.
Huttenlocher, P. R. (1961): Evoked and spontaneous activity in single units of medial brain stem during natural sleep and waking. *J. Neurophysiol.,* 24:451–468.
Jacobs, L., Feldman, M., and Bender, M. B. (1971): Eye movements during sleep. I. The pattern in the normal human. *Arch. Neurol.,* 25:151–159.
Jacobson, A., Kales, A., Lehmann, D., and Hoedemaker, F. S. (1964): Muscle tonus in human subjects during sleep and dreaming. *Exp. Neurol.,* 10:418–424.
Johnson, L. C. (1969): Psychological and physiological changes following total sleep deprivation. In: *Sleep. Physiology and Pathology. A Symposium,* edited by A. Kales, pp. 206–220. J. B. Lippincott Company, Philadelphia.
Johnson, L. C. (1970): A psychophysiology for all states. *Psychophysiology,* 6:501–516.
Johnson, L. C., and Lubin, A. (1966): Spontaneous electrodermal activity during waking and sleeping. *Psychophysiology,* 3:8–17.
Jones, E. (1949): *On the Nightmare.* Hogarth, London.
Jouvet, M. (1961): Telencephalic and rhombencephalic sleep in the cat. In: *Ciba Foundation Symposium on the Nature of Sleep,* edited by G. E. W. Wolstenholme and M. O'Connor, pp. 188–208. Little, Brown and Company, Boston.
Jouvet, M. (1962): Recherches sur les structures nerveuses et les mécanismes responsables des différentes phases du sommeil physiologique. *Arch. Ital. Biol.,* 100:125–206.
Jouvet, M. (1963): The rhombencephalic phase of sleep. In: *Progress in Brain Research, Vol. 1: Brain Mechanisms,* edited by G. Moruzzi, A. Fessard, and H. H. Jasper, pp. 406–424. Elsevier Publishing Company, New York.
Jouvet, M. (1967): Neurophysiology of the states of sleep. *Physiol. Rev.,* 47:117–177.

Jouvet, M. (1972): The role of monoamines and acetylcholine-containing neurons in the regulation of the sleep-waking cycle. *Ergeb. Physiol.,* 64:166–307.

Jouvet, M., and Delorme, F. (1965): Locus coeruleus et sommeil paradoxal. *C. R. Soc. Biol. (Paris),* 159:895–899.

Jouvet, M., and Jouvet, D. (1963): A study of the neurophysiological mechanisms of dreaming. In: *Electroencephalography and Clinical Neurophysiology, Suppl. 24: The Physiological Basis of Mental Activity,* edited by R. Hernández Péon, pp. 133–157. Elsevier Publishing Company, New York.

Jovanović, U. J. (1971): *Normal Sleep in Man. An Experimental Contribution to our Knowledge of the Phenomenology of Sleep.* Hippokrates Verlag, Stuttgart.

Jovanović, U. J., Dogan, S., Dürrigl, V., Gubarev, N., Hajnšek, F., Rogina, V., and Stojanović, V. (1973): Changes of sleep in manic-depressive patients dependent on the clinical state. In: *The Nature of Sleep. International Symposium, Würzburg, September 23–26, 1971,* edited by U. J. Jovanović, pp. 208–211. Gustav Fischer Verlag, Stuttgart.

Kaelbling, R. (1971): REM sleep suppression and rebound after antidepressant therapy. In: *Research in Comprehensive Psychiatry. Festschrift for a Tribute to Ralph M. Patterson. May, 1971,* edited by H. Goldman, pp. 61–75. Ohio State University Press, Columbus, Ohio.

Kahn, M., Baker, B. L., and Weiss, J. M. (1968): Treatment of insomnia by relaxation training. *J. Abnorm. Psychol.,* 73:556–558.

Kales, A., Hanley, J., Rickles, W., Kanas, N., Baker, M., and Goring, P. (1972): Effects of marijuana administration and withdrawal in chronic users and naive subjects. *Psychophysiology,* 9:92. (*Abstr.*)

Kales, A., Hoedemaker, F. S., Jacobson, A., and Lichtenstein, E. L. (1964): Dream deprivation: An experimental reappraisal. *Nature (Lond.),* 204:1337–1338.

Kales, A., Malmstrom, E. J., Scharf, M. B., and Rubin, R. T. (1969): Psychophysiological and biochemical changes following use and withdrawal of hypnotics. In: *Sleep. Physiology and Pathology. A Symposium,* edited by A. Kales, pp. 331–343. J. B. Lippincott Company, Philadelphia.

Kapen, S., Boyar, R., Hellman, L., and Weitzman, E. D. (1973a): Episodic release of luteinizing hormone at mid-menstrual cycle in normal adult women. *J. Clin. Endocrinol. Metab.,* 36:724–729.

Kapen, S., Boyar, R., Perlow, M., Hellman, L., and Weitzman, E. D. (1973b): Luteinizing hormone: Changes in secretory pattern during sleep in adult women. *Life Sci.,* 13:693–701.

Karacan, I. (1969): A simple and inexpensive transducer for quantitative measurements of penile erection during sleep. *Behav. Res. Methods Instrument.,* 1:251–252.

Karacan, I. (1970): Clinical value of nocturnal erection in the prognosis and diagnosis of impotence. *Med. Aspects Hum. Sexual.,* 4:27–34.

Karacan, I., Finley, W. W., Williams, R. L., and Hursch, C. J. (1970): Changes in stage 1-REM and stage 4 sleep during naps. *Biol. Psychiatry,* 2:261–265.

Karacan, I., Goodenough, D. R., Shapiro, A., and Starker, S. (1966): Erection cycle during sleep in relation to dream anxiety. *Arch. Gen. Psychiatry,* 15:183–189.

Karacan, I., Hursch, C. J., and Williams, R. L. (1972a): Some characteristics of nocturnal penile tumescence in elderly males. *J. Gerontol.,* 27:39–45.

Karacan, I., Hursch, C. J., Williams, R. L., and Littell, R. C. (1972b): Some characteristics of nocturnal penile tumescence during puberty. *Pediat. Res.,* 6:529–537.

Karacan, I., Hursch, C. J., Williams, R. L., and Thornby, J. I. (1972c): Some characteristics of nocturnal penile tumescence in young adults. *Arch. Gen. Psychiatry,* 26:351–356.

Karacan, I., Rosenbloom, A. L., Londono, J. H., Williams, R. L., and Salis, P. J. (1975a): Growth hormone levels during morning and afternoon naps. *P.D.M.,* 5–6:26–29.

Karacan, I., Rosenbloom, A. L., Williams, R. L., Finley, W. W., and Hursch, C. J. (1971): Slow wave sleep deprivation in relation to plasma growth hormone concentration. *Behav. Neuropsychiatry,* 2:11–14.

Karacan, I., Salis, P. J., and Williams, R. L. (1973): Clinical disorders of sleep. *Psychosomatics,* 14:77–88.

Karacan, I., Thornby, J. I., Booth, G. H., Okawa, M., Salis, P. J., Anch, A. M., and Williams, R. L. (1975b): Dose-response effects of coffee on objective (EEG) and subjective measures of sleep. In: *Proceedings of the Second European Congress on Sleep Research,* edited by W. P. Koella and P. Levin. S. Karger, Basel. (*in press*).

Karacan, I., and Williams, R. L. (1970): Current advances in theory and practice relating to postpartum syndromes. *Psychiatry Med.,* 1:307–328.

Kay, D. C. (1973): Sleep and some psychoactive drugs. *Psychosomatics,* 14:108–118.

Kleitman, N. (1963): *Sleep and Wakefulness* (rev. ed.). University of Chicago Press, Chicago.

Kleitman, N. (1967): The basic rest-activity cycle and physiological correlates of dreaming. *Exp. Neurol.,* 19:2–4.

Kleitman, N. (1969): Basic rest-activity cycle in relation to sleep and wakefulness. In: *Sleep. Physiology and Pathology. A Symposium,* edited by A. Kales, pp. 33–38. J. B. Lippincott Company, Philadelphia.

Koella, W. P. (1967): *Sleep. Its Nature and Physiological Organization.* Charles C Thomas, Springfield, Illinois.

Koella, W. P. (1969): Neurohumoral aspects of sleep control. *Biol. Psychiatry,* 1:161–177.

Koella, W. P. (1973): The physiology and pharmacology of sleep. In: *Biological Psychiatry,* edited by J. Mendels, pp. 263–296. John Wiley & Sons, New York.

Kohler, W. C., Coddington, R. D., and Agnew, H. W., Jr. (1968): Sleep patterns in 2-year-old children. *J. Pediatr.,* 72:228–233.

Koresko, R. L., Snyder, F., and Feinberg, I. (1963): "Dream time" in hallucinating and non-hallucinating schizophrenic patients. *Nature (Lond.),* 199:1118–1119.

Kretschmar, J. H., and Peters, U. H. (1973): Schlafentzug zur Behandlung der endogenen Depression. In: *The Nature of Sleep. International Symposium, Würzburg, September 23–26, 1971,* edited by U. J. Jovanović, pp. 175–177. Gustav Fischer Verlag, Stuttgart.

Kumashiro, H., Sato, M., Hirata, J., Baba, O., and Otsuki, S. (1971): "Sleep apnoea" and sleep regulating mechanism. A case effectively treated with monochlorimipramine. *Folia Psychiatr. Neurol. Jap.,* 25:41–49.

Kupfer, D. J., and Foster, F. G. (1972): Interval between onset of sleep and rapid-eye-movement sleep as an indicator of depression. *Lancet,* 2:684–686.

Kupfer, D. J., and Heninger, G. R. (1972): REM activity as a correlate of mood changes throughout the night. Electroencephalographic sleep patterns in a patient with a 48-hour cyclic mood disorder. *Arch. Gen. Psychiatry,* 27:368–373.

Kupfer, D. J., Himmelhoch, J. M., Swartzburg, M., Anderson, C., Byck, R., and Detre, T. P. (1972): Hypersomnia in manic-depressive disease. (A preliminary report). *Dis. Nerv. Syst.,* 33:720–724.

Kupfer, D. J., Wyatt, R. J., Scott, J., and Snyder, F. (1970): Sleep disturbance in acute schizophrenic patients. *Am. J. Psychiatry,* 126:1213–1223.

Legendre, R., and Piéron, H. (1912): De la propriété hypnotoxique des humeurs développée au cours d'une veille prolongée. *C. R. Soc. Biol. (Paris),* 72:210–212.

Lester, B. K., Burch, N. R., and Dossett, R. C. (1967): Nocturnal EEG-GSR profiles: The influence of presleep states. *Psychophysiology,* 3:238–248.

Loomis, A. L., Harvey, E. N., and Hobart, G. (1935): Further observations on the potential rhythms of the cerebral cortex during sleep. *Science,* 82:198–200.

Lowy, F. H., Cleghorn, J. M., and McClure, D. J. (1971): Sleep patterns in depression. Longitudinal study of six patients and brief review of literature. *J. Nerv. Ment. Dis.,* 153:10–26.

Luby, E. D., and Caldwell, D. F. (1967): Sleep deprivation and EEG slow wave activity in chronic schizophrenia. *Arch. Gen. Psychiatry,* 17:361–364.

Lucke, C., and Glick, S. M. (1971): Experimental modification of the sleep-induced peak of growth hormone secretion. *J. Clin. Endocrinol. Metab.,* 32:729–736.

Magnes, J., Moruzzi, G., and Pompeiano, O. (1961): Synchronization of the EEG produced by low-frequency electrical stimulation of the region of the solitary tract. *Arch. Ital. Biol.,* 99:33–67.

Maron, L., Rechtschaffen, A., and Wolpert, E. A. (1964): Sleep cycle during napping. *Arch. Gen. Psychiatry,* 11:503–508.

Mayer-Gross, W. (1954): The diagnosis of depression. *Br. Med. J.,* 2:948–950.

Mellette, H. C., Hutt, B. K., Askovitz, S. I., and Horvath, S. M. (1951): Diurnal variations in body temperatures. *J. Appl. Physiol.,* 3:665–675.

Mendels, J., and Hawkins, D. R. (1967a): Sleep and depression. A controlled EEG study. *Arch. Gen. Psychiatry,* 16:344–354.

Mendels, J., and Hawkins, D. R. (1967b): Sleep and depression. A follow-up study. *Arch. Gen. Psychiatry,* 16:536–542.

Mendels, J., and Hawkins, D. R. (1968): Sleep and depression. Further considerations. *Arch. Gen. Psychiatry,* 19:445–452.

Mendels, J., and Hawkins, D. R. (1971a): Longitudinal sleep study in hypomania. *Arch. Gen. Psychiatry,* 25:274–277.

Mendels, J., and Hawkins, D. R. (1971b): Sleep and depression. IV. Longitudinal studies. *J. Nerv. Ment. Dis.,* 153:251–272.

Mendels, J., and Hawkins, D. R. (1972): Sleep studies in depression. In: *Recent Advances in the Psychobiology of the Depressive Illnesses. Proceedings of a Workshop Sponsored by the Clinical Research Branch, Division of Extramural Research Programs, National Institute of Mental Health.* D.H.E.W. Publication No. (HSM) 70–9053, edited by T. A. Williams, M. M. Katz, and J. A. Shield, Jr., pp. 147–170. U.S. Government Printing Office, Washington, D.C.

Monnier, M., Koller, T., and Graber, S. (1963): Humoral influences of induced sleep and arousal upon electrical brain activity of animals with crossed circulation. *Exp. Neurol.,* 8:264–277.

Monroe, L. J. (1967): Psychological and physiological differences between good and poor sleepers. *J. Abnorm. Psychol.,* 72:255–264.

Morrison, A. R., and Pompeiano, O. (1965): Vestibular influences on vegetative functions during the rapid eye movement periods of desynchronized sleep. *Experientia,* 21:667–668.

Moruzzi, G. (1964): Reticular influences on the EEG. *Electroencephalogr. Clin. Neurophysiol.,* 16:2–17.

Moruzzi, G. (1966): The functional significance of sleep with particular regard to the brain mechanisms underlying consciousness. In: *Brain and Conscious Experience,* edited by J. C. Eccles, pp. 345–388. Springer-Verlag New York Inc., New York.

Moruzzi, G. (1972): The sleep-waking cycle. *Ergeb. Physiol.,* 64:1–165.

Moruzzi, G., and Magoun, H. W. (1949): Brain stem reticular formation and activation of the EEG. *Electroencephalogr. Clin. Neurophysiol.,* 1:455–473.

Moskowitz, E., and Berger, R. J. (1969): Rapid eye movements and dream imagery: Are they related? *Nature (Lond.),* 224:613–614.

Muzio, J. N., Roffwarg, H. P., and Kaufman, E. (1966): Alterations in the nocturnal sleep cycle resulting from LSD. *Electroencephalogr. Clin. Neurophysiol.,* 21:313–324.

Naitoh, P., Johnson, L. C., and Austin, M. (1971): Aquanaut sleep patterns during Tektite 1: A 60-day habitation under hyperbaric nitrogen saturation. *Aerosp. Med.,* 42:69–77.

Newman, E. A., and Evans, C. R. (1965): Human dream processes as analogous to computer programme clearance. *Nature (Lond.),* 206:534.

Nichols, C. T., and Tyler, F. H. (1967): Diurnal variation in adrenal cortical function. In: *Annual Review of Medicine, Vol. 18,* edited by A. C. De Graff and W. P. Creger, pp. 313–324. Annual Reviews, Inc., Palo Alto, California.

Onheiber, P., White, P. T., DeMyer, M. K., and Ottinger, D. R. (1965): Sleep and dream patterns of child schizophrenics. *Arch. Gen. Psychiatry,* 12:568–571.

Ornitz, E. M., Ritvo, E. R., and Walter, R. D. (1965a): Dreaming sleep in autistic and schizophrenic children. *Am. J. Psychiatry,* 122:419–424.

Ornitz, E. M., Ritvo, E. R., and Walter, R. D. (1965b): Dreaming sleep in autistic twins. *Arch. Gen. Psychiatry,* 12:77–79.

Oswald, I. (1968): Drugs and sleep. *Pharmacol. Rev.,* 20:273–303.

Oswald, I. (1969): Sleep and dependence on amphetamine and other drugs. In: *Sleep. Physiology and Pathology. A Symposium,* edited by A. Kales, pp. 317–330. J. B. Lippincott Company, Philadelphia.

Oswald, I. (1970): Effects on sleep of amphetamine and its derivatives. In: *Amphetamines and Related Compounds. Proceedings of the Mario Negri Institute for*

Pharmacological Research, Milan, Italy, edited by E. Costa and S. Garattini, pp. 865–871. Raven Press, New York.

Oswald, I., Berger, R. J., Jaramillo, R. A., Keddie, K. M. G., Olley, P. C., and Plunkett, G. B. (1963): Melancholia and barbiturates: A controlled EEG, body and eye movement study of sleep. *Br. J. Psychiatry,* 109:66–78.

Oswald, I., Evans, J. I., and Lewis, S. A. (1969): Addictive drugs cause suppression of paradoxical sleep with withdrawal rebound. In: *Scientific Basis of Drug Dependence. A Symposium,* edited by H. Steinberg, pp. 243–257. Grune & Stratton, Inc., New York.

Parker, D. C., and Rossman, L. G. (1971): Human growth hormone release in sleep: Nonsuppression by acute hyperglycemia. *J. Clin. Endocrinol. Metab.,* 32:65–69.

Parker, D. C., Sassin, J. F., Mace, J. W., Gotlin, R. W., and Rossman, L. G. (1969): Human growth hormone release during sleep: Electroencephalographic correlation. *J. Clin. Endocrinol. Metab.,* 29:871–874.

Parkes, J. D., and Fenton, G. W. (1973): Levo(−)amphetamine and dextro(+)amphetamine in the treatment of narcolepsy. *J. Neurol. Neurosurg. Psychiatry,* 36:1076–1081.

Parmeggiani, P. L., and Franzini, C. (1970): Activity of hypothalamic units during sleep. *Experientia,* 26:682. (*Abstr.*)

Pesikoff, R. B., and Davis, P. C. (1971): Treatment of pavor nocturnus and somnambulism in children. *Am. J. Psychiatry,* 128:778–781.

Pflug, B., and Tölle, R. (1971): Disturbance of the 24-hour rhythm in endogenous depression and the treatment of endogenous depression by sleep deprivation. *Int. Pharmacopsychiatry,* 6:187–196.

Pflug, B., and Tölle, R. (1973): Die Wirkung des Schlafentzuges auf die Symptomatik der endogenen Depression. In: *The Nature of Sleep. International Symposium, Würzburg, September 23–26, 1971,* edited by U. J. Jovanović, pp. 177–180. Gustav Fischer Verlag, Stuttgart.

Pickering, G. W., Sleight, P., and Smyth, H. S. (1967): The relation of arterial pressure to sleep and arousal in man. *J. Physiol. (Lond.),* 191:76P–78P.

Piéron, H. (1913): *Le Problème Physiologique du Sommeil.* Masson et Cie, Paris.

Pivik, T., and Dement, W. C. (1970): Phasic changes in muscular and reflex activity during non-REM sleep. *Exp. Neurol.,* 27:115–124.

Pivik, R. T., Zarcone, V., Dement, W. C., and Hollister, L. E. (1972): Delta-9-tetrahydrocannabinol and synhexyl: Effects on human sleep patterns. *Clin. Pharmacol. Ther.,* 13:426–435.

Pompeiano, O., and Morrison, A. R. (1965): Vestibular influences during sleep. I. Abolition of the rapid eye movements of desynchronized sleep following vestibular lesions. *Arch. Ital. Biol.,* 103:569–595.

Pranikoff, K., Karacan, I., Larson, E. A., Williams, R. L., Thornby, J. I., and Hursch, C. J. (1973): Effects of marijuana smoking on the sleep EEG. Preliminary studies. *J. Florida Med. Assoc.,* 60:28–31.

Rechtschaffen, A., and Kales, A., editors. (1968): *A Manual of Standardized Terminology, Techniques and Scoring System for Sleep Stages of Human Subjects.* U.S. Government Printing Office (Public Health Service), Washington, D.C.

Rechtschaffen, A., Schulsinger, F., and Mednick, S. A. (1964): Schizophrenia and physiological indices of dreaming. *Arch. Gen. Psychiatry,* 10:89–93.

Richardson, D. W., Honour, A. J., Fenton, G. W., Stott, F. H., and Pickering, G. W. (1964): Variation in arterial pressure throughout the day and night. *Clin. Sci.,* 26:445–460.

Roffwarg, H. P., Dement, W. C., Muzio, J. N., and Fisher, C. (1962): Dream imagery: Relationship to rapid eye movements of sleep. *Arch. Gen. Psychiatry,* 7:235–258.

Roffwarg, H. P., Muzio, J. N., and Dement, W. C. (1966): Ontogenetic development of the human sleep-dream cycle. *Science,* 152:604–619.

Rohmer, F., Schaff, G., Collard, M., and Kurtz, D. (1965): La motilité spontanée, la fréquence cardiaque et la fréquence respiratoire au cours du sommeil chez l'homme normal. Leurs relations avec les manifestations électroencéphalographiques et la profondeur du sommeil. In: *Le Sommeil de Nuit Normal et Pathologique. Études Élec-*

troencéphalographiques, edited by La Société d'Électroencéphalographie et de Neurophysiologie Clinique de Langue Française, pp. 192–207. Masson, Paris.

Rosenthal, S. H. (1972): Electrosleep: A double-blind clinical study. *Biol. Psychiatry,* 4:179–185.

Ross, J. J., Agnew, H. W., Jr., Williams, R. L., and Webb, W. B. (1968): Sleep patterns in pre-adolescent children: An EEG-EOG study. *Pediatrics,* 42:324–335.

Rubin, R. T., Kales A., Adler, R., Fagan, T., and Odell, W. (1972): Gonadotropin secretion during sleep in normal adult men. *Science,* 175:196–198.

Saletu, B., and Itil, T. M. (1973): Digital computer "sleep prints"—an indicator of the most effective drug treatment of somnambulism. *Clin. Electroencephalogr.,* 4:33–41.

Sampson, H. (1966): Psychological effects of deprivation of dreaming sleep. *J. Nerv. Ment. Dis.,* 143:305–317.

Sassin, J. F., Frantz, A. G., Kapen, S., and Weitzman, E. D. (1973): The nocturnal rise of human prolactin is dependent on sleep. *J. Clin. Endocrinol. Metab.,* 37:436–440.

Sassin, J. F., Frantz, A. G., Weitzman, E. D., and Kapen, S. (1972): Human prolactin: 24-hour pattern with increased release during sleep. *Science,* 177:1205–1207.

Sassin, J. F., Parker, D. C., Johnson, L. C., Rossman, L. G., Mace, J. W., and Gotlin, R. W. (1969*a*): Effects of slow wave sleep deprivation on human growth hormone release in sleep: Preliminary study. *Life Sci.,* 8:1299–1307.

Sassin, J. F., Parker, D. C., Mace, J. W., Gotlin, R. W., Johnson, L. C., and Rossman, L. G. (1969*b*): Human growth hormone release: Relation to slow-wave sleep and sleep-waking cycles. *Science,* 165:513–515.

Schnedorf, J. G., and Ivy, A. C. (1939): An examination of the hypnotoxin theory of sleep. *Am. J. Physiol.,* 125:491–505.

Schwartz, B. A., and Rochemaure, J. (1973): Syndrome pickwickien: Traitement par la chlorimipramine. *Nouv. Presse Méd.,* 2:1520.

Shapiro, A., Goodenough, D. R., Biederman, I., and Sleser, I. (1964): Dream recall and the physiology of sleep. *J. Appl. Physiol.,* 19:778–783.

Shurley, J. T., Pierce, C. M., Natani, K., and Brooks, R. E. (1970): Sleep and activity patterns at South Pole Station. A preliminary report. *Arch. Gen. Psychiatry,* 22:385–389.

Snyder, F. (1966): Toward an evolutionary theory of dreaming. *Am. J. Psychiatry,* 123:121–136.

Snyder, F. (1968): Electrographic studies of sleep in depression. In: *Computers and Electronic Devices in Psychiatry,* edited by N. S. Kline and E. Laska, pp. 272–303. Grune & Stratton, Inc., New York.

Snyder, F. (1969): Sleep disturbance in relation to acute psychosis. In: *Sleep. Physiology and Pathology. A Symposium,* edited by A. Kales, pp. 170–182. J. B. Lippincott Company, Philadelphia.

Snyder, F. (1972): NIH studies of EEG sleep in affective illness. In: *Recent Advances in the Psychobiology of the Depressive Illnesses. Proceedings of a Workshop Sponsored by the Clinical Research Branch, Division of Extramural Research Programs, National Institute of Mental Health.* D.H.E.W. Publication No. (HSM) 70–9053, edited by T. A. Williams, M. M. Katz, and J. A. Shield, Jr., pp. 147–170. U.S. Government Printing Office, Washington, D.C.

Snyder, F., Hobson, J. A., and Goldfrank, F. (1963): Blood pressure changes during human sleep. *Science,* 142:1313–1314.

Snyder, F., Hobson, J. A., Morrison, D. F., and Goldfrank, F. (1964): Changes in respiration, heart rate, and systolic blood pressure in human sleep. *J. Appl. Physiol.,* 19:417–422.

Snyder, F., and Scott, J. (1972): The psychophysiology of sleep. In: *Handbook of Psychophysiology,* edited by N. S. Greenfield and R. A. Sternbach, pp. 645–708. Holt, Rinehart and Winston, Inc., New York.

Sollberger, A. (1965): *Biological Rhythm Research.* Elsevier Publishing Company, New York.

Stern, M., Fram, D. H., Wyatt, R., Grinspoon, L., and Tursky, B. (1969): All-night sleep studies of acute schizophrenics. *Arch. Gen. Psychiatry,* 20:470–477.

Takahashi, Y., Kipnis, D. M., and Daughaday, W. H. (1968): Growth hormone secretion during sleep. *J. Clin. Invest.,* 47:2079–2090.

Underwood, L. E., Azumi, K., Voina, S. J., and Van Wyk, J. J. (1971): Growth hormone levels during sleep in normal and growth hormone deficient children. *Pediatrics*, 48:946–954.

Vogel, G. W., Thompson, F. C., Jr., Thurmond, A., and Rivers, B. (1973): The effect of REM deprivation on depression. *Psychosomatics*, 14:104–107.

Vogel, G. W., and Traub, A. C. (1968): REM deprivation. I. The effect on schizophrenic patients. *Arch. Gen. Psychiatry*, 18:287–300.

Vogel, G. W., Traub, A. C., Ben-Horin, P., and Meyers, G. M. (1968): REM deprivation. II. The effects on depressed patients. *Arch. Gen. Psychiatry*, 18:301–311.

Wageneder, F. M., and Schuy, S., editors. (1967): *Electrotherapeutic Sleep and Electroanaesthesia. Proceedings of the First International Symposium, Graz, Austria, September 12–17, 1966.* Excerpta Medica International Congress Series No. 136. Excerpta Medica Foundation, Amsterdam.

Wageneder, F. M., and Schuy, S., editors. (1970): *Electrotherapeutic Sleep and Electroanesthesia, Vol. 2. Proceedings of the Second International Symposium, Graz, Austria, September 8–13, 1969.* Excerpta Medica International Congress Series No. 212. Excerpta Medica Foundation, Amsterdam.

Walsh, J. T., and Cordeau, J. P. (1965): Responsiveness in the visual system during various phases of sleep and waking. *Exp. Neurol.*, 11:80–103.

Webb, W. B. (1969): Partial and differential sleep deprivation. In: *Sleep. Physiology and Pathology. A Symposium*, edited by A. Kales, pp. 221–231. J. B. Lippincott Company, Philadelphia.

Webb, W. B., editor. (1972): Sleep deprivation: Total, partial and selective. In: *Perspectives in the Brain Sciences, Vol. 1: The Sleeping Brain*, edited by M. H. Chase, pp. 323–361. Brain Information Service/Brain Research Institute, UCLA, Los Angeles.

Webb, W. B., and Agnew, H. W., Jr. (1967): Sleep cycling within twenty-four hour periods. *J. Exp. Psychol.*, 74:158–160.

Webb, W. B., Agnew, H. W., Jr., and Sternthal, H. (1966): Sleep during the early morning. *Psychonom. Sci.*, 6:277–278.

Weiss, B. L., McPartland, R. J., and Kupfer, D. J. (1973): Once more: The inaccuracy of non-EEG estimations of sleep. *Am. J. Psychiatry*, 130:1282–1285.

Weitzman, E. D., Fukushima, D., Nogeire, C., Roffwarg, H., Gallagher, T. F., and Hellman, L. (1971): Twenty-four hour pattern of the episodic secretion of cortisol in normal subjects. *J. Clin. Endocrinol. Metab.*, 33:14–22.

Weitzman, E. D., Goldmacher, D., Kripke, D., MacGregor, P., Kream, J., and Hellman, L. (1968): Reversal of sleep-waking cycle: Effect on sleep stage pattern and certain neuroendocrine rhythms. *Trans. Am. Neurol. Assoc.*, 93:153–157.

Weitzman, E. D., Kripke, D. F., Goldmacher, D., McGregor, P., and Nogeire, C. (1970a): Acute reversal of the sleep-waking cycle in man. Effect on sleep stage patterns. *Arch. Neurol.*, 22:483–489.

Weitzman, E. D., Kripke, D. F., Kream, J., McGregor, P., and Hellman, L. (1970b): The effect of a prolonged non-geographic 180° sleep-wake cycle shift on body temperature, plasma growth hormone, cortisol, and urinary 17 OCHS. *Psychophysiology*, 3:307. (*Abstr.*)

Weitzman, E. D., Schaumburg, H., and Fishbein, W. (1966): Plasma 17-hydroxycorticosteroid levels during sleep in man. *J. Clin. Endocrinol. Metab.*, 26:121–127.

Whybrow, P. C., and Mendels, J. (1969): Toward a biology of depression: Some suggestions from neurophysiology. *Am. J. Psychiatry*, 125:1491–1500.

Williams, H. L., Holloway, F. A., and Griffiths, W. J. (1973): Physiological psychology: Sleep. In: *Annual Review of Psychology, Vol. 24*, edited by P. J. Mussen and M. R. Rosenzweig, pp. 279–316. Annual Reviews Inc., Palo Alto, California.

Williams, H. L., and Salamy, A. (1972): Alcohol and sleep. In: *The Biology of Alcoholism, Vol. 2: Physiology and Behavior*, edited by B. Kissin and H. Begleiter, pp. 435–483. Plenum Press, New York.

Williams, R. L., Agnew, H. W., Jr., and Webb, W. B. (1964): Sleep patterns in young adults: An EEG study. *Electroencephalogr. Clin. Neurophysiol.*, 17:376–381.

Williams, R. L., Agnew, H. W., Jr., and Webb, W. B. (1966): Sleep patterns in the young adult female: An EEG study. *Electroencephalogr. Clin. Neurophysiol.,* 20:264–266.

Williams, R. L., Agnew, H. W., Jr., and Webb, W. B. (1967): Effects of prolonged stage four and 1-REM sleep deprivation. EEG, task performance, and psychologic responses. *SAM Reports,* Sam-TR-67–59.

Williams, R. L., Karacan, I., and Hursch, C. J. (1974): *Electroencephalography (EEG) of Human Sleep: Clinical Applications.* John Wiley & Sons, New York.

Williams, R. L., Karacan, I., Hursch, C. J., and Davis, C. E. (1972*a*): Sleep patterns of pubertal males. *Pediatr. Res.,* 6:643–648.

Williams, R. L., Karacan, I., Thornby, J. I., and Salis, P. J. (1972*b*): The electroencephalogram sleep patterns of middle-aged males. *J. Nerv. Ment. Dis.,* 154:22–30.

Witkin, H. A., and Lewis, H. B., editors. (1967): *Experimental Studies of Dreaming.* Random House, New York.

Wolpert, E. A. (1960): Studies in psychophysiology of dreams. II. An electromyographic study of dreaming. *Arch. Gen. Psychiatry,* 2:231–241.

Wyatt, R. J., Fram, D. H., Kupfer, D. J., and Snyder, F. (1971): Total prolonged drug-induced REM sleep suppression in anxious-depressed patients. *Arch. Gen. Psychiatry,* 24:145–155.

Wyatt, R. J., Kupfer, D. J., Scott, J., Robinson, D. S., and Snyder, F. (1969): Longitudinal studies of the effect of monoamine oxidase inhibitors on sleep in man. *Psychopharmacologia,* 15:236–244.

Zarcone, V. (1973): Narcolepsy. *N. Engl. J. Med.,* 288:1156–1166.

Zarcone, V., and Dement, W. (1969): Sleep disturbances in schizophrenia. In: *Sleep. Physiology and Pathology. A Symposium,* edited by A. Kales, pp. 192–199. J. B. Lippincott Company, Philadelphia.

Zarcone, V., Gulevich, G., Pivik, T., and Dement, W. (1968): Partial REM phase deprivation and schizophrenia, *Arch. Gen. Psychiatry,* 18:194–202.

Zung, W. W. K. (1970): The pharmacology of disordered sleep: A laboratory approach. In: *International Psychiatry Clinics, Vol. 7: Sleep and Dreaming,* edited by E. Hartmann, pp. 123–146. Little, Brown and Company, Boston.

Zung, W. W. K., Wilson, W. P., and Dodson, W. E. (1964): Effect of depressive disorders on sleep EEG responses. *Arch. Gen. Psychiatry,* 10:439–445.

Biological Foundations of Psychiatry,
edited by R. G. Grenell and S. Gabay.
Raven Press, New York © 1976.

Neurobiological Aspects of Memory

James L. McGaugh

Department of Psychobiology, School of Biological Sciences, University of California, Irvine, California 92664

I. INTRODUCTION

It is a fact of experience that we are changed by our experiences. Everything that we, as humans, do involves memory. In the most general sense, the term memory is used to refer to the consequences of past experience. It is generally assumed that memory is due to changes in the central nervous system (CNS). But the problem of understanding the neural bases of memory —or the nature of the *engram* (Lashley, 1950)—is not simply one of determining the neural residua of experience. Memory involves a complex set of processes by which experiences alter the nervous system in ways such that the changes endure and affect subsequent experience and behavior.

An analysis of one's attempts to recall information that was well learned at some previous time will illustrate some of the complexity of memory processes. Recall for example the numbers from 1 to 10 in a foreign language that you have not used for some time. In order to do this, it is not sufficient that you have the information "stored." You must be able to understand the request, remember the request, search for the particular words needed, discriminate them from all other words you have stored, and use this information to generate motor responses—either speaking or writing. The recalled information does not, of course, consist simply of words or static images or discrete responses. We remember the context in which particular experiences occurred and, as part of that context, the affective tone.

Obviously memory involves enormously complex processing systems. An understanding of the neurobiological bases of memory will require an understanding of the processing systems involved in storing and retrieving experiences as well as the specific neural changes that are produced by experience. Thus the general question concerning the neural basis of memory must be considered as referring to a series of questions concerning the way in which the nervous system processes experiences.

II. CRITICAL QUESTIONS CONCERNING MEMORY

A brief review of some of the major questions of memory will serve to emphasize the complexity of the problem of understanding memory. Subsequent sections in this chapter will consider recent research findings that bear on some of these questions.

A. What Experiences Are Stored?

We are continuously bombarded by stimulation from all of our senses as well as from our thinking, dreaming, and planning. Is the nervous system changed by every experience? If so, then what kinds of changes are produced? It seems that the changes would have to be extremely subtle since the number of nerve cells and their potential for change is not infinite. If all experiences are not stored, then what processes determine the selection of information for storage? If we do not store instant-by-instant information about pressures on different regions of the body for example, or transient levels of auditory stimulation, then why do we store other kinds of information? We do in fact appear to select information for storage (Weinberger, 1971) but the processes underlying selection are poorly understood.

Memories come in different forms. We remember isolated experiences, complex events, and skills. It is extremely important to note that memory does not consist simply of responses that are made during the course of learning. We readily learn by observing others learning and performing. What is it that is stored that enables us to learn by observing and to acquire complicated skills such as language or the ability to read music? Obviously simple models of the nervous system in which memories are formed only as a

consequence of repetitive activation of the same neural units in precise sequence will not provide an explanation of memory for such complex skills
(Lashley, 1951; John, 1967). Understanding the processes by which information is selected and sequenced is well beyond the current state of knowledge but is essential for a complete understanding of the neurobiological bases
of memory.

B. How Are Experiences Stored?

This question refers to several problems. Are all experiences stored in the
same way or are there different kinds of storage processes? Are memories of
recent experiences stored in the same way as long-term memories or are
memories of different ages based on different mechanisms? Although this
problem has been the subject of extensive study for over 25 years (Hebb,
1949), it has not yet been resolved (McGaugh, 1968a; Wickelgren, 1973;
Gold and McGaugh, 1975). What processes are involved in the consolidation of long-term memory? This fundamental question is examined in detail
in a subsequent section. Are the same processes involved in the consolidation
of different kinds of memories such as those involved in conditioning, habituation, and language learning? Are the same processes used by different species
of animals (see Horn, Rose, and Bateson, 1973)?

Much recent research on the neurobiology of memory has used "model
systems" such as simple forms of learning in invertebrates (Kandel and
Spencer, 1968) and in restricted regions of the nervous system such as the
spinal cord (Groves and Thompson, 1970). Such research is based on the
assumption that knowledge of the basis of plasticity in simpler systems will
be useful in understanding how memory works in higher systems. But this
view remains an assumption at the present time. It is of course also an assumption that studies of memory in laboratory animals such as mice, rats,
cats, and monkeys will provide an understanding of memory processes in
general. The validity of these assumptions will ultimately have to be examined.

C. How Are Memories Retrieved?

At any moment we are capable of recalling an enormous amount of information based on our past experiences. What processes occur when you
decide to recall a particular phone number from all sequences of numbers
that you have experienced or the name of a friend out of all of the names
that you know? And, how do you know whether you are correct or incorrect? At a conceptual level, some clues are provided by studies of subjects'
attempts to recall information that is not readily remembered but is on the
tip-of-the-tongue (Brown and McNeill, 1966). The speed of recall clearly
indicates that the information is categorized. It is not searched simply in

terms of order of storage or alphabetically but in terms of other features such as word length and whether the word is common or unusual, in the case of names, for example.

At a physiological level, it has been clearly demonstrated that memory retrieval is state dependent (Overton, 1971). Learned responses are more easily retrieved if the physiological state at the time of retrieval is similar to that which existed at the time of learning. State dependency can readily be demonstrated by training and testing animals under different drug states. However, beyond such demonstrations very little is known about the neuronal processes involved in the retrieval of memories of past experiences.

D. How Are Memories Integrated?

This question also refers to a series of questions. How do memories of recent experiences activate well-established memories? This is of course the major function of memory systems—to provide continuity of experience and behavior. Why does repetition generally produce stronger memories (Ebbinghaus, 1885)? That is how does the nervous system add new memories to old memories? Is the strengthening of memory by repetition based on additive changes in the same neural elements, or does each experience produce a change in different neural elements? How do memories of a series of experiences summate to produce a skill in which responses can occur in different and novel sequences?

Sperry and his associate (Sperry, 1968; Gazzaniga, 1970) have shown that the two cerebral hemispheres differ in their capacity to process different types of information. How are memories processed in the left hemisphere (such as speech) integrated with those processed in the right hemisphere (such as memory for tactile experiences)?

Are some kinds of experiences easier to integrate into memory systems? Different animal species appear to be specifically "prepared" to learn certain kinds of information (Seligman, 1970). Is this true for humans as well? If so, is this "preparedness" due to the organization of neurons and neural systems? What is there about the human brain that makes it possible for us to learn the complex skill of language, even though we often struggle to learn other types of responses and skills?

E. Why Do We Forget?

Just as memory is a fact of experience, so is forgetting. Part of the problem of forgetting is caused by temporary problems of retrieval. In fact much of what we call forgetting is simply temporary. We forget to do some task or forget someone's name. Understanding the mechanisms of retrieval will provide an explanation of this kind of forgetting. However, we forget for other reasons as well. We learn new responses that interfere with older responses—the well-studied phenomenon of retroactive interference. As is discussed in detail below, memory losses are produced by a variety of treatments that affect neuronal functioning, such as drugs and electrical stimulation of the brain, if the treatments are administered shortly after training. Presumably such treatments interfere with the consolidation of new memories. However, much if not most forgetting appears to occur as a function of time. Is all such forgetting due to new learning or interference with consolidation or is forgetting a normal neurobiological process? Is forgetting in part a consequence of ongoing processes of cellular metabolism?

These are but some of the important questions concerning the nature and neurobiological bases of memory. At the present time we do not have detailed answers to any of these questions. Some of the questions deal with problems that are well beyond current research ability. But some of these questions are the focus of much recent and current research. Greatest progress has been made in understanding the neurobiological changes associated with the acquisition of new memory and the physiological conditions that are effective in modulating the consolidation of memory.

III. NEUROBIOLOGICAL CHANGES ASSOCIATED WITH MEMORY

When new memories are acquired, the nervous system is, we assume, altered in specific ways. Consequently it should be possible to discover what the changes are and just where they are located. Although the locus (or loci) of memory traces or engrams has been vigorously and imaginatively sought for decades (see Lashley, 1950), the research on this problem has not yet been fruitful. The technique used most commonly in such studies is that of making lesions in different brain regions following training in order to see whether memory losses might result from damage to specific neural structures. The results of such studies have been difficult to interpret. In experiments where deficits in retention are produced, it is difficult to dissociate the effects of the lesions on memory from effects on other processes that influence behavior, such as sensory processes, motivation, arousal levels, and locomotor activity (see Isaacson, *in press*). If a particular brain lesion does not affect retention, it cannot be concluded that the particular region destroyed has no function on memory in intact subjects. Lesion studies only indicate what animals' behavior is like when the brain is damaged. They do not readily reveal the function of the lost tissue. Recent findings indicate that the nervous system may become reorganized following lesions. Axons from undamaged cells can sprout and innervate synaptic regions vacated by damaged cells (Lynch, Deadwyler, and Cotman, 1973; Lynch, Stanfield, and Cotman, 1973). Because of these problems, it seems likely that lesion studies, by themselves, are not likely to provide an understanding of the neural systems involved in memory.

It is clear, however, from recent studies using other experimental approaches that the nervous system is altered by training experiences. There is extensive evidence that training produces electrophysiological, neurochemical, and neuroanatomical changes in the CNS (John, 1967; Glassman, 1969; Greenough, *in press*). Although the physiological significance of the observed changes is not yet determined, such findings are encouraging and suggest that detailed examination of such correlates may eventually lead to an understanding of the nature and locus of the neurobiological traces of experiences.

IV. ELECTROPHYSIOLOGICAL CORRELATES OF TRAINING

When animals are trained to make new responses, many kinds of electrophysiological changes in brain activity can be recorded. Numerous experiments have demonstrated that training produces changes in EEG activity, slow cortical potentials, evoked potentials, multiple unit discharges, and single unit activity (Morrell, 1961; John, 1967; Thompson, Patterson, and Teyler, 1972). There is no doubt that such changes are correlated with learning. The problem faced by these studies is that of determining whether the changes directly reflect neural changes underlying the formation of new memories. When animals are trained, many physiological systems are affected. Training affects physiological processes involved in sensory systems, arousal, motivation, mood, and motor responsiveness as well as memory. Thus neural correlates of training are, or at least may be, correlates of any of these processes. Research in this area has gone beyond the problem of simply demonstrating that electrophysiological changes occur with training. Recent research has focused on an attempt to determine whether such changes are uniquely associated with the formation of memory. This has been, and will continue to be, a difficult task. A brief review of a selection of some recent experiments will illustrate the current strategies, problems, and progress in this area.

As I noted above, a number of investigators (see Kandel and Spencer, 1968; Groves and Thompson, 1970) have proposed that progress in understanding the neural basis of memory will be furthered by investigations of simple forms of learning in simple systems such as invertebrates or restricted regions of the nervous systems of mammals. One of the simpler forms of learning is habituation—the decrease in response to a specific stimulus with repetition of the stimulus. Habituation has been observed in all species of animals that have been studied. In an attempt to discover the neural basis of this simple form of learning, Groves and Thompson (1970) studied behavioral and neuronal habituation in spinal cats. When a mild shock was delivered to the animal's skin, a muscle contraction was produced. With repeated stimulation the response habituated. A number of control procedures were used to demonstrate that the decrease in responsiveness was not due to fatigue or illness and that the habituation was specific to the stimulus used. During the habituation trials, the activity of interneurons in the spinal cord was recorded (extracellularly) by means of microelectrodes. Three types of cells were found. One type showed no change in firing during the habituation. A second type first increased its rate of firing when the stimulation was repeated and then decreased. In cells of the third type, the firing rates showed habituation; firing rates decreased with repetition of the stimulus. Thus the response of the third type of cell was similar to that of the animal's behavior. However, it is not yet known just what properties of the cell are responsible for the neuronal habituation or whether the cells that habituate are the ones responsible for the behavioral habituation. This type of simple system approach appears to be quite promising for investigating simple forms of learning. It remains to be seen whether such research will lead to an understanding of more complex forms of learning.

Many studies have examined the effects of different kinds of training procedures on the firing patterns of neurons (Morrell, 1967; Gabriel, Wheeler, and Thompson, 1973a,b; Woody, 1974). For example, in a series of recent experiments, Fuster (1973) has studied the activity of simple units in the prefrontal cortex of monkeys as the animals performed a delayed response task. The activity was recorded from chronically implanted microelectrodes. In these experiments the monkeys were extensively trained to perform the delayed-response. On each trial the monkeys had to observe which of two containers contained a bit of food. Then a screen was lowered to block the animal's view of the food and was raised 18 sec later. After they were trained, unit responses were recorded throughout the delay and the subject's accuracy of choice was observed. Several patterns of unit activity were observed. In some cells, unit activity increased during the delay, whereas in others unit activity decreased. Other cells showed various patterns of increase and decrease in firing rates during the delay. Comparable patterns were not observed in animals tested without prior delayed-response training. Fuster (1973) has interpreted these results as suggesting that the cells in this region of the brain are involved in processes that play some critical role in short-term memory. This interpretation is consistent with other findings (Fuster and Alexander, 1970) that delayed-response performance is impaired if this brain region is depressed by cooling. These interesting results raise a number of questions concerning the significance of the changes in firing patterns. What functions do the changes serve? But the fact that such correlations are observed makes further inquiry promising.

Most studies of neural correlates of memory have been concerned with the changes associated with long-term memory. Olds (1973) has adopted an interesting and unique strategy. It is, as he has emphasized, extremely difficult to determine whether an observed correlate is causally related to the changes in learning and memory. The pattern of a neuron's firing may change merely because the neuron under study is stimulated by neurons that are changed by training. As Olds (1973, p. 42) has put it, "How can we, from an enormous number of changes fed back upon changes in a confusing web of neuron behavior cycles and neuron-neuron epicycles, sort out the critical changes which come first, and being at the sites of the learning, cause the others?" Olds suggests that the critical measure is the latency of a neuron's response to a new stimulus. If a unit changes its rate of firing during training and if the latency of the response of the unit is very short, then the unit is likely to be directly rather than indirectly involved in the learning process. In a series of studies, Olds and his colleagues have studied, in many brain regions, the latencies of cells (multiple units) whose patterns of activity are changed during a simple learning task. Only latencies of less than 80 msec were studied. In these studies rats were trained simply to orient toward a pellet dispenser at the onset of a tone. The rats learned the response within 10 to 20 trials and the latency of the response was about 200 msec. Cells in a large number of brain regions showed short latency increases in firing rates as training progressed. Units in some regions required more than 30 trials to "learn," whereas units in other regions "learned" in fewer than 10 trials. In particular, in cells in the hypothalamus medial forebrain bundle, signs of learning were observed before behavioral changes were seen. Olds' findings appear to point to some regions of the brain in which cellular activity may be causally related to the behavioral change. The fact that the cells' responses precede the behavior makes it possible for the cells' activity to be causally related to the learning. If the cells are involved, what is their role? Are they part of a neural circuit that *is* the engram? Or are the cells important because of other influences such as possibly modulating cells with longer response latencies? For the present the changes in unit activity must be regarded as correlates of learning. It remains to be determined whether the neural changes are critically involved in the learned behavior.

In studies such as these, in which changes in the nervous system are to be interpreted as reflecting associative changes, i.e., alterations in the meaning of the stimulation, it is essential that other factors that might influence the amplitude or pattern of the evoked neural acivity be held constant. This is a complicated but important problem in studies of learning, since factors such as changes in the intensity of the stimulus at the receptor as well as the animal's state of excitability might produce changes that could be regarded as being due to memory processes (Oleson, Ashe, and Weinberger, *in press*). In a series of recent experiments, Oleson et al. (*in press*) have recorded multiple unit activity from several brain regions during the classical conditioning of a pupillary dilation response in paralyzed cats. Under these conditions, the sensory stimulation could be kept constant and, thus, ruled out as a cause of changes in the neural activity. Using the pupil response as the measure of learning, the animals showed evidence of conditioning, discrimination between two auditory signals, and reversal learning. Evoked multiple unit activity in the auditory cortex, somatic cortex, and even the cochlear nucleus also showed essentially similar results. Thus these findings indicate that systematic changes in evoked multiple unit activity occur during treatments that produce learning as indicated by the pupillary response. However, the role of such changes is not at all clear since the acquisition of neural changes sometimes followed rather than preceded the behavioral changes. As Oleson et al. note, it may be that some of the observed neural changes are involved in establishing changes in somatic systems and might therefore not be involved in systems mediating autonomic conditioning. These findings, like those of Olds, serve to emphasize the need for careful examination of the relationship between development of behavioral changes and the development of changes in neuronal activity. This type of information can of course only be obtained when the behavioral and neural responses are observed in the same subjects.

A number of recent studies have shown that animals can be trained to alter rates of unit activity through the use of rewards. For example Shinkman, Bruce, and Pfingst (1974) reported that the rate of firing of cells in cat visual cortex following the presentation of a visual stimulus could be increased if the cats were rewarded (with brain stimulation) on trials in which the cells responded with increases in firing rates. Since the cats were paralyzed during the experiment, the changes could not have been caused by changes in sensory stimulation or feedback from motor responses. However, the changes might have been caused by alterations in levels of arousal and thus caused indirectly by changes occurring elsewhere in the brain. Consequently, without additional information concerning the specificity of the changes, studies of this kind can only serve to show that changes in cellular activity can be instrumentally, as well as classically, conditioned.

One of the major purposes of studies of changes in the activity of neurons as a consequence of training is to find cells that are directly involved in the learning. Thus the electrophysiological studies of unit activity are frequently conducted in an attempt to locate cells that are parts of neural circuits, which provide the basis of a memory trace. The basic assumption of this approach is that memories are based on neural circuits. Although this assumption is appealing and therefore widely accepted, it is not beyond question. John (1972) has argued that the "switchboard" view of learning—that is the view that learning is based on the formation of specific connections—between nerve cells is not well supported by existing evidence. For example, as was discussed above, lesion studies have not shown that specific memories are lost when brain tissue is destroyed. Sometimes even very large lesions fail to cause retention losses. Furthermore, when an animal is trained, changes in firing patterns can be recorded in a large proportion of cells (from 10 to 70% in various studies). This suggests that each cell is affected by many experiences. Given this degree of complexity, how are specific circuits formed? John suggests that specific circuits are not formed. Rather he proposes that information is represented by a common mode of activity in units located in many regions of the brain. The important feature of firing is the coherence of firing patterns in ensembles of neurons. The coherence can be measured in patterns of evoked potentials or as statistical averages of unit discharges. In a series of studies, John and his colleagues have shown that training produces highly specific changes in the wave shapes of evoked potentials that can be recorded from several brain regions. Furthermore the response of a trained animal to a stimulus is predicted by the shape of the evoked potential, which is elicited by the stimulus. For example cats were first trained to respond when a flicking (10 Hz) light was presented. The animal was then tested with lights flicking at different frequencies. When the cats responded to the test lights, the evoked potentials were similar to those elicited by the 10-Hz training light. When the cats failed to respond, the evoked potentials were not similar to those elicited by the 10-Hz light. On the basis of findings such as these, John suggests that information about an experience is represented by coherent activity in ensembles of cells and that the information will be activated or "readout" when a stimulus—even a novel one—activates the representative system, ". . . in such a way as to cause release of a common mode of activity like that stored during the learning experience" (John, 1972, p. 863).

These theoretical arguments and experimental findings provide difficulty for theories that assume that memories are based on the formation of specific circuits. However, John's alternative theory raises a number of questions. In particular what is the basis of the alteration in the coherence of firing in ensembles? Are the changes due to stable changes at specific synaptic sites of specific cells? Are the ensembles merely more complex circuits? How do the ensembles activate specific units that control behavior? If the activity released during readout is like that stored during experiences, it should be difficult to distinguish sensory experience from a memory of experience.

Some of the major facts provided by studies of learning, such as those emphasized by John, make it difficult to imagine how specific memory circuits can be formed. Yet the dominant view of memory is that memory is based on the formation of circuits. Is each new hypothesis of circuit formation really a new article of "clothing for the Emperor?" It is too early to tell whether John's view provides a satisfactory alternative interpretation or whether it is merely another type of wardrobe.

V. NEUROCHEMICAL CORRELATES OF TRAINING

The electrophysiological changes produced by training are, of course, merely signs that something has changed in the nervous system. If it is assumed for the moment that a change in unit activity is due to alterations in the particular cells whose discharges are recorded, the fundamental question is, "What is the basis of the change?" What are the alterations that cause the cells to increase or decrease their firing rates? It seems reasonable to assume that the activation of a neuron during training triggers chemical changes that alter the cell's probability of firing. Such changes might, for example, produce a stable increase in transmitter substances in presynaptic terminals. Or they might alter the receptive properties of postsynaptic sites on dendrites. In either case the changes would presumably require the synthesis of ribonucleic acid (RNA) and protein. It might even be, as some investigators have suggested (Hyden and Lange, 1970; Ungar, 1972), that training causes the synthesis of specific species of RNA and protein.

During the past 15 years, a large number of studies have investigated the effects of training on the synthesis of RNA and protein. The findings of these experiments are summarized in several recent reviews (Glassman, 1969; Booth, 1973; Uphouse, MacInnes, and Schlesinger, 1974). Although many of the findings and interpretations are controversial (Horn et al., 1973), the overall evidence does support the general view that training stimulates RNA and protein synthesis. In these experiments animals, usually rats or mice, are trained on a task. Control animals are given some kind of stimulation but are not trained. Immediately after the experience the animals are sacrificed and the brains are analyzed for changes in RNA or protein. Studies focusing on RNA have measured changes in the ratios of bases in the RNA (Hyden and Egyhazi, 1964) as well as the incorporation of radioactive precursors into RNA (Glassman, 1969). For example, in the well-known studies by Hyden and Egyhazi (1962), rats were trained to climb a sloping wire for a food reward; then the RNA in cells in the vestibular nucleus of the trained rats was compared with that of control rats subjected to stimulation produced by rotation. The results suggested that the training increased RNA and altered the composition of RNA in the cell nucleus.

In a series of experiments, Glassman, Wilson, and their colleagues (see Glassman, 1974) investigated the effects of active avoidance training on the incorporation of radioactively labeled uridine into RNA. Mice were trained to jump to a small platform in order to avoid a footshock. "Yoked" controls received the conditioned stimulus (light and buzzer) and the unconditioned stimulus (footshock) but were not allowed to learn to avoid the shock. The findings suggested that the training increased the incorporation of the uridine into RNA, particularly in the hippocampus and diencephalon. Comparable results have been obtained by other investigators (Bowman and Strobel, 1969; Uphouse, MacInnes, and Schlesinger, 1972). For example Matthies, Lossner, Ott, Phole, and Rauca (1973) reported that in rats training on a visual discrimination task increased the incorporation of radioactive precursors into RNA. The effect was particularly pronounced in the cells of the hippocampus and visual cortex.

The findings of these kinds of experiments suggest that training increases RNA in neurons in specific regions of the brain. Thus it would seem that RNA synthesis is a correlate of learning. However, both the biochemical and the behavioral findings of these experiments are difficult to interpret. In many of the incorporation studies, it is not clear that the changes measured reflect increased synthesis of RNA (Horn et al., 1973). For example recent evidence (Entingh, Damstra-Entingh, Dunn, Wilson, and Glassman, 1974) indicates that in mice training on an active avoidance response decreases the amount of radioactivity measured in uridine monophosphates (UMP). Since UMP radioactivity has in many studies been used as the correction factor for measuring the incorporation of labeled uridine into RNA, the conclusion that training increases RNA synthesis is seriously questioned by these findings. It is clear nonetheless that the training procedures affect brain biochemistry. At the behavioral level, it is important to consider whether the neurochemical changes are associated with the formation of memory or whether they reflect changes caused by sensory stimulation, arousal stress, or performance of the response. That is, what are the changes correlates *of* (Bateson, 1970)?

In a series of experiments, Horn et al. (1973) have attempted to clarify both the biochemical and behavioral questions concerning the effects of training on RNA synthesis. In their studies newborn chicks were subjected to imprinting procedures. A flashing yellow light was presented for 60 min. This training produces a strong and sustained approach response. Thus the behavior is changed by the imprinting training. The training also produces an increase in incorporation of labeled precursors into what is presumed to be RNA (and protein). However, what aspects of the imprinting procedure produce the chemical changes? In order to attempt to answer this question, Horn et al. (1973) produced split-brain chicks by surgically severing the supraoptic commissure. The chicks were then exposed to the flashing light while one eye was covered with a patch. Thus, only one side of the brain received the imprinting information, but both sides of the brain were influenced by other factors such as arousal and stress. The chicks' brains were then analyzed for incorporation of labeled uracil into acid-insoluble substances presumed to be RNA. The incorporation in the trained side of the brain was higher than in the untrained side. The effect was obtained only in the forebrain "roof." Other brain regions were not affected. Other experiments showed that in chicks with intact brains, monocular imprinting does not differentially affect incorporation in the two halves of the brain. Furthermore incorporation is not enhanced by stimulation with the flashing light if the chicks are given imprinting training on the previous day. Overall these findings suggest that the changes in incorporation are related to the learning that occurs during the imprinting session and are not caused simply by arousal, stress, or sensory stimulation. It may be, as Horn et al. (1973) note, that there are alternative interpretations that have not been tested. The effects may be due for example to some nonmemorial consequences of the flashing light (Glassman, 1974). But these findings strongly suggest that the chemical changes may be critically involved in learning.

Numerous recent studies have also reported that training increases the incorporation of labeled amino acids into protein. For example Hyden and Lange (1970) reported that when rats are forced to learn to use a non-preferred paw there is an increase in synthesis of a particular protein (S100) in the region of the hippocampus. Other experiments suggest that protein synthesis is increased by visual discrimination learning (Matthies et al., 1973) and imprinting (Horn et al., 1973).

Glassman drew the following conclusion in his review of this research in 1969:

> It seems well established that certain types of stimulation and nerve activity cause changes in RNA and protein of the nerve cell. . . . The evidence, however, that RNA and protein are involved directly in the storage of memory is not convincing. There is little question that chemical changes have been observed during learning, but it is not clear whether they are directly associated with the storage of memory, or with general sensory or motor stimulation, or with other processes.

Although many studies in this area have been published in the last 6 years, Glassman's conclusion is appropriate for the more recent research as well. None of the observed chemical correlates of training can, as yet, be regarded as part of the mechanisms of memory.

Most of the research in this area has, as I have emphasized, investigated the possible role of the synthesis of macromolecules. There is, however, other evidence that brain chemistry is altered by experience. Rosenzweig, Bennett, and Diamond (1972) have shown that environmental stimulation can alter the activity of enzymes involved in the regulation of cholinergic transmitters. Furthermore Lewy and Seiden (1972) have reported that training alters the turnover of brain norepinephrine. Obviously, much research is needed to provide an understanding of the specific chemical changes involved in memory storage.

VI. ANATOMICAL CORRELATES OF TRAINING

There is now little doubt that the brain is changed by experience. Studies of the electrophysiological and neurochemical correlates of training indicate that many different kinds of neural changes are produced. A number of recent studies indicate that experiences also produce anatomical changes in the brain. The changes that have been observed include increases in brain weight, thickness of the cortex, complexity of dendritic branching, number of dendritic spines, and size of synapses in certain regions of the cerebral cortex. All of these changes are correlates of experience. The question is: are these changes involved in the neural mechanisms of memory, or are they consequences of other influences of experience?

In an extensive series of studies conducted over the past two decades, Krech, Rosenzweig, Bennett, Diamond, and their colleagues (see Rosenzweig, Bennett, and Diamond, 1972; Bennett, Diamond, Krech, and Rosenzweig, 1964) have studied the effects of different kinds of environmental stimulation on the brain biochemistry and anatomy of rats. The brains of rats reared in large cages containing numerous objects that provided visual stimulation and encouraged exploration were significantly heavier than were those of littermates reared in isolation as well as under normal colony conditions. The largest effects were found in the occipital cortex. In comparison with the rats reared in isolation, the occipital cortices of enriched rats were about 6% heavier, 6% thicker, and cell bodies of the neurons were about 13% larger. Studies of Greenough and his colleagues (Greenough, *in press*) indicate that environmental enrichment increases the number of branches on the dendrites of neurons, particularly in basilar dendrites of pyramidal cells (Greenough, Volkmar, and Juraska, 1973). In general the cortical regions in which branching is seen correspond fairly well to the brain regions in which cortical weight and thickness is increased by environmental complexity. Globus, Rosenzweig, Bennett, and Diamond (1973) found that enriched rats have a greater number of spines on the basal dendrites of cortical pyramidal neurons. Furthermore detailed analyses of electron micrographs of isolated and enriched rats (West and Greenough, 1972) indicated that the synapses in the visual cortex of the enriched rats were larger.

Although it is quite clear that these changes in brain structure are produced by environmental stimulation, it is not yet established that they are related to memory processing. It is particularly difficult to interpret the findings of studies in which the animals are subjected to environmental stimulation over a period of months. However, recent findings indicate that brain changes are produced by very short (30 min) daily periods of environmental stimulation over a short time period (15 days). The effects are enhanced if the animals are given CNS stimulants (amphetamine or pentylenetetrazol) before each stimulation session (Bennett, Rosenzweig, and Chang Wu, 1973).

Recent evidence from several studies indicates that formal training of rats also produces changes in dendritic branching in the apical dendrites of pyramidal cells in rats (Greenough et al., 1973) and cats (Rutledge, *in press;* Rutledge, Wright, and Duncan, *in press*). Rutledge et al. (*in press*) trained cats to make a foreleg flexion in response to brain stimulation. The conditioned stimulus (CS) was stimulation of the suprasylvian gyrus. The unconditioned stimulus (US) was a shock to the foreleg. Twenty training trials were given each day for 50 days. Controls received unpaired presentations of the CS and US. The total duration of the brain stimulation was 40 sec/day, or a total of just over a half hour during the 50 days. The animals were then sacrificed, the brains stained using the Golgi method, and the pyramidal cells on the stimulated and contralateral sides were analyzed. In the trained animals, the pyramidal cells on the contralateral side had more dendritic branches and more spines on the apical and oblique branches. Some effects were produced by stimulation in the untrained animals but the magnitude of the effects was smaller.

Thus, these recent findings indicate that specific training as well as general environmental enrichment produces changes in the fine structure of the nervous system. It is not yet clear whether these changes are involved in learning. But as Greenough (*in press*) has pointed out, "It is hard to imagine that such alterations play no role in the functioning of the brain. Assessment of the role(s) will almost certainly require a more detailed knowledge of the circumstances under which such effects do and do not occur."

VII. IMPLICATIONS REGARDING CORRELATES OF TRAINING

As the findings of studies summarized here indicate, the brain is changed by experience. The role of the various changes remains to be determined by further research. There are undoubtedly other changes that are of importance in establishing the neural traces of experience. Although these findings must be interpreted with a great deal of caution they are highly interesting and suggest that progress in understanding the neural basis of memory is likely to result from further studies of correlates of training.

VIII. MODULATION OF MEMORY STORAGE PROCESSES

It seems likely that the storage of newly acquired information requires processes that occur over a period of time after the information is received. Whereas some processes must occur quickly in order to provide immediate memory for very recent experiences, the development of changes underlying stable long-term traces seems to require time. The neurobiological changes such as the electrophysiological, neurochemical, and anatomical correlates of training already discussed are not instantaneous products of training. Furthermore there is extensive evidence that memory storage processes can be modulated by treatments that affect brain functioning for a period of time following learning. It is well known that memory losses are produced by brain injury. The fact that brain injury generally has greater effects on memories of experiences that occurred just prior to the injury (i.e., retrograde amnesia) has suggested that brain injury can interfere with the consolidation of the recently acquired information (Whitty and Zangwill, 1966). Electro-convulsive therapy (ECT) sometimes produces memory losses (Fink, Kety, McGaugh, and Williams, 1974). Some of the impairment is no doubt temporary and may be due to an inability to retrieve recent as well as older information (Squire, 1974). But, under some conditions, ECT appears to produce retrograde amnesia (Dornbush and Williams, 1974).

Studies of memory in laboratory animals have confirmed and extended the findings that treatments such as electrical stimulation of the brain affects memory storage processes (Glickman, 1961; McGaugh and Herz, 1972; McGaugh, 1974). In these studies, the animals—usually mice, rats, or cats—are first trained on some simple task. Then they are given a treatment either immediately after the training or after an interval of time. At a later time, usually at least a day or longer after the training, the animals are tested to see whether they remember the training experience. In general the treatments are most effective if they are administered immediately after training. The degree of modulation of retention observed decreases as the time interval between training and posttraining treatment is increased.

Experimental studies of the effects of posttraining treatments on retention of learned responses address several questions. First, at the descriptive level, what kinds of treatments affect retention? Second, at a neurobiological level, what effects of the treatment are responsible for the memory effects? Third, are the effects seen on the retention test due to influences on memory processes, or to other influences on behavior? The findings or research in this area have been summarized in a number of recent papers (McGaugh and Herz, 1972; Jarvik, 1972; McGaugh and Gold, *in press;* DeWied, 1974; McGaugh, 1973). The basic assumption guiding this research is that an understanding of the nature and neurobiological bases of the effects of the treatments on memory will provide some insights into the processes involved in memory storage. Eventually this research approach should be useful in helping to determine which of the many correlates of training are, in fact, involved in memory storage. A brief review of some of the recent findings will indicate some of the more promising research approaches in this general area.

IX. EFFECTS OF ELECTRICAL STIMULATION OF THE BRAIN

Research in this area was initiated by the studies of Duncan (1949) and Gerard (1949) who reported that retrograde amnesia could be produced in rats by passing electrical currents through the animals' heads by means of electrodes attached to their ears. Such electroconvulsive shock (ECS) treatments elicit brain seizures and bodily convulsions. However, subsequent research has shown that neither the convulsions nor the brain seizures play any critical role in producing the amnesic effects (McGaugh, 1974). If the current is applied directly to the surface of the brain cortex in rats, the length of the gradient of retrograde amnesia varies directly with the intensity of the electrical current (Zornetzer, 1974). Different gradients can be obtained with different experimental treatments. For example Gold, Macri, and McGaugh (1973a) stimulated different cortical regions with currents of varying intensity at an interval varying from a second to several hours after the rats were trained on an inhibitory avoidance task. On the training trial, the rats were punished with a mild footshock as they stepped from one compartment to another compartment of a straight alley. The following day the rats were tested for retention of the experience. With lower intensities (2 to 4 mA) of cortical stimulation, retention was affected only if the current was applied within seconds after the training. With a higher intensity (8 mA), amnesia was produced even if the treatments were administered at an interval of 1 hr following training. Even longer gradients of retrograde amnesia can be produced with ECS by varying the intensity and duration of the treatment and by administering several treatments after the training (Mah and Albert, 1973). Memory storage processes appear to remain susceptible to modulating influences of brain stimulation for at least several hours following training. It is clear that no single treatment condition can provide a measure of "storage time." Retrograde amnesia gradients are products of the specific experimental conditions under which they are obtained.

When electrical stimulation is delivered either by means of peripheral electrodes or directly to the brain cortex, memory effects are usually produced when the current also elicits brain seizure activity. Currents that elicit seizures also have other effects, such as inhibition of brain protein synthesis (Cotman, Banker, Zornetzer, and McGaugh, 1971; Dunn, Ginditta, Wilson, and Glassman, 1974). However, electrical stimulation applied to some subcortical brain regions produces alteration in memory even if the stimulating current is well below the seizure threshold. Amnesic effects have been obtained with low-intensity (subseizure) stimulation of several structures including the caudate nucleus, substantia nigra, hippocampus, mesencephalic reticular formation (MRF), and the amygdala (Wyers, Peeke, Welliston, and Herz, 1968; Routtenberg and Holzman, 1973; Haycock, Deadwyler, Sideroff, and McGaugh, 1973; Gold et al., 1973b; Kesner and Wilburn, 1974; Sideroff, Bueno, Hirsch, Weyand, and McGaugh, 1974). Such findings have been interpreted by some investigators as suggesting that the electrical stimulation interferes with neural processing of information which is occurring in the region stimulated. For example, Kesner and Conner (1974) have reported that, in rats, recent memory is disrupted by MRF stimulation, and the formation of long-term memory is impaired by posttraining stimulation of the hippocampus. On the basis of these findings, Kesner has argued that the two neural structures have different functions in short- and long-term memory (Kesner, 1973). There are of course other possible interpretations of these results (cf. Gold and McGaugh, 1975; McGaugh and Gold, in press). The memory effects might be produced because stimulation of these two structures produces quite different effects in other regions of the brain. Or it might be that stimulation produces the same effects in the two regions, but that the two regions have different thresholds for response to the stimulation. With other experimental conditions for example, posttrial stimulation of the MRF and hippocampus produces enhancement rather than disruption of retention (Bloch, 1970; Landfield, Tusa, and McGaugh, 1973; Destrade, Soumireu-Morat, and Cardo, 1973). Furthermore, Gold, Hankins, Edwards, Chester, and McGaugh, (1975) have shown that both disrupting and facilitating effects of amygdala stimulation depend upon the motivating conditions used in the training task. With low-footshock posttraining amygdala stimulation enhances retention. With high-footshock posttraining amygdala stimulation disrupts retention. Thus the stimulation appears to interact in a complex way with the physiologic processes elicited by the training situation. Gold, Edwards, and McGaugh (*in press*) have also shown that the amygdala stimulation is most effective if the current is delivered to a restricted region of the amygdala (in or near the basomedial nucleus). However this finding does not mean that memory processing occurs in this brain region. It seems more likely that activation of this region leads to widespread changes that have a modulating influence on memory storage processes. In view of evidence (discussed below) that pituitary hormones may affect memory storage it could be that brain stimulation modulates memory through the release of pituitary hormones. Or, the brain stimulation might cause the release of transmitters at the terminals of the neurons stimulated. If the stimulated structures project throughout the brain, then numerous brain regions could be affected by stimulation of a restricted brain region (see Kety, 1972).

It is clear that brain stimulation can modulate retention. The fact that the effects are time-dependent provides strong support for the view that the stimulation alters memory storage processes. Comparable effects have been obtained with several kinds of learning tasks including inhibitory avoidance (Gold et al., 1973b), active avoidance (Handwerker, Gold, and McGaugh, 1974), and discrimination learning tasks. It is also clear that there is considerable anatomic specificity in the stimulation effects. However, brain stimulation experiments have not located "memory neurons" or even "memory structures." They have located structures that when stimulated produce modulating influences on memory storage. With more information of this kind it should eventually be possible to determine which of the effects of brain stimulation are critical for producing the modulating influence.

X. EFFECTS OF NEUROCHEMICAL INFLUENCES

There are undoubtedly many ways in which treatments might influence neuronal functioning so as to modulate memory storage. As indicated above some treatments might be effective because they cause the release of substances such as transmitters or circulating hormones. Others might act by influencing the synthesis of chemicals involved in producing changes underlying memory. Numerous experiments have attempted to investigate the possible roles of RNA and protein synthesis in memory storage by administering antibiotic drugs that interfere with the synthesis of RNA and proteins. There is substantial evidence that drugs such as puromycin, cycloheximide, acetoxycycloheximide, and anisomycin disrupt retention if they are administered either before or shortly after training (Luttges, Andry, and MacInnes, 1972; Andry and Luttges, 1972; Uphouse, et al., 1974). Generally, behavioral effects are obtained only if the protein synthesis is reduced by more than 90%. Under some conditions the amount of memory impairment seems to be related to the duration of inhibition of protein synthesis (Flood, Bennett, Rosenzweig, and Orme, 1973).

Recent evidence also indicates that memory is impaired by reversible inhibition of RNA synthesis (Thut, Hruska, Kelter, Mizne, and Lindell, 1973; Kobiler and Allweis, 1974). Under some conditions the memory losses produced by inhibitors of RNA and protein synthesis are temporary, whereas under others the losses appear to be permanent (Agranoff, 1972; Barondes and Squire, 1972). These findings suggest that the treatments may affect the retrieval as well as the storage of memory processes. However, the fact that the degree of retention loss depends upon the training treatment interval indicates that the effects are not due to nonspecific influences such as illness. Some inhibitors of RNA and protein synthesis do appear to cause illness, so the findings of such experiments must be interpreted with caution (Nakajima, 1973).

These experiments are also difficult to interpret in terms of the mechanism responsible for the amnesia. The findings that inhibitors of RNA and protein synthesis impair retention are of course consistent with the findings reviewed above, suggesting that training stimulates RNA and protein synthesis. However, it could be that these drugs influence learning because of other influences on neuronal functioning. It could be that memory storage is disrupted by any treatment that disrupts cellular metabolic processes. Further studies are needed to determine the biochemical bases of the effects of these drugs on memory.

A variety of drugs, including CNS stimulants such as strychnine, picrotoxin, pentylenetetrazol, bemegride, and amphetamines, enhance retention when they are administered to animals either shortly before or shortly after training (McGaugh, 1968b, 1973; Dawson and McGaugh, 1973). Enhancing effects of stimulants have been obtained in many tasks and with several species of animals. Furthermore, as is the case with brain stimulation, the degree of modulation of retention decreases as the time between the training and the drug injection is increased. These findings suggest that the drugs act in some way to modulate memory storage processes (McGaugh, 1973). It is not yet clear what processes underlie the effects of these drugs on memory. It could be that the drugs affect hormonal systems. Or it could be that the drugs directly influence synaptic mechanisms. This latter possibility is of interest in view of evidence that retention is influenced by treatments that affect both cholinergic (Ilyutchenok and Yeliseyeva, 1972) and adrenergic (McGaugh, 1973) systems. Fulginiti and Orsingher (1971) have shown, for example, that the enhancing effects of posttraining injections of amphetamines are blocked by alpha-methylparatyrosine (α-MPT), a compound that interferes with dopamine, the precursor of norepinephrine. In addition, recent research indicates that retention is impaired by posttrial administration of diethyldithiocarbamate (DDC), an inhibitor of dopamine beta hydroxylase, the enzyme that converts dopamine to norepinephrine (Randt, Quartermain, Goldstein, and Anagnosti, 1971). Studies from my laboratory (McGaugh, Gold, Van Buskirk, and Haycock, 1975) indicate that, in mice, retention is enhanced by posttrial intraventricular administration of low doses of norepinephrine and dopamine. These findings are consistent with evidence that retention is enhanced by posttrial injections of amantadine, a drug that appears to release catecholamines from CNS neurons. Other recent evidence (Stein, Belluzi, and Wise, 1975) indicates that the amnesic effects of DDC are blocked by posttraining intraventricular administration of norepinephrine.

All of these results are consistent with Kety's (1972) hypothesis that catecholamines play some role as modulators of memory storage in neuronal systems activated by a training experience. At a general level, all of the treatments that affect retention might do so by influencing the nonspecific physiological changes produced by training (Gold and McGaugh, 1975). According to this general hypothesis, training may produce two kinds of effects, which are important for learning. First, the training elicits temporary changes in the neuronal systems activated by the training stimulation. Second, the stimulation activates a number of physiological changes such as the release of catecholamines in diffuse brain systems and the release of pituitary hormones. These chemicals then act to potentiate the changes produced in the specific neuronal systems activated by the training. It could be that only one type of nonspecific effect (e.g., catecholamine release) is central for the modulating influences. Or it might be that many kinds of endogenous chemical substances play a role in modulating memory storage.

This latter view is supported by evidence from de Wied's laboratory (de Wied, 1974) that retention of learned responses is influenced by pituitary hormones. Most of the studies of this problem have investigated the effects of adrenocorticotropic hormone (ACTH) and ACTH analogues, particularly the 4 to 10 peptide sequence of the ACTH molecule. ACTH or $ACTH_{4-10}$ both retard the extinction of learned avoidance responses. The fact that the 4 to 10 peptide has effects that are similar to ACTH is interesting because $ACTH_{4-10}$ does not affect the adrenal cortex. This suggests that ACTH may influence retention by directly influencing brain processes. Recently Gold, Van Buskirk, and McGaugh (1975) have reported that ACTH affects retention when administered immediately after training on an inhibitory avoidance task. Thus, ACTH appears to modulate memory storage processes. It is not known whether these modulating influences are independent of the adrenal effects of ACTH. Hormones of the posterior pituitary may also play some role in modulating memory. Van Wimersma, Bohus, and de Wied (1975) reported that rats with a genetic defect in the ability to synthesize vasopressin are unable to learn an inhibitory avoidance response. However, the animals of this strain (Brattleboro) were able to learn the response if vasopressin was administered immediately after training. Furthermore the learning of normal animals was impaired by intraventricular injections of vasopressin antibodies.

The findings of these recent studies strongly suggest that pituitary hormones have regulatory influences in memory storage in addition to their other well-known endocrine influences.

XI. MODULATING INFLUENCES OF SLEEP

The evidence from several lines of research suggests that memory storage processes are modulated by endogenous physiological processes. For years many investigators have suspected that processes occurring during sleep may be important for memory. There is evidence to support these suspicions. For example Fishbein, McGaugh, and Swarz (1971) found that the gradient of retrograde amnesia produced by ECS was greatly extended if mice were deprived of sleep during the interval between the training and the ECS treatment. The deprivation procedures largely influenced the "paradoxical" or rapid-eye-movement (REM) stage of sleep, but slow-wave sleep was also affected. Other studies (Leconte and Bloch, 1970; Pearlman and Becker, 1973) have found that retention is impaired simply by depriving animals of sleep shortly after they are trained.

In a series of studies, Bloch and his colleagues have obtained extensive evidence that REM sleep may have a critical function in memory processing (Leconte, Hennevin, and Bloch, 1973; Leconte and Hennevin, 1973; Bloch, *in press*). Their findings indicate that REM sleep is increased immediately after animals are trained and that REM sleep decreases as the animals learn the task (active avoidance). Furthermore, if REM sleep is prevented for a period of time following training, learning is retarded even though REM sleep occurs within 90 min following the training. Learning is markedly retarded if the period of REM sleep is delayed for 3 hr following each training session. It is not yet known which aspects of REM sleep are responsible for these modulating influences. It might be that hormones secreted during REM sleep affect neuronal processes involved in learning. Or it might be that the effects are due to general influences on cellular metabolism. There is some evidence that the effects involve catecholamines. Hartmann and Stern (1972) have reported that the learning deficits produced by REM sleep deprivation can be reversed by administration of L-DOPA, the precursor of dopamine. Whatever the basis of the effects, it seems likely that processes occurring during sleep have important influences on memory storage. These are highly intriguing findings and further studies of the effects of REM sleep on learning should increase our understanding of the role of endogenous physiological processes in the modulation of memory storage.

XII. BRAIN PATHOLOGY AND MEMORY: SOME IMPLICATIONS

A number of conditions that affect brain functioning seem to produce defects in memory storage. Part of the Korsakoff syndrome seems to be a defect in acquiring new information (Talland, 1968). Other types of CNS diseases and injuries result in learning defects (Barbizet, 1970). Senility seems to involve in some cases a decline in the ability to acquire new information (Talland, 1968). There is also evidence (Warrington and Weiskrantz, 1973) that some defects of memory are due to impaired retrieval processes rather than to an impairment of memory storage processes. These findings (brain pathology associated with learning defects) have been interpreted as suggesting that particular neural structures play specific roles in memory storage. For example, since lesions of the hippocampus produce learning deficits in humans, numerous experiments have attempted to determine the role of the hippocampus in memory storage. It might be that the hippocampus does in fact play some important role in learning. Alternatively it might be that damage to the hippocampus (or some other structure thought to be involved in learning) results in learning deficits because the remaining structures have abnormal modulating effects on memory storage. It might be that the hippocampus normally inhibits other structures that control catecholamine or hormonal systems and the lesion produces a loss of control of such modulating influences. According to this interpretation of the effects of brain lesions on memory in humans, it might be possible to correct memory deficits by appropriate treatments with pituitary hormones or drugs that affect catecholamine metabolism.

XIII. CONCLUDING COMMENTS

In the introduction to this chapter, I stressed the fact that memory involves a complex set of neurobiological processes. In this chapter, I have only touched on a selected sample of the research concerned with neurobiological correlates of training and treatments that modulate memory storage processes. It is clear that progress is being made in understanding both correlates and modulation of memory. But it is also clear that, at the present time, we are far from having even a coherent theory of how information is stored in the brain. At the neurobiological level we need to be able to determine the specific influences responsible for the modulating influences of electrical and chemical stimulation of the brain on memory. Furthermore we need better understanding at a behavioral level of memory as an information processing system. We will not find engrams until we are certain that we will recognize them when we find them.

ACKNOWLEDGMENTS

Some of the recent research findings summarized here were based on research supported by U.S. Public Health Service Grants MH 12526 and MH 25384 from the National Institute of Mental Health, HD 07981 from the

National Institutes of Health, and GB 42746 from the National Science Foundation.

REFERENCES

Agranoff, B. W. (1972): Further studies on memory formation in the goldfish. In: *The Chemistry of Mood, Motivation and Memory,* edited by J. L. McGaugh, pp. 175–185. Plenum, New York.

Andry, D. K., and Luttges, M. W. (1972): Memory traces: Experimental separation by cycloheximide and electroconvulsive shock. *Science,* 178:518–520.

Barbizet, J. (1970): *Human Memory and Its Pathology.* Freeman, San Francisco.

Barondes, S. H., and Squire, L. R. (1972): Slow biological processes in memory storage and "recovery" of memory. In: *The Chemistry of Mood, Motivation and Memory,* edited by J. L. McGaugh, pp. 207–216. Plenum, New York.

Bateson, P. P. G. (1970): Are they really the products of learning? In: *Short-Term Changes in Neural Activity and Behavior,* edited by G. Horn, and R. A. Hinde, pp. 553–564. Cambridge University Press, Cambridge.

Bennett, E. L., Diamond, M. C., Krech, D., and Rosenzweig, M. R. (1964): Chemical and anatomical plasticity of brain. *Science,* 146:610–619.

Bennett, E. L., Rosenzweig, M. R., and Chang Wu, S. (1973): Excitant and depressant drugs modulate effects of environment on brain weight and cholinesterases. *Psychopharmacologia,* 33:309–328.

Bloch, V. (1970): Facts and hypotheses concerning memory consolidation. *Brain Res.,* 24:561–575.

Bloch, V. Brain Activation and memory consolidation. In: *Neural Mechanisms of Learning and Memory,* edited by M. Rosenzweig and E. Bennett. Cambridge: The MIT Press, *in press.*

Booth, D. A. (1973): Protein synthesis and memory. In: *The Physiological Basis of Memory,* edited by J. A. Deutsch, pp. 27–58. Academic Press, New York.

Bowman, R. E., and Strobel, D. A. (1968): Brain RNA metabolism in the rat during learning. *J. Comp. Physiol. Psychol.,* 67:448–458.

Brown, R., and McNeill, D. (1966): The "tip-of-the-tongue" phenomenon. *J. Verbal Learn. Verbal Behav.,* 5:325–337.

Cotman, C., Banker, G., Zornetzer, S., and McGaugh, J. L. (1971): Electroshock effects on brain protein synthesis: Relation to brain seizures and retrograde amnesia. *Science,* 173:454–456.

Dawson, R. G., and McGaugh, J. L. (1973): Drug facilitation of learning and memory. In: *The Physiological Basis of Memory,* edited by J. A. Deutsch, pp. 77–111. Academic Press, New York.

Destrade, C., Soumireu-Mourat, B., and Cardo, B. (1973): Effects of posttrial hippocampal stimulation on acquisition. *Behav. Biol.,* 8:713–724.

de Wied, D. (1974): Pituitary-adrenal system hormones and behavior. In: *The Neurosciences,* edited by F. O. Schmitt and F. G. Worden, pp. 653–666. MIT Press, Cambridge, Mass.

Dornbush, R. L., and Williams, M. (1974): Memory and ECT. In: *Psychobiology of Convulsive Therapy,* edited by M. Fink, S. Kety, J. McGaugh, and T. A. Williams, pp. 199–207. Winston, Washington, D.C.

Duncan, C. P. (1949): The retroactive effect of electroshock on learning. *J. Comp. Physiol. Psychol.,* 32–44.

Dunn, A., Ginditta, A., Wilson, J. E., and Glassman, E. (1974): The effect of electroshock on brain RNA and protein synthesis and its possible relationship to behavioral effects. In: *Psychobiology of Convulsive Therapy,* edited by M. Fink, S. Kety, J. L. McGaugh, and T. A. Williams, pp. 185–197. Winston, Washington, D.C.

Ebbinghaus, H. (1885): *Uber das Gedachtniss.* Drucker and Humblat, Leipzig.

Entingh, D., Damstra-Entingh, T., Dunn, A., Wilson, J. E., and Glassman, E. (1974): Brain uridine monophosphate: reduced incorporation of uridine during avoidance training. *Brain Res.,* 70:131–138.

Fink, M., Kety, S. S., McGaugh, J. L., and Williams, T. A., editors (1974): *Psychobiology of Convulsive Therapy.* Winston, Washington, D.C.

Fishbein, W., McGaugh, J. L., and Swarz, J. R. (1971): Retrograde amnesia: Electroconvulsive shock effects after termination of rapid eye movement sleep deprivation. *Science,* 172:80–82.

Flood, J. F., Bennett, E. L., Rosenzweig, M. R., and Orme, A. E. (1973): The influence of duration of protein synthesis on inhibition of memory. *Physiol. Behav.,* 10:555–562.

Fulginiti, S., and Orsingher, O. A. (1971): Effects on learning, amphetamine and nicotine on the level and synthesis of brain noradrenalin in rats. *Arch. Int. Pharmacodyn.,* 190:291–298.

Fuster, J. M. (1973): Unit activity in prefrontal cortex during delayed-response performance: Neuronal correlates of transient memory. *J. Neurophysiol.,* 36:61–78.

Fuster, J. M., and Alexander, G. E. (1970): Delayed response deficit by cryogenic depression of prefrontal cortex. *Brain Res.,* 20:85–90.

Gabriel, M., Wheeler, W., and Thompson, R. F. (1973a): Multi-unit activity of the rabbit cerebral cortex in single-session avoidance conditioning. *Physiol. Psychol.,* 1:45–55.

Gabriel, M., Wheeler, W., and Thompson, R. F. (1973b): Multiple unit activity of the rabbit cerebral cortex during stimulus generalization of avoidance behavior. *Physiol. Psychol.,* 1:313–320.

Gazzaniga, M. S. (1970): *The Bisected Brain.* Appleton-Century-Crofts, New York.

Gerard, R. W. (1949): Physiology and psychiatry. *Am. J. Psychiatry,* 106:161–173.

Glassman, E. (1969): The biochemistry of learning: An evaluation of the role of RNA and protein. *Ann. Rev. Biochem.* 38:605–646.

Glassman, E. (1974): Macromolecules and behavior: A commentary. In: *The Neurosciences,* edited by F. O. Schmitt and F. G. Worden, pp. 667–677. MIT Press, Cambridge, Mass.

Glickman, S. E. (1961): Perseverative neural processes and consolidation of the memory trace. *Psychol. Bull.,* 58:218–233.

Globus, A., Rosenzweig, M. R., Bennett, E. L., and Diamond, M. C. (1973): Effects of differential experience on dendritic spine counts in rat cerebral cortex. *J. Comp. Physiol. Psychol.,* 82:175–181.

Gold, P. E., Edwards, R., and McGaugh, J. L. Amnesia produced by unilateral subseizure electrical stimulation of the amygdala in rats. *Behav. Biol., in press.*

Gold, P. E., Hankins, L., Edwards, R., Chester, J., and McGaugh, J. L. (1975): Memory interference and facilitation with posttrial amygdala stimulation: Effect on memory varies with footshock level. *Brain Res.,* 86:509–513.

Gold, P. E., Macri, J., and McGaugh, J. L. (1973a): Retrograde amnesia gradients: Effect of direct cortical stimulation. *Science,* 179:1343–1345.

Gold, P. E., Macri, J., and McGaugh, J. L. (1973b): Retrograde amnesia produced by subseizure amygdala stimulation. *Behav. Biol.,* 9:671–680.

Gold, P. E., and McGaugh, J. L. (1975): A single-trace, two-process view of memory storage processes. In: *Short Term Memory,* edited by D. Deutsch and J. A. Deutsch. pp. 355–378. Academic Press, New York.

Gold, P. E., Van Buskirk, R. B., and McGaugh, J. L. (1975): Effects of hormones on time-dependent memory storage processes. In: *Hormones, Homeostasis and the Brain. Progress in Brain Research,* Vol. 42, edited by W. H. Gispen, Tj. B. van Wimersma Greidanus, B. Bohus, and D. de Wied. pp. 210–211. Elsevier, Amsterdam.

Greenough, W. T. (*in press*): Enduring effects of differential experience and training. In: *Neural Mechanisms of Learning and Memory,* edited by M. Rosenzweig and E. Bennett. The MIT Press, Cambridge.

Greenough, W. T., Volkmar, F. R. and Juraska, J. M. (1973): Effects of rearing complexity on dendritic branching in frontolateral and temporal cortex of the rat. *Exp. Neurol.,* 41:371–378.

Groves, P. M., and Thompson, R. F. (1970): Habituation: A dual process theory. *Psychol. Rev.,* 77:412–450.

Handwerker, M. J., Gold, P. E., and McGaugh, J. L. (1974): Impairment of active avoidance learning with post-training amygdala stimulation. *Brain Res.,* 75:324–327.

Hartmann, E., and Stern, W. C. (1972): Desynchronized sleep deprivation: learning deficit and its reversal by increased catecholamines. *Physiol. Behav.,* 8:585–587.

Haycock, J. W., Deadwyler, S. A., Sideroff, S. I., and McGaugh, J. L. (1973): Retrograde amnesia and cholinergic systems in the caudate-putamen complex and dorsal hippocampus of the rat. *Exp. Neurol.,* 41:201–213.

Hebb, D. O. (1949): *The Organization of Behavior.* Wiley, New York.

Horn, G., Rose, S. P. R., and Bateson, P. P. G. (1973): Experience and plasticity in the central nervous system. *Science,* 181:506–514.

Hyden, H., and Egyhazi, E. (1962): Nuclear RNA changes in nerve cells during learning experiment in rats. *Proc. Natl. Acad. Sci. USA,* 48:1366–1372.

Hyden, H., and Egyhazi, E. (1964): Changes in RNA content and base composition in cortical neurons of rats in a learning experiment involving transfer of handedness. *Proc. Natl. Acad. Sci. USA,* 52:1030–1035.

Hyden, H., and Lange, P. W. (1970): Brain-cell protein synthesis specifically related to learning. *Proc. Natl. Acad. Sci. USA,* 65:898–904.

Illyutchenok, R. Y., and Yeliseyeva, A. G. (1972): Cholinergic mechanisms of memory: analysis of the amnestic effects of anticholinergic drugs. *Int. J. Psychobiol.,* 2:177–192.

Isaacson, R. L. (*in press*): Experimental brain lesions and memory. In: *Neural Mechanisms of Learning and Memory,* edited by M. Rosenzweig and E. Bennett. The MIT Press, Cambridge.

Jarvik, M. E. (1972): Effects of chemical and physical treatments on learning and memory. *Ann. Rev. Psychol.,* 23:457–486.

John, E. R. (1967): *Mechanisms of Memory.* Academic Press, New York.

John, E. R. (1972): Statistical versus switchboard theories of memory. *Science,* 177: 850–864.

Kándel, E. R., and Spencer, W. A. (1968): Cellular neurophysiological approaches in the study of learning. *Physiol. Rev.,* 48:65–134.

Kesner, R. (1973): A neural system analysis of memory storage and retrieval. *Psychol. Bull.,* 80:177–203.

Kesner, R. P., and Conner, H. S. (1974): Effects of electrical stimulation of rat limbic system and midbrain reticular formation upon short- and long-term memory. *Physiol. Behav.,* 12:5–12.

Kesner, R. P., and Wilburn, M. W. (1974): A review of electrical stimulation of the brain in the context of learning and retention. *Behav. Biol.,* 10:259–293.

Kety, S. (1972): Brain catecholamines, affective states, and memory. In: *The Chemistry of Mood, Motivation, and Memory,* edited by J. L. McGaugh, pp. 65–80. Plenum, New York.

Kobiler, D., and Allweis, C. (1974): The prevention of long term memory formation by 2,6-diaminopurine. *Pharmacol. Biochem. Behav.,* 2:9–17.

Landfield, P. W., Tusa, R., and McGaugh, J. L. (1973): Effects of posttrial hippocampal stimulation on memory storage and EEG activity. *Behav. Biol.,* 8:485–505.

Lashley, K. S. (1950): In search of the engram. *Symp. Soc. Exp. Biol.,* 4:454–482.

Lashley, K. S. (1951): The problem of serial order in behavior. In: *Control Mechanisms in Behavior,* edited by L. A. Jeffres. Wiley, New York.

Leconte, P., and Bloch, V. (1970): Deficit de la retention d'un conditionnement après privation de Sommeil paradoxal chez le Rat. *C. R. Acad. Sci. (Paris),* 271:226–229.

Leconte, P., and Hennevin, E. (1973): Characteristiques temporelles de l'augmentation de sommeil paradoxal consecutif a l'apprentissage chez le Rat. *Physiol. Behav.,* 11: 677–686.

Leconte, P., Hennevin, E., and Bloch, V. (1973): Analyse des effets d'un apprentissage et de son niveau d'acquisition sur le sommeil paradoxal consecutif. *Brain Res.,* 49: 367–379.

Lewy, A. J., and Seiden, L. S. (1972): Operant behavior changes norepinephrine metabolism in rat brain. *Science,* 175:454–455.

Luttges, M. W., Andry, D. K., and McInnes, J. W. (1972): Cycloheximide alters the neural and behavioral responses of mice to electroconvulsive shock. *Brain Res.,* 46: 411–416.

Lynch, G., Deadwyler, S., and Cotman, C. (1973): Postlesion arousal growth produces permanent functional connections. *Science,* 180:1364–1366.

Lynch, G., Stanfield, B., and Cotman, C. W. (1973): Developmental differences in post-lesion axonal growth in the hippocampus. *Brain Res.,* 59:155–168.

Mah, C. J., and Albert, D. J. (1973): Electroconvulsive shock-induced retrograde amnesia: An analysis of the variation in the length of the amnesia gradient. *Behav. Biol.,* 9:517–540.

Matthies, H., Lossner, B., Ott, T., Phole, W., and Rauca, C. (1973): The intraneuronal regulation of neuronal connectivity. In: *Pharmacology and the Future of Man. Proceedings of the Fifth International Congress on Pharmacology, 1972, Vol. 4,* pp. 29–38. Karger, Basel.

McGaugh, J. L. (1968a): A multi-trace view of memory storage. In: *Recent Advances on Learning and Retention,* edited by D. Bovet, F. Bovet-Nitti, and A. Oliverio, pp. 13–24. Roma Accademia Nazionale Dei Lincei, Quaderno N. 109 Anno CCLXV.

McGaugh, J. L. (1968b): Drug facilitation of memory and learning. In: *Psychopharmacology: A Review of Progress. 1957–1967,* edited by D. H. Efron et al., pp. 891–904. U.S. Government Printing Office: Washington, D.C., PHS Publ. No. 1836.

McGaugh, J. L. (1973): Drug facilitation of learning and memory. *Ann. Rev. Pharmacol.,* 13:229–241.

McGaugh, J. L. (1974): Electroconvulsive shock: effects on learning and memory in animals. In: *Psychobiology of Convulsive Therapy,* edited by M. Fink, S. Kety, J. L. McGaugh, and T. A. Williams, pp. 85–97. Winston, Washington, D.C.

McGaugh, J. L., and Gold, P. E. (*in press*): Modulation of memory by electrical stimulation of the brain. In: *Neural Mechanisms of Learning and Memory,* edited by M. Rosenzweig, and E. Bennett. The MIT Press, Cambridge.

McGaugh, J. L., Gold, P. E., Van Buskirk, R. B., and Haycock, J. W. (1975): Modulating influences of hormones and catecholamines on memory storage processes. In: *Hormones, Homeostasis, and the Brain. Progress in Brain Research, Vol. 42,* W. H. Gispen, Tj. B. van Wimersma Greidanus, B. Bohus, and D. de Wied. (Eds.), pp. 151–162. Elsevier, Amsterdam.

McGaugh, J. L., and Herz, M. J. (1972): *Memory Consolidation.* Albion, San Francisco.

Morrell, F. (1961): Electrophysiological contributions to the neural basis of learning. *Physiol. Rev.,* 41:443–494.

Morrell, F. (1967): Electrical signs of sensory coding. In: *The Neurosciences,* edited by G. C. Quarton, T. Melnechuk, and F. O. Schmitt. Rockefeller Press, New York.

Nakajima, S. (1973): Biochemical disruption of memory: a re-examination. In: *Current Biochemical Approaches to Learning and Memory,* edited by W. B. Essman and S. Nakajima, pp. 133–146. Halsted, New York.

Olds, J. (1973): Brain mechanisms of reinforcement learning. In: *Pleasure, Reward, and Preference,* edited by L. D. E. Berlyne and K. B. Masden, pp. 35–63. Academic Press, New York.

Oleson, T. D., Ashe, J. H., and Weinberger, N. M. (*in press*): Modification of auditory and somatosensory activity during pupillary conditioning in the paralyzed cat. *J. Neurophysiol.*

Overton, D. A. (1971): Discriminative control of behavior by drug states. In: *Stimulus Properties of Drugs,* edited by G. Thompson and R. Dickens, pp. 87–110. Appleton-Century-Crofts, New York.

Pearlman, C., and Becker, M. (1973): Brief posttrial REM sleep deprivation impairs discrimination learning in rats. *Physiol. Psychol.,* 1:373–376.

Randt, C. T., Quartermain, D., Goldstein, M., and Anagnosti, B. (1971): Norepinephrine biosynthesis inhibition: Effects on memory in mice. *Science,* 172:498–499.

Rosenzweig, M. R., Bennett, E. L., and Diamond, M. C. (1972): Brain changes in response to experience. *Sci. Am.,* 226:22–29.

Routtenberg, A., and Holzman, N. (1973): Memory disruption by electrical stimulation of substantia nigra, pars compacta. *Science,* 181:83–86.

Rutledge, L. T. (*in press*): Synaptogenesis: Genetic considerations and the effect of synaptic use. In: *Neural Mechanisms of Learning and Memory,* edited by M. Rosenzweig and E. Bennett. MIT Press, Cambridge.

Rutledge, L. T., Wright, C., and Duncan, J. (*in press*): Morphological changes in pyramidal cells of mammalian neocortex associated with increased use. *Exp. Neurol.*

Seligman, M. E. P. (1970): On the generality of the laws of learning. *Psychol. Rev.,* 77:406–418.

Shinkman, P. G., Bruce, C. J., and Pfingst, B. E. (1974): Operant conditioning of single-unit response patterns in visual cortex. *Science,* 184:1194–1196.

Sideroff, S., Bueno, O., Hirsch, A., Weyand, T., and McGaugh, J. L. (1974): Retrograde amnesia initiated by low-level stimulation of hippocampal cytoarchitectonic areas. *Exp. Neurol.,* 43:285–297.

Sperry, R. W. (1968): Mental unity following surgical disconnection of the cerebral hemispheres. *Harvey Lect.,* 62:293–323.

Squire, L. (1974): Amnesia for remote events following electroconvulsive therapy. *Behav. Biol.,* 12:119–125.

Stein, L., Belluzzi, I. P., and Wise, D. C. (1975): Memory enhancement by central administration of norepinephrine. *Brain Res.,* 84:329–335.

Talland, G. A. (1968): *Deranged Memory.* Academic Press, New York.

Thompson, R. F., Patterson, M. M., and Teyler, T. J. (1972): Neurophysiology of learning. *Ann. Rev. Psychol.,* 23:73–104.

Thut, P. D., Hruska, R. E., Kelter, A., Mizne, J., and Lindell, T. J. (1973): The effect of α-amanitin on passive and active avoidance acquisition in mice. *Psychopharmacologia,* 30:355–368.

Ungar, G. (1972): Molecular approaches to neural coding. *Int. J. Neurosci.,* 3:193–200.

Uphouse, L., MacInnes, J. W., and Schlesinger, K. (1972): Effects of conditioned avoidance training on the incorporation of uridine into polyribosomes of parts of mouse brain. *Physiol. Behav.,* 9:315–318.

Uphouse, L., MacInnes, J. W., and Schlesinger, K. (1974): Role of RNA and protein in memory storage: A review. *Behav. Genet.,* 4:29–81.

van Wimersma Greidanus, T. B., Bohus, B., and de Wied, D. (1975): The role of vasopressin in memory processes. In: *Hormones, Homeostasis, and the Brain. Progress in Brain Research, Vol. 42,* edited by W. H. Gispen, Tj. B. van Wimersma Greidanus, B. Bohus, and D. de Wied. Elsevier, Amsterdam.

Warrington, E. K., and Weiskrantz, L. (1973): An analysis of short-term and long-term memory defects in man. In: *The Physiological Basis of Memory,* edited by J. A. Deutsch, pp. 365–395. Academic Press, New York.

Weinberger, N. M. (1971): Attentive processes. In: *Psychobiology: Behavior from a Biological Perspective,* edited by J. L. McGaugh, pp. 129–198. Academic Press, New York.

West, R. W., and Greenough, W. J. (1972): Effect of environmental complexity on cortical synapses of rats: preliminary results. *Behav. Biol.,* 7:279–284.

Whitty, C. W. M., and Zangwill, O. L., editors (1966): *Amnesia.* Butterworths, London.

Wickelgren, W. A. (1973): The long and the short of memory. *Psych. Bull.,* 80:425–438.

Woody, C. D. (1974): Aspects of the electrophysiology of cortical processes related to the development and performance of learned motor responses. *Physiologist,* 17:49–69.

Wyers, E. J., Peeke, H. V. S., Welliston, J. S., and Herz, M. J. (1968): Retroactive impairment of passive avoidance learning by stimulation of the caudate nucleus. *Exp. Neurol.,* 22:350–366.

Zornetzer, S. F. (1974): Retrograde amnesia and brain seizures in rodents: Electrophysiological and neuroanatomical analyses. In: *The Psychobiology of Convulsive Therapy,* edited by M. D. Fink, S. S. Kety, J. L. McGaugh, and T. A. Williams. Washington, D.C.: V. H. Winston and Sons, Inc.

Biological Foundations of Psychiatry,
edited by R. G. Grenell and S. Gabay.
Raven Press, New York © 1976.

The Neuropsychological Analysis of Cognitive Deficit

M. Kinsbourne

Hospital for Sick Children, 555 University Avenue, Toronto, Ontario, Canada M5G 1X8

I. INTRODUCTION

When we try to understand any disease process, we first describe it and then relate its symptomatology to the underlying disorder of physiological functioning. Faced by a pattern of symptoms, we seek to determine which part of the body, by virtue of its incapacity, is responsible. Having correctly identified the bodily part, we then investigate the pathogenesis of its malfunction. In doing this, we assume that clinical phenomena bear one-to-one relationships to disordered bodily functions. We do so on the basis of extensive knowledge of the way different parts of the body are specialized to cater for different requirements of the organism. With respect to disordered cognitive function and underlying disordered brain, we similarly assume causal relationships and therefore seek to establish a set of brain-behavior correspondences. However, this lengthy enterprise has not yet yielded anything even remotely resembling an exhaustive inventory of such relationships. This is because the relationship between a behavioral deficit and the area of brain damage that gives rise to the deficit is not direct.

One cannot relate cognitive deficit to cerebral locus by mapping categories of behavior established by man-made convention. Rather one must first analyze the defective activity in terms of its nature and of the stages of information flow that underlie it. What, for instance, are the component processes that in concert support sophisticated skills, such as reading, writing, or recognizing a face? Each such skill results from the coordination in series and in parallel of a great number of component processes (Neisser, 1967). Also a single component process may be deployed for purposes of several different performances. For instance the ability to remember sequences is necessary, if not sufficient, for mastery of spelling and for arithmetic calculation. A selective disorder in the use of sequential information will prejudice both spelling and arithmetic ability. Thus, if brain damage occurs at the point where seriation is localized, both of these skills will be impaired. Conversely either spelling or arithmetic can be impaired for reasons that are unconnected with seriation and spare its cortical locus.

It is apparent that, if one attempts to accumulate evidence about the central locus of a skill, such as spelling or arithmetic, while disregarding the need to analyze it into its components, then the results will become cumulatively confusing. Evidence will pile up to implicate more and more cortical areas, as the presumptive localizations of these skills increasingly overlap. Component analysis of such data would reveal that different cerebral loci contribute different ingredients to a complex skill. Differently located lesions, when they implicate the same ability, do so for different reasons and therefore in different ways. Thus, if one confines oneself to a standard measure of spelling ability, then one cannot distinguish among the various possible causes of spelling disability. Spelling demands correct letter choice (item information) and correct letter sequence (order information). An analysis of errors will in some cases reveal a predominance of item errors, in other cases a predominance of order errors (Kinsbourne and Warrington, 1964a).

One must avoid the temptation to assume that a complex skill is localized at one specific point simply because one has observed patients with lesions at that point who were impaired as regards that skill. By the same token, if one collects information about the function of a particular part of the brain by noting the manner in which different human activities are affected by damage to it, then one might assign responsibility for many complex functions to one locus. But component analysis may reveal that in each of these apparently diverse activities (such as spelling and arithmetic) the same component process (such as seriation) is involved.

Hence it is not enough to note brain-behavior relationships. One has to perform a neuropsychological analysis. Neuropsychological analysis has the goal of identifying the simplest building blocks of behavior and locating the cerebral locus uniquely responsible for it. This approach to brain function holds promise for both clinical and fundamental insights into brain function. The clinician is offered more specific and reliable means for diagnosing and localizing organic cognitive deficit. The investigator achieves a better understanding of the principles and details of information flow in the brain.

The neuropsychologist is linked with the human experimental psychologist, who studies cognitive processes in normal people, by a circular logic. The cognitive psychologist supplies a sophisticated methodology that can be used to study many aspects of behavioral deficit. The neuropsychologist uses methodology usually applied to the study of normal people but applies it to the study of separately localized and therefore differentially vulnerable cognitive processes in cases of focal brain pathology. Focal brain damage teases out uncorrelated processes by generating disparities between preserved and impaired abilitites. The most informative type of result in neuro-psychology is a double dissociation between processes and cerebral loci. Lesion at locus a impairs process p more than process q; lesion at locus b impairs q more than p. Thus, for example, left-hemisphere lesions impair verbal more than spatial processes, and the reverse is true of right-hemisphere lesions. The majority of neuropsychological investigations are designed to uncover such double dissociations. The most popular comparisons are between the effects of damage to the left hemisphere and of damage to the right. The extent to which the results of these investigations are neuropsychologically relevant depends on the accuracy with which one can specify the crucial dimensions in which performances p and q differ. If they differ in many or imponderable ways, brain-behavior relationships may have been established, but fundamental advances in neuropsychology will not have been made. If they differ in a few definite or ideally in a single, crucial way, then knowledge of cerebral specialization of function is enlarged.

The discussions that follow are intended to illustrate the way in which cognitive deficits can be analyzed and interpreted. They demonstrate a problem-solving approach to the cerebral organization of higher mental processes.

II. PERCEPTION

In this section we discuss the two types of derangement that may impair any communication system—the transmission of misleading information and the failure to transmit information. At the cerebral level, irritative lesions may generate spurious experiences, whereas destructive lesions may deprive patients of the ability to recognize particular types of input. Damage to the two hemispheres gives rise to different types of recognition defect.

At each level of neural organization, neurons may fire excessively or not at all, depending on the nature of the damage. At the cerebral level, lack of neuronal firing typically does not so much deprive patients of experience of the outside world, as preclude them from categorizing that experience in particular ways. Clinically these disabilities are classed as agnosias (recognition defects). In contrast excessive or even spontaneous neuronal firing at high levels of organization generate subjective experiences that lack reference to related external change. Perceptual distortions, elaborations, and hallucinations may occur. Insofar as perceptual systems make "inferences" from the information given (Bruner, 1957), perceptual disorder may appear as unbridled and unwarranted inference.

Some of the more elementary of the "positive" manifestations of perceptual derangement can be thought of simply as undamped or unstable firing of specialized cortical analyzers. Such phenomena include persistent after-images (Kinsbourne and Warrington, 1963a) and illusory reduplication (monocular diplopia) of stimuli in cases of occipital lobe damage. Macropsia and micropsia, transitory distortions in apparent size, and metamorphopsia (distortions in shape) perhaps also reflect the excessive firing of relevant neurons (usually because their blood supply is restricted). More challenging are the elaborate visual hallucinations that are apt to occur in the presence of pathologically discharging neuronal populations in the temporal-occipital borderland. Patients report "remembered" objects or even complete scenes. Curious parallels can be found in the phenomenology of mescaline and lysergic acid intoxication, as well as in the reports of some subjects under conditions of perceptual deprivation. A mechanism common to these diverse situations could be an instability of neurons at a relatively high level of perceptual processing, compounded with biased expectancy or impaired critical sense. Specifically patients appear to over-interpret certain externally presented or spontaneously generated perceptual cues, filling in detail to form a highly refined percept. A similar mechanism may be at work in mystical experience.

A recognition defect (agnosia) is an impairment of recognition (identification) out of proportion to, and not accounted for, by any rise in detection threshold. The stimulus is detected but not recognized. A formal proof of the existence of such a situation was presented by Kinsbourne (1966), working with a series of veterans of World War II who had sustained penetrating missile wounds of the brain. Both detection and recognition duration thresholds were measured at the same loci in the visual field (for simple shapes and silhouette drawings). A dissociation between these two measures was found, such that for a given level of detection threshold recognition threshold was higher the more posteriorly the lesion was located. Thus the elevation of recognition threshold was not simply a function of visuo-sensory impairment. It indicated involvement of some posteriorly located processing mechanism active subsequent to the detection of the stimulus.

Failure to respond correctly may indicate error of omission or of commission, no response or wrong response. These two types of mistake differ in significance. A degree of ambiguity attaches to the errors of omission. An observer will fail to respond if insufficiently sure of his information. Now the decision as to how definite information must be to warrant a response (the response criterion according to Green and Swets, 1966) is itself subject to individual variation and also possibly to pathologic shift. A very liberal criterion of response could well give rise to the various perceptual illusions and hallucinations. An unduly conservative criterion would simulate perceptual deficit.

Irritation of the calcarine (visual) cortex causes positive phenomena such as flashing lights and whirling forms. Destruction of the calcarine cortex has been thought to result in blindness. However, there was a recent case report in which a patient with left hemianopia caused by right visual cortex excision could accurately point to, and even discriminate (by forced choice), signals in his "blind" half-field (Sanders, Warrington, Marshall, and Weiskrantz, 1974). This suggests that the patient was not blind but instead that a shifting detection criterion might at least play a role in amblyopia of cortical origin. It becomes necessary to reexamine this and other well-established cortical sensory deficits by forced choice or by signal detection theoretic methodology. A patient may be thoroughly uncertain of the accuracy of his actually correct response, but if he is forced to choose between it and an even less promising alternative, he will respond correctly. This need for reexamination of findings even extends to the now classical "split-brain" situation, in which after callosal section a patient, if informed through one hemisphere, cannot respond differentially with an effector controlled exclusively by the other disconnected hemisphere. We now need assurance that if forced to choose, the disconnected hemisphere would not reveal a hitherto unsuspected ability to communicate.

The effects discussed up to this point can occur with lesions of either cerebral hemisphere. The more categorically specific visual recognition defects (agnosias) arise either from left or from right posterior cerebral lesions, depending upon their relationships to the functional specialization of the two hemispheres. Left-sided lesions are apt to disturb acts of recognition that depend on specific associations. Right-sided lesions impair recognitions that depend upon spatial contextual relationships (Jackson, 1876; Paterson and Zangwill, 1944). The left-sided disease can give rise to object agnosia (and its minor form, simultaneous agnosia) and to color agnosia; right-sided disease causes spatial agnosia and agnosia for faces. Simultaneous agnosia is a case in point. Caused by anteroinferomedial left occipital disease (Kinsbourne and Warrington, 1963b), it presents clinically with reading and picture-identification difficulties. On brief (tachistoscopic) exposure, recognition thresholds for simple stimuli are not raised, but identification of multiple stimuli in sequence takes a remarkably long time (Kinsbourne and Warrington, 1962a). This is either because the processing of such stimuli is abnormally time-consuming or because sequential processing is interrupted by transitory periods of abnormal refractoriness. The defect is not limited to any one category of stimulus but affects both graphic and representational figures.

Color agnosia on the contrary is categorically selective. The problem is not sensory. Color matching and sorting are normally done. But the association of color with the color name is hopelessly confused, to the point that subjects can neither consistently match up a color and a name nor associate colors or color names with any other information (Kinsbourne and Warrington, 1964b; Oxbury, Oxbury, and Humphrey, 1969). Curiously enough, white, black, and shades of grey and their names are exempt from this disability—a bizarre instance of the selectivity of some recognition defects.

Various and selective although the visual agnosias of left-hemispheric origin are, they can all be classified as difficulties in relation to some aspect of the process of identification. After one processes a stimulus as a pattern (although not without influence on that processing), one classifies it in the context of previously experienced events. This is concurrently a process of association (to previous, similar events) and differentiation (from less similar categories of experience). In the visual agnosias this process fails with respect to the relevant category in input. The visual agnosic cannot fit the display into his inventory of possible and meaningful events (i.e., his semantic memory; see our later discussion of memory).

Although classifiable in this way, the visual agnosias differ not only along a monotonic dimension of increasing severity but also with respect to the particular classification in question. A color agnosic may have little difficulty with letters; an alexic may classify colors with facility. We derive a general picture of cerebral organization in which some sector of cortex is dedicated to a particular form of processing, such as classification. However, within that zone there are further dissociations of function between diverse cerebral loci, so that one locus might be more concerned with classification of one category of event, another with the classifying of a different type of experience. We shall see that the left-sided language area is similarly subdivided. Does a similar principle govern the organization of those abilities for which the right hemisphere is dominant?

Initially suggested on the basis of a single case report by Jackson (1876), the notion of right ("minor") hemisphere dominance was propagated by Brain (1941), Paterson and Zangwill (1944), Bogen (1969), Hécaen (1969), Newcombe and Russell (1969), Levy-Agresti and Sperry (1968), and many others (Kinsbourne and Smith, 1974; Kinsbourne, 1976b). The various tasks on which patients with right-hemisphere lesions have been found to be disproportionately handicapped all have some spatial or spatio-temporal ingredient, and they share the attribute that verbal coding seems unlikely to be of practical use (Kimura, 1963). Again the question may be asked: Are the different spatial deficits the result of different degrees of impairment along a monotonic dimension of spatial intelligence, and can the ostensibly diverse classical pictures be explained on the basis of incidental concomitant deficits?

Most of the tasks on which patients with left-hemisphere lesions show the greater disability are verbal. Most of those that reveal disproportionate handicap in right-hemisphere disease can be described as nonverbal and in some sense spatial or spatiotemporal. But it has become obvious that a formulation of these differences should be made in more basic terms. Of the many attempts at this that have been made, the suggestion of Semmes (1968) remains the most persuasive. As compared to the organization in the left hemisphere, in the right "unlike units would more frequently converge, and therefore one might predict heteromodal integration to an extent surpassing that possible in a focally organized hemisphere. In contrast to functions that may depend upon a high degree of convergence of like elements, spatial function might depend instead on convergence of unlike elements—visual. kinesthetic, vestibular, and perhaps others—combining in such a way as to create a single supramodal space." Elaborating on this speculation, we might describe the analytical bent of the left hemisphere as concerned with the reduction of differences, the right with the integration of differences. Presented with a sequence of words, the left hemisphere abstracts their common import or allocates them to categories, thereby rejecting their individual richness in favor of a rational organization. The right hemisphere in contrast integrates the units into a supraordinate configuration. Instead of sorting them, it combines them. An unanswered question of basic importance remains. Does the right hemisphere proceed in analogue fashion, forming and maintaining a faithful representation of the input? Or does it, in its way, also dismiss redundancy from awareness, abstracting from the unique situation the best-fitting available spatial schemata?

A case in point is the intriguing and apparently highly specific agnosia for faces (prosopagnosia, Hécaen and Angelergues, 1962). The selectivity of some right posterior cerebral lesions for recognition of faces is consistent with the spatial specialization of the right hemisphere. Faces differ from each other primarily in terms of relational cues (relative size, shape, and position of the features) rather than the features themselves. Just as reading is the most demanding exercise of the left-sided visual processing faculty, so face recognition puts particular strain on right-sided visual processing skill. A subtle difficulty in spatial perception could account for agnosia for faces (Hécaen and Angelergues, 1962), but it has been claimed that agnosia for faces is highly dissociable from other spatial deficits (Yin, 1970). Indeed correlations among the various right-sided spatial deficits are low (Newcombe and Russell, 1969), suggesting that different sectors of the spatial cortex are specialized for the application of spatial organization to different tasks. Right-hemisphere lesions cause agnosia for faces, and the right hemisphere of commissurotomized patients is more adept at recognizing faces than the left (Levy, Trevarthen, and Sperry, 1972). Agnosia for faces is very rare, much more so than a more general difficulty with spatial relationships. Patients with right-hemisphere disease often lose their way (topographical agnosia of Paterson and Zangwill, 1945) and fail to observe, retain, or use spatial relationships. The effect of this difficulty on the ability to sketch and copy drawings is discussed in the section on performance. A kindred disability has been reported in relation to the binocular disparity mechanism of depth perception, which is selectively vulnerable to right-hemisphere damage (Carmon and Bechtoldt, 1969; Benton and Hécaen, 1970).

Since they deal with different aspects of reality, are spatial skills in addition different in kind from the classificatory abilities of the left hemisphere, or do they differ only in the nature of the coding they use—nonverbal grouping as opposed to verbal labeling?

One can readily distinguish among at least three kinds of spatial processing. These are the retention in rich detail of a direct representation of perceived spatial relationships (as in the extreme case of eidetic imagery); the imaginative manipulation of spatial relationships (e.g., the mental rotation studies by Shepard and Metzler, 1971); and the ability to recode (organize) a spatially complex array into groupings that weigh less heavily on memory capacity. Although these three aspects of spatial processing are often spoken of as if interchangeable (Ornstein, 1972), there is very little evidence that direct representational spatial memory is even lateralized on the right side. Therefore we shall not consider it further as a right-hemisphere function. The mental rotation and organization functions seem to be definite right-hemisphere functions. Mental rotation is little understood. In particular it is not clear to what extent it involves the flexibly adaptive use of previous experiences. Mental organization of space certainly is most easily conceptualized as the assimilation of information into preexisting schemata (Piaget and Inhelder, 1956). The notion is well illustrated by an experiment, which compared the ability of expert and novice chess players to memorize the arrangement of pieces on a chess board (DeGroot, 1965). When the arrangement represented a stage in the playing of a particular game (although this was unknown to the subject), the chess master was able to reconstruct it after little more than a glance. When the pieces were randomly placed about the board, there was, in contrast, no difference in performance between the two groups. Thus the experts did not have a superior general spatial memory. But they were much better able to take advantage of the spatial constraints of a realistic position in chess to regroup the data into a form less taxing to their representational memory than the random display (Chase and Simon, 1973). Although such processing is not verbal, it is nevertheless semantic. If it characterizes right-hemisphere functioning, then we can no longer assume that, whereas the left hemisphere codes information in new forms, the right hemisphere represents it directly, without transformation. Instead, the hemispheres would seem to differ in that they apply different coding operations to the processing of information.

We conclude that wide areas of the cerebrum are specialized to perform particular basic operations. Within each area proper to a particular operation are subareas, in each of which the basic operation is performed with respect to a different type of input-output transformation. The two hemispheres contribute different basic ingredients to behavior. The left hemisphere abstracts attributes from input and groups according to these abstracted dimensions. The right hemisphere organizes input into superordinate spatial configurations. Thus the right hemisphere provides a contextual framework in which the left performs its focal analysis.

III. ATTENTION

In this section we discuss how people deploy their attention in space and over time. Lateral cerebral lesions distort the lateral distribution of attention through imbalance between opposing control systems. The focus of attention, varying between narrowly concentrated and widely diffused, is also vulnerable to brain disorder. Uncontrollable approach tendencies may cause continual switching of attention. Exaggerated avoidance may cause obliviousness of any stimulus outside the current focal point of attention.

Behavior is compounded of selection and processing. The organism picks up from the environment (or from its memory of the environment) a subset of the total accessible input. The amount of information picked up for processing reflects the organism's state of arousal or alertness. The choice of subset reflects its selective attention. Arousal is determined by cortical-brainstem interactions, which are outside the scope of our discussion. But selective attention is central to the topic of cognitive deficit, because restricted or anomalous selection produces aberrations in cognitive functioning.

Holding constant the amount of information processed per unit time, a person can decide whether to focus this attention or to spread it thin, and if to focus, then on what. We will first discuss the quantitative control of attentional processes.

Except in certain rare states of artificial perceptual isolation, people are constantly surrounded by far more sensory stimuli than they can possibly handle in the available time. Although an observer can hardly process everything, it is open to him either to orient to a relatively large subset of possible relevant events or to exclude most stimuli while processing a few in detail (i.e., to vary the range of cue utilization). A normal person can vary this range widely at will, although individual differences in personality cause different people to have different preferences in this respect. Range of cue utilization can be modified temporarily by drugs and more enduringly by brain damage.

Virtually from moment to moment, people change the degree to which they focus their attention. One strolls through a country lane, focus wide open; listens intently to one voice among many, focus clamped down; scans the horizon for sight of a sail; virtually excludes all input while pondering a difficult problem. These changes in focus are not necessarily effortless. Some people find it difficult to focus down and in preparation for doing so they minimize potential distraction. Others have trouble keeping focus open and constantly have to guard against drifting obliviously into some personal train of thought. The former are attending in an extraverted, the latter in an introverted manner. There is a correlated difference in personality. The extravert is not only open to a wide range of stimuli, but he also goes out to meet them halfway; he is a stimulus seeker. The introvert not only fails to attend to more than a small subset of events, but he also does his best to avoid exposure to more than that small range. The former has a predominant search tendency; the latter tends toward avoidance behavior. These closely linked cognitive and personality variables can be modified by drugs (Kinsbourne, 1973c).

Barbiturates (Laverty, 1958) and alcohol in subsedative dosage have an extraverting effect. They decrease avoidance, make for sociability, and impair the ability to focus attention. Given to introverts, they help in social situations that demand some degree of readiness to approach. The same dosage given to extraverts could make them overimpulsive, even aggressive, and soon sends them to sleep. Conversely, stimulants (caffeine, amphetamine, methylphenidate) are introverting. They focus attention, minimize the distracting effect of incidental happening, reduce the temptation to socialize, and help concentration for support of sustained mental or physical effort. Given to extreme extraverts, they correct distractibility. In the case of introverts, a similar dose might generate a socially undesirable degree of withdrawal.

The brain basis of this balance between diffuse and focused attention, approach and avoidance tendencies, is uncertain, as is the locus of the drug effects. There is some reason to hold the frontal lobes responsible for focusing down, the parietal lobes for diffusing attention, each in relation to different brainstem structures (Gray, 1973). If these attributions are approximately correct, certain brain-behavior relationships become explicable.

Whereas it is easy to discern cognitive deficits in patients with posterior cerebral disease, it has proven quite difficult to demonstrate adverse cognitive consequences of frontal lobe lesions anterior to those areas involved in control of speech output and facial praxis. Indeed neurosurgeons have felt free to excise these prefrontal areas for reasons that would have been judged insufficient had it been the parietal lobes that were in question. But cumulatively, a picture of deficit has in fact emerged from the literature on frontal lobe disease, which is best summarized in terms of defective focus of attention and unbridled approach tendency.

It proves quite difficult to maintain a frontal lobe patient's application to a task that is given him. Indeed he tends to make short shrift of it by breaking rules, as shown by Milner (1964) in her attempt to examine maze-solving skills in such patients. This unbridled approach to problem solving is paralleled by social disinhibition. Patients are casual and even insulting toward people who have influence over them and who would not normally be targets for impulsive behavior. They are indolent and hard to employ. They seem not to focus down spontaneously on any one task, even when it would serve their interests to do so (Petrie, 1952).

Prefrontal leucotomy appears to be most effective when used to counteract pathologic reflectiveness and avoidance, the extremes of introversion (as in the diagnostic categories of anxiety and obsessive states and religious mania). Patients who have been operated on sometimes actually overshoot into a psychopathic indifference to the very factors that previously weighed unduly heavily in their decision making.

Three entities for which there is no direct evidence of frontal lobe involvement bear certain resemblances to frontal lobe states. Organic or developmental hyperactivity (Wender, 1971) is a childhood syndrome characterized by an obtrusive mobility, which is exaggerated orienting to ambient stimuli. These children have a pathologically wide open focus of cue utilization. When they try to focus on any particular relevant subset of input, such as a task set in the classroom, they can barely control their stimulus-seeking tendency, which causes them to switch prematurely from stimulus to stimulus. This switching can be seen as disinhibited approach behavior untempered by any consideration of possible hazards of approach that normally enters into one's calculation in approach-avoidance conflicts. Correspondingly they exhibit the social evils of extreme extraversion. They are seen as blustering, blundering intruders, the fools who rush in where introverted angels fear to tread. Their resulting unpopularity, compounded with school failure caused by inadequate concentration, sets up a serious situation. The harmful disinhibited approach tendency is substantially reduced by use of stimulant medication. In such cases one might speculatively invoke underdevelopment of frontal-lobe control of cue utilization and avoidance tendencies.

Less is known about the postconcussional syndrome. After closed head injuries that leave their victims neurologically intact, the patients often complain of difficulties in concentrating, with depression, loss of sense of purpose, and unaccountable loss of employment. Psychogenesis of such complains, for instance "compensation neurosis," has not been substantiated. It might be appropriate to classify this as a disorder of attention, incorporating maladaptive extraverting bias. If this classification is appropriate, it would suggest that stimulant therapy should be tried.

Finally it is a commonplace observation among gerontologists that barbiturates are unsuitable as hypnotics for many old people, because their use results in confused and disoriented behavior during the night. Impaired frontal-lobe control of attention could explain this. Again stimulants would be the logical antidote for such nighttime confusion (and would not necessarily cause insomnia, see Kinsbourne, 1973a).

Most tantalizing of all is the rare condition of infantile autism. With respect to the repetitive and stereotypic behavior, gaze avoidance, and need for sameness, the syndrome suggests a pathologically heightened and inflexible introversion. Whether a remedy as simple as sedative therapy could be of benefit remains to be seen.

Tenuous as the attribution of frontal-lobe deficit may seem in conditions like hyperactivity, the role of the parietal lobe in diffusing attention is supported by even less definitive, merely circumstantial evidence. Inability to defocus attention is hard to test for in patients who also have a miscellany of extraordinary cognitive deficits and the argument has to rest on anecdotal observations. These do suggest that patients with parietal disease (right-sided or particularly bilateral) find it difficult to shift attention (Balint, 1909; Tyler, 1968). At this point we can wonder whether focusing of attention in space might constitute the only or major spatial function of the right hemisphere, and whether this attentional difficulty alone might account for the inferior performances of patients with right-hemisphere damage on a variety of spatial tasks. Perhaps all parts of the right hemisphere regulate spatial attention, but different parts of the hemisphere regulate different kinds of spatial attention. Thus, a lesion in one section of the right hemisphere would cause topographical agnosia, because the patient cannot attend to the relevant features of the city roadways; a lesion in another area would cause prosopagnosia, because the patient cannot attend to the relevant spatial relationships among the features of people's faces, and so on.

In order to form an internal representation of the spatial relationships of landmarks in the environment, one must at the very least attend to a sufficiently wide range of such features. Is it this early stage that is lacking in severe right-sided parietal disease, or is it some subsequent operation by means of which the spatial relationships are ordered and related to the organism's focus of attention and specific acts? Perhaps the attentional function is biparietal, the framework more right parietal. Parietal patients often seem oblivious of surreptitious changes made just outside their immediate focus of attention. They also seem to be unable to incorporate observed spatial relations into performance. They certainly are apt to lose the ability to search the environment in a systematic and nonredundant manner. At any rate observations of parietal and, particularly, bi-parietal, disease are consistent with the notion that the diffusion of attention is a parietal function.

Given a modicum of flexibility of focus of attention, a patient may still be constrained by cerebral disease in selecting what to attend to. Evidence from pathology suggests that one consequence of lesions of the "association cortex" may be a withdrawal of attention from particular input or output channels (whether or not they are themselves impaired as stimulus-analyzing mechanisms).

Cerebrally damaged patients at times manifest unusual attitudes toward their cerebral symptomatology. They will be surprisingly uncomplaining about hemianopia, even about hemianesthesia and hemiparesis. They may protest unawareness of a deficit or even dispute its existence. In extreme cases even complete blindness, when cortical in origin, will be denied (Anton, 1899), and a similar denial of aphasia has been observed (Kinsbourne and War-rington, 1963c). Correspondingly there may be disuse of a weakened or numbed limb quite out of proportion to the mechanical disability imposed by the lesion. We can relate these manifestations to the difference between interruption of centrally directed information flow and destruction of the cortical analyzers that extract information from the sensory channels.

One may conceive of the cortex as containing a number of modality-specific neuronal systems whose function it is to extract information from the sensory messages that reach the cortex. These cortical analyzers are instruments of selective attention. They extract information, not wholesale but selectively, according to the adaptive needs of the moment. The organism is oblivious of information not extracted by the analyzers. This is the basis of not noticing. If an analyzer is set to receive certain kinds of input, and these are not forthcoming, then that fact is registered in conscious awareness. If analyzers specialized for this input are inactivated, the lack of that mode of input is not registered in awareness. If the analyzer is destroyed, then not only is the sensory or motor deficit not noticed, but also it cannot even be imagined (imagining being conceived of as endogenous activation of appropriate analyzers). Thus the patient is in a unique quandary. He has, of old, a set of concepts relative to a particular type and source of input, but he has no immediate experience to go along with these concepts. How he resolves the paradox is a function of his personality and intellect. Denial is an obvious mechanism in such a predicament, and indeed both explicitly in words and implicitly in deeds such patients tend to deny their disabilities (Weinstein and Kahn, 1955).

Quite commonly inattention involves to a greater or lesser degree much of the input from one side of space, usually the left. This unilateral neglect of person and of space (the latter sometimes called unilateral spatial agnosia) indicates a lesion of the parietal lobe contralateral to the affected side. Unilateral neglect and inattention effects are a subset of the disorders of selective attention relative to the spatial location of the focus of attention, along the horizontal (left-right) axis. The properties of these phenomena reveal the nature of the mechanism of selectively attending within the right-left axis of space. We will begin discussion of these properties by considering how selective attention normally develops ontogenetically.

Selective attending may be usefully regarded as an elaborated derivative of gross orientational motor response, as it for instance can be observed in babies. As explained by Vygotsky (1962), immature organisms tend to act out their thought processes in gross movement patterns; overt behavior and thought are synonymous in babies. In the further course of ontogenesis, the organism becomes capable of programming internal representations of overt acts. Thus, where the infant would babble and the toddler would speak, an older child might think the words without uttering them. There is evidence that this verbal thought involves the same central motor program that would be used for spoken speech, if clarified. When people think in words, submotor electrical changes can be detected in the articulatory musculature (McGuigan, 1966). Presumably thought is an elaboration on motor behavior, in that the motor consequences are inhibited downstream of the motor program. Similarly we regard submotor attentional shifts as premotor and inhibited gross motor responses.

When the infant selectively attends to a stimulus, or searches for a stimulus, to the right or left, he uses a gross orientational synergism (termed the asymmetrical tonic neck response), which consists of lateral turning of head and eyes, pointing of the index finger of the extended ipsilateral arm, and flexion of the ipsilateral foot, representing incipient approach, while the body pivots on the contralateral leg. In the course of differentiation of the motor system, elements of this synergism come under selective control, so that the finger can point or the eyes swivel, whereas the other elements of the synergism are inhibited from motor expression. Our model proposes a further sophistication of this mechanism, by means of which attention can shift from central fixation prior to any overt deviation of gaze. However, as in the case of verbal thought, the motor suppression is imperfect. Subjects move their eyes in the direction of a lateral stimulus that has appeared very briefly, after it has disappeared (Bryden, 1961). Another type of orientational overflow is observed when subjects listening to simultaneous messages arriving at two earphones are asked to attend selectively to one of the two message. They turn their eyes to its side (Kahneman, 1973), even though there is nothing to look at or for. Even when selective attention is purely imaginative, within the framework of a remembered spatially extended display, shifts of gaze occur, as if the display were physically present and being scanned. This kind of circumstantial evidence gives us license to speculate that the same motor facility that programs gross lateral orienting also programs submotor lateral shifts of attention. We are now equipped to account for the otherwise inexplicable characteristics of unilateral neglect of space.

Patients with lesions implicating the right posterior-inferior parietal lobe often appear oblivious of the objects and events to their left, to an extent which cannot be accounted for on sensorimotor grounds. Not only do they fail to compensate for any hemianopia by shifting their fixation point to the left and by sending frequent exploratory glances to that side (as do patients with more peripherally located lesions that cause field defect); they actually deviate gaze maladaptively to the intact side, thereby further limiting the range of their useful field of vision. This gaze deviation is exaggerated if there are multiple stimuli in the visual field. Gaze appears drawn to the rightmost side in such a display. Curiously patients seem unaware of deficits to the left of that fixation point, even though they might just have been seen to glance across a rich array in search of its extreme right end. In the modality of touch, stimulation on the left is often ignored or meets with a very casual, nonurgent response. Spatial localization in hearing is far less exact than in vision or touch, and the auditory field is usually less populated by stimuli than the visual; but in this modality, the same principles apply. Of two competing messages, patients attend to the rightmost.

These effects imply that neglect is not simply a matter of rivalry between stimulation of the right and the left sensory field. Rather it relates to the *relative* location of multiple simultaneous stimuli along the horizontal plane. Regardless of which visual field is stimulated, the right extreme of a display captures conscious awareness. This suggests an imbalance of opponent processes that are specialized to swing attention in contrary directions along the horizontal plane. Each cerebral hemisphere is known to incorporate several areas that are specialized to deviate the axis of gaze and head position, predominantly in a contralateral direction (Crosby, 1953). In mutual inhibitory balance, these paired facilities control the moment-to-moment direction of orientation for purposes of looking and listening (and are linked to the manual component of exploration within the tonic neck response). Our model provides for a shift in balance when a novel stimulus appears to one or other side of fixation. Rightward shift of attention involves increased ascendancy of the left- over the right-hemispheric gaze mechanism, and vice versa. When the stimulus has appreciable lateral extent in space, the left hemisphere tends to shift attention to its right-sided border, whereas the left influences attention toward the left extremity of the stimulus. Normally the balance of excitation of the cerebral hemispheres can be voluntarily manipulated so as to permit selective fixation of gaze on any part of the stimulus or systematic exploration of it. When one hemisphere is damaged, the other may gain an ascendancy that, in the presence of a display, swings attention compulsorily to its contralateral margin. The effect is grossly obvious when the visual angle of shift is substantial and the stimulus remains visible for awhile. If the exposure of a visual stimulus is too brief to permit gaze to shift and fixate the target, a high-speed, implicit scan takes place. In the face of a unilateral lesion, this scan may be biased in the same way as is gaze. This implicit scan can be regarded as a shifting focus of awareness. The corollary is that awareness in such patients, rather than being flexibly available for voluntary disposition in any direction along the horizontal axis, inertly adheres to one side. The patient is unaware of the rest of the display and remains unaware of it. This is unilateral neglect of space. The patient's disability is far greater than it would have been if there had merely been loss of ability to retrieve information from one side of space. For instance, if such a patient tries to read a newspaper, he is not able to read as much as half of it. Rather, he obligatorily focuses on the extreme right vertical column of words and reads them out, expressing his bewilderment at the senseless communication.

Failure to attend may result not only in ignoring but also in taking for granted the input at the locus of inattention. An illustration that has been studied experimentally is the "completion" effect, first described by Poppelreuter (1917) in cases of posterior cerebral gunshot wounds. Patients with visual half-field defects reported seeing stimuli, although they were presented to blind sectors of field in a specific circumstance. The blind field was stimulated by part of a single, coherent figure, which also overlapped the intact field. The effect was further clarified by presenting a fragment of a figure to the intact field in such a way as to have the missing section overlie impaired visual field. Subjects "completed" the incomplete figure, reporting it as a whole (Warrington, 1962). The same effect is demonstrable with use of incomplete words (Kinsbourne and Warrington, 1962b). The mechanism of the completion effect, which occurs contralateral to a parietal lesion (Warrington, 1962) or to either side after corpus callosum section (Kinsbourne, 1971; Levy et al., 1972), appears to be as follows.

When presented visual information, people do not view it exhaustively but only up to the point at which their chances of a correct identification exceed some preset criterion (Green and Swets, 1966). Spurious identification can result either if the criterion is set pathologically low (as may be the case in drug intoxication) or if the predictive value of certain kinds of cues is overestimated and others are underestimated as sources of information. With lesions that unbalance the attentional system, the pathologic bias in attention results in exactly such a shift. Information contralateral to the lesion is undervalued, and an overambitious perceptual judgment is based on ipsilateral cues alone. The absence of corresponding cues on the other side (of the incomplete figure) should disconfirm the judgment, but because of the attentional shift the absence of cues is as little noticed as their presence would have been. Like unilateral inattention, completion is a disorder of selective attention. In the former the presence of a stimulus goes unnoticed; in the latter it is its absence that escapes attention.

Unilateral neglect tends to be frequent and gross with right-hemisphere disease, rare and mild with damage on the left. Our proposed explanation for this phenomenon introduces another principle of cerebral organization.

The brain is neuronally a highly-linked system. There are only a few synapses between any two neurons in the cortex. This organization, which is so different from that of a computer, perhaps has to do with the different uses to which brains and computers are customarily put. Powerful computers simultaneously perform totally uncorrelated tasks, and the multiple outputs are totally distinct and independently valid. Organisms rarely make, or could usefully make, more than one output at a time. Unlike computers, however, they do have to be able to shift mental set at great speed, varying their plan, and thus the range of relevant information, from moment to moment in response to contingencies that cannot be fully foreseen. The high level of linkage results in a tendency for spill-over from system to system. Left-lateralized control systems manifest cross-talk to each other (Kinsbourne and Cook, 1971), and this would presumably be true also of multiple simultaneously active systems on the right. There is for intelligible reasons

(Kinsbourne, 1975a) a particularly rich linkage between cognitive processing facilitated in a hemisphere and that hemisphere's control system for contralateral deviation of attention. Thus, if a person thinks in words (left-hemisphere function), his eyes tend to shift contralaterally to his active hemisphere, i.e., they move to the right, and they shift in the opposite direction if he thinks spatially (Kinsbourne, 1972a). When patients with hemisphere lesions are examined, they are usually communicating with the experimenter and are, therefore, verbally active, either overtly or in thought. This would tend to push attention rightward and would both minimize any neglect to the right caused by left-sided bias and accentuate neglect of the left caused by right-sided disease, accounting for the discrepancy in observed incidence of clinically obvious neglect of left and of right (Kinsbourne, 1970a).

A similar bias of attention can be demonstrated in "split-brain" patients, in whom the corpus callosum has been surgically sectioned and the cerebral hemispheres thus disconnected from one another. If only one visual half-field of such a patient is stimulated, the patient seems aware of the stimulus, as judged by the fact that he responds quite reliably with the left hand to left-sided stimulation or with the right hand or with his voice to right-sided stimulation. However, if subjects are simultaneously stimulated on both sides, in the context of an attention-demanding task that is verbal in nature, they show a striking abnormality. They tend to be oblivious of left-sided input. Consistent with the mechanism proposed alone we would regard this as an instance of left-sided neglect. The verbal activity in the left hemisphere biases attention to the right, causing neglect of the left side of space. The fact that this gross phenomenon seems to be released by callosal section suggests that one of the functions of the corpus callosum is normally to hold such biases in check. In normal subjects, verbal set does swing attention to the right, but the effects are quite subtle and on a small scale (Kinsbourne, 1970b, 1973b, 1975a).

A relatively mild variant of attentional imbalance apt to result from unilateral posterior cerebral damage is the so-called "sensory inattention." A stimulus, which is detected in isolation elicits no response if paired with a similar stimulus on the other side of the body. Such effects are frequent in visual, auditory, and tactile modalities. They can be mimicked by the effects of a relatively raised sensory threshold at an affected location. However, not all instances can be accounted for in this way. Sensory inattention may occur although the visual (Kinsbourne and Warrington, 1961) or tactile (Birch, Belmont, and Karp, 1964) thresholds at both of the simultaneously stimulated parts are identical. A directional imbalance of mutual inhibition between the relevant loci constitutes a reasonable model of this effect. A corollary is that attention is not only diverted away from the inattended stimulus but also is abnormally intensely focused on its attended rival. There are similar effects in the more flagrant but related phenomenon of unilateral neglect of space. But it is worth noting that some types of sensory inattention can be elicited in normally developing children. This warrants the speculation that as the nervous system matures, it becomes more adept at stabilizing laterally inhibitory interactions.

Much less is known about the way in which attentional shifts on the vertical axis are effected. There is some slight reason to suppose that posterior-lateral cerebral disease biases attention downward. It may be that there is a balance between bilateral posterior facilities that drive attention up and bilateral anterior ones that drive it down, functioning on the same general lines as the balance between the hemispheres with respect to lateral shifts of attention. But this is at present no more than a speculative possibility.

We have discussed instances in which pathologic bias enters into the systems that control the dispersion of selective attention in space and time. These biases do not selectively eliminate particular learned strategies. They hamper particular forms of selection, whether learned, innate, or only potential in the individual's repertoire. The actual strategies acquired during development are relatively invulnerable to disease, and this fact, outstandingly, differentiates the cognitive limitations of the brain-damaged adult from those of the child.

Brain disease may strike at any time during the life span, but only among the elderly is a degree of brain damage more the rule than the exception. Having gained control over his behavior in the course of childhood, the individual maintains his level of control during his adult years. But at any stage a variety of impairments may disturb that control by making mental capacity unavailable. Focal brain lesions selectively, and diffuse brain disease more generally, degrades control over cognitive processes. Anxiety makes prior claim on mental capacity and restricts behavior to well-practiced and automatized operations that can proceed with minimal mental effort. Thought disorder does not reduce mental capacity but diverts it from effective use toward the pursuit of idiosyncratic goals. In each of these diverse cases, an adult who has acquired a previously effective repertoire of cognitive plans and attentional strategies for deploying his mental capacity now finds that capacity ineffective when deployed. He selects as before, but he can no longer process.

The limitations that circumscribe the behavior of the immature organism (and the mental retardate in his perceptual immaturity) are different in nature. During development children learn to look, listen, and move according to what they have observed. They learn to search systematically, economically where it is sufficient, exhaustively where it is required; to select the most relevant, rather than the most salient, perceptual dimension or feature; to attend analytically; to use organization available in the display or to impose organization of their own making on it; and to set their response criterion in a way that reconciles desired speed with needed precision. The landmarks of cognitive development are the acquisition of diverse skills. The anomalous and ostensibly idiosyncratic ways that children go about tasks may represent nothing more than the way any human being would approach a task that is totally novel. The adult, too, learning a new skill, has to discover how and at what to look, where and when to listen. In the process, he runs through a developmental sequence analogous to the progression of events in childhood. He has to learn how to deploy his processing capacity before he is in a position to try out its power.

Selective attention deploys processing capacity in space and time. Even if an adult whose capacity is reduced by disease brings his processors to bear in the usual way, he can no longer effectively process the information to which he has gained access. The child's failures are quite different. He has not yet learned how best to deploy his mental capacity. He does not yet know how to go about the task.

These considerations explain why brain damage, although it may reduce overall level of performance to child-like levels, does not, as regards the mechanism of that reduction, roll back the developmental sequence from sophistication to innocence. Cerebral disease may slow down or knock out an information pick-up system, but there is no way by which it can so damage it as to divest it of learned bias, while leaving it functional. One can only unlearn by undergoing new and contradictory learning. As cerebral gray matter is thinned in the cortical atrophies of old age, such new learning becomes increasingly difficult to institute, and the intellectually deteriorated patient is increasingly locked into a rigid, overlearned behavioral repertoire. He represents not a comparable but the opposite case to the child, who has a wide range of available options but does not yet know how to decide among them. Only when faced with what is for him a novel task does an intellectually deteriorated person seem as helpless as a child. He has no preformed plans for the contingency, and his improverished cerebrum cannot adapt existing plans to the purpose. In this instance, he, like a young child, hardly knows where to begin.

We conclude that sideways shifts of attention represent a refinement of a basic mechanism by which each half of a bisymmetrical nervous system is in charge of turning the body toward the opposite side of space. The two halves are in balance. In man, verbal processing is superimposed on the left and spatial on the right half of the brain. Verbal activity therefore tends to swing attention right, and spatial tends to swing it left. When the corpus callosum is severed, these tendencies are amplified, and each hemisphere, when active, swings attention contralaterally and takes total charge of voluntary behavior, unchecked by the other, inactive hemisphere.

People's preferred disposition of attention may be focal or diffuse, their behavior reflective or impulsive, their social style introverted or extraverted. Organic hyperactivity is a state of pathologically extreme diffusion of attention, impulsivity, and extraversion. This aberration can be minimized by use of amphetamines. Normal children have to learn how to attend, because all tasks are new to them. Demented or otherwise brain-damaged adults often can still attend but have lost capacity to process the incoming information.

IV. MEMORY

We now distinguish between semantic and episodic amnesia. The semantic amnesias result from focal cerebral damage and render the patient unable to use particular categories of information that he previously knew well. Episodic amnesia is different. In it, people forget autobiographic detail, the various combinations of circumstances occurring uniquely at one or another time, which in sequence constitute a person's life experience. Insight into the mechanism of this forgetting could suggest ways of strengthening the flagging memory that characterizes those of advanced age.

Patients who suffer from a wide range of organic and functional disorders complain of or seem to have poor memory. The memory difficulty may be general, or it may be selective, with reference either to the category of items to be remembered or to the time at which the relevant events occurred. It may be persistent, progressive, fluctuating, or intermittent. We will present a classification of memory disorder, which will guide us toward first allocating a given memory difficulty to its probable pathology and then evaluating the mechanism of that difficulty.

Broadly speaking, two kinds of learning occur during human (and presumably all animal) life. Information may be entered either into "semantic" or "episodic" memory (Tulving, 1972). Episodic memory refers to our awareness of what happened on one occasion. Semantic memory refers to our knowledge of things independent of when we learned or observed them.

As a person grows up, he acquires a vast repertoire of information. In the course of perceptual learning, he learns to scan the environment effectively and economically, and to listen selectively to potentially important sounds, ignoring those that are adventitious. During motor development he becomes able to fragment and recombine patterns of muscular action in goal-directed ways. He acquires the vocabulary and rules of one or more languages, learns the unspoken rules of social behavior, and acquires facility with mathematical and logical reasoning. All this knowledge is acquired by dint of repetition, to the point when its exercise becomes second nature (automatic) to the individual. Much of it he learned without explicit awareness of learning anything. Much he learned during early childhood, the events of which he has quite forgotten. If asked specifically when and under what circumstances he learned any one such item of information he would be hard pressed for an answer.

This is semantic memory; it represents a fund of knowledge common to individuals within a species, an ethnic, economic, or social group, rather than information of private significance to a single individual. It is "context free" (Pribram, 1969) in that the manner and circumstances under which the information is acquired are irrelevant to its validity or use. To the best of our knowledge, deficits in semantic memory are attributable to cerebral cortical damage.

In contrast to semantic memory is episodic memory. Each individual, throughout his life, encounters and participates in a succession of uniquely personal and never-to-be repeated events. The sum of such episodes, perfectly recalled, would comprise an exhaustive biography. The episodes have no general validity; they are "context bound" (Pribram, 1969) and only make sense in the appropriate time frame and the specific situation in which they occurred. Whereas semantic learning arises from repetition of the essentials of what is being learned, episodic memory cannot derive strength from such external repetition but only from repeated recollection (mental reenactment) of the episodes. A few episodes may indeed take on some of the characteristics of semantic memoranda in this way, but mostly episodic remembering is based, not on virtually effortless resort to overlearned decision processes, but rather on a cued retrieval or search process that demands appreciable attention or effort. Episodic memory deficit ensues if patients fail to allocate attention to the search (as in a variety of functional and emotional disorders), or if they are unable by using appropriate cues to recreate enough of the relevant context to permit retrieval of the context-bound information (as in the case of limbic lesions).

A. Disorders of Semantic Memory

The semantic memory store contains the full inventory of information-processing strategies available to the individual. Thus virtually the full range of possible disorders of higher mental function consequent upon focal cerebral injury lends itself to classification as category-specific semantic memory deficit. The agnosias, failures to recognize familiar (i.e., repeatedly experienced) stimuli in one or another modality, represent such a deficit. The apraxias, failures to program effectively overlearned motor acts and sequences, represent another. Aphasic disorders such as word-finding difficulty and agrammatism, are dramatic instances of foreclosed access to "semantic" information relevant to vocabulary and syntax, respectively. To illustrate the simplifying power of this perspective, let us discuss how much of the difficulty that patients experience in receptive aphasia can be made intelligible in terms of unavailability of verbal grouping skills based on overlearned knowledge of the constraints of the language.

Decoding of spoken language is conventionally evaluated by asking patients either to repeat or to act in accord with the meaning of a word, a phrase, a sentence. Now the ability of normal adults to repeat verbatim a list of unrelated words is severely limited to around seven, the so-called memory span. Yet when in conversation people often listen to sequences of words far greater than seven in number before gathering the gist of the message, and they store or otherwise respond to the information, dismissing its exact wording from their minds. How is this done?

Words in any language are grouped according to rules that generate varying levels of probability for different groupings. An implicit knowledge of these probabilities, such as is acquired by virtue of experience both as listener and speaker, over many years, enables the listener to minimize the load on his short-term memory by treating highly probable word clusters as if they were single, superordinate units. Thus familiar phrases might use up not several, but only one of the about seven slots available in short-term memory (Miller, 1956). Lists that avoid familiar word groups or violate sequential probabilities are harder to remember. Beyond this a second opportunity for economy is afforded at the level of meaning. If the proposition is familiar or easily accepted, it can be classified in terms of the individual's existing inventory of possible, probable, or acceptable propositions. Again this process constitutes a form of instant repetition or rehearsal, and the message is remembered better than the limited capacity of short-term memory might have led one to expect. If what is being said is implausible and contradicts the individual's semantic expectations, it is harder to repeat.

It is well known that even when a simple vocabulary is used, the words of which they can easily decode when they appear one at a time, aphasics show a rapidly gathering decoding difficulty for sentences as they increase in length.

The mechanism of this effect was explored by Kinsbourne (1972b). As spoken messages he used the letter names, presenting them by tape recorder in sequences varying in length and in transitional probability, which is the extent to which a given letter sequence conforms to spelling patterns prevalent in the language. As expected young adults were able to repeat an increasing number of letter names as conformity of the letter sequence to English spelling increased (although no meaningful words were used). Elderly subjects had substantially shorter memory spans, but proportionately they derived about as much benefit from closer approximation to the language as did the young subjects. Aphasics, however, not only had a curtailed memory span, they also derived no significant benefit at all from the presence of English spelling patterns within some of the sequences. We conclude that even though aging quantitatively diminished the efficiency of processing, the young and old both took advantage of their over-learned knowledge of English spelling to enhance their baseline span. However, aphasics were unable to make use of this information. Their semantic memory for transitional probability in English could not be put to work. The information was unavailable, and the grouping process could not be implemented.

These data suggest a model for receptive aphasia. Aphasics may be unable to combine words in groups. Thus their short-term memory (which itself may be limited) is soon flooded with information. Words spill over into oblivion, and neither the verbatim text of the message nor its meaning can be rendered in response.

Semantic memory deficits are characteristically highly selective. Whereas an aphasic patient may fail to organize word sequences in ways that represent his long-term experience with the language, he may remain well able to organize his visual environment in terms that make use of expected relationships. But the patient with visuospatial agnosia (Paterson and Zangwill, 1944) caused by right posterior cerebral disease unaffected in his semantic memory for language instead has extreme difficulty in piecing together fragmentary visual impressions with respect to their perfectly lawful and expected relationships. Space has its own semantics, as does language. We learn the rules during perceptual development; but, in the presence of a strategically located cortical lesion, these rules may become unavailable for use (or for relearning).

As we have seen, semantic memories are established by repetition (practice). Only on early trials is their acquisition in any way linked with the episodic context of those trials. Patients with episodic memory deficits may be slow in assuming and reassuming task orientation and have trouble keeping instructions in mind. Whereas in the amnesic syndrome or in aging the memory deficit is mostly episodic, skill learning is initially slow not for semantic but for episodic reasons; but it then may progress substantially, even though the subject is at each trial totally oblivious of the fact that he has been similarly engaged at any time before.

B. Disorders of Episodic Memory

Perhaps the most common single complaint by people suffering from any type of psychopathology is of impaired memory. Almost always this implicates memory for events, and recent events are usually said to be particularly difficult to remember. As people age they complain of failing memory. It is the most common initial symptom of dementia of any age. Forgetting is often accounted for by hypothesizing repression or denial. It is common in depression. In mental retardation it is only one instance of a whole range of relatively inefficient mental processes, but in the postconcussional state and in the amnesic syndrome (whether due to alcoholism, bitemporal encephalitis, infarction, or excision) it is the most prominent, even defining, manifestation.

Episodic memory loss is as intractable as it is prevalent. Semantic memories can, in many cases, be inculcated even in impaired individuals, by the simple device of training to criterion, however many trials that should take. Thus, even grossly mentally retarded people can be taught a variety of skilled acts. But one can hardly train episodic memory by practice, as its essence is the retrieval of unique rather than repeating events. The elderly person who has misplaced his spectacles can tell which are the usual places he puts them in. That is semantic memory. But he cannot remember which of these he last used. In general episodic remembering involves specifying a particular, often arbitrary, subset of events that could as well have grouped themselves in some other way (e.g., a particular sequence of digits one to nine, which measures episodic digit span, rather than the full inventory of digits one to nine, which constitutes semantic information about number).

The way in which people have tried to strengthen episodic memory has implications for understanding its mechanism. An ancient "Art of Memory" has trained its devotees to generate "bizarre images" in relation to specific memoranda. In other words the subject encodes the item to be remembered with some striking and unusual context. When the item is to be retrieved, he uses this contextual cue to find his way to the item in question.

"An event is remembered only when a retrieval cue makes contact with the stored representation of the event" (Watkins, 1974). Items are remembered by the company they keep. An item is forgotten either if at the time it was represented in awareness the subject failed to attend to its context in space and time, or if at the time of retrieval, the subject fails to evoke contextual cues in sufficient richness to make remembering possible. Contextual cues vary in efficiency insofar as they vary in frequency. The more frequently a cue occurs, the less useful it is in helping people sort out the right remembered event from others. A bizarre image is an infrequent context, allowing for minimal confusion with comparable events at other points in time. An everyday cue, such as at breakfast time, has little specifying value for those who breakfast daily.

Patients with amnesic syndrome (caused by damage within a circuit running from hippocampus along fornix to mammillary bodies to anterior thalamus and by the cingulate bundle back to hippocampus, as discussed by Victor, 1969) have extreme difficulty in recollecting any event once it has left the focus of their immediate awareness. There is no evidence to incriminate their immediate memory span, and, as they understand conversation normally (Lackner, 1974), they must be capable of normal encoding and grouping of verbal sequences. Their problem relates to the retrieval of episodic information.

An experiment by Kinsbourne and Wood (1975) illustrates the point. It applies the Peterson method of interference to the investigation of amnesic forgetting. Peterson and Peterson (1959) described a way of investigating forgetting over short periods of time by showing subjects a to-be-remembered unit of information and then having them perform an irrelevant distraction task for a fixed number of seconds. Very rapid forgetting ensues. Amnesics forget even more rapidly than normals under these conditions (Cermak and Butters, 1972). This is not unexpected, as clinicians have for many years remarked on the fact that in severe amnesia, it is not so much time as change of mental set that causes forgetting. Once the experience has left the ambit of immediate awareness, the "primary memory" of Waugh and Norman (1965), it is lost.

A clue to the mechanism of that loss is afforded by studying the effect on amnesic forgetting of a variant on the Peterson paradigm, called "release from proactive inhibition" (Wickens, 1970). After several interference trials, during which performance customarily falls to very low levels, the category of the to-be-remembered item is without warning changed. For instance, after four successive trials using animal names, the fifth might introduce the name of a flower. This category shift results in a substantially greater probability of recall than when the previous category is again drawn from on that trial. Clearly subjects note the category of the test items, and a change in category is for some reason of benefit. Cermak, Butters, and Moreines (1974) have shown that amnesics do not benefit as expected from the category shift. They fail to show "release from proactive inhibition." The authors suggest that this reveals an amnesic encoding deficit. The patients have failed to encode the categorical nature of the test items and therefore cannot benefit from a change in that category. A simple extension of this experiment disposes of this notion. Kinsbourne and Wood (1975) replicated Cermak et al.'s (1974) design but continued for a few more trials in the new category. They found that proactive inhibition release does occur. But it is delayed as compared to the normal, appearing more typically on trial six or seven than five. For it to occur at all, "category" must after all have been encoded. Instead the finding is explained as follows. In order to recall the test item, it has to be discriminated from the other previous test items. The more salient the difference between it and them, the easier the discrimination. Hence category shift is of benefit. Therefore, when an amnesic at trial five attempts to retrieve the correct test item, he will only be helped by its categorical nature if he can use that as a retrieval cue. But this he cannot do. As he thinks back in time, his ability to make distinctions based on recency in a sequence of events proves blunted, and the massed (four times repeated) experience of the original category prevails over the single experience of the new one. Only after the new category has been repeated once or twice does it become sufficiently salient to impress itself upon the patient for use as a retrieval cue. It then is of expected benefit to recall.

We are now in a position to understand the tendency that amnesics have to perseverate with previous, once correct but now outdated, responses. Superficially this perseveration resembles that known to occur after frontal-lobe lesions (Milner, 1964). But the mechanism is different. The frontal-lobe case, human or operated monkey, perseverates in his response to a particular target or cue, even if the context is totally changed. The amnesic (or hippocampally lesioned animal, as demonstrated by Winocur and Breckenridge, 1973) does not perseverate with a response so much as continue his task orientation when he should change it. When relatively minor changes in context are used to indicate changes in task, these are not retrieved, and the patient proceeds as if the situation had not altered. But if context is radically changed, then he will not perseverate (even if the "positive" target or cue is included in the new test situation). Thus amnesics cannot appropriate cues to support a search for contextually bound information. If they are specifically supplied with cues at retrieval time, this improves their remembering. If they are given these cues both at encoding and at retrieval time, no further improvement ensues (Kinsbourne and Wood, 1974). Thus it is not a matter of imperfectly noting cues at encoding; cues not registered at that time could hardly be of use if later supplied for retrieval. The problem then is in setting the context. If context is supplied, at least some remembering could occur.

We can now decide among the various major interpretations of the mechanism of amnesia. Are amnesics unable to register new information? No. At times they register only too successfully and even perseverate. Are they unable to encode verbally or semantically? No, because they have a normal working memory for speech comprehension and because giving cues at retrieval has effects that are not further enhanced by helping patients encode at registration. Are they precluded from retrieving specific memories by an onrush of disinhibited competing recollections? No. When given freedom to tell of any episode within a wide range, they merely come up with generalities. Do they have greater than normal need for time to rehearse information merely to drive it into memory? No, because merely engaging their attention does not make them forget. One has to distract them with a task that uses ideas similar, indeed comparable, to the items to be remembered. The amnesic defect is in retrieving unique and unrehearsed items of information on the basis of contextual cues that would normally permit a differentiation between the sought-for item and the ones competing with it. For instance amnesics learn a paired associate list. They are then given a second list in which the responses are categorically similar to those in the first list. They erroneously continue to give first list responses. They are given a further list in which the responses are categorically quite different. Now there are no longer any previous list intrusions (Winocur and Weiskrantz, 1975).

Recognition is sometimes regarded as not necessitating retrieval (Kintsch, 1970). Given that amnesics have conspicuous recognition as well as recall difficulties, it would follow that retrieval difficulty alone could not account for amnesic forgetting. But this is illogical. In recall, an event consists of a target item and its context. A target item is retrieved through access to certain of its contextual specifications. In recognition specifications are retrieved through access to the stimulus they specify. Aspects of an event are retrieved by use of the "target item" as the retrieval cue (Tulving and Thompson, 1971). Recall is generally more difficult than recognition only because of the way in which these two types of task are usually set up. Recall typically involves a large or open-ended set of alternatives, recognition perhaps as little as a binary choice ("have you seen this before or not?"). The difficulty of recognition also depends on the length of the list. The longer the list, the worse the overall performance will be on recognition. Where old people have been found unimpaired in recognition though impaired in recall (Schonfield and Robertson, 1966), this is to say no more than that they were relatively less impaired when choice was between fewer alternatives and the test list short. When the number of alternatives is substantial and the list long, then old people can be shown actually to have a relatively greater recognition than recall deficit (Kinsbourne and Wilson, 1975). A retrieval model will accommodate both types of remembering.

Huppert and Piercy (1974) have reported that amnesics who have great trouble in recognizing common words previously presented find it far easier to recognize rare words and show no inferiority as compared to controls in recognizing sets of pictures presented under similar experimental conditions. The effect of frequency on word recognition has in normals been shown to be due to the difference that recent extraexperimental occurrences of test items make for retrieval processes (Kinsbourne and George, 1974). When a subject sees a rare word, he may not have experienced it at all recently except in the context of the test presentation. If he is shown a common word, he may have recently experienced it repeatedly and may be unsure in which context, experimental or extraexperimental, he last saw it. This retrieval requires a fine discrimination among recent events. Such a discrimination presents particular difficulty to amnesics, who are selectively handicapped in their ability to retrieve on the basis of relatively minor changes in context, which they would then have to use as cues for retrieval. When rare words or unfamiliar pictures are used, then the discrimination in time is far less exacting, and the coarse grain of amnesics' temporal discrimination of successive events may prove adequate.

As would be expected of patients with selective weakness in episodic memory, amnesics are able to learn a wide range of skills—perceptual (Milner, Corkin, and Teuber, 1968; Warrington and Weiskrantz, 1968, 1970), motor (Milner, 1965; Corkin, 1968), and logical (Kinsbourne and Wood, 1975). The fact that this is regarded as at all unexpected or surprising demonstrates the power of words to obstruct thought. When different situations are labeled with the same name, this blurs awareness of differences between them (Whorf, 1965) by so-called "acquired equivalence of cues." The word "memory" is used both for the retrieval of unique episodes and for perfection of practiced skill, and the word "learning" has found similarly promiscuous application. In fact amnesics should be able to learn virtually anything, given sufficient practice. The confusion is most acute in animal learning (Iverson, 1973). A recent review (Kimble, 1968) illustrates the confusion caused by unqualified acceptance that amnesics forget the incidents of daily life as fast as they occur (Scoville and Milner, 1957). In this field, "memory" and "learning" are almost exclusively applied to situations in which animals are given the opportunity, over repeated trials, to test hypotheses till they hit on the one behavior that is substantially rewarded. These procedures relate to an aspect of semantic memory. They do not test episodic memory, and bilateral inferomedial temporal excisions would not be expected to affect this kind of performance.

A series of experiments by Gaffan (1972), although differently interpreted by that investigator, illustrates the type of learning difficulty that one would expect of animals with limbic lesions, if analogous to human amnesia. Rats with bilateral fornix lesions were run in a T maze. From trial to trial, one limb of the T was changed in color. Normal animals explored the novel segment of runway. The lesioned animals indifferently entered either the changed or the invariantly colored limb. This would be expected if lesioned animals, like amnesics, fail to use context in remembering. The color of the runway is a contextual cue. This is not used to guide subsequent behavior. Also it is when animals are asked to change problem-solving strategy on the basis of changed context that the hippocampal deficit is revealed as analogous to that in amnesics (Winocur and Breckenridge, 1973).

Our discussion of the amnesic deficit has been detailed, because it is an unusually striking illustration of a neuropsychologic phenomenon that has been clarified by applying insights from contemporary experimental psychology. However, such microanalysis of mechanism could have important practical implications. For instance how can an amnesic be taught a complex (multistep) skill?

In the initial stages of such teaching, our understanding of the syndrome suggests that there would be little difficulty in teaching the patient individual movements but great difficulty in teaching him their sequence. Orderly succession of movements must eventually depend on each movement acting as contextual cue for the next. The amnesic might instead perseverate on the same movement. But we would have recourse to our control over context in an attempt to help him make the appropriate transition. If we stage major contextual changes in time with each component of the skilled movement sequence, the patient's weakened retrieval power might still be sufficient, given such salient contextual cues, to perform as desired. Over time, the movement sequence would become practiced, and thus enter "semantic memory," with which the patient has greater facility.

The potential social significance of this method is clearer when one considers how like amnesia, although in a minor form, is the memory difficulty that so often attends aging. The elderly person's forgetfulness for recent mundane events is notorious, as is the preservation of his semantic memory and his tendency to rely on highly rehearsed memories. The amnesic syndrome may prove to be a testing ground for an approach to the problem of why old people forget.

We must also discuss two prominent characteristics of some amnesics and of people who have suffered severe head trauma: confabulation and retrograde amnesia.

Sharpening contextual contrasts improves performance. In the early stages of recovery from the devastating Wernicke's encephalopathy that ushers in the amnesic syndrome of alcoholic etiology, patients have often been observed to "fill in" gaps in recent memory by spurious recollection. That this is no inevitable consequence of severe amnesia is shown by its absence in nonalcoholic cases (Scoville and Milner, 1957) and in alcoholic cases in the long term (Talland, 1965). Two views are tenable. One would regard confabulation as a deficit characterized by uncontrolled access to memories, which is not part of, but can complicate, amnesia caused by limbic lesions. Lesions in the brainstem in Wernicke's encephalopathy are quite widespread, and perhaps some transitory brainstem involvement accounts for the confabulatory phase of the alcoholic amnesic syndrome. A more economic account takes cognizance of the fact that no objective evidence for multiple variants of the amnesic syndrome exists. Confabulation could be explained as an initial response of alcoholics, typically plausible and verbally adept people, to their predicament, a response that is extinguished by consistent social disapproval. At any rate, when amnesics are asked to retrieve certain types of episodes from memory at random (e.g., when did you last see a bird?) far from responding with profuse detailed episodes, they seem devoid of memories altogether and try to evade the task by drawing on their semantic memory instead ("birds have wings. One sees them in the air") (Kinsbourne and Wood, 1975).

Amnesics forget not only episodes that occurred subsequent to the onset of their illness, but also events that occurred well before that time. This retrograde amnesia is said to extend a number of years into the past but to spare memory of very early experiences. This phenomenon is particularly stressed in reports of retrograde amnesia following head injury (Russell and Nathan, 1946). Soon after the impact, retrograde amnesia usually exists for that day, and sometimes for much longer into the past. Typically it shrinks, until only the circumstances immediately preceding the impact remain shrouded in oblivion.

This account of retrograde amnesia does not survive close scrutiny. A controlled study showed that amnesics could in fact not remember public events better the earlier (longer ago) they occurred (Sanders and Warrington, 1971). When retrograde amnesia resolves, it does not do so in any orderly fashion (Williams and Zangwill, 1952). Rather memories reappear in patchy, disjointed fashion, and only by their subsequent confluence reestablish an orderly recession of remembered events. Consistent with our account of retrieval from episodic memory is the view that as patients recover the ability to generate and use those categorical and relational cues that make retrieval possible so, one by one, they remember the events of the past. Whereas semantic memories are characteristically enduring, episodic memory is typically evanescent. In recognition of this fact, clinicians and investigators typically tend to ask different questions about recent and more distant personal experience. Questions about the very day of interview will center on episodes—what did you have for breakfast? Questions about the distant past will tap rehearsed and overlearned recollection—where did you live as a child? This difference in type of questioning elicits a spurious impression of better memory for long ago. Actually the episodic memory deficit of retrograde amnesia is not delimited in time, but extends back to the early limits of conscious experience.

Until some reason develops for rejecting this simple account, it is unnecessary to adopt Wickelgren's (1968) post hoc assumption that memory traces gain strength (resistance to disruption) by some hypothetical spontaneous molecular change over time. A striking illustration of the importance of interference in retrograde amnesia is provided by a recent report of retrograde amnesia on the football field (Lynch and Yarnell, 1973). Concussed players were asked about events leading to the injury within 30 seconds, and then again later. There was more retrograde amnesia at subsequent than initial questioning. This is striking evidence against consolidation theory. Our interpretation (which deviates from that offered by the authors) is that initial questioning took place in the same context as the injury, and so cues were available. Later questioning was off the field, and because of the appropriate injury, the previous context could not again be conjured up; hence the forgetting.

The phenomenon of retrograde amnesia proves that retrieval is impaired in amnesia. Premorbid events must have been normally encoded. In fact, if an amnesic is given retrieval cues, this helps him remember. He must therefore have experienced the corresponding events at registration. If he is cued at registration as well as at retrieval, no further benefit accrues (Kinsbourne and Wood, 1975). Encoding was correctly performed in the first place.

Memory tasks in clinical use perhaps fortuitously take cognizance of the episodic/semantic dichotomy. The neurologist asks his patient to remember a name, an address, and the name of a flower, after one hearing. He is testing episodic memory. The clinical psychologist administers a test of paired associate learning. This starts out episodic, but with rehearsal acquires some attributes of semantic memory. The two types of memory are confounded. Does the patient know where he lives, whether he is married? Amnesia may contribute somewhat to error here, but a confusional state much more.

Difficult as it is to remember episodes from any time in childhood, it is virtually impossible to do so from infancy and early childhood. This childhood amnesia has been referred to a process of psychodynamic repression. Do we need this assumption? Let us remind ourselves of what is involved in remembering (Mandler, 1967). To remember we recreate to some partial extent, the context and spirit of the episode for which we search. In a way, we think ourselves back into the past, and conjure up its cognitive attributes and emotional flavor. The infant is so different from the adult in how he thinks and feels that such an act of imaginative regression is hardly possible, except under the special circumstances of psychotherapy and particularly hypnotic regression. (Reiff and Scheerer, 1959).

We conclude that focal cortical lesions may deny people the use of particular ways of handling information available to all healthy adults. Limbic lesions in contrast spare highly practiced skills, but render patients unable to remember particular episodes in their lives. Each event enters memory as an episode labeled by its specific context. The more context is supplied at retrieval, the easier it is to recall the episode. In order to recall the correct episode, that context has to be discriminated from the context of other episodes. Amnesics are impaired in their ability to make that discrimination and therefore select episodes at random from within broad contextual bands. A possible practical solution would be to sharpen contextual transitions between separate memoranda that need to be separately remembered.

V. PERFORMANCE

In this section we consider how skilled performance is programmed in the cerebral cortex. What are the specialities of the two hemispheres, and how do they interact?

The programming facilities for skilled movements are located anteriorly to the decoding mechanisms for sensory input. As might be expected, they lie in the neighborhood of the motor strip, from which originates the final common pathway for specific instructions to the somatic musculature. Thus relatively anterior cerebral damage is more apt to impair performance than posterior insult, except for activities for which monitoring of sensory feedback is crucial. Feedback-dependent activities would be vulnerable to posterior as well as anterior cerebral disease.

All purposeful movements are initially conducted under close perceptual surveillance. The infant's early efforts to make even gross and simple, individual, goal directed movements are conspicuously wide of the mark. In time, his aim improves. This improvement derives from trial and error, with correction of the motor program so as to minimize the discrepancy between the intended and the actual outcome. The discrepancy must be perceived if it is to be eliminated. This "closed-loop" control is involved when people acquire a new skill at any age. Motor learning may be disrupted not only by lesions that deplete or disconnect the neuronal loci of the necessary motor programs but also by lesions that interrupt the neuronal connections that constitute the feedback loop, by means of which the action becomes refined. The effects of the two kinds of impairment are different. Destruction of the programming area eliminates the act in question from the repertoire of voluntary skills. Interruption of the closed loop control leaves the skill intact if it has already been automatized, but if it has not then it renders it capable of adaptive refinement with practice.

When a program has already been written, the case is different from when it is still being developed. Although close continuous sensory scrutiny is needed initially, this need is progressively relaxed with practice. Initially, the operator uses the external feedback to build up an internal representation of these changes in movement patterns that most effectively meet the objective. Further practice increases the operator's facility in bringing these motor changes about. What he now monitors is no longer the environment but rather his own motor program. This internal (reafferent) scrutiny can occur without knowledge of external results (Adams, 1971). An occasional "observing response" suffices to ascertain that there have been no unforeseen changes in the formulated cause-effect relationship. The movement sequence is automatized. At the endpoint of full automatization, control is virtually exclusively open loop, so that demands on attention are minimal, and the automatized act can proceed concurrently with other activities that do demand attentive monitoring. One can talk and think while walking, driving, cycling, or knitting. Activities that are sufficiently automatized to permit such "time sharing" are not very vulnerable to focal lesions in association cortex, although they can naturally be disrupted by lesions of motor cortex and consequent paresis of essential moving parts. When, as in the rare apraxia of gait, cortical lesions do selectively impair an automatized skill, it is as if the automatization were undone, and the patient closely monitors his hesitant and halting steps. He can no longer improve with practice. Another deficit of automatized skill is apraxic agraphia, in which the highly overlearned ability to write by hand is selectively implicated. The far more common deficit of stuttering bears tantalizing resemblance to an intermittently deautomatized skill. All stutterers have periods of normally fluent speech. Their language development, which in other respects also is quite normal, must therefore have resulted in the usual automatization of spoken speech. However, whereas this verbal programming normally breaks down only in circumstances of extreme embarrassment or emotional turmoil, the stutterer is readily reduced to a characteristic state of dysfluency in which movement sequences are decomposed, either with block on an initial articulatory gesture or with its pointless rapid repetition. The unifying description of all situations in which stutterers stutter is that they involve the focusing of attention on speaking. The more public and deliberate the speech act, the more likely it is to be dysfluent. In all of the following situations, the speaker is distracted from monitoring his own speech: speaking or singing in chorus, speaking while subject to masking noise, speaking under the pressure of strong emotion, and speaking while engaged in some concurrent unrelated activity; all of those situations minimize stuttering. Perhaps failure to withdraw attention—the pathologic closing of what should be an open loop—is the agent of stuttering disruption of speech. A simple account of its mechanism would be the maladaptive persistence or recurrence of observing responses. During an observing response, motor activity ceases, whereas the feedback is circulated pending any necessary reprogramming of the motor sequence. Although they are initially necessary, as performance becomes more fluent these observing responses arrest the smooth flow of the motor sequence. The patient either blocks or repeatedly starts over.

The cause or causes of inconsistent automatization of speech are uncertain. In some cases abnormal patterns of cerebral dominance obtain (Jones, 1966), which lend themselves to speculations about disruptive competition between two language-competent cerebral hemispheres. However, it is perfectly plausible to suppose that in other cases other causes, including psychogenic ones, might be in operation.

Just as the stutterer can under certain conditions speak fluently, so the patient rendered apraxic by left-hemisphere disease, can, when acting automatically, smoothly and easily perform the very movements that he is quite incapable of carrying out if he is instructed to do so. The ideational apraxic has a seemingly inexplicable difficulty in programming movement sequences, such as the maneuvers involved in reaching for cigarettes, picking up a match box and then lighting up, although he can perform each constituent movement with customary skill. Typically component acts are omitted, and the act is telescoped, so that the otherwise quite unconfused patient finds himself lighting a cigarette case or smoking a match. Motor apraxia is a simpler and more common deficit with similar characteristics. Simple individual movements are unsuccessful when attempted in response to an order, but they appear normal when involuntary. Asked to wave goodbye, the motor apraxic does not wave ineptly but rather does something else instead. His difficulty is not in implementing or correcting a movement, but rather in retrieving the appropriate movement. The facial apraxic smiles spontaneously, but when he tries to smile he grimaces. Even coughing on order may be too difficult, although he coughs as usual when his pharynx is stimulated. A model for motor performance developed by Bernstein (1967) is applicable. Movements are hierarchically organized in the brain. At a relatively low level, each component is separately represented. Inaccessibility to volition of a subset of component movements at this level produces motor apraxia. At a higher level of organization, a superordinate control system activates the components at a proper rate in proper sequence. Impaired communication between the levels of organization understandably results in omission of components in complex sequences. In contrast there is no rationale in this model for reversal in time of component movements, and this in fact does not occur.

The various motor programming failures described as apraxias typically result from left-hemisphere lesions. Right-hemisphere disease can also interfere but in an intelligibly different manner.

For purposes of everyday use, it is not sufficient to develop an adaptive repertoire of motor programs. The activity must be carried out in the face of a variety of environmental contingencies of which abrupt shifts in equilibrium are the most obvious. Shooting while standing is one thing; shooting while riding quite another. To meet the latter challenge, the movement program is equipped with a set of subroutines that approximately align the primarily moving parts with a set of possible alternative base states of bodily position. Thus positional information, suitably organized into a representation of the person in space, must be made available. This appears to be contributed mostly by the right hemisphere.

The patient with right parietal disease is subject to spatial disorientation. He loses his way on familiar streets, in his house, or the hospital, and he experiences undue difficulty with map reading. He may miss in pointing, lose his way on a printed page, write crazily up or down a sheet of paper. The nature of his difficulty is well illustrated by the difficulty he experiences in copying simple drawings.

The most common and most exhaustively studied performance deficit referable to cerebral disease is the inability to copy simple line drawings. This impairment is for no valid reason (Benton, 1967) customarily subsumed with a miscellany of other difficulties of spatial thinking under the category of constructional apraxia. Drawing difficulties can derive both from left- and right-sided lesions (Paterson and Zangwill, 1944; Piercy, Hecaen, and Ajuriaguerra, 1960), making this a tempting candidate for impairment of a bilaterally represented skill (Piercy and Smyth, 1962). This view is disconfirmed by the observation that left- and right-sided lesions give rise to qualitatively different drawing difficulties (Warrington, James, and Kinsbourne, 1966).

When a patient with left-hemisphere disease experiences difficulty in copying geometrical figures, his attempt bears a rough and ready resemblance to the model. But it lacks refinement and detail. Topological relationships are preserved. Closed figures are not rendered open, separate elements are not made to overlap, and the number of enclosed areas is held constant. However, angles are rounded off or simplified into right angles. The rendering often resembles the best efforts of a normal 5-year-old child, suggesting that some tactic that normally enters the behavioral repertoire at about age 5 years is unavailable to these patients.

Patients with right-hemisphere disease do not typically show this coarsening of the model and reduction of its intricacy. Indeed, if the patient does not lose heart and desist after drawing a few lines, his version may be more complex still than the model itself. Nor does he reduce the number of angled junctions of lines. Rather the problem is related to the spatial articulation of the elements of the figure. Each element of the model is often recognizably represented, but they are in spatial disarray. The patient's effort is decomposed, even exploded in space.

The explanation of these contrasting error patterns is to be found in the complementary contributions that the dominant and subdominant hemispheres make to cognition. The left contributes analyses and plans; the right contributes alignment within a spatial framework. The left-lesion patients cannot analyze the model into manipulable components. They therefore content themselves with a cruder but roughly appropriate analysis. The right-sided cases can analyze accurately, as is shown by their efforts. But they cannot properly arrange the components with respect to each other and to surrounding space. Thus, like other skills, copying is revealed as depending both on correctly planned, specific action and on correct reference to a spatial framework. A task analysis thus reveals that subsumed under the label "constructional apraxia" are quite diverse and variously localized cerebral processes.

We conclude that sequential actions are programmed by the left hemisphere, and they are interpreted into a spatial context by the right hemisphere. Just like perceptual analysis, the programming of skilled movement is hierarchic. Superordinate programs are implemented at a lower level by activation of component movements in correct sequence.

VI. REASONING

Is the ability to reason a separate and localizable function, or is it an aspect of efficient functioning of large expanses of cortex? How is reasoning ability affected by focal cerebral lesions, and how is it affected by generalized cerebral involvement in extreme aging and dementia?

Logical operations involve processing of input, planning, and the mental manipulation of verbal propositions and of nonverbal images. They may make considerable demands on primary memory (the ability to keep multiple thoughts concurrently in mind), or on secondary memory (the ability to recall material back to the focus of awareness) (Waugh and Norman, 1965). But primarily they require subjects to reject obvious and habitual responses and to change set in favor of novel concepts. A modicum of perceptual, executive, memorial, and linguistic skill is necessary for the exercise of logic, because one cannot manipulate ideas in a vacuum. However, careful analysis will reveal instances in which failure to solve problems is attributable not to some extraneous although relevant deficit but rather to the inadequate exercise of reason itself. The patient persists with a disconfirmed response and cannot recombine the information available to him in a sufficiently radical way.

Two models of the cerebral representation of reasoning power may be entertained. One states that reasoning is represented in differentially distributed fashion across wide areas of cerebral cortex and certainly bilaterally. The other states that reasoning is no entity in its own right but that it represents the most sophisticated level of use of each and every mental process. On the first view, verbal reasoning will be left lateralized, spatial reasoning will be right lateralized, and so forth. Reasoning tests that reveal deficit after both right- and left-sided damage, such as Raven's Progressive Matrices (Warrington et al., 1966) might be sensitive to loss of distinct right- and left-sided contributions to the problem-solving situation (cf. Zaidel and Sperry's,

1973, work with split-brain patients). Goldstein's (1948) views as to the lapse of "brain-injured" persons from "abstract" to "concrete" attitude with respect to the involved function is an instance of the second approach.

Claims for a differential cerebral distribution of various forms of reasoning range from the localization of ability to change set in the frontal area (verbal set left, spatial-temporal right), to the allocation of verbal reasoning to left parietal, spatial reasoning to right parietal loci. But in no such case has it been formally demonstrated that the problem is one of reasoning per se, rather than one of its essential vehicles—language, space perception, etc. The converse proposition, that "thought" is exclusively tied to some form of processing such as language (Luria, 1969), can be refuted with some confidence. Once they are helped to understand what is required, aphasics do not behave unintelligently but in fact often approach tests such as the Raven's Progressive Matrices (a test of general intelligence) with remarkable success. Posteriorly damaged aphasics have more trouble than those with anterior damage, but it is not clear that this reflects anything but that more patients in the posterior group have substantial difficulty in understanding what is said.

Formal or experimental studies of deficit in reasoning are few and inconclusive. Clinical experience permits only a few general statements. It is overwhelmingly clear that strictly focal cerebral lesions do not appreciably compromise the patient's ability to respond adaptively to novel situations or to observe the social amenities. People who are generally confused and bewildered (rather than puzzled about specific problems) and who generally behave in a socially inappropriate manner (rather than just in a specific context) invariably have bilateral cerebral disease. Dementia cannot be elicited by destruction of any one limited cerebral territory. It involves widespread neuronal depletion. The etiology of the dementia may vary, one case caused by chronic ischemia, another by slow virus infection, a third by recurrent concussion. Its rate of progress may be fast, as in certain presenile and arteriosclerotic dementias, or very slow, as in what some would consider "normal aging." But no one has shown that these variants differ behaviorally, except in degree.

Intellectual impairment may be accompanied by changes in mood—depression, euphoria, or most characteristically a labile alternation between the two. As critical faculties are lost, people decreasingly comprehend their predicament and increasingly lapse into inert passivity. They become readily suggestible, frightened by novelty, and subject to misperceptions and even hallucinations under perceptually difficult conditions, such as nighttime or when the eyes are kept covered (as after cataract operations). All these problems result from their inability, by use of reason, to adjust to or even contradict the import of immediate perception.

Inability to reject misleading perceptual impressions is not unique to the demented state. It is the basis of the much-studied phenomenon of "nonconservation" in young children (Piaget, 1953). This is the situation in which children, having judged two quantities equal, are content a moment later, when one has been spread out or otherwise rearranged to look greater, to judge them unequal. He either sees no inconsistency in this, or the inconsistency does not bother him. It has been reported that old people tend to regress into errors of nonconservation (Papalia, 1972), but it is not clear whether this is because they are subject to increasingly powerful perceptual distortion, have impaired memory, or really have lost "conservation logic" itself. At any rate, the analogy between childhood and old age—intellectual descent recapitulating its ascent (so-called regression theory)—remains unsubstantiated. Indeed the intellectual limitations of old people and young children are in more striking ways different than similar. It is as difficult and dubious to make general statements about old people as it is easy and valid to make them about the young. Children of a given mental age really are quite similar in the way they think (excluding only those at the lowest extreme of the range of intelligence). When a particular mental age is allocated to a group of old people because they score comparably on some acceptable test, two individuals are found to vary tremendously in their scores on most other test procedures. Aging is no homogeneous decline but is instead a highly irregular and idiosyncratic loss of abilities over time. General statements about how old people think, whether optimistic or resigned, must be wrong (except at the extreme of senile deterioration). The only reliable proposition is that they vary. Thus no common approach to the elderly, comparable to the relatively homogeneous approach to children, can be entertained. The individual must first be studied, so that his specific needs can be defined and met.

Overall intelligence quotients are particularly misleading in the aged. Intelligence tests share the common goal of attempting to measure a person's ability to respond adaptively to cognitive challenges in the environment. But they attempt this in either of two ways or a mixture of both. Only sometimes do tests confront the subject with a novel challenge to his reasoning abilities (tests of "fluid intelligence"). Often they proceed more indirectly, by testing his fund of knowledge of information or problem-solving strategies ("crystallized intelligence"). It is correctly argued that the more someone knows, the more likely it is that he is a good problem solver; but this relationship has important limitations. A person who knows little (scores low on tests of crystallized intelligence) either was not intelligent enough to take advantage of his opportunities or else had substandard opportunities (Cattell, 1965). Many old people received education as children that would be classed as inadequate by contemporary standards. This would depress their scores on tests of crystallized intelligence. Still more misleading is a contrasting source of error. A person's fund of knowledge, even if it represents his mental efficiency at its peak (when the information was absorbed) does not necessarily represent mental efficiency at the time of testing. Many old people remember things they previously learned but which they would have been incapable of learning in their old age. Typically old people score less well on tests of fluid than of crystallized intelligence. The former represent the efficiency of their current thinking; the latter represent the efficiency of their thinking at its previous peak. When tests of fluid intelligence only are considered, there is no evidence that any one type of mental process is more affected by age-related deficit than another. In particular the widely held view that verbal processes suffer less than spatial is probably an artifact of the fact that verbal intelligence tests tend to involve crystallized intelligence to a relatively large degree. When spatial and verbal problems are closely matched as regards the manner of testing, verbal processes appear not necessarily to be spared (Elias and Kinsbourne, 1972).

Focal cerebral damage impairs specific abilities while sparing general intelligence; diffuse damage does the reverse. A group of alcoholics, as compared to matched controls, showed deficits only on tests of reasoning (Stevens and Kinsbourne, 1975). In many states of diffuse cerebral impairment, adaptive and flexible behavior suffers much more than any focally localized mode of information processing.

We conclude that reasoning ability is not localizable, not limited to any particular mode of processing. Rather, the ability to change set, reject preconceptions, and entertain improbable alternative solutions is a general property of the cerebral cortex. Neuronal depletion impairs reasoning power more than it impairs specific cognitive processes, and the reverse is true of focal cerebral lesions.

VII. PHYLOGENY OF CEREBRAL DOMINANCE

In this section we consider why cerebral asymmetry evolved. Were certain processes indispensible for the elevation of man from other primates only feasible if lateralized, or was lateralization a fortuitous result of some asymmetry antecedent to language or other lateralized human cognitive skills?

Most discussion of the evolution of cerebral dominance implicitly presupposes that neurological asymmetry is a uniquely human phenomenon. In fact there are many exceptions to the rule of complete bisymmetry among vertebrates (Morgan, 1976). In all cases but one, the neurological asymmetry corresponds to a somatic asymmetry. Fishes are frequently asymmetrically structured; their right-sided pectoral and pelvic fins have more radii and more powerful musculature than those on the left (Hubbs and Hubbs, 1945). This asymmetry is extreme between flukes and flounders. It is not purely incidental but rather appears to be associated with some factor or factors that have survival value. In a right-biased species, individuals who manifest the opposite bias tend toward greater morbidity and earlier mortality. Asymmetry is also prominent among crustaceans such as crabs. Curious asymmetries in brain structure and function have been reported in amphibia (Braitenberg and Kemali, 1970).

Among mammals and birds, gross physical inequalities between right and left do not seem to occur (but note the asymmetry of the gorilla's skull, as reported by Groves and Humphrey, 1973). One intriguing instance of asymmetry of neurological control was reported by Nottebohm (1970). Bird song shows some similarities to prespeech babbling in infants (Petrinovich, 1972). Nottebohm found that chaffinch song is chiefly controlled by the left side of the bird's brain. The chaffinch has right and left syringeal muscles, each controlling the tension of a membrane that is instrumental in generating the bird's song. The hypoglossal nerves on each side control the respective syringeal muscles. Nottebohm found that left hypoglossal section grossly depleted the chaffinch's song; right section had only minor effect. An intriguing parallel to the early plasticity of human cerebral dominance is provided by Nottebohm's further finding that if left hypoglossal section precedes the initiation of bird song, then the song develops nonetheless. Presumably the other side assumes a controlling role after left hypoglossal section (or the left side now exerts its control by crossed pathways).

A curious asymmetry of cerebral function has been noted in mice (Collins and Ward, 1970). Although there have been numerous reports of paw preferences among dogs, cats, and monkeys, there has been only a little evidence of cerebral dominance in the stricter sense of a superior control mechanism for a particular type of behavior on one side than the other (Hamilton, Tieman, and Farrell, 1974). Hamilton and Lund (1970) and Trevarthen (1976) in monkeys, and Webster (1972) and Robinson and Voneida (1973) in cats, with use of complex discriminations, found that in a given split-brain animal one hemisphere was superior to the other (although both together serve better than either one alone). However, it was as often the right hemisphere as the left that was the more efficient.

The relationship of this phenomenon to human cerebral dominance is uncertain. Certainly most animal learning experiments do not involve a type of cognitive activity that resembles lateralized abilities in man. Usually the task set is a matter of confirming or disconfirming hypotheses about the relevant (experimenter-selected) dimension or concept. This, if anything, more resembles human general intelligence (reasoning power) than any lateralized ability. It will be necessary to design and use custom-made tasks (coding to simulate human left-hemispheric abilities and spatial orientation to simulate human right-hemispheric abilities) before it can be securely stated that the nonhuman mammal is wholly bereft of the cerebral double dissociation of function that characterizes most humans.

Language asymmetry is the prototype of cerebral dominance in humans; indeed it is usually assumed that minor-hemisphere dominance represents a rearrangement that only occurred after left cerebral space was preempted by verbal processes (e.g., Annett, Lee, and Ounsted, 1961). It differs from recorded nonhuman asymmetries in that it is a primarily asymmetric control over a bisymmetrically innervated musculature, the articulatory apparatus. Whereas previous instances of asymmetry could be parsimoniously (although not necessarily correctly) explained as representing the need to choose and practice a skill with one of paired effectors, either of which in principle would have worked, we here have an instance in which the control facility is one of a pair, whereas the effector is not. Two main alternative explanations could account for this development in phylogeny. Either there was an adaptive advantage for unilateral control of the vocal mechanism, i.e., the neural organization is in some sense more effective if confined or largely limited to one hemisphere (utility theory, UT), or the asymmetry in itself is not necessary but was superimposed on an antecedent skill which was asymmetrical (superimposition theory, ST).

Utility theory can itself follow either of two alternative lines of argument. One (present utility) states that departure from asymmetry is of present demonstrable disadvantage. That disadvantage, viewed in evolutionary perspective, could have biased natural selection against the bisymmetric distribution of the relevant control system. The other argument (antecedent utility) states that originally there was such an advantage, but in modern society it is no longer operative.

Present UT can refer to a miscellany of reports of inferiority of left-handed and ambidextrous persons on a wide range of tasks (Hécaen and Angelergues, 1964). Since non-right-handers are known to include more ill-lateralized subjects than right-handers, one can infer that lack of lateralization is apt to penalize performance in these heterogeneous respects. More convincingly antecedent UT (or atavistic theory) can be supported as follows: The very heterogeneity of problems related to sinistrality and the relatively low frequency of any one of them, argues against a flaw inherent in bihemispheric organization. If bilateral organization is inefficient, why is this usually not apparent? Satz (1972) has argued that a substantial contribution to the incidence of sinistrality derives from left-sided early brain damage (see Churchill, 1966). If pathologic left-handedness is indeed common, then a high incidence in left-handers of various deficits of cerebral control needs no further explanation. The difficulties that left-handers experience relatively often are not due to their anomalous cerebral dominance but rather to the cause of that anomaly, which is the brain damage that brought it about. Were we to study familial, nonpathologic left-handers exclusively, would they show a higher incidence of any disability than does a comparable right-handed sample?

If then there is a suspicious lack of evidence for deleterious effects of disturbed dominance relationships, this again could be explained in two quite different ways. Either there are such effects but we have not looked for them in the right way, or there are indeed no such effects.

When human faculties are evaluated, an attempt is made to define the faculty under examination—verbal, spatial, etc. But in real-life situations, the ability to combine modes may be at a premium. Even if there is, in fact, little difference between right- and left-handers as regards the efficiency with which they solve problems in any particular mode, they perhaps differ in the extent to which they can function in multiple modes concurrently. An extreme case is the split-brain patient, who at any given moment is locked into either a right- or a left-hemisphere mode (Kinsbourne, 1975a). There are phenomena that could speculatively be interpreted as suggesting that some left-handers function out of either one or the other hemisphere at a given time (Kinsbourne, 1972a; Gur, Gur, and Harris, 1975). From the point of view of natural selection it might be argued that in specialized human societies (whether western or some other societies) people can seek employment to suit their preferred thinking mode, but that primitive men needed a combination of faculties for survival and would in this respect have been ill served by anomalous cerebral dominance (ST). This matter remains to be definitively tested.

ST would dismiss those equivocal indications and regard nonpathologic cerebral dominance variants as essentially equivalent in their ability to support intelligent behavior. ST assumes that there never was any biologic necessity to lateralize control of a midline structure such as the articulatory apparatus. It further postulates that lateralization was, however, already an accomplished fact at the time when spoken language originated.

The purpose of communication is to reduce uncertainty. What is the simplest, ontogenetically earliest means by which human beings accomplish such an increase in entropy? Pointing. But we cannot suppose that a newborn baby can make a discrete, uncluttered pointing movement. The head and eyes turn sideways, mouth opens (later in infancy to vocalize in concert with the somatic synergism), ipsilateral leg flexes, contralateral leg extends, contralateral arm flexes. As a synergism in its passively elicited form, it is familiar as the asymmetric tonic neck reflex. As a reflex it is inconstant in infants. As spontaneous behavior it is frequent and clear and with a marked bias to the right (Siqueland and Lipsitt, 1966); Turkewitz, Gordon, and Birch, 1968). As in ontogeny, so in phylogeny? Was the pointing gesture the earliest language?

Hominids used tools at a stage when they were not fully erect and when their voice box was as yet unsuited to speech (Liberman, Klatt, and Wilson, 1969). A tool user who is not erect must hold on with three limbs while he manipulates with the fourth. Dropping the tool, does he indicate and imitate (Hewes, 1973)? And then in pictures (frozen gesture), ideographs, and writing, does he put his gesture on permanent record? If language began before man was bipedal and was by gesture, he had to choose a preferred limb. Biologically, as we have seen, there is much precedent for choice of the right. The left cerebral hemisphere is the primary repository of the control skills (whereas the right provides context as the left hand holds the anvil while the right strikes it with hammer blows). Then, when glottal evolution makes a further facility available, the already preferred left hemisphere is available for the job.

We conclude that, whereas many vertebrate species have asymmetric bodies, brain asymmetry of function is rare and most developed in man. Higher mental processes are characteristically internalized. They differ from simpler operations in lacking reference to specific points in space, and they therefore do not need to be bilaterally represented. But lateralization does not seem to be necessary; anomalies in human cerebral dominance are not rare, and they do not seem to entail substantial cognitive disadvantage. It may be that the verbal system is lateralized because it became superimposed on a more primitive system of communication based on the right-hand gestures and programmed by the left hemisphere.

VIII. ONTOGENY OF CEREBRAL DOMINANCE

The brain mechanisms that control human behavior are represented in only rudimentary form in the newborn child. They progressively gain sophistication in the course of childhood and are thought to reach a stable endpoint of maturity in adolescence. Although all forms of behavior evolve with increasing age, ranging from sensorimotor control to the use of elaborate codes for problem solving and communication, it is the latter that undergo the most conspicuously prolonged development and are most reliably known to be lateralized cerebrally in the mature brain. What is the ontogeny of that lateralization?

Two possibilities exist. One is that asymmetry becomes superimposed on an originally symmetrical neural substrate. The other is that the developmental sequences that culminate in hemispherically lateralized higher mental processes are from the start asymmetrically represented. For each relevant mental process, it is necessary separately to establish which of these two situations—emerging or constant asymmetry—actually obtains.

Each model can claim a plausible biological rationale. Emerging asymmetry can be regarded as ontogeny recapitulating phylogeny. Lateralization of function is seemingly a recent development in evolution, and it would be reasonable to suppose that ontogeny begins by recapitulating the neurally symmetric precursors of human brain organization. The contrary view of constant asymmetries can also claim a reasonable basis. To have become the nearly universal blueprint for human brain organization, asymmetry must have brought with it some behavioral advantage. In what crucial respect does the bisymmetric nonhuman primate differ from asymmetric man? Perhaps the transition involved the development of processes that depend on asymmetry for their neural basis. Language is the obvious human characteristic to invoke at this point. It would follow that language should be lateralized, probably from its very beginnings, both in evolution and in the developing child. But then again, what is the very beginning of language? Maybe it precedes the first uttered word.

Motor development consists in the fragmentation and selective suppression of elements of the few generalized primitive synergisms that characterize the behavior of the newborn child and the progressive internalization and dissociation from overt motor manifestation of these components. This formulation admits of no discontinuity in time at which asymmetry is grafted on brain organization. Asymmetry, if present at all, should be present from the start. Indeed it should be more readily apparent in overt behavior than later in life, as it is only later that mental processes internalize and thus evade direct inspection. In the case of spatial skill the problem is harder to define than with language, in which it is relatively easy to trace back the developmental sequence. In a general sense, the infant inhabits and negotiates space. But in his ability to orient to stimuli, to localize and manipulate objects, antecedent in a developmental sequence to the right-lateralized spatial problem-solving ability of the adult? It is not necessarily so. We cannot necessarily assume that the infant's tactic in manipulating space is antecedent in manner to the adult's. For all we know, he uses quite a different strategy.

The best we can do in the face of these logical difficulties is to trace back, as far as present knowledge permits, the developmental origins of lateralized higher mental processes. Then we can list asymmetries observed in the infant. Finally we can consider which, if any, of the latter could be regarded as antecedent to the former in developmental sequence. Evidence for lateralization of function can derive from the sources listed below, each of which we shall then discuss in detail.

A. Abnormal function—asymmetric vulnerability of a function to brain damage or irritation
B. Normal function
   1. Asymmetrical orientation to stimuli, depending on their category
   2. Asymmetry in the efficiency with which inputs are processed, depending on their category
   3. Asymmetrical motor concomitants of thought processes in particular modes
   4. Anatomical and electrophysiologic signs of brain asymmetry (only interpretable in the context of definitely established behavioral correlates)

Most of the evidence on the ontogeny of asymmetry derives from the effects of brain damage on developing language skills. Lateralized cerebral hemisphere disease is quite common at or soon after birth and again in middle age. It is relatively rare during the early years of language development, so that the evidence from this source is sparse. Nevertheless it is clear that left-hemisphere disease is liable to disrupt language processes at any time after the child begins to talk. There are conspicuous differences in the severity of the deficit: the earlier the insult, the less severe and shorter lasting the dysphasia.

Basser (1962), Lenneberg (1967), Krashen (1972), and Kinsbourne (1975*b*) have mustered evidence for a change over time in the relationship between the laterality of a cerebral insult and the probability that it will disrupt language functioning. Whereas only two or three of 100 adults with right-hemisphere damage become aphasic, children in the first 2 or 3 years of language development are reputed to manifest language impairment almost as often after right- as after left-hemisphere damage (see Basser, 1962, for a review). After age 5 right-hemisphere damage no longer interrupts language development. These older children do become aphasic after left-hemisphere damage, but the degree and duration of the aphasia seem mild as compared to what one would expect in adults who sustained lesions of comparable size and location (Guttmann, 1942). Taken at face value, these considerations suggest that in children language is at first under bilateral control and then, over time, becomes increasingly lateralized. In fact, the extent to which language representation in young children is bilateral has probably been exaggerated, and the extent to which it is irrevocably lateralized in adults has certainly been overstated. We will discuss the latter point first.

When a particular performance is defective, this could be explained in either of two ways. It might be that the cerebral area responsible for the function is subserving it in a limited way on account of damage. Or, it might be that the damaged area has relinquished its function, which has been taken over by some other area less fitted for the purpose.

Long ago Hughlings Jackson (see Riese, 1965) attributed residual automatic utterance of global aphasics to the right hemisphere, and claims for right-hemisphere compensation for language area damage have been occasionally made on clinical grounds (Moutier, 1908; Nielsen and Raney, 1939). Right-hemisphere compensation was directly demonstrated in three aphasics by intracarotid amobarbital injection (Kinsbourne, 1971), and these findings have since been replicated (Czopf, 1972). First one and then the other hemisphere can in this way be temporarily inactivated (Wada and Rasmussen, 1960). In three cases aphasic speech was left unaffected by left-sided anesthesia, and in two of these subsequent right-sided injection confirmed the inference that the right hemisphere had assumed responsibility for language behavior. All three patients showed substantial impairment in language skill over time. It remains to be determined whether such recovery depends on restitution of left-sided control of language or whether the right hemisphere has substantial potential for language even in adult-acquired disease. Furthermore it may have implications for the planning of remedial therapy to know whether a sophisticated damaged or a naive intact hemisphere is being trained.

Aphasia caused by localized structural disease relatively spares the receptive function (Alajouanine and Lhermitte, 1965). One obvious conclusion would be that, whereas a single hemisphere is responsible for expression, either hemisphere is sufficient for comprehension. Clinical impressions have suggested that receptive aphasia becomes more common with increasing age of the patient at the time of insult (Brown and Jaffe, 1975). If this is substantiated, we could suppose that lateralization for decoding of speech lags behind lateralization for encoding, but that it finally also occurs.

However, there are reasons to doubt this, and the facts can be otherwise explained. For instance, Wada testing relies on the subjects' ability to understand spoken commands irrespective of the side of amobarbital injection. If receptive function is ultimately lateralized, there should be reports that older patients cannot follow instructions under left-hemisphere anesthesia. There are no such reports. In any case there is another age-related variable that could be used more simply as an explanatory principle. This is the plasticity diminishing with age of the immature brain.

Suppose that the right hemisphere is capable of compensating for left-sided language area impairment. Its ability to do so might well diminish over time, as the brain becomes less plastic (and perhaps additionally, as alternate specializations become increasingly elaborated). Early left-sided damage is immediately compensated by assumption of the necessary language processing by the right side of the cerebrum (permanently if the left-sided damage is extensive and irreversible, but otherwise temporarily). The older the individual, the slower the right side is to take over, and the less perfect its compensatory functioning.

Thus the facts of the interaction between brain damage causing aphasia and age can be accounted for without assuming any change over time in left-hemisphere dominance for language (i.e., predominant role in moment-to-moment language functioning), with one exception. This is the claim of several case reports, collected by Basser (1962), that below age 5 years, right-hemisphere damage prejudices language function with nearly as high a probability as left-hemisphere damage. That an occasional episode of right-hemisphere damage in childhood might impair language would in itself not be surprising, as this might represent that 1 or 2% of the population which, at any age, is right-dominant (Hécaen and Angelergues, 1964). But if the probabilities as presented are correct, one would have to assume that the right hemisphere participates actively in normal language functioning in many, if not most, young children. One account would be that language representation begins by being bilateral and only gradually becomes lateralized. The rate of such lateralization then becomes a potentially significant dependent variable in relation to such entities as delayed language development and the specific learning disabilities (Kinsbourne, 1974c). However, before accepting the notion of developing lateralization and attempting to use it as an explanatory principle, what reliance can we place on that clinical evidence?

Very little. Apart from the obvious sampling difficulties that arise when one tries to compile prevalence statistics out of sporadic clinical reports, the reports themselves do not survive scrutiny. So little is the language disorder after right-hemisphere disease documented in these reports reviewed by Basser (1962) that it might be no more than a severely sick child in hospital withholding speech. Not one case report supplies the minimal documentation that is needed to sustain the diagnosis of organic language impairment.

The evidence from brain damage does not at this time justify departure from the simple proposition that the left cerebral hemisphere is primarily responsible for language function at all ages. A corollary is that the right hemisphere, whether by virtue of cumulative suppression by the left or by virtue of its own divergent specialization, becomes over time less adept at compensating for sudden loss of left-sided language capability.

What then about the evidence from studies of normal development? A variety of behavioral and electrophysiologic indices of right-left asymmetry have been assumed to represent the degree of hemisphere asymmetry for cognitive processes. Notably, dichotic asymmetry has been invoked.

In the dichotic listening paradigm, subjects listen through earphones to pairs of different messages. One goes to each ear, and they are synchronized in time. When asked to report what they hear, right-handers more commonly report words first from the right ear, then from the left (Kimura, 1961). Holding ear order of report constant, they still make fewer errors with respect to the right-sided message (Bryden, 1964). Asked to listen for the presence of a target word, they respond faster when it occurs on the right (Springer, 1971; Fisher and Kinsbourne, 1973). Significantly the asymmetry is reversed when the dichotic messages are musical, not verbal (Kimura, 1961). Clearly, since the left hemisphere primarily processes words, and the right processes music, the channel opposite the hemisphere specialized for processing the message is favored. Even though there are both ipsilateral and contralateral connections between each ear and the auditory cortex, the asymmetry is easily explained as due to the fact that each hemisphere is specialized to subserve attention to the contralateral side of space. Thus language processing is most compatible with attending to the right and musical (right-hemisphere) processing with attending to the left (Kinsbourne, 1970b, 1973b).

Is this dichotic asymmetry as pronounced in children as in adults? A gradual increase in any asymmetry during the life span might well support the view that lateral specialization itself increases. There is disagreement about whether the dichotic data show such an effect, in relation to some differences on how to calculate the index of asymmetry (Krashen, 1972). What is certain is that significant right ear advantage can be observed at least as early as age 3 (Nagafuchi, 1970; Geffner and Hochberg, 1971; Ingram, 1973; Kinsbourne, Hoch, and Sessions, 1974), a finding that is discouraging for the notion that the hemispheres function symmetrically at that age. More recently a very simple and clear-cut index of ongoing distribution of hemispheric activity has become available in the form of grossly obvious eye and head turning while subjects think of how to answer questions (Kinsbourne, 1972a, 1974b). Rightward gaze and head turning indicates predominantly left-sided cerebral activity, and leftward gaze and head turning indicates a predominance of activity on the right. We have now been able to show that this index is applicable to normal 5-year-old children and that during verbal tasks such children look mostly to the right while thinking verbally.

On the output side, we have recently been able to document substantial lateral specialization at age 5 (Kinsbourne and McMurray, 1975). A group of 5-year-olds was asked to tap with one index finger at a time. As a group children are able to tap more rapidly on the right (Knights and Moule, 1967). But when asked to speak while tapping, their tapping rate decreased much more on the right than on the left. This was predicted by a model that postulates interference between two motor programs if they are run in the same cerebral hemisphere (Kinsbourne and Cook, 1971). The results are in principle similar to those found in adults (although with them one has to use a more difficult motor task, see Kinsbourne and Cook, 1971; Hicks, 1975), and similarly indicate left lateralization of speech programs.

Insofar as structure is a guide to function, the anatomic evidence to date favors the notion of constant asymmetry. In the adult a section of the left temporal lobe known to be related to language processes, the *planum temporale,* is known to be more frequently larger on the left than on the right (Geschwind and Levitsky, 1968). Similar asymmetry has been demonstrated in newborns (Witelson and Pallie, 1973; Wada, Clark and Hamm, 1974).

Finally there is electrophysiologic evidence for asymmetry of response to speech and nonspeech stimuli even in young infants. Crowell, Jones, Kapunia, and Nakagawa (1973) found EEG asymmetries in newborns favoring the right hemisphere. Molfese (1973) found higher amplitude evoked response on the left for speech sounds and on the right for musical sounds. Very early preprogramming for lateralization seems proven by these findings. What is the nature of such preprogramming? Possibly some processing is occurring already at this early stage, and the relevant hemisphere is more effective than its mate (although we know both to have language potential). However, an alternative possibility has gone unnoticed. Perhaps the preprogramming is attentional—rightward turning for verbal, leftward for non-verbal stimuli (on the lines described by Kinsbourne, 1972a, in adults). Asymmetry in evoked potential cannot at present be equated with any particular brain operation, and it could have picked up differential turning that went unnoticed by the investigator. Such differential turning, with attendant inhibition of the hemisphere toward which turning is directed, could be the mechanism of ascendancy of each hemisphere over the other, with respect to its specialized functions.

We conclude that one hemisphere can compensate for damage to the other to some extent at any age but decreasingly with increasing age. It seems unjustified to relate these facts to any increase over time in cerebral dominance, and evidence from behavioral asymmetry suggests that the developmental sequences that culminate in mature verbal and spatial thought are lateralized from the start. If lateralization is not necessary for efficient cognitive function, and if this lateralization is a stable rather than emergent characteristic, the present emphasis on relating lack of lateralization to various mental disabilities and seeking to modify it is misplaced.

IX. DISCONNECTION OF THE CEREBRAL HEMISPHERES

In this section, we consider how behavior changes when the cerebral hemispheres are disconnected by severing the interconnecting forebrain commissure. Can disconnected hemispheres communicate? Can they function independently and, in parallel, sustain separate continuity of awareness?

The blueprint of the bisymmetrical nervous system is strikingly constant across a wide evolutionary span. Each of the two mirror-image components is hierarchically organized, with the more rostral levels in charge of more complex behavioral control, which they exert by influencing the subordinated caudal levels. At each level the two halves of the central nervous system are interconnected by transverse commissures. These have a communicative function and a control function.

The freely moving organism can, by orienting in different directions, rather easily inform both halves of its nervous system about most external events (other than those that occur very briefly) that occur on one side. When stimulation is limited to pathways that lead to one side of the brain only, the transverse commissures share information with the unstimulated side of the brain. This is the communicative function.

Should more than one event occur at a time, the organism has to choose between alternatives, which often amounts to deciding whether to orient to the right or to the left. When there are competing lateral response tendencies, transverse commissures pit these against one another, so that one prevails, and attention shifts accordingly (Ingle, 1973). This is the control function.

For us the point of interest is to apply these principles to the most rostral, highest-level transverse commissure, the corpus callosum. The cerebral hemispheres communicate with each other across the great forebrain commissure. If this pathway is sectioned, each hemisphere is deprived of information gathered by the other, precluded from use of the specialized processing facilities of the other, and released from contralateral influences on its own level of activation. The information-transmitting function of the corpus callosum was first revealed by experiments on dogs who had been conditioned to respond with salivation to touch on one forepaw. In intact animals the conditioned response generalized to the opposite paw; generalization did not occur when the conditioning followed section of the corpus callosum (Bykov, 1924; Bykov and Speransky, 1924).

Later work has greatly extended knowledge in this area. Myers (1956) sectioned the monkey corpus callosum and the optic chiasm and used each eye as an input channel with access only to the cerebral hemisphere on the same side. Training performed while one eye was occluded did not generalize to the disconnected hemisphere. There were no savings in training after the occluder was moved to the other eye. The disconnected hemisphere was totally uninformed. As for response after callosal section, this is best done by the limb contralateral to the active hemisphere. Ipsilateral hand-eye coordination is defective (Downer, 1959).

Humans have undergone operative section of the corpus callosum in order to stop spreading to the normal hemisphere of epileptic discharge from the hemisphere with an actively discharging epileptic focus (Akelaitis, 1944). Lateral somesthetic stimulation or lateral visual stimulation can be so short that eye movements cannot disperse the information to both sides of the brain. Such brief stimulation will exclusively communicate to the contralateral cerebral hemisphere. Under these circumstances the findings closely parallel those in animals. Sectioned patients with left-lateralized language cannot respond verbally to left-sided stimulation; they can only respond to it with the left-sided limbs (Gazzaniga and Sperry, 1967). Left-sided stimulation is initially transmitted to the right hemisphere. For verbal responding it has to be passed on to the left hemisphere; but it cannot be passed on, because the forebrain commissure, which would conduct it, has been sectioned. In fact when asked, the patient will deny (verbally) that anything happened. When it is pointed out to him or if he happens to notice that his own left hand moved (because it entered his right visual field), he will try somehow to explain this away. As has already previously been reported in cases of anterior callosal interruption caused by brain disease (Dejerine, 1914; Geschwind and Kaplan, 1962), writing is similarly affected, in that the patient cannot spell correctly with his left hand (whether by writing or by picking out letters from an ensemble). The left hand is also apraxic to verbal commands and fails to carry them out. (It is curious that more recent studies show that surgical anterior callosectomy, sparing only the posterior extremity—the splenium of the corpus callosum—causes virtually no permanent disconnection. Evidently projection across the commissure either is not "point to point" or is capable of substantially rerouting after anterior section.)

Thus callosectomized persons are unable to share information between cerebral hemispheres by the direct callosal route. Except perhaps in agenesis of the corpus callosum (Jeeves, 1965; Kinsbourne and Fisher, 1971), extra-callosal transverse pathways appear to be relatively ineffective in man. The uninformed hemisphere retains the following options: separately to orient toward the locus of external change and thus independently to gain information; to orient toward the response generated by the intact hemisphere (cross-cueing) and make the appropriate inferences (Gazzaniga, 1970); or to make inferences based on such partial cues as are directly available to it, inadequate although they might be. In fact all three types of behavior are effectively used, and as a result the comportment of a split-brain person outside the laboratory is in no obvious sense abnormal. The true state of affairs is only revealed when specific steps are taken to counteract these compensatory strategies. The unstimulated hemisphere cannot orient fast enough when stimulation is very brief. Cross-cueing is minimized when the selected response is distal (such as a finger press), soundless, and well away from the line of sight. Behavior based on hypothesis-making is unmasked if stimuli are designed to violate the contingencies learned over many years of perceptual experience.

A salient finding that arises from the facts of split-brain behavior is that each hemisphere has internalized a spatial framework not just for one-half but for the whole of observable external space (Trevarthen, 1974). Each hemisphere receives detailed information about events that appear in the contralateral visual half-field. But the behavior it generates operates in the context of visual space as a whole. Thus one hemisphere can initiate well-coordinated reaching by either or both forelimbs for objects in either half of visual space (Mark and Sperry, 1968). It follows that each hemisphere has available to it and registers input and output against an internalized representation of the spatial environment. It populates this visuospatial framework with information picked up in the course of successive glances in various directions. Thus a hemispherectomized person, or animal with divided callosum and optic chiasm and one eye covered, is limited as regards his effective visual receptor surface; however, he can find his way about the world in a manner that is not grossly abnormal. Indeed the very notion of the callosum as an interhemispheric communication channel has this implication. For how could one hemisphere be informed about an event in ipsilateral as well as contralateral space except with reference to a spatial framework that represents both sides of space? We think of cortical analyzing systems that are specialized to process detailed information about both personal and extrapersonal space by two routes: from the environment by way of the sensory projection systems and from the other hemisphere transcallosally. When these sources of information are depleted by surgical intervention or natural disease, the analyzing system is itself intact but is short of data. It then populates its spatial framework with such inferences as it can base on the sparse cues available. But the inference, once made, is directly and vividly experienced. This process may be illustrated from the behavior of callosally sectioned humans.

In the absence of transcallosal input, the hemisphere dominant for speech (usually the left) can encode a verbal response only to information projected directly to it. Thus, at any moment the "speaking hemisphere" is disconnected from and unable to comment on events in the left visual half-field; it is similarly "anesthetic" over much of the left body surface. Yet these impairments are never complained of, either by explicit statements or implicitly in action. The hemisphere is "unaware" of these restrictions on input available to it. Is this because, as in unilateral neglect of space due to lateralized hemispheric damage, the patient is altogether unaware of or even denies the existence of these receptor surfaces? No, because far from denying the existence or his possession of one side of his body, the patient is fully ready to discuss these parts and to plan action that involves them. He experiences a convincing array of percepts in ipsilateral visual and somatosensory space. It is only that these perceptions are unduly fallible because they are based for the most part on tenuous inference. But that makes them no less real or vivid subjectively.

Why then does a hemisphere cut off by callosal section from information about ipsilateral events show only minimal neglect of that side, when a hemisphere opposite to an area of damage may generate behavior that is highly biased in lateral space? In the latter circumstance, there is gross imbalance of lateral orienting impulse, due to corresponding imbalance at brainstem level through loss of tonic excitation from the damaged cerebral hemisphere. The direction of attention is the direction in which one responds, attention and therefore response (including verbal) being withdrawn from the opposite direction. For this reason the unilaterally injured patient is literally oblivious of the affected side of person and of space.

In the case of the cerebrally split person, on the other hand, the tonic influence of the two hemispheres on the brainstem remains bilaterally intact, and the changes that do occur are more in the nature of superimposed, undamped phasic irregularities in situations (usually experimental) in which one hemisphere is predominantly or even exclusively active. In the natural environment, this dominance will oscillate between the two sides, with a multitude of accompanying orienting responses in both lateral directions, resulting in information pick-up through both visual half-fields from large expanses of the visual world, and no observable neglect of space.

What then does the corpus callosum contribute to the distribution of lateral attention as expressed by patterns of lateral gaze? By its function in distributing information between the hemispheres, it provides each hemisphere with the sum total of available information, so that priorities may be determined and result in unequivocal command to the centrencephalic motor control mechanism. If this is true, it should be demonstrable that scanning eye movements of split-brain subjects lack regularity and instead are at the command of whichever hemisphere happens to dominate the moment. Reciprocally they would reflect the distribution of activation between the hemispheres at any time and would deviate contralateral to the more active hemisphere even when its activity, such as speech, is not inherently related to any particular location in visual space (Kinsbourne, 1974a)

While little is as yet known about these patients' strategies and capabilities in sequential visual search, we do know something about their response to brief, nonrecurrent visual events. When detailed visual information is presented to one half-field exclusively, only the contralateral hemisphere is capable of programming discriminative response to that input (Sperry, Gazzaniga, and Bogen, 1969). But if information is simultaneously presented to both sides, can both hemispheres simultaneously attend?

Kinsbourne (1975a) had split-brain patients perform visual search. A target letter might briefly appear in either visual half-field. Subjects responded by lifting an index finger if they detected a match with a predetermined target letter (this is the C reaction of Donders).

We know from experiments on callosally sectioned monkeys that the two disconnected hemispheres can be taught different, and even logically incompatible, responses. For example, one hand can be trained to move an object forward on cue, while the other hand can be trained to move it backward on the same cue. But can they perform simultaneously in tasks that require awareness and draw upon so-called "mental capacity"? This point cannot be settled by work with overlearned responses, which can be produced automatically. Cognitive psychologists have developed an experimental technique called the visual search paradigm, which affords an exact test of the notion of parallel awareness in the two hemispheres. If both can attend simultaneously, then it should take no more time to scan visually two stimuli for presence of a target than one, as long as one is presented to each hemisphere (i.e., to each visual half-field). Similarly it should take less time to search through two stimuli if they are presented to either side of fixation than if both are presented in one half-field.

The results of the Kinsbourne (1975a) experiment were quite different. Bilateral presentation was by far the most difficult, to the extent that in most sessions subjects failed to respond at all to many left-sided stimuli. Evidently callosally sectioned people have much greater difficulty than normals in distributing their attention across the midline of space. Perhaps the corpus callosum aids in distributing mental capacity between the hemispheres, so that both are capable of rapid response. When the callosum is severed, this distribution must rely on less stable brain stem mechanisms, which tend to invest one hemisphere or the other with the available capacity, leaving the unsupplied one inert and either unresponsive or only crudely responsive at the automatic level. Whereas normal people can draw upon their various cerebral facilities in any required combination, irrespective of lateralization, split-brain subjects are constantly confronted with a choice between those on the right and those on the left. Effectively they are in a state of variably lateralized hemispherectomy.

We conclude that the corpus callosum has both a communicative and a control function. It mediates the spread of information from one hemisphere to the other in those special experimental situations in which stimulation is set up so as to impinge on one hemisphere only. In everyday life head and eye movements and bimanual handling spread information across *both* sides, and the loss of callosal information flow is inconsequential. But the control function of the corpus callosum, which enables people to use any combination of right- and left-hemisphere processors at will is not so readily dispensed with. The split-brain patient is virtually reduced to using just one or the other of the two hemispheres at any one time for all but highly habitual and automatic behavior patterns.

X. NEUROPSYCHOLOGICAL MECHANISMS

The limits of our understanding of cerebral neuropsychology are not methodological nor are they related to any scarcity of relevant case material. Appropriate methodologies are provided by contemporary cognitive psychology as regards function, and modern methods of neurological diagnosis, pre- and postmortem as regards structure. Cerebral symptomatology is profuse among the major disease entities. The limits are conceptual. An investigator cannot know what he will discover until the evidence is in. But the limits of what he discovers are inherent in the experimental questions that he asks. These will to a large degree be determined by the investigator's implicit or explicit model of the brain. Qualitative advance in neuropsychology results from application of a novel concept that makes it possible to view familiar manifestations in new and productive ways.

For a century neuropsychology has subsisted on a very simple conceptual framework. There are loci (centers, decision points) in the brain, at which information is processed, and tracts (connections, communication channels), along which the proceeds of processing are communicated from decision point to decision point. Destruction of a decision point correspondingly depletes the patient's behavioral repertoire. Disconnection of the decision points renders the proceeds of a particular form of processing unavailable to some or all forms of decision making. Thus, whereas the behavioral repertoire is not depleted, it is rendered less flexible by disconnection, in that certain processes are restricted in their applicability. This telephone exchange model has yielded surprisingly rich insights into brain function, and coincidentally it is the dominant model also in contemporary cognitive psychology (Broadbent, 1958). It is a hierarchical model of information flow, in which input is dispersed and reintegrated in adaptive recombination for purposes of ultimate, definitive decision making.

Another type of hierarchical model was long ago proposed by Hughlings Jackson (see Riese, 1965). He suggested that functionally higher and evolutionarily younger mechanisms are superimposed on less well differentiated and more primitive facilities. High-level central nervous system lesions not only deplete and restrict the behavioral repertoire, as the telephone exchange model postulates, but they also release from inhibition more primitive forms of behavior, which then become manifest. This model received striking physiological support through the classic studies of Sherrington (1906), but, except in the work of Denny-Brown (1966) and his colleagues (Denny-Brown and Chambers, 1958) has been little applied in neuropsychology. A model that orders the hierarchy of processing not from input to output, but in terms of depth (complexity) of processing, has recently been reviewed by Brown (1972). Equipotentiality models of brain organization have been largely discredited after Lashley's (1929, 1931) overambitious formulation; but they could in fact illuminate certain aspects of behavior, such as mental processes that appear not to fall victim to sharply localized cerebral diseases. Finally cybernetic models of cerebral organization involving the basic principles of positive and negative feedback are now receiving some overdue attention in the context of neuropsychological studies (Kinsbourne, 1975a, 1976a).

It is not suggested that investigators should import models from other disciplines and attempt to reorganize neuropsychological data accordingly. Cerebral symptomatology has always proved recalcitrant to alien notions; it can only be elucidated on the basis of hypotheses that derive from direct observation. However, the observer who is equipped with more than the prevalent simple notions of brain organization will be more inventive not only in explaining known facts but also in revealing new ones. What a neuropsychologist who observes behavior can successfully study depends upon the physiologic organization of the brain basis of the behavioral system. If we accept the currently popular view of cognitive function as composed of a sequence of component operations $A, B, \ldots, n$ (Sternberg, 1969) we do not necessarily arrive at a system that can be analyzed neuropsychologically. If we observe behavioral inadequacy in n, the neuropsychologist cannot discover whether this was due to a shortcoming in A or B (electrophysiologic studies would be necessary for that). The latter type of conclusion can only be reached by demonstrating a parallel element $A, B', \ldots, n$. If behavior B is preserved A is excluded from responsibility for deficit in n. The principle can be illustrated by considering a recently elucidated neuropsychologic microcosm, the complex of highly specialized neurons in visual cortex that underlies perception of patterns. Microelectrode studies of mammalian cortical neurons have revealed a wiring plan of information flow in visual and auditory systems that, if generally applicable, could generate cerebral specialization of function to a degree consistent with the strictest localizationist approach to neuropsychology. They validate the telephone exchange model and also point to the need to incorporate cybernetic ways of thinking into models by demonstrating positive (difference amplifying) feedback in the form of reciprocal inhibition between processors.

Hubel and Wiesel (1962) have described "simple" cells, maximally sensitive to a particular length, width, and orientation of stimulus within a specific sector (receptive field) of visual space. "Complex" cells are more sensitive to direction of movement and less restricted as regards visual field than simple cells. Hypercomplex cells of type I are particularly sensitive to the length of the stimulus and of type II to the angle of the stimulus. Thus each cell extracts a particular aspect of visual input. The outputs of these cortical analyzers are presumably reintegrated at a postcalcarine level of cerebral functioning. Not only are there neurons with different trigger features (Barlow, Narasimham, and Rosenfeld, 1972) in the visual cortex, but cells of different types are also anatomically segregated; this provides a simple instance of the anatomic segregation of like-functioning cerebral elements analogous to that revealed by neuropsychological investigations. But does it follow that a focal lesion within such a system would necessarily selectively deprive the organism of a subset of its pattern detection ability? Does this system have B' branches, making it amenable to neuropsychological investigation?

The columnar organization of neurons in the visual cortex (Hubel and Wiesel, 1963) suggests that there are separate pattern extraction mechanisms for different sectors of visual field as well as a serial organization of processing within each columnar processor. Thus it is often assumed that simple cells feed into complex, complex into hypercomplex I, and hypercomplex I into hypercomplex II. If information flow were completely restricted to this A, B, . . . , n pattern of communication, then lesions at any level within a processor would have the identical effect on perceptual awareness, just as damming a tributary at any point will deprive the mainstream of the tributary's contribution. However, this is not how the system works. The axons that cross the corpus callosum represent receptive fields corresponding to all of the neuron types (Hubel and Wiesel, 1967). So at the very least, cells at one level of visual organization communicate not only with the next level, but also laterally with each other and to extracalcarine centers. This means that a focal lesion can selectively eliminate particular trigger features, while preserving others.

The notion that the individual neuron represents a microcosm of a particular aspect of perception has generated enthusiasm among reductionist psychologists (Weisstein, 1969). However, it is incorrect. Even the cell at the first cortical relay in the visual system, the simple cell, has an output that in itself confounds change in stimulus length, width, and orientation. At no cerebral level does it seem to be correct to claim that "abstract aspects of stimulus qualities are coded by simple nerve cells" (Thompson, 1967). Even to code the simplest stimulus dimension, interaction of multiple neurons is necessary. Thus, although it may well be proper to challenge particular reports that suggest such extreme localization of cerebral function on methodological ground, it is no longer possible to sustain the sweeping view that "the brain just does not work that way."

Neuropsychology is more than a methodology for establishing brain-behavior relationships. It is a means for studying cerebral organization. In this respect it is a corrective to the prevalent reductionism that would discover principles of behavior in the properties of the individual neuron. Ultimately the reductionist policy is as self-defeating as is the converse heresy of emphasizing the complex and multifactorial nature of human behavior to such an exaggerated extent that one despairs of ever organizing the onrush of unique events into any account that has explanatory value. No one level of explanation is inferior to or can be replaced by another, nor is any one unamenable to systematic observation and experimental test. The opportunity now exists to devise a behavioral map of cerebral space.

REFERENCES

Adams, J. A. (1971): A closed-loop theory of motor learning. *J. Mol. Beh.,* 3:111–150.
Akelaitis, A. J. (1944): A study of gnosis, praxis and language following section of the corpus callosum and anterior commissure. *J. Neurosurg.,* 1:94–102.
Alajouanine, T., and Lhermitte, F. (1965): Acquired aphasia in children. *Brain,* 88: 653–662.
Annett, M., Lee, D., and Ounsted, C. (1961): Intellectual disabilities in relation to lateralized features in the EEG. In: *Hemiplegic Cerebral Palsy in Children and Adults, Little Club Clinics in Developmental Medicine.* Heinemann, London.
Anton, G. (1899): Uber die Selbstwahrnehmung der Herderkrankungen des Gehirns durch den Kranken bei Rindenblindheit und Rindentaubheit *Arch. Psychiatr. Nervenkr.,* 32:85–127.
Balint, R. (1909): Seelen lahmung des Schauens, optische Ataxie, raumliche Storung der Aufmerksamkeit. *Monatschr. Psychiatr. Neurol.,* 25:51–81.
Barlow, H. B., Narasimham, R., and Rosenfeld, A. (1972): Visual pattern analysis in machines and animals. *Science,* 177:567–575.
Basser, L. S. (1962): Hemiplegia of early onset and the faculty of speech with special reference to the effects of hemispherectomy. *Brain,* 85:427–460.
Benton, A. L. (1967): Constructional apraxia and the minor hemisphere. *Confin. Neurol.,* 29:1–16.
Benton, A. L., and Hécaen, H. (1970): Stereoscopic vision in patients with unilateral cerebral disease. *Neurology,* 20:1084–1089.
Bernstein, N. (1967): *Co-ordination and Regulation of Movement.* Pergamon Press, Oxford.
Birch, H. G., Belmont, I., and Karp, E. (1964): The relation of single stimulus threshold to extinction in double simultaneous stimulation. *Cortex,* 1:19–39.
Bogen, J. E. (1969): The other side of the brain—II. An appositional mind. *Bull. L.A. Neurol. Soc.,* 34:135–162.
Brain, W. R. (1941): Visual disorientation with special reference to lesions of the right hemisphere. *Brain,* 64:244–272.
Braitenberg, V., and Kemali, M. (1970): Exceptions to bilateral symmetry in the epithalamus of lower vertebrates. *J. Comp. Neurol.,* 138:137–146.
Broadbent, E. (1958): *Perception and Communication.* Pergamon, New York.
Brown, J. (1972): *Aphasia, Apraxia and Agnosia.* Thomas, Springfield.
Brown, J., and Jaffe, J. (1975): Hypothesis on cerebral dominance. *Neuropsychologia,* 13:107–110.
Bruner, J. S., (1957): On perceptual readiness. *Psychol. Rev.,* 64:123–152.
Bryden, M. P. (1961): The role of post-exposural eye movements in tachistoscopic perception. *Can. J. Psychol.,* 15:220–225.
Bryden, M. P. (1964): The manipulation of strategies of report in dichotic listening. *Can. J. Psychol.,* 18:126–138.
Bykov, K. M. (1924): Versuche an Hunden mit Durchschneiden des Corpus Callosum. *Zentralbl. Gesamte Neurol. Psychiatr.,* 39:199.

Bykov, K. M., and Speransky, A. D. (1924): Observations upon dogs after section of the corpus callosum. In: *Collected Papers of the Physiological Laboratory. I.* edited by P. Pavlov, Vol. 1, pp. 47–39.

Carmon, A., and Bechtoldt, H. P. (1969): Dominance of the right cerebral hemisphere for stereopsis. *Neuropsychologia,* 7:29–40.

Cattell, R. B. (1965): *The Scientific Analysis of Personality.* Penguin, Baltimore.

Cermak, L., and Butters, N. (1972): The role of interference and encoding in the short term memory deficits of Korsakoff patients. *Neuropsychologia,* 11:85–94.

Cermak, L. S., Butters, N. ,and Moreines, J. (1974): Some analyses of the verbal encoding deficit in alcoholic Korsakoff patients. *Brain and Language,* 1:141–150.

Chase, W. G., and Simon, H. A. (1973): The mind's eye in chess. In: *Visual Information Processing,* edited by W. G. Chase. Academic Press, New York.

Churchill, J. A. (1966): On the origin of focal motor epilepsy. *Neurology,* 16:49–58.

Collins, R. W., and Ward, R. (1970): Evidence for an asymmetry of cerebral function in mice tested for audiogenic seizures. *Nature,* 226:1062–1063.

Corkin, S. (1968): Acquisition of motor skill after bilateral medial temporal-lobe excitation. *Neuropsychologica,* 6:255–265.

Crosby, E. C. (1953): Relations of brain centers to normal and abnormal eye movements in the horizontal plane. *J. Comp. Neurol.,* 99:437–479.

Crowell, D. H., Jones, R. H., Kapunia, L. S., and Nakagawa, J. K. (1973): Unilateral cortical activity in newborn infants: an early index of cerebral dominance. *Science,* 180:205–208.

Czopf, J. (1972): Uber die Rolle der nicht dominanten Hemisphere in der Restitution der Sprache des Aphasischen. *Arch. Psychiatr. Nervenkr.,* 216:162–171.

DeGroot, A. (1965): *Thought and Choice in Chess.* Mouton, The Hague.

Dejerine, J. (1914): *Semiologie des Affections due Systeme Nerveux.* Masson, Paris.

Denny-Brown, D. (1966): *The Cerebral Control of Movement.* Thomas, Springfield, Ill.

Denny-Brown, D., and Chambers, R. A. (1958): The parietal lobe and behavior. *Publicat. Soc. Res. Nerv. Ment. Dis.,* 36:35–117.

de C. Downer, J. L. (1959): Changes in visually guided behavior following midsaggital division of optic chiasm and corpus callosum in monkey (Macaca mulatta). *Brain,* 82:251–259.

Elias, M. F., and Kinsbourne, M. (1972): Time-course of identity and category matching by spatial orientation. *J. Exp. Psychol.,* 95:177–183.

Fisher, M., and Kinsbourne, M. (1972): Processing dichotic stimuli: Latency vs. order of report. Paper delivered to the Psychonomic Society, St. Louis.

Gaffan, D. (1972): Loss of recognition memory in rats with lesions in the fornix. *Neuropsychologia,* 10:341–377.

Gazzaniga, M. S. (1970): *The Bisected Brain.* Appleton-Century-Croft, New York.

Gazzaniga, M. S., and Sperry, R. (1967): Language after section of the cerebral commissures. *Brain,* 90:131–148.

Geffner, D. S., and Hochberg, I. (1971): Ear laterality preference of children from low and middle socio-economic levels on a verbal dichotic listening task. *Cortex,* 7:193–203.

Geschwind, N., and Kaplan, E. (1962): A human cerebral deconnection syndrome. *Neurology,* 12:675–685.

Geschwind, N., and Levitsky, W. (1968): Human brain; left-right asymmetries in temporal speech region. *Science,* 161:186–187.

Goldstein, K. (1948): *Language and Language Disturbances.* Grune and Stratton, New York.

Gray, J. A. (1973): Causal theories of personality and how to test them. In J. Royce (Ed.) *Contributions of Multivariate Analysis to Psychology.* Academic Press, London.

Green, D., and Swets, J. (1966): *Signal Detection Theory and Psychophysics.* Wiley, New York.

Groves, C. P., and Humphrey, N. K. (1973): Asymmetry in gorilla skulls: evidence of lateralized brain function? *Nature,* 244:53–54.

Gur, R. E., Gur, R. C., and Harris, L. J. (1975). Cerebral activation, as measured by subjects' lateral eye movements, is influenced by experimenter location. *Neuropsychologia,* 13:35–44.

Guttmann, E. (1942): Aphasia in children. *Brain,* 65:205–219.

Hamilton, C. R., and Lund, J. S. (1970): Visual discrimination of movement—Midbrain or forebrain? *Science,* 170:1428–1430.

Hamilton, C. R., Tieman, J. B., and Farrell, W. S., Jr. (1974): Cerebral dominance in monkeys. *Neuropsychologia,* 12:193–197.

Hécaen, H. (1969): Aphasic, apraxic and agnosic syndromes in right and left hemisphere lesions. In: *Handbook of Clinical Neurology,* Vol. 4, edited by P. J. Vinken and G. W. Bruyn, pp. 291–311. North Holland, Amsterdam.

Hécaen, M., and Angelergues, R. (1962): Agnosia for faces (prosopagnosia). *Arch. Neurol.,* 7:92–100.

Hécaen, H., and de Angelergues, R. (1964): *Left-handedness. Manual Superiority and Cerebral Dominance.* Grune and Stratton, New York.

Hewes, G. W. (1973): Primate communication and the gestural origin of language. *Curr. Anthropol.,* 14:5–32.

Hicks, R. E. (1975): Interhemispheric response competition between vocal and unimanual performance in normal adult human males. *J. Comp. Physiol. Psychol.,* 89: 50–60.

Hubbs, C. L., and Hubbs, L. C. (1945): Bilateral asymmetry and bilateral variation in fishes. Paper of the Michigan Academy of Sciences, Arts and Letters, Vol. 30, pp. 229–310.

Hubel, D. H., and Wiesel, T. N. (1967): Cortical and callosal connections concerned with the vertical meridian of visual fields in the cat. *J. Neurophysiol.,* 30:1561–1573.

Hubel, D. H., and Wiesel, T. N. (1962): Receptive fields, binocular interactions and functional architecture in the cat's visual cortex. *J. Physiol.,* 160:106–154.

Hubel, D. H., and Wiesel, T. N. (1963): Shape and arrangement of columns in the cat's visual cortex. *J. Physiol.,* 165:559–568.

Huppert, F. A., and Piercy, M. T. (1974): Recognition memory for words and pictures in organic amnesia. Paper delivered to the Experimental Psychology Society, London.

Ingle, D. (1973): Selective choice between double prey objects by frogs. *Brain Behav. Evol.,* 7:127–144.

Ingram, D. (1973): Motor asymmetries in young children. *Research Bulletin,* Vol. 269, University of Western Ontario, London, Ontario.

Iverson, S. D. (1973): Brain lesions and memory in animals. In: *The Physiological Basis of Memory,* edited by J. A. Deutsch. Academic Press, New York.

Jackson, J. H. (1876): *Case of Large Cerebral Tumour Without Optic Neuritis and with Left Hemiplegia and Imperception.* Royal London Ophthalmic Hospital Reports, No. 434.

Jeeves, M. A. (1965): Psychological studies of three cases of congenital absence of the corpus callosum. In: *The Functions of the Corpus Callosum,* edited by W. Etlinger. Churchill, London.

Jones, R. K. (1966): Observations on stammering after localized cerebral injury. *J. Neurol. Neurosurg. Psychiatry,* 29:192–195.

Kahneman, D. (1973): *Attention and Effort.* Prentice-Hall, Englewood Cliffs, N.J.

Kimble, D. P. (1968): Hippocampus and internal inhibition. *Psychol. Bull.,* 70:285–295.

Kimura, D. 1961. Cerebral dominance and the perception of verbal stimuli. *Canadian Journal of Psychology,* 15, 166–171.

Kimura, D. (1963): Right-temporal lobe damage. *Arch. Neurol.,* 8:264–271.

Kinsbourne, M. (1966): Limitations in visual capacity due to cerebral lesions. *Eighteenth International Congress of Psychology, Symposium* 26:120–127.

Kinsbourne, M. (1970a): A model for the mechanism of unilateral neglect of space. *Trans. Am. Neurol. Assoc.,* 95:143–145.

Kinsbourne, M. (1970b): The cerebral basis of lateral asymmetries in attention. *Acta Psychol.,* 33:193–201.

Kinsbourne, M. (1971): The minor cerebral hemisphere as a source of aphasic speech. *Arch. Neurol.,* 25:302–306.

Kinsbourne, M. (1972a): Eye and head turning indicates cerebral lateralization. *Science,* 176:539–541.

Kinsbourne, M. (1972b): Contrasting patterns of memory span decrement in aging and aphasia. *J. Neurol. Neurosurg. Psychiatry,* 35:192–195.

Kinsbourne, M. (1973a): Stimulants for insomnia. N. Engl. J. Med., 288:1129.

Kinsbourne, M. (1973b): The control of attention by interaction between the cerebral hemispheres. In: Attention and Performance, Vol. IV., edited by S. Kornblum. Academic Press, New York.

Kinsbourne, M. (1973c): Personality correlates of hyperactivity and the effect of stimulant therapy. Paper delivered to the Annual Meeting of the American Psychological Association, Montreal.

Kinsbourne, M. (1974a): Mechanisms of hemispheric interaction in man. In: Hemispheric Disconnection and Cerebral Function, edited by M. Kinsbourne and W. L. Smith. Thomas, Springfield, Ill.

Kinsbourne, M. (1974b): Direction of gaze and distribution of cerebral thought processes. Neuropsychologia, 12:279–281.

Kinsbourne, M. (1974c): Disorders of mental development. In: Textbook of Clinical Pediatric Neurology, edited by J. Menkes. Lea and Feibiger, Philadelphia.

Kinsbourne, M. (1975a): The mechanisms of hemispheric control of the lateral gradient of attention. In: Attention and Performance, Vol. V, edited by R. M. A. Rabbitt and S. Dornic. Academic Press, London.

Kinsbourne, M. (1975b): Minor hemisphere language and cerebral maturation. In: Development of Language, edited by E. Lenneberg and E. Lenneberg. Excerpta Medica, Amsterdam.

Kinsbourne, M. (1976a): Mechanisms of hemispheric interaction. In: The Assymetrical Function of the Brain, edited by M. Kinsbourne. Cambridge University Press, New York.

Kinsbourne, M. (Ed.). (1976b): The Asymmetrical Function of the Brain. Cambridge University Press, New York, in press.

Kinsbourne, M., and Cook, J. (1971): Generalized and lateralized effects of concurrent verbalization on a unimanual skill. Q. J. Exp. Psychol., 23:341–345.

Kinsbourne, M., and Fisher, M. (1971): Latency of uncrossed and crossed reaction in callosal agenesis. Neuropsychologia, 9:471–472.

Kinsbourne, M., and George, J. (1974): The mechanism of the word-frequency effect on recognition memory. J. Verb. Learn. Verb. Behav., 13, 63–69.

Kinsbourne, M., Hoch, D., and Sessions, T. (1974): In preparation.

Kinsbourne, M., and Jardno, D. M. (1974): The relationship between eye lateralization and cerebral dominance. Unpublished manuscript.

Kinsbourne, M., and McMurray, J. (1975): The effect of cerebral dominance on time sharing between speaking and tapping by preschool children. Child Dev., 46, 240–242.

Kinsbourne, M., and W. L. Smith (Eds.). (1974): Hemispheric Disconnection and Cerebral Function. Thomas, Springfield, Ill.

Kinsbourne, M., and Warrington, E. K. (1961): A tachistoscopic study of visual inattention. J. Physiol., 156:33–34.

Kinsbourne, M., and Warrington, E. K. (1962a): A disorder of simultaneous form perception. Brain, 85:461–486.

Kinsbourne, M., and Warrington, E. K. (1962b): A variety of reading disability associated with right hemisphere lesions. J. Neurol. Neurosurg. Psychiatry, 25:339–344.

Kinsbourne, M., and Warrington, E. K. (1963a): A study of visual perseveration. J. Neurol. Neurosurg. Psychiatry, 26:468–475.

Kinsbourne, M., and Warrington, E. K. (1963b): The localizing significance of limited simultaneous visual form perception. Brain, 86:697–702.

Kinsbourne, M., and Warrington, E. K. (1963c): Jargon aphasia. Neuropsychologia, 1:27–38.

Kinsbourne, M., and Warrington, E. K. (1964a): Disorders of spelling. J. Neurol. Neurosurg. Psychiatry, 27:296–299.

Kinsbourne, M., and Warrington, E. K. (1964b): Observations on colour agnosia. J. Neurol. Neurosurg. Psychiatry, 27:296–299.

Kinsbourne, M., and Wilson, J. M. (1975): Frequency effect on recall and recognition in relation to age. In preparation.

Kinsbourne, M., and Wood, F. (1975): Short-term memory processes and the amnesic syndrome. In: Short-Term Memory, edited by D. Deutsch and J. A. Deutsch. Academic Press, New York.

Kintsch, W. (1970): Models for free recall and recognition. In: *Models of Human Memory,* edited by D. A. Norman. Academic Press, New York.

Knights, R. M., and Moule, A. D. (1967): Normative and reliability data on finger and foot tapping in children. *Percept. Mot. Skills, 25,* 717–720.

Krashen, S. (1972): *Language and the Left Hemisphere. Working Papers in Phonetics. Vol. 24.* University of California at Los Angeles.

Lackner, J. R. (1974): Observations on the speech processing capabilities of an amnesic patient—several aspects of H.M.'s language function. *Neuropsychologia,* 12:199–208.

Lashley, K. S. (1929): *Brain Mechanisms and Intelligence.* University of Chicago Press, Chicago.

Lashley, K. S. (1931): Mass action in cerebral function. *Science,* 73:245–254.

Laverty, S. G. (1958): Sodium amytal and extraversion. *J. Neurol. Neurosurg. Psychiatry,* 21:50–54.

Lenneberg, E. H. (1967): *Biological Foundations of Language.* Wiley, New York.

Levy-Agresti, J., and Sperry, R. W. (1968): Differential perceptual capacities in major and minor hemispheres. *Proc. Nat. Acad. Sci. USA,* 61:1151.

Levy, J., Trevarthen, C., and Sperry, R. W. (1972): Perception of bilateral chimeric figures following hemispheric deconnexion. *Brain,* 95:61–78.

Lieberman, P., Klatt, D. L., and Wilson, W. A. (1969): Vocal tract limitations in the vowel repertoire of rhesus monkey and other non-human primates. *Science,* 164:1185–1187.

Luria, A. R. (1969): Speech development and the formation of mental processes. In: *A Handbook of Contemporary Soviet Psychology.* Basic Books, New York.

Lynch, S., and Yarnell, P. R. (1973): Retrograde amnesia: delayed forgetting after concussion. *Am. J. Psychol.,* 86:643–645.

Mandler, G. (1967): Organization and Memory. In: *Advances in the Psychology of Learning and Motivation; Research and Theory, Vol. II,* edited by N. Spence and J. Spence. Academic Press, New York.

Mark, R. E., and Sperry, R. W. (1968): Bimanual coordination in monkeys. *Exp. Neurol.,* 21:92–104.

McGuigan, F. S. (1966): *Thinking: Studies of Covert Language Processes.* Appleton, New York.

Miller, G. A. (1956): The magical number seven, plus or minus two: Some limits on our capacity for processing information. *Psychol. Rev.,* 63:81–97.

Milner, B. (1964): Some effects of frontal lobectomy in man. In: *The Frontal Granular Cortex and Behavior,* edited by J. M. Warren and K. Ackert. McGraw-Hill, New York.

Milner, B. (1965): Visually-guided maze learning in man: effects of bilateral hippocampal, bilateral frontal, and unilateral cerebral lesions. *Neuropsychologia,* 3:317–338.

Milner, B., Corkin, S., and Teuber, H. L. (1968): Further analysis of the hippocampal amnesic syndrome: 14-year follow-up study of H.M. *Neuropsychologia,* 6:215–234.

Molfese, D. L. (1973): Cerebral asymmetry in infants, children and adults: Auditory evoked responses to speech and musical stimuli. *J. Acoust. Soc. Am.,* 53:363 (A).

Morgan, M. J. (1975): The ontogeny of asymmetry. In: *The Asymmetrical Function of the Brain,* edited by M. Kinsbourne. Cambridge University Press, New York.

Moutier, R. (1908): *L'Aphasie de Broca.* Steinheil, Paris.

Myers, R. E. (1956): Functions of corpus callosum in interocular transfer. *Brain,* 79:358–363.

Nagafuchi, M. (1970): Development of dichotic and monaural hearing abilities in young children. *Acta Otolaryngol.* (Stockh), 69:409–414.

Neisser, U. (1967): *Cognitive Psychology.* Appleton, New York.

Newcombe, F., and Russell, W. R. (1969): Dissociated visual perceptual and spatial deficits in focal lesions of the right hemisphere. *J. Neurol. Neurosurg. Psychiatry,* 32:73–81.

Nielsen, J. M., and Raney, R. B. (1939): Recovery from aphasia studied in cases of lobectomy. *Arch. Neurol. Psychiatry,* 42:189.

Nottebohm, F. (1970): Ontogeny of bird song. *Science,* 167:950–956.

Ornstein, R. E. (1972): *The Psychology of Consciousness.* Freeman, San Francisco.

Oxbury, S., Oxbury, L., and Humphrey, N. K. (1969): Varieties of colour anomia. *Brain,* 92:847–860.

Papalia, D. E. (1972): The status of several conservation abilities across the life-span. *Human Development,* 15:229–243.

Paterson, A., and Zangwill, O. L. (1944): Disorders of visual space perception associated with lesions of the right cerebral hemisphere. *Brain,* 67:331–358.

Paterson, A., and Zangwill, O. L. (1945): A case of topographical disorientation associated with a unilateral cerebral lesion. *Brain,* 68:188–212.

Peterson, L. R., and Peterson, M. J. (1959): Short-term retention of individual verbal items. *J. Exp. Psychol.,* 58:193–198.

Petrie, A. (1952): *Personality and the Frontal Lobes.* Routledge and Kegan, London.

Petrinovich, L. (1972): Psychological mechanisms in language development. *Adv. Psychobiol.,* 1:259–285.

Piaget, J. (1953): *Origins of Intelligence in Children.* International Universities Press, New York.

Piaget, J., and Inhelder, B. (1956): *The Child's Conception of Space.* Humanities Press, New York.

Piercy, M., Hecaen, H., and de Ajuriaguerra, D. (1960): Constructional apraxia associated with unilateral cerebral lesions; left and right sided cases compared. *Brain,* 83:225–242.

Piercy, M. F., and Smith, V. (1962): Right hemisphere dominance for certain nonverbal intellectual skills. *Brain,* 85:775–790.

Poppelreuter, W. (1917): *Die psychischen Schädigungen durch Kopfschuss im Kriege 1914–1916: die Storungen der niederen und hoheren Schleistungen durch Verletzungen des Okzipitalhirns.* Voss, Leipzig.

Pribram, K. M. (1969): The amnesic syndromes: disturbance in coding? In: *The Pathology of Memory,* edited by G. A. Talland and N. Waugh. Academic Press, New York.

Reiff, R., and Scheerer, M. (1959): *Memory and Hypnotic Age Regression.* International Universities Press.

Riese, W. (1965): The sources of Hughlings Jackson's view on aphasia. *Brain,* 88:811–822.

Robinson, J. S., and Voneida, J. R. (1973): Hemispheric differences in cognitive capacity in the split-brain cat. *Neuropsychologia,* 38:123–134.

Russell, W. R., and Nathan, P. W. (1946): Traumatic amnesia. *Brain,* 69:280–300.

Sanders, H., and Warrington, E. K. (1971): Memory for remote events in amnesic patients. *Brain,* 94:661–668.

Sanders, H., Warrington, E. K., Marshall, J., and Weiskrantz, L. (1974): "Blindsight." Vision in a field defect. *Lancet,* 1:707–708.

Satz, P. (1972): Pathological left-handedness: An explanatory model. *Cortex,* 8:121–135.

Schonfield, D., and Robertson, B. A. (1966): Memory storage and ageing. *Can. J. Psychol.,* 20:228–236.

Scoville, W. B., and Milner, B. (1957): Loss of recent memory after bilateral hippocampal lesions. *J. Neurol. Neurosurg. Psychiatry,* 20:11–21.

Semmes, J. (1968): Hemispheric specialization: a possible clue to mechanism. *Neuropsychologia,* 6:11–26.

Shepard, R. N., and Metzler, J. (1971): Mental rotation of three-dimensional objects. *Science,* 171:701–703.

Sherrington, C. S. (1906): *Integrative Action of the Nervous System.* Yale University Press, New Haven.

Siqueland, E. R., and Lipsitt, L. P. (1966): Conditioned head turning in human newborns. *J. Exp. Child Psychol.,* 4:356–377.

Sperry, R. W., Gazzaniga, M. S., and Bogen, J. E. (1969): Interhemispheric relationships: the neocortical commissures: syndromes of hemisphere disconnection. In: *Handbook of Clinical Neurology, Vol. 4,* edited by P. J. Vinken and G. W. Bruyn. North Holland, Amsterdam.

Springer, S. (1971): Ear asymmetry in a dichotic listening task. *Percept. Psychophys.,* 10:239–241.

Sternberg, S. (1969): The discovery of processing stages: extensions of Donder's method. *Acta Psychol.,* 30:276–315.

Stevens, J., and Kinsbourne, M. (1975). Alcoholism compared to ageing as a cause of cognitive deficit. *In preparation.*

Talland, G. A. (1965): *Deranged Memory.* Academic Press, New York.

Thompson, R. (1967): *Foundations of Physiological Psychology.* Harper and Row, New York.

Trevarthen, C. W. (1974): In: *Hemispheric Disconnection and Cerebral Function,* edited by M. Kinsbourne and W. L. Smith. Thomas, Springfield, Ill.

Trevarthen, C. W. (1976): Manipulative strategies of baboons and the origins of cerebral dominance. In: *The Assymetrical Function of the Brain,* edited by M. Kinsbourne. Cambridge University Press, New York.

Tulving, E. (1972): Episodic and semantic memory. In: *Organisation of Memory,* edited by E. Tulving and W. Donaldson. Academic Press, New York.

Tulving, E., and Thompson, D. M. (1971): Retrieval processes in recognition memory: effects of associative context. *J. Exp. Psychol.,* 87:116–124.

Turkewitz, G., Gordon, B. W., and Birch, M. G. (1968): Head turning in the human neonate: effect of prandial condition and lateral preference. *J. Comp. Physiol. Psychol.,* 59:189–192.

Tyler, H. R. (1968): Abnormalities of perception with defective eye movements (Balint's syndrome). *Cortex,* 4:154–171.

Victor, M. (1969): The amnesic syndrome and its anatomical basis. *Can. Med. Assoc. J.,* 100:1115–1125.

Vygotsky, L. S. (1962): *Thought and Language.* MIT Press, Cambridge.

Wada, J. A., Clark, R., and Hamm, A. (1975): Cerebral hemispheric asymmetry in humans: Cortical speech zones in 100 adult and 100 infant brains. *Arch. Neurol, 32,* 239–246.

Wada, J., and Rasmussen, T. R. (1960): Intracarotid amytal for the lateralization of cerebral speech dominance. *J. Neurosurg.,* 17:266–282.

Warrington, E. K. (1962): The completion of visual forms across hemianopic field defects. *J. Neurol. Neurosurg. Psychiatry,* 25:208–217.

Warrington, E. K., James M., and Kinsbourne, M. (1966): Drawing disability in relation to laterality of cerebral lesion. *Brain,* 89:53–82.

Warrington, E. K., and Weiskrantz. (1970): Amnesic syndrome: consolidation or retrieval? *Nature,* 228:628–630.

Warrington, E. K., and Weiskrantz, L. (1968): New methods of testing long-term retention with special reference to amnesic patients. *Nature,* 217:972–974.

Watkins, M. J. (1974): When is recall spectacularly higher than recognition? *J. Exp. Psychol.,* 102:161–163.

Waugh, N., and Norman, D. (1965): Primary memory. *Psychol. Rev.,* 76:89–104.

Webster, W. G. (1972): Functional asymmetry between the cerebral hemisphere of the cat. *Neuropsychologia,* 10:75–87.

Weinstein, E. A., and Kahn, R. L. (1955): *Denial of Illness.* Thomas, Springfield, Ill.

Weisstein, N. (1969): What the frog's eye tells the human brain: single cell analyzers in the human visual system. *Psychol. Bull.,* 72:157–176.

Wender, P. M. (1971): *Minimal Brain Disfunction in Children.* Interscience, New York.

Whorf, B. L. (1965): *Language, Thought and Reality.* MIT Press, Cambridge.

Wickelgren, W. A. (1968): Sparing of short-term memory in an amnesic patient: Implications for strength theory of memory. *Nature,* 6:235–244.

Wickens, D. (1970): Encoding categories of words: an empirical approach to memory. *Psychol. Rev.,* 77:1–15.

Williams, M., and Zangwill, O. L. (1952): Memory defects after head injury. *J. Neurol. Neurosurg. Psychiatry,* 15:54–58.

Winocur, G., and Breckenridge, C. B. (1973): Cue-dependent behavior of hippocampally damaged rats in complex maze. *J. Comp. Physiol. Psychol.,* 82:512–522.

Winocur, G., and Weiskrantz, L. (1975): An investigation of paired-associate learning in amnesic patients. *Neuropsychologia,* in press.

Witelson, S. F., and Pallie, W. (1973): Left hemisphere specialization for language in the newborn: neuroanatomical evidence of asymmetry. *Brain*, 96:641–646.

Yin, R. K. (1970): Face recognition by brain-injured patients: a dissociable ability. *Neuropsychologia*, 8:395–402.

Zaidel, D., and Sperry, R. W. (1973): Performance on the Raven's Colored Progressive Matrices. Test by subjects with cerebral commissurotomy. *Cortex*, 9:34–39.